A NEW HISTORY OF THE ISLE OF MAN

Volume 4 – Part II

The Isle of Man, 1405–1830

Social and Economic History

A NEW HISTORY OF THE ISLE OF MAN

A New History of the Isle of Man is a Millennium project which began in 1997 as a collaboration between the Isle of Man government and Liverpool University's Centre for Manx Studies. The books in the series are:

1 *A New History of the Isle of Man – The Evolution of the Natural Landscape*, edited by Richard Chiverrell and Geoffrey Thomas (Liverpool University Press, 2007)
2 *A New History of the Isle of Man – Prehistory*, in preparation
3 *A New History of the Isle of Man – The Medieval Period, 1000–1406*, edited by Sean Duffy and Harold Mytum (Liverpool University Press, 2015)
4.i *The Isle of Man, 1405–1830 – Political and Constitutional History*, edited by Tim Thornton, Harold Mytum and Michael Hoy (Boydell Press, 2025)
4.ii *The Isle of Man, 1405–1830 – Social and Economic History*, edited by Tim Thornton, Harold Mytum and Michael Hoy (Boydell Press, 2025)
5. *A New History of the Isle of Man – The Modern Period, 1830–1999*, edited by John Belchem (Liverpool University Press, 2001)

A NEW HISTORY OF THE ISLE OF MAN

Volume 4 – Part II

The Isle of Man, 1405–1830

Social and Economic History

Edited by
TIM THORNTON,
HAROLD MYTUM AND
MICHAEL HOY

Culture VANNIN

THE BOYDELL PRESS

First published 2025
The Boydell Press, Woodbridge

ISBN 978 1 83765 178 8

The Boydell Press is an imprint of Boydell & Brewer Ltd
PO Box 9, Woodbridge, Suffolk IP12 3DF, UK
and of Boydell & Brewer Inc.
668 Mt Hope Avenue, Rochester, NY 14620–2731, USA
website: www.boydellandbrewer.com

Our Authorised Representative for product safety in the EU is Easy Access System Europe – Mustamäe tee 50, 10621 Tallinn, Estonia, gpsr.requests@easproject.com

A CIP catalogue record for this book is available from the British Library

This publication has been supported by Culture Vannin. Culture Vannin has provided funding only and the views, opinions, findings and conclusions or recommendations expressed are strictly those of the authors. Culture Vannin takes no responsibility for any errors or omissions or for the correctness of the information contained in this publication

In Memoriam

William Cain
Ulla Corkill
Nigel G. Crowe
Harold Dickinson
Ann Harrison
Jennifer Platten
Constance Radcliffe
J.R. Roscow
J.A. Sharpe
Rosalie Stott
R.L. Thomson
Nigel Yates

Contents

Illustrations

Full credit details are provided in the captions to the images in the text. The editors, contributors and publisher are grateful to all the institutions and persons for permission to reproduce the materials in which they hold copyright. Every effort has been made to trace the copyright holders; apologies are offered for any omission, and the publisher will be pleased to add any necessary acknowledgement in subsequent editions.

Preface

This volume forms the second element of the fourth volume of the new history of the Isle of Man, produced under the auspices of the Centre for Manx Studies at the University of Liverpool. It covers the period from the early fifteenth century to 1830 and is focused on social and economic aspects of the Island's history. Companion volumes covering the evolution of the natural landscape (edited by Richard Chiverrell and Geoffrey Thomas), the medieval period (edited by Seán Duffy and Harold Mytum), and the modern period (edited by John Belchem) have previously been published by Liverpool University Press.

As will immediately be clear, this volume and its companion are a collaborative effort involving a large group of scholars from the Island and beyond. In some cases, their contributions are worthy of particular note as we record with sadness that they did not live to enjoy the publication of their work: William Cain, Ulla Corkill, Nigel Crowe, Jennifer Platten, J.R. Roscow, R.L. Thomson and Nigel Yates. This preface also allows for recognition to be given to those who have helped coordinate the efforts of the contributors, especially amongst the editorial team: Professor Harold Mytum has deftly maintained the momentum of the project overall; Dr Mike Hoy has taken particular trouble to support the development of the Island-based contributions and played a pivotal role in coordinating support for the project there, including working with Charles Guard (formerly Administrator of the Manx Heritage Foundation, now Culture Vannin, whose generosity and commitment to the project is also acknowledged) on the identification of the extensive range of illustrations which support the text and ensuring the necessary permissions were secured; Dr Fenella Bazin has coordinated and contributed to a wide ranging chapter on Arts and Culture; and Dr Catriona Mackie has written a comprehensive account of the Island's landscape and built environment drawn from a number of specialist sources.

Thanks are due to many organizations and individuals who have made the project possible: to Manx National Heritage, and the universities of Liverpool and Huddersfield. Generous funding for this publication specifically has been received from Culture Vannin.

Libraries and archives have supported the work, notably the Manx National Heritage Library and Archives, the British Library, the National Archives of the United Kingdom, and the university libraries of Huddersfield, Leeds, Liverpool and Manchester.

A companion volume, covering the Island's political and constitutional history across the same period, is also published by Boydell and Brewer.

TIM THORNTON

Acknowledgements

We would like to thank the following people for their invaluable assistance during the research carried out for this volume:

Fenella Bazin
Michael Bridson
William Cain †
Mike Clague
Frances Coakley
Ulla Corkill †
Yvonne Cresswell
Nigel Crowe †
Peter Davey
Colette Davies
Harold Dickinson †
Kit Gawne
Tim Grass
Andrew Johnson
Nick Johnson
Brenda Kennaugh
Sue King
Christopher Lewin
Priscilla Lewthwaite
Catriona Mackie
Pat McClure
Stephen Miller
Chris Page
Jennifer Platten †
Deann Powell
Carola Rush
J.A. Sharpe †
Patricia Tutt
Penelope Wilson

We would like to thank Charles Guard for his help in compiling the illustrations.

We would also like to thank the librarians, archivists and curators at Manx National Heritage:

Edmund Southworth, formerly director of the Manx Museum
Roger Sims and Paul Weatherall, former librarian-archivists, Manx National Heritage

Wendy Thirkettle, librarian-archivist
Steve Blackford, Sarah Christian, Yvonne Cresswell, Jude Dicken, Allison Fox, Alan Franklin, Pat Griffiths, Suzi Heslan, Kim Holden, Kirsty Neate, Matthew Richardson and Andrea Roberts

We would also like to thank the librarians and archivists at the Blair Atholl Collection; British Library; Cheshire Archives and Local Studies, Chester (formerly Cheshire Record Office and Chester City Record Office) Chester; Derby Collection, Knowsley; Durham University Library; ; Lancashire Record Office, Preston; Leeds Castle Foundation; Liverpool City Libraries; National Archives, Kew; National Archives of Scotland, Edinburgh; National Galleries Scotland; National Museums Liverpool; North East Wales Archives – Flintshire, Hawarden; Sydney Jones Library, University of Liverpool; Wallasey Central Library.

Contributors

FENELLA BAZIN, formerly director of post-graduate studies, Centre for Manx Studies, University of Liverpool

MIKE CLAGUE, independent researcher

FRANCES COAKLEY, independent researcher

ULLA CORKILL, independent researcher †

YVONNE CRESSWELL, honorary visiting fellow, University of Leicester, formerly curator of social history, Manx National Heritage

NIGEL G. CROWE, independent researcher †

PETER DAVEY, honorary research fellow, Centre for Manx Studies, University of Liverpool

COLETTE DAVIES, lecturer in fine art, critical and contextual studies, University College Isle of Man

J.R. DICKINSON, independent researcher

ALLISON FOX, curator of archaeology, Manx National Heritage

KIT GAWNE, independent researcher

TIM GRASS, senior research fellow, Spurgeon's College, London

MICHAEL HOY, research assistant, University of Huddersfield

ANDREW C.C. JOHNSON, curator, field archaeology, Manx National Heritage

NICK JOHNSON, independent researcher

SUE KING, independent researcher

CHRISTOPHER LEWIN, postdoctoral research fellow, University of Edinburgh

PRISCILLA LEWTHWAITE, independent researcher

CATRIONA MACKIE, programme leader for history and heritage, University College Isle of Man

PAT MCCLURE, independent researcher

STEPHEN MILLER, independent researcher

HAROLD MYTUM, professor of archaeology, University of Liverpool

CHRIS PAGE, independent researcher

JENNIFER PLATTEN, independent researcher †

Edmund Southworth, formerly director, Manx National Heritage

Tim Thornton, deputy vice-chancellor and professor of history, University of Huddersfield

Patricia A. Tutt, independent researcher

Nigel Yates, late professor of ecclesiastical history at the University of Wales, Lampeter †

Editors

Tim Thornton, Harold Mytum and Michael Hoy

Contributing Editors: Fenella Bazin and Catriona Mackie

Abbreviations

AP	Atholl Papers (MNH)
AW	Archidiaconal Wills (MNH)
BAR	British Archaeological Reports, Oxford
BL	British Library
Bodl	Bodleian Library, Oxford
Charities	*The Isle of Man Charities*, J. McHutchin & G. Quirk (eds), 1831 (Liverpool)
CJ	*The Journals of the House of Commons*
CRP	Castle Rushen Papers (MNH)
CSPD	*Calendar of State Papers Domestic*
CTB	*Calendar of Treasury Books*
DD	Diocesan Deposits (MNH)
DP	Derby Papers (MNH)
EcHR	*Economic History Review*
EP	Ellesmere Papers (MNH)
EPR	Episcopal Probate Records (MNH)
EW	Episcopal Wills (MNH)
FLS	Manx Folk Life Survey (MNH)
HKJ	House of Keys Journals (MNH)
HMC	Historical Manuscripts Commission
ICBS	Incorporated Church Building Society files (Lambeth Palace Archives)
JMM	*Journal of the Manx Museum*, 88 numbers, 1924-1980 (Douglas)
Lib.Assed.	Libri Assedationis (Manorial & Bishop's Barony setting books) (MNH)
Lib.Canc.	Libri Cancellarii (Chancery Court actions) (MNH)
Lib.Caus.	Libri Causarum (Ecclesiastical causes and church court proceedings) (MNH)
Lib.Irrot.	Libri Irrotulamentorum (Commissions of officials) (MNH)
Lib.Mon.	Libri Monasteriorum (Abbey setting books) (MNH)

Lib.Plit.	Libri Placitorum/Plitor (Books of Common Pleas) (MNH)
Lib.Scacc.	Libri Scaccarii (Court of Exchequer Books) (MNH)
Lib.Vast	Libri Vastarum ('Wast' books) (MNH)
LRO	Lancashire Record Office, Preston
MNH	Manx National Heritage Library, Douglas
Monumenta	*Monumenta de Insula Manniae, or a Collection of National Documents relating to the Isle of Man*, J.R. Oliver (ed), Manx Society, 4, 7, 9 (1867)
Moore, *Isle of Man*	A.W. Moore, *A History of the Isle of Man* (2 vols, London 1900)
NADFAS	National Association of the Decorative and Fine Art Societies
NEWAF	North East Wales Archives – Flintshire, Hawarden
ODNB	*Oxford Dictionary of National Biography*
PIMNHAS	*Proceedings of the Isle of Man Natural History and Antiquarian Society*
PR	Parochial (Parish) Records (MNH)
Presentments	Presentments to the Church courts (MNH)
QBHP	Quayle Bridge House Papers (MNH)
Records of Convocation	*Records of Convocation 1: Sodor and Man 1229–1877*, G. Bray (ed), 2005 (Woodbridge)
RSLC	Record Society of Lancashire and Cheshire
SPCK	The Society for Promoting Christian Knowledge
Statutes	*Statutes of the Isle of Man*, J.F. Gill (ed), vol. 1, 1883 (London)
THSLC	*Transactions of the Historical Society of Lancashire and Cheshire*
TNA	The National Archives of the United Kingdom (London). Formerly PRO – Public Record Office (London)
VR	Episcopal Visitation Returns (MNH)
Warwick CRO	Warwickshire County Record Office
YLM	*Yn Lioar Manninagh* (*Proceedings of the Isle of Man Natural History and Antiquarian Society* – early series)

Introduction

CATRIONA MACKIE

The 425 years covered by this volume represent a formative period in the Isle of Man's history. Key external events had a significant impact on the Island, including the dissolution of the monasteries, the English Civil War, England's developing trade routes, and the revestment of the Island's sovereignty and customs rights to the British Crown. While the first volume of this series explores the political and constitutional position of the Island during this period, this volume explores the impact of these events, and others, on the Island's economy, society, and culture during the late medieval and early modern periods. The chapters in this volume are broadly thematic and, in taking such an approach, there is necessarily some overlap between the subjects covered.

Chapter 1 details what we know of the Island's population, settlement distribution, land tenure, and the basis of the Island's economy in the early part of this period, before exploring the development of the 'running trade' and its impact on the Island.

Chapter 2 explores the status of religion and the established Island church, with additional sections on Methodism and non-conformism, Roman Catholicism and the Quakers.

Chapter 3 describes practical elements of daily life on the Island during this period. Material culture and aspects of family life are explored, in particular looking at the role of women and the life of children and adolescents. A major section of this chapter describes the provision of education on the Island, highlighting the roles of Bishops Barrow (1663–1671), Wilson (1698–1755), and Hildesley (1755–1772) in developing education and literacy in Manx and English.

Chapter 4 looks at those aspects of intangible culture which would have imbued the everyday life of the population, such as Manx language, music, and folklore, as well as developments in publishing and popular entertainment that emerged towards the end of this period. The importance of art and literature as sources of evidence for Manx history are also highlighted in this chapter.

Chapter 5 explores the development of towns and villages on the Island, also touched upon in Chapter 1, and examines the impact of daily life on the environment and on settlement morphology, as well as the development of rural and urban architecture.

These chapters draw on evidence from a range of narrow and imperfect sources. This is especially so for the early period covered in this volume. Documentary sources are primarily political and administrative and there is limited archaeological evidence to help elucidate the development of the Island during the late medieval period outside of the key defensive, executive and monastic centres at Peel, Castletown and Rushen Abbey.

In the medieval and early modern periods, apart from the main political base at Castle Rushen, the Isle of Man did not have local centres of administration or municipal buildings of the kind that existed, for example, in England. This means that traditional sources of evidence for medieval towns and villages are largely absent. There are no reliable accounts of the Island's population until the first census of 1821. Sources indicate that between 1405 and 1660, the population may have been in the region of 12,000 inhabitants, and the first ecclesiastical census of 1726, itself not completely reliable, lists a population of just over 14,000. The 1831 census recorded a population of 41,000.

The early sixteenth century rent books show that there were only three significant settlements on the Island at the time: Castletown, Douglas, and Peel. Each of these possessed a natural harbour but had their own distinctive characteristics. In Castletown and Peel, the settlements expanded from their respective castles along the shoreline. In Douglas, the settlement developed from the north side of the harbour and gradually moved inland. The construction of bridges in the mid-eighteenth century allowed for the expansion of Castletown and Douglas across their river, while harbour developments in Douglas helped to cement its position as the Island's primary trading centre. Outside of these towns, there is no evidence for nucleated settlements during the sixteenth century. By the mid-seventeenth century, Ramsey had become a significant community, and Laxey and Ballasalla could be described as villages. Unlike traditional English villages, most villages in the Isle of Man did not develop around the site of a parish church. Instead, they were centred on highways, particularly crossroads or bridges. Ballasalla, in contrast, likely emerged from a settlement established to house those working at Rushen Abbey farm.

Throughout most of the period covered in this volume, farming and fishing, particularly herring fishing, were fundamental to the Island's economy. These industries were primarily subsistence-based and, until the mid-seventeenth century, external trade was minimal. Exports were limited to the products of farming and fishing, such as wool, animal hide, and herring, while imports were mainly of items that were either unavailable on the Island, such as coal and salt, or in short supply, such as timber.

It is unsurprising that the Island's central position among the key trading routes of the Irish Sea was crucial to the way in which its economy and society developed in the seventeenth and eighteenth centuries. With the expansion of England's international trade and the introduction of legislation to regulate it, the Isle of Man finally developed into a thriving trading post for enterprising merchants engaged in the 'running trade,' where goods were landed on the Island and customs duties paid, before leaving the Island and being smuggled into Britain. The Island's newfound mercantile success led to economic prosperity and helped to establish a new 'middling' class of residents, comprising merchants, retailers, and professionals, both Manx-born and incomers. This increasing wealth is reflected in the construction of some of the Island's early Georgian buildings, such as 2 Parliament Square in Castletown, built in 1719, and the Douglas Hotel, built in the late 1750s. The attraction of the Island to new residents continued after the Revestment in 1765, with the Island seen as a place where living was relatively cheap and, for some, a jurisdictional refuge.

While the seventeenth and eighteenth centuries saw the rise of the Island's urban middle class, life did not change considerably for the majority of those in rural communities. Analysis of probate inventories indicates that the contents of most Manx homes as late as the early-nineteenth century were not dissimilar to those in the early-seventeenth century. Rural tenants generally worked their own small parcels of land or laboured on the larger, 'quarterland' farms, or for the lord of Man's officers. Many tenants were also involved in the herring fishing, which provided additional food for the winter months as well as money to help pay rent.

Throughout the Stanley period (1405–1736), the Derby lords of Man and their families spent relatively little time on the Isle of Man but were keen to maximise their income from the Island. In the seventeenth century they made a relatively unsuccessful attempt to introduce leaseholds, in place of the customary 'tenure of the straw' whereby tenants exchanged and passed on land without paying any dues. The lengthy dispute between tenants and lord was finally resolved with the Act of Settlement of 1704 which strengthened the position of the tenants and finally convinced the earls of Derby that rental income from the Isle of Man would always be relatively inconsequential in comparison with that obtained by other means.

Agricultural improvement was not seriously attempted on the Island until the latter part of the eighteenth century when model farms, demonstrating some of the new farming technologies, were established by wealthy Manx and incoming landowners. However, developments in agriculture were slow to filter down to the majority of the rural population and widespread changes in farming practices were not seen until the nineteenth century.

It is not until the early nineteenth century that sustained development in the Isle of Man's built environment can be seen. The lords of Man had not invested in substantial property development on the Island and, unlike England, the Isle of Man lacked any significant domestic buildings until the construction of Castle Mona in 1803/04. The work of architects George Steuart and Thomas Brine in the first decades of the nineteenth century helped to introduce new architectural elements to the Island, and Georgian neo-classicism became fashionable for domestic dwellings of all classes. The impact of this can be seen across the Manx countryside in the symmetrical three- and five-bay cottages and farmhouses which predominate.

Religion and education on the Island were closely intertwined. When Bishop Barrow took up his episcopate on the Island in 1663, he was dismayed at the lack of education to be found among both the general populace and the clergy. The majority of the population spoke only Manx Gaelic and most of the clergy were therefore also local. Remuneration for clergymen was poor and most derived a second income from farming or some other occupation. Bishops Barrow (1663–1671) and Wilson (1698–1755) both committed to improving the education of islanders and clergy by setting up petty schools, which would be available to all residents, regardless of income. Secondary education was also established, beginning with the grammar school in Castletown. Additional secondary schools followed, in Douglas, Ramsey, and Peel, along with a mathematical school in Peel, providing navigation and technical skills. Secondary schools for girls, teaching practical subjects such as sewing and spinning, as well as reading, were established in the 1760s and 1770s. However, the path towards general education on the Island was not a smooth one. Funds to pay for teachers and the upkeep of buildings were not always readily available, not all teachers or clergy were equally capable or dedicated, and not all islanders were willing or able to send their children to school. For rural tenants, sending a child to school often meant losing out on their work or support at home. Despite these challenges, by the end of the eighteenth century, literacy rates in the Isle of Man seem to have been higher than those in rural England and Wales, albeit many on the Island were literate in Manx, rather than English.

Bishop Phillips (1605–1633) had attempted to introduce a Manx translation of the Book of Common Prayer in 1610, but without success. At that time, the Manx clergy was content with improvising in Manx the English liturgy for their congregations. Bishop Wilson was responsible for the first publication in Manx Gaelic, a translation of his *Principles and Duties of Christianity*, published in 1707, and he intended to produce further works in Manx. However, it was Bishop Hildesley (1755–1772) who championed the use of Manx in schools and ultimately brought to fruition the translation and publication of the bible and prayer book in Manx Gaelic from the 1760s, supported by the SPCK.

The established Anglican church on the Isle of Man appears to have been more flexible than in England and Wales, absorbing influences that, elsewhere, provoked division, thereby providing the Island with an element of religious stability that was not seen in other bishoprics. For example, there is evidence of the adoption and survival of certain puritan influences in the Manx church and, while Methodism had a significant impact on the Island, it developed within the established church, rather than in opposition to it. Indeed, many Islanders attended both churches, with efforts being taken by both denominations not to overlap the times of their services. The influence of the church on the publication of sacred texts in Manx extended to Methodism, with the publication of a Manx translation of hymns by Wesley and Watts in 1795.

While the islanders, for the most part, conformed to the established church, traditional folk beliefs and customs were retained by the majority of the population throughout this period. Although sources for these beliefs and customs during the late medieval period are rare, there are some references to the Island as a place where witchcraft was practised. However, only three cases of witchcraft were prosecuted by the secular courts and in only one case was a death sentence carried out. The Isle of Man seems to have followed Ireland, Wales, and the Gaelic-speaking regions of Scotland in its reluctance to prosecute those accused of witchcraft. It has been suggested that this may be due to the strong belief in these regions in a malignant class of supernatural beings that could be responsible for misdeeds which, elsewhere, might be attributed to witchcraft. The ecclesiastical records suggest a strong acceptance of charming and cursing on the Island, particularly during the seventeenth and early eighteenth centuries. Because medical provision was only available to those who could afford it, it is unsurprising that most people would rely on folk medicine, charmers and bonesetters, rather than professionally qualified doctors.

The ecclesiastical records are also a valuable source of information regarding daily life and relationships within the community. For example, they highlight the type of activities that people undertook for amusement with numerous examples of people presented to the church for engaging in entertainments on a Sunday. Fines issued by the ecclesiastical courts for such indiscretions were often used for poor relief, as were donations from wealthier residents. The Isle of Man had no formal poor relief system until the latter part of the nineteenth century. Prior to this, those in need were looked after by relatives or by the church. One peculiarity of the Manx system, seemingly unique in Britain, was the acceptance of a 'choice child' who would be exempt from any form of prescribed work because they were looking after a sick or elderly relative. By the late eighteenth century, Friendly Societies began to be established for those who could afford to contribute, and charitable societies were established for those who could not.

The Isle of Man experienced significant growth during the period covered by this volume. The population perhaps trebled, the economy expanded, the Island's towns and villages spread out, and new ideas in agriculture and architecture were introduced and adopted. The Island's development did not, however, follow a consistent or straightforward trajectory but rather witnessed ebbs and flows in both economic situation and the efficacy of religious, educational, and social endeavours.

The Island's relationship with its nearest neighbours also changed significantly during this period, not only constitutionally, but also economically and socially. While the economic prerogative dictated that the Island face toward England, socially and culturally there remained a strong connection to Britain's Celtic-speaking regions. With its central location in the Irish Sea and its proximity to the surrounding nations, the Island was not only responsive to their influence, but it also absorbed several waves of British and Irish immigrants, from the late medieval militia stationed at the garrisons in Castletown and Peel, to the seventeenth- and eighteenth-century merchants and customs officers, to those who sought to benefit from the Island's higher standard of living in the late eighteenth and early nineteenth centuries.

While immigration from Britain and Ireland was critical to the economic and social development of the Isle of Man, a distinctive feature of the Manx experience is the way the Island absorbed incomers into its community and adapted the established structures and practices of neighbouring territories to best suit the unique society, culture, and economy of the Island. In this way, through the late medieval and early modern periods, the Isle of Man began to lay the foundations for the creation of an evolving sense of Manx identity.

1 *Society and Economy in the Stanley Period, 1572–1736*

J.R. DICKINSON

WITH CONTRIBUTIONS BY NIGEL G. CROWE † AND J.R. ROSCOW †

When the Royalist refugee William Blundell landed in the Isle of Man in 1646, he discovered a land which was in some ways quite different from his native Lancashire.[1] While there were some superficial similarities in that agriculture and fishing were, and had long been, the main occupations of the inhabitants of the Island, as they were of the people living on or near the coasts of the Irish Sea, there were many striking contrasts which Blundell observed. One of the most obvious of these was that the majority of the natives of the Island spoke primarily, if not exclusively, Manx, but their clothing and customs were also unfamiliar to the Englishman. Nearly all of the population lived in isolated houses, scattered throughout the countryside, in much the same way as those who eked out a living in the upland areas of England, but even the larger landholders, those regarded by Blundell as gentry, lived on their estates rather than in any of the four recognized towns, the number of residents in which scarcely exceeded that of many English villages. One similarity of which Blundell was perhaps not aware was that the population seems to have been rising steadily, if slowly, in the Island, as it certainly had been in England and elsewhere in Europe, since at least the early sixteenth century. Whereas this upward trend levelled off in England in the second half of the seventeenth century, the rise in the number of inhabitants in the Island appears to have continued equally steadily into the eighteenth century and beyond, partly as a result of the changes to the Island's economy which began to develop during the last eighty years of the Stanley lordship. The rise of trade between England and its overseas colonies from the middle of the seventeenth century onwards and English legislation to regulate its conduct led directly to the increasing importance of the Isle of Man to merchants who were determined to increase their profits from this traffic by circumventing the duties imposed on their cargoes. The expansion of the running trade had a significant beneficial impact on the Island, providing employment opportunities for seamen and those in the trades which supported maritime commerce, encouraging at least some foreign merchants to establish a base in one of the ports and creating a limited market

1 M. Blundell (ed), *Cavalier. Letters of William Blundell to His Friends* (London, 1933), 19.

within the Island itself for some of the luxuries which were carried from the colonies, such as tobacco. This 'smuggling' activity also drew the unwelcome attentions of the government in London, which was as determined to prevent what it considered 'abuses in the Plantation trade' as the merchants engaged in the running trade were set on continuing to reap the benefits from it.

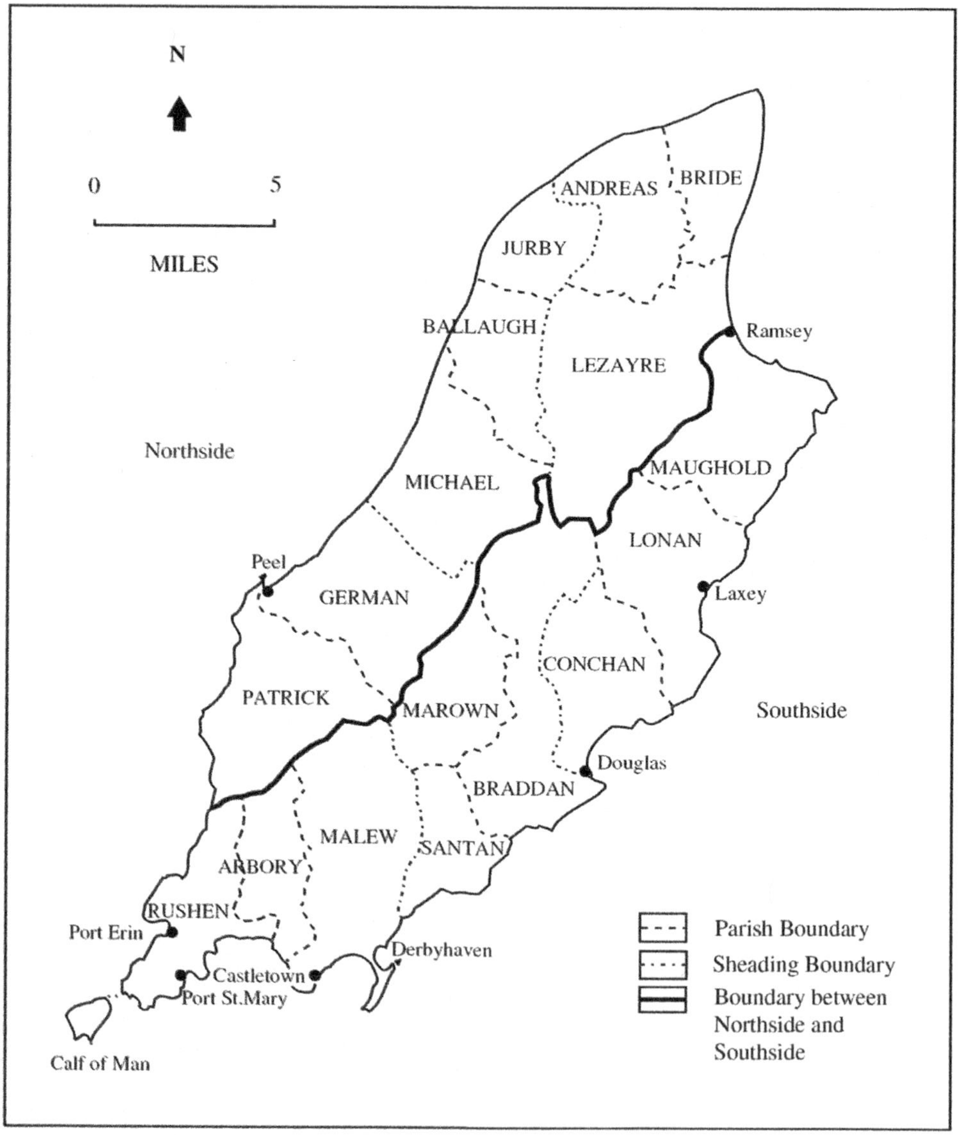

Fig. 1.1 *Administrative divisions of the Isle of Man in the Stanley period.*

POPULATION AND SETTLEMENT

Sources of information about the population of the Isle of Man during the Stanley period are scarce before the early eighteenth century and even then are far from plentiful. Parish registers, the most basic source for the historical demographer, survive in only one of the Island's seventeen parishes from the very end of the sixteenth century and in only nine parishes for at least part of the first half of the seventeenth century; the situation is slightly better by 1700, at which point only three parishes have no extant registers at all. Clear evidence of under-recording, however, such as in Andreas between 1686 and 1700, and the evident failure to make entries at all in some years make the registers difficult to use for estimating the population of the Island, even towards the end of the period.[2] The absence of the sort of lists drawn up for fiscal, ecclesiastical or military purposes in England presents a further problem in attempting to calculate the population of the Island and it is only at the end of the Stanley period that this type of record makes an appearance. While there are inevitably serious questions about its reliability and there is the significant omission of the total number of 'souls' for the parish of Marown, the 'census' apparently drawn up by order of Bishop Wilson in 1726 does nevertheless constitute the first set of almost complete demographic data for the parishes and towns of the Island and it was followed by similar exercises, both at a local and Island-wide level, in the eighteenth century.[3]

When Elizabethan writers on the topography and history of the British Isles described the Isle of Man, they did not concern themselves particularly with the size of the Island's population, even though some, like Camden, were able to avail themselves of first hand information. Bishop Meyrick's letter to the author of *Britannia* was, however, more concerned with refuting some of the statements made by William Harrison in Holinshed's *Chronicles* than in providing any detailed account of the Island and an assessment of the number of its inhabitants.[4] Harrison, who, like most of his contemporaries in the field, relied on existing authorities, maps and information supplied by acquaintances for his accounts of the distant parts of the British Isles, did nevertheless claim that there were 'some time 1300 families' in the Isle of Man, 'of which 960 were

2 MNH MS 09992 (PR), Andreas parish registers: baptisms, 1691; marriages, 1687; burials, 1686.

3 T. Quayle, *A General View of the Agriculture of the Isle of Man* (London, 1812), Appendix H, no. I; A.W. Moore, *A History of the Isle of Man*, 2 vols (1900, London), vol. 1, 412. Later ecclesiastical censuses were undertaken in 1757, 1784 and 1792. T. Quayle, *General View*, Appendix H, nos II-IV.

4 J.R. Oliver (ed), *Monumenta de Insula Manniae, or a Collection of National Documents relating to the Isle of Man*, Manx Society, vol. 1 (1867), 87–99; BL Cotton MS Julius F10, fols 124–25.

in the West halfe, and the rest in the other.'[5] Since there are no indications of the sources which he may have used to come to this conclusion or the date or period to which his estimate refers, it is hard to give much weight to Harrison's speculative total or his suggestions as to population distribution. Furthermore, the fact that the size of the 'average' Manx family unit throughout the early modern period has yet to be established with certainty makes it hard to have any confidence in using these figures even to produce an estimate of the Island's population in the mid-sixteenth century.

Seventeenth-century accounts of the Island were written almost exclusively from the author's own experiences, a trend in such works in keeping with the dawning emphasis on experiment and observation rather than 'reference to authority and revelation' which characterised the Restoration period and beyond, but not all of these writers devoted much energy to ascertaining the number of inhabitants.[6] Writing probably in the late 1640s, Blundell stated that 'the Island of Man is at this day in a mean populous; it neither wanteth nor aboundeth, much less is it overburthened by its natives.'[7] Beyond noting that the militia numbered 1,500 men and that if necessary the Island might muster between 5,000 and 6,000 in all, James Chaloner offered little insight in his *Treatise*, which appeared in 1656, and Thomas Denton, who visited the Island in the late 1680s, recorded rather vaguely that each parish 'comprehends at least an 100 families, many more.'[8] William Stout, a Lancastrian Quaker, was in the Isle of Man at about the same time as Denton and commented in passing on the size and distribution of the population in the countryside and the towns. He found that the Island as a whole was 'thinly inhabited ex[c]ept in and about the aforesaid towns.'[9] Several years later, however, William Sacheverell, who served in the Island as both deputy governor and later governor between 1691 and 1695, estimated that 'there may be there 16,000 soules or thereabouts,' a figure which, if even only slightly inflated, obviously suggests that Denton's assessment was too conservative. The population of the Island was stated as 'more than twenty thousand People' in a petition from Governor

5 R. Holinshed, *Chronicles of England, Scotlande, and Irelande* (London, 1577), vol. 1, 37; W. Harrison, *The Description of England*, G. Edelen (ed) (Washington, D.C., 1968, reprinted 1994), xviii, xx.

6 E.G.R. Taylor, *Late Tudor and Early Stuart Geography, 1583–1650* (London, 1934, reprinted New York 1968), v.

7 W. Blundell, *A History of the Isle of Man*, W. Harrison (ed), Manx Society, 25: vol. 1 and 27: vol. 2 (1876, 1877), vol. 1, 54.

8 J. Chaloner, *A Short Treatise of the Isle of Man*, 1653–66, Manx Society, vol. 10 (1864), 55; T. Denton, *A Description of the Isle of Man and its Customes* (1681), G.W. Wood (ed), *YLM*, 3 (1898–99), 495.

9 J.D. Marshall (ed), *The Autobiography of William Stout of Lancaster, 1665–1752*, Chetham Society, third ser., 14 (1967), 86.

Fig. 1.2 *Estimates of the population of the Isle of Man, 1405–c.1692 and the ecclesiastical 'census' of 1726.*

Year	Total
1405–1660	c. 12,000 on average
c.1550?	1,300 families
c.1670	10,464
1687-8	1,700+ families
c.1692	16,000
1705	more than 20,000
1726	14,426

Sources: 1405–1660: Moore, *Isle of Man*, vol 1, 302; c.1550?: [W. Harrison in] R. Holinshed, *Chronicles*, i, 37; c.1670: Dickinson, *Lordship of Man*, 10; 1687–8: A.J. Winchester and M. Wane (eds.), *Thomas Denton. A Perambulation of Cumberland, 1687–1688, including descriptions of Westmorland, the Isle of Man and Ireland*, Surtees Society, ccvii/Cumberland and Westmorland Antiquarian and Archæological Society record series, xvi (2003), 495; c.1692: Sacheverell, *Account*, 15; 1705: MNH MS 06523 (DP), MD 401/1720/11/1; 1726: T. Quayle, *A General View of the Agriculture of the Isle of Man* (1812), Appendix H, no. I; Moore, *Isle of Man*, vol 1, 412.

Robert Mawdesley and the officers to Earl James in 1705, but this is probably no more than a very general estimate by those who drafted the document.[10]

The difficulty of using the available primary sources has not prevented historians from making their own estimates of the number of inhabitants of the Island during the Stanley period. More than a century ago, A.W. Moore came to the conclusion from the number of tenants recorded in the *Libri Assedationis* (the setting books or 'manorial roll') that between the first grant of the Island to the Stanleys in 1405 and the restoration of Earl Charles in 1660 the population 'probably averaged about 12,000.'[11] Unfortunately, it is not entirely clear how Moore arrived at this figure. More recently, a simple exercise was carried out to produce a figure for the total population of the Island in c.1670, using the burial registers from nine parishes, a notional figure derived from the mean number of burials in these parishes over a decade applied to parishes without registers and a multiplier employed by the seventeenth-century English demographer John Graunt to calculate living persons from the total of burials. This yielded

10 W. Sacheverell, *An Account of the Isle of Man* (c.1694), J.G. Cumming (ed), Manx Society, vol. 1 (1859), 15; LRO DDKe 84/79, Mr Sacheverells computacons about the Isle of Man (n.d., 1692?); MNH MS 06523 (DP), MD 401/1720/11/1.

11 Moore, *Isle of Man*, vol. 1, 302.

Fig. 1.3 *The 'number of souls' in the Isle of Man from the ecclesiastical 'census', 1726.*

Sheading	Parish/Town	Souls
Michael	Michael	643
	Ballaugh	806
	Jurby	483
Ayre	Andreas	967
	Bride	612
	Lezayre	1,309
Garff	Maughold	525
	Ramsey	460
	Lonan	547
	Onchan	370
	Douglas	810
Middle	Braddan	780
	Marown	499
	Santan	376
Rushen	Malew	890
	Castletown	785
	Bally Sally [Ballasalla]	360
	Arbory	661
	Rushen	813
Glenfaba	Patrick	745
	German	510
	Peeletown [Peel]	475
Total		14,426

Sources: T. Quayle, *A General View of the Agriculture of the Isle of Man* (1812), Appendix H, no. I; estimate calculated by Moore, *Isle of Man*, vol. 2, 646.

a total of 10,464 which, even allowing for some margin of error, may seem somewhat low in relation to the figure of 14,426 produced by Wilson's census a little more than fifty years later.[12]

12 J.R. Dickinson, *The Lordship of Man under the Stanleys: Government and Economy in the Isle of Man, 1580–1704* (Chetham Society, 3rd ser., 41, 1996), 10–11; Moore, *Isle of Man*, vol. 1, 412–13. The total of 499 for Marown in 1726 was calculated by Moore. Moore, *Isle of Man*, vol. 2, 646.

Applying some of the sophisticated techniques developed by historical demographers over the last sixty years to the limited sources available may help future researchers both to arrive at more plausible estimates of the Island's population before 1700 and to identify more accurately underlying trends, but for the present even the contemporary estimates and the tentative figures suggested above indicate that there was a definite upward movement in the number of inhabitants during the Stanley period as a whole. Even assuming that Moore's assessment of the population in the first two hundred and fifty years of the Stanley lordship is more than simple conjecture, it appears to admit of little significant change, though there must necessarily have been some fluctuations and definite trends over such a long timespan. The estimates of Harrison and Denton, while more than a century apart and drawn up in very different circumstances, nevertheless hint at sustained growth of the Island's population between perhaps the middle of the sixteenth century and the late seventeenth century, though clearly not on the scale experienced in England. The impact of any setbacks to this upward trend, for example in the form of epidemics, such as occurred with the outbreaks of smallpox in 1656, 1685 and 1704, appears to have been short-term and limited.[13] This steady, if unspectacular, growth seems to be confirmed by the evident pressure on property resources in the towns in the Island during this period which is revealed by the general upward trend in the number of rent-payers, who were not necessarily actual residents.

Sacheverell's figure of 16,000 inhabitants in c.1692 may well be purely speculative, though it is possible, of course, that the population of the Island was then actually declining, paralleling the fall in England in the same period, and only began a period of renewed and sustained growth in the eighteenth century.[14] In any event, there were clearly definite limits on the extent to which the Island's population could grow during this period. It has long been acknowledged that restricted agricultural output will inevitably determine the limits of population growth – in effect a form of Malthusian preventive check – and, according to Basil Quayle, writing in the last decade of the eighteenth century, it was only 'within these thirty years' that the value of landed estates had risen 'for want of a spirit of improvement, which circumstances have now changed.'

13 For the trends in English, Scottish and Irish population figures in this period and the methodologies developed for working with parish registers, see M.W. Flinn (ed), *Scottish Population History from the Seventeenth Century to the 1930s* (Cambridge, 1977); E.A. Wrigley and R.S. Schofield, *The Population History of England, 1541–1871* (1981, revised edn, 1989); R.A. Houston, *The Population History of Britain and Ireland, 1500–1750* (1992). MNH MS 09767 (PR), Malew parish registers: burials, 1656, 1685, 1704. Other parishes, such as German and Michael, also record burials of victims of smallpox in the latter years. On other epidemics, see Moore, *Isle of Man*, vol. 1, 411–12.

14 T. Quayle, *General View*, Appendix H, nos I–IV; Moore, *Isle of Man*, vol. 2, 646.

Fig. 1.4 *Rent-payers in the towns of the Isle of Man, 1506–1705.*

Year	Castletown	Douglas	Peel	Ramsey
1506	87	51	-	-
1511	82	57	-	2
1526	-	-	31(+15)[1]	-
1539	113	-	30(+15)[1]	-
1540	-	66	37+8(+5)[1]	8
1542	-	-	23(+15)[1]	-
1557	111	-	-	-
1559	-	-	28(+15)[1]	-
1561	-	53	-	12
1578	-	47	-	-
1600	160	-	-	19
1620	-	-	94(+25)[1]	-
1643	188	111	-	-
1651	-	-	-	33
1654	-	-	89(+25)[1]	-
1703	154	-	114(+5)[1]	80
1705	-	117	-	-

Sources: MNH MS 10057, Lib.Assed.; N.G. Crowe, *The Survey of Douglas*, vol. i: *The Quarterland and Cottage Rents of Douglas, c.1705* (Douglas 2001); N.G. Crowe, *The Survey of Douglas*, vol. ii: *Origins of an Island Port: Douglas before 1705* (forthcoming); J.R. Roscow, 'The development of sixteenth-century Castletown: studies from contemporary documents', *PIMNHAS*, x, 4 (1998), 317–323; J.R. Roscow, 'The development of Castletown, 1601 to 1703', *PIMNHAS*, xi, 1 (2000), 16–28; T. Talbot (ed.), *The Manorial Roll of the Isle of Man, 1511–15* (Oxford 1924); P.J. Davey and J.R. Roscow, *Rushen Abbey and the Dissolution of the Monasteries in the Isle of Man*, Isle of Man Natural History and Antiquarian Society, Monograph 1 ([Douglas] 2010), 150, 168; MNH MD401/1715/4; manxroots (http://www.manxroots.com/1540/GERMANROLL.htm), date accessed: 17 June 2009; Manx Note Book (http://www.isle-of-man.com/manxnotebook/towns), date accessed: 17 June 2009; C.K. Radcliffe, *Ramsey, 1600–1800* (Douglas 1986), 16, 144–6.

Note

[1] The figures for Peel represent primarily rent–payers with unique names paying Lord's rent only. The town also contained cottage and other rents on Abbey land and a small part of the bishop's barony. The mean number of Abbey rent–payers with unique names up to about the middle of the sixteenth century has been estimated as ten and from the later sixteenth century onwards for the rest of this period as twenty; the mean number of bishop's tenants was perhaps five throughout. Therefore to arrive at an overall, albeit notional, total of rent-payers for Peel, the figures in the table above should be increased by fifteen before c.1560 and by twenty-five thereafter, except in 1540 and 1703. In 1540 the actual number of Abbey rent-payers with unique names is stated. In 1540 and in 1703, where the number of Abbey rent-payers and that of Lord's rent-payers are combined, the respective totals above should be increased by five, the estimated mean number of rent-payers in the bishop's barony.

Fig. 1.5 *Cottage above the shore, Port Mooar: MNH PG/3125/140.*

The landed proprietors who had paid 'particular attention to agriculture' after c.1760 quite literally reaped the rewards in the form of increased output and profits and enabled the Island to support more readily the growing population of the later eighteenth century.[15]

The vast majority of the Manx population lived in houses or cottages scattered throughout the countryside rather than in villages or towns. Blundell recorded that in 'travailing from one town to another you discover their country houses, or rather hovels, almost at the end of every other acre of ground, solely seated and dispersed, yet scarce 2 flightshot distant the one from the other.'[16]

15 M. Overton, *Agricultural Revolution in England* (Cambridge, 1996), 198; B. Quayle, *A General View of the Agriculture of the Isle of Man* (London, 1794), 10; Moore, *Isle of Man*, vol. 2, 646. On the complexity of the relationship between growing towns and agricultural output, see E.A. Wrigley, 'Urban growth and agricultural change: England and the Continent in the early modern period', *Journal of Interdisciplinary History*, 15 (1985), 683–728.

16 Blundell, *History*, vol. 1, 54.

These 'hutts and sleight buildinges' were largely of the single-unit type, consisting of one room for both family and animals, with walls made from stone, sods or puddled clay mixed with chaff and a thatched roof of broom. There were also some two-unit houses, comprising a single-storey dwelling and conjoined barn, similar to the house-and-byre homestead type common in the north and west of England and in Wales, but overall 'very few have 2 rooms, have no upper rooms,' Blundell observed, 'nor any ceiling but the thatch itself.'[17] Richard Tyldesley subsequently noted that these houses had 'not as much as a doore of tymber for the generality to their houses, but a bundle or greate faggott of bryers, gorses, heath or such like stuffe reared upp in their doore[way]s ... which manner of doore is called in the Manish or Manske tounge a *ska*.' Tyldesley also remarked on the absence of chimneys on these houses, which had 'only a hole left in the roofe and thatch on the topp of the house aboute the midle therof, for a vent for the smoake and out of one of the doores.'[18]

In the opinion of Bishop Meyrick at the end of the sixteenth century, the wealthier sort who 'possess the larger farms' and resided on their estates, did 'approach ... in their refinement of manners' and otherwise emulate 'the Lancashire gentry in splendid living,' building houses in keeping with their status, such as those of the Christians at Milntown in Lezayre and the Stevensons at Balladoole in Arbory.[19] 'There is not one of these,' Blundell agreed, 'that beareth the title of a gentleman in the Isle of Man that doth pride it to live in any of the townes or villages, but have their mansion houses built upon their own lands in the country, and these for the major part have high handsome well-built houses after the English fashion.'

It would certainly seem that the compact two-storey house which was fashionable in England throughout the seventeenth century was adopted in the Island, although recent research suggests that those whom Blundell regarded as gentry were equally influenced by Scottish and continental European fashions in interior design. Even so, it seems that some of these houses retained thatched roofs long after slates came into fashion in the Island in the later seventeenth century.[20]

17 Blundell, *History*, vol. 1, 56–57; N.G. Crowe, 'Manx houses of the seventeenth century: a hidden heritage?', *PIMNHAS*, 12:1 1 (2008), 67–70; I.M. Killip, 'Mrs. Gilrea of the East Nappin', *JMM*, 6 (1957–65), plate 277; P. Smith, 'Rural building in Wales, 1640–1750', in M. Barley (ed), *The Buildings of the Countryside, 1500–1750* (Cambridge, 1990), 257–58.

18 NEWAF D/NA/905, Account of the Isle of Man, c.1665, 8, 18.

19 *Monumenta*, vol. 1, 98; W. Camden, *Britannia*, E. Gibson (ed) (London 1695), 1051; Crowe, 'Manx houses', 72, 75, 77, 83; N.G. Crowe, 'Architectural Development of Milntown, Lezayre' (unpublished research papers); MNH MS 10216 (EW) 6, Inventory of Richard Stevenson of Balladoole, 1623.

20 Blundell, *History*, vol. 1, 55, 69; Crowe, 'Manx houses', 72–73, 75–76, 90.

Fig. 1.6 *Knockaloe Beg (two-storey country farmhouse): Photo Charles Guard.*

Blundell was not entirely accurate in suggesting that those who aspired to genteel status only built their houses in the countryside, for there were at least some merchants resident in the Island's four towns who grew comparatively wealthy from overseas trade, particularly from the later seventeenth century onwards, and invested some of their profits in raising substantial houses in the growing settlements. These houses were few in number, but were clearly impressive, such as the Murrey house in the later Duke Street in Douglas, which was extended considerably by David Murrey, the son of the merchant responsible for the initial building, about the time of the Restoration, and the Balcony House or 'Murrey's New Building' in Church Street (Malew Street) in Castletown, built by David Murrey and completed after his death in 1677 by his widow, Katherine, and her second husband, Nicholas Williams.[21] The lord's officers also resided in the towns, chiefly Castletown, the administrative centre of the Island, and not surprisingly some lived in houses commensurate

21 Crowe, 'Manx houses', 75, 89–91; MNH MS 09767 (PR), Malew parish registers: burials, 1678. Some articles of agreement for the building of houses do survive, such as that made between Mary, wife of Isaac Harrison, late of Dublin and then of Douglas and Ewan Kerruish of the same town, carpenter, in September 1719. This document provides information about the number and size of the rooms, the materials to be used and the type of windows which were to be fitted. MNH MS 10071 (Lib.Canc.), 1722, *inter* 34–37 [2].

Fig. 1.7 *Castletown, town and castle, from the west, c.1656: Daniel King, fol. 20r. © The British Library Board: BL, Add 27362, fol. 20r.*

with their position, the house occupied by the receiver William Smyth between 1644 and at least 1648 adjacent to the later Balcony House, or 'Murrey's New Building,' in Church Street (Malew Street) being a particularly striking example.[22] Blundell identified a trend towards improving the appearance of houses in the towns, since 'example inviteth imitation,' with tiles or slates beginning to replace thatch and the addition of 'a garret unto their lofts, so as now they begin to see the commodity of building three stories high.'[23]

The less affluent townspeople lived in houses of a much more modest type, which had some significant differences from those found outwith the towns. Blundell described these houses as 'of one fashion, low built … of small stones and lime … and thatch'd,' but observed that the difference between them and those in the countryside was that 'these are 2 stories high, that is, they have an upper room above the lower, which the country houses for the most part have not; the lower rooms they call cellars, for they have none underground; their upper rooms they call lofts, and they are long and narrow.' He also claimed that 'Every towns' man there, tho' never so poor hath commonly 2, but some which are shopkeepers have 3 of these houses,' the latter having one for domestic needs, a second to serve as a shop, the loft being employed as a warehouse, and a third to be used as a storehouse for barrels, with the loft being let out

22 Crowe, 'Manx houses', 77.
23 Blundell, *History*, vol. 1, 69.

to accommodate strangers.[24] Although Daniel King's drawings of Castletown and Douglas indicate that most houses in these towns had chimney stacks at least by c.1650, 'the generall want of chimneys throughout this Isle, and more especially in Markett and other townes' occasioned an order by Governor Nicholas Sankey in October 1696 to erect chimneys to counter the 'smoke comeing out of the doores' which proved 'a very great Inconvenience both to the Inhabitants and passers by.'[25]

One individual who was characteristic of late sixteenth-century England yet apparently almost totally absent from both town and countryside in the Island was the sturdy vagabond. The homeless poor were a major concern to the Elizabethan authorities, but were never a concern for the earl of Derby's officers in the Isle of Man. The Island had a relatively small, if growing, population, the movement of which could, at least in theory, be regulated quite closely. This ensured that, alongside the efforts of the clergy, the other, largely informal methods of supporting those who required assistance, by doles to the poor paid out of the lord's income, by personal charitable donations, frequently in the form of a bequest, and through kinship networks, were mostly sufficient to meet any needs that arose.[26] Sacheverell attributed this partly to 'an universal plenty and cheapness,' which might be construed as a generally low, though adequate, standard of living, for 'as there are few that can be properly said to be rich, so neither are there many that can be said to be miserably poor.'[27] Any man bringing beggars or vagabonds into the Island risked the forfeit of his boat, according to customary law, though on one of the apparently few occasions when the law was tested, it is not known whether John Crellin and his partners lost their vessel after landing four female Irish beggars in early 1643.[28] In general, however, begging, either by natives or strangers, was an issue which rarely troubled the Lord's officers. Nevertheless, in June 1658, Governor Chaloner and the officers ordered that 'all fforraigne beggars of any other countrey that are not natives doe transport themselves out of the Isle by the next opportunetie' or face arrest; Manx beggars were to be relieved 'by their owne parishioners,'

24 Blundell, *History*, vol. 1, 68.

25 Dickinson, *Lordship of Man*, *inter* 189–91, 3; J.R. Roscow, 'The development of Castletown, 1601 to 1703', *PIMNHAS*, 11:1 (2000), fig. 4, 11; MNH MS 10071 (Lib. Scacc.), 1696, 66–67.

26 A.L. Beier, *Masterless Men. The Vagrancy Problem in England, 1560–1640* (London, 1985); MNH MS 10192, Book of allowance, Castle Rushen, 1624 ... Book of allowance, Castle Rushen, 1649: Rewards and pensions; MNH MS 10071 (Lib.Scacc.), 1687, 81; MNH MS 10216 (EW) 20, will of John Thompson, vicar of Rushen, 11 March 1664; MS 10216 (EW) 1699, will of Jane Harrison *alias* Caesar of Malew, 1 October 1699. For the important role of the Church and parish clergy in supporting the poor, see chapter 2, 'Religion and the Island church, 1405-1838'.

27 Sacheverell, *Account*, 7.

28 *Statutes*, vol. 1, 20; MNH MS 10071 (Lib.Scacc.), 1643, *inter* 14–15, 15.

being punished and returned to their native parish if found wandering.[29] Even though he apparently saw few in the Island who were in desperate straits and therefore presumably equally few vagrants, Sacheverell himself presided at a session of the Tynwald court in June 1692 at which directions were given for the erection of a public workhouse as part of the plan for the creation of a linen manufactory in the Island. The workhouse was designed for the punishment of 'not only all lazie persons, vagabonds and all publick beggars, but also all fornicators, Adulterers, Drunkards, common swearers, vicious, lewd and such like persons,' but it is not clear whether it was, in fact, ever established.[30]

While small by the standards of the adjacent kingdoms, the four towns of the Island clearly began to be transformed during the Stanley period, particularly in the years after 1700. Establishing the size of the population of these towns at any point before the nineteenth century censuses and identifying the periods during which the towns experienced particularly rapid growth or short-term declines will never be possible with any degree of certainty, but at least the 'censuses' conducted by the clergy in the eighteenth century do offer a clear indication of the continuing expansion of the towns after the mid-1720s. Before then, the evidence for the size of the towns is limited. In the mid-seventeenth century, Blundell was dismissive of the claims of these settlements to urban status, remarking that 'I suppose a cat's skin so extended wou'd treble encompass the greatest of these 4 towns, there being divers villages in England equalling and some surpassing the best of these in bulk,' but by the third decade of the eighteenth century, each had already grown into something rather more substantial and together the towns accounted for twenty per cent of the entire population.[31]

When Wilson drew up the 'census' of the number of souls in the Island in 1726, Douglas, then the largest of the four towns, had a population of 810. The town developed on the northern bank of the Douglas River, where the river flowed into a wide, crescent-shaped bay. Despite the presence of rocks in the bay, on the landward side of which 'a little small fort' was constructed, Douglas became the most important of the Island's ports and as a result the cottages and chambers of the town expanded northwards along the shore of the bay and up the rising ground behind the strand. In c.1540 it had perhaps twenty-one dwellings, but by the early 1640s, this number had risen to about one hundred. Camden stated that Douglas was the 'most populous town ... for it has the best harbour ... and is frequented by the French and other foreigners.'[32]

29 MNH MS 10071 (Lib.Scacc.), 1658, 67.

30 MNH MS 06523 (DP) MD 401/1719/8; Moore, *Isle of Man*, vol. 1, 408–09.

31 Blundell, *History*, vol. 1, 67; T. Quayle, *General View*, Appendix H, no. I.

32 N.G. Crowe, *The Survey of Douglas*, vol. 1: *The Quarterland and Cottage Rents of Douglas, c.1705* (Douglas, 2001), ix; N.G. Crowe, 'Origins of an Island Port: Douglas

Fig. 1.8 *Douglas, from the west, c.1656: Daniel King, fol. 26r. © The British Library Board: BL, Add 27362, fol. 26r.*

Writing about seventy years later, Blundell agreed about the town's importance as a port, though he considered that at that time Douglas had fewer inhabitants than Castletown.[33] In the late 1680s, Denton described the town as 'larger and much more populous' than Castletown and emphasized that it was 'a place of the greatest resort in the whole iland because the haven is commodious' and was 'a safe road for ships.'[34] By this time, the town had also assumed some administrative importance as the regular venue for the Garff sheading courts in the late spring and autumn. Bishop Wilson noted in about 1720 that Douglas was 'much the richest town, the best market, and most populous of any in the whole island' and that the recent increase in its overseas trade was mirrored in its growth. He lamented that 'anybody that sees it would wish that authority had interposed to have made the buildings and streets more regular.'[35] A survey of the town's population was carried out by local clergy in 1730, when it was reported that there were at least 825 residents, as well as seventy-eight lodgers and strangers, in 213 households. This survey provides the

before 1705' (unpublished research papers, n.d., deposited with MNH); MNH MS 10057 (Lib.Assed.); Camden, *Britannia*, Gibson (ed), 1051.

33 Blundell, *History*, vol. 1, 75.

34 Denton, *Description*, 500–01. Denton's account is clearly influenced by Camden.

35 T. Wilson, 'History of the Isle of Man', in W. Harrison (ed), *The Old Historians of the Isle of Man*, Manx Society, 18 (1871), 102. The form of the town can be seen on the map in Crowe, *Survey of Douglas*, vol. 1, 2.

first information about the number of individuals in households in the town, indicating that the mean size, excluding transients, was then 3.9 persons.[36]

The second largest town in Wilson's census was Castletown, the administrative centre of the south side of the Island, which could boast only 785 inhabitants in 1726. The town was located on a gravel bank overlying limestone at the tip of a peninsula of dry land stretching from Rushen Abbey to the sea, with bogs to the west and, even in the seventeenth century, the substantial waters of Ballalough to the north-west. The Silverburn River runs down the east side of this peninsula and forms a tidal harbour on the west of which an earlier, possibly twelfth-century, fortified tower evolved into the fortress of Castle Rushen, complete with curtain wall and glacis by the later sixteenth century.[37] Castletown grew up around the castle and market place, principally along Church Street (Malew Street) and West Street (Arbory Street), and expanded notably between the 1540s, when it comprised seventy-three houses and cottages, and the 1560s, when it had grown to about ninety-six dwellings. It also boasted a large number of chambers and other premises, with seventy-one buildings so described in c.1540, three more than Douglas at that time, though the number in Castletown declined thereafter.[38] Blundell acknowledged Castletown as 'the principal and court town' of the Island because not only did the earl of Derby take up residence in Castle Rushen 'when he pleaseth to be there,' but the sheading courts for Middle and Rushen and the sessions of the Island's court of criminal justice, the court of general gaol delivery, were also held in the castle. 'If any of the towns cou'd deserve the title,' Blundell observed, 'this town above the rest might merit to be called the metropolis of the island.'[39] Castletown was, however, a less significant port than Douglas, since it lacked a good harbour for trading vessels. Sacheverell was merely speaking the truth when he remarked that Castletown had 'a poor creek (where small ships sometimes venture in)' and even when they did, any passengers found it, as Denton complained, 'very troublesome landing in regard of rocks of rough, uneaven limestones.'

36 The mean houseful size was 4.27 persons. The list of 1730 is, however, defective in part in the column enumerating 'lodgers and strangers.' MNH MS 09888 (PR), (DG ma/pa 1), St Matthew's parish registers, 1730; Crowe, 'Origins of an Island Port'. On the problems of counting household size, see P. Laslett, 'Introduction: the history of the family', in P. Laslett and R. Wall (eds), *Household and Family in Past Time* (Cambridge, 1972), especially 23–40.

37 J.R. Roscow, 'The development of sixteenth-century Castletown: studies from contemporary documents', *PIMNHAS*, 10: 4 (1998), 301. Ballalough appears on the map of the Island by Speed (1610, after Durham, 1595). N. Nicholson and A. Hawkyard (eds), *The Counties of Britain. A Tudor Atlas by John Speed* (London, 1998), 210–11.

38 Roscow, 'Sixteenth-century Castletown', 306, 307 and fig. 4; MNH MS 10057 (Lib. Assed.).

39 Blundell, *History*, vol. 1, 74–75.

Fig. 1.9 *Castletown, mouth of the Silverburn – 'The Face of the Burne', c.1656: Daniel King, fol. 44r. © The British Library Board: BL, Add 27362, fol. 44r.*

Nevertheless, he reported that 'Some gentry do frequently retire hither from Ireland,' though he claimed this was for 'privacy and parcimony,' whereas those that came in the late 1680s were, in fact, fleeing the Jacobite wars across the Irish Sea.[40] Although Douglas attracted some affluent incomers as a place of residence during the eighteenth century, Castletown continued to have a sizeable contingent of residents of English origin, as is evident from the clerical survey of the town in 1755–56, when the population had reached 888, with a mean household size of 3.78 persons, or 915, according to the Island-wide ecclesiastical census carried out in that year.[41]

Peel was the third largest of the Island's towns in the 1726 census, with a population of 475. The town was the administrative centre of the north side of the Island and stood on a wide, crescent-shaped bay at the southern end of which, where the River Neb flowed into the sea, was situated St. Patrick's Isle. This small island was the location of Peel Castle, the other principal fortress of

40 Sacheverell, *Account*, 16; Denton, *Description*, 498, 499, 501. Sacheverell claimed 'many thousands of Irish Protestants' had been hospitably received in the Island after 'these (1689) last devastations', in Ireland. Sacheverell, *Account*, 7.

41 D. Robertson, *A Tour Through the Isle of Man* (Newcastle upon Tyne, 1970), ch. 4; MNH MS 1770C, List of inhabitants of Castletown, 1751 [*recte* 1755–56]; T. Quayle, *General View*, Appendix H, no. II. In c.1756, the mean household size in Castletown, excluding transients, was 3.78 and the mean houseful size was 4.23 persons.

the lord of Man, which also encompassed the cathedral church of St German. Part of the town was Abbey land for which the early records have perished, but the surviving lord's setting books indicate that there may have been at least fifty-nine dwellings there by the mid-1590s and in 1607 there were forty-one cottage rents on the Abbey land in the town.[42] Known often as Holmtown before the eighteenth century, Peel was both a market and a court town, three separate sheading court sessions for Glenfaba, Michael and Ayre being held there twice each year.[43] The castle also housed the ecclesiastical prison in the crypt beneath the chancel of the cathedral, 'the common prison for all offenders within the whole Island,' as Blundell proclaimed it somewhat inaccurately.[44] Most of Peel's maritime trade was conducted with Ireland, for which it was well situated, but its harbour could not accommodate large vessels because the channel between the town and St. Patrick's Isle was very narrow and the sea was consequently 'too boisterous at this haven' to encourage regular traffic.[45]

The smallest of the Island's towns, according to the census of 1726, was Ramsey, which had a recorded population of 460 (fig. 1.3), although two years later it was claimed that 'about five hundred souls' lived there.[46] Perhaps surprisingly, in c.1650 Blundell stated that 'Ramsey hath always heretofore been accounted the 3d town of the Island, but,' he noted, 'it is at this day the least and poorest of them all.'[47] Ramsey developed on the treen of that name and on the Mooragh, especially to the south of the mouth of the Sulby River.[48] In 1511, there were only two tenants paying lord's rent in the treen, though the number in the town had increased to twelve by c.1560 and to nineteen by the end of the century (fig. 1.4). Ramsey continued to grow during the seventeenth century despite periodic inundations by the sea. Following one such instance, in 1630, the inhabitants petitioned Lord Strange's commissioners for assistance 'for the manteyninge yearly of a fence for the saffegard of the sayd towne' and thereafter boats coming to the fishing in Ramsey Bay brought two boat loads of stones apiece for the maintenance of a stone bulwark along the Mooragh. The fence did not, however, prevent further damage caused by storms or high tides, such as in January 1644, after which the townspeople requested that the whole Island aid them in raising a defence against the sea, 'for divers times we are overflowed by the sea to our great losses alreadie past and standeth in danger

42 MNH MS 10057 (Lib.Assed.); MNH MS 06523 (DP), MD 401/1715/4.

43 Blundell, *History*, vol. 1, 77; Chaloner, *Treatise*, 32.

44 D. Craine, 'The Dungeon of St. German's. Sidelights on Church Discipline, 1600–1800', *PIMNHAS*, 5:1 (1942–1956), 161, 163; Blundell, *History*, vol. 1, 93.

45 Dickinson, *Lordship of Man*, 310; Blundell, *History*, vol. 1, 92.

46 MNH MS 10071 (Lib.Scacc.), 1728, Petition of inhabitants of Ramsey to Thomas Horton, Governor, 13 March 1728.

47 Blundell, *History*, vol. 1, 76.

48 The treen is a land division. See Dickinson, *Lordship of Man*, 84.

and dayly feare of every springe tides when they doe raise.' The sea continued to cause problems for the town in 1659, 1660 and 1671, but while the fence required repairs throughout the period, the threat of flooding apparently did little to hinder the development of Ramsey or interfere for long with its modest, but fairly regular, overseas trade.[49]

Apart from the towns, there were several village settlements in the Island. The largest of these and the only one which was noticed separately in 1726 was Ballasalla, which then had a hundred fewer inhabitants than Ramsey. It had grown up to serve Rushen Abbey, but survived after the Reformation, when it had perhaps twenty-five dwellings, and continued to prosper (fig. 1.3).[50] Tracing the development of Port Erin and Port St. Mary is complicated by the fact that both grew up partly on Abbey land for which the early records are not extant, but it is clear that both were well established by the sixteenth century, with nine chambers possibly at Port St. Mary in 1506 and perhaps twenty shared between the two Rushen villages in 1540. Both were well enough established to be specified among the half dozen landing places officially sanctioned for overseas trade in 1692.[51] Laxey was a lesser port, included with Douglas in the waterbailiff's accounts on most occasions, but a settlement which in 1540 nevertheless comprised seven dwellings and sixteen chambers.[52]

THE LAND QUESTION

There has never been any doubt that the attempts to convert the customary form of Manx land tenure, the tenure by the straw, to leasehold were a source of friction between the earls of Derby as lords of Man and the inhabitants of the Isle of Man, especially after 1643. What is surprising, however, is that the circumstances in which this policy was introduced and pursued, and indeed in which it failed, have never been the subject of detailed examination. Even A.W. Moore, the most influential of Manx historians, only provided a comparatively

49 MNH MS 10071 (Lib.Scacc.), 1644, 36, *inter* 37–38 [1]; MNH MS 09862, Rolls Office, Charles, earl of Derby to the Deputy Governor and officers, 10 July 1669; MNH MS 09862, Rolls Office, Petition of the inhabitants of Ramsey to Governor Kenyon upon their being required to show their leases, [c.1692]; MNH MS 09862, Rolls Office, Disbursement of the ten pounds received out of the Lord's treasury by Captain Nicholas Christian and Captain Wattleworth to defend the town of Ramsey 'from the voyalence of the sea,' April 1721; C.K. Radcliffe, *Ramsey, 1600–1800* (Douglas, 1986), 26–27, 45, 55–56.

50 Crowe, 'Origins of an Island Port'.

51 MNH MS 06523 (DP) MD 401/1715/2; Crowe, 'Origins of an Island Port'; Dickinson, *Lordship of Man*, 243–44; MNH MD401/1719/9.

52 Dickinson, *Lordship of Man*, 224; Crowe, 'Origins of an Island Port'.

brief account of the events in a chapter in his *History of the Isle of Man*, without any substantive investigation of the background.[53] Although there is still much that is not known in detail, a good deal of research has been done on the finances, if not so much the estate policies, of the great noble families of England and the evolution of land tenures since Moore's *History* appeared and in the light of such work it is now possible to provide a more detailed context in which to view the events in the Island and to analyse the reasons for the introduction and for the ultimate failure of the Stanleys' policy of conversion of the customary tenure to leasehold.

The origins of the system of land tenure in the Isle of Man are obscure. It has been assumed on the basis of rather limited evidence that during the period of the Norse kingdom of Man and the Isles (1098–1265) the inhabitants of the Island held their lands by a form of allodial tenure.[54] This would effectively mean that they would have been freeholders. In 1423, the second Stanley lord of Man, Sir John Stanley II, was informed that under the rule of the kings of Man and the Isles, the Keys, including the sixteen drawn from the Island itself, were 'xxiiij free Houlders,' but it is clearly not possible to determine from this solitary reference the basis of this tenure or indeed the rights and duties which characterised it, nor is it possible to draw any conclusions about the tenure by which the rest of the inhabitants held their tenements in this period.[55] What is more certain, however, is that either after the Island had passed into the hands of the Scottish kings in 1265 or after it had finally become subject to the English Crown after 1333, a form of tenure was introduced which, as might be expected, shared many of the characteristics of specific types of land tenure in operation in parts of Scotland and England.[56] This should come as no surprise, since forms of tenure, while often in retrospect appearing to be fixed and immutable, evolved and changed, frequently as a result of initiatives from above.[57] Although local circumstances may have shaped its operation in detail, the terminology and practices of the system of land tenure in the Island at the time of the advent of the Stanleys in 1405 were broadly similar to those of which Sir John Stanley already had long experience in England.

53 Moore, *Isle of Man*, vol. 2, 871–909.

54 Moore, *Isle of Man*, vol. 1, 155; R.D. Farrant, *Mann. Its Land Tenure, Lord's Rent and Deemsters* (Oxford, 1937), 1–3, 6–11.

55 *Statutes*, vol. 1, 11.

56 This is disputed by Farrant, who asserts that the Scandinavian *odal* system persisted, a feature of this system being that no obligation to perform military service was imposed on the inhabitants. Farrant, *Mann*, 54–55. If that were ever the case, however, the situation had demonstrably changed by the Stanley period, by which time parish companies or militia on the same model as in England may have long been in existence. Moore, *Isle of Man*, vol. 1, 329–32.

57 C.M. Gray, *Copyhold, Equity and the Common Law* (Cambridge, Mass. 1963), 8; E. Kerridge, *Agrarian Problems in the Sixteenth Century and After* (London, 1969), 53.

It is not until the end of the fifteenth century that more tangible information about the system of land tenure becomes available. From the surviving evidence it appears that at this time the lord's lands were being let to tenants for specific terms of years, the terms being almost certainly renewable, with rents paid partly in money and partly in kind.[58] Since almost none of the lord's demesne was cultivated directly, the payments in kind were apparently in lieu of the labour services normally required for this purpose.[59] These were characteristics which this form of tenure in the Island shared with the range of customary tenures which had evolved from villein tenure in England in the later fourteenth and early fifteenth century and which would later be recognized as copyhold or tenure by copy of court roll, with the name of the tenant in the *Libri Assedationis* (setting books) constituting sufficient proof of his or her title.[60] More particularly, since tenements often remained in successive generations of the same family, the tenant was, in effect, a copyholder of inheritance with a fee simple interest and *de facto* 'owner' of the land. In the Island this tenure became known as tenure by the straw, the latter being the symbolic token used to convey seisin of a tenement when it was alienated or sold.[61]

The rents which the tenants paid were apparently not then fixed by custom, though in real terms in the later fifteenth century the tenants were probably benefiting from a decline in rents brought on by a generally stagnant economy. Although the rental incomes of some of the greater English landlords were recovering from the mid-fifteenth century slump, it is possible that Thomas, first earl of Derby, was still suffering from the effects and that these extended to the Isle of Man as well.[62] It seems 'verie lyke [he] had receyved informacon that yf order weare not taken his Rents would come to no chardge' and in the later fifteenth century the *Libri Assedationis* did often record a 'decrease or decay of rents [though] sometymes increase of rents,' leaving the earl with an uncertain rental income.[63] In 1490, Earl Thomas therefore appointed a commission,

58 NEWAF Nantlys MS D/NA/905, Account of the Isle of Man, c.1665, 1.

59 Moore, *Isle of Man*, vol. 2, 874–75.

60 Gray, *Copyhold*, 13; G.H. Tupling, *The Economic History of Rossendale*, Chetham Society, new ser., 86 (1927), 72.

61 Gray, *Copyhold*, 7; R.H. Britnell, *The Commercialisation of English Society, 1000–1500* (Cambridge, 1993), 221–22; Kerridge, *Agrarian Problems*, 37–38. The procedures for conveying freeholds and copyholds, such as lands held by the straw, were not dissimilar. Freeholds were almost always conveyed by livery of seisin, by physically handing over a stick or clod of earth to symbolize the transfer of possession. Copyholds were generally conveyed by the delivery of a similar token, a verge or wand in England and a straw in the Isle of Man. Gray, *Copyhold*, 15; Tupling, *Rossendale*, 74–75; R. Sherwood, *Manx Law Tenures* (Douglas, 1899), 37.

62 C. Dyer, *Standards of Living in the Middle Ages. Social Change in England, c.1200–1520* (Cambridge, 1989), 41–43.

63 NEWAF Nantlys MS D/NA/905, Account of the Isle of Man, c.1665, 1.

including the lieutenant of the Island, to set his lands for such rents as the commissioners thought fitting, but they were constrained to reduce the rents on all tenements, so that each treen, the principal unit into which cultivable land was divided, was henceforth yielding between 20s. and 30s. less each year than previously.[64] It may be that the reductions were made in an effort to retain tenants for, while it was against the law of the Island to depart without licence, there was in practice nothing to prevent a determined individual from leaving Manx shores in the expectation of better prospects abroad and replacement tenants were not necessarily easy to find. Furthermore, while some rents were raised thereafter, others declined in the interval before the next commission from the lord to review the setting of lands, in 1505. A few rents were even lost altogether, as in Jurby in 1499, where two rents, totalling 16s., disappeared for unexplained reasons.[65]

From the lord's point of view, this state of affairs was clearly far from ideal, since rental income from the Island, which in any case inevitably varied from year to year, appeared to be in decay. After the death of the first earl in 1504, a commission was soon despatched to the Island with the intention of bringing the lord's rent 'to some certaintie.' The commissioners were directed to raise rents and authorized to set the lands for terms of ten years, though in the event the term was generally limited to seven.[66] It was clearly the purpose of this commission to deal with the decay of the lord's rents, but not perhaps by establishing a distinct and novel form of land tenure. Writing in the mid-1660s, Richard Tyldesley, comptroller and clerk of the rolls, who had searched the existing archives for such information, stated that he did 'heare not of [the] Lord or Comissioners that came over to create or setle such a Tenure as is pretended, viz. a tenure by the Strawe.'[67] Nevertheless, it seems clear that from the beginning of the sixteenth century rents for specific tenements became more or less fixed and evolved into fixed customary rents. Tenants paid a certain annual rent and a single rent or benevolence at the succession of a new lord or at the end of a period of twenty-one years. The benevolence represented, in effect, the fine which was normally paid elsewhere on copyholds on the entry of a new tenant and consequently gave the form of tenure in the Island all the appearance of tenant right, the customary land tenure common in northern England. It is not clear whether the sums paid as benevolences in the Island were fixed or arbitrary, the latter being nevertheless governed by accepted rules which were not to be transgressed and therefore not truly at the will of the lord. The entry of the tenant's name on the court roll served as both proof of title

64 NEWAF Nantlys MS D/NA/905, c.1665, 1; Dickinson, *Lordship of Man*, 84–86
65 NEWAF Nantlys MS D/NA/905, c.1665, 1–2.
66 NEWAF Nantlys MS D/NA/905, c.1665, 2.
67 NEWAF Nantlys MS D/NA/905, c.1665, 2.

and of payment of the fine. In addition, tenants paid rent in kind, although the latter was finally commuted permanently to a money payment in 1601.[68]

The lord's income had thus to some extent been stabilised, with benefits consequently to both the lord and the tenants. The latter knew exactly how much rent and other dues were to be paid and the lord received a certain income, the more so as rental income was in effect guaranteed by the setting quest, a jury in each parish which assisted the governor and officers in ensuring that only able tenants entered upon vacant tenements, paying the rent themselves if the tenant defaulted.[69] This system worked reasonably well until the Island was affected by inflation in the century after c.1540. As prices rose, so the fixed rents in money payable on the lord's lands fell in value in real terms; by contrast, the rents paid in kind rose in value. In times of hardship, as in years following harvest failures, notably in the later 1590s, for example, payments in kind only increased the difficulties which the inhabitants of the Island had to endure.

Once the rents in kind had been converted into a money rent, so that the tenants paid a so-called double rent, the problem remained for the Stanleys that the only way in which the rental income of the Island could be increased significantly was through raising entry fines. This was something which could be done most effectively on leaseholds. Rents on copyholds were fixed *secundum consuetudinem manerii* (according to the custom of the manor) and, although some rents were nevertheless increased to a limited extent, income from this source could really only be increased when licences were granted for the enclosure of waste land or intacks. From about 1540 onwards, possibly stimulated by the rising population in the Island, there is evidence that the number of intacks rose significantly. In Lezayre, for example, there were only seven intacks in 1540; by 1554 that total had risen to sixty-four; and just over a decade later, in 1568, there were 160 intacks in the parish. The rents accruing to the lord from these enclosures increased from 5s.8d. in 1540 to £18 5s.7d. in 1568.[70] Intacking continued throughout the Island in the later sixteenth and early seventeenth centuries, but the increased amount of revenue which it could generate was still comparatively limited.[71] The replacement of

68 NEWAF Nantlys MS D/NA/905, c.1665, 2; Kerridge, *Agrarian Problems*, 38–39; R. Hoyle, 'An ancient and laudable custom: the definition and development of tenant right in north-western England in the sixteenth century', *Past and Present*, 116 (1987), 26; MNH MS 09862, Rolls Office, Act to confirm tenures, 1682, 2; MNH MS 06523 (DP) MD401/1716/4, Articles of agreement between the Crown and its officers and the inhabitants of the Isle of Man to commute customary payments in kind to a money rent, 3 August, 43 Eliz. (1601).

69 Dickinson, *Lordship of Man*, 71–72.

70 MNH MS 10057 (Lib.Assed.) GL 825, GL 826.

71 See, for example, MNH MS 10057 (Lib.Assed.) GL 838, A Book of new intacks and enclosures of ground pres[ented by] the great Inquests of the severall sheading[s] within the [Isle] of Manne viewed and Rents thereuppon imposed to be payd yearlie to his

customary tenure with leaseholds, however, offered the opportunity both for more regular and higher levels of income and was a policy widely adopted by landlords in England after 1540 until the outbreak of the civil wars a century later, not least by the Crown. Furthermore, there is evidence that the Stanleys were following the same strategy on their English and Welsh estates from at least the late sixteenth century onwards. Leases for three lives or twenty-one years were generally renewed on the death of the first life or after seven years, at which time the entry fine could be adjusted, by negotiation, though in practice this usually meant an increase in the amount paid.[72]

It is not clear when leases were first introduced into the Island, but it is evident from an examination of those remaining extant among the Derby papers that leases for three lives or twenty-one years were being made at least from about the middle of the sixteenth century onwards. According to a supposedly comprehensive record of all the leases of tenements in the Island made by the earls of Derby, which was drawn up in 1609, the earliest extant leases made during the Stanley lordship date from 1541,[73] but it is not until the 1560s that any significant number of leases was made (figure 1.10). Although the precise reason for the peak of leasing activity in this decade is less certain than in subsequent instances, it is surely no coincidence that all but one of the leases made in the 1560s date from the two years following the arrival of commissioners from Earl Edward. This commission, headed by Sir Richard Shireburne, undertook a rigorous examination of the Island's establishment and produced a book of orders which focused on eliminating waste and tightening up fiscal procedures.[74] It was no doubt part of a general review of Stanley estate administration prompted by the financial problems affecting Henry, Lord Strange, as a result of the spendthrift nature of his wife, Lady Margaret Clifford. Her

---

majesties use, and assessed in particuler uppon every severall parcell, by John Ireland, Esquier, governor of the sayd Isle under the kings Royall majestie And with the consent of thofficers in the sayd Isle in the year of our lord god 1609. Ireland's activities in August 1609 record a total of seventy-seven new intacks, the largest number of new enclosures being in Malew (thirteen) and Andreas (eleven).

72 R.H. Tawney, *The Agrarian Problem in the Sixteenth Century* (London, 1912), 301–02; Kerridge, *Agrarian Problems*, 53; E. Kerridge, 'The movement of rent, 1540–1640', *EcHR*, 2nd ser., 6 (1953), 20; R. Hoyle, 'The management of the estates of the earls of Derby, 1575–1640: some new sources', *Northern History*, 39 (2002), 25–36.

73 Knowsley Hall MS H/45, Leases in the Isle of Man: A breeffe Colleccon off all such leases within the Isle of Mann as have beene formerly graunted by anie of [the] Erles of Derby to thinhabitants thereof with theire several dates, what acres they doe contayne, what rentes are reserved, what estates are in beinge, and what is the true valuacon of every particuler rated by the oathes of an especiall Jurie Impanelled onlie for that service, who vewed each severall demyse and valued the same, Anno Domini 1609, unfoliated [11, 15].

74 *Statutes*, vol. 1, 31–37.

Fig. 1.10 *Leases made by, or on behalf of, the earls of Derby in the Isle of the Man, 1541–1630 (by decade).*

1541–1550	3
1551–1560	0
1561–1570	16
1571–1580	1
1581–1590	60
1591–1600	11[1]
1601–1610	216[1]
1611–1620	71
1621–1630	324
Not datable	32[2]
Total	734

Source: Knowsley Hall, MS H/45, 'Leases in the Isle of Man'

Notes

1 1595–1609: Isle of Man held directly by the Crown. Of the leases made in 1610, seventeen are of lands in more than one parish.

2 Twenty-seven leases dating from before c.1593 can not be dated; a further five have problematic dates: two from the governorship of Thomas Stanley (c.1552), two from the lordship of Earl Henry (1572–93) and one made by certain unnamed commissioners.

casual attitude to money led Strange to resort to moneylenders in the 1560s, borrowing at least £2,000 between 1562 and 1568, and even persuaded him to order the sale of estates to the value of £1,500 to pay off her creditors.[75] With inflation already affecting the returns from the estates in general, it is hardly surprising that efforts would be made to raise additional income by encouraging tenants, including the inhabitants of the Isle of Man, to take leases. This initial attempt, however, clearly had limited success and little further effort was made in this direction until two decades later.

The second peak of leasing activity in the sixteenth century came in the 1580s and was undoubtedly prompted by the continuing financial difficulties for the Stanleys. Under the governorship of Sir Richard Shireburne, a handful of leases was made in the Island in the early 1580s, but the financial burdens resulting from Earl Henry's two embassies, to France in 1585 and to Flanders in 1588,

75 B. Coward, *The Stanleys, Lords Stanley and Earls of Derby, 1395–1672: The Origins, Wealth and Power of a Landowning Family* (Chetham Society, 3rd ser., 30, 1983), 28–33.

led to renewed efforts in the middle of the decade, with nineteen leases being made in the latter year.[76] Of course, even the total for the decade is comparatively small, given the number of tenements in the Island, but it may well reflect the relative poverty of many of the inhabitants or simply a reluctance to take a lease. It does not, however, indicate the absence of an active land market in the Island, as is evident from frequent changes in the names of incumbent tenants on any particular property. This in itself makes it clear, as Nigel Crowe has suggested, that at least some tenants were able to build up reserves of capital which they could employ either to add to their existing property or to take out a lease.[77] The land market between tenants who alienated property without seeking a licence from the lord was sufficiently active to cause the deputy and Council to issue an order in October 1582 berating those who had ignored previous directions to desist from effectively making 'common Merchandize' of the lord's land. Thereafter, a licence was required for all such transactions to be valid and some took the opportunity to have the indentures of bargain and sale enrolled as a guarantee.[78]

The dispute over the succession to the Stanley estates following the death of Ferdinando, fifth earl of Derby, in 1594, brought leasing activity to an end for a time. Although the Island remained in the hands of the Crown until restored to Earl William and Countess Elizabeth in July 1609, it appears that it was included in the general survey of the Crown lands instituted by the lord treasurer, the earl of Dorset, five years before.[79] The Crown surveyor entrusted with the task of visiting the Island was Richard Hoper, who had previously performed a similar duty in Jersey and Guernsey between August and October in 1607.[80] Hoper's survey was undertaken in the following year and also seems to have formed the basis of the collection of leases compiled in 1609.[81]

At about the same time as the Isle of Man was returned to the Stanleys, Hoper, together with the recently appointed governor, John Ireland, was commissioned by Salisbury, then lord treasurer, and Suffolk, the lord chamberlain, to make

76 Coward, *The Stanleys*, 34; Knowsley Hall MS H/45, Leases in the Isle of Man: A breeffe Colleccon ... 1609, *passim*.

77 N.G. Crowe, 'The Moores of Ballakilley, Marown', *PIMNHAS*, 10:2 (1994), 35.

78 MNH MS 10071 (Lib.Scacc.) 1583, 5–6; *Statutes*, vol. 1, 58–59.

79 R. Hoyle, '"Vain projects": the Crown and its copyholders in the reign of James I', in J.A. Chartres and D. Hey (eds), *English Rural Society, 1500–1800* (Cambridge, 1990), 76–77.

80 *HMC Salisbury*, xix, 284.

81 MNH MS 06523 (DP) MD 401/1715/5; Knowsley Hall, MS H/45, Leases in the Isle of Man: A breeffe Colleccon ... 1609. As comprehensive as this collection claims to be, there is evidence that some leases were not recorded in its pages. Several leases omitted have to date been found enrolled in the Island's court books and it is very likely that there are others. MNH MS 10071 (Lib.Canc.), 1595, 8; MNH MS 10071 (Lib.Scacc.), 1603, 23–25, MNH MS 10071 (Lib.Scacc.),1604, 33.

leases in the Island for terms of nineteen years from Michaelmas in 1610.[82] The policy of enfranchising copyholders on Crown lands drafted by Dorset and continued by Salisbury was being applied to the Island as to other Crown estates.[83] Whether leasing would have been encouraged quite so vigorously in the Island in the absence of Crown stewardship between 1594 and 1609 remains to be seen, but this commission nevertheless marked something of a turning point. Hoper and Ireland oversaw the making of 216 leases in the summer of 1610 and this policy was continued when the Stanleys, in the person of Countess Elizabeth, Salisbury's niece, took effective charge of the Island shortly afterwards. The financial burdens resulting from the disputed succession to the Stanley estates demanded careful exploitation of all the family's assets and it was inevitable that this policy of raising income from the Island would be pursued in an effort to help restore and maintain the Stanley finances. Although not quite as successful as Hoper and Ireland, Countess Elizabeth's commissioner, Edward Rigby, and the officers negotiated a further seventy-one leases between 1611 and 1619 (Fig. 1.11).[84]

Some progress towards establishing leaseholds in the Island had been made by the time this phase of activity drew to a close, but the vast majority of the inhabitants continued to hold their property by the tenure of the straw. Renewed efforts to encourage tenants to take leases did not begin until after James, Lord Strange, assumed the lordship on the death of his mother in 1627. His main concern appears to have been that the lord was not receiving his dues as a result of unlicensed exchanges of land, a practice which had attracted the attention of the authorities in the later sixteenth century, as has been mentioned previously. Strange later urged his son to continue his plans to replace tenure by the straw 'Whereby Men thinke their Dwellings are their owne auntient Inheritances, and that [they may] passe the same to any, and dispose thereof without License of the Lord, but paying him a bare small Rent like unto a Fee-Farme in England:

82 Knowsley Hall MS H/45, Leases in the Isle of Man: A Booke containing the particular grants of leases for the terme of xix years from Michaelmas 1610, of lands and tenements within the said Isle to the several Persons heerafter mentioned: The Parishes in which the same lands do ly, their ancient Rents reserved, and fines to be paid for the same: Made by John Ireland, lieutenant of the Isle, and Richard Hoper, by vertue of a commission to them in that behalf directed by the Right Honourable Robert Earle of Salisbury Lord Treasurer of England and Thomas Earle of Suffolk Lord Chamberlaine of his Majesties houshould (interested in the state of the Isle by his Highnes letters Patents) bearing date the xth day of July 1610.

83 Hoyle, '"Vain projects"', 77–79.

84 Knowsley Hall MS H/45, Leases in the Isle of Man: The names of the Tenants, with the Fines, who compounded with Edward Rigby Esquire Commissioner and with the Officers of the Island, [1611–19].

Wherein they are much deceived.'[85] Shortly after Strange effectively became lord of Man, in September 1629, the leases made by Hoper and Ireland in 1610 determined. He was then presented with an opportunity to renew these leases and to create new ones and accordingly appointed Gabriel Houghton, Peter Winn and Alexander Rigby as his commissioners to undertake the task in addition to the more general supervisory duties normally entrusted to such officials. The overall total number of leases made with the inhabitants was only increased to 324, but most, if not all, of those contained a specific proviso preventing the lessee from demising the land to another party for any period longer than the term of the lease.[86]

The commissioners had less success in 1630 than had been expected, not least because some of those inhabitants who had at first seemed inclined to take a lease had, for one reason or another, withdrawn from the arrangement. In at least eight cases, leases of tenements were drawn up, but were ultimately not executed. It is difficult to determine any specific cause for this in any of the surviving cases on record, although in one instance in Patrick, possession of the land in question was in dispute and a court hearing was pending.[87] Perhaps more surprising is the fact that two of the unexecuted leases involved officers. Deemster Henry Ratcliffe of Gordon, Patrick, died not long after the lease he made with the commissioners, which may explain why the lease of Gordon was not executed,[88] but while Edward Fletcher, the receiver, may not have been in good health in 1630, there seems to be no particular reason for him to decline the lease he initially took for the Old or Lord's Close in the Lezayre Curraghs.[89] Strange was far from satisfied with the achievements of the commissioners, later remarking that as a result of his own inexperience in such matters they were 'ill chosen' and 'lavish to spend my Moneys' and blamed their lack of success on 'their merrie Times and bad Reckonings.'[90] His early efforts to ensure that lands were not alienated by tenants without licence also proved less successful than he had hoped, to the extent that

85 F.R. Raines (ed), 'James Stanley, Earl of Derby, History and Antiquities of the Isle of Man', in F.R. Raines (ed), *The Stanley Papers*, pt 3, vol. 3, Chetham Society, Old Series, vol. lxx (1867), 37.

86 Knowsley Hall MS H/45, Leases in the Isle of Man: A Breviate contayninge the particular Grauntes of leases for the terme of xxj yeares from the Annunciacon of the blessed virgin Marie [25 March] 1630 of lands and tenements within the said Isle ... ; MNH MS 10071 (Lib.Scacc.), 1630, 23, 24; MNH MS 10071 (Lib.Canc.), 1630, 13.

87 MNH MS 06523 (DP) MD 401/1725/10; Knowsley Hall H/45, Leases in the Isle of Man: A Breviate ... [25 March] 1630, f. 8r.

88 MNH MS 06523 (DP) MD 401/1725/9; Knowsley Hall H/45, Leases in the Isle of Man: A Breviate ... [25 March] 1630, f. 8v.

89 MNH MS 06523 (DP) MD 401/1725/12; Knowsley Hall H/45, Leases in the Isle of Man: A Breviate ... [25 March] 1630, f. 21v.

90 'History and Antiquities', 32, 34.

Strange complained in April 1638 that 'many of my Tennants in the Iland have sould, bargaynd or exchanged their tenancyes or some partes thereof without lycense of mee, or of you my officers.'[91]

The apparent failure to extend the leaseholds in the Island in 1630 raises questions as to why the commissioners did not make greater efforts to achieve Strange's desired goal. It could be argued that there was entrenched resistance because the lord had no right to make such tenurial changes by the laws of the Island, but since the laws recorded in writing were scarcely comprehensive when it came to matters of tenure and interpretation of law was largely a matter for the deemsters and Keys, all of whom had vested interests in maintaining the *status quo*, that was a defence which was unlikely to carry much weight with the Stanley lord of Man. Tenurial changes had clearly been made at some point since the end of the Norse kingdom of Man and the Isles and the plan of the Stanleys to convert the customary copyholds by which the inhabitants held their tenements to leaseholds was merely another such change. Besides, tenurial changes had occurred as recently as the beginning of the sixteenth century and the key tests of the legal validity of customary tenures was generally whether they had existed, unchanged, from beyond the memory of man. This was evidently not the case in this instance. Moreover, there seems not to have been a great deal of vocal opposition to the policy of conversion until some time following the wholesale introduction of leaseholds after 1643.

There is also the question of whether Strange, as lord of Man, was a good landlord or whether he was attempting to squeeze unreasonable fines out of the inhabitants of the Island. Strange himself advised his son to be 'alwayes good unto the People, and to all Tenants under you, Consideringe your selfe is but Tenant for Life unto the Lord of Life, who hath committed this Land and People to your Stewardship.'[92] Faced in Weeton and Trayles in Lancashire by tenants who had been advised not to accept leases, he confided to his officer, William Farrington, that they 'will enforce me to be a severe landlord, which I am loath to bee.'[93] Commendable as these sentiments may appear, there is some evidence to suggest that Strange, who became seventh earl of Derby in September 1642, had perhaps a less virtuous side as a landlord. The Parliamentarian steward of the former Stanley estate of West Derby claimed in 1647 that Earl James had raised the entry fines there, despite the fact that they were fixed by custom at one third of the annual rent.[94] Although unlikely to be popular with the tenants, this was, however, far from being evidence that the earl was an oppressive

91 MNH MS 10071 (Lib.Scacc.), 1638, 37.

92 'History and Antiquities', 40.

93 James, Lord Strange to William Farrington, 15 October 1637, F.R. Raines (ed), *The Stanley Papers*, pt ii, vol. iii, Chetham Society, lxvii (1867), ccclxxvi.

94 Colonel Edward Moore to William Lenthall, Speaker of the Commons, 24 April 1647. *HMC 10th Report, Appendix IV*, 81.

landlord. The dearth of extant information relating to the seventh earl's estates in Lancashire nevertheless makes it difficult to come to any general conclusions about his policy on fining in the county. An examination of the relationship between annual rents and entry fines payable to the Stanleys on leaseholds in the Isle of Man up to 1640 may therefore give some idea of the usual Stanley practice of setting the level of fines on their estates. Such an exercise indicates that in the period 1541–1609, the amount payable was generally in keeping with the mean total in England at the beginning of the sixteenth century, that is, the leaseholder paid the equivalent of one to two years' rent (figure 1.11).[95] By Elizabeth's reign, landlords in England were often imposing much heavier entry fines, frequently in the region of twenty times the annual rent.[96] Even the mean level of fines payable by tenants making leases in the Isle of Man in 1630 – more than seventy per cent of tenants paid less than ten times their annual rent – compares favourably with the fines imposed on leasehold tenants by other Lancashire gentry families between 1600 and the outbreak of the civil wars. The average fine as a multiple of the annual rent payable by tenants of the Hesketh of Rufford, for instance, was 27.5, but this appears to have been at the low end of the scale. Tenants of the Scarisbricks of Scarisbrick and the Chorleys of Chorley could expect to pay in the region of 41.8 and 44.8 times their annual rent respectively.[97]

The circumstances confronting Earl James in 1643 encouraged him to extend leaseholds in the Island still further. Having landed in the Island in July to deal with Edward Christian's insurrection and to regroup after the Royalist setbacks in Lancashire, the earl planned to build up the Island's defences and

95 B.G. Blackwood, 'The Lancashire cavaliers and their tenants', *THSLC*, 117 (1965), 23 and n. 17; P.J. Bowden, 'Agricultural prices, farm profits and rents, 1500–1640', in idem (ed), *Economic Change: Wages, Profits and Rents, 1500–1750* (Cambridge, 1990), 105–06.

96 Bowden, 'Agricultural prices, farm profits and rents', 106; J.C.K. Cornwall, *Wealth and Society in Early Sixteenth Century England* (London, 1988), 161. In 1600, the fines payable on leaseholds on the Abbey lands were said to be four times the annual rent, but in 1607 the majority of fines (59.6 per cent) were set at between five and ten times that amount. This was also true for the leases made on the Abbey lands in c.1611, when 75 per cent of fines fell within this range. MNH MS 00510 C, J. Quayle, *A Book of Precedents*, 78; MNH MS 06523 (DP) MD 401/1715/4; MNH MS10057 (Lib.Mon.), 243–44, 255a-b.

97 B.G. Blackwood, 'The economic state of the Lancashire gentry on the eve of the civil war', *Northern History*, 12 (1976), 61, table 3. Some landlords in England extracted even higher entry fines from their tenants. For example, in c.1612, one Yorkshire landlord, Sir Henry Saville of Methley, imposed increased fines on the copyholders there 'amounting to eighty- or a hundredfold more than the former rate.' J.T. Cliffe, *The Yorkshire Gentry. From the Reformation to the Civil War* (London, 1969), 38–40.

Fig. 1.11 *Mean rent multiplier on the Lord's leasehold lands in the Isle of Man, 1541–1630. (Fine = n x rent).*

Multiplier	1541–1609		1611–19		1630	
Not known	10	(8.1%)	–		4	(1.2%)
Less than 1 x	53	(43.0%)	1	(1.4%)	4	(1.2%)
1–1.9x	26	(21.1%)	3	(4.1%)	20	(6.2%)
2–2.9x	16	(13.0%)	5	(6.9%)	34	(10.5%)
3–3.9x	8	(6.5%)	4	(5.5%)	39	(12.0%)
4-4.9x	3	(2.4%)	3	(4.1%)	28	(8.6%)
5-9.9x	3	(2.4%)	24	(32.9%)	103	(31.8%)
10–14.9x	4	(3.25%)	10	(13.7%)	40	(12.3%)
15–19.9x	–		14	(19.2%)	14	(4.3%)
20–29.9x	–		6	(8.2%)	22	(6.8%)
30–39.9x	–		3	(4.1%)	7	(2.2%)
Over 40x	–		–		8	(2.5%)
Total	123		73		324	

Source: Knowsley Hall, MS H/45, 'Leases in the Isle of Man'.

prepare to rejoin the king's cause at the appropriate moment.[98] To fulfil those plans he needed money and requiring his tenants to take leases for three lives or twenty-one years was one way in which he tried to raise the necessary funds. A commission was issued on 10 December to the governor, John Greenhalgh, Deemster John Cannell, William Smyth, the receiver, and John Sharples, the comptroller, and so successful were these commissioners that about £3,000 in fines was raised over the next five years.[99] Earl James also attempted to raise money by a variety of other means, including 'loans' and compulsory assessments to buy weapons, all of which served to increase discontent with Stanley government of the Island, especially as at least some of these were implemented at the same time as harvests in the Island failed in the late 1640s.[100]

98 J.R. Dickinson, 'The earl of Derby and the Isle of Man, 1643–1651', *THSLC*, 141 (1991), 39–70.

99 *Statutes*, vol. 1, 100; NEWAF Nantlys MS, D/NA/905, Account of the Isle of Man, c.1665, 3.

100 Dickinson, 'Derby and the Isle of Man', 59–62. See also D.M. Powell, '"Considering the extraordinary dearth and scarcity of bread ..." Aspects of life on the Isle of Man in the years, 1647 to 1651' (MA thesis, University of Liverpool Centre for Manx Studies, 2001).

The additional financial burdens imposed in this decade were mostly of limited duration, but the continuing possibility of ever heavier entry fines payable on the renewal of leases meant that the inhabitants would doubtless be only too pleased to retain or revert to the customary tenure by which they had held their tenements in the past.

The policy of encouraging tenants to take leaseholds was continued after the restoration of the Stanleys in 1660, but, in spite of the advantages to the tenant, there was apparently still a reluctance to accept leases. The benefits were not inconsiderable. Leaseholders enjoyed freedom from customary burdens which they had previously rendered, such as the custom beef delivered from each quarterland every year to one of the castles, and purveyance, the lord's prerogative right to purchase goods from tenants at a low price, well below market value. Leaseholders were also freed from the payment of benevolences.[101] Once they had paid the entry fine and so long as they paid the annual rent, the benefit from the land belonged entirely to them. Nevertheless, there was a perceived degree of certainty about the rents and services payable under customary tenure which, combined with ingrained conservatism, made many tenants reluctant to take a lease. Inevitably, concerns over the heritability of land were a major influence, even though leases were almost always subject to automatic renewal, particularly when replacement tenants were hard to come by. The fact that entry fines were likely to rise unpredictably was, however, even more of a deterrent. If tenants could not pay the fine when it fell due, they risked the loss of their property. Deficient or worse harvests on occasion and the apparent failure of the herring fishery in the last quarter of the seventeenth century made it difficult for many tenants to pay their rent, never mind an entry fine which they might be bound to pay as often as every seven years.[102] It was the frequency with which such fines had to be paid which lay at the heart of the resistance to leaseholds.

In an effort to resolve the friction caused by the question of land tenure in the Island, legislation was proposed by the Keys in 1682 which would enable tenants to hold their tenements by the straw, if they so desired, on payment of a benevolence on the death of the lord and at the end of a period to be determined, possibly thirty-one years. Leasehold tenants were to enjoy the same rights of heirship as those holding by customary tenure and, crucially, the level of fines was to be fixed at two years' rent on quarterlands and four years' rent on mills, cottages and intacks.[103] William, ninth earl of Derby, rejected the proposals. Although, so far as fines were concerned, his position was not dramatically

101 R. Sherwood, *Manx Law Tenures* (Douglas, 1899), 8.
102 Dickinson, *Lordship of Man*, 102–05, 119–23.
103 MNH MS 09862, Rolls Office, Act to confirm tenures, 1682.

different from that of his opponents, Earl William was intransigent enough that it was not until after his death in 1702 that agreement was reached.[104]

The Act of Settlement passed in February 1704 was both an acknowledgement of the failure of the policy of converting customary copyholds to leaseholds and a clearer recognition of the tenant's estate of inheritance in his or her tenements. While undoubtedly and understandably regarded as a great benefit and relief for the inhabitants of the Island, the provisions of the Act also underlined the fact that the income from rents in the Island was of limited interest to the Stanleys. Leases were introduced in the Island by the Stanleys in the same way as on their estates in England and Wales in an effort to combat the effects of inflation and particularly the heavy burdens on the family's finances after 1580. Any enhancement in income that increases in entry fines in the Isle of Man produced was eventually considered too insignificant to offset the difficulties confronting the lord's officers in imposing and collecting them and the cost of sending commissioners to the Island periodically to check on the process. Encouraging signs that customs revenue offered a much less contentious means of raising income from the Island merely fuelled the Stanley determination to resolve the thorny question of land tenure and estates in the Island.

FARMING AND FISHERIES

In the Isle of Man, no less than in other maritime regions around the Irish Sea, the most important parts of the economy were agriculture and fisheries. Whether on their own smallholdings or working as labourers in the fields on quarterland farms, most of the inhabitants of the Island were engaged in the cultivation of crops and the care of livestock for a large part of the year. Corn and other crops were grown to feed the farmer's family and provide seed for the following year, with any surplus being sent to the nearest market to be sold. Cattle and sheep were kept wherever possible to provide milk and wool for use on the farm and further produce for sale. Farmers also reared poultry, pigs and other livestock for their own use and for market, though for most, meat was still something of a luxury. Between July and October in particular, during the annual herring fishery off the Manx coast, men spent some time fishing, the catches from which helped to supplement the diet of the majority of the population. Much depended on the success or failure of both the harvest and the fisheries, though to some extent the amount of grain harvested and the size of the catches landed lay outside the control of the inhabitants of the Island. If the yields from both were good, the inhabitants could expect to have enough to

104 MNH MS 00485 C, Plea of the landholders to the earl of Derby to retain the tenure of the straw [c.1701].

eat, but if either were deficient or worse, serious hardship might ensue unless imports could make up the shortfall. Writing in the late sixteenth century, Bishop Meyrick was clear that in good years the Island 'not only produces sufficient for its own consumption, but annually exports a great deal,' but pointed out that while 'it is rich in flocks, fish, and corn, [this was] more through the industry of man than on account of the kindliness of the soil.'[105]

Mixed farming with an emphasis on the rearing of livestock was probably the most common type of farming activity in the Island, although the exact balance between the growing of crops and the keeping of animals was determined by the size and location of the landholding. The Island was small enough for climatic differences to be more the result of elevation above sea level than any other single factor so that, once the limitations imposed by a temperate climate with a heavy annual rainfall and frequent strong winds were taken into account, it was the nature of the land and the soil which dictated the type of farming practised.[106] Consequently, sheep farming predominated on the thin soils of the upland and plateau areas, much of which was intack or common land beyond the Feldike, the boundary wall which marked the upper limit of intacking. These were also the areas which experienced the heaviest rainfall. Blundell was the first to note that sheep 'thrive best in this Island,' although he neglected to specify which breeds were kept, apart from an apparently small number of Loaghtan sheep. In general, though 'they are as fat and their flesh as well tasted as our mutton,' the sheep were 'not so great of body' as English sheep and their wool, though very good in quality, was 'not to be compared to our Cotswold or Leicester,' with the exception of the 'grayish coloured' wool or 'yellow tawny fleece' from the Loaghtan. Denton also found the sheep in the Island 'both smaller bodied then in England and less headed, more like unto Irish cattle.'[107] Cattle were grazed on parts of the plateaux and in the lowlands, on the 'most healthy [heathy] and gravelly ground' in the north of the Island which Blundell compared to 'the mountainous parts of Wales,' the meadow and pasture land in the south and where possible along the coast. The animals remained outside all year round and were not fed hay or other fodder but left to graze on grass and seaweed. Access to seaweed and 'sea tangle' was certainly of considerable benefit to the farmer, since cattle which habitually fed on such grazing were 'far fairer, bigger-bodyed, fatter and yield more milk than those of the inland.' For the most part, however, the cattle were 'little,

105 BL Cotton MS Julius F10, fols 124–25.

106 Dickinson, *Lordship of Man*, 79–80.

107 Blundell, *History*, vol. 1, 42–43; Denton, *Description*, 496. The land beyond the Feldike was part of the lord's forest in which, as in the lord's warrens in the north and south of the Island, only the lord had the right to hunt. All the game, including the puffins (Manx shearwaters), on the Calf of Man was also protected by law. Dickinson, *Lordship of Man*, 21 n.39 and 40; *Statutes*, vol. 1, 140.

low, small, and poor (but not in any extremity), resembling those of Ireland, but nothing near our breed of England.'[108] Pigs were also kept, not least in and adjacent to the towns, in which they were wont to be found straying, as in Douglas in 1696, when five men were presented by the *moar* of Onchan for 'not keeping their swine up in swine corts, but letting them (in a contemptious manner) ramble up and down the towne.' Blundell considered 'the hoggs of an ordinary grandure,' but it was Sacheverell who not only remarked on the large number of pigs in the Island, but was also the first to make reference to the native Manx pig, 'a small mountain kind called Purs, which are admirable meat.'[109] In addition, farmers kept goats and poultry of various sorts and, on the larger farms at least, a small number of horses. The Manx breed of horse Blundell described as 'low and little ... and withal frightfully poor,' although he readily admitted that 'In enduring labour and hardness they exceed others.'[110]

While sheep farming was the main activity in the uplands and cattle were reared on poorer land elsewhere, barley and oats were the principal grain crops grown on the more fertile soils of some parts of the plateaux and in the lowland regions. Wheat was also grown, but only in limited quantities in a few favoured areas because of the difficulties in producing good yields in the Manx climate. 'All parts of the Island, as well the north as the south, yieldeth store of all sorts of grain,' Blundell found, 'both barley, wheat, rye and oats (yet of the last the most), but not only of each satisfying the inhabitants' necessity, but also affording an overplus for exportation into other parts.' He was also impressed with the quality of the corn, esteeming it 'so purely good as that you shall not find, no, not in England, either better bread or better beer than is here commonly sold.'[111] Denton recorded that the most common variety of oats grown in the Island was white oats, which produced the heaviest grain and which was best for both bread and potage, 'in so much that most of the inhabitants eat onely oat bread.' This may have been the variety recognized by Richard Tyldesley as the 'excellent oates called plackett,' grown particularly on land where turf had previously been extracted on the north side.[112] Nevertheless, barley was also grown widely because of its versatility for use in bread, malt and animal feed. Three main varieties were grown in the seventeenth century, of which the two-rowed was the most productive on poorer land and

108 Blundell, *History*, vol. 1, 39, 40–41.

109 MNH MS 10071 (Lib.Scacc.), 1696, 69; Blundell, *History*, vol. 1, 45; Sacheverell, *Account*, 13.

110 Blundell, *History*, vol. 1, 41–42.

111 Dickinson, *Lordship of Man*, 84–87, 89; B. Quayle, *General View*, 30; Blundell, *History*, vol. 1, 39.

112 Denton, *Description*, 496; J. Thirsk, 'Farming techniques, 1500–1640', in J. Thirsk (ed), *Agricultural Change: Policy and Practice, 1500–1750* (Cambridge, 1990), 25; NEWAF Nantlys MS, D/NA/905, Account of the Isle of Man, c.1665, 8.

from which the Manx made 'their best mault and of it the strongest ale, not inferior to Milford ale.' Flax and hemp were also produced in considerable quantities and, by the late seventeenth century at least, some land was given over to the growing of legumes, such as peas and beans.[113]

Although Meyrick had informed Camden that at least in years when the harvest was good the Island could produce 'sufficient for its own consumption,' Manx agriculture faced problems which seriously limited its ability to increase productivity in the face of a rising population. These disadvantages, as Moore termed them, arose largely from entrenched farming practices. It has long been accepted that there were similarities between the system of cultivation in the Isle of Man and those in use in Ireland and the Hebrides. This is largely because of the similarities in shape between many quarterlands and the strips of land characteristic of both the Irish and Hebridean systems, which, it has been argued, involved the annual reallocation of holdings. There seems to be a good deal of doubt as to whether this annual redistribution actually took place or whether the strips were in fact allocated permanently, as was certainly later the case in the Island, but what is certain is that there were some features of the Manx system of agriculture which inhibited productivity.[114] The practice of erecting fences only for the duration of the summer growing season was one of the most significant of these disadvantages. It persisted into the later eighteenth century, despite the efforts of the lord's officers from the early years of the Stanley lordship to compel the tenants to keep their lands in severalty throughout the year and legislation increasing the size of the 'sod hedges' or fences to be raised to protect crops and prevent the straying of animals. Every spring, banks of earth and sometimes stones were raised to a height which was eventually set by law in 1691 at five and a half feet, with a trench one and a half feet deep and three feet in breadth; where trenches could not be made, fences were to be six feet in height. These banks were then thrown down after All Hallows (1 November) so that, as in Jurby, even as late as perhaps the 1760s, 'the greater part of the parish ... was an open common in the winter season.' Hedgerows and more permanent, stone walls only became features of the Manx landscape after the Act of Settlement.[115] In addition to wandering

113 Thirsk, 'Farming techniques', 24; B. Quayle, *General View*, 23; Dickinson, *Lordship of Man*, 91; Denton, *Description*, 496.

114 Moore, *Isle of Man*, vol. 1, 48–55, 2, 916–17; F.J. Shaw, *The Northern and Western Isles of Scotland* (Edinburgh, 1980), 88, 90–91; G. Whittington, 'Field systems of Scotland', in A.R.H. Baker and R.A. Butlin (eds), *Studies of Field Systems in the British Isles* (Cambridge, 1973), 537–42.

115 Moore, *Isle of Man*, vol. 2, 918–19; MNH MS 06676, J. Parr, *An Abridgement or Short Tract of the most usefull Lawes Actes and Ordinances conteyned in the Statute Book of the Isle of Man* (1679), 69; I.M. Killip, 'The development of the Manx nineteenth-century field pattern', in P.J. Davey (ed), *Man and Environment in the Isle of Man*, British Archaeological Reports: British series, 54 (1978), 401–02; Dickinson, *Lordship*

livestock, crops were also endangered by exposure to strong winds through the general lack of trees in the Island. Although trees were protected by law, there appears to have been little effort to plant more to improve the situation and trees remained comparatively few in number. Blundell remarked that he 'cou'd not observe one tree to be in any place but what grew in gardens.'[116]

Even though there was a growing population during this period, there appears to be little evidence of experiments either with new methods of farming or new crops to increase the yields from the land. Writing at the end of the eighteenth century, Basil Quayle admitted that the idea of rotating crops was 'little understood or practised, it being almost the universal custom to crop the lands after manuring, as long as they are able to bear corn.' This approach to cultivation was typical of the infield-outfield system common throughout north-western Europe in areas where good arable land was in short supply and which continued in use in the Isle of Man and Scotland into the eighteenth century.[117] The manuring of land continued to be carried out by a combination of folding animals on the land and, in the south of the Island at least, employing seaweed. The use of marl, of which there were large deposits in the north, was apparently only begun by the example of Governor John Greenhalgh in the 1640s 'for [the Manx people] now marle their arable ground with lime, which was never there put in practice before.'[118] Denton recorded that attempts had been made to grow the poor quality six-rowed barley or *bigg*, but it was not a success as it was 'a sort of grain which doth not like in this soyl.' One notable change was that, once marling had become popular, wheat-growing largely replaced the cultivation of rye; another was the popularity of the potato by the late eighteenth century.[119] It is difficult to determine how successful the cultivation of any crop in the Island actually was in the general absence of relevant information from sources such as probate inventories, though what little has so far come to light – the projected yield of plackett from Red Gap in Malew in 1639 – suggests that farmers might only expect a break-even harvest.[120]

---

of Man, 106–08; *Statutes*, vol. 1, 110, 151, 293, 302; MNH MS 10071 (Lib.Scacc.),1770, cited by A.W. Moore, 'The early land system of the Isle of Man', *Yn Lioar Manninagh*, 2 (1901), 44.

116 Moore, *Isle of Man*, vol. 2, 919–20; Dickinson, *Lordship of Man*, 80; *Statutes*, vol. 1, 82, 134; Blundell, *History*, vol. 1, 46–47.

117 B. Quayle, *General View*, 30; I.D. Whyte, *Agriculture and Society in Seventeenth-Century Scotland* (Edinburgh, 1979), 60.

118 Moore, *Isle of Many*, vol. 2, 921; T. Quayle, *General View*, 93; Blundell, *History*, vol. 1, 40.

119 Denton, *Description*, 496; Thirsk, 'Farming techniques', 24; B. Quayle, *General View*, 34, 35.

120 MNH MS 10216 (EW), 1639, Inventory of Sir Charles Gerrard, kt., 14 July 1639; Whyte, *Agriculture and Society*, 74–79; Dickinson, *Lordship of Man*, 92–105.

Agricultural productivity was also limited by the generally poor standard of livestock and a lack of capital to invest in new tools and improvements, such as drainage. As contemporary observers noted, the quality of the livestock in the Island, particularly the cattle and horses, was such that imported animals were necessary to raise the standard and there are indications that some of the larger farmers were already endeavouring to 'improve their breed' of the former by the late seventeenth century 'as likewise that of their horses, which are not yet arrived to any great perfection.'[121] Less progress had been made in providing farms with the tools and equipment necessary to boost productivity. At the end of the eighteenth century, Basil Quayle had to confess that until recently 'the instruments and geers used in agriculture were few in number, and badly constructed.' Although farming equipment, such as ploughbeams and scythes, had been imported since at least the sixteenth century, it seems that it was only by the early nineteenth century that tools imported from England and Scotland were becoming common.[122] One of the most fundamental improvements for cultivation was drainage, though this did not begin on any significant scale until the mid-seventeenth century, when the Great Enquest of Michael sheading met Governor Greenhalgh and the other officers to consider 'some convenient remedie and redresse for the drayninge of the waters from the corraghlands.' This led to the cutting of the Lhen trench, which was so successful that the adjacent lands, once regarded as of limited value for agriculture, soon became some of the more fertile parts of the Island. Elsewhere, however, there were still bodies of water which required draining, but this work was not undertaken until the second half of the eighteenth century.[123]

Together with agriculture, fishing, and in particular the herring fishery, was the foundation of the Manx economy throughout the Stanley period. 'The sea feedeth more of the Manksmen than of the soil,' wrote Blundell, and while the Irish Sea offered 'divers sorts of fish, [it provided] of no one sort so much as of herrings in their season.' Whether consumed fresh or salted, the herring was a major part of the diet of the Island's population. Fishermen took other varieties, such as salmon, cod, haddock and mackerel, but it was the herring fishery, which the ninth earl's secretary, Robert Roper, called 'the Gould Mine of that Place,' on which they relied to supply most of the Island's needs.[124] The importance of the fisheries to the Island had long been recognized and this was reflected by the interest taken in them by the authorities. The first documentary

121 Moore, *Isle of Man*, vol. 2, 917–18; Sacheverell, *Account*, 12–13.

122 B. Quayle, *General View*, 19; T. Quayle, *General View*, 36–41; Dickinson, *Lordship of Man*, 108–09.

123 MNH MS 10071 (Lib.Scacc.), 1648, 34; B. Quayle, *General View*, 29–30; Moore, *Isle of Man*, vol. 2, 922.

124 Blundell, *History*, vol. 1, 52; Sacheverell, *Account*, 14; BL Add MS 33589, fol. 238 r. Roper to James, Duke of Ormonde, 17 March 1674.

evidence of this, however, only dates from the end of the thirteenth century, when it was recorded that the Church claimed a tithe of all fish landed in the Island. The Lord of Man also claimed a proportion of each catch, as stated in one of the earliest customary laws set down in the early fifteenth century – one maze of 620 fish in every five – though this levy, known as the *castle mazes*, was, as its name suggests, used as provisions for the garrisons of Castle Rushen and Peel Castle rather than by the Stanley household. It was finally commuted to a money payment by at least the 1660s at the rate of 5s. for each maze.[125]

Though of much less importance than the sea fisheries, the Island's rivers provided an additional source of fish and of revenue for the lord. Leases were granted of the fishing in the Island's main rivers, of which the salmon fishery in the Douglas River was the most productive and bore the highest rent. In 1660, for example, Richard Joyner of Douglas agreed to pay a fine of 40s. for this fishery and an annual rent of 13s.4d., thus permitting him to issue licences to anybody wanting to catch salmon legally. In view of the temptation that such fisheries presented, it is not surprising that many people did not bother to obtain licences to fish in the rivers and that presentments for poaching were consequently not all that uncommon.[126]

Such was the importance of the herring fishery, both to the Island and to the lord, that it was carefully regulated. The earliest extant regulations date from June 1610, when the lieutenant or governor, John Ireland, and Keys issued orders specifying the burthen of the herring boats called 'Scowtes' as four tons. This was a requirement which was probably widely disregarded, since a century later herring boats were said to be about half that tonnage. The regulations also directed that all tenants 'shall have alwayes in Redines prepared for the Hearing Fishing eight Fathomes of Netts furnished with Corckes or Boyes.' Any farmer who lacked nets was given a month to obtain them or risk a fine at the court's discretion. Further orders, which may well have been merely a restatement of customary practice, covered the detailed organization of the fishery which began after proclamation at the Tynwald Court held annually in June. No fishing was allowed to take place before 16 July, although this date varied slightly in later years. There was no time limit set for the duration of the fishing season since, as it was acknowledged that 'the Herring Fishing is

125 A.W. Moore, *Sodor and Man,* SPCK Diocesan Histories (London, 1893), 65; *Statutes*, vol. 1, 5; NEWAF Nantlys MS, D/NA/905, Account of the Isle of Man, c.1665, 21; Dickinson, *Lordship of Man*, 110–11; MNH MS 10192, Book of Charge of the Isle of Man, 1665.

126 MNH MS 10071 (Lib.Scacc.), 1660, *inter* 82–84; Dickinson, *Lordship of Man*, 124–25; Quayle, *Book of Precedents*, 98; MNH MS 10071 (Lib.Scacc.), 1639, 9, 61; MNH MS 10071 (Lib.Scacc.), 1645, 96; MNH MS 10071 (Lib.Scacc.), 1655, *inter* 94–95 (8); MNH MS 10071 (Lib.Scacc.), 1661, 28; MNH MS 10071 (Lib.Scacc.), 1678, 43; MNH MS 10071 (Lib.Scacc.), 1681, 15; MNH MS 10071 (Lib.Scacc.), 1696, 44.

as great a Blessing as this poor Island receives,' it was considered advisable to exploit the presence of the herring shoals for as long as possible. In practice, it seems as though in the mid-seventeenth century the season closed at the end of September, but it appears to have been extended subsequently, as by c.1720, Bishop Wilson recorded that the 'time of fishing is between July and All-hallow's tide' (1 November). It was the duty of the water bailiff to assemble the boats, maintain order among the crews, see that no fishing took place on Sundays and oversee collection of the lord's quota. He was also to hold an Admiral Court every Saturday afternoon during the 'Herring Fishing Time' to 'reform all Wrongs committed through the Fleet.'[127] Close supervision was clearly necessary since irregularities in the fishery were not unusual, with fishermen attempting to avoid paying their full customs and sometimes neglecting the fishery altogether. On occasion, herring boats crossed the Irish Sea to fish in Scottish or Irish waters, though this was not always done without official licence. When fishermen engaging in this practice and endeavouring to evade customs payments did become a problem, as was clearly the case in the early 1680s, Governor Robert Heywood eventually issued orders in June 1687 that all those returning from such expeditions should pay customs as if they had fished in Manx waters.[128]

The regulations for the fishery prescribed the conduct and detailed the practices of the fishermen, but provide very little information about the number of boats and the size of the crews engaged in the actual business of fishing. The evidence for the size of the herring fleet, if it can be so called, is fragmentary before the later eighteenth century. The first surviving record of the number of Manx vessels indicates that there were 222 boats at the fishery in 1636, along with forty-eight from elsewhere in the British Isles. In April 1653, Isaac Birkenhead reported to the Council of State in London that 'at every herring fishing in the Isle of Man, which happens once every summer, the natives employ 400 boats.'[129] In 1672, it was reported that slightly fewer Manx crews had caught herring that year, when there were 'about 200 fishing botes in the Island.' Twenty-five years later there were only 142 boats at the fishery, which was estimated to be 'near three score boates less then [there] was eight or nine yeares agoe.'[130] Information about the number of men in these fishing vessels

127 MNH MS 10071 (Lib.Scacc.), 1610, 24; *Statutes*, vol. 1, 73, 74–6, 141; B.R.S. Megaw and E. Megaw, 'Early Manx fishing craft', *Mariner's Mirror*, 27 (1941), 93; MNH MS 10071 (Lib.Scacc.), 1687, 61; Dickinson, *Lordship of Man*, 112, 114–16.

128 *Statutes*, vol. 1, 34, 141; Dickinson, *Lordship of Man*, 111, 117–18, 120–24; MNH MS 10071 (Lib.Scacc.), 1677, 42–43; (Lib.Scacc.), 1688, 43; MNH MS 10058, Ingates and outgates, Book of Licences, 1578.

129 *CSPD*, *1652–53*, 271.

130 Megaw and Megaw, 'Early Manx fishing craft', 104; MNH MS 06523 (DP) MD401/1717/23; Dickinson, *Lordship of Man*, 112–14.

is equally scarce. In the mid-seventeenth century, Blundell stated that 'in every boat that goeth out to fish there be 4 fishermen,' though this number may not have included the owner of the boat, who may also have been the same person who supplied the nets. In his report to London about the size of the herring fleet in 1653, Birkenhead noted that the boats had crews of 'five to seven men in each, all made seamen.'[131] By the late eighteenth century, in Ballaugh at least, all the vessels involved in herring fishing were open boats, with twenty to twenty-four foot keels and 'navigated generally by 8 hands each boat.'[132]

Evidence about the size and fluctuations of the annual herring catch during the Stanley period is about as limited as that for other aspects of the fishery before the eighteenth century. Often the only indication of the success or failure of the enterprise before c.1700 comes from very occasional comments made by contemporaries or the response of the lord's officers to complaints about the scale of the impositions laid on the fishermen. In 1612, both natives and strangers 'refrayned to come to the late ffisshinge' because of the 'great Imposicon' incurred by payment of the 'customes heyringes' and consequently the rate was reduced 'during the tyme of this next heyring ffisshinge.' Payment of the castle mazes does not appear to have caused such difficulties thereafter, but there were other reasons for the fishery to fail, not least a limited number of fish in the shoals or even the non-appearance of the fish at the expected time, though such occurrences are not generally recorded. It was obviously particularly serious when the herring fishery was deficient or failed for several years at a time. In c.1650, Blundell recorded that 'of late years they have not taken half the quantity of herring which they used to take in former times,' although it is not clear to which specific years he was referring.[133] Few records of the herring custom payments before 1700 have so far come to light, but one such account has been discovered which reveals that in 1665 the lord received revenue for the equivalent of 890 mazes of herring. A detailed account of the fishery for 1697 reveals that the Manx herring boats landed 754 mazes during that year's season.[134] In general, however, the herring fishery seems to have been deficient or worse for much of the last quarter of the seventeenth century. Sacheverell recorded in the 1690s that

131 *CSPD, 1652–53*, 271.

132 Blundell, *History*, vol. 1, 85; 'Description of Ballaugh parish in the year 1774', Document 194, *JMM*, 4 (1938–40), 18; Dickinson, *Lordship of Man*, 114. Moore estimated the mean number of men in a crew in the late eighteenth century as seven. Moore, *Isle of Man*, vol. 2, 951, n. 1.

133 MNH MS 10071 (Lib.Scacc.), 1613, 49; *Statutes*, vol. 1, 79–80; Blundell, *History*, vol. 1, 87.

134 MNH MS 10192, Receipts and Disbursements, Book of Charge of the Isle of Man, 1665; MNH MS 10058, Book of the Custom of ingates and outgates, 1698; Dickinson, *Lordship of Man*, 119–21.

Fig. 1.12 *Herring customs revenue of the Isle of Man, 1705–55.*

Year	Total	Year	Total
1705	8	1731	38
1706	–	1732	53
1707	23	1733	53
1708	26	1734	44
1709	9	1735	58
1710	3	1736	66
1711	40	1737	60
1712	49	1738	72
1713	56	1739	84
1714	60	1740	90
1715	–	1741	95
1716	48	1742	119
1717	37	1743	129
1718	56	1744	98
1719	48	1745	119
1720	47	1746	117
1721	52	1747	115
1722	–	1748	109
1723	–	1749	112
1724	–	1750	112
1725	–	1751	112
1726	–	1752	96
1727	–	1753	117
1728	63	1754	157
1729	45	1755	170
1730	–		

Source: MNH MS 10058, Ingates and outgates, 1705–55 (gross totals, to the nearest pound)

Notes
1706, 1715, 1730: Missing accounts
1722–27: Customs at farm: no accounts

> neither in truth is there near the quantity of fish they had in former ages; for since their herring fails, (of which formerly they had such quantities that five hundred have been sold for a groat, and yet the fishery worth £3000 *per annum*) all other fish declines, for herring is the universal prey, so that this only want has reduced the country to great extremities.[135]

Although there may have been a degree of exaggeration in Sacheverell's estimate of the plenty and value of the fishery in previous years, his overall assessment appears to be borne out by the subsequent statement of Governor Robert Mawdesley and the rest of the officers in a petition sent to Earl James in 1705, when they reported that 'the Fishing about this Island (which was its chief subsistence) has fail'd us for near thirty years past.'[136] Information about the revenue from the herring customs is extant after 1705, but because there is some doubt about the way in which it was calculated at this time, it is difficult to use the data as a means for determining the herring catch in the first half of the eighteenth century. Nevertheless, on the assumption that there were no significant changes to rates during the period covered by these records, the totals from the water bailiff's accounts alone show clearly enough that the fishery was not prospering in the first decade of the century, enjoyed moderate, if variable, success thereafter until the end of the 1730s and then entered a phase when it maintained a steady, somewhat higher income for the lord for at least fifteen years.

OCCUPATIONS, MANUFACTURES AND MARKETS

Few people in a pre-industrialised economy had only a single occupation and in this respect the Isle of Man was no exception. Only a small percentage of the population, which included the lord's officers, the bishop, the archdeacon and perhaps a few members of the clergy, the wealthier landholders and merchants, enjoyed this privilege.[137] The vast majority of the inhabitants, however, could

135 Sacheverell, *Account*, 14.

136 MNH MS 06523 (DP) MD401/1720/11/1.

137 Although it is generally accepted that clerical incomes in the Island during this period were low, there is evidence that at least some offered perhaps at least enough to avoid the need to engage in a secondary occupation. In 1633, a report drawn up by Sir Hugh Cannell, vicar of Michael, on the state of the bishopric recorded that 'the revenewes of severall Churches are that 9 or 0 of them [are] not worth above 4 *li.* [£] *per annum* by reason the meanes of the Church is in the hands of laye men. The rest of the parishes, which are 7, one or two of them are worth 40 *li.* [£] *per annum*, the rest 20 *li.* [£] or 20 markes or thereabouts.' TNA SP 16/265/45. A decade or so later Blundell suggested that benefices provided sufficient income for all of the clergy, though he must surely have been misled when he claimed that '[y]e least yt I did hear of was of threescore

not survive without supplementing the income from their main occupation with a second or even a third source of money. The principal occupation for much of the year was almost always agriculture, although because caring for livestock was not generally labour-intensive and the growing and harvesting of corn and other crops was very much a seasonal activity, there was ample opportunity to engage in other work to bring in additional income. Fishing was another important occupation, though this, too, was probably only a seasonal activity for many. During the summer months, at least some men were involved in the herring fishery, with perhaps more than 1,300 fishermen among the crews of the fleet in 1636. While the numbers declined towards the end of the seventeenth century – possibly as few as about 570 were engaged in the fishery in 1697 – Moore estimated that, by the end of the eighteenth century, 2,500 men were employed in the herring fishing.[138] For the remainder of the year, the bulk of the population devoted their time either to general labouring work or to some form of manufacturing, which largely involved the processing of the Island's primary produce – corn, fish, wool and hides – mostly for domestic consumption, while some, particularly in the towns, also operated as alehouse keepers. Many town-dwellers pursued a trade, such as weaving, which accounted for a substantial part of their income. Some of the small number of craftsmen, such as carpenters and smiths, who were also based mainly in the towns, had to rely to a large extent on imports, since the Island could not supply the necessary raw materials which they needed. Generally less than a hundred men served in the lord's garrisons in the Island, yet even many of these officers and soldiers had one and sometimes two other occupations, perhaps following a trade and selling ale alongside their police duties.[139]

Manufacturing in the Island was conducted on a very modest scale. While many of a family's requirements for food and other necessities could be supplied by the tenants themselves, particularly on larger farms, those on smaller holdings and in the towns in particular relied to some extent on what they could purchase in the town markets, at the periodic fairs, or even at the

pounds *per annum*;' he also maintained that Earl James supplemented the stipends of the clergy with funds from all of the church revenues which the latter held after the mid-1640s. Blundell, *History*, vol. 2, 167. By contrast, after his arrival in the diocese in 1663, Bishop Barrow found 'their livings not amounting to five or six pounds *per annum*, which forced them to engage in all mechanical sources, even in keeping of ale-houses, to procure a livelihood.' Moore, *Sodor and Man*, 157.

138 Figures based on the number of vessels in these years as noted above and the size of the crews as estimated by Blundell – see pp. 46–47, 47 n. 132. Megaw and Megaw, 'Early Manx fishing craft', 104; Dickinson, *Lordship of Man*, 113–14; Blundell, *History*, vol. 1, 85; Moore, *Isle of Man*, vol. 2, 951.

139 Dickinson, *Lordship of Man*, 127–31, 135–36; D. Craine, *Manannan's Isle* (Douglas, 1955), 42–43; MNH MS 10192, Receipts and disbursements, Books of Allowance, Castle Rushen and Peel Castle, *passim*.

handful of retail shops maintained by a few of the Island's merchants. Whereas some of the items on sale were imported, many, if not most, were produced by craftsmen in the Island, though there were few enough of the latter and inevitably they produced only essential goods. Blundell found this to be the case in the mid-seventeenth century, when the Island had 'none but the poorest trades, and such as are meerly for necessity.' He claimed that each town had 'an ordinary taylor, shoemaker, a weaver, and a smith' and no more than one of each, emphasising the paucity of materials available to such craftsmen by suggesting that when a farmer needed to have his ploughshare repaired or a horseshoe replaced, he had to 'bring the coals to make the fire, and the iron to make the shoe or nail, as the smith is not provided with either.' There was also a suggestion that the smith exploited his position to 'exact extreamly for his labour, because he is assured you must make use of him.'[140] However unflattering a picture this account presents, there are some doubts about Blundell's claims about the number as well as the range of craftsmen working in the towns, even if he did correctly identify the most important trades. Court records alone reveal that in the 1640s and 1650s, Castletown, for example, had at least two tailors, as many as three shoemakers and three weavers, perhaps two masons, two blacksmiths and four glovers and furthermore, due to the presence of the castles, there were one or more slaters, glaziers, coopers, carpenters and joiners resident in both Castletown and Peel, who could, in addition, offer their services to the rest of the town. At different times in the seventeenth century, Douglas could also boast a pewterer and a goldsmith.[141] By contrast, contemporary observers paid scant attention to manufacturing activity outwith the towns, in spite of the fact that there were some craftsmen in each parish. Lists of licensed and unlicensed measures belonging to millers, tailors, weavers and those dealing in corn of all sorts dating from 1640 demonstrate clearly that the towns were by no means the only centres of economic activity. Between them, the three northern parishes of Andreas, Lezayre and Bride, for example, had no fewer than fifty-four weavers at that date and most parishes in the Island then had at least one tailor. Some parishes even had slightly more specialist craftsmen, such as Andreas, which in 1661 appears to have been the residence of John

140 Dickinson, *Lordship of Man*, 191–98; MNH MS 10216 (EW) 1, inventory of Jeffrey Galloway of Castletown, 1610; MNH MS 10216 (EW) 7, inventory of Michael Bowtch of Douglas, 1619; MNH MS 10057 (Lib.Assed.), inventory of John Black of Ramsey, 1665; MNH MS 10216 (EW) 20, inventory of John Ottiwell of Castletown, 1675; Blundell, *History*, vol. 1, 83.

141 Dickinson, *Lordship of Man*, 131, 139–42; FRO Nantlys MS D/NA/905, Account of the Isle of Man, c.1665, 4; MNH MS 09767 (PR18): Malew parish registers: baptisms, 1656.

Norris, hatmaker.[142] Although brewing activity tended to be concentrated in the towns, surviving alehouse licences reveal that it was certainly not absent from the countryside. As might well be expected, some trades were probably even based exclusively outside outside the towns, such as tanning and the fulling of cloth.[143]

Despite the apparently low level of manufacturing activity in the Island, efforts were made to ensure that all craftsmen and those engaged in any retail trade were properly regulated. In England in the sixteenth century the responsibility for regulating trades still belonged to the craft gilds in corporate towns, but in the Island, there were no such bodies and it was left to the Lord's Council to oversee the practices of all those engaged in 'any Arte, Mysterye or Manuell Occupation.' This regulatory responsibility seems to have included ensuring that apprentices underwent a sufficient period of training and although no record of such an order remains extant, it is likely that a term of apprenticeship similar in length to the seven years specified in England by law after 1563 and which was generally practised in Scottish burghs and elsewhere was also adopted in the Isle of Man. The authorities certainly took action when unqualified craftsmen were found trying to exploit or defraud potential customers, as in 1534, when several weavers were charged with not doing their work and cheating the lord's tenants and in 1595, when the Great Enquest of Glenfaba presented Finlo Quayle of Patrick for plying the trade of a weaver while 'not being sufficiently instructed in the sayd occupacon or mystery.'[144] The problem of craftsmen setting themselves up in business without completing an apprenticeship continued, not least because apprentices 'becoming thus to be Tradesmen, assumes [*sic*] an Exemption from being Servants,' that is, from yarding, the custom by which the lord's officers could select almost any labourer as a servant on half wages for a year, the only exceptions being those working for a member of the Keys or the clergy. In an attempt to address this issue, new regulations were introduced in 1665 which directed that an apprentice must serve a term of five years while learning his chosen trade or forfeit a bond in £10 if he failed to do so. This legislation also declared that a newly-qualified apprentice was to be prohibited from himself taking on apprentices or getting married for a year.[145] To conduct their trade, some qualified craftsmen – weavers, tailors and millers – were also required to have licensed measures, bearing the lord's arms, while alehouse

142 MNH MS 10071 (Lib.Scacc.), 1640, 79–98, 110–11; Dickinson, *Lordship of Man*, 133–34; MNH MS 10071 (Lib.Scacc.), 1661, 47.

143 Dickinson, *Lordship of Man*, 135–36, 143–44.

144 5 Eliz., c.4; M.G. Davies, *The Enforcement of English Apprenticeship, 1563–1642* (Cambridge, Mass. 1956), 10; I.F. Grant, *The Social and Economic Development of Scotland before 1603* (Edinburgh, 1930), 422; Quayle, *Book of Precedents*, 29; MNH MS 10071 (Lib.Plit.), 1595, 17.

145 *Statutes*, vol. 1, 50, 128–29; Moore, *Isle of Man*, vol. 1, 290–91; Craine, *Manannan's Isle*, 47–48.

keepers needed a licence to operate legally, but many flouted the law and were presented to the courts as a result. Having such a licence was no guarantee of fair dealing, however, as, for instance, the inhabitants of Castletown found when dealing with Robert Gelling, the miller at the 'wheele mill' near the town in 1655. Gelling was prosecuted for a list of offences, mostly fraud in delivering short measure after grinding the townspeople's corn.[146]

The wages of tradesmen and labourers were undoubtedly set and carefully monitored in the Isle of Man in the same way as in other countries, although there are no extant regulations concerning wage levels before the early seventeenth century. The number of people in the Island who relied solely on income from wages was small, but these were the very individuals who would have been most exposed to the effects of an increasing population and the concomitant rise in the prices of foodstuffs and raw materials. In such a situation, demands for higher wages were perfectly understandable. In October 1609, either to record and fix existing wage rates or to set maximum levels for servants, labourers and certain craftsmen for the future, Governor John Ireland, the officers and Keys issued a schedule of the wage rates to be paid. A comparison between these wage rates and those current in different parts of England at the same time suggests that Manx carpenters, joiners and masons received very similar wages to their counterparts in Lancashire at 4d. *per diem*, though 1d. less than tradesmen in those professions in Rutland. Slaters and thatchers in the Island were even paid at a slightly higher level than the winter rate in Wiltshire.[147] Inflationary pressures may have eased gradually during the seventeenth century, but no adjustments were made to the official wage levels in response to such developments. Nevertheless, there is evidence that by the 1660s higher rates were already being paid to some and not just to those retained by the lord. Agricultural labourers were demanding and apparently being paid at rates above those set in 1609, claiming that the old rates only applied to those former vagrants set to work as labourers by the jury for servants. Some were even said to have refused 'of late Yeares [to] hire for double the Wages.' This was a state of affairs to which many of the members of the Keys, often farmers of large estates themselves, strongly objected. Consequently, in September 1667, the maximum wages which could be paid to ploughmen, drivers and horsemen were set down, but in practice this was little more than a reiteration of the earlier schedule of rates, since there was only one relatively minor increase over the levels fixed nearly sixty years before. There was one further reasonably comprehensive statement of wage rates in the Island during the Stanley period,

146 Dickinson, *Lordship of Man*, 132–38, 148–55; MNH MS 10071 (Lib.Scacc.), 1655, 59–62, 64–65, 67–68.

147 MNH MS 10071(Lib.Scacc.), 1609, 69; *Statutes*, vol. 1, 70–71; Dickinson, *Lordship of Man*, 167–69. In both England and the Isle of Man meat and drink were supplied in addition to the money wage.

Fig. 1.13 *Wage rates in the Isle of Man in the seventeenth century.* (Daily rates unless stated.)

		1609	1667	1679	1691
Tailor	head tailor	4d.	-	-	4d.
	apprentice	-	-	-	2d.
Weaver	wool, per yard	0.5d.	-	-	0.5d
	kere or russett, 'Great Hundred Breadth,' per yard	-	-	-	0.75d.
	medley or mixed cloth, 'being five Hundred,' each hundred	0.25d.	-	-	1.25d.
	linen, per 'Great Hundred'	2d.	-	-	2d.
	per 'Great Hundred,' 'according to fineness or courseness of yarn	-	-	-	0.25d.
Walker or fuller	blanket cloth, 'Great Hundred'	0.5d.	-	-	0.5d.
	kere or russett, per yard	0.75.d.	-	-	0.75d
	medley or mixed cloth, per yard	1.5d.	-	-	1.5d.
	white cloth	-	-	-	1d.
Mason Carpenter Shipwright Hooper Slater Thatcher 'all other such Tradesmen or Handycraftmen'	(with meat and drink)	4d.	-	-	4d.
	(without meat and drink)	-	-	-	8d.
Smith	coulter, laying of, each	1d.	-	-	1d.
	coulter, making new, each	2d.	-	-	2d.
	suck, making new	2d.	-	-	2d.
	wing, making and laying, each	0.5d.	-	-	0.5d.
Labourers (gardeners, hedgers, reapers, corn- and haymakers)					
	(with meat and drink)	-	-	-	2d.
	(without meat and drink)	-	-	-	4d.
Ploughman		13s.4d. p.a.	15s.0d. p.a.	-	-
Driver		10s.0d. p.a.	10s.0d. p.a.	-	-
Horseman		8s.0d. p.a.	8s.0d. p.a.	-	-
Mower	(with meat and drink)	-	-	4d.	4d.
	(without meat and drink)	-	-	12d.	12d.
Maid servant		-	9s. p.a.	-	-
Household fisherman		-	13s.0d. p.a.	-	-

Source: *Statutes,* vol. 1, 70–71, 132–33, 137, 148.

in 1691, yet apart from the significant addition to the list of more specific types of agricultural labourers, this was effectively just another republication of the schedule drawn up in 1609.[148]

It was no doubt more than mere coincidence that the list of wage rates was reissued in 1691, since this was done at the beginning of a decade throughout which plans were being considered for the establishment or revitalization of manufacturing enterprises in the Island. If there was one man who gave the impetus to these projects it was William Sacheverell, who approached William, ninth earl of Derby, at about this time with an idea for the creation of a linen manufactory, the encouragement of similar projects and the establishment of a trading company, supported by the lord, to manage the Island's trade. The earl was clearly impressed enough with Sacheverell's plans to appoint him as one of the commissioners of the revenue in April 1692, deputy governor in the following month and to promote him to the office of governor in June 1693. The crux of Sacheverell's textile scheme was that every woman in the Island, 'without distinction of quality,' should spin some quantity of wool or flax, perhaps twenty pounds in weight, with prizes for the finest yarn and the largest amount spun. He aimed to stimulate the growth of crafts by advocating laws 'in favour of all Artisans' and by encouraging strangers to settle in the Island, granting them long leases on waste land properties at low rents to ensure that they stayed. Sacheverell had chosen his moment well, as the Island had in the past few years apparently suffered several poor harvests, the catch from the herring fishery during the same period had also been disappointing and his plan seemed to offer an opportunity to provide work and much-needed income for the inhabitants. Many of his proposals were adopted in an Act of Tynwald 'for setting up a Linnen manufacture' in June 1692, though not always without some modification. Only able-bodied women between fifteen and fifty were to spin sufficient linen yarn for twelve yards of cloth and though the incentive of prizes remained, the reward for the best yarn was set at 20s. rather than Sacheverell's inspired choice of a spinning wheel. Nevertheless, having secured the support he wanted, Sacheverell proceeded to contact John Scanfield, a non-conformist clothier, whom he hoped would supervise the project. Initial negotiations seemed to go well, but in the end it appears that Scanfield's demand for a house and four or five hundred acres of land for his own use proved to be the stumbling block which brought this stage of Sacheverell's plan to an end. Despite this setback, however, the linen manufactory did get under way before the end of the seventeenth century, though not perhaps quite in the form Sacheverell had intended.[149]

148 *Statutes*, vol. 1, 128–29, 132–33, 137, 148–49; Dickinson, *Lordship of Man*, 158 n. 95, 170–74.

149 Knowsley Hall H44C, Sacheverell's proposals to Lord Derby for erecting a Company for the Isle of Man, [1691?]; LRO DDKe 84/17, 73, 76, 78, 79; Sacheverell, *Account*,

Other manufacturing activity, particularly a revival of trades which had fallen dormant, was stimulated by Sacheverell's efforts, though much of this renewed interest was in enterprises which were not well established and appears in most cases to have been short-lived. Brickmaking, for example, had been undertaken in Malew, probably in 'The Brickfield' on Red Gap Farm, just outside Castletown, between c.1650 and c.1680, in spite of the unsuitability of local clays for the purpose and an absence of readily available coal. After his arrival in May 1692, Sacheverell supervised the construction of a kiln and the preparation of 100,000 bricks, which the comptroller, John Rowe, reported to Earl William in August had been 'burnt in the Ovens.' Production using both kilns and clamps continued at least until the end of that month, but the brickmaker, who had been brought to the Island, probably from England, then departed.[150] Although there are indications that the pottery he had promised to organize was still operating in 1700, it is not clear whether it survived for long afterwards. Soap-boiling and the construction of a brewhouse and malthouse were among the new enterprises which were planned in the 1690s, although it is by no means certain whether any of them prospered.[151]

One area in which considerable efforts were made to revive activity in the last decade of the seventeenth century was mining. The rights to the lead and iron mines in the Island had been a part of the grant to Sir John Stanley in 1406 but, with the exception of the grant to the bishop of the right to the mineral deposits on the episcopal estates in 1505, there is no record of any sustained interest in mine workings or successful exploitation of mineral deposits in the Island during the Stanley period before the seventeenth century. By this point, the mineral rights had clearly been revested in the Crown, since, in May 1627, Charles I granted full mineral rights in the Island to James, Lord Strange, as *de facto* lord of Man, but for twenty-one years only. Strange quickly endeavoured to secure a return on his interest by attempting to bring in skilled mining engineers to search for and exploit any mineral deposits. Contact was made with Daniel and Joseph Höchstetter, the German engineers working in Cumberland, but although they agreed to a seven-year lease of the rights in 1628, it appears that they abandoned the project after a preliminary survey.[152] At about the same time, Governor Edward Christian was said to have 'experimented' with the lead ore from 'Mine-hough' or Bradda Head in Rushen, perhaps because it

ix-x; *HMC Kenyon*, 269–70; MNH MS 06523 (DP) MD 401/1718/87/2, Ferdinando Calcott to Robert Roper, 12 January 1691, MD 401/1719/8; MD 401/1719/63; Dickinson, *Lordship of Man*, 176–82.

150 T.A. Bawden, L.S. Garrad, J.K. Qualtrough and J.W. Scatchard, *Industrial Archaeology of the Isle of Man* (Newton Abbot, 1972), 132; Dickinson, *Lordship of Man*, 144, 182–83.

151 MNH MS 06523 (DP) MD 401/1719/63.

152 MNH MS 06523 (DP) MD 401/1725/3.

was reputed 'to hold much Silver,' but there is little evidence that these deposits were worked seriously at all. Sacheverell reported that there were signs of other minerals at 'Mine-haugh,' including copper, but only limited operations seem to have been undertaken there before the early eighteenth century.[153] Attempts to interest speculators in investing in mining projects continued, but were not particularly successful, partly perhaps because those enterprises which did begin quickly came to an unprofitable end. Such was the fate of the project to work the copper mines in the Island undertaken by Middleton Shaw of Uttoxeter in April 1700; by February 1703, the twenty-one-year lease was a dead letter, Shaw 'being broke and having left the mines.'[154] In spite of this catalogue of failures, there were some working mines in the Island in the 1690s, the output of copper and lead amounting to about 163.25 tons in 1699 and the iron mines at Dhyrnane in Maughold producing 227.5 tons in the following year.[155] It was this productivity which seems to have convinced potential investors to continue to risk their capital. In 1708, John Murrey of Douglas leased all the lead and copper mines in the Island and built a smelthouse at Derbyhaven, but although he seems to have achieved a degree of success in the early years of his lease, apparently producing about 30–40 tons a year in total, it was not long before he, too, abandoned his project. In October 1713, to encourage the search for new deposits and at the instance of Earl James, Governor Charles Stanley issued a reward of 30s. for the discovery of new veins of lead and copper and offered preferential rates for those willing to undertake the workings, an inducement which was augmented by the earl himself in May 1714, when he raised the reward to 40s. A steward or overseer of the mines was also appointed to ensure that the lord's share of the ore was collected properly and to monitor the operation of the mines which continued to operate.[156]

Towards the end of the Stanley period, the outlook for mining seemed somewhat mixed, with the efforts to encourage investment achieving some initial success, only to be apparently undermined by financial problems and fluctuating output. In May 1723, a twenty-one-year lease of the lead and copper mines 'between Douglas and Peale Town' was negotiated with a group of investors, including Richard McGwire of Dublin, to whom the earl had leased the customs of the Island in 1722. The lessees undertook to invest £400 each year, but it seems that this arrangement, like so many previous mining

153 Chaloner, *Treatise*, 8; Sacheverell, *Account*, 14.
154 Dickinson, *Lordship of Man*, 186–88; MNH MS 06523 (DP) MD401/1720/6, William Ross to James, earl of Derby, 11 February 1703.
155 Dickinson, *Lordship of Man*, 187; Moore, *History*, vol. 2, 962.
156 Moore, *Isle of Man*, vol. 2, 960, 962; J.R. Bruce, 'John Murrey's Smelt-House, Derbyhaven', *JMM*, 6 (1957–65), 152- 54; MNH MS 10071 (Lib.Scacc.), 1713, 26, 27; MNH MS 10071 (Lib.Scacc.), 1714, 36, *inter* 36–37. A.W. Moore, *Notes and Documents from the Records of the Isle of Man* (Douglas, n.d.), 4–5.

projects, came to nothing, partly due perhaps to the difficulties McGwire had in maintaining his other commitments to the earl.[157] The limited productivity of the mines may also have caused sufficient uncertainty about future output to discourage speculators. The deputy governor, John Sandforth, reported to Earl James in 1724 that though 'the prospect I take to be the best [was] in copper oar, of which a reasonable quantity is weekly raised,' the returns from the lead mines in particular were not promising. 'The work for lead at Kirk Christ [Rushen] has been at a stand still all winter,' Sandforth lamented, 'but shortly it will be carryed on again.' It may be, however, that these workings did not continue much longer, since when the Company of Mine Adventurers of England surveyed the area in 1740, it was reported that it was so long since the mines at Bradda had been in use that it was not possible to discover the extent of the underground workings there. Sandforth also informed the earl that 'Foxdayle hath from the first been worked as vigorously as possible and with the least success' and feared that 'I shall be forced to give it up, for the longer we work it the worse it grows.' It was not until the nineteenth century that the fortunes of the Island's mines, particularly those at Foxdale and Laxey, were transformed.[158]

While some of the manufacturing activity which the authorities were attempting to stimulate at the end of the seventeenth century was directed primarily towards producing exports, most of the existing operations were focused on the domestic market and this, too, was closely regulated. This was obviously a necessity, since all but the largest farmers were to an extent dependent on the markets for their food and while some of the inhabitants' clothing and even the *carranes* (shoes made from salted hide) may have been produced at home, the markets provided a much-needed alternative source for the purchase of essential items as well as offering the opportunity to buy imported goods. Each of the four towns had a market which was probably held twice a week, on Wednesday and Saturday, as well as two or three annual fairs. At Douglas, for instance, three fairs were held each year within a month – on 28 April, 3 May and 24 May; Ramsey also had three fairs, on 24 August, 28 September and 15 November; the other towns had only two each: at Castletown fairs were held on 3 May and 15 October and at Peel on 17 March and 13 July. Fairs also took place in each parish at least once a year – the patronal fair on the parish saint's day – so that most people did not have to travel too far to purchase necessities as well as perhaps the occasional frivolity. None of the fairs appears to have

157 MNH MS 06523 (DP) MD 401/1726/12, MD 401/1726/14, MD 401/1726/16; J.R. Dickinson, 'The overseas trade of the Isle of Man, 1576–1755', *THSLC*, 154 (2005), 28.

158 Moore, *Notes and Documents*, 5; Moore, *Isle of Man*, vol. 2, 964–68; Bawden, *et al.*, *Industrial Archaeology of the Isle of Man*, 52.

specialized in particular commodities.[159] Although there were no restrictions on attending markets and fairs, there were strict regulations on where goods could be sold, at least in certain circumstances. It is not known when such orders were first issued, but they were first recorded in June 1594 and reissued in October 1595, perhaps in the wake of poor harvests in each of the preceding years, and required the inhabitants of specific parishes to bring their goods to the market in a prescribed town. It seems that for the purposes of supplying the markets, the Island was divided into four quarters, each centred on one of the towns, with penalties for those who failed to comply. The parishioners of Rushen, Arbory, Malew, Santon and Marown, for example, were directed to deliver their goods to Castletown market or face imprisonment and a fine unless there were mitigating circumstances.[160] The comptroller was the officer responsible for supervision of the markets and fairs, but in the towns, it was the Captain of the Town who actually exercised the office as deputy clerk of the market. It was his task to nominate a market jury of two or four residents who served for a year. These were the individuals who had to make sure that all transactions were carried out after the market bell had been rung, to see that only weights and measures carrying an official seal were used by vendors and to examine merchandise brought for sale to ensure that it was of marketable quality. The jurors also had the important duty of checking the quality and prices of bread and ale, both staples of the inhabitants' diet. They were further charged with the associated task of preventing forestalling and regrating – the buying up of goods away from the market and doing so with the intention of selling later at a profit. Outside the towns the duties of the market jurors were assumed by the Great Enquests, the coroners and their parish deputies, the lockmen, although it appears that at least on one occasion, in 1569, four men were appointed in each sheading specifically to investigate the problem of selling away from the open markets.[161] Presentments for market offences seem to have been few and far between, but were taken no less seriously for all that, especially if the accused was one of those responsible for enforcing the market regulations. Such a case occurred in July 1609, when Edward Fletcher of Ballafletcher in Braddan, one of the Great Enquest of Middle and very likely the same man who went on to become receiver of the Island in 1616, was presented by his colleagues because

159 Dickinson, *Lordship of Man*, 192–95; Moore, *Isle of Man*, vol. 1, 315; B. Quayle, *General View*, 24; MNH MS 10071 (Lib.Scacc.), 1587, 25; MNH MS 10071 (Lib.Plit.), 1587, 69; MNH MS 10071 (Lib.Scacc.), 1648, *inter* 76–77 [2]; J.J. Kneen, 'Manx fairs and festivals', *PIMNHAS*, 3:1 (1927–32), 59–80.

160 Statutes, vol. 1, 65–66; MNH MS 10071 (Lib.Canc.), 1595, 17; Dickinson, *Lordship of Man*, 151 n.68, 198–99; MNH MS 10071 (Lib.Scacc.), 1653, 4.

161 Dickinson, *Lordship of Man*, 201–08; Quayle, *Book of Precedents*, 41.

he 'did contrarie to thorders provided for observance of the markett sell certen oxen at his house and served not the markett.'[162]

MARITIME TRADE AND SMUGGLING

In years when harvests were good and the herring were abundant, the Island was probably able to meet its requirements for food, but when the harvest was deficient or worse or the herring fishery failed, then the shortfall in foodstuffs could only be supplied by reliance on imports. Trade with the countries around the Irish Sea was also the only way in which raw materials, such as timber, iron and coal, and many manufactured goods which were not produced in the Island could be obtained. Clothing and shoes were imported to supplement domestic production, farming tools and equipment in limited quantities were brought in for use on Manx farms and an increasingly diverse range of luxury items was introduced to meet the small but growing demand among the more affluent farmers and merchants and the lord's officers. Until the late seventeenth century, the overseas trade of the Isle of Man was, however, conducted on a fairly modest scale, as is revealed by the surviving water bailiff's accounts, but it was clear to James, Lord Strange, several decades earlier that an expansion of maritime commerce would be of great potential benefit, both to the Island and to the lord. 'This Isle will never flourish until some Trading be,' he declared, suggesting that he himself would invest money to encourage such a development and claiming that 'I will rather sell Land in England, than misse so excellent a Designe.'[163] In the event, the Island's overseas trade was transformed towards the end of the seventeenth century, but this was as a result of changing external circumstances rather than any particular project inspired by the Stanleys to stimulate trade.

The earliest extant water bailiff's accounts show that in the late sixteenth century the export trade of the Island was based on primary products. Livestock, particularly cattle, and livestock products, such as skins, tallow and wool, were the most important commodities in this trade and were shipped to all the countries of the Irish Sea littoral, but especially to England. The ports of north-west England were the principal destination of these shipments, not only because of the link between the Island and the region where the Stanleys had their power base, but also because of the development of manufacturing in south Lancashire, particularly from the late seventeenth century onwards. The growing towns in the south of the county were an expanding market for Manx products as well as being the source of many of the manufactured goods for which there was an increasing demand in the Island.

162 MNH MS 10071 (Lib.Scacc.), 1609, 69; Dickinson, *Lordship of Man*, 359.
163 MNH MS 10058, Ingates and outgates, 1576–1755; 'History and Antiquities', 17–18.

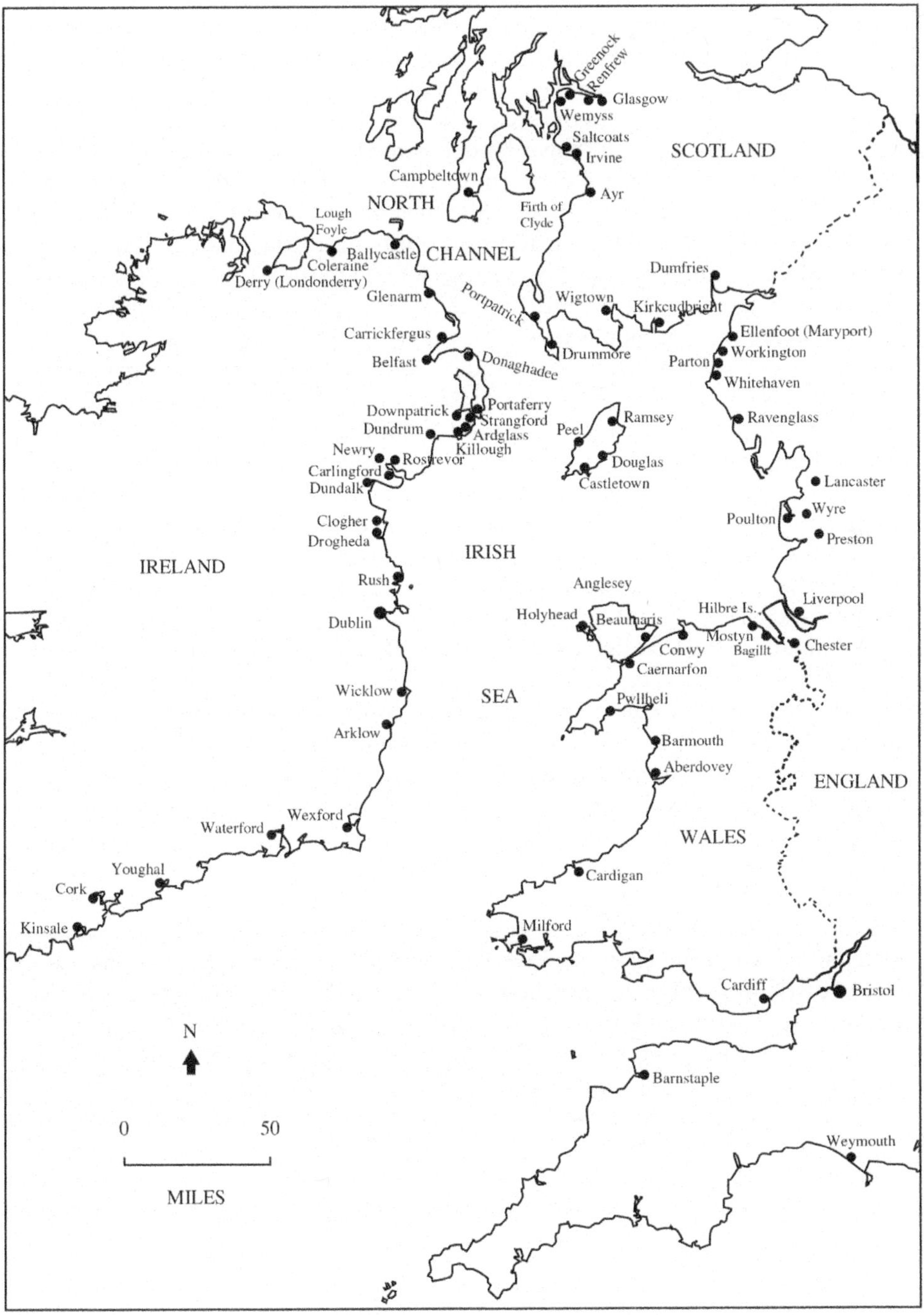

Fig. 1.14 *Maritime trade: ports trading with the Isle of Man, 1576–1736.*

It is likely that shipments of cattle, whether as quick beasts or as carcases, often with the associated tallow, had been a significant part of the Island's export trade since at least medieval times, though the earliest known reference to this traffic dates only from the second half of the sixteenth century. In March 1566, Thomas Lea of Castletown landed three hogsheads and five barrels of beef at Chester and in the following month returned to the same port with five hogsheads and a quarter of beef.[164] Significantly perhaps, these are the only entries found in the Chester customs accounts up to this date and although some small quantities of salted beef were shipped to the city and to Beaumaris thereafter, it seems that this trade remained at a low level until the end of the sixteenth century.[165] It may very well be that the export trade in live cattle and other livestock was restricted by the requirement to make customary payments of cattle, sheep and pigs in kind, a practice which was clearly a tremendous advantage to the lord during a period of inflation. A temporary break in this system in 1593–94, when the payments were rendered in money, gave the trade a marked boost and after such customary payments were finally ended in 1601, shipments of live cattle as well as carcases were in general notably higher, a situation which continued for much of the next sixty years. Exports of sheep and pigs, however, quickly declined after 1600 and, in common with shipments of horses, came to an end by about 1700.[166]

Although most of the livestock exports in the early seventeenth century were probably destined for English ports, it is not possible to be certain that this was so because the water bailiff's accounts do not record the port for which the cargoes were cleared and the corresponding English port books do not always survive. It is tempting to assume that Chester and Liverpool were the destinations for most shipments, since both ports had existing links with the Island as well as an important place in the growing trade in live cattle from Ireland, but in view of the problems with the sources it is difficult to demonstrate this and, in fact, the extant port books seem to indicate that this may not have always been the case. In 1603–04, for example, twenty-one live cattle were landed from the Island at Liverpool, while in 1619–20, only twenty-two Manx cattle were imported at Chester.[167] Nevertheless, at whichever ports the animals were landed, there is no question but that the imports of Manx cattle became associated with the much larger trade in cattle between Ireland and the ports of north-west England and north Wales. Many English and Welsh merchants engaged in the business, as well as some among the political classes,

164 K.B. Wilson (ed), *Chester Customs Accounts, 1301–1566*, RSLC, 111 (1969), 78, 79.
165 D.M. Woodward, *The Trade of Elizabethan Chester*, University of Hull Occasional Papers in Economic and Social History, 4 (Hull, 1970), 35; E.A. Lewis (ed), *The Welsh Port Books, 1550–1603*, Cymmrodorion Record Series, 12 (1927), 244, 256, 258.
166 Dickinson, *Lordship of Man*, 247–51, 259–60; MNH MS 06523 (DP) MD 401/1716/4.
167 TNA E190/1328/11, E190/1332/1.

Fig. 1.15 *Exports of livestock from the Isle of Man. Years ending at 24 June (before 1701); 29 Sept. (after 1700).*

Year	Cattle	Sheep	Pigs	Horses
1579	378	110	226	28
1594	749	515	263	16
1600	405	383	42	67
1605	454	152	66	65
1610	714	8	124	101
1618	895	50	48	14
1630	589	24	30	43
1647	890	–	9	40
1667	18	20	–	–
1685	4	12	5	32
1696	582	8	–	6
1710	577	–	–	13
1721	–	–	–	–
1738	–	–	–	–

Sources: MNH MS10058, Port Customes for the Isle of Man, 1579; Customs book, 1594; Waterbailiff's accounts, 1594; Ingates and outgates (Port Customs), 1600; Ingates and outgates, 1605; Ingates and outgates, 1610; Waterbailiff's accounts, 1618; Waterbailiff's accounts, 1630; Waterbailiff's accounts, 1647; Customs book, 1667; Customs book, 1685 ; Customs book, 1696; Book of customs of ingates and outgates, 1710; Book of customs of ingates and outgates, 1721; Charge of the customs of ingates and outgates, 1738.

believed that the Manx beasts were, in fact, merely Irish cattle which had been re-exported from the Island. When the question of a ban on Irish cattle imports was debated in the House of Commons in 1621, Richard Kippax, the member for Newton, near Wigan, therefore proposed an addition to the bill 'to provide against the Importation [of Irish cattle] out of the Isle of Man.'[168] While the bill did not, in the end, become law, this erroneous belief had serious implications for the Island's cattle export trade. When the question of Irish cattle imports resurfaced in the early 1660s, the position of the Isle of Man was consequently carefully considered. The Island was not directly affected by the first Irish Cattle Act (1664), but after this had failed to stem the number of cattle shipped to

168 *HCJ*, i, 615b; C.A. Edie, 'The Irish cattle bills: a study in Restoration politics', *Transactions of the American Philosophical Society*, 60, pt 2 (1970), 8.

England, a second Act (1667) was passed which did extend to the Isle of Man. This Act limited the number of cattle which could be imported into England from the Island to six hundred beasts of the native breed and these could only be landed at Chester 'or some of the Members thereof.'[169] Although there is some evidence that the number of cattle for export was already being restricted at this time, at least temporarily, by order perhaps from Earl Charles and certainly later from his widow, in order to ensure a supply both for the lord's use and for the garrisons, the second Irish Cattle Act added a further disincentive to ship animals overseas. Despite exceptional years when shipments nearly reached the quota set by the Act, such as in 1695–96, the export trade in Manx cattle in general seems to have slumped after the mid-1660s and to have all but ended by the early eighteenth century.[170]

The trade in skins, hides and wool was closely associated with livestock exports, but experienced somewhat different fortunes. There can be little doubt that the trade in skins and hides was quite as long established as that in livestock and there is evidence that it flourished throughout the sixteenth century. As in the case of livestock exports, Chester was the destination for many of the shipments of skins and hides. In 1524, William Offlay, a prominent Chester merchant, purchased two consignments of hides in the Island and there seems to have been a fairly regular trade between the Island and the city, as is clearly demonstrated in the later part of Elizabeth's reign. This trade seems to have reached its peak in the last decade of the sixteenth century, when, in 1592–93 alone, 8,080 sheepskins, fifty goatskins and 4.5 dickers of hides were imported into Chester, accounting for almost all of the Island's skin and hide exports in that year. Shipments were also made to other ports, including Liverpool, but it seems likely that Chester remained the most important market for merchants dealing in skins and hides.[171] After 1600, the export trade continued, though generally at a much lower level than in the previous decade, until the 1660s when, perhaps as a result of the restrictions on livestock exports, it seems to have gone into something of a decline. Although there were years in the late seventeenth century when the trade appeared to be unaffected by this trend, by the 1720s it had ceased altogether.

Like skins and hides, wool was regularly shipped from the Island until the third decade of the eighteenth century. Whether exported as wool or as fleeces along with the skins in the form of sheepfells, most of these shipments were probably destined for the ports of north-west England, where imports of Irish wool also increased to feed the demands of south Lancashire's growing textile

169 15 Chas. II, c.5, 18 Chas. II, c.2; Edie, 'Irish cattle bills', 17–35.

170 Dickinson, *Lordship of Man*, 254–59; MNH MS 10071 (Lib.Scacc.), 1673, 1.

171 A. Crosby, 'A Chester merchant buys leather from the Isle of Man in 1524', *Cheshire History*, 44 (2004–05), 37–41; D.M. Woodward, 'The Chester leather industry', 1558–1625, *THSLC*, 119 (1967), 71, 72.

Fig. 1.16 *Exports of skins and hides from the Isle of Man. Years ending at 24 June (before 1701); 29 Sept. (after 1700).*

Year	Sheep skins	Lamb skins	Calf skins	Rabbit skins	Goat skins	Kid skins	Mixed skins	Hides(dickers)[1]	
								Raw	Tanned
1579	1548	5540	24	724	–	36	2674	–	–
1594	5292	3356	–	360	126	384	2580	157.8	–
1600	2308	4434	–	240	–	–	2040	77.7	24.0
1605	2400	5076	24	660	–	–	1353	48.2	–
1610	1348	3120	343	540	–	–	2086	64.8	–
1618	1886	5112	126	360	–	–	2100	66.5	–
1630	528	1536	60	240	–	–	2100	54.6	76.0
1647	2106	3124	–	600	1	–	1118	2.0	26.0
1667	900	720	–	480	24	–	900	16.0	2.0
1685	–	1080	139	708	170	–	750	29.8	25.7
1696	144	3012	234	1698	570	–	998	76.8	8.4
1710	–	–	872	410	424	–	84	71.8	–
1721	–	–	–	100	–	–	–	32.3	–
1738	–	–	–	–	–	–	–	–	–

Sources: See Fig. 1.15.

1 The number of hides to the dicker varied. There were eight ox hides to the dicker, but ten cow hides. Since a distinction is not always drawn, hides of an unspecified nature have been taken to be cow hides.

manufactures. Although Liverpool was more important than Chester in the Irish wool trade, there seems to be little evidence that it received the majority of Manx wool shipments and it may well be that, as far as sheepfells were concerned at least, the city on the Dee offered a readier market.[172]

In addition to livestock and livestock products, the Island exported a range of other commodities. This included various types of corn, some of which could have been re-exported grain. Exports of wheat, oats, barley and malt reached a high point in the first half of the seventeenth century before falling dramatically after about 1640. In 1609–10, for instance, 215.5 bolls and 103.5 barrels of wheat, 643 bolls and 24 barrels of barley, 232 bolls of oats and 224.5 bolls and 6 barrels of malt were shipped from Manx ports. Towards the end of the century, exports were generally much less than a hundred bolls of each.[173] Perhaps surprisingly, fish, including herring, do not appear often as exports in the water bailiff's accounts, although it should be remembered that the payments of the castle mazes were accounted for separately and strangers wanting to obtain herring might do so without their catch appearing among the official exports. Nevertheless, imports of fish from the Island are recorded at Chester during the reigns of Henry VIII and Elizabeth.[174] In the sixteenth century, considerable quantities of cloth were licensed for export from the Island, most of which was reportedly 'course frize.' 6,761 yards of 'raw cloth' were exported in 1578–79 in addition to 808 yards of what was specifically recorded as 'Manske cloyth.' Shipments of all types of cloth dwindled fairly steadily after 1600, but there were signs that exports of woollen cloth had begun to recover by c.1690. The establishment of the linen manufacture after 1692 helped to stimulate textile exports in general so that, even by 1695–96, exports had risen to 2,602 yards of linen and 2,127 yards of woollen cloth and Manx textiles continued to prosper in the eighteenth century.[175] Another product of the projects begun in the last decade of the seventeenth century was increased output from the Island's mines and small quantities of iron, copper and lead were exported, but the failure of the various mining enterprises brought this trade to an end in the early eighteenth century.[176] Ale and beer were fairly regular

172 N.G. Lowe, *The Lancashire Textile Industry in the Sixteenth Century*, Chetham Society, third series, 20 (1972), 10–19; Woodward, *Elizabethan Chester*, 8; Dickinson, *Lordship of Man*, 263–65; Dickinson, 'Overseas trade', 12.

173 Dickinson, *Lordship of Man*, 266–68.

174 J. Kermode, 'The trade of late medieval Chester, 1500–1550', in R.H. Britnell and J. Hatcher (eds), *Progress and Problems in Medieval England: Essays in honour of Edward Miller* (Cambridge, 1996), 290; Woodward, *Elizabethan Chester*, 35.

175 LRO DDKe 84/14, John Rowe, Bishop Wilson *et al.* to James, earl of Derby, 4 August 1709; MNH MS 10058, Port Customes for the Isle of Man, 1579; Dickinson, *Lordship of Man*, 268–69; Moore, *Isle of Man*, vol. 2, 592 n. 4.

176 Dickinson, 'Overseas trade', 13–14; Dickinson, *Lordship of Man*, 187–88; Moore, *Isle of Man*, vol. 2, 962.

Fig. 1.17 *Exports of wool and herring from the Isle of Man. Years ending at 24 June (before 1701); 29 Sept. (after 1700).*

Year	Wool stones	Herring tons	Herring hogsheads	Herring barrels	Herring maze
1579	634	1.5	–	16	–
1594	1,665	1	–	–	–
1600	439	–	1	1	–
1605	435	–	8	–	–
1610	113	–	–	–	–
1618	614	54.5	–	71	3
1630	684	2	–	139	1
1647	175	–	–	60	–
1667	39	54.5	–	485	339
1685	335	–	–	388	1
1696	395	–	–	–	–
1710	130	0.05	–	1	–
1721	54	–	–	–	–
1738	–	–	–	–	–

Sources: See Fig. 1.15.

exports from the Island and appear to have gained something of a reputation in England and further afield. In 1673, Richard Walmsley of Clayton-le-Moors wrote to Deputy Governor Henry Nowell, asking him to send some 'excellent sort of strong beer made in your island, such as my Lord of Derby drinks, some times, at Knowsley.' Manx ale was also enjoyed in Scotland, to which country all but two of the 41.75 barrels of ale exported from the Island was shipped in 1695–96.[177] An export trade in slates and flagstones developed at the end of the seventeenth century and grew to such an extent that, in 1709, the officers estimated it could easily account for 200,000 slates and 5,000 flagstones in a single year. This proved to be only a slightly exaggerated assessment. In 1709–10, although shipments of flags, some for use as tombstones and mainly

177 Dickinson, *Lordship of Man*, 270; *HMC Kenyon*, 95; MNH MS 10058, Customs book, 1696.

cleared from Poyll Vaaish and Castletown, fell far short of this figure, exports of slates in this year amounted to 136,500.[178]

Until the late seventeenth century, the nature of the Island's import trade was largely dictated by the need for raw materials which could not be obtained by any other means. Timber, iron and coal were the most important commodities which the Island lacked. The limited amount of woodland in the Island meant that all the wood needed for maintenance and construction work had to be brought in from outside and for this reason timber features regularly in the water bailiff's accounts in a variety of forms and often in very substantial quantities. Boards of deal, ash and oak, poles of different types, joists, staves, spars and boat stems were among the types of timber landed in the Island's ports in their hundreds, occasionally thousands, probably mostly from Ireland, for use in repairing boats, making barrels and building houses. The scarcity of wood is underlined by the fact that the customs duty on shipments was frequently paid in kind rather than in money.[179] Although the Isle of Man had some iron deposits of its own, these were worked only infrequently, as already observed, and were clearly not a reliable source to supply the Island's needs. Small amounts, usually between four and ten tons *per annum*, were imported regularly from Ireland, Spain and very occasionally England to answer the modest requirements of the Island's smiths, though the quantity seems to have increased after the middle of the eighteenth century, with 77.8 tons being unloaded on Manx quays in 1751–52. The demand for coal in the Island was limited because, whereas peat was readily available, all coal had to be imported and it was therefore expensive. This restricted its use to the houses of the lord's officers, the higher clergy and the larger landowners as well as the garrisons and those who required it in manufacturing. Nevertheless, by the end of the sixteenth century, large quantities – approximately 440 tons in 1593–94 – were being imported, much, if not most, from Parton in Cumberland. After 1600, imports were also landed from Workington and Whitehaven, both ports assuming greater importance as sources for coal after the destruction of the pier at Parton in a gale in the early 1630s and the failure to build a replacement until six decades later. By 1700, Whitehaven was supplying at least half and probably more of the Island's coal. Coal imports fluctuated considerably during the seventeenth century but rose to a generally higher level of more than 100 tons *per annum* after c.1660 and began to increase more markedly in the early eighteenth century.[180]

The fisheries of the Island and the herring fishery in particular created a considerable demand for salt. Although the salt produced by brine evaporation was not perhaps ideal because of the bitter taste, at least some of the salt used

178 LRO DDKe 84/14, John Rowe, Bishop Wilson *et al.* to James, earl of Derby, 4 August 1709; MNH MS 10058, Book of Customs of ingates and outgates, 1710.

179 Dickinson, *Lordship of Man*, 275–76; Dickinson, 'Overseas trade', 14.

180 Dickinson, *Lordship of Man*, 270–75, 292, 299; Dickinson, 'Overseas trade', 14–15.

Fig. 1.18 *Imports of coal and iron into the Isle of Man. Years ending at 24 June (before 1701); 29 Sept. (after 1700).*

	Coal			Iron	
Year	Tons	'Loads'[1]	Part loads	Barrels	Tons
1579	–	7	–	12	20.8
1594	–	11	–	–	9.35
1600	26	2	–	20	4.35
1605	38	5	–	–	1.2
1610	74	7	–	–	6.25
1618	46	5	–	2	6.8
1630	49	8	–	–	4.5
1647	86	19	6	–	5.6
1667	110	10	5	–	7.65
1685	–	12	–	–	6.1
1696	119	–	–	5	9.25
1710	100	–	–	–	4.1
1721	161	–	–	–	9.75
1738	514	–	–	–	7.5
1752	1,035	–	–	–	77.8

Sources: See Fig. 1.15.

1 A 'load' may have been a variable amount depending on the size of the ship or it may have been an abbreviated form of 'keel load.' This was a measure of twenty chaldrons or forty tons before 1676, when it was changed to sixteen chaldrons or thirty-two tons. R. Zupko, *British Weights and Measures. A History from Antiquity to the Seventeenth Century* (Madison 1977), Appendix B, 151.

by Manx fishermen was probably obtained in this way, since it was a lot less expensive than purchasing the salt which was imported mainly from England, but also from France, Portugal and Spain.[181] Imports varied from year to year, very likely in response to the success or failure of the herring fishery, but perhaps not surprisingly, given the importance of fish in the Manx economy in general, there were few occasions when the amount of salt landed in the Island fell below fifty tons *per annum* in total.

181 S.G.E. Lythe, *The Economy of Scotland in its European Setting, 1550–1625* (Edinburgh, 1960), 49; A. Fenton, *The Northern Isles: Orkney and Shetland* (Edinburgh, 1978, reprinted East Linton, 1997), 211; TNA SP 16/539/120, A Breife Description of the Isle of Man (n.d., c.1642).

Fig. 1.19 *Imports of salt, soap, hops, tobacco and wine into the Isle of Man. Years ending at 24 June (before 1701); 29 Sept. (after 1700).*

	Salt		Soap		Tobacco	Hops	Wine
Year	Tons	Barrels	Firkins	lbs.	lbs.	lbs.	Tuns
1579	47.25	8	3	56	–	336	70.25
1594	27	155	10	–	448	1,240	19
1600	5	171	31	–	–	874	29
1605	25	22	11	–	–	304	25
1610	1	368	41	–	112	838	21
1618	5.5	629	32	–	448	1,086	18
1630	67	204	46	–	104	1,646	21
1647	12	145	59	–	2,354	2,102	18
1667	10	94	13	–	1,046	2,296	2
1685	59	6	3	–	6,613	2,980	25
1696	108	14	–	–	23,870	2,584	–
1710	130.5	31	–	4,374	356,461	2,731	11.5
1721	104	43.5	–	2,744	200,079	3,561	155.9
1738	153	–	–	7,196	22,147	6,961	57.9
1752	305.25	1.5	–	5,625	235,818	14,545	62.6

Sources: See Fig. 1.15.

Demand increased in the eighteenth century, but this was no doubt partly the result of the Island's rising population and therefore rising demand, as well as the sustained level of larger herring catches which the higher revenue from the fishery after 1740 in particular clearly suggests.

In addition to necessary raw materials, a generally modest number of horses and sometimes substantial amounts of wheat, oats and barley when circumstances dictated, the Island imported a diverse range of commodities, though usually in small quantities. Most of these items were manufactured goods which supplied deficiencies in the Island's ability to produce sufficient for domestic requirements or which fulfilled needs which Manx manufacturing could not. Farming tools, particularly scythes and sickles, but also including ploughs and plough beams, clothing and shoes, especially Irish brogues, made up a large part of the imports recorded each year by the water bailiff and his deputies. Haberdashery wares were imported in plenty, as well as limited amounts of cloth, chiefly linen. Foodstuffs, such as butter, cheese and fruit, constituted a small part of the import trade, but the quantity of hops brought in to support the brewing of Manx beer increased steadily until, at the end of the Stanley period, imports were exceeding 5,000 pounds in weight *per annum*. Goods which might be regarded as luxury items in the sixteenth century, but which had become more commonplace two hundred years later, also made up part of some merchants' cargoes. Soap, especially the Castilian variety, pepper, spices, drinking glasses and glass in general, books, locks and silk handkerchiefs were just some of the commodities which began to find a growing market in the Island's towns and among the larger landowners.[182]

Of far greater value to the merchants and equally greater importance to the Island's economy from the later seventeenth century onwards, however, was the rise of the trade in valuable commodities from the East Indies, the Caribbean and the American colonies. This was a development which had less to do with schemes and projects instigated by speculators sponsored or encouraged by the Stanleys and far more to do with the impact of political events in western Europe.

The outbreak of war between England and France in 1689 led to an increase in tariffs imposed by the English government to meet the financial demands of conducting campaigns in Ireland and continental Europe and, together with the existing restrictions on trade with the colonies embodied in the Navigation Acts of 1651, 1660 and 1671, encouraged merchants to find ways to circumvent these imposts. Because of the Island's peculiar constitutional status in relation to the Crown and its low customs duties, even by previous English standards, the Isle of Man was in a perfect position to benefit from this commercial situation. Imports of tobacco, which had previously been fairly negligible, began to rise significantly in the 1680s, a fact which was not lost on the English government. The effect of the Navigation Acts was to restrict the destination of shipments from the colonies finally to English ports alone and similar limits were put on trade with the Far East in 1706, when it was ordered that such shipments could only be unloaded at a port in Great Britain.[183] Resourceful merchants discovered that they were able to get around these strictures by taking advantage of a provision which allowed them to claim back some of the duty which they paid on inward shipments when they re-exported the goods to a foreign destination. The procedure was fairly simple. If a Liverpool merchant wanted to supply his customers in the burgeoning market of industrialising south Lancashire, he landed a cargo of tobacco or rum from the colonies at an English port and paid the applicable duty. He then entered his goods for export to a destination which was outside the British Isles and obtained a debenture to claim a 'drawback' or refund of part of the duty he had paid on the inward shipment. The cargo was then shipped to the Isle of Man and if, by chance, the vessel carrying it was intercepted *en route* by a revenue cutter in the Irish Sea, the merchant or

182 Dickinson, *Lordship of Man*, 282, 283, 288–90; Dickinson, 'Overseas trade', 17–18.
183 Dickinson, *Lordship of Man*, 334; Dickinson, 'Overseas trade', 18–19; 6 Anne, c.3.

his factor would offer some reason for the vessel's presence off the Manx coast, 'distress of weather' being a frequent and often plausible and genuine excuse. Once the vessel had arrived in the Island and the appropriate duty paid to the water bailiff or his deputy, the cargo could be broken up and shipped in smaller vessels back across the Irish Sea to the Cumbrian or Lancashire coast, along which there were numerous estuaries and creeks into which the boats could be run. The end result was that the merchant could now distribute his goods to his customers, having paid considerably less in customs duty than if he had simply imported the cargo at an English port and sold the cargo there. He was thus also naturally able to enjoy a larger profit.

As far as the lord and his officers were concerned, this practice was entirely lawful, since the lord's customs duty had been paid and no Manx laws had been broken, but the authorities in London, Edinburgh and Dublin took a quite different view. From their perspective, this was clearly smuggling. Soon after the government in London resumed collection of customs duties in its own right in 1671, it was clear that the potential for the growth of contraband traffic had been recognized. In 1673, the lord treasurer proposed that an itinerant officer should be sent to the Isle of Man and Ireland 'to prevent abuses in the Plantation trade,' but for reasons which are not entirely clear, this was not acted upon for almost another decade. In April 1682, however, the first of a succession of resident customs officers was appointed for the Island to ensure that the king was not defrauded of his customs by merchants eager to avoid paying their duty.[184] Strictly speaking, the commission of these Crown officers had no force in the Island, but they were allowed to continue to monitor trading activity there. Clashes between the officers of the lord and of the Crown over jurisdiction were inevitable. One of the most notable involved the Spanish vessel *St. Stephen*, which arrived at the Island in April 1691 with a cargo of brandy and wines. According to the depositions of the ship's crew, the ship had been *en route* from its home port of San Sebastian to Dublin when it was forced by 'distresse of weather' to take refuge in Derbyhaven. The Crown officers considered this story to be highly dubious since there was a suspicion that the brandy and wine were French and therefore contraband. The fact that the pilot of the vessel and its owner were both French, though the latter was a recently naturalized Englishman, only added to the doubts about the origin and ultimate destination of the cargo. The Crown officer, Benjamin Dewey, disputed the right of Governor Roger Kenyon to seize the vessel and objected to the removal of a sample of the wine for testing by the authority of the earl of Derby. Although the brandy was considered to be of French origin, the English

184 Dickinson, 'Overseas trade', 20; *CTB, 1673–75*, 144; *CTB, 1681–85*, 449, 452.

government nevertheless ordered the release of the vessel, no doubt because it came from a country allied to William III.[185]

While the possibility continued to exist that merchants would employ such schemes to avoid paying customs duty and run their cargoes into any of the countries of the Irish Sea littoral covertly, the authorities in London and Dublin remained equally determined to try to stop them and prevent them from claiming fraudulent drawbacks. Similar abuses occurred in the tobacco trade between Scotland and Ireland and in an effort to stamp out the practice, the Scottish customs commissioners suggested in 1708 and 1709 that drawbacks should not be issued for any exports to Ireland until a certificate was received that the cargo had actually been landed at its stated destination and this was passed into law.[186] In an effort to deal with the problem in the Island, proposals were made that merchants should have to enter into bonds which would only be discharged once the certificate from the customs officers at the cargo's destination port had been produced. The officers and Keys objected to this, claiming that 'the taking of bonds will intirely sink our trade here,' even though acceptance of such a system might have been linked to an agreement to allow at least some of the Island's produce to be imported into Britain without paying duty.[187] Exports of Manx products did indeed dwindle in the early eighteenth century, though most probably because of the greater profits which could be made from re-exported goods rather than for any other particular reason. By the end of the Stanley period such exports had practically ceased, while imports and duty-free re-exports had expanded dramatically.[188]

In spite of the efforts of the English and later British government and its revenue officers, the running trade in the Irish Sea prospered. The government had endeavoured to nip the problem in the bud by securing a lease of the Island's customs in the 1680s, but Earl William had steadfastly refused to entertain such proposals, which eventually foundered in 1688.[189] When his successor did agree to lease the Island's customs in 1722, it was to Richard McGwire, a Dublin merchant, and not surprisingly this short-lived experiment, which came to an end five years into the twenty-one-year term when the lessee and his partner could not make the agreed payments to Earl James, had no discernible effect on the running trade. It was reported, however, that McGwire and his partner, Josiah Poole of Liverpool, appeared to be at the very least in league with those engaged in the trade, if not involved directly themselves. The commander of the *Royal George*, a vessel in government service, informed the collector of customs

185 Dickinson, 'Overseas trade', 21–22; LRO DDKe 84/24, 28, 32.
186 *CTB, 1709*, 2, 414, *CTB, 1710*, 2, 179–80; L.M. Cullen, *Anglo-Irish Trade, 1660–1800* (Manchester, 1968), 145; 8 Anne, c.13.
187 MNH MS 06523 (DP) MD 401/1720/18.
188 Dickinson, 'Overseas trade', 22–28.
189 Dickinson, *Lordship of Man*, 336–37.

at Liverpool in August 1726 that McGwire and Poole did 'exasperate and spirit up the people [in the Island] to make the officers and all persons employed in the service of the [British] government as uneasy as they possibly can to deter them from doing their duty.' In an apparent effort to subvert the effectiveness of the policing effort by the revenue cutters, Poole even succeeded in getting some of his tenants who were sailors to join the brigantine *Moncaster*, hired to patrol the Manx coast, as members of the crew. Understandably, the captain had 'great reason to believe they were corrupted by Poole and his partner to betray his design.'[190]

Imports of all the high-value commodities which featured in the running trade increased significantly after 1700 and brought great profits to many merchants and their associates based in the Island. The trade in tobacco was the longest established, with some inward shipments even recorded before 1600, but imports only reached levels of more than 1,000 pounds in weight *per annum* after about the middle of the seventeenth century. By 1700, imports were approaching twenty-five times that amount and during the first half of the eighteenth century inward shipments sometimes reached in excess of 200,000 pounds in weight in a single year. Wine had always been imported into the Island to some extent, but even when the running trade was its height, the amounts landed in Manx ports were not particularly great. The profits which could be made from brandy were such, however, that the import trade grew quickly after 1700 to about 800 tuns *per annum*. Sugar and rum, especially the former, were commodities in demand, but the trade in both only really expanded after the end of the Stanley lordship. The most important trade besides that in tobacco during these years was that in tea. This had not even existed before the end of the seventeenth century, but it developed rapidly towards the end of the Stanley period and by the late 1730s imports were reaching in excess of 10,000 pounds in weight *per annum*.

More than a few merchants, both natives and foreigners, as well as their agents, benefitted from the running trade, but there were a handful of merchants who, from the frequency of their appearances in the water bailiff's accounts shipping large quantities of tobacco and similar goods, clearly profited very considerably from the trade in these valuable commodities.

Among this group were the Murreys of Douglas, a dynasty of Scottish origin which was established in the Island in the early seventeenth century and which, by 1700, had members in Chester and Liverpool as well, the Moores of Douglas and John Bignall of Ramsey, a merchant of Irish origin.[191]

190 R.C. Jarvis (ed), *Customs Letter-Books of the Port of Liverpool, 1711–1813*, Chetham Society, third series, 6 (1954), 28–30.

191 Dickinson, *Lordship of Man*, 312–15; MNH MS 10058, Customs book, 1696; Book of Customs of ingates and outgates, 1710; Book of Customs of ingates and outgates, 1721; Charge of the Customs of ingates and outgates, 1738; MNH MS 10216 (EW) 27, inventory of David Murrey, 1709.

Fig. 1.20 *Imports of brandy, rum, sugar and tea into the Isle of Man. Years ending at 24 June (before 1701); 29 Sept. (after 1700).*

Year	Brandy tuns	Rum tuns	Sugar lbs.	Tea lbs.
1579	–	–	–	–
1594	–	–	200	–
1600	–	–	–	–
1605	–	–	–	–
1610	–	–	–	–
1618	–	–	–	–
1630	–	–	–	–
1647	0.64	–	78	–
1667	0.25	–	–	–
1685	2.87	–	956	–
1696	–	–	255	–
1710	98.1	–	852.5	–
1721	774.5	–	4,336	–
1738	858.1	72.2	2,557	12,957
1752	1,588.6	651.1	175,841	83,635

Sources: See Fig. 1.15.

Fig. 1.21 *Merchant's house, Peel (Castle Street) - Photo: Carola Rush.*

By the end of the Stanley period, the running trade had long since become the most important part of the Island's maritime trade. Indeed, during the 1730s, but especially after 1736, it rapidly came to account for almost all of the Island's maritime trade by value. In the early years of the Atholl lordship, the value of imports rose to previously unimaginable levels, so much so that, with perhaps only slight exaggeration, Edmund Burke could later refer to the Isle of Man at this time as 'the very head quarters, the very citadel of smuggling,' and it was this escalation in the running trade which made the British government determined to purchase the rights to the Island vested in the Duke of Atholl, something which was not finally achieved until 1765. This, it was hoped, would finally bring the heyday of the running trade from the Isle of Man to a close.[192]

NOTE – DATES AND CURRENCY

Dates are Old Style, but the year is taken to begin on 1 January instead of 25 March.

Before the late seventeenth century there seems to have been an equivalence between the English pound sterling and the Manx currency of account. The appearance of the description 'Manx' or 'English' on occasion and in rare instances the mention of the 'Manx mark' (worth 4s. by comparison with the English mark, worth 13s. 4d.) in the records suggests that a distinction, if not a differential, existed. (Dickinson, *Lordship of Man*, 163–64; MNHL MS 10071 (Lib.Plit.), 1588, 3.)

12d. = 1 shilling

20s. = £1 (240d.)

In 1692, in an effort to stem an outflow of sound coinage, the Manx currency of account was apparently devalued: English crowns (5s.) were henceforth to circulate at the value of 5s. 4d., English half crowns (2s. 6d.) at 2s. 8d. (MNH MD401/1719/8)

In April 1703, there was a further devaluation. The Keys advised the deputy governor Robert Mawdesley that English crowns should henceforth pass for 5s. 10d., English half crowns at 2s. 11d., one shilling sterling for 14d. and a guinea (21s. sterling) for 24s. 6d. (Lib.Scacc. 1703, *inter* 20–21 (3)). One pound sterling would therefore circulate at the value of 23s. 4d. Manx.

192 Dickinson, 'Overseas trade', 27–30; E.J. Payne (ed), *Burke: Selected Works*, 3 vols (Oxford, 1874), vol. 1, 114; Jarvis, *Customs Letter-Books*, xx-xxi; E. Carson, *The Ancient and Rightful Customs: A History of the English Customs Service* (London, 1972), 72–73; 5 Geo. III, c.26.

This relationship between sterling and the Manx currency of account remained in effect until the introduction of a new coinage with the same values as that of the United Kingdom in 1840. (Moore, *Isle of Man*, vol. 1, 416–17.)

2 *Religion and the Island Church 1405–1838*

NIGEL YATES †

WITH CONTRIBUTIONS BY FRANCES COAKLEY, PRISCILLA LEWTHWAITE AND JENNIFER PLATTEN †.

ADDITIONAL SECTIONS ARE BY PETER DAVEY (PRE-REFORMATION CHURCH LIFE), TIM GRASS (ROMAN CATHOLICISM, THE QUAKERS AND DISSENT) AND PAT MCCLURE (EARLY MODERN CHURCH FURNITURE, CLERICAL DRESS AND TWO EXEMPLAR PARISHES)

INTRODUCTION

Michael Hoy

A.W. Moore, in his two volume *History of the Isle of Man* and his diocesan history *Sodor and Man*, written at the end of the nineteenth century, is the first historian to give a comprehensive history of the Island church and its contribution to the ordering and administration of insular and parochial society, together with accounts of customary religious practice, biographical sketches of some bishops and other ecclesiastical figures, and descriptions of key buildings and other aspects of church life.[1] Before Moore's work, the historiography of accounts of religion and the church in the Isle of Man is for the most part limited to studies of the established church as a political and administrative instrument in the context of the Stanley, Atholl and Crown lordships, and biographies of a handful of Island bishops which are limited in scope and design. Three biographies of Bishop Wilson – Clement Cruttwell's late eighteenth-century account, tagged on to his eight-volume collection of Wilson's works, and two more detailed nineteenth-century accounts by Hugh Stowell and John Keble – and Weedon Butler's *Memoirs of Mark Hildesley* are for the most part merely descriptive and hagiographical, and none offers any critical reflection on or contextual evaluation of their subjects.[2]

1 A.W. Moore, *Sodor and Man*, SPCK Diocesan Histories (London, 1893); A.W. Moore, *A History of the Isle of Man*, 2 vols (London, 1900).

2 C. Cruttwell, *The Works of the Right Reverend Thomas Wilson, DD, Lord Bishop of Sodor and Man, with his Life*, 8 vols, 3rd edn (Bath, 1784); H. Stowell, *The Life of the Right Reverend Thomas Wilson, D.D., late Lord Bishop of Sodor and Man* (London, 1819); J. Keble, *Life of the Right Reverend Father in God Thomas Wilson, D.D., Bishop of Sodor and Man*, 2 vols (Oxford, 1863); W. Butler, *The Memoirs of Mark Hildesley, DD, Lord Bishop of Sodor and Man* (London, 1799).

There is little modern biographical writing, although a more recent authoritative account of the Island's bishops and clergy, with factual and anecdotal notes on personalities and parish life, may be found in John Gelling's *History of the Manx Church, 1698–1911*, published in 1998. This begins relatively late in the period of this volume with the arrival of Bishop Wilson, however, and the work is not referenced.[3]

A number of well-researched accounts of events, personalities and places of significant interest in the Island's religious life, such as studies of the spiritual courts by Anne Ashley and Jennifer Platten, David Craine's description of clerical life in the parishes and Pat McClure's work on the archaeology of Manx church interiors, broaden the historiographical perspective, while Thomas Hodgkin's early account of the fortunes of the Quakers is a particularly valuable insular and contextual study.[4]

The historiography of published work on religion and the church in the Isle of Man is limited and fragmentary, and in consequence in many ways this chapter has presented the editors and contributors with more challenges than any other in this volume. The main body of the chapter – the story of the established church in the Isle of Man from the Reformation to the mid-nineteenth century – was written by the distinguished ecclesiastical historian Nigel Yates. Other scholars have widened the perspectives of the Island story with sections on pre-Reformation church life, recusancy, dissent, and Quakerism, and there are descriptions of significant aspects of the established church's contribution to community and family life in the operation of the church courts, the provision of parochial care for the needy and the preservation of moral order. A view of liturgical tradition, reflected in architecture, furniture, vestments and priestly practice, and a focus on two exemplar parishes, are also included. Other key areas of service provided by the church, such as schools, education and poor relief, are described in detail in other chapters.

In a chapter which attempts a comprehensive overview of such a broad subject there are inevitably some significant omissions which reflect the absence of relevant scholarly research. Most notable of these is the story of Methodism, which came to dominate religious life and observance in the Island from the late eighteenth century onwards. Rex Kissack, building on William

3 J.D. Gelling, *A History of the Manx Church, 1698–1911* (Douglas, 1998).

4 A. Ashley, 'The spiritual courts of the Isle of Man, especially in the seventeenth and eighteenth centuries', *English Historical Review*, 72 (1957), 35–59; J.A. Platten, 'The Church Court System: Presentments to the Manx Church Courts, 1640–1799' (PhD thesis, University of Liverpool, 2010); D. Craine, 'Manx Clerical Life, 1600–1800', *PIMNHAS*, 5:4 (1954), 368–84; P.T. McClure, 'The Archaeology of Manx Church Interiors: contents and contexts 1632–1925' (PhD thesis, University of Liverpool, 2013); T. Hodgkin, 'Ruillick-Ny-Quakeryn: notes on the history of Friends in the Isle of Man', *Friends Quarterly Examiner* (October 1908), 457–95.

Radcliffe's views, argued that the Reformation never really happened in the Island in the sixteenth century.[5] He claimed that the reforming role in church life was eventually undertaken by Methodism, which focussed on evangelism and individual spirituality and service throughout this period. While some work has been done on aspects of Methodism in Island life, there is a wealth of documentary evidence in the Island's national archive and elsewhere awaiting the attention of scholars. A full academic history of Methodism in the Isle of Man is long overdue.[6]

Outside the mainstream of church life in the Island, not all pre-Reformation ideas and traditions disappeared. Popular reverence for holy wells, for example, usually sited near keeills, as places of healing continued long into the twentieth century, and talismans like the fifteenth century Mylecharaine pectoral cross (figure 2.3) preserved echoes of the Island's old Celtic past through subsequent centuries.[7] Some insight into these and other aspects of belief and tradition are given elsewhere, for example in the 'Arts and Culture' chapter, but much still awaits the attention of future researchers.

THE ISLAND CHURCH BEFORE THE REFORMATION

Peter Davey

Introduction

The Manx church entered fully into the world of western European Christianity in the twelfth century. This was as a result of three main events. Firstly, the arrival of Olaf I (1113–1153) as king of Man and the Isles. He had been educated in the English court and, whilst remaining a Norwegian petty king, had acquired an English and, therefore, a continental understanding of developments in religious doctrine and practice. His introduction of one of the reformed monastic orders, the Savignacs, in 1134 with the foundation of Rushen Abbey – the first in any of the Norse kingdoms – is evidence of this. Then, secondly, in 1154, following a papal review of the church in Scandinavia, a new metropolitan was established at Nidaros (Trondheim) within which new dioceses were created along political lines, including that of the 'Southern Isles'

5 W.T. Radcliffe, *Ellan Vannin* (London, 1895), 139–52; R. Kissack, 'The contribution of Methodism to the culture of the Isle of Man', *Manx Methodist Historical Society Newsletter*, 17 (1993), 9: summary of lecture.

6 Tim Grass is currently researching the Reformation in the Isle of Man in the 16th and 17th centuries. See T.G Grass, 'The Reformation in the Isle of Man', *Isle of Man Studies*, 17 (2021), 89–102.

7 G.E. Quayle, *Legends of a Lifetime: Manx Folklore* (Douglas, 1973), 107; the Mylecharaine Cross: MNH 1954-4622.

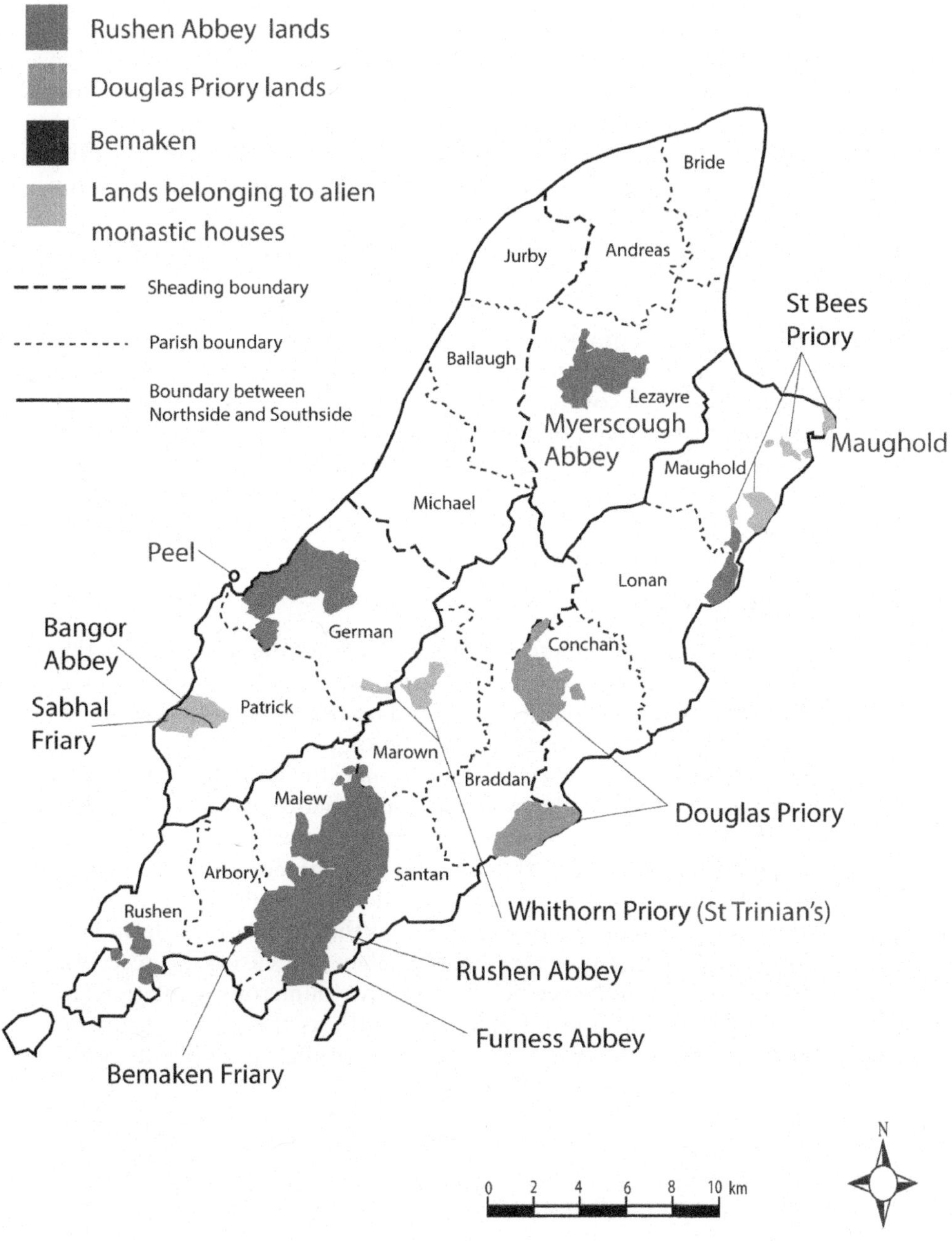

Fig. 2.1 *Monastic lands of the Isle of Man. Graphic by Peter Davey.*

(*Sodorensis* in contemporary records) that consisted of Man and the Hebrides.[8] Finally, an important outcome of this change appears to have been the creation of parishes. Initially 16 in number, with Marown added later, they formed the basis for both ecclesiastical and secular administration until the nineteenth century. Monastic institutions both insular and alien owned around one third of the ploughed land in the Island (Fig. 2.1) and made a significant contribution to religious life until their dissolution in 1540.[9]

The evidence

The nature of religious practice in the period 1400 to 1540 is difficult to determine, due to lack of contemporary ecclesiastical documentation, such as records of synods, church courts or registers. The subject can be approached, albeit rather obliquely from a number of directions: the earlier ecclesiastical and contemporary administrative, legal, and financial documents, literature, architecture, art history and archaeology. The following text is an attempt to sketch some sort of picture of religious life in the century and a half before the Reformation using a combination of these sources.

Earlier ecclesiastical sources

Three medieval synodal ordinances have survived for the diocese, together with a 'Confirmation of the church's liberties by Thomas, earl of Derby, Lord Stanley, 28 March 1505'.[10] The three statutes date from 1229/30, 1291/92 and 1350/51 respectively. The next recorded synod took place in 1577.

The three sets deal with a variety of issues, especially with the collection of monies due to the church, but also with religious practice within the churches and the behaviour of the clergy, as well as practical matters such as how priests are to be housed and the fabric of the churches maintained. They are accumulative, that is each adds to the previous one. A detailed study of the surviving texts and their context in the wider church shows that many of the ordinances were borrowed from other dioceses, but that they had clearly been written down afresh on the Island. Nevertheless, there are 'numerous regulations for which no parallel has been found elsewhere' such as the 1230/1 ordinance (para 3) on mortuaries, the 1291/2 arrangements for the churching of women

8 A. Woolf, 'The early history of the diocese of Sodor', in S. Duffy and H. Mytum (eds), *A New History of the Isle of Man*, vol. 3: *The Medieval Period, 1000–1406* (Liverpool, 2015), 336.

9 P.J. Davey and J. Roscow, *Rushen Abbey and the dissolution of the monasteries in the Isle of Man*, IMNHAS Monograph 1 (Douglas, 2010), 63–115.

10 G. Bray (ed), *Records of Convocation: Sodor and Man 1229–1877*, 2 vols (Woodbridge, 2005), vol. 1, 23–63.

(para 28) and the 1350/1 rules for how a rector is to be commemorated after his death (para1).[11]

In terms of its possible implication for the period after 1400, the third set of ordinances is of particular interest. The second of these 'additions made by the venerable father lord William Russell, bishop of Sodor' includes detailed instructions about preaching God's word and faith and the conduct of the sacraments. There is a specific instruction to all the clergy to:

> … instruct their subjects diligently in the articles of the faith, and admonish and persuade them to learn the Apostle's Creed in their mother-tongue and to expound the faith to their children and teach them the articles.[12]

Whilst Latin remained the language of the liturgy, preaching in Manx an understanding of the key tenets of faith, to adults and within the family, was intended to be the norm. It seems likely that this movement towards individual piety and the vernacular would have progressed further during the fifteenth century.

The earlier ordinances show a degree of Scottish influence which is not surprising given the origins of some of the key bishops but following the loss of the Hebrides in 1374 and under the influence of the Montacutes from 1333 and the Stanleys from 1406 the diocese became increasingly English in its orientation.[13]

Administrative, legal, and financial

The Manx customary laws were first set down in writing from 1417. This *lex scripta*, amended and added to, still forms the basis of the Manx legal system today. The very first statute deals with the organization of Tynwald Court. It is addressed to the king by the deemsters as being of the 'constitution of old time' and describes how he must 'come hither in his royal array', sit in a chair on the top of the hill 'covered with royal cloth and cushions' surrounded by the barons on the next tier down, with clerks, knights, esquires and yeomen below them. Then, 'the commons to stand without the circle of the hill, with three clerks in their surplices', with, as the earliest surviving version of the text in a Sloane MSS in the British Library indicates, 'the three relics of Man, there to be before you in your presence, and three clerks bearing them in your presence'.[14]

11 C.R. Cheney, 'Manx synodal statutes: A.D. 1230(?)–1351 part 1: introduction and Latin texts', *Cambridge Medieval Celtic Studies*, 7 (1984a), 70–71.

12 C.R. Cheney, 'Manx synodal statutes: A.D. 1230(?)–1351 part 2: translation of Latin texts', *Cambridge Medieval Celtic Studies*, 8 (1984b), 61.

13 Cheney, 'Manx synodal statutes, part 1' (1984a), 66.

14 BL Add MS 4149, fol. 331; W. Mackenzie (ed), *Legislation by three of the Stanley Kings of Man*, Manx Society, 3 (1860), 69, 194; W.W. Gill, 'The three relics of Man', *JMM*, 5:69 (1943), 125; M.A. Mills, *The ancient ordinances and statute laws of the Isle of Man* (Douglas, 1821), 5; *Statutes*, vol. 1, 4, Statute 1. This reference to three relics has

The possession of relics was of the essence in late medieval piety. They provided concrete reference points for individuals, affirmed the legitimacy of special sites and, as the objects of pilgrimage, created important sources of income for their owners. In the context of Tynwald Court, the three priests each holding a relic created a circle of awesome holiness around the hill, separating the king and law makers from the people and creating a strongly religious context and legitimacy to the secular proceedings.

There has been some discussion as to the nature of these relics, but the consensus is that they probably included St Maughold's staff and possibly those of St Patrick and St German. In other words, a staff 'belonging' to each of the Island's adopted national saints.[15]

Literature

The so-called 'Manx traditionary ballad' provides a contemporary 'folk' history of the Island with many references to its religion. This, the earliest surviving example of the Manx language, entitled *Account of the Isle of Man in Song*, only survives in two eighteenth-century copies, but on structural, linguistic and internal historic grounds the first 57 of the 62 stanzas are thought to have been written in the period 1490 to 1530.[16] The interpretation of the kind of popular piety implied in this text is made tricky by its pervading tone of ambiguous, self-deprecating cynicism – a feature well represented by the most recent free translation.[17]

The *Song* sets out a traditional insular amphictyony of conversion and dedication giving priority to Patrick who hounded 'Manannan from his seat' (9), followed by German who is credited with creating the keeills and building the cathedral (13) and then Maughold who was the supposed author of the parochial system (18). Lonan, Onchan and Marown are then mentioned but at this point the writer becomes bored: 'so that's enough of holy men' (21) and then turns to the Island's secular history which is full of complaints about taxes and witty asides about many rulers, especially the Scots.

A feature of the naming of the Island in the *Song* is its use of the term *Ellan Sheeant* meaning 'holy island' beginning even in the first stanza which announces that the subject of the song to be sung is the history of *Ellan Sheeant*. Later on, the writer asks how the Manx themselves could have created such

been omitted from later printed versions of the *Statutes* (e.g. Mills and Gill above) presumably because of their overtly papist connotations.

15 Gill, 'Three relics', 126.

16 R.L. Thomson, 'The date of the Traditionary Ballad', *JMM*, 6:75 (1958), 53–54; R.L. Thomson, 'The Manx Traditionary Ballad (suite et fin)', *Etudes Celtiques*, 10 (1962), fascicule 1, 86.

17 J. Kewley Draskau, *Account of the Isle of Man in Song* (Douglas, 2006).

bad laws in *Ellan Sheeant* (26). This name for the Island apparently survived in use until at least 1628.[18]

That the Island was known more widely for its holiness is stated in a letter from Pope Pius II to Thomas Stanley dated January 20, 1459:

> At the said petition therefore of the said Thomas, who alleges that the said isle has from very old times been enriched with the relics of many saints, and commonly called to the present day a holy isle (*insula sancta*), etc.[19]

Although this statement should be seen in the context of Thomas trying to enlist the assistance of the pope, it can hardly have been an invention and reflects how the Island was viewed by itself, by Thomas Stanley and the wider world, in contrast to neighbouring lands.

The pope's letter, quoting Stanley, also provides confirmation of the presence of relics, in the plural, almost certainly referring to those used publicly on Tynwald Day. Other possible relics seem to have resided at Rushen Abbey. At the Dissolution, Edward Stanley's officers removed the *jocalia* before the auditor from London had arrived to oversee the process of asset stripping the sites. They are not mentioned in the earl's own accounts but a list of them, for both abbey and priory, in English, has been tacked on to the Court of Augmentation accounts for that year, but without a valuation. They include a typical range of religious and domestic silver items that could be melted down for their metal such as chalices, crosses, sensors, spoons, salts, and ale-pots. But at Rushen there is also a 'hand of silver' and a 'bishop's head' which almost certainly refer to relics that provided a spiritual focus for the abbey itself. The value of all these items, £28 14s. 0d., was not admitted until the 1542/43 accounts and not paid, along with the earl's other debts to Henry VIII resulting from the Dissolution, until 1546.[20] In 1543 the lists for both abbey and priory contain the same items in the same order but some of them are more fully described. For example, the second object on the Rushen 1540 list is described as a 'crouche'. In 1543 it is the 'abbot's pastoral staff' valued at 16s. 0d. The apparent incongruity of melting down a preserved bishop's head is explained in the 1543 accounts where, following the 'silver hand' at 3s. 0d., the 'bishop's head' has become a 'reliquary' at 3s. 4d. The silver value is relatively low, and the reliquary would

18 R.L. Thomson, 'The Manx Traditionary Ballad, *Etudes Celtiques*, 9 (1961), fascicule 2, 523.

19 Vatican Regesta 470: 1459, f 441; J.A. Twemlow, *Calendar of Papal Registers Relating To Great Britain and Ireland: Volume 11, 1455–1464* (London, 1921), 379–82; *British History Online,* https://www.british-history.ac.uk/cal-papal-registers/brit-ie/vol11/pp379-382 [accessed 4 July 2020].

20 TNA, SC6/Henry VIII/5678, 5680, 5681; Davey and Roscow, *Rushen Abbey*, 26–30, 161.

have to have been big enough to contain a human head so was presumably made of wood or copper alloy and covered with silver or gold sheeting.

Although the earl may have removed the monastic *jocalia* for the same reason as Henry, to provide ready cash, given the conservative piety seen in his correspondence over the future of the church at Burscough Priory, for example, it seems quite likely that, for these two relics at least, he took them in order to preserve them.[21] What happened to them and their Tynwald counterparts? Nothing is known; but their presence demonstrates the contemporary centrality of these locally possessed symbols of faith.

Architecture and archaeology

There is little extant medieval architecture that might be used to help understand religious usage during this period, except perhaps its simplicity. The parish churches all appear to have been single-celled structures, some remaining so up to the present, others enlarged in the nineteenth century, and others replaced by new buildings nearer to the centres of population. Rushen Abbey is a rare example of a Cistercian monastery with no aisles and the cathedral itself only possessed a south aisle which was not part of the original design and was demolished in the fifteenth century. Arbory church had a rood screen, separating the nave from the chancel, placed there by Thomas Radcliffe, the abbot of Rushen who had the advowson of the parish, sometime between 1508 and 1539. The eagle and child references in its inscription also reflect the strong, penetrating influence of the Stanley family on the Manx church.[22]

The contemporary screen from Douglas priory church also survived on the site but was not incorporated into the owner's reconstituted 'chapel' in the 1870s. Both medieval screens are now in the Manx Museum.[23]

There are a handful of exceptions to this otherwise architectural simplicity. In Castletown, an aisle was added to St Mary's chapel. Its semi-circular arches are difficult to date precisely. On technical grounds they are not Romanesque in style, albeit semi-circular, and do not date from the period AD 1190 to 1230, as suggested by Cubbon.[24] They are a secondary feature, renaissance in influence,

21 T.N. Toller (ed), *Correspondence of Edward, third earl of Derby, during the years 24 to 31 Henry VIII* (Chetham Society, new ser., 19, 1890), 128–29. Although most properly used for ornaments worn by women, at the Dissolution the term *jocalia* was employed for any items, whether religious or secular, that contained enough precious metal to be melted down for money.

22 William Sacheverell, *An Account of the Isle of Man, its Inhabitants, Language, Soil, Remarkable Curiosities, the Succession of its Kings and Bishops, down to the Eighteenth Century*, c.1692 (London, 1702), 121.

23 MNH MM 1954-0541; L22221.

24 A.M. Cubbon, 'The mediaeval chapel of St Mary's Castletown, later the Castletown Grammar School', *PIMNHAS*, 7:3 (1968–70), 332–34.

Fig. 2.2 *Rood screen c.1500, probably commissioned by Thomas Radcliffe, abbot of Rushen. The inscription reads: Bloud the best cuyn of the chylde fun in the egle nest Thomas Radclyf Abbot (Blood the best scion of the child found in the eagle's nest. Thomas Radclyf Abbot). MNH L22221.*

so must represent an enlargement of the chapel at sometime within the period of this essay.[25]

In the middle ages St Patrick's Island held the parish churches for both Patrick (the chapel) and German (the cathedral). An entry in the 1428 garrison roll refers to a meeting in the 'chapel in the holme town', which probably refers to an earlier manifestation of what was to become St Peter's church in the centre of the town, right next to the market place.[26] There are no surviving architectural details that are certainly medieval in date, though the masonry used in the so-called piscina may just possibly have functioned as the voussoir of a medieval window frame.[27] The aisles are late seventeenth- and eighteenth- century in date. But with the new stone curtain wall of the castle being constructed between 1432 and 1460, it seems likely that the inhabitants of both parishes had moved to the church in the town by the first half of the fifteenth century.[28]

The main structural walls of other parish churches, such as Malew, may well be medieval and may have been enlarged during this period but there is no direct evidence for this.[29] An exception is Maughold which experienced a second extension and rebuilding of its east end, given the detail of the new perpendicular east window and its glass, early in the fifteenth century.[30]

25 P.J. Davey, *After the Vikings: medieval archaeology of the Isle of Man AD 1100–1550* (Douglas, 2013), 86–88; J. Kewley, 'The old grammar school', in J Kewley (ed), *Annual conference 2014: the Isle of Man conference notes*, London: The Society of Architectural Historians of Great Britain (London, 2014), 129–32.

26 MNH MS 09862, garrison roll, 1428.

27 J.J. Joughin, 'St Peter's church, Peel', *PIMNHAS*, 2:4 (1924), 425–46.

28 H.G. Slade, 'Architectural interpretation', in D. Freke, *Excavations on St Patrick's Isle, Peel, Isle of Man 1982–88* (Liverpool, 2002), 213.

29 J. Kewley, 'Malew church', in J. Kewley (ed), *Annual conference 2014: the Isle of Man conference notes*, London: The Society of Architectural Historians of Great Britain (London, 2014), 146–48.

30 F. Logan, 'Maughold parish church: an attempt at structural analysis', *Isle of Man Studies*, 17 (2021), 49–50, phase 6 (BA thesis, University of Chester, 2012), 12–13; *Manx Archaeological Survey Fourth Report* (Douglas, 1915; reprinted Glasgow 1968), 14–15.

All these examples seem to be the product of population increase, which can be seen in the surviving rent books, rather than any change of religious practice. They show, albeit on a small scale, that the Island remained in the mainstream of western European architectural development during this period. In Castletown and Peel in particular, the practice of religion was becoming more urban with larger numbers of people from wider socio-economic backgrounds worshiping together.

A particularly interesting and unique contemporary artefact at Maughold is its early fifteenth-century high cross which has been the subject of a recent architectural study.[31] It is a very high-quality sculpture with very few contemporary parallels in Britain or Ireland of the same standard or complexity and contains both religious and secular imagery, the meaning of much of which is obscure. The Manx connection is clear from the three-legs symbols on one of its faces. But why was such a unique artefact erected in Maughold? As some of its imagery may have been considered papist, was perhaps the upper part removed from a more prominent position, say in the centre of Castletown or Peel, to a more remote location for its own safety?[32] Given its high quality, was it, for the same reason, brought to the Island from Lancashire at the reformation by Edward, the third earl? Whatever the answer, a number of later medieval crosses seem to have survived into the early modern period or, at least, the use of standing crosses in market places and elsewhere continued to act as communal focal points, for example the one in Ballasalla.[33]

A few smaller ecclesiastical items survive from this period, in particular the very fine silver chalice from Jurby, apparently made in Lancashire and essayed in London in 1521/2, and the Mylecharaine early fifteenth-century silver cross which is likely to have been the possession of a senior cleric, possibly an abbot, given its discovery on Myerscough abbey land in Lezayre where it was preserved by a local farming family.[34]

The detail of the window and its glass is still visible in a late 19th century photograph in the Manx Museum: PG11545.

31 D. Allwood, 'The Maughold high cross and its symbolism', *Isle of Man Studies*, 16 (2019), 39–54.

32 Joughin, 'St Peter's church, Peel', 427; E. Wilson, *A book of prospects … seventeenth-century prints and drawings of the Isle of Man* (Castletown, 2014), 42–43.

33 P.J. Davey, 'Towards the 16th-century topography of Ballasalla', *PIMNHAS*, 12:3 (2012), 380, fig. 7.

34 J. Feltham, *A Tour through the Island of Mann, in 1797 and 1798* (Bath, 1798), 182; E.L. Barnwell, 'Church furniture in Malew church, Isle of Man', *Archaeologia Cambrensis*, 3rd ser., 48 (Oct 1866), 475 (MNH M 02333; P.J. Davey, *After the Vikings* (Douglas, 2013), 77–78; W. Harrison, 'The Mylecharaine silver cross', Manx Society, 21 (1873), 106–07; C. Radcliffe, 'Mylecharaine: the tune and the treasure', *PIMNHAS*, 10:1 (1989–91), 49–62. Constance Radcliffe tracked the cross down to 1720 and the family that preserved it to 1607, but she did not have access to the Court of Augmentations

Fig. 2.3 *Mylecharaine silver cross: MNH 1954-4622.*

At Malew, the parish church still retains three medieval items: part of a copper alloy thurible, a small bronze crucifix, possibly twelfth century and a paten dating, on formal and decorative grounds, from between 1500 and 1525.[35] It is inscribed with the legend SANCTE LUPE ORA PRO NOBIS and appears to have been in continuous use in the communion service until late in the nineteenth century when, because the details had become worn, the parish had an exact copy made.[36]

The survival of these artefacts and the continued use of some of them is evidence of a religious conservatism only partially swayed by changes in doctrine.

The role of music in the Manx church of this period is unclear. The people were described in the seventeenth century as 'much inclined to music' and music was clearly important within the Stanley entourage.[37] It seems likely that to plainchant would have been added the new polyphonic forms widely adopted in this period, especially in the cathedrals and major monasteries. Direct evidence of this is contained in a detailed indenture drawn up in 1503 by John Faragher, abbot of Rushen, and the authorities of Chester abbey for one John Darse to

---

Manx accounts or the 1540 Liber Assedationes (Lib.Assed.), which show that the same family (with a variety of spellings) were monastic tenants in 1540, so that the cross may well have been held by them since the Dissolution. See Davey and Roscow, *Rushen Abbey*, 143–76.

35 E.A. Jones, *The old church plate of the Isle of Man* (London & Derby, 1907).

36 Barnwell, 'Church furniture in Malew', 472.

37 Sacheverell, *Account*: Introduction.

Fig. 2.4 *Malew silver paten: Malew parish church. Photo: Peter Davey, courtesy of the vicar and wardens, Malew parish church.*

study there for six years with William Park; the musical part of the agreement was to teach him:

> ......to synge prykkytsong, Descant of all man[ner] mesurs & to sygn upon a pryksonge fawburdon to cownter of ev[er]y mesur, & to set a songe of thre p[ar]ts iiij or v sbstancyally, and also to play upon the organs any man[ner] playsong or prykkytsonge two pts or thre.[38]

The abbot is paying for musical education that includes plainchant, part writing and playing the organ. This strongly suggests that liturgical polyphony had arrived at the abbey and that it possessed an organ. The same was probably true of the cathedral and possibly in some of the parish churches. No contemporary musical instruments of any kind survive.

Summary

Manx religious beliefs, practices, and institutions in the period between 1400 and the Reformation appear to have been similar to those of the surrounding lands and, through Derby influence, increasingly close to those in north-west England. The ecclesiastical structure was simpler, less hierarchical and its rules contained some insular elements. In terms of popular belief and perception

38 J. Flynn, 'Thomas Mulliner: an apprentice of John Heywood?', in S. Boynton and E. Rice (eds), *Young choristers, 650–1700*, Studies in medieval and renaissance music, 7 (Martlesham, 2008), 175.

Man was seen as a 'holy island' not especially because of the faithfulness or piety of its inhabitants but because of its possession of holy relics. Their significance and the unusually deep integration of the religious with the secular appeared with the greatest clarity and force on Tynwald Day when the law givers and church officials were surrounded by a saintly force field. Man functioned as a Lindisfarne, a Durham and a Westminster rolled into one.[39]

Some elements of late medieval belief and a few artifacts survived beyond the Reformation. The *Song*, with its history of the saints of the Manx early church, continued to be remembered and not rejected. The Jurby chalice continued in use, as did the Malew paten with its Latin invocation to St Lupus; and the Mylecharaine cross was preserved by successive generations of a Lezayre family. The survival of many holy wells, with their individual saintly dedications and their uses for healing into the recent past is evidence, perhaps, of a continuity from even further in the past.[40]

THE IMPACT OF THE REFORMATION

Nigel Yates †

Until the late 1570s it is unlikely that much attempt was made to promote the Reformation in the Isle of Man. Edward Stanley, third earl of Derby, who held the lordship of Man for over 50 years (1521–72), was a religious conservative who had assisted in the suppression of the northern rebellion against the dissolution of the monasteries in 1536–37 but protested in the House of Lords against the legalisation of clerical marriages in Edward VI's reign.[41] In 1570 a bishop of similar conservative views was appointed to the diocese of Sodor and Man when John Salisbury (1570–73) was translated from the suffragan bishopric of Thetford. Salisbury, a former Benedictine monk, had been an early supporter of the Reformation, but by 1550 his Protestant opinions had cooled and he could be described as 'an ex-monk of steadily more conservative religious outlook'.[42] He held in plurality the deanery of Norwich and is not known to have visited his diocese.[43]

39 In other words, a place set apart for its holy relics (Lindisfarne), the centre of an episcopal see (Durham) and a law giving centre (Westminster).

40 Davey, *After the Vikings*, 91–93, fig. 72.

41 *ODNB*: Stanley, Thomas, 3rd earl of Derby, 52, 175–77.

42 D. MacCulloch, *Thomas Cranmer* (New Haven and London, 1996), 458.

43 For Salisbury's career see *ODNB*: Salisbury, John, 48, 710–11; A. Jessop, *One Generation of a Norfolk House: A Contribution to Elizabethan History*, 3rd edn (London, 1913), 67–68; R. Houlbrooke, 'Refoundation and Reformation, 1538–1628', in I. Atherton, E. Fernie, C. Harper-Bill and H. Smith (eds), *Norwich Cathedral: City, Church and Diocese, 1096–1996* (London, 1996), 510–11; M.C. McClendon, *The Quiet Reformation:*

In 1576 a committed Welsh Protestant, John Meyrick (1576–99) was consecrated bishop. Though he retained his living of Hornchurch in Essex, he visited the Isle of Man; in 1594 the vicars-general were to 'inquire of and present all such as carry bells or banners before the dead, or pray upon the graves of the dead'.[44] However, it was not until 1610 that the children of married clergy were formally legitimised. Bishop Parr complained in 1635 'that the grossest superstitions were practised in church' and in 1688 Bishop Levinz noted the survival of 'reliques of popish superstition', including prayers for the dead.[45] This, however, was not formal recusancy but more a case of debased and popular survivals, on a par with the widespread belief in the efficacy of charms and fairy doctors, and which had its counterparts in Ireland, Scotland and Wales, where similar survivals were noted well into the nineteenth century.[46] Ronald Hutton has argued that these represent a kind of impromptu replacement for the rites which a priest was no longer able to perform.[47] Indeed, by the late sixteenth century the Manx Church was being subjected as much to puritan as to recusant influences. The fourth earl of Derby (lord of Man 1572–93), though not himself a puritan, was strongly anti-Catholic and vigorous in exposing recusants and is known to have invited puritan clergy to preach before him at Knowsley and Lathom.

Meyrick's successor as bishop, George Lloyd (1600–04), who combined the bishopric with the living of Heswall in Cheshire, was sympathetic to puritan demands for a more Protestant liturgy, but his successor, John Phillips (1604–33), was not.[48] Phillips was the first post-Reformation bishop to really make his mark on the diocese, though his episcopate was not without controversy. He is said to have been appointed archdeacon of Man in 1587 and retained this when he became bishop; until 1619 he also held the archdeaconry of Cleveland, the rectory of Slingsby in the diocese of York and other benefices.[49] In 1610

Magistrates and the Emergence of Protestantism in Tudor Norwich (Stamford, 1999), 79–80, 138–39, 203.

44 Wright, S., 'Meyrick, John (1537/8–1599), bishop of Sodor and Man', *ODNB*, 38, 5–6; Bray (ed), *Records of Convocation*, vol. 1, 75.

45 Moore, *Sodor and Man*, 97–98, 174; H.R. Trevor-Roper, *Archbishop Laud 1573–1645*, 2nd edn (London, 1965), 189; Ashley, 'Spiritual courts', 37.

46 D. Craine, *Manannan's Isle* (Douglas, 1955), 28. For the lack of survival of formal recusancy in the Isle of Man see W.S. Dempsey, *The Story of the Catholic Church in the Isle of Man* (Billinge, 1958), 128–36, and J. Bossy, *The English Catholic Community 1570–1850* (London, 1975), 111.

47 R. Hutton, 'The English Reformation and the evidence of folklore', *Past and Present*, 148 (1995), 89–116.

48 *ODNB*: Lloyd, George, 34, 123–24.

49 *ODNB*: Phillips, John, 44, 116–17. The earliest evidence for Phillips as archdeacon is the fact that he was deprived in favour of Curwen by the fifth earl of Derby, who was

Fig. 2.5 *Bishop Phillips' Manx Gaelic translation of the Prayer Book (handwritten, bound): MNH MS 00003.*

Phillips attempted, unsuccessfully, to impose a Manx translation of the *Book of Common Prayer* on the Manx Church.

This would have completed the arrangements whereby all parts of the British Isles which used this liturgy had an official version in the language used by a majority of the inhabitants: similar translations had been made into French, for use in Calais and the Channel Islands, in 1553, into Welsh in 1567 and Irish in 1571.[50] The Manx clergy, however, preferred to maintain their existing practice of making an *extempore* translation of the English services. Whether this was religious conservatism, the influence of puritan objections to a set form of liturgy or, perhaps more likely in the light of recent scholarship, simply differences in orthography, is not clear.

Certainly there is evidence of some puritan influence in the Isle of Man in the early seventeenth century. John Woods, the parish clerk of Michael refused to 'attend the minister in the chancel where Divine Service is usually read' in 1616, or to help him with his surplice, 'but would have the communion table and the Byble removed down into the body of the church, where he himself sayt, and there onlie he sayd he would do and execute these services'.[51] Another possible indication of puritan influence is the interesting survival of communion beakers, in place of chalices, in several Manx churches. Beakers are exceptionally rare survivals in England, though common in parts of presbyterian Scotland, and are, almost invariably, associated with known puritan clergy or congregations, or the meeting houses of foreign or dissenting English Protestants. The earliest

lord of Man from1593 until his death on 16 April 1594. See MNH MS 00509, 22; MS 00510, 71 (both Lib.Canc., 1595).

50 W.K.L. Clarke and C. Harris (eds), *Liturgy and Worship: A Companion to the Prayer Books of the Anglican Communion* (London, 1932), 814–15; D.N. Griffiths, *The Bibliography of the Book of Common Prayer 1549–1999* (London, 2002), 510.

51 MNH MS 10071/3/3 (Lib.Scacc.), 1616, fol. 36.

surviving of these Manx beakers is one of 1591–92 at German (see Fig. 2.32). However, eight other Manx churches have between them a total of ten beakers dating from between 1703 and 1789.[52] Although none of these gifts came from other than orthodox Anglican sources, they may represent the popular survival of a type of communion vessel that had been introduced to the Isle of Man through earlier puritan influences. James Chaloner recorded in 1656 that 'now that Episcopacy, with Ecclesiastical Jurisdiction accompanying the same, is put down in England, the same is by their example laid here aside', but also went out of his way to praise two former bishops, Phillips and Parr, as 'very eminent for Piety and Learning' and 'excellent Patterns for the Clergie under them'.[53] The evidence for possible efforts to deprive and replace members of the Manx clergy is not clear cut; while there is no indication of a dramatic high-profile and systematic campaign to remove ministers, the funeral sermon preached for Fairfax by his chaplain Richard Stretton suggests that efforts were made to displace some men who were considered unacceptable.[54] Of the fifteen named holders of Manx benefices in 1642, five were still holding the same or another Manx benefice in 1663, two had moved elsewhere in the Island, five had died in office, one was displaced and the details of two others are unknown. None of their successors was, however, deprived in 1662.[55] This argues for the absorption of non-extremist puritan influences into the Manx Church in such a way as to provide for religious stability, and a relative lack (with one exception) of Protestant dissent, in the Isle of Man, unique in the British Isles, until the late eighteenth century.[56]

52 Jones, *Old Church Plate*; J. Gilchrist, *Anglican Church Plate* (London, 1967), 59–71.

53 J. Chaloner, *A Short Treatise of the Island of Man, digested into six chapters, by James Chaloner, one of the commissioners under Lord Fairfax, for settling the affairs of the Isle of Man in 1652; and afterwards Governor of the island, from 1658 to 1660. Originally published in 1656, as an appendix to 'King's Vale Royal of England; or, the County Palatine of Chester, Illustrated with Severall Prospects of the Island, by Daniel King* [written 1653, published 1656] (London) (MNH MS 12587), 7,9.

54 Bodleian, MS Fairfax 33, fols 24r–v.

55 MNH MS 09309; W. Harrison, *An Account of the Diocese of Sodor and Man*, Manx Society, 29 (1879), 73–138. New research suggests that Harrison's lists of parish clergy are not always accurate.

56 Feltham noted fifteen Methodist 'meeting houses' in the landscape in 1797–98: J. Feltham, *A Tour Through the Island of Mann in 1797 and 1798* (Bath, 1798), 206; see also J. Rosser, *The History of Wesleyan Methodism in the Isle of Man: with some account of the Island, and of the life and labours of Bishop Wilson; in a series of letters* (Douglas, 1849), letters 4, 6, 7.

THE DIOCESE AND ITS BISHOPS, 1661–1827

Nigel Yates † with contributions by Frances Coakley, Priscilla Lewthwaite and Jennifer Platten †

Before the death of Bishop Parr in 1643 the bishops of Sodor and Man had invariably combined their episcopal duties with the holding of another benefice, normally one in England. This pattern continued after the restoration of the bishopric in 1661. Of the eleven bishops between then and 1827, only four were not pluralists. Samuel Rutter (1661–62) combined the bishopric with the archdeaconry of Man he had held since 1644.[57]

Isaac Barrow (1663–71) was also rector of Downham, in Cambridgeshire, and for his last year in office combined the diocese with that of St Asaph.[58] Henry Bridgeman (1671–82) was also dean of Chester, John Lake (1683–84) a prebendary at St Paul's and York, and Baptist Levinz (1685–93) a prebendary at Wells and Winchester.[59] Thomas Wilson (1698–1755) was the first post-Reformation Manx bishop to refuse a benefice *in commendam*, but his example was not followed by his two immediate successors: Mark Hildesley (1755–72) was rector of Holwell, in Hertfordshire, until 1767 and thereafter master of Sherburn Hospital, Durham; Richard Richmond (1773–80) combined the bishopric with the Lancashire rectory of Walton-on-the-Hill.[60] This pluralism was not, in and of itself, detrimental to the interests of the Manx Church. The diocese was much smaller than any others in the provinces of Canterbury and York and the bishop, unlike all his episcopal colleagues in both provinces, had a seat but no vote in the House of Lords, so did not have to undertake the parliamentary duties that occupied all other bishops for most of the winter months. Such pluralism could also be justified by the poverty of the bishopric, which was roughly on a par with those of Bristol, Llandaff, Oxford and Rochester, all valued at between £450 and £600 *per annum* in 1762. All these bishoprics, and four others valued between £900 and £1000, were held with other preferment *in commendam* in order to increase the annual incomes to the levels that were

57 Rosser, *Wesleyan Methodism*, 65; J. Davies, *The Caroline Captivity of the Church: Charles I and the Remoulding of Anglicanism* (Oxford, 1992), 326, where his surname is given incorrectly as 'Rutler'. Rutter swore the oath of allegiance as archdeacon in Feb 1643/4, just before Parr died: MNH MS 09864, GR1/24.

58 J.R. Dickinson, 'Barrow, Isaac (1612/13–1680), bishop of St Asaph', *ODNB*, 4, 97–98. See also M.J. Hoy, *Isaac Barrow: his Life and Legacy* (Douglas, 2010).

59 J.R. Dickinson, 'Bridgeman, Henry (1615–1682), bishop of Sodor and Man', *ODNB*, 7, 566–67; J. Stephens, 'Levinz, Baptist (c.1644–1693), bishop of Sodor and Man', *ODNB*, 32, 244–46; 33, 548–49.

60 Gelling, *Manx Church*, 29, 36; J. and J.A. Venn, *Alumni cantabrigienses: a biographical list of all known students, graduates and holders of office at the University of Cambridge, from the earliest times to 1900*, 10 vols (Cambridge, 1922–54), vol. 1, 3, 456.

Fig. 2.6 *Bishop Samuel Rutter, unknown artist: MNH 1954-7824.*

Fig. 2.7 *Bishop Isaac Barrow, unknown artist: Peterhouse, Cambridge. Image courtesy of the Master and Fellows, Peterhouse, Cambridge.*

needed to enable bishops to afford the expense of carrying out their episcopal duties.[61] In the case of the diocese of Sodor and Man, the financial inducement of holding other benefices *in commendam* also helped to compensate the bishops for the difficulties caused by the geographical remoteness of the Isle of Man and the hazardous nature of the journey by sea. When the younger Thomas Wilson visited his aged father in 1750, he noted in his diary several days of fierce winds and driving rain even at the height of summer.[62] In July 1757 Bishop Hildesley was prevented from carrying out his planned visitation of Lonan Church by 'the severity of the weather' and it was carried out on his behalf by the registrar.[63]

Undoubtedly the Manx bishop with the highest reputation over the years has been Thomas Wilson, whose record-breaking episcopate of 57 years was regarded as a model by the early Tractarians. His pastoral writings were republished by them in *The Tracts for the Times* and his more profound theological works re-issued in *The Library of Anglo-Catholic Theology.* The life by John Keble, published to accompany the latter, remains the standard biography of Wilson, replacing two earlier works.[64] Wilson had been promoted to the bishopric after a five-year vacancy in the see which was widely felt to be an abuse. In September 1695 the governor of the Isle of Man, William Sacheverell, wrote in obvious frustration to Archbishop Tenison of Canterbury:

> The Charge with which the Earl of Derby has entrusted Me in the Government of his Isle of Man forces Me to lay before Your Grace the Necessity the poor Church of that place labours under, not only in the want of a Bishop by the Decease of our Late Reverend Prelate Dr Levinz, but at my coming over I found the ancient Cathedral down, and several Churches ruinous, to ye Repairing whereof the Earl of Derby has kept the Bishoprick vacant for near three years, and tho' the Churches are already repaired, yet the Necessity of

61 W. Gibson, *The Achievement of the Anglican Church, 1689–1800: The Confessional State in Eighteenth Century England* (Lampeter, 1995), 199–201.

62 C.L.S. Linnell (ed), *The Diaries of Thomas Wilson, DD, 1731–7 and 1750* (London, 1964), 242–47.

63 MNH MS 00791 C.

64 J. Keble, *The Life of Thomas Wilson*, 2 vols (Oxford, 1863); C. Cruttwell, *The Life of the Right Reverend Thomas Wilson, DD, Lord Bishop of Sodor and Man,* 8 vols, 4th edn (Bath, 1797), vol. 1; H. Stowell, *The Life of the Right Reverend Father in God Thomas Wilson, DD, Lord Bishop of Sodor and Man* (London, 1819). For the most recent re-assessment of Wilson see J.O. Mann, 'Thomas Wilson and Anglicanism: A Study of the Theology, Spirituality and Pastoral Practice of Thomas Wilson, Bishop of Sodor and Man (1698–1755) with reference to his place within the development of Anglicanism, examined chiefly on the basis of his written works' (MA thesis, Queen's University Belfast, 1998). In the portrait, Wilson holds a map of the Isle of Man in place of a traditional bible which is thought to represent his great love of the Island and its people.

Fig. 2.8 *Bishop Thomas Wilson, unknown artist: MNH PG/5947/2.*

> a Chappel in Castletown will force his Lordship to continue the Vacancy at least 'til Easter next ... but were these our only misfortunes they ought to be born without Complaint, but the poor Clergy here so absolutely depend on His Majesty's Benefaction of £100 a year, which has for more than two Years been unpaid, so y[t] the Greatest Part are fallen into poverty and Debt, and three Churches are already vacant... 3 of the hopefullest of our Young Men y[t] ever ye Island bred have deserted Us, for fear they should be impos'd on them. I know I need no other argument to so great a Patron of the Church than to open ye misery of our Condition, and y[t] Your Grace would at least be pleas'd to retrieve his Majesty's Benefaction.[65]

No such vacancy occurred on Wilson's death and his reforming agenda was continued by his immediate successor, Mark Hildesley, also the subject of an almost contemporary biography.[66]

Hildesley achieved what his predecessor John Phillips had failed to achieve 150 years earlier, the provision of both a complete Bible and the *Book of Common Prayer* translated into Manx. Although this work had been begun by Wilson, it had proceeded very slowly. On 2 October 1761, Hildesley informed the clergy that this was now a matter of the highest priority and by 10 November he was pleased to inform them that a Manx translation of the psalms was now available. Hildesley was greatly encouraged in his work by the archbishop of York, Robert Hay Drummond, who wrote to him on 14 August 1762 to draw comparison with Wales, where the service was always read in the language the parishioners best understood: 'the people have a right to this and to every effort of that sincere affection for the salvation of souls'. At a convocation held on 23 September 1762 responsibility for translating the proper collects, epistles and gospels in the *Book of Common Prayer* was divided out among the Manx clergy, each taking four or five Sundays or holy days. At a subsequent convocation, on 21 May 1767, a similar division was made for the translation of the books of the Old Testament.[67] A complete translation of the *Book of Common Prayer* was first published in 1765 and of the Bible, three years after Hildesley's death, in 1775.[68]

The praise which has been lavished by historians of the diocese on Bishops Wilson (1698–1755) and Hildesley (1755–72) is in marked contrast to the contempt expressed for the three occupants of the bishopric between 1773 and

65 Lambeth Palace Library MS 941, f.74. The 1695 dating is derived from a librarian's annotation to the ms; others have dated it to 1693, which is when Sacheverell was appointed.

66 W. Butler, *Memoirs of Mark Hildesley, DD, Lord Bishop of Sodor and Man and Master of Sherburn Hospital* (London, 1799).

67 Bray (ed), *Records of Convocation*, vol. 1, 267–76, 295–96; Gelling, *Manx Church*, 34.

68 *The Book of Common Prayer ... translated into Manks* (London, 1765) (MNH M 02680); *Yn Vible Casherick* (Whitehaven, 1775) (MNH M 02581).

Fig. 2.9 *Bishop Mark Hildesley, unknown artist: MNH L21814.*

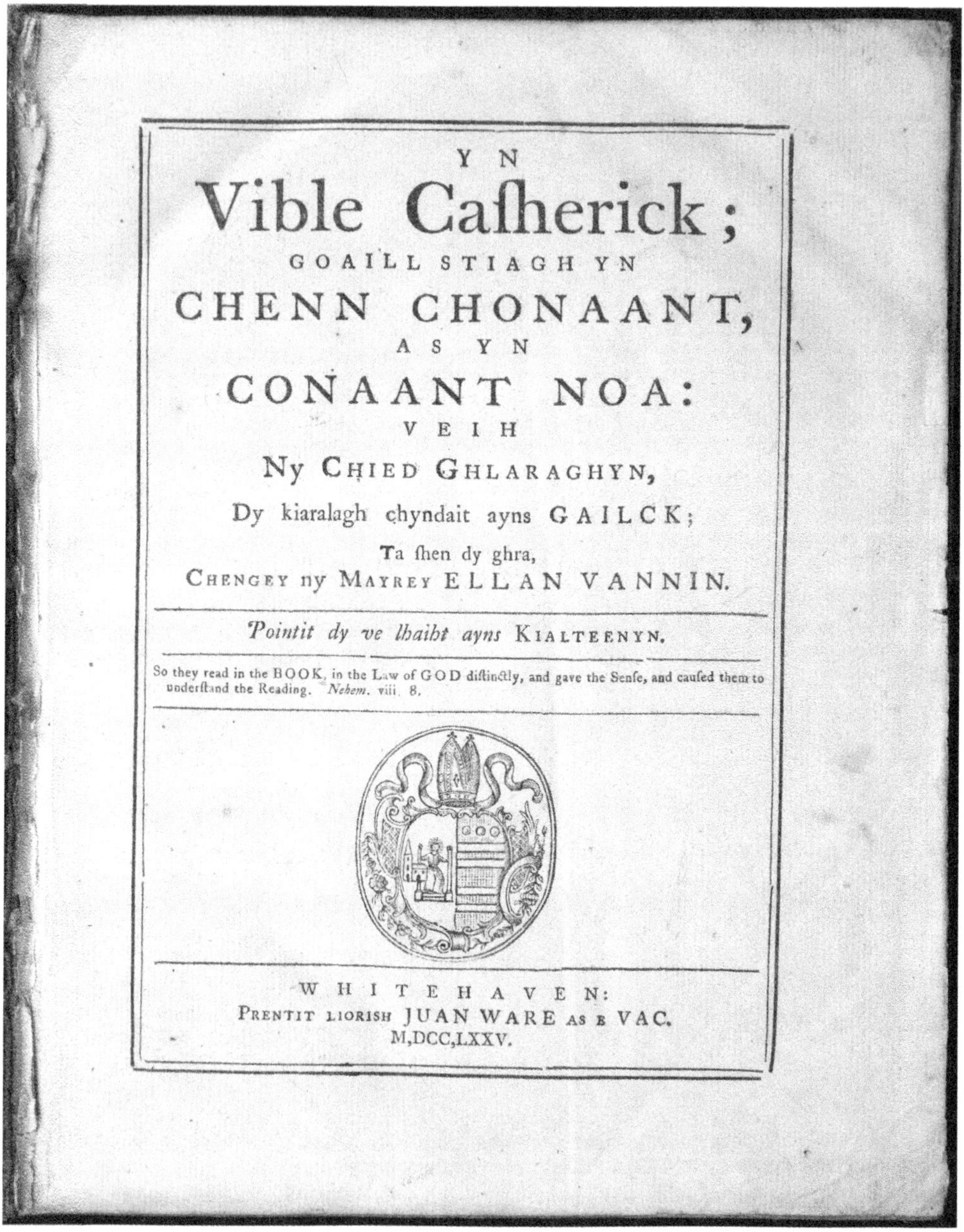

Y N

Vible Casherick;

GOAILL STIAGH YN

CHENN CHONAANT,

AS YN

CONAANT NOA:

VEIH

Ny CHIED GHLARAGHYN,

Dy kiaralagh chyndait ayns GAILCK;

Ta shen dy ghra,

CHENGEY ny MAYREY ELLAN VANNIN.

Pointit dy ve lhaiht ayns KIALTEENYN.

So they read in the BOOK, in the Law of GOD distinctly, and gave the Sense, and caused them to understand the Reading. *Nehem.* viii. 8.

WHITEHAVEN:

PRENTIT LIORISH JUAN WARE AS E VAC.

M,DCC,LXXV.

Fig. 2.10 *Yn Vible Casherick (Bible in Manx Gaelic), completed and published in 1775: MNH M 02581.*

1813, much of which is unjustified. Bishop Richmond's acknowledged lethargy was largely the result of poor health, as one of his clergy, Philip Moore, noted during his final illness in 1780:

> Last winter he was tap'd in four different parts of the Abdomen – but not above a quart of any Liquid obtained – it was all converted into a thick Gelatinous Matter like Jelly. He had a miserable time of it for years with Gout, Asthma and Dropsy. When stripped for the operation no man on earth would take him for a human creature but for his face, he was such a monstrous figure of Fat and Blubber – like a Whale.[69]

Dr Thomas Wilson noted of Bishop Mason (1780–83) that 'I have heard a very good account of him and the poor Church of Man never stood more in need of a Worthy Prelate, but his early death meant that he made little impact on the diocese.[70] Much of Claudius Crigan's long episcopate, between 1784 and his death in 1813, was disrupted by allegations of simony spread against him by Charlotte, Baroness Strange and duchess of Atholl, to the effect that he had offered her money for the appointment which he had then refused to pay, in an effort to discredit him. Crigan vigorously denied both the allegations and attributed them to his refusal to ordain 'certain characters without proper certificates' who happened to be friends or protégés of the duchess or her allies, at a time of division between her and her son, the fourth duke of Atholl, with whom Crigan had good relations.[71] The statements made by Crigan against the duchess seem to be confirmed in a peremptory letter she wrote to the bishop on 18 November 1791:

> It is with great surprise I hear you have refused to induct Mr N. Christian to KK Arbory, in stating an Act of Parliament which cannot exist, as I have an undoubted Right of Patronage in the Isle of Man, you are the Second Bishop of my own making, and whenever you make a Vacancy I shall undoubtedly make a Third. Your ingratitude has often shewed itself, once in particular you may remember refusing Mr Crawford Priest Orders tho' particularly desired to ordain him by myself … I expect to hear Mr Christian is inducted to KK Arbory by Return of Post.[72]

69 Quoted in Linnell (ed), *Diaries,* 22.

70 Linnell (ed), *Diaries*, 22–23.

71 MNH MS 09707, Atholl Papers, 116 (2nd) – 2, 3, 4, 16; letters from Bishop Crigan to his godmother, Mrs Colquitt, 18 and 22 June 1792, 12 December 1792 and 31 August 1795.

72 MNH MS 04600 C. The letter raises some interesting discrepancies: Gelling, *Manx Church,* 225, 243, 251, notes that John Christian became vicar of Arbory and Nicholas Christian became chaplain of St Matthew's Douglas, both late in 1791. Had Bishop Crigan got his own way or had the duchess of Atholl got her names mixed up?

In the same letter the duchess repeated to Crigan the allegations she was circulating against him:

> Your God Mother Mrs Colquit promised in y^{r} name and which you solemnly promised to perform the first time I saw you at Bath, and which you would have gone down on your knees to swear to … that I might depend on y^{r} word, had I known either her or you as well as I do at present, it wd not have been in y^{r} power to have shewed any Ingratitude.[73]

There is no doubt that Crigan's apparent failure to dispel the allegations circulating against him were immensely damaging to his standing in the Island and effectively prevented him from exercising his episcopal office in a proper manner.[74]

The view held by some later historians of the Manx church, that the fourth duke of Atholl acted improperly after Crigan's death by keeping the diocese vacant for 11 months so that his nephew, George Murray, could reach the minimum canonical age for consecration as a bishop, was not shared by contemporaries.[75] Daniel Mylrea, rector of Ballaugh, wrote to the duke to say 'that it gives me the sincerest pleasure to find that your Grace has thought of appointing your nephew Mr Murray to be Bishop of this diocese, a Man who I am confident will fulfil the Duties of his high Office, with the greatest dignity and Integrity, and it will be a high Honor to the Diocese of Mann to have its See filled with so worthy a Character'. It is clear that Bishop Crigan's troubles had led to serious neglect, not just of the episcopal duties but of the episcopal property as well, Bishopscourt being described as 'very much infested with rats … as I never saw a place that has so much of that kind of Vermin about'.[76] Tribute was also paid to Murray's work by his successor, William Ward, who described him in his first charge as 'a great benefactor in this neighbourhood. He promoted industry and virtue, and suppressed vice all around him, and his benevolence and charity to the poor amounted to a high degree of liberality'. However, Ward clearly took the view that Murray had not acted wisely in the 'unhappy variance that rose between the Bishop and the people' over the matter of tithes during his episcopate, referred to later in this chapter, and which had led to his translation, for his own safety, to the see of Rochester in 1827.[77]

73 MNH MS 04600 C.

74 See W.T. Gibson, '"Sully the lawn sleeves": the appointment of Claudius Crigan as bishop of Sodor and Man, 1784', *Journal of the British Records Association*, 23 (1998), 41–50.

75 Gelling, *Manx Church*, 52.

76 MNH MS 09707, Atholl Papers 107–30, letter from Daniel Mylrea to the duke of Atholl, 21 April 1813.

77 MNH MS 09309.

THE ISLAND CLERGY

Nigel Yates †

When Isaac Barrow became bishop of Sodor and Man, he described the inhabitants as having

> no means of instruction, or of being better acquainted with the very principles of Christianity. Their ministers, it is true, took upon them to preach; but were themselves much fitter to be taught, being very ignorant and wholly illiterate; having had no other education than what that rude place afforded them: not many books among them, nor they intelligent of any but English books, which come rarely thither. The poverty of the clergy gave no encouragement to such merchandise, their livings not amounting to above five or six pounds *per annum*, which forced them to engage in all mechanical courses, even in keeping ale-houses to procure a livelihood.[78]

Barrow's remedy for the problems he had analysed was 'to acquaint the people with the English tongue … and for this purpose to set up an English school in every parish' and to establish 'a Grammar School which is also wanting'.[79] He banned the clergy from keeping alehouses with penalties of suspension for the first offence 'and for the second made incapable of any spirituall preferment in this Island'.[80] These were not new problems. In 1634 it had been noted that 'all the clergy except two or three are illiterate men, brought up in the island in secular professions' and in 1639 Bishop Parr stated that 'most of the Ministers were of no better ability than to read distinctly divine service'.[81] Complaints against the vicar of Maughold, Robert Allen, in 1642, alleged that

> there is no Manx sermon in our Church … There is no catechising or only a little in Lent; the sick are not visited; the parties dying without prayers, exhortation and the Holy Communion, though much desired by the sick. Children … have to be taken to other parishes for their christendom and to pay for it.[82]

On the other hand, William Blundell recorded positive assessments of the clergy during his time in the Island (1648–56), and in 1666 the churchwardens of Arbory described their vicar, John Crellin, in glowing terms:

> He observes holydays, fasting days, Ember weeks and yearly perambulations. He instructs children diligently, preparing them to be confirmed. He never

78 MNH MS 09782 (CRP), assorted ecclesiastical documents (Box 2 of 3 at 2014).

79 MNH MS 09782 (CRP), (Box 2 of 3).

80 Moore, *Sodor and Man,* 156–58.

81 Moore, *Sodor and Man,* 134.

82 Craine, *Mananan's Isle,* 114.

> neglects to visit the sick nor baptize any children. He preaches true and sound doctrine to his congregation in knowledge, faith and obedience.[83]

It would appear that, as in all other parts of the British Isles, the Manx clergy could furnish examples of both extreme diligence and extreme negligence, but that most fell into neither of these categories.

There were, however, particular problems facing the bishop of Sodor and Man, which Barrow and his successors made strenuous efforts to address. One was the poverty of the Manx livings. This, together with the need to be able to conduct services in Manx, made them unattractive to anyone who was not a native of the Isle of Man, in which the facilities for the education of both clergy and laity were so poor. In the late seventeenth century most Manx clergy were also farmers, frequently farming land additional to their own glebe. John Huddleston, curate of Andreas during the 1660s, owned four draught oxen, ten other cattle, six horses, 70 sheep, four pigs, 11 stocks of bees and a fishing boat. His inventory at his death, however, recorded ownership of no books, though his contemporaries, Charles Crowe, vicar of Santon, and John Crellin, vicar of Arbory, died leaving about 30 and 70 books respectively.[84] There is no doubt that the Island's livings were poor. Lezayre was worth £25 in 1725 and had increased to £90 in 1831, an increase somewhat below the average 400% calculated by Virgin for England and Wales between 1700 and 1840, though still in excess of the estimated 100% inflation figure in the same period.[85] In 1763 and 1773 the values of the 14 Manx vicarages ranged from a low of £17 10s. at Rushen to a high of £53 11s. 2d. at Michael.[86] To put these figures in perspective, Bishop Woodward of Cloyne calculated in 1787 that the average annual income of a beneficed clergyman of the Church of Ireland was £148 and that even in the poorest diocese, Killala and Achonry, the average reached £90.[87] By 1831 the Manx vicarages were worth an average of about £100 and the rectories about double that figure, but this still compared poorly with figures in the rest of the British Isles. In the poorest diocese, St David's, the benefice average was £137. In England and Wales only 37% of livings were worth less than £200 and in Ireland the figure was 33%.[88] The problem of clerical poverty extended to the widows and dependents of former clergy. Bishop Wilson endeavoured

83 W. Blundell, 'A history of the Isle of Man, 1648–56', 2 vols (unpublished MS: MNH MS 00049 C & MS 00050 C), vol. 2, fols 728–34; Craine, *Mananan's Isle*, 118.

84 Craine, *Mananan' s Isle*, 119–21.

85 Gelling, *Manx Church*, 23, 49; P. Virgin, *The Church in an Age of Negligence* (Cambridge, 1989), 73–74.

86 MNH MD 00436, folder 17/20.

87 D.H. Akenson, *The Church of Ireland: Ecclesiastical Reform and Revolution, 1800–1885* (New Haven and London, 1971), 61–62.

88 Gelling, *Manx Church*, 64, 68; M. Cragoe, *An Anglican Aristocracy: the Moral Economy of the Landed Estate in Carmarthenshire, 1832–1895* (Oxford, 1996), 192;

to resolve these through the establishment of 'a fund for the desolate widows and children of clergymen in this island'. The fund was established initially by gifts of £100 from the widow of Bishop Crowe of Cloyne, £50 from the widow of Bishop Levinz and £30 from Sir John Philipps, the Pembrokeshire baronet who was the benefactor of many schools in south-west Wales. Bishop Wilson himself donated £100 to the fund, and another benefactress of good causes, Lady Elizabeth Hastings, gave £25 6s. 8d. The fund became operative in 1731.[89]

The poverty of its livings, however, secured some advantages for the Manx church. Although the evils of pluralism and non-residence in other parts of the British Isles have been greatly exaggerated in the past and are now being seen in better perspective, the situation in the Isle of Man was even better.[90] There were very few incidences of pluralism. The archdeaconry of Man was always held with the rectory of Andreas, which provided its endowment, and at least 11 of the 17 occupants of the post between 1587 and 1839 held no other preferment at the same time. Of the 154 known holders of the other 16 Manx rectories and vicarages between the end of the sixteenth century and the death of Bishop Ward in 1838, only ten combined two or more preferments at the same time, and five held adjacent cures which they could have served personally without difficulty.[91] The virtual absence of pluralism in the Isle of Man meant that the vast majority of incumbents resided on their cures, although most parishes seem to have had curates as well, at least for some of the time. Residence was also assisted by the plentiful supply of parsonage houses in the Isle of Man, some in a good state of repair, although some were very modest buildings. Bishop Wilson noted on 26 March 1739 that 'we have at last got a very pretty vicarage House built near the new church at Kirk Lonan and I hope to see a more regular curate in it (or vicar) than at present I have been able to get'.[92]

F. Knight, *The Nineteenth Century Church and English Society* (Cambridge, 1995), 131–32; Akenson, *Church of Ireland*, 87.

89 Bray (ed), *Records of Convocation*, vol. 1, 177–78, 180, 183–86.

90 For recent reassessments of the impact of pluralism and non-residence in different parts of the British Isles see A.R. Acheson, *A History of the Church of Ireland 1691–1996* (Dublin, 1997), 19–24; W. Gibson, *Church, State and Society, 1760–1850* (London, 1994), 19–25; J. Gregory, *Restoration, Reformation and Reform, 1660–1828: Archbishops of Canterbury and their Diocese* (Oxford, 1999), 171–73; W.M. Jacob, *Lay People and Religion in the Early Eighteenth Century* (Cambridge, 1996), 21–22; Knight, *Nineteenth Century Church*, 3–4, 118–22; F.C. Mather, *High Church Prophet: Bishop Samuel Horsley (1733–1806) and the Caroline Tradition in the Late Georgian Church* (Oxford, 1992), 149–55, 194–95; Virgin, *Age of Negligence*, 191–214; and J. Walsh, C. Haydon and S. Taylor (eds), *The Church of England c.1689–c.1833: From Toleration to Tractarianism* (Cambridge, 1993), 7–9, 90–94, 105–07.

91 Information extracted from lists of clergy and benefices in Gelling, *Manx Church*, and Harrison, *Sodor and Man*.

92 MNH MS 09309.

Between 1740 and 1742 a total of £6 12s. 9½d. was spent on repairs to the vicarage at Rushen, and in 1744–5 £12 2s. 5d. on building a new vicarage at Arbory.[93] Only the rector of Bride and the chaplains of Castletown, Ramsey and St Matthew's, Douglas, did not have parsonage houses. Comparison can be made with the situation in Anglesey in 1837 where the 76 parish churches in the Island were served by only 34 incumbents, with frequently two and sometimes as many as five churches being served by the same clergyman. Only 13 of these 34 incumbents were resident, the remainder employing curates.[94] In 1801 only nine out of 36 incumbents were resident and only 14 benefices had parsonage houses in repair.[95] On the Isle of Wight ten of the 28 parish churches and chapelries had either pluralist or non-resident incumbents in 1725 and this figure had risen to 18 by 1788; in the latter year the rector of Binstead was also rector of Yarmouth, vicar of Shalfleet, chaplain of Carisbrooke Castle and master of Newport Grammar School.[96] The close proximity of both Anglesey and the Isle of Wight to mainland Britain meant that a few island incumbents also held mainland benefices, but the majority of the pluralist incumbents on both Anglesey and the Isle of Wight were holding more than one island benefice in a way that was only rarely the case in the Isle of Man.

The main problems facing the Manx Church were not pluralism, non-residence or the absence of parsonage houses, but the difficulties of finding suitable candidates for the ministry and providing for their education. All but seven out of the 19 parish churches and chaplaincies had at least one period in the early eighteenth century when the benefice was vacant. The situation was so serious that on 27 April 1751 Bishop Wilson wrote to his son, Dr Thomas Wilson

> The circumstances of this church are in such a condition as are enough to distract a younger head than one of near 90. Three of our parishes are destitute of pastors. One is dead, another (Mr More) is more disordered in his understanding than ever, K. Bride is 80 and quite Blind, and Marown has been for more than 2 years confin'd by sickness, ... I must therefore (much against my wish) beg of you (being myself not able) to speak or write to His Grace our Metropolitan to permit me to put 2 or 3 sober young men into Deacons Orders tho' not above 21 or 22 yeares of Age ... The Archdeacon continues ill of a Palsy, so that I can have no assistance from him in any

93 Bray (ed), *Records of Convocation*, vol. 1, 209–12, 218–19.
94 National Library of Wales, B/QA/26.
95 National Library of Wales, B/QA/14.
96 Isle of Wight visitation returns for 1725 and 1788 in W.R. Ward (ed), *Parson and Parish in Eighteenth Century Hampshire: Replies to Bishops; Visitations*, Hampshire Record Series, 13 (1995), *passim*.

> shape and Mr Mores case growing worse every day has almost distracted his Brother of Douglas.[97]

Even when clergy could be found, their training was another serious problem, since few could afford the cost of an education at either Dublin, Oxford, Cambridge or one of the Scottish universities. Bishop Barrow made an attempt to remedy this situation by improving the stipends of his clergy and creating an endowment for 'the maintenance of three boys at an academical school', who were to be ordained as clergy in the diocese. Barrow also made the first moves towards the provision of more general education in the Isle of Man with the establishment of parochial schools and a grammar school in Castletown.[98]

A major and sustained campaign for the improvement of the education of the Manx clergy was one of the most significant features of Bishop Wilson's episcopate. He established an arrangement whereby those seeking ordination would, in addition to their education in one of the grammar schools, spend some time in the bishop's household and might also be licensed as lay assistants to elderly or infirm clergy, by 'reading the Lessons and Psalms, and now and then a homily'.[99] Wilson, however, thought that the best means of training the clergy was to provide for their continued education beyond ordination, and determined to achieve this in two ways, by issuing guidance on reading to the clergy and by establishing libraries in every parish for their use.[100] In his guidance to the clergy Wilson recommended books that explained the liturgy of the *Book of Common Prayer* and defended the doctrine of the Church of England, as well as more general theological works such as Hammond's *Practical Catechism*. He told the clergy that 'these will serve your best purposes and when you are master of the learning contained in them, you may be able to choose your own studies'. Wilson's more advanced reading guide included, for 'School Divinity', the *Summa Theologica* of St Thomas Aquinas in Latin. His final piece of advice to the clergy was that 'when you are at leisure and can find

97 Borthwick Institute of Historical Research, Bp. C&P XV/7. The clergy referred to are William Bridson, rector of Ballaugh 1729–51; Edward Moore, vicar of Michael 1735–51; Matthias Curghey, rector of Bride 1729–54; Thomas Christian, vicar of Marown 1734–52; Archdeacon John Kippax, rector of Andreas 1727–60; and Philip Moore, chaplain of Douglas and master of Douglas grammar school 1736–65, succeeding Bridson as rector of Bride, in addition to his other preferment, in 1751.

98 See chapter 3, pp. 201–20, on 'Education and Literacy'.

99 Keble, *Wilson*, vol. 2, 796–99.

100 For the interesting comparison between Wilson's innovations and those of Bishops Horsley and Burgess at St David's see W.N. Yates, 'An Opportunity Missed? The Provision of Education and Training for a Non-Graduate Clergy: Comparative Case Studies of the Dioceses of St David's and Sodor and Man in the Eighteenth and Nineteenth Centuries', *Dutch Review of Church History*, 83 (2004), 319–29.

time read the Fathers of the first 300 years: they are few and the surest guides'.[101] The first step to establish parochial libraries was taken in 1699, within a year of Wilson's consecration, and in close association with the leader of the parochial library movement, Thomas Bray, and the Society for the Promotion of Christian Knowledge.[102] In that year Wilson made a gift of ten titles to each parish to form the nucleus of a parochial library. Further books were given in subsequent years so that by 1725 Wilson had arranged that each library had at least 30 titles.[103] Wilson gave a further four titles between 1725 and 1735 and a more significant benefaction in 1740. Whereas the 34 titles given up to 1735 had been common to all the libraries, those given in 1740 varied from one library to another. Each of the 17 parishes received additional titles ranging from two at Michael to ten at Lonan. The 17 parishes received 82 titles altogether.[104] Wilson also established or improved more extensive libraries at Castletown and Douglas, where the chaplains acted as the masters of the grammar schools in which most of the Manx clergy were educated. The Castletown library was completed in 1710 at a cost of £83 5s. 6d., the majority of which had been personally subscribed by Wilson.[105] A catalogue compiled in 1716 shows that the library then had a total of 872 volumes and was by far the most extensive library in the Island, with major works by classical authors as well as books on theology, which provided the main content of the other parochial libraries.[106] The Douglas library was substantially expanded after the appointment of Philip Moore as chaplain and master of the grammar school in 1736. He inherited only 41 books, but this number had been increased to 108 by 1748 and to 174 by 1772. The library was then substantially augmented by the bequest of a further 233 books from the library of the late Bishop Hildesley, the total value of which was given as £27 14s. 10d. In addition to books on theology, the library contained works on history, law, medicine, editions of classical authors and philosophical treatises in French. Hildesley's bequest included his books on gardening.[107]

Unfortunately, the surviving records show that the efforts made by Wilson and Hildesley to establish and augment these libraries were not always fully appreciated. By 1738, a list of the contents of 12 out of the 17 parochial libraries shows that only one, at Jurby, still held the full complement of 34 titles given by

101 MNH MS MD 00436, folder 2/3.

102 See Jacob, *Lay People and Religion*, 174–76. A library of 217 books had been sent to the Island by Fairfax during his lordship. See Moore, *Isle of Man*, vol. 1, 274n.

103 Keble, *Wilson*, vol. 1, 250–58; for a list of these titles see Bray (ed), *Records of Convocation*, vol. 1, 159–61.

104 J.P. Ferguson, *The Parochial Libraries of Bishop Wilson* (Douglas, 1975), 6–9.

105 Cruttwell, *Wilson*, vol. 1, 85. Cruttwell also notes, vol. 1, 59, that in respect of the seventeen parochial libraries, Wilson also 'gave to each a proper bookcase'.

106 Ferguson, *Parochial Libraries*, 83–106.

107 MHN MS 00832 A.

Wilson.[108] By 1757 only 15 of the original titles survived at Andreas; the highest survival rates were at Ballaugh (31), Jurby (28), Lezayre (32) and Onchan (30). Of the ten parishes which returned catalogues of their libraries at Hildesley's visitation in that year, all had acquired additional titles, not given by Wilson, ranging from two titles at Andreas to nine at Jurby. The largest libraries were those at Ballaugh, Jurby and Lezayre, each containing 42 titles.[109] By 1833, although 15 chapelry and parochial libraries still existed in the Isle of Man, most were in poor condition and rarely used, and even the books at Douglas were described as 'old and many of them mutilated'. The former libraries at Lonan, Marown, Patrick and Ramsey no longer existed. At Braddan the 15 titles surviving from the 'old parochial library' were described as 'considerably damaged'. However, a new collection of 104 titles had been given in recent years by Miss Harrison of Sheffield, and to these a further 11 titles had been added in 1829–31. These were described as

> still in good order. The parishioners have access to the library and discover much fondness for reading the Books bestowed by Miss Harrison these being not only newer to the People but of a more spiritual and edifying character than the works of which the library consisted previously.[110]

An examination of the books listed as having been given by Miss Harrison show these to have been strongly evangelical in character, and this reflected the personal sympathies of both the vicar, Thomas Howard, and his curate, Robert Brown. Further losses occurred from the Manx parochial libraries after 1833.[111]

Wilson's educational efforts seem to have paid off. Hildesley described the clergy he had inherited as 'in general a very sensible, regular, decent set of men almost without exception', though he insisted that they wore proper clerical dress and wigs.[112] There were, however, cases of indiscipline and immorality, as there had been earlier in the seventeenth century. Wilson had had to suspend the vicar of Michael, Henry Norris, for unchastity in 1699. Robert Fletcher, vicar of Braddan, was first charged with a similar offence in 1698 and again

108 Ferguson, *Parochial Libraries,* 36–62.

109 MNH MS 00791 C.

110 MNH MS 00794 C.

111 M. Perkin, *A Directory of the Parochial Libraries of the Church of England and the Church in Wales* (London, 2004), 405–09. The most recent survey of books surviving from parochial libraries throughout England, Wales and the Isle of Man has recorded the survival of 17 volumes from the Jurby parochial library and 18 volumes from the former library at Douglas. There are even more fragmentary remains of six other parochial libraries totalling only 17 books altogether.

112 Moore, *Sodor and Man,* 223; Butler, *Memoirs of Hildesley,* 99; Bray (ed), *Records of Convocation*, vol. 1, 256–57.

in 1702, being deprived after a third allegation was proved in 1704.[113] During the late eighteenth and early nineteenth centuries there were four major cases of indiscipline. Thomas Corlett, vicar of Lezayre, was suspended by Bishop Mason in 1780 'for an offence with another man's wife'.[114] Even the reputedly lethargic Bishop Crigan was obliged to take action against Thomas Christian, vicar of Marown, who fathered at least five illegitimate children and who was, on various occasions, accused of drunkenness and violence, though he was also the author of a Manx paraphrase of *Paradise Lost*. Christian was, after several years of ineffective legal action, finally deprived of his living in 1799.[115] Bishop Murray took action against two of his clergy, John Cottier and William Christian, vicars of Patrick and Malew respectively. In 1827 Cottier was deprived for drunkenness and Christian suspended for three years for neglect of duty. In 1830, having failed to convince his churchwardens that he was fit to resume office, he was deprived by Bishop Ward.[116]

Although he was a strong disciplinarian, Bishop Murray was also keen to improve the economic status of the Manx clergy and saw an opportunity to do this through the more efficient collection of tithes. The attempt to collect those on fish and potatoes had been abandoned during the eighteenth century, but Murray filed a suit for the collection of the tithe on potatoes in 1817. As in all other parts of the British Isles, tithes were unpopular in the Isle of Man, and Murray had to resort to the courts to achieve a judgement in his favour.[117] An appeal against this judgement failed in 1826, but Murray's insistence on collection led to massive public protests, which began in Jurby and quickly spread to the other parishes. Since it was impossible to enforce the claim, Murray had no option but to abandon it. In order to protect him from further outbursts of opposition, the British government offered Murray translation to the see of Rochester late in 1827, an offer which he accepted.[118] It has been suggested that Murray had a low opinion of the Manx clergy and was keen to attract to the Isle of Man clergy of better, 'social and educational qualifications' from England, though the only clergy to be so attracted were Thomas Thimbleby, appointed chaplain of Castletown in 1818, and Benjamin Philpot, whose initial appointment in 1827 was as chaplain of St George's, Douglas,

113 Keble, *Wilson,* vol. 1, 142–45.

114 Gelling, *Manx Church,* 44.

115 R.L. Thomson (ed), *Pargys Caillit, an Arrangement of John Milton's Paradise Lost by Thomas Christian with the Anonymous Translation of Thomas Parnell's The Hermit,* Centre for Manx Studies Research Report 3 (Douglas, 1995), 11–16.

116 Gelling, *Manx Church,* 61–62.

117 See E.J. Evans, *The Contentious Tithe* (London, 1976).

118 There are detailed accounts of the tithe dispute in Craine, *Mananan's Isle,* 197–209, and Gelling, *Manx Church*, 53–58, the former's account being somewhat more sympathetic to Murray than the latter's.

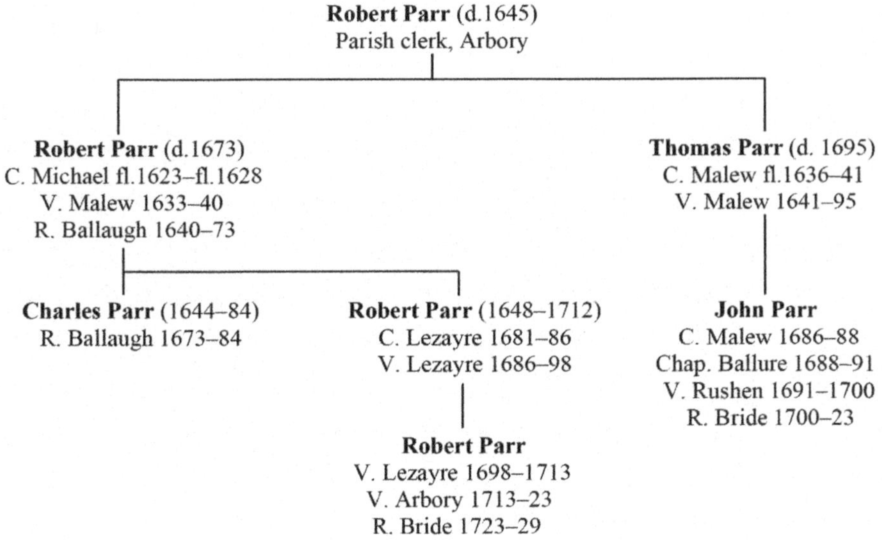

Fig. 2.11 *Members of the Parr family holding Manx benefices 1633–1729.*

but who succeeded to the archdeaconry of Man in 1832.[119] However, when he left the diocese in 1827, Murray's farewell letter to the clergy expressed 'the sincere regret with which I separate myself from a Body of Clergy ... for whom collectively and individually (with few exceptions) I shall ever entertain an affectionate regard'.[120]

The poverty of the Manx livings and the requirement for clergy to be proficient in the Manx language had ensured that, with very few exceptions, the clergy had been born, bred and in most cases wholly educated in the Isle of Man.[121] There were many cases of sons succeeding their fathers in the same benefice and five generations of Allens held the vicarage of Maughold between 1625 and 1754. There were several clerical dynasties on the Island and some of these were closely related to each other (see Figs 2.11, 2.12 and 2.13).

Although, apart from the three rectories of Andreas, Ballaugh and Bride, there was relatively little difference in the benefice income of the 14 vicarages, there was a surprising degree of movement between them. Samuel Gell moved from Jurby to Onchan in 1748, and from Onchan to Lonan in 1759. Thomas Cubbon held successively the vicarages of Santon (1765–9), Maughold

119 Virgin, *Age of Negligence*, 84.
120 MNH MD 00436, folder 4/6.
121 This section is based on the lists of Manx clergy published by Gelling and Harrison, with much useful supplementary information supplied by Priscilla Lewthwaite.

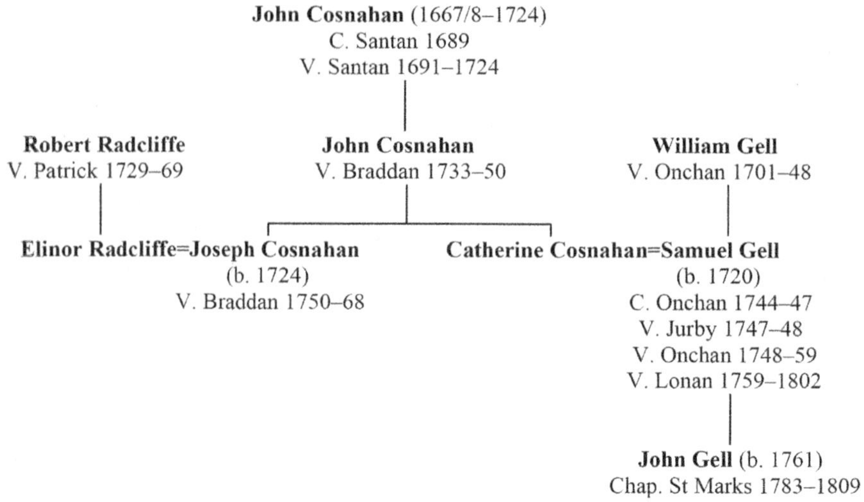

Fig. 2.12 *Relationship of Cosnahan and Gell families 1691–1809.*

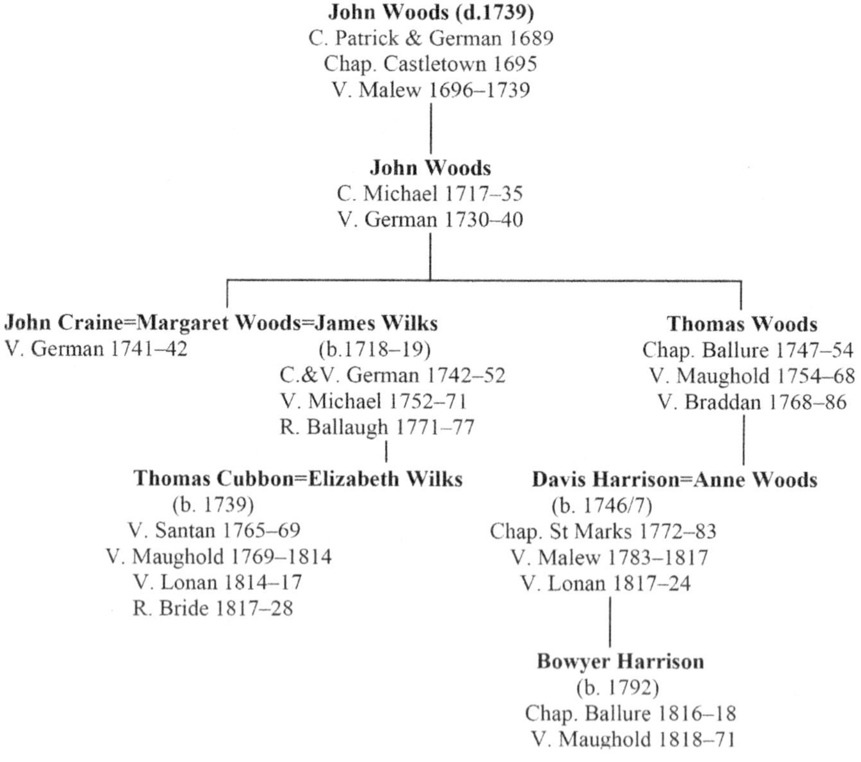

Fig. 2.13 *Relationship of Woods and other families 1696–1871.*

(1769–1814) and Lonan (1814–17), before his preferment to the rectory of Bride at the advanced age of 78. This pattern of the movement of local-born clergy to neighbouring livings of relatively equal value appears to have been replicated in the Channel Islands, where remarkably similar clerical careers to those of the Manx clergy are indicated in the lists of clergy compiled for Bishop Sumner in 1827.[122]

THE PIETY OF THE ISLAND COMMUNITY

Nigel Yates †

Directions to the clergy and laity of the Isle of Man on religious observances were contained in the formal constitutions issued by Bishop Phillips in 1610:

> To read the service of the Church on Sundays and Holy Days soberly and distinctly, and in due time. To preach one sermon every Sunday (having no lawful impediment) in such Language or Tongue as shall be to the best edification of the people. To catechize the youth of the parish every Sunday in the afternoon, and to explain some part of the Church Catechism after so plain and familiar a manner as may be to the edifying of the Parishioners. To suffer none to come to the Holy Sacrament of the Lord's Supper until such time as they be confirmed ... To visit the Sick, to marry none without Banns or Licence, nor at any time but betwixt the Hours of Eight and Twelve in the forenoon: and to live so soberly as to be a Pattern of Religion and Virtue to his whole Parish.[123]

These instructions were reinforced from time to time by the advice given by individual bishops. On 17 March 1664 Bishop Barrow, 'hoping I shall be at liberty to return to ye Island very shortly', advised the clergy

> to settle all things in good order that concerne your office ... that you would also make it your business to see your Churches repaired, the Communion table decently placed at the east end, with carpets on them, and all the seats that are about the table ... removed, and for the better performance of the Church Service, I have sent over 17 Common prayer bookes ... that the office be exactly celebrated according to the Rubrick by all the Clergy.[124]

122 Hampshire Record Office 21M65/B5/1. The majority of the clergy listed had French surnames.
123 Moore, *Sodor and Man,* 121–25.
124 MNH MS 10216 (EW) 17.

Three years later Barrow, who was a strong high churchman, ordered 'that there be a communion in the church at least eight times in the year ... and all at fourteen years to receive ... or be presented, unless a lawful cause appear'.[125]

Bishop Wilson laid down clear standards for the behaviour and duties of the clergy, and the response required from the laity, in the ecclesiastical constitutions adopted by the convocation of the Clergy of the diocese on 3 February 1704. The constitutions comprised ten articles. The first placed a duty on the clergy to notify the bishop of those 'desirous and fit to be confirmed' and to ensure that they were instructed 'in the necessary parts of Christian knowledge' and had learned both the church catechism and set forms of 'short prayers for morning and evening'. The second article laid down that only confirmed persons were to be admitted to Holy Communion. The third article required that no person should 'be admitted to stand as Godfather or Godmother, or to enter into the holy state of Matrimony, till they have received the Holy Sacrament of the Lord's Supper'. The fourth article required all unconfirmed children and servants to attend the afternoon service and that the minister instruct them in the church catechism. The sixth article required the clergy to refuse to admit those 'whose lives are blemished with the vices of drunkenness, tippling, swearing, profaning the Lord's Day, quarrelling, fornication, or any other crime' to Holy Communion and to present them before the church courts. The seventh article forbade the collection of rents or other payments on Sundays. The ninth article required all parents to send their children 'to some petty school ... until the said children can read English distinctly', and the tenth required the clergy to make lists on the last Sunday of every month of those who absented themselves from church or who did not send their children to be catechized or to school.[126]

Bishop Wilson used his annual convocation charges to offer advice to his clergy. In 1715 he recommended each clergyman to keep a register of every family in his parish, noting 'when he visited any of them, and in what state he found them, and what hopes he had of reforming what he found amiss in them'. He stressed the importance of family prayers and urged the clergy to encourage the laity to confess their sins to them in cases where they were deeply troubled. This he specifically recommended in order to prevent suicide; since suicides could not be given Christian burial, clergy who did not offer spiritual comfort to disturbed parishioners might unwittingly be denying them the benefits of Christian burial.[127] Wilson also offered more private advice to his clergy. In two sets of instructions, one dated 1738 and the other undated, of which manuscript copies survive, Wilson had recommended that they

125 Moore, *Sodor and Man*, 112–13.
126 Bray (ed), *Records of Convocation*, vol. 1, 206–09.
127 Cruttwell, *Wilson*, vol. 1, 90–95.

> neglect not to stir up the Grace of God – By diligent reading of the Holy Scriptures ... By instructing your People, and catechising the youth – By reading the Service of the Church, and administering both the Sacraments after the devoutest manner, and especially by a conversation becoming a Priest of the most high God ...
>
> As to y^{r} Sermons, do not ... make choice of subjects out of Fancy, or Laziness, but consider what is most proper and necessary for the Wants of y^{r} own people ... A Clergyman forgets the end of preaching, when he preaches upon a subject that is not practical ...
>
> Without a great deal of pains in Catechising, your Sermons will be of little use ...
>
> I hope you will take some special Pains with every Family in your parish to have Family Prayers ... for the blessings they have rec^{d}
>
> Endeavour to have the Sacram^{t} administer'd oftner than 3 times a Year. The Rubric wch requires every Parishioner to receive at least so often, supposes that they may have an Opportunity to do it oftner.[128]

Wilson also warned his clergy against 'reading the Service of the Church after an Hasty, careless and Indecent manner' and the similar indecency of parish clerks who 'hurry over the responses, and psalmes, and hymns as fast as ever they can', pointing out that 'if there were Dissenters meeting here, as in England', they would 'see their churches much thinner of people than at present ... But who knowes how soon we may be punish'd by some such judgm^{t}, if this matter is not soon mended'.[129] Wilson's dedication to the importance of catechising, reflected in his 1747 convocation charge, led him to refuse permission for a Sunday evening lecture at the chapel in Douglas, since he feared that this would compromise the afternoon catechising which he regarded as essential. This charge also noted that 'we have of late ... broke through a bad custom of having the Lord's Supper administered in country parishes only three times a year'.[130]

Wilson's advice to his clergy through private instruction and convocation charges was given further weight by his publications on pastoral theology, beginning in 1707 with his *Principles and Duties of Christianity*, written in Manx Gaelic.[131]

128 MNH MD 00436, folder 2/4.
129 MNH MD 00436, folder 2/13.
130 Cruttwell, *Wilson*, vol. 1, 174–76, 191–98.
131 T. Wilson, *The Principles and Duties of Christianity with Short and Plain Directions and Prayers* (London, 1707).

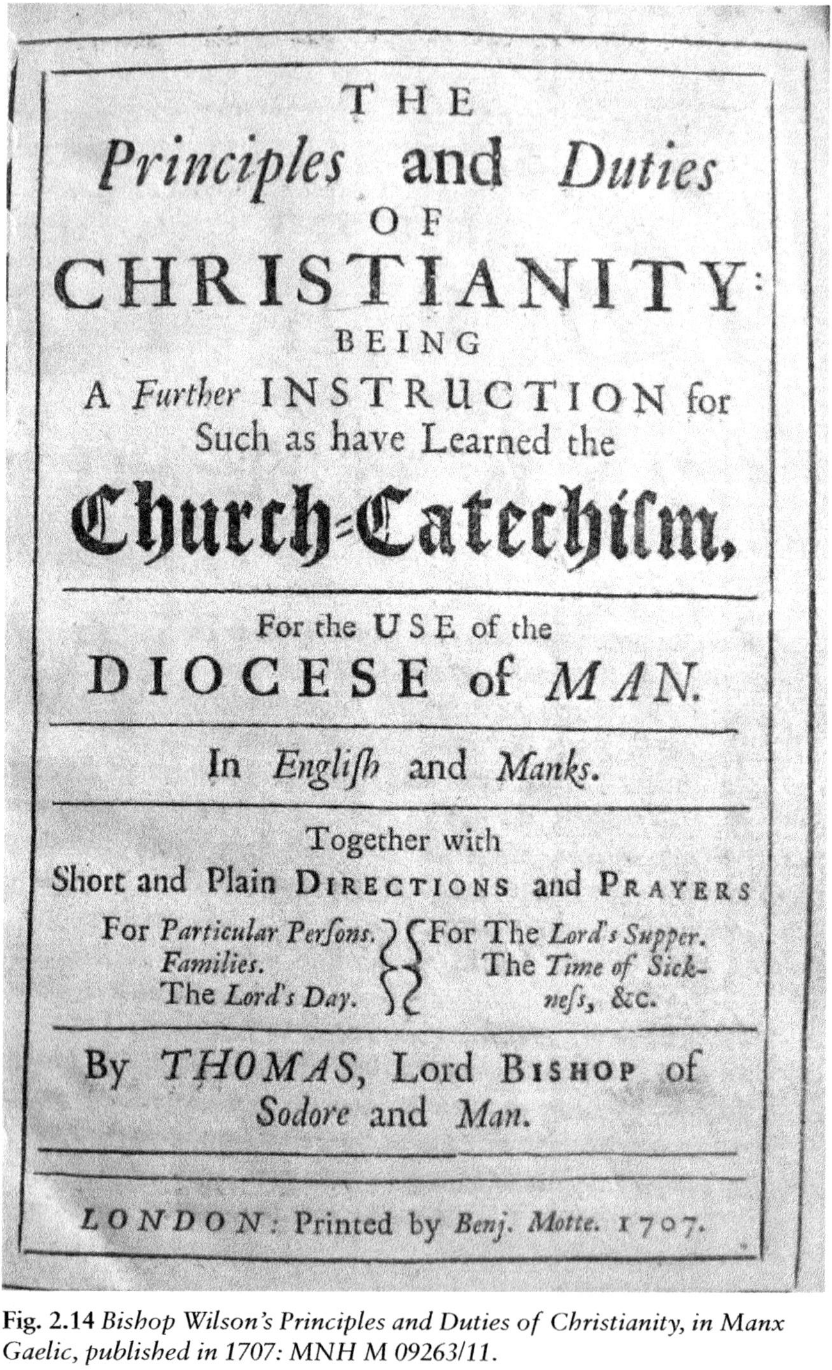

THE

Principles and *Duties*

OF

CHRISTIANITY:

BEING

A *Further* INSTRUCTION for
Such as have Learned the

Church-Catechism.

For the USE of the

DIOCESE of *MAN.*

In *English* and *Manks.*

Together with
Short and Plain DIRECTIONS and PRAYERS

For *Particular Persons.*
Families.
The *Lord's Day.*
For The *Lord's Supper.*
The *Time of Sickness*, &c.

By *THOMAS*, Lord BISHOP of
Sodore and *Man.*

LONDON: Printed by *Benj. Motte.* 1707.

Fig. 2.14 *Bishop Wilson's Principles and Duties of Christianity, in Manx Gaelic, published in 1707: MNH M 09263/11.*

Wilson recommended that the clergy read sections of this book every Sunday after catechising, and also included forms for both private and family prayers, morning and evening, devotions to be read before morning and afternoon service on Sundays, and instructions for the 'worthy receiving of the Lord's Supper' and 'for such as are sick or under any affliction'. He also recommended fasting as 'a punishment and expiation for past sins, a remedy for present temptations, and a preservative against future [ones]'.[132] His popular work on the eucharist recommends the use of sacramental confession in appropriate cases and provides meditations on the text of the Communion Service in the *Book of Common Prayer*.[133]

Bishop Hildesley was full of praise for the spiritual condition of his diocese:

> Never did I see more justice done to our excellent Liturgy in any place than in the congregations of this Isle, whether it be in Manx or English, the responses duly made, and the directions of the rubric punctually and regularly attended to, in kneeling and rising in proper time and place ... the adult natives, to a man, I think I may say, are conformists of the established communion of the Church of England; and so exact and punctual, for the most part, in their attendance on the public offices of divine worship, and especially at the sacrament ... that there is little or no occasion for presentments on this head.[134]

Hildesley was, however, concerned about the proper keeping of fast days, especially Ash Wednesday and Good Friday, and issued instructions to his clergy in both 1760 and 1761 to secure the observation of these fasts by the laity. In both years the non-observance of both days had been brought home to him by the sight of people ploughing the fields.[135] Whilst the frequency of communion services was not as high as either Wilson, or probably Hildesley, would have desired, the communicant figures were exceptionally high, as figure 2.15 shows, especially at Easter, even allowing for the absence of dissent on the Island or the admission of those under the age of sixteen to communion.

Numbers at confirmations were high also, Hildesley noting in a letter to Philip Moore, chaplain at Douglas, on 31 October 1763 that there were 'two hundred and thirty three catechumens, confirmed by your poor old friend at Lezayre last Friday'.[136]

132 T. Wilson, *Sacra Privata* (Bath, 1792), 112.

133 T. Wilson, *A Short and Plain Instruction for the Better Understanding of the Lord's Supper*, 24th edn (London, 1796).

134 Quoted in Moore, *Sodor and Man*, 213–14.

135 Bray (ed), *Records of Convocation*, vol. 1, 251–52, 261–64.

136 MNH MS 09309; the parish registers of German (MNH MS 10974 PR12–13) give details of Easter communicants in the late 18th and early 19th centuries. There were three celebrations, on Good Friday and Easter Eve in Manx and on Easter Day in English. The number of communicants rose from 696 in 1767 to 1175 in 1790 but began to decline thereafter.

Fig. 2.15 *Manx communion statistics 1757.*[137]

Parish	Population over Age sixteen	Easter Communicants	Communicants at other sacraments
Andreas	652	400	80
Arbory	526	400	80–90
Ballaugh	496	494	107
Braddan (including Douglas chapel)	1897	about 1250	260–500
Bride	371	313	78
Jurby	305	300	no return
Lezayre	903	600	140–200
Lonan	417	261	56–78
Marown	360	350	200
Maughold (including Ballure chapel)	1019	632	60–82
Michael	597	380	135–150
Onchan	280	254	60–80
Rushen	633	520	130–150

The chief source for making an assessment of the levels of Manx piety, in respect of both clergy and laity, are the surviving records of episcopal and archidiaconal visitation. There are a few responses to visitation questions in 1634 and 1665, but the main surviving documents record one archidiaconal and nine episcopal visitations between 1743 and 1835.[138] All the returns have been analysed for 1757 and 1833 when visitations were carried out by, respectively, Bishop Hildesley and Archdeacon Philpot. In the first of these visitations, questions were asked about benefactions, collections, the frequency of

137 MNH MS 00791 C, Episcopal visitation records, 1757.

138 Episcopal visitations in 1743, 1748 and 1754 (MNH MS 00790 C), 1757 (MS 00791 C), 1766 (MS 00792 C), 1782 (MS 00797 C), 1786 (MS 00793 C), 1830 (MS 00798 C) and 1835 (MS 00795 C); archidiaconal visitation in 1833 (MS 00794 C). The section that follows is based on the evidence contained in these visitation returns. Whereas most English and Welsh visitation returns were made on printed forms, those for the diocese of Sodor and Man are entirely in manuscript. The returns for both 1757 and 1766 make it clear that the questions were forwarded from one clergyman to another and copied out about six weeks before the visitation took place. The visitations in 1757 and 1766 involved episcopal visits to up to three parishes or chapelries a day over a period of eight days. In 1833 Archdeacon Philpot visited up to six parishes or chapelries a day over a period of six days: see Gelling, *Manx Church*, 66.

the sacrament and preaching in Manx, numbers of communicants, catechising and how often the incumbent visited his parish school. In 1833 more detailed questions were asked about preaching and the services, whether schoolchildren were taken to church and the moral welfare of the parishioners. The replies, analysed in figure 2.16 show a generally acceptable situation in most parishes, though with some room for improvement in all but a small minority.

Fig. 2.16 *Pastoral provision in the parishes of the diocese of Sodor and Man as revealed in the replies to visitation queries in 1757 and 1833.*

	1757	1833
Total number of returns	15	23
Benefactions/ Charities	12	17
For poor	1	6
For schools	1	2
For other purposes		
Holy Communion	4	12
More than quarterly	10	11
Quarterly	1	
Less than quarterly		
(3) Service/ Preaching in Manx	4	1
Every Sunday	8	15
Alternate Sundays	1	3
Occasional	2	4
Never		
(4) Weekday Services		9
Catechizing	2	7
Every Sunday	10	5
Some Sundays	2	6
Before Confirmation	1	5
Never		
Schools	10	17
Separate buildings	3	22
Held in church		
Sunday schools		

Source: MNH MS 00791C and MS 00794C

The chief trends are fairly clear. There had been a modest increase in the number of communion services, with monthly celebrations in all six town churches, by 1833; all three churches in Douglas, the chapels at Castletown and Ramsey, and the parish churches at Andreas, Arbory, Ballaugh and Michael also had regular or occasional weekday services by 1833. The curate of Braddan excused the lack of weekday services on the grounds that

> the country people here are so constantly employed during the morning and afternoon of every weekday whether holy day or not that it would be utterly impossible to assemble a congregation either at the morning or the afternoon service of a saints day ... a weekday lecture would have been established by me at this church were it not that I was informed of Mr Howards having been obliged to relinquish one which he had commenced owing to the non-attendance of the parishioners.[139]

Although the number of Manx services had declined, the drop was not as great as might have been expected. Bishop Ward's wife recorded that

> there is a reluctance (deserving consideration) in the old native clergy to drop, or diminish, the use of the Manx Language ... though . . the people are so rapidly learning English, and such numbers of settlers arriving.[140]

It is also clear that by 1833 catechising was being seen as outmoded by many clergy following the rapid increase in the number of Sunday schools. The curate of Braddan opined that

> to catechize on Sundays would be impracticable in this parish owing to the mass of occasional duty which in addition to the Services of the Day the minister of this Parish has almost every Sabbath to perform.

The only parish not to have a Sunday school was Lezayre, where the vicar reported that

> we had lately a Sunday School but in consequence of a few good teachers having left the Parish who regularly attended the same it is discontinued but I hope in April next it will be open again.[141]

Church music in the 1830s maintained its traditional form with lined psalm-singing, frequently in Manx, and with anthems on special occasions, the musical settings of which were provided by a small orchestra housed in the west gallery.[142] The first organ to be installed in a Manx church was at St George's, Douglas, where an organ 'was purchased in Dublin ... from the Musical Academy' in 1788, the cost being defrayed by an annual rent on the pews.[143]

139 MNH MS 00794 C.

140 MNH MS 09309, 'An account of Bishop Ward's work by his wife' (29 September 1832).

141 MNH MS 00794 C.

142 F. Bazin, 'Cultural history: music', in *A New History of the Isle of Man*, vol. 5: *The Modern Period*, J. Belchem (ed) (Liverpool, 2000), 384–85. See chapter 4, F. Bazin, 'music'.

143 L. Craine, *St George's and St Barnabas' Church* (Douglas, 1974: pamphlet), 2–3.

An organ was installed at Castletown chapel in 1811, in a gallery placed over the altar, at a cost of £432.[144] Bishop Ward's wife noted, after the rebuilding of Michael church in 1833, that 'we do not despair of obtaining an Organ, and much improving the Psalmody in this church before the end of the next year'.[145]

CHURCH BUILDING AND RESTORATION

Nigel Yates †

If the spiritual life of a diocese can be judged by the amount of work carried out on church fabrics and furnishings, and the frequency of gifts of plate to churches, between the late seventeenth and the early nineteenth centuries, then the diocese of Sodor and Man was in a remarkably healthy condition, as figures 2.17 and 2.18 show. Among the plate given to Manx churches were complete sets (chalice, paten, flagon and almsdish) given to the new chapel of St George at Douglas, by the fourth duke of Atholl, in 1777 and to Santon in 1832.[146]

Fig. 2.17 *Renovations of church buildings and gifts of church plate in the Isle of Man 1660–1840.*

	1660–1720	1720–80	1780–1840
Churches renovated/rebuilt	8	14	19
Churches receiving gifts of plate	11	13	8
Number of items given	18	37	19

Between the consecration of Bishop Wilson in 1698 and the translation of Bishop Murray in 1827 every single parish church and existing chapelry was either rebuilt or renovated as shown in figure 2.18, and new churches built at Douglas and St Mark's.[147]

144 D. Thompson, *A History of the Parish Church of St Mary's* (Castletown, 1964), 6–7.
145 MNH MS 09309, 'Bishop Ward's work'.
146 Jones, *Old Church Plate*, 20–24.
147 Recent research suggests some errors in Gelling's account of church buildings at Ballure, Braddan and Santon. In 1775 it was clarified that 'a church, once consecrated, may not be consecrated again' (Burns, *Ecclesiastical Law*, 3rd edn (1775), vol. 1, 309). In the eighteenth century the building of a new church generated a considerable amount of official paperwork related to the necessary Act of Tynwald, the lord of Man's assent, churchwardens' accounts, and its consecration. Because of their official nature, most related documents have survived. But no paperwork associated with a complete rebuild and consecration related to Braddan or Santon after 1747 has been found (Pat McClure, pers. comm., 15 April 2015).

Fig. 2.18 *New churches and renovations of existing churches in the Isle of Man 1698–1827.*

Andreas	New church consecrated 1821
Arbory	New church consecrated 1759
Ballaugh	Church enlarged 1717
Braddan	Church extensively renovated 1773–4[148]
Bride	New gallery 1772
Castletown	New chapel consecrated 1701; organ installed 1811; chapel rebuilt 1824–6
Douglas (St Matthew)	New chapel consecrated 1708
Douglas (St George)	New chapel consecrated 1781
German	Church repaired 1820
St John's	New chapel built 1699–1706; repaired 1739; rebuilt 1792–8; repaired 1814
Jurby	Church repaired 1751 and 1757; new church consecrated 1813
Lezayre	Church rebuilt 1704–23; repaired 1760
Lonan	New church consecrated 1735
Malew	Church enlarged 1781
St Mark's	New chapel consecrated 1772
Marown	Church repaired 1754
Maughold	Church repaired 1708; new gallery c.1774
Michael	Chancel rebuilt 1776
Onchan	Church enlarged 1757–60
Patrick	New church consecrated 1714

148 Gelling notes that there were major restorations at Braddan, c.1774, but there was no change of location (as at Arbory and Jurby) and no documentary evidence of a new consecration has been found. Brown noted in 1887 that the churchyard level 'has been raised so that the church is almost in a hollow,' further evidence that the church has been in the same place for a long time. See Brown, *Hugh Stowell Brown*, 12. Kermode refers to twelfth-century remains, and cross-slabs from the seventh century found in the walls, to a probable keeill, not to a pre-eighteenth century successor (P.M.C. Kermode, 'The parish church of Kirk Braddan', in *The Manx Archaeological Survey Fifth Report*, 1918 (Douglas, 1935; reprinted Glasgow, 1968), 13).

Ramsey	Ballure chapel repaired 1706 and 1743–5 and new chapel consecrated 1747. New church at St Paul's, Ramsey, consecrated 1822[149]
Rushen	Church enlarged 1775–90
Santon	Church renovated 1730 and at least partially re-built in 1774; refitted 1797[150]

Source: J.D. Gelling, *A History of the Manx Church 1698–1911*, Douglas 1998; L.D. Butler, 'An Architectural History of the Churches of the Isle of Man', Typescript 1970 (MNH MD 492).

Nigel Yates' table has been amended to reflect recent research.

It was a record that almost certainly surpassed that of any other diocese in England, Ireland or Wales in the same period. The only blot on this distinguished record was the failure to maintain in repair the cathedral of St German on St Patrick's Isle but its abandonment has to be seen in context. Its exposed site made it difficult both to use and to maintain, and expenditure on such a problematical building was seen as a waste of resources. By 1765 'every part … except the choir, was … in a dilapidated state, and unfit for divine service' but 'the chancel was roofed in, the windows and seats entire, a stone altar entire and railed in'. By 1791 even the choir had 'gone completely to ruin, is in most places unroofed, and the doors and windows and everything within, have been taken away'.[151]

The best survey of the condition of churches in the Isle of Man in the eighteenth century was that carried out as part of Bishop Hildesley's primary visitation in 1757. Although most churches required some repairs to the fabric or furnishings, they were generally of a fairly minor nature. One church omitted from this survey was Arbory, which was in the process of being rebuilt. When this was completed, Hildesley inspected the church and, on 2 June 1761, noted that '… the Pulpit is at present so situated as [if] the officiating min^r^ has not at all times suff^t^ Light.' He ordered that the pulpit be moved nearer a north window, and enlarged, that the altar rails be extended, and that a new

149 A new chapel was consecrated at Ballure in 1747 (MNH MS 09946 (PR18), St Paul's Ramsey and Ballure; St Paul's, Ramsey, was consecrated in 1822 (MNH MS 09946 (PR18)).

150 No documentary evidence has been discovered to support ideas that a new church was consecrated in 1774, although there are many references about plans to repair, enlarge and improve this building at that time. Body parts found under the nave in the twentieth century suggest burial inside the church prior to the eighteenth century; also Feltham noted that he saw the 1725 steeple when he visited in 1797–98. See MNH MS 10855 (DD), Santon red file; see Feltham, *Tour*, 256.

151 Harrison, *Sodor and Man*, 16.

Fig. 2.19 *St German's Cathedral, 1775: from David Robertson, A Tour through the Isle of Man (London, 1794) – MNH.*

communion table be purchased and raised on one step, to be 'covered with a good matting'. Hildesley was very keen on the provision of proper facilities for kneeling, both around the communion table and within the seats. At Marown, where the church had recently been rebuilt, he commented that

> inasmuch as the inhabitants of this parish have shown a laudable zeal in the expensive repairs and enlargement of their church, it is hoped and accordingly recommended that kneeling boards be procured by the Wardens and fixed in the several seats of the church for the greater decency and convenience of the parishioners.

On 26 May 1759 the vicar confirmed that the majority of the bishop's directions had been implemented with the exception of 'kneeling boards, which my parishioners have through necessity at this time posponed [*sic*], for the great expense they have been at, in rebuilding their church'. Marown was not the only church where Hildesley recommended the installation of kneeling boards; the same direction, couched in similar terms, was given at Ballaugh, Braddan, Jurby, Lezayre and Michael. At Santon, as at Marown, the vicar pleaded for time to carry out the bishop's directions for repairs to the roof,

> As the carpenters, who new seated the Church in the Month of March last, observed great defects in several parts of the roof, which is intended to be stript off and fully repaired, in order to make the work more perfect, and durable ... timber is, at present, both scarce and dear, in the Island, and ... the new seating of the Church has been very expensive.

The two most scandalous cases of neglect were at German and Malew where 'human bones and pieces of coffin lie scattered in different parts of the church ... and old rotten boards and pieces of coffins in many of the pews or seats, to the great offence of the parishioners'.[152]

Hildesley's main contributions to church building in his diocese were the new chapel at St Mark's and the beginnings of a second chapel for the expanding town of Douglas. In a letter to Archbishop Drummond of York he complained that

> By the benefactions from the living and the dead, the people have been enabled to rebuild and enlarge three of their parish churches [Arbory, Marown and Onchan]. And there we stop, and must stop, till Providence shall be pleased to raise up more friends to assist us in so desirable and charitable a work as this, of erecting places, moderately convenient for the reception of a well-disposed people to attend the offices of religious worship, in a country where there is no law for briefs, for the purpose of rebuilding churches, as in England; and where, if there were any such method appointed, the circumstances of the inhabitants, especially in the country parishes, are far too low to raise a sum of any significance towards it. This is one of the grievances which the diocese of Mann at present labours under.[153]

St Mark's chapel was built largely at Hildesley's own expense, he and his sister contributing £500 to the total cost of £716 2s. 7½d. for the purchase of glebe, and the building of the chapel and a house for the chaplain.[154]

The petition from the inhabitants of Douglas for a second chapel was a slight problem for Hildesley, as he was at the same time endeavouring to improve provision at Braddan parish church to which the new chapel would be subservient.

> If the good people of Douglas think I have been wanting in my good will for their Service, because I have not made them the sole object of my attention, they may please to be reminded that they are but a part of my Charge ... If I shall be enabled, as if God prosper my application I trust I shall, to enlarge the conveniences in the parish church of KK Braddan, for the more commodious

152 MNH MS 00791 C, 1757 visitation record.
153 Moore, *Sodor and Man*, 233–34.
154 Gelling, *Manx Church*, 38–39.

Fig. 2.20 *'Old Kirk Braddan', by Thomas Howard c.1825: MNH 1954-5144.*

> and easy assembling of the people who frequent divine service there, I can't help supposing, that even in that view, I shall approve myself a friend even to the town of Douglass, or at least to sundry of the inhabitants there.[155]

In fact, Hildesley and his successors were eventually able to meet both needs. The church at Braddan was extensively renovated, shortly after Hildesley's death, in 1773–74, and it remains the most complete example of eighteenth-century church building and furnishing on the Isle of Man.

Work on the new chapel-of-ease at Douglas (St George's) began in 1761 but had to be suspended in 1765 when the trustees appointed by Hildesley to raise the necessary funds ran out of money. In 1775 Bishop Richmond launched an appeal in Bath, Liverpool and London, which raised £418, and new trustees were appointed to supervise the building work. The new chapel was completed in 1780 and consecrated by Bishop Mason in 1781, though the trustees were still nearly £300 in debt when the organ was installed in 1788.[156]

A useful snapshot of the condition of Manx churches in the late 1790s is given by John Feltham, who recorded the details of buildings he visited. On

155 MNH MS 09309, letter from Hildesley, probably to Philip Moore, chaplain at St Matthew's, Douglas, 30 September 1762.

156 Craine, *St George's and St Barnabas' Church*, 1; Gelling, *Manx Church*, 43.

Fig. 2.21 *'St George's Douglas 1822', by Will Latham: MNH 1954-7403.*

the whole, he was impressed by what he saw. German church, condemned by Bishop Hildesley for its disgraceful condition in 1757, was 'neatly pewed', Santon church 'was new seated last year', and at Castletown chapel 'the pulpit has a satin damask cloth of crimson colour'; St George's chapel at Douglas 'has spacious pews and galleries, and a handsome organ'. Though the chapel at St John's had 'been lately rebuilt … It has no pews, being used only occasionally'. Feltham described the church at Bride as 'badly seated' but he noted that Bishop Hildesley had erected a new west gallery there, with 'a handsome painted front, with [his] arms on it' in 1772.[157]

In addition to Braddan, two other Manx churches, Malew and Santon, retain substantial remains of their late eighteenth-century fittings. Of the three churches built or rebuilt during the episcopate of George Murray (1814–27), that at Andreas retains its original box pews, re-used and simply re-ordered, no doubt to save expense, when the church was again largely rebuilt in 1864–69. The new chapels at Castletown and Ramsey had galleried interiors with the pulpit and reading desk placed in a central position directly in front of the altar. The little-altered interior of the former was lost after the church was closed in 1975, and the interior of the latter was significantly re-ordered in 1869–74.[158] The chapel at Castletown had been a relatively expensive building for its date, costing £1675 16s. 8½d., one third of the cost being provided by the government and the remainder being raised through the sale or auctioning of the pews.[159]

157 Feltham, *Tour*, 172–73, 207, 213, 222, 225, 259, 268.
158 Gelling, *Manx Church,* 130–31, 183.
159 Thompson, *St Mary's,* 8.

EARLY MODERN FURNISHINGS INSIDE MANX CHURCHES

Pat McClure

The installation of seating clustered around a pulpit inside early modern churches reflected the change from the medieval services that once focused on the sacrament of mass celebrated at a stone altar. Protestants placed an emphasis on communal worship with everyone being able to hear and understand the Word of God delivered in the vernacular. By 1657 it was officially recognized in the Isle of Man that congregational seating, the main component of nave furnishings, was to be funded by the quarterland farmers, intack holders, and the townspeople 'according to their abillityes.'[160] Pew holders were ordered 'to take a speedy course for the repairing and making up of their respective seats and pewes, in some handsome and orderly manner [...]'.[161] Maintenance of chancels was funded by the clergy, although high status quarterland tenants who occupied chancel pews also contributed.

Lack of local timber must have been a logistical and economic challenge to providing decent seating for everyone, as evidenced in Malew parish church, where the 1698 congregation had to make do with benches resting on 'great stones.'[162] The Island's involvement with international trade became more visible from the eighteenth century. For instance, Norwegian timber was being advertised for sale in Douglas in 1733.[163] This was reflected in Santon parish church when uniform seating made from pine sourced off-island was installed in 1796.[164]

Typically, there was little material definition between chancel and nave inside a Manx church. The small, wooden holy table that parishioners gathered around for infrequent commemorative celebrations of Holy Communion was inconspicuously located at the east end of a short chancel. The plain, high-sided, doored seating which provided privacy and protection from draughts focused onto a large, triple-decker pulpit which was deliberately situated by a window to source its precious, natural light.

Candles were probably a luxury in the context of the earthen floors which continued to be a feature of many rural churches and chapels.[165] The heights of the top two pulpit desks reminded those present of the authority of the

160 MNH MS 10071/3/9, Lib.Scacc., 1657.
161 R.D. Kermode, 'Parish of Trinity Ayre now called Kirk Christ Lezayre', *PIMNHAS*, 4 (1939), 3, 347.
162 MNH MS 10216 (EPR), 1698.
163 *Manks Mercury*, 23 July 1733.
164 Feltham, *Tour*, 'Kirk St Ann, or Santon', 259; Atkinson, A., *et al.*, 'Woodwork' in 'St Sanctain's Church', *NADFAS Record of Church Furnishings*, 2005 (MNH MS 11165).
165 J.T. Clarke, *A History of St Mark's Chapel, Malew from the Year of Our Lord 1771 to the year 1843* (Douglas, 1861), 28.

Fig. 2.22 *Old Kirk Braddan triple pulpit. Photo Charles Guard.*

clergyman and of the Bible. The lowest desk was occupied by a clerk who led the responses from an English Book of Common Prayer in the absence of a fully-literate congregation or a Book of Common Prayer, which was only published in the vernacular in 1765 (see Fig. 2.10). Similar arrangements were still being installed in the mid-1830s, as when a new church was built at Lonan.[166] The triple-decker pulpit was only removed from Ballaugh parish church in 1852.[167]

Seat occupation reflected acceptance of social segregation, apparently supported by the church officials who regulated the seating. The clergy and those residing on the most prestigious quarterlands were allocated large family pews in the chancel or at the east end of the nave. Space in the body of the nave was more limited. There was not always room to kneel. In 1762 Bishop Hildesley expressed his concerns about arrangements in Bride church: '... it is not without the greatest inconvenience and uneasiness they [parishioners] comply with the appointed custom of *kneeling*: insomuch, that we have frequent instances of persons carried out sick [...] owing to an exceeding *close crowd*.'[168] The

166 MNH MS 10855 (DD), Lonan red file.
167 MNH MS 10457 (PR).
168 Butler, *Memoirs of Hildesley*, 69.

least fortunate were allocated places furthest from the prestigious east end. For example, the Santon poor were allocated the steps of the font to sit on in 1727.[169]

Ecclesiastical court transcripts and related seating plans indicate where members of congregations sat and that in the rural parishes this continued to be strongly related to land tenancy until well into the nineteenth century. In 1818, 32 seats in Marown parish church were allocated to the quarterlands and intacks.[170] In 1832 all the seating in Ballaugh parish church was allocated to landholdings.[171] This also applied in Lonan in 1836.[172] In contrast, by 1788 all the seats in the urban St Mary's chapel in Castletown had been assigned to named persons.[173] This reflected that many were businessmen, rather than farmers. It was some time before the latter style became visible in the rural churches, as in Lezayre where, by 1838 some of the seats that had been allocated to landholdings in 1766 were transferred to named heads of families occupying local intacks.[174]

There was a perception of pew ownership and related prestige. The 1781 construction of a north transept in Malew parish church was financed by the sale of the new pews which were to remain the property of the proprietors 'for ever without the interference of any General or parochial Regulation in the Church.'[175] 'Sittings were owned, bought, sold, bequeathed, and inherited like other real property.'[176] In 1818 Marown parish church officials wrote 'The Vicar's seat at the entrance of the door opposite the vestry is appropriated to the use of the families of the Vicars of K Marown for ever.'[177] On 12 October 1820 the subscribers to the new St Paul's chapel-of-ease in Ramsey discussed the seats as 'the property of subscribers' even though they were subject to an annual rent. The contemporary seating plan was 'to be considered binding as to the allotment of Pews to Subscribers forever.'[178]

Even so, some Manx parishes pre-empted Cambridge Camden Society changes, evident in English churches from the early nineteenth century, by providing limited free seating within their churches. In 1781, 30 of the 1,300 seats installed in the newly-built chapel of St George's in Douglas were reserved

169 MNH MS 10855 (DD), Santon red file.
170 MNH MS 10855 (DD), Marown red file.
171 MNH MS 10855 (DD), Ballaugh red file.
172 MNH MS 10855 (DD), Lonan red file.
173 P.G. Ralfe, *Parish Church of St Mary, Castletown* (Castletown, 1924: pamphlet in bound volume *Castletown*), 46.
174 R.D. Kermode, *The Annals of Kirk Christ Lezayre: sometime known as Trinity Ayre* (Douglas, 1954), plate 2; MNH MS 10855 (DD), Lezayre red file.
175 MNH 10855 (DD), Malew red file.
176 Ralfe, *St Mary's Castletown*, 19.
177 MNH MS 10855 (DD), Marown red file.
178 MNH MS 09946/10 (PR), 5–10.

for the poor.[179] This probably reflected the large numbers of destitute in the town. Around 1823 the Incorporated Church Building Society made a donation of £300 to the new chapel being built in Castletown 'on the understanding that a certain number of seats should be free.'[180] An 1826 ground plan of St Paul's chapel-of-ease in Ramsey shows sixteen free pews at the rear of the nave.[181] When the rural new Ballaugh parish church opened in 1832, a free seat was provided directly under the pulpit.[182] This reiterated widely-shared Protestant ideals that everyone should be able to hear the sermon clearly. At the same time St Barnabas' Church in Douglas designated 500 out of its 1500 seats as free.[183]

In conclusion, the material arrangements inside early modern Manx churches reflected land tenancy in the Isle of Man where a shared, conservative, mildly-puritan paradigm tolerated by Anglican officials prevailed until well into the nineteenth century.

CLERICAL DRESS

Pat McClure

Eighteenth-century clothing defined social rank. Manx Anglican clergy were required to dress in dark clothing according to their office, to distinguish them from laity.[184] Even light-coloured stockings were not allowed in public.[185] Presumably this included natural un-dyed fabrics bleached during long use outdoor that might imply involvement in low-status manual occupations. Another prescription required each Manx church or chapel-of-ease to own a surplice for the priest to wear 'at the times both of prayer and preaching'.[186]

Most eighteenth-century families made woollen clothing for personal use, as in Ballaugh in 1774.[187] Once dyed black and made into clothing, the resultant broadcloth represented authority and rank. The costly processes involved in manufacture and maintenance made the results impracticable for use by those involved in outdoor manual labour.

179 C.W. Gawne, *A History of St George's Church, Douglas, Isle of Man* (church leaflet, 2006), 3.
180 MNH MS 10855 (DD), box 98.
181 T. Brine, 'Ramsey, St Paul, Man, Isle of' (Lambeth Palace Church Plans Online, 1818-1826), accessed 30 May 2012.
182 MNH MS 10855 (DD), Ballaugh red file.
183 MNH MS 10052, box 2, religious census returns, 1851.
184 G. Bray (ed), 1998, *The Anglican Canons, 1529–1947* (Woodbridge, 1998), 721, 723.
185 Bray (ed), *Anglican Canons*, 369.
186 Bray (ed), *Anglican Canons*, 297.
187 MNH MS 00197 C: 1–3, James Wilks, 'Description of Ballaugh parish in the year 1774', 1.

Despite the official rules, Manx clergy sometimes dressed more simply than their English contemporaries. In 1665 vicar of Arbory John Crellin's dress was 'but baire, though grave; and according to the country, and the colour poore.'[188] This probably reflected his low stipend and involvement in husbandry or other manual tasks to make ends meet. In the Island there may have been a smaller social gap between literate and illiterate natives who shared use of vernacular language than between islanders and outsiders. It must have been difficult in small, isolated communities to maintain the required perception of clerical 'otherness.' In 1761 Bishop Hildesley still thought Manx clergy lax in distinguishing themselves from the laity in dress, and local clergy continued to challenge hierarchical expectations.[189] Although Philip Moore, chaplain of St Matthew's chapel-of-ease in Douglas in 1769, complained of the financial strain of meeting expectations for the way he should dress, these requirements were perpetuated.[190] When John Clarke went to Castletown grammar school in 1818, he purchased a 'new set of clothes.'[191] This major, unusual event in the context of his family's limited means, as expressed in his reflective diary, publicly marked his transition from farmer's son to prospective clergyman.

Parishioners were responsible for the funding and maintenance of parochial surplices. Records of periodic visitations from Church officials indicate that a relatively large proportion of eighteenth-century surplices were in a less than acceptable condition. The 1757 Santon visitation return declared that the Santon surplice was 'foul and dirty.'[192] This was not an isolated incident. Island-wide, prescriptive orders to amend shortfalls suggest a reactive attitude towards caring for and replacing these garments. Reluctance to make the associated expenditure may have been associated with perceptions that surplices had Catholic connotations.

Although the manufacture of linen was a significant Island cottage industry, the transformation of flax into linen cloth was protracted, involving large numbers of people and long, uncomfortable, wet, cold processes. Presumably locally-woven linen was sourced for surplices so, rather than being snowy-white displays of divine ecclesiastical, and/or priestly purity, the majority of Manx rural parochial surplices were probably creased, rust-marked, pocked with insect and rodent damage, and a pale shade of grey. Difficulties in overcoming

188 MNH MS 10216, Ecclesiastical Probate Records (EPR).

189 Bray (ed), *Records of Convocation*, vol. 1, 256–57.

190 MNH MS 10855 (DD), box 104; MNH M 02880, Philip Moore, c.1763–69, 'Letters of the Rev. Philip Moore' reprinted in 1897/8 in *Ramsey Church Magazine*, 1 and 2 (in one volume), 1758, n.p.

191 MNH MD 10141/B1, J.T. Clarke, 'A journal', 1817–19, 34.

192 MNH MS 00791 C, Episcopal Visitation Return (VR), 1757.

storage problems in a damp climate must have been almost insurmountable in the face of requirements that surplices 'shall be proper and fitting'.[193]

Another factor that influenced how surplices were cared for must have been the apparent reluctance of the clergy to wear the surplice. For example, in 1634 the Santon minister 'usually' wore his surplice.[194] This suggests that sometimes he did not. On 17 March 1663 Isaac Barrow wrote to the Manx clergy saying that he hoped 'to find you all ... officiating in your Surplices [...],' implying they probably had not been. This may have been influenced by earlier puritan activity. Malew had not acquired a surplice by 1665. Nor had Arbory which, it was reported, had 'noe surplus as yet'.[195] Although an apparently optimistic remark, it is unclear whether this reflected an intention of the bishop or of the parish that Arbory would acquire one soon. Continued mildly dissident activity within the Anglican Church and self-assurance to challenge the bishop in the context of the Island's exclusion from the 1662 Parliamentary Act of Uniformity may have encouraged non-compliance. It became the Manx custom 'to take off the surplice at the pulpit steps, put on a black gown, then put the surplice on again afterwards.'[196] Manx clergy were also required to attend annual Tynwald Day ceremonies in their 'proper habit and garb.'[197] Although Chaloner reported that the governor and Keys were accompanied at Tynwald by 'three clerks [priests] in their ſurplices', nearly two centuries later a visitor from England complained that the way the clergy wore their surplices at Tynwald contributed to an unimpressive ceremony.[198] In the first half of the nineteenth century the Manx clergy often wore only a black gown in the pulpit.[199] However, surplices were perceived differently in Castletown. Generous patronage by successive lords of Man supported lavish amounts of imported French and Irish linen to be made into surplices destined for use in the lord of Man's chapel.[200] This suggests that the local product was perceived to be of a lower quality. Wilks inferred that most locally-woven linen remained coarse.[201]

Records in the secular Castle Rushen Papers provide an insight into the considerable resources made available to the congregation of the Castletown

193 Bray (ed), *Anglican Canons*, 713.
194 MNH MS 09756 (VR).
195 MNH MS 10216 (EPR).
196 Gelling, *Manx Church*, 154; *Act of Uniformity 1662* (14 Car 2 c. 4).
197 Bray (ed), *Records of Convocation*, vol. 1, 256.
198 Chaloner, *Treatise*, fol. 20; Anon, [probably John Welsh], 'Tynwald Hill' in 'Fourth Day' in *A Six Days Tour through the Isle of Man by a Stranger* (c.1836), 131.
199 A.E. Lamothe, 'Humorous stories of the clergy', in *Manx Yarns* (1905), 4, 9; Gelling, *Manx Church*, 154, 253.
200 MNH MS 09782 (CRP), 1701–1801.
201 Wilks, 'Ballaugh parish', 1.

chapel-of-ease which were unavailable elsewhere.[202] The fine surplices in use formed part of the hierarchical trappings of governance. When in 1722 long-standing tensions between church and state came to a head, the governor confiscated the Castletown chapel key and surplice, and suspended services. Clearly the surplice expressed power and wealth. Three years later the chapel remained locked; a letter sent from the governor to Bishop Wilson in 1725 reminded him that it was secular power that had closed the chapel and retained the surplice.[203] This overruled any religious authority that item of dress implied. Eventually the chapel reopened and distinctively dressed clergymen continued to practise there, an outward manifestation of the Church's involvement in Island governance, despite the gradual but inevitable transfer of power from religious to civil leadership that took place during this period.

Acceptance of the use of surplices in Castletown was probably also linked with the economic opportunities related to their construction and maintenance that the patronage of successive lordships afforded them.[204] This patronage did not extend to the same extent to the mother church at Malew, even though it actually enjoyed seniority.

Black broadcloth and snowy surplices were supposed to reiterate social order and governmental support of Anglican practice, personified in its clergymen. Dark outdoor apparel that implied elevated social status when worn was often impractical in the context of the economic and practical constraints of the office of rural, eighteenth-century Manx clergyman. Neither did the homespun linen used in the surplices funded by congregations represent the intended social division between the rural clergy and the laity. Conversely, in Castletown, finely-clothed merchants and government officials were more familiar, and the regularly-laundered surplices of fine imported linen worn by the chapel chaplains ensured the townspeople recognized the clergy as their betters and the Church's link with civil governance.

THE OPERATION OF THE CHURCH COURTS

Jennifer Platten † and Nigel Yates †

The argument that the continued operation of the church courts in the Isle of Man into the nineteenth century was fundamentally different from the operation of ecclesiastical jurisdiction in other parts of the provinces of

202 The Castle Rushen Papers are a strong source since they are contemporary, secular (not written by the clergy), countersigned and formal.

203 MNH MS 10855 (DD), Castletown red file, governor to Bp Wilson, 1725.

204 MNH MS 09782 (CRP), 1701–65.

Canterbury and York can no longer be sustained.[205] They did, however, have some peculiar characteristics. There was even less distinction than on the mainland between the respective jurisdictions of the episcopal and archidiaconal courts; the practice was for each year to be divided into two halves, with jurisdiction vested in the bishop for one half and the archdeacon for the other, though the more serious offences, such as adultery or witchcraft, were usually tried in the bishop's court; in practice the courts were presided over by the same officers, the vicars-general.[206] Although the most common punishments imposed in the ecclesiastical courts were, as in England, public penance and, for severe offences, excommunication, the Manx jurisdiction sanctioned other punishments as well: fines; imprisonment, in the bishop's prison at St German's cathedral until 1780, and thereafter in the governor's prison at Castle Rushen until 1825; the use of the bridle for serious cases of slander; the occasional use of the pillory, stocks, or whipping; and 'to be drawn after a boat in the sea' for prostitution, a sentence only rarely imposed and meted out for the last time in 1734 but not carried out.[207] Jennifer Platten argued that the differing degrees of severity of punishment in the Manx system slowed the decline of the ecclesiastical courts into disrepute.[208]

The enforcement of ecclesiastical discipline in the Isle of Man received strong encouragement from successive bishops. In March 1664 one of the first tasks undertaken by Isaac Barrow at the beginning of his episcopate was to issue instructions to his clergy to 'be careful and diligent in their places and callings' and to assist him in improving the pastoral and spiritual welfare of the diocese.[209] On 15 May 1675 Bishop Bridgeman, 'that the many vices and especially those three deadly sins of Whoredom, Drunkenness and swearing ... might be utterly extirpated from among us', appointed three, rather than the customary two, vicars-general 'to take frequent notice of the offences Committed within their respective precincts, either against morality ... or the Cannons of the Church'.[210] The rector of Bride was made responsible for the

205 See the excellent discussions of this topic in Jacob, *Lay People and Religion*, 135–54, and W. Gibson, *The Church of England 1688–1832* (London, 2001), 127–36. Public penance was commonplace in the Church of Scotland until the 1820s: see C.G. Brown, *Religion and Society in Scotland since 1707* (Edinburgh, 1997), 69ff.

206 Ashley, 'Spiritual courts', 38–40.

207 Ashley, 'Spiritual courts', 54–55; Moore, *Sodor and Man,* 108–11, 121–22; Craine, *Mananan's Isle*, 136.

208 J.A. Platten, 'The Church Court System: Presentments to the Manx Church Courts, 1640–1799' (PhD thesis, University of Liverpool, 2010), 226–27.

209 MNH MS 10216 (EW), Barrow to Vicars General, 17 March 1664; M.J. Hoy, 'Isaac Barrow: builder of foundations for a modern nation' (PhD thesis, University of Liverpool, 2015), 35–41.

210 Bishop Barrow appointed three vicars general: see MNH MS 06448 MD 335 (Lib. Testam.), Barrow's commission to vicars general John Harrison, Thomas Parr and Patrick Thompson, 3 July 1668.

parishes of Andreas, German, Jurby, Lezayre, Maughold and Patrick; the rector of Ballaugh for those of Braddan, Lonan, Michael and Onchan; and the vicar of Malew for those of Arbory, Marown, Rushen and Santon; 'the ministers of the respective parishes and chapels of this Island to bring in their Presentments every 3 weeks ... to the president of that Circuit wherein they live'.[211] On 26 July 1683, at a meeting of the convocation of the clergy, Bishop Lake issued four decrees tightening up on church attendance, catechising, the repair of churches and the keeping of registers, all of which he clearly regarded as being below acceptable levels. At a meeting of convocation on 17 August 1685 Bishop Levinz repeated the decrees on all these matters and added new ones on preaching, the proper reading of the church service, visiting the sick, presenting 'all crimes and misdemeanours ... so that all sins may be timely punished', and requiring all clergy in benefices in receipt of augmentation money for that purpose 'to teach an English school respectively in his respective parish, under the penalty of forfeiting his said augmentation'.[212] Discipline was further tightened in the ecclesiastical constitutions drawn up by Bishop Wilson and approved at a meeting of the convocation of the clergy on 3 February 1704 and ratified by Tynwald on the following day. In particular, the practice 'of exempting persons ... from penance and other punishment appointed by law, on account of paying a sum of money, or doing some charitable work, shall for the future cease'.[213] The practice of commutation had been discouraged earlier by Bishop Barrow, who favoured forms of penance rather than payment of fines.[214] Even the lethargic Bishop Richmond requested his vicars-general on 25 May 1774 'to send to me an account in writing, signed by them both, of the state in which they find all Ecclesiastical matters ... in their Circuit Courts to be holden throughout this Isle, and Diocese, within 14 days after said Circuits are ended'. A report was duly returned on 22 June 1774 listing all the presentments. There were 52 cases of non-payment of the church assessments; 11 of breaches of sabbath discipline, either by working or not attending divine service; six cases of cursing, swearing or slander; two each of drunkenness and failing to keep the church in repair; and one each of adultery and 'keeping a lewd and disorderly house'. The vicar of Maughold was presented 'for performing the whole of divine service in ye Chancel' and at Andreas 'many of the parishioners for not attending divine service on Holy-days'.[215]

211 MNH MD 00436, folder 8/8.

212 Bray (ed), *Records of Convocation*, vol. 1, 111–14. The amount of each augmentation, provided by royal bounty in 1676, was recorded at the convocation held on 9 June 1715: see Bray (ed), *Records of Convocation*, vol. 1, 146.

213 The constitutions are printed in full in Bray (ed), *Records of Convocation*, vol. 1, 206–09.

214 Hoy, 'Isaac Barrow', 49.

215 MNH MD 00436, folder 7/19, 20.

Research by Jennifer Platten has shown that, far from decreasing, the number of cases considered by the church courts in the Isle of Man increased substantially between the middle years of the seventeenth and the last decade of the eighteenth centuries, as shown in figure 2.23.[216]

Fig. 2.23 *Number of cases considered by the Manx Church Courts 1640–1800.*

Years	Average Number of Offences	Sexual Offences	Verbal Offences	Breaches of Sunday Observance
1640	96	16	10	35
1659	132	54	15	41
1667–8	138	33.5	30	53
1678–9	100	20.5	17.5	37
1695–1704	120	20	18	49
1730–9	219.5	47	32	66
1760–9	186	54	23	38
1790–9	202	71	51	38

During the 1650s the system of imposing penances on those found guilty was temporarily replaced by fines or more secular forms of physical punishment, such as a period in the stocks, but the more traditional system of penances had been reintroduced by the late 1660s.[217] Adultery and fornication, however, usually led to a period of imprisonment. These sanctions remained the standard pattern for regulating moral behaviour throughout the eighteenth century. The use of the bridle in cases of slander was, however, not sanctioned after 1701. Throughout the whole period the most common offences were those of a sexual nature, cases of slander, cursing or swearing, and non-attendance at church or working on Sundays. Other offences prosecuted in the church courts were drinking, fighting or playing games on Sundays, habitual drunkenness, irreverence in church and omitting to send children to school or catechism. Persistent failure to repair one's pew in church or one's section of the churchyard wall or fence, or any other repeated offences, meant that the offender was likely to be threatened with imprisonment. The most severe sentence, that of excommunication, was usually reserved for persistent adulterers and fornicators. Despite the penalties, if presented and found guilty, non-attendance at church

216 This section is based on J.A. Platten, 'Mid-Seventeenth Century Church Court Presentments in the Isle of Man: Social Control or Salvation for Sinners?' (MA thesis, University of Liverpool, 1999), and 'The Church Court System' (2010).

217 Bishop Wilson commended Isaac Barrow for this reform: see Keble, *Wilson*, vol. 1, 140.

was frequently reported to the courts, the most serious case occurring in 1762 when 172 parishioners of Andreas were presented for non-attendance.[218]

However, by the second quarter of the nineteenth century, although both Bishop Ward and Archdeacon Philpot were keen to maintain the ecclesiastical discipline of former years, it is clear that they were beginning to face opposition to it from some clergy and churchwardens, and this appears to be at least partly associated with the growth of Evangelicalism within the Manx church during the early nineteenth century. These divisions were clearly revealed in the replies to Philpot's query about discipline at his visitation in 1833. The rector of Ballaugh noted that 'few presentments have been made of late years in consequence of no notice being taken of them'. At Malew adulterers and fornicators were only presented when the charges could be supported by the evidence of illegitimate children. At Onchan presentments had been 'for many years discontinued'. It was the evangelical curate of Braddan who stated that

> I have never yet presented any person to the ecclesiastical court. I have used no other than spiritual weapons in contending against the strongholds of Satan and weapons of this kind are I believe the only weapons that will ever be found mighty to the pulling down of those strongholds.

There were, however, some parishes such as Lezayre, Maughold and Rushen, in which presentments were still being made in the traditional manner.[219]

As Jacob has noted, the survival of ecclesiastical discipline implies public acceptance.[220] The only occasion on which this seems to have been in doubt was in the dispute between Bishop Wilson and Governor Horne, though the issues were more complicated. There seems to have been a personal antipathy and degree of power struggle between the two men, which may have been exacerbated by Horne's suspicion that Wilson sided with the British government in its efforts to prevent the Isle of Man being a haven for smugglers.[221] Nevertheless, the issue that provoked the dispute, and resulted in Wilson's brief imprisonment in Castle Rushen, revolved around the question of ecclesiastical discipline.[222] On 5 June 1716, Mary Henricks or Hendrick and Isaac Allgood of Douglas were sentenced to perform public penance for adultery. Allgood submitted, but Henricks did not and was sentenced to excommunication and imprisonment.

218 This figure has been omitted from the calculations in Table 1 in order not to produce a false impression of the number of offences in this category in the 1760s.

219 MNH MS 00794 C.

220 Jacob, *Lay People and Religion*, 136.

221 This suggestion is put forward by G. Every, *The High Church Party 1688–1718* (London, 1956), 170–72.

222 The most detailed account of the dispute, and the one on which all subsequent accounts are based, is provided by Keble, *Wilson*, vol. 1, 364–71, 374–405, 415–45; and vol. 2, 454–616.

She then appealed through Governor Horne to have her case heard by the earl of Derby, which Horne accepted. Wilson, however, refused to accept the validity of this appeal, which he stated, correctly, should have been referred not to the earl of Derby but to the archbishop of York. Horne responded by accusing two of Wilson's clergy of holding Roman Catholic doctrines, charges which Wilson investigated and dismissed. On 19 February 1719 the governor's court fined Wilson ten pounds for refusing to attend the appeal hearing before the earl of Derby, though this fine was later remitted. Wilson had the full support of the clergy in the stand he took. At the meeting of convocation on 9 June 1720, all the clergy present, including two who later opposed him, Archdeacon Robert Horrobin and William Bridson, vicar of Marown, supported an address to the archbishop of York expressing 'most humble and unfeigned thanks for your Grace's zealous Concern in behalf of this church and its Discipline, and for Countenancing and Supporting our Excellent Bishop in the regular Government of the One and due Execution of the Other'. In forwarding this address to the archbishop, Wilson noted that the governor's officers 'refuse to give us the legal assistance to commit obstinate People, unless we ask it after a way y^{t} is neither agreeable to law nor former practice'.[223]

There the matter might have stood but for a complaint against Archdeacon Horrobin for preaching false doctrine in a sermon at Castletown. This complaint was investigated by Bishop Wilson, who informed the archbishop of York on 23 June 1721 that Horrobin 'spoke very suspiciously of the Athanasian Creed, and said it gave great offence to many good men'. He also enclosed some papers to show that 'we still keep up our discipline, notwithstanding the discouragements we meet with'.[224] Whilst the complaint was still being investigated, Horrobin refused Holy Communion to one of his parishioners on the grounds that she was conducting an improper relationship with a fellow parishioner. It transpired that this information had been supplied to Horrobin by Governor Horne's wife. Upon investigation it became clear that Mrs Horne could produce no witnesses to substantiate her allegations. She was formally censured and required to 'acknowledge her offence accordingly ... asking forgiveness for the great injury done' or face imprisonment. Horrobin was also censured for arbitrarily excluding a parishioner from Holy Communion 'without any previous notice or admonition'.

On 17 May 1722, Bishop Wilson delivered his judgement on the complaint against Horrobin for preaching false doctrine, which he found to have been proved, and the archdeacon was suspended from his office, the rectory of Andreas and the chaplaincy of Castletown. Governor Horne responded by having the chapel at Castletown locked up so that no services could be held

223 Borthwick Institute of Historical Research, Bp. C & P. XV/2.
224 Borthwick Institute of Historical Research, Bp. C & P. XV/5.

there, and by ordering Wilson to reinstate Horrobin or be fined £50 and the vicars-general £20 each. This time it was not only the clergy who supported the bishop but also the Keys, who rejected the charges of 'spiritual tyranny' that Horne had levelled against Wilson. Wilson and the vicars-general refused to pay the fines and were imprisoned at Castle Rushen from 29 June until 31 August 1722, being released after pressure was brought on Horne by the British government. On 31 October 1723, Archdeacon Horrobin submitted to the bishop and his suspension was lifted. During his imprisonment Wilson had submitted an appeal to the Privy Council against the behaviour of the governor and his officers and on 4 July 1724, sentence was given in his favour. Difficult relations between the secular and the ecclesiastical authorities in the Isle of Man were, however, to continue for several more years. Whilst one must beware of some of the more hagiographical assessments of Wilson, it is hard not to conclude that the course of action he pursued was entirely defensible. Indeed, it could be argued that the failed attempt to curtail the powers of the Manx church was a factor in maintaining the jurisdiction of the ecclesiastical courts well into the nineteenth century.

THE ISLAND CHURCH IN TWO CONTRASTED PARISHES

Pat McClure

This section considers material aspects of two Manx places of worship as dynamic microcosms of their eighteenth-century congregations. The early modern parochial system in Man reflected rural human activity because the townships and their urban chapels-of-ease fell within the jurisdiction of the incumbents of mother churches located in the countryside. The eighteenth-century Church continued to intrude into, and record, many aspects of everyday family life. Consideration of characteristics of Anglican buildings and their internal liturgical arrangements provides much evidence about the activities of, and relationships between, those involved.

Kirk Arbory (otherwise St Cairbre's and later St Columba's) parish church, Arbory (SC 246705)[225]

Kirk Arbory occupies an earlier Christian site.[226] The only surviving source of how the predecessor of the eighteenth-century building that survives may have looked is a nineteenth-century copy of a c.1700 drawing showing a small

225 Gill (ed), *Statutes*, vol. 1, 285: 'And the said new Church … shall be called, esteemed, and taken as the Parish Church of Kirk Arbory.'

226 D.S. Dugdale, *Manx Church Origins* (Lampeter, 1998), 140.

Fig. 2.24 *Kirk Arbory: Miss Oliver's copy of c.1700 sketch. MNH.* Oliver (Miss), Drawings of Manx churches as they were c.1700. Manx Society, vol. 14 (1868), facing 81.

vernacular building with undefined chancel and single south entrance accessed from the only pathway into the churchyard leading from the minor roadway into the hills to the east of the church.

Although the simple internal arrangements reflected prevalent local living conditions, there is evidence that a few families enjoyed higher economic status.[227] For instance, by 1719 the parish had acquired some silver communion plate.[228] Although the donors of this plate are unknown, it seems unlikely this remote rural community could have afforded such prestigious items without patronage from within the parish.

Baptism remained a central tenet of Protestant faith, despite the disruption of the Commonwealth period when, probably, many fonts were removed, including that at Kirk Arbory. Although by 1665 it was reported that the newborn were being baptized inside the church, likely this statement probably does not tell the whole story. In 1748 Kirk Arbory officials were reminded to pour water into the font at baptisms, which suggests a different vessel was being used.[229]

The dearth of gravestones around the church in Oliver's copy of c.1700 sketch probably represented the customary practice of burying the dead inside the building under the family pews. The resultant, often shallow, burials in the earthen floor contributed to the deterioration of this building. By 1743 the pulpit, reading desk, and many of the seats were also broken.[230] Instructions to churchwardens at periodic visitations confirm that officials perceived that

227 MNH MS 10216 (EPR).
228 MNH MS 00791 C (VR).
229 MNH MS 00791 C (VR).
230 MNH MS 00791 C (PR).

Fig. 2.25 *Kirk Arbory before the erection of a tower in 1915. Courtesy Peter Kelly Collection.*

parishioners were responsible for the maintenance of their nave. Despite the contemporary population explosion which allowed for wider sharing of this responsibility, the Kirk Arbory interior remained dilapidated. It seems expectations were low, and parishioners had difficulties in accessing even basic resources to make repairs.

The old church was declared too small to accommodate all the new residents, but formal procedures associated with its enlargement or rebuilding were protracted. A group of parishioners became impatient and began to pull down the old church anyway, without permission.[231] The church was finally rebuilt adjacent and immediately to the north of the old site, a practical solution to the logistical problems created by the burials under the old church. Detailed accounts record the many other challenges overcome by the builders, most of whom lived within parish boundaries.[232] Eventually, in 1759, the new church was completed, furnished, and consecrated.

A drawing commissioned by Bishop Ward c.1830 indicates the new church was another vernacular build.[233] Its white exterior had a dual role. Any intended message about Christian purity also became a local landmark. The church's

231 MNH MS 10855 (DD), Arbory red file.
232 MNH MS 10855 (DD), Arbory red file.
233 MNH M 17096.

high visibility in the landscape facilitated rural travel on foot before a time of street lighting and vehicular transport along surfaced roads. The absence of a seat in this parish church for the lord of Man's representative, and of the Royal Arms, is a reminder that eighteenth-century Arbory remained a relatively landlocked outpost despite its actual proximity to Castletown. Even so, these logistical obstacles were challenged and a new church with numerous, large windows was erected. These windows suggest increased parochial literacy, despite continued economic constraints. Parishioners were ordered to move the pulpit nearer to a window in 1761, presumably to take advantage of the free light afforded.[234]

The new triple-decker pulpit was also declared too small to meet official expectations. Other tensions about the new internal arrangements arose. Ordinary churchgoers insisted on sitting in the high-status Stevenson family's new pew, allocated because of required changes to the communion rail.[235] It seems this congregation had a self-confident, challenging element, perhaps supported by the parish's relative isolation. The Anglican hierarchy's reaction, an order to enlarge the pulpit, was a material prompt that reiterated clerical authority every Sunday. Another directive instructing parishioners to cease their invasion of the Stevenson pew reminded them that the eighteenth-century Church supported social segregation.[236]

No surviving records document the installation of a font into the new church, whereas the font from the old church lay outside in the churchyard until the middle of the nineteenth century.[237] So, although contemporary visitation and baptismal records indicate that baptisms did take place publicly inside Kirk Arbory, parishioners and incumbents may have expressed their moderate dissidence by using a tin basin through much of this period, as occurred elsewhere in the Island, for example in Braddan parish church.[238]

Although Methodist meetings were being held in Colby by 1798, it was only after 1822 that a house in Colby was converted into a Primitive Methodist meeting room.[239] This relatively late innovation in the context of Welsh and

234 MNH MS 10855 (DD), Arbory red file.
235 MNH MS 10855 (DD), Arbory red file.
236 MNH MS 10855 (DD), Arbory red file.
237 J.M. Neale, 'The Isle of Man' in *Ecclesiological Notes on the Isle of Man, Ross, Sutherland and the Orkneys; A Summer Pilgrimage to S. Maughold and S. Magnus* (1848), 35.
238 H.S. Brown, 'Notes of my life' in *Hugh Stowell Brown His Autobiography His Commonplace Book and Extracts from his Sermons and Addresses*, W.S. Cain (ed), 2nd edn (Glasgow and New York, 1887), 13; J.G. Cumming, *The Isle of Man, its History, Physical, Ecclesiastical, Civil and Legendary* (London, 1848), 19–20.
239 MNH M 11397, C.C. McFee, *Colby Methodism and its buildings* (1972: pamphlet), 6, 9.

English Nonconformity was another reflection of the continued acceptance of restrained puritanism within the Manx Church as described by Yates above.

Around the same time, the eighteenth-century parish communion silver was stolen.[240] The church's earliest silver survivor is a small mug dated 1812/13.[241] In the context of the poor condition of Kirk Arbory in 1830, these must have been huge losses, in spite of their infrequent use. Communion was only being celebrated four times a year.[242] Despite the centrality of this building within the local community, its serial neglect suggests inaction from even the highest ranking within the congregation, implying shared mildly-puritan ideas and/or a more general lack of access to the resources necessary to make changes. The stolen silver was not replaced until the second half of the nineteenth century. Acquisition of replacements in silver seems to have been beyond parochial means at that time. However, one wonders if items of less monetary, but of considerable practical value, were donated soon after the robbery. A pewter goblet and plain plate manufactured in Sheffield, both dated 1806, survive, as does a more-decorative pewter flagon of the same date made in Exeter.[243] Clearly these items were not purchased as a communion set. Rather, the material suggests possible previous domestic use; the style, quality and access to off-Island commodity markets. Such a donation would have been a timely and very acceptable gift to this rural congregation.

By 1830, English must have been in common use in this parish, because services were only read in Manx twice every month.[244]

It was not until well into the last quarter of the nineteenth century that the material liturgical changes so familiar to today's churchgoers, like a large altar and a single-decker pulpit, were made. These arrangements were installed long after they had become fashionable in England. The 1851 census recorded that only 12 of the 327 seats were perceived as 'free.' New pews were installed in 1886.[245] However, the fact that these still had doors suggests that the new convention of free seating was not popular. The 1759 building exterior, albeit altered, remains a local landmark.

240 MNH MS 09756 (PR).

241 Jones, *Old church plate*, plate XIII, facing 19.

242 MNH MS 00798 C (VR).

243 W. Creer, 2017, 'Metalwork' in 'St Columba, Arbory parish church, Ballabeg, Isle of Man' in *NADFAS Record of Church Furnishings* (MNH MS 11165), 48, 50 and J. Latimer *et al.*, 2017, 'Metalwork' in 'St Cairbre, Belle Abbey Church, Colby, Isle of Man' in *NADFAS Record of Church Furnishings* (MNH MS 11165), 18.

244 MNH MS 00798 C (VR).

245 MNH MS 10855 (DD), Arbory red file.

St Matthew's Chapel, Douglas (SC 382753)

St Matthew's chapel-of-ease to Braddan parish church, consecrated in 1708, stood in Douglas Market Place facing James Street.[246] Despite financial support from the tenth earl of Derby and others, the resulting structure was simply constructed without foundations.[247] Its proximity to the harbour and the market place facilitated interactions with the townspeople. John Murrey's 1706 gift of a belfry clock must have provided a much needed public service. The chapel bell also had a civic role when rung to announce services or 'when any of the townsfolk died [...]'.[248]

St Matthew's was built on land that had belonged to the Church in earlier times, which ensured the new chapel's exemption from the lord of Man's rent. Lintel graves found nearby were consistent with an earlier Christian graveyard.[249] Those who died in eighteenth-century Douglas were taken to Braddan parish church for burial.

Worshippers entering St Matthew's through the north wall were met with a nave crowded with simple, high, lockable pews clustered either side of a central aisle around a massive triple-decker pulpit which was the focus of the eighteenth-century liturgies.[250] A low ceiling loomed over the whole space. In later years many windows were partially obscured, perhaps to segregate increasing secular activity outside from the sacred space within. The pulpit would have overshadowed a small, covered table against the east gable where communion was almost certainly celebrated infrequently. In 1782 communion was only celebrated six times in the mother church at Braddan.[251]

In contrast with rural Kirk Arbory, there was no shortage of patronage for the early requirement that St Matthew's should acquire appropriate communion plate.[252] Although the sizable and valuable silver items largely provided by several generations of the prestigious, merchant Murrey family for use on the holy table between 1704 and 1742 might seem to contrast with the more overall simplicity of other liturgical arrangements inside St Matthew's, the style of most items was very plain.[253] The simplicity, which reflected shared

246 MNH PG/4729; H.S. Taggart, *The Story of St Matthew's, Douglas, Isle of Man* (Douglas, c.1923), 56 in MNH M 09210/1-126, *Douglas Churches Scrapbook*, 1.

247 MNH MS 09782 (CRP); Taggart, *St Matthew's Church*; *Isle of Man Examiner*, 29 January 1943.

248 Brown, *Hugh Stowell Brown*, 6.

249 P.M.C. Kermode, 'The Douglas Chapel', *The Manx Archaeological Survey Fifth Report*, 11.

250 MNH PG/4735, 1890; Taggart, *St Matthew's Church*, 4.

251 MNH MS 00797 C (VR).

252 'The Churchwardens' Charge' in Bishop Wilson's Strict Regulations 6 September 1700, *JMM*, 2:40 (1934), doc. 86: 203, 204 (MNH) A 365 1/2.

253 Jones, *Old Church Plate*, plate IX.

Fig. 2.26 *'Old St Matthew's Douglas', by G. Pickering, 1832: MNH 1955-0361.*

mild puritanism, was not shared by all. At least one piece of eighteenth-century silver was ornate, which challenged the building's lowly chapel-of-ease status, its location within a poor urban district, and Braddan's known low-church paradigm. The Braddan communion plate was relatively austere.[254] In contrast, the St Matthew's plate acknowledged perceptions of the worth of those within the Douglas congregation with high enough social and economic capital to access off-island commodity markets and artisanship. The large box pews that filled the prestigious east end of the chapel reiterated official approval of these arrangements. This seating was formally allocated to the congregation's highest-ranking families.[255] The duke of Atholl's pew in the west gallery, decorated with the Royal Arms, raised its occupants even higher, level with the chaplain in the triple-decker pulpit, which was in use until at least 1878.[256] This seat's position and size expressed perceptions that the lord of Man or his representatives shared equal authority with the Church, whilst providing a paternalistic view of all proceedings and actors involved. Surrounding drapes ensured the privilege of personal privacy denied to all others present.

The upsurge in Douglas' population during the first half of the eighteenth century raised issues about St Matthew's seating capacity.[257] The chapel was enlarged in 1818 but it is unclear how.[258] Seating for 300, allocated since at least between 1735 and 1739 to specific homes and individuals, did not facilitate integration of newcomers.[259] The lack of Anglican accommodation in Douglas surely contributed towards the building of Douglas's first Non-conformist chapel opposite Thomas Street in 1786, long after such an event would have been noteworthy in England or Wales.[260]

Brown remembered St Matthew's lighted by candles 'that spluttered abominably'.[261] The 1824 proposal that gas light be installed at St Matthew's, well before the 1836 Douglas Gas Act was passed, reflected the centrality of this edifice to the local population.[262] Hugh Taggart recalled yellow walls, perhaps a consequence of long years of smoking candles and gas fumes.[263] They were undecorated except for the single memorial plaque to Philip Moore, chaplain

254 Jones, *Old Church Plate*, plate V.
255 MNH PG/4735, 1890.
256 MNH MS 10855 (DD), St Matthew's red file.
257 MNH MS 10855 (DD), box 104; MNH M 02880, Philip Moore, 'Letters'.
258 J. McHutchin and G. Quirk (eds), *The Isle of Man Charities* (Liverpool, 1831), 113.
259 Pigot, *Directory and Topography of the Isle of Man* (Douglas, 1837), 830; MNH MS 10855 (DD), box 104.
260 MNH M 17591, E240, E.V. Chapman, 'The Story of Manx Methodism in the Isle of Man', incomplete interim report for the Manx Methodist Society (c.1971), revised by F. Coakley (1997), 'Introduction – Early Days', 3.
261 Brown, *Hugh Stowell Brown*, 6.
262 *Rising Sun*, 21 December 1824.
263 Taggart, *St Matthew's Church*, 4.

Fig. 2.27 *Methodist, Independent and Roman Catholic churches in Douglas – composite illustration incorporating Wesleyan Methodist Chapel, Thomas Street, Primitive Methodist Chapel, Factory Lane, Scotch Kirk, Finch Road, Independent Chapel, Athol Street and Roman Catholic Chapel, Athol Street – MNH P.6410.*

of St Matthew's and master of Douglas Grammar School 1736–65, sponsored by Bishop Wilson, on the east gable.[264]

The absence of other monuments and the rank of the plaque's patron surely reflected the importance placed by the Church on education as well as community acceptance of rigid, contemporary, top-down paradigms. The latter was reiterated in the two other panels on the east gable, which probably contained the Decalogue, Creed, and Lord's Prayer in English. These expressions of ecclesiastical power prevailed even though many of the poor assembled during the eighteenth century probably could not read them. The fact that weekly services in Manx were still taking place in 1830 reflected this building's largely-Manx, Protestant congregation.[265] St Matthew's chapel was demolished in 1899.[266]

To conclude, although the two Anglican buildings explored above represented growing Manx populations in town and country and replaced or supplemented part of the earlier built ecclesiastical culture, insular parochial governance continued to be directed rurally. The liturgical arrangements within these two structures perpetuated earlier conventions representative of long, revered memories and an island-wide conservative paradigm. However, new technologies ensured that change was inevitable, albeit introduced and accepted later and more slowly in the Island than elsewhere. It was not until after 1830 that churches designed by English architects to replicate medieval ideas began to appear in Manx landscapes. Changes to internal material arrangements in English churches began to reflect proposals made by the Cambridge Camden Society, which was formed in 1839.[267] These modifications were not implemented inside Manx churches until much later.

BISHOP WARD'S REFORM PROGRAMME

The Anglican Church in the Isle of Man in the early nineteenth century

Nigel Yates †

When Bishop Murray was translated to Rochester in 1827, the right of nomination to the vacant diocese of Sodor and Man was exercised for the first time by the Crown. The person appointed was in some ways an unusual choice. William Ward, then aged 65, a non-graduate who had been promoted

264 MNH PG/3470, 1899.

265 MNH MS 00798 C (VR); J. Train, *An Historical and Statistical Account of the Isle of Man from the earliest times to the present date*, 2 vols (Liverpool, 1845), vol. 1, 374.

266 *Examiner*, 4 February 1899.

267 See C. Webster (ed), '*Temples ... worthy of His presence*': *the early publications of the Cambridge Camden Society* (Ecclesiological Society, c.2003), 13.

by Bishop Porteous of London, was then the incumbent of two Essex parishes, Alphamstone and Great Horkesley, which he retained after his consecration.

In addition to his establishment of King William's College at Castletown, which opened in 1833, he also launched a programme of church building in the Isle of Man which outdid that of all his predecessors in the diocese. This programme has to be seen in the context of church building programmes in other parts of the British Isles in the early nineteenth century. From 1808 there had been one of building new churches and glebe houses in Ireland, funded by parliamentary grants through the Irish Board of First Fruits. In 1818, funds were made available to a Church Building Commission to provide money for building additional churches in parishes with populations in excess of 4000 people, in which there was inadequate church accommodation, in England and Wales. In the same year, the Incorporated Church Building Society was established to provide grants towards the extension or reseating of existing church buildings in England and Wales. In 1823 a parliamentary grant of £50,000 was made available for building additional churches and manses in the highlands and islands of Scotland.[268] Ward had hoped that it might be possible to obtain financial support for his own programme of church building, in the form of grants, from either the Church Building Commission or the Incorporated Church Building Society, but discovered that provision of such support to a diocese outside England and Wales 'was found to be neither within the rules of the former, nor the charter of the latter'. In 1829 he therefore launched an appeal, with collecting offices in Liverpool and London, and sent the rector of Ballaugh, Hugh Stowell, 'to solicit and receive contributions':

> The population of the Island has of late years increased considerably, and the number of the poor has increased in an equal proportion, whilst the Churches within the Diocese are quite inadequate to the accommodation of such augmented numbers. The population of the Island is not less than 50,000 souls, and the existing churches do not afford room for more than about 9000 ... The inhabitants of this little Island, though blessed by a kind Providence with various advantages, yet labour under many privations. They enjoy few of the benefits of Commerce and Manufacturies. They have little access to the sources of national wealth and prosperity; and few of them possess any other riches than the riches of contentment. They are, consequently, much circumscribed in their means, and obviously unable of themselves, to meet the great spiritual exigencies of the Diocese ... An appeal, therefore, to public liberality, is the last and only resource of the inhabitants of this little Island ... They appeal to their wealthier neighbours of the United Kingdom in behalf of the many thousands of their poor brethren, who desire to join with them in the same Liturgy, to imbibe the same doctrines, and to participate

268 S.J. Brown, *The National Churches of England, Ireland and Scotland 1801–1846* (Oxford, 2001), 65, 68–73.

Fig. 2.28 *Bishop William Ward, unknown artist: courtesy of the Principal and Council, King William's College.*

in the same communion. Their object is Christian unity, and their appeal is to Christian charity.[269]

Fig. 2.29 *Details of population and church accommodation in the diocese of Sodor and Man 1829.*

Parish/Town	Population	Church Accommodation	Shortfall (%)
Andreas	2729	650	76.2
Arbory	1775	300	83.1
Ballaugh	1487	350	76.5
Braddan	2154	400	81.4
Bride	1220	250	79.5
Castletown	2486	1150	53.7
Douglas	8530	1300	84.8
German	4608	700	84.8
Jurby	1348	280	79.2
Lezayre	2709	250	90.8
Lonan	2256	300	86.7
Malew	2239	730	67.4
Marown	1475	250	83.1
Maughold	1854	260	86.0
Michael	1737	300	82.7
Onchan	1701	150	91.2
Patrick	2485	320	87.1
Ramsey	1863	500	73.2
Rushen	3138	400	87.3
Santon	980	250	74.5
TOTALS	48,774	9090	81.4

The details of population and church accommodation, with sketches of the Island's churches which was produced to accompany the appeal, illustrated, as Figure 2.29 shows, that the established church could only offer accommodation in its churches for about a fifth of the population, and also that many of its

269 MNH M 08977, E 205/5(1), *An Appeal in Behalf of the Poor Churches in the Diocese of Sodor and Mann* (c.1830).

buildings appeared to be in poor condition.[270] In fact, there is clear evidence that Ward may have exaggerated the problems. The official population of the Isle of Man according to the 1831 census was only 41,000, or 84.1% of that in Ward's statistics.[271] The detailed visitation of the Island's churches carried out by Archdeacon Philpot in 1833, well before most of Ward's building programme had been completed, suggested that the majority of them were then in good condition, certainly compared with the much more extensive schedules of repairs ordered by Bishop Hildesley in 1757.[272]

Fig. 2.30 *Relation of church provision to acreage and population in Anglesey, Isles of Man and Wight, and Channel Islands 1831.*

	Anglican Churches	Acreage per Church	Population per Church
Anglesey	76	2324.1	570.1
Isle of Man	23	6141.9	1815.6
Isle of Wight	34	2822.4	1042.1
Guernsey	15	1291.1	2195.2
Jersey	18	1595.4	2642.0

Although, as figure 2.30 shows, the number of churches in relation to the geographical extent of the Island was fewer in the Isle of Man than in any other British island community in which the Church of England was the established church, in terms of the size of population the Isle of Man had better provision than the densely populated Channel Islands, though poorer than that of Anglesey or the Isle of Wight. The other issue which Bishop Ward did not take into account was whether it was really lack of accommodation, and especially free or unappropriated sittings, that was preventing the population from attending the services of the established church. As a result of the labours of Ward and his successors, Anglican church accommodation was increased by 64.8% between 1829 and 1851, but the evidence of the religious census of the latter year, summarized in figure 2.31, shows that the whole of this increase had been unnecessary.[273] Overprovision had been extensive by both Anglicans and Methodists (though more so with Wesleyans than Primitives) with the former reaching only 42.3%, and the latter only 50.7%, capacity at their best attended services.

270 See Gelling, *Manx Church,* plate 5.

271 J. Beckerson, 'Statistical Appendix', in J. Belchem (ed), *New History of the Isle of Man,* vol. 5: *The Modern Period, 1830–1999* (Liverpool, 2000), 417–36.

272 MNH MS 00794C.

273 *British Parliamentary Papers: Population 11*, 604–05.

Fig. 2.31 *Sittings and attendances at Anglican and Methodist places of worship in the Isle of Man 1851.*

		Attendances		
Denomination	Sittings (Free)	Morning	Afternoon	Evening
Church of England	14,978 (5304)	6329	2497	3132
Wesleyan Methodists	11,827 (5993)	2042	3233	4505
Primitive Methodists	5,258 (2353)	1289	1483	4105

There was certainly a view at the time that Bishop Ward's church building programme was a waste of money. A correspondent to one of the local newspapers took him to task:

> The unnecessary pulling down of our Parish Churches (most of which, if they were properly repaired, are sufficiently commodious) is a very oppressive tax upon the parishioners ... the present church of Kirk Christ Lezayre is such as is suitable for the Parish and will afford room for a larger congregation than it is probable will ever assemble there. From my knowledge I can say that I have never known it (even when best attended) more than two thirds full.[274]

Ward's wife noted rows over the new church at Lonan which 'have I fear prevented its being so compleat as it ought to have been', and defended the rebuilding at Lezayre on the grounds that 'the old Church [was] dangerous to enter'.[275]

Whilst some of the contemporary justifications of Bishop Ward's church building programme may have been open to question, there is no doubt that its architectural legacy is one of exceptional interest. The churches at Lezayre, Lonan, Michael and Onchan were rebuilt and new churches built at Ballaugh and Douglas during Ward's espiscopate. Three chapels-of-ease in the parishes of Braddan, Lezayre and Patrick were planned by Ward but only that at Baldwin was completed before his death in 1838. Those at Dalby and Sulby were completed in 1839. All these churches were designed by one of three architects, the partnership of J.A. Hansom (1803–82) and Edward Welch (1806–68) and Edward's younger brother, John Welch, born in 1810 but dead by 1857.[276] Bishop Ward also purchased in 1829 a building in Ramsey which had been opened as an Independent chapel in 1822. His wife described this building, reopened as St

274 *Manx Sun*, 2 June 1830, quoted in Kermode, *Annals of Kirk Christ Lezayre*, 61.

275 MNH MS 09309, 'Bishop Ward's work'.

276 MNH MS 06679, MD 492, L.D. Butler (1970: typescript), 6–11, and the entries in H.M. Colvin, *A Biographical Dictionary of British Architects 1600–1840* (London, 1978), 877–79.

Peter's chapel, as 'a very neat little place of Worship and well attended', but it had closed by 1842 and became a National School in 1850.[277] She was also very proud of her husband's achievement at St Barnabas', Douglas:

> This chapel admits fourteen or fifteen hundred persons, seven hundred seats being free and constantly filled with the poor. That this chapel proves the greatest blessing that could be bestowed on this Town is generally felt and acknowledged. The excellent clergyman who has been appointed to it, the Revd. W. Carpenter, besides the most popular talents from the pulpit, proposes the true Christian act of conciliation and makes all who desire and promote religion his friends. The families who have taken seats by a unanimous agreement greatly added to the beauty of the Church by fitting up the interior in a uniform and handsome manner. It is well lighted, and altogether a commodious and excellent Church.[278]

The abandonment of St German's cathedral in the late eighteenth century led to successive bishops of Sodor and Man making improvements to their domestic chapel at Bishopscourt. Bishop Hildesley 'constantly performed divine service, and preached every Sunday in his own chapel; where, from his first coming to the Isle of Man till his death, he had formed a small choir, of twenty poor children, viz. ten boys and ten girls, educated and clothed at his own expense'.[279] Bishop Ward had daily services in the chapel at Bishopscourt at 8.30am and 3.00pm, read by his chaplain, and had two candlesticks made for the chapel altar.[280]

Since its formation in the late Middle Ages, the diocese of Sodor and Man had been the smallest diocese in the British Isles. The one diocese of comparable size in Ireland, that of Dromore, with only 26 parishes and 27 churches, had been united with the larger neighbouring diocese of Down and Connor under the provisions of the Irish Church Temporalities Act of 1833.[281] Before the revolution in France in 1789, there had been a few dioceses, such as Agde, Mirepoix, Orange, Senez, Toulon and Vence, with between 20 and 30 parishes each, but the post-revolutionary ecclesiastical settlement, and the subsequent concordat of 1801 with the papacy, had made the French dioceses coterminous with the *départments*, resulting in the creation of much larger dioceses and an

277 MNH MS 09309, 'Bishop Ward's work'; C. Radcliffe, *Shining by the Sea: A History of Ramsey, 1800–1914* (Douglas, 1989), 125.
278 MNH MS 09309, 'Bishop Ward's work'.
279 Butler, *Memoirs of Hildesley*, 198.
280 E.C. Wilson, *An Island Bishop 1762–1838: Memorials of William Ward, DD, Bishop of Sodor and Mann, 1828–1838* (London, 1931), 125, 129.
281 Akenson, *Church of Ireland*, 56.

overall reduction in their number.[282] It was therefore not surprising that when, as part of the political and ecclesiastical reform programme of the 1820s and 1830s, the British government looked at diocesan organization in the provinces of Canterbury and York, it should have regarded the continued existence of such a small diocese as Sodor and Man as something of an anomaly. The government's intentions were not, as they had been in Ireland, to reduce the total number of bishoprics, but to permit the creation of new dioceses in areas of expanding population by amalgamating some of the smaller dioceses with their neighbours, specifically Bangor with St Asaph, Bristol with Gloucester, and Sodor and Man with Carlisle. The fact that Bristol had fallen vacant through the translation of its bishop to the diocese of Ely allowed that union to be effected and the new diocese of Ripon to be created. There was strong opposition to the two other proposed unions and both were eventually abandoned. In the case of the merger of Sodor and Man with Carlisle, the legislation was passed by the British Parliament, but a determined campaign by the ailing Bishop Ward to reverse this decision resulted in it being repealed shortly after the bishop's death in 1838. Bishop Ward's arguments against the abolition of a separate Manx diocese, which had never been deliberately created in the first place but had resulted from an episcopal schism, were, looked at objectively, fairly specious, but they played well to those in parliament whose antiquarian sympathies made them keen to preserve unique institutions, and the government decided that the benefits of the proposed union were not worth the outrage it would provoke in some influential quarters.[283] Thus the diocese was saved.

Bishop Ward was the last of the old-style bishops of Sodor and Man. The isolation of the Manx church, which the political status of the Island had encouraged, was not maintained with the preservation of the diocese, but rather an attempt was made to integrate it more fully into the ecclesiastical province of which it was a part. It is notable that whereas only four out of 19 bishops of Sodor and Man between 1542 and 1838 were translated to bishoprics in England and Wales, seven out of ten were translated in the much shorter period between 1838 and 1912. Indeed, with short episcopates averaging less than eight years, the diocese became the sort of training ground for English bishops that the Welsh dioceses had been in the eighteenth century.[284]

282 J. McManners, *Church and Society in Eighteenth Century France*, 2 vols (Oxford, 1998), vol. 1, 178.

283 *Memorial of the Bishop of Sodor and Man to his Majesty's Commissioners Appointed to Consider the State of the Established Church with Reference to Ecclesiastical Duties and Revenues* (Colchester 1837), reprinted in Wilson, *An Island Bishop*, 164–81.

284 E.B. Fryde (ed), *Handbook of British Chronology*, 3rd edn (1996), 274, 292, 294, 296–99.

Fig. 2.32 *Communion beakers and communion plate: St German's Cathedral. Photo: Carola Rush. Left to right: Commonwealth chalice and paten with arms of Sodor and Man and Bishop Henry Bridgeman, London 1650; St German's Elizabethan communion beaker with a spray of roses, London 1591–2; William III communion beaker 'Ecclesiae Christi de Rishen acrum Insula Man 1703', Chester 1695.*

THE IMPACT OF METHODISM

Nigel Yates †

The most significant religious development in the Isle of Man during the last quarter of the eighteenth century was that of Methodism. It is important to emphasize that Methodism began as a movement within the established church and stemmed from the much wider pietist or evangelical movement that had an impact on many of the European Protestant churches during the eighteenth century.[285] One of those attracted to pietism was Bishop Wilson himself, who had close associations with the Moravians, accepting an honorary presidency of their General Synod.[286] It is perhaps significant that the two members of the

285 See especially W.R. Ward, *The Protestant Evangelical Awakening* (Cambridge, 1992), for the best overview of this movement. See also D. Bebbington, *Evangelicalism in Modern Britain: A History from the 1730s to the 1980s* (London, 1989) and D. Hempton, *Methodism: Empire of the Spirit* (New Haven, Conn. and London, 2005).

286 C. Podmore, *The Moravian Church in England, 1728–1760* (Oxford, 1998), 194–95, 212–15.

Manx clergy most closely associated with Methodism, Henry Corlett (vicar of German 1761–1801) and Daniel Gelling (vicar of Malew 1761–77 and rector of Ballaugh 1777–1801), had been trained by Wilson and spent time as members of his household. The effective beginning of Methodist preaching in the Isle of Man can be dated to the mission of John Crook in 1775, funded by Methodists in Liverpool. John Wesley himself paid two visits to the Island, in 1777 and 1781. On his first visit, Wesley preached in the open air at Castletown and Douglas and also 'in our own room' at Castletown on Sunday 1 June. At Peel, 'Mr Corlett said he would gladly have asked me to preach, but that the Bishop had forbidden him; who had also forbidden all his clergy to admit any Methodist preacher to the Lord's Supper', so Wesley preached there after divine service in 'a large malthouse'.[287]

Bishop Richmond's opposition to Methodism, which was shared by the rector of Bride, Philip Moore, and many other Anglican high churchmen throughout the British Isles, was on three grounds. In the first place they were keen to protect the established church from a revival of the Calvinism it had largely rejected in the early seventeenth century;[288] though Wesley and his followers were not Calvinists, some other groups of Evangelicals within the established church, notably in Wales, were. In the second place, they thought that the emotionalism, what they would term the 'enthusiasm', of Methodist worship was un-Anglican, and in the third they were concerned about the potential schisms from the established church which were already beginning to happen. Richmond's concerns were made clear in a pastoral letter issued in 1776, in which he described the Methodist preachers as 'unordained, unauthorized, and unqualified persons' holding 'private meetings, assemblies and congregations contrary to the divine government, Rites and Ceremonies of the Established Church'. Richmond advised the clergy to dissuade their parishioners from attending Methodist services 'for the prevention of schism and the re-establishment of the uniformity of religious worship which so long hath subsisted among us' and to prevent them from being led astray 'and misguided by such incompetent teachers'.[289] It is clear that Richmond's successors took a more relaxed line on Methodism, which was specifically criticised by Bishop Short in 1841; he condemned those clergy who had aimed 'to live on friendly terms with the dissenters ... imitating dissenting practices and plans', and

287 J. Wesley, *The Journal of the Rev John Wesley*, N. Curnock (ed), 8 vols (London, 1909–16), vol. 6, 150–53.

288 For the background to this, see N. Tyacke, *Anti-Calvinists: the Rise of English Arminianism c.1590–1640* (Oxford, 1987).

289 Moore, *Sodor and Man*, 246–51; for the text of Richmond's letter see Bray (ed), *Records of Convocation*, vol. 1, 326–27.

especially one clergyman 'who rented a seat in the [Methodist] chapel in his own parish, and was in the habit of attending evening service there'.[290]

Wesley's second visit to the Isle of Man in 1781 was more prolonged than his first one. He preached in all the main towns of the Island and at several locations in the countryside, mostly in the open air but also in the preaching houses which had been established in Ballaugh and Peel: 'here is no opposition, either from the Governor (a mild, humane man), from the Bishop [Mason] (a good man) or from the bulk of the clergy'. At Ballaugh the rector, Daniel Gelling, attended the evening service in the Methodist chapel with his wife, sister and daughter, and Wesley breakfasted with them on the following morning. He estimated that the total number of Methodists in the Isle of Man at that date was over two thousand, or more than a tenth of the total adult population: 'what has been seen like this, in any part of either Great Britain or Ireland'.[291] The Methodist societies in the Isle of Man were attached to the Whitehaven circuit until 1778, when a separate Manx circuit was formed with John Crook as superintendent. He was joined by another very able preacher, Robert Dall, who had previously worked in Scotland, and who married the widowed daughter of a Douglas flour merchant.[292] The chief need was for Manx-speaking preachers who were clearly in place by the late 1780s and attracting large congregations. George Holder's wife noted in 1788 that 'in the evening we went to hear a Manx preacher, and I was struck with surprise at seeing the people flock to chapel'.[293] John Feltham, who visited the Isle of Man in 1797–8, stated that there were then 2700 Methodists with 'three travelling preachers, sixty Manks preachers, and fifteen meeting houses'. At Onchan he 'heard an English sermon delivered with an animated elocution; and one in Manks, by a native no less fervent and devout'.[294] By 1800 there were some 15 Methodist chapels on the Isle of Man and on the 1813 circuit plan 67 meetings were listed, of which 54 were in specially built chapels.[295] However, apart from brief increases in the 1790s, possibly a reaction to the alleged scandals surrounding Bishop Crigan, and the 1830s, a reaction to an outbreak of cholera, the numbers of Wesleyan Methodists in the Isle of Man did not normally exceed three thousand before the death of Bishop Ward in 1838. In 1801 the Island was divided into two circuits, Douglas

290 Moore, *Sodor and Man*, 271–73.

291 Curnock (ed), *Wesley*, vol. 6, 318–22.

292 The most authoritative account of the growth of Wesleyan Methodism in the Isle of Man is still J. Rosser, *History of the Wesleyan Methodism in the Isle of Man* (Douglas, 1849). See D. Jackson, 'Early Manx Methodism and the Eighteenth Century' (BA dissertation, London Bible College, 1989) and Chapman, 'Manx Methodism' (report c.1971).

293 A.M. Harrison, 'New light on Methodism in the Isle of Man', *Proceedings of the Wesley Historical Society*, 19 (1938), 195–201.

294 Feltham, *Tour*, 239–40.

295 MNH M 07461, E 240f, 1813.

and Ramsey, with roughly equal memberships. The first Primitive Methodist meetings were established on the Isle of Man in 1823 and the membership of these quickly grew to about two thirds of the Wesleyan membership.[296]

Whilst there is no doubt that Methodism had made a substantial impact on the Isle of Man by the first quarter of the nineteenth century, it needs to be placed in context.

Fig. 2.33 *Comparisons of communicant figures in selected Manx parishes 1757 and 1833.*

Parish	1757	1833
Andreas	80, Easter 400	100, more at Easter
Arbory	80 to 90, Easter 400	50 to 80, Easter 280
Ballaugh	107, Easter 494	400
Braddan (inc. Douglas)	260 to 500, Easter 1250	305 to 355
Bride	78, Easter 313	100
Jurby	Easter 300	50 to 100, Easter 300 to 600
Lezayre	140 to 200, Easter 600	100 to 140, Easter 640
Lonan	56 to 78, Easter 261	100, Easter 200
Marown	200, Easter 350	100, Easter 200
Maughold (inc. Ramsey)	60 to 72, Easter 632	280
Onchan	60 to 80, Easter 264	60, Easter 150
Rushen	130 to 150, Easter 520	200, Easter 400

For example, as figure 2.33 shows, though there had been an overall decline in the number of communicants, especially in relation to the increase in population, in most Manx parishes, it was far from the collapse experienced in most Anglesey parishes as the result of the separation of the Calvinistic Methodists from the established church in 1811.[297]

296 W. Curry, 'A Kingdom Won. The story of Primitive Methodism in the Isle of Man', published in *Primitive Methodist World* between 20 December 1906 and 4 April 1907.

297 Manx figures for 1757 and 1833 from visitation returns in MNH MS 00791 C and MS 00794; Anglesey figures based on a comparison of the visitation returns from 1801 and 1837 in National Library of Wales, B/QA/14 and 26. The interesting increase in the number of regular communicants at Ballaugh dates from the late eighteenth century: in 1786 (MNH MS 00793C) there were 569 communicants at Easter, 268 at Whitsun, 309 at Michaelmas and 226 at Christmas.

Fig. 2.34 *Established church sittings and attendances in selected island communities 1851.*

Islands	Sittings (%)	Attendances (%)
Isle of Man	46.0	40.0
Jersey	51.3	48.7
Guernsey	41.1	44.7
Orkney/ Shetland	41.6	27.3
Isle of Wight	50.6	44.8
Anglesey	31.3	14.1

A comparison of the statistics from the 1851 religious census for several British island communities in figure 2.34 shows that, though in the Isle of Man the established church had a minority of both sittings and attendances, the pattern of attendances, especially in relation to sittings, was much closer to that in the southern islands of Britain, where the established church was relatively strong, than in either Anglesey, where Anglican attendances were less than a quarter of the Calvinistic Methodist ones, or Orkney and Shetland where the attendances in the non-established churches were double those in the established Church of Scotland.

It is very clear that Methodism in the Isle of Man had grown not in opposition to the established church, but as a pressure group within that church, sometimes actively encouraged, mostly quietly tolerated, only occasionally condemned, by the clergy. Wesley himself had noted in 1781 that the local preacher at Lonan, where a chapel had been erected the year before, was none other than the parish clerk. The surviving diary of an anonymous Wesleyan local preacher covering the years 1826–8 indicates that, even though he attended class, and preached or exhorted almost every evening, he still regularly attended his parish church. He also attended Primitive chapels when a known good, or especially female, preacher was announced.[298] The two Anglican clergy who commented on the strength of Methodism in their parishes at Archdeacon Philpot's visitation in 1833 recognized that this was at least partly the fault of the established church. At Andreas, parents were 'very remiss in sending' their children to Sunday school, 'preferring in general the Methodist meeting houses, where reading and writing are taught'. The vicar of Patrick attributed his poor congregations to the situation of the parish church 'in a corner of the parish' remote from the principal centres of population at Dalby and Foxdale 'nearly 5 miles distant and where the population attend the Methodist chapels'.[299] Chapels-

298 MNH MS 00994 C.
299 MNH MS 00794 C.

of-ease were eventually built to serve both these areas, in 1839 at Dalby and 1850 at Foxdale.[300] The generally good relations between Methodism and the established church, and the fact that many people attended both Anglican and Methodist services fairly indiscriminately, is shown in the unwillingness of the different bodies to hold services at the same times as one another, a widespread early Methodist practice. In 1841 it was recorded that the decision of the rector of Andreas to change 'the hour of evening service from 3 to 6 … has raised a great deal of dismay among the Wesleyans whose service is at the same hour'.[301] Even in 1851 the religious census returns show that, of the 39 Anglican places of worship in the Isle of Man, only nine had services on Sunday evenings, whereas only 17 out of 59 Wesleyan, and four out of 27 Primitive, Methodist places of worship had services on Sunday mornings.[302]

The main tensions within Manx Methodism were caused by the relationship between it and the Wesleyan Methodist conference. Crook had set up a system whereby the local preachers had 'established themselves as an unofficial Manx conference',[303] but it was an arrangement much criticised by John Mercer in a letter to Jabez Bunting in 1820:

> He [Crook] established good order in all the Societies; and had everything among them as regular as clockwork. However he set up one rule, which in my opinion has been, and still is, a great evil. I mean his giving so much power into the hands of the Local Preachers. He began by meeting them regular every Quarter, but instead of giving it the simple and proper name of Local Preachers' Meeting he gave it the high sounding name of Manks Conference, and adopted most of the phraseology used in the Minutes of the English Conference. But the evil did not consist so much in the name, as in the nature of that meeting. For instead of attending to the simple business of a Local Preachers' Meeting, they also transacted the business of the Quarterly Meeting too, and I may say almost everything which belongs to the Leaders' Meeting. And at last grew to such a height of despotism, that no man, however well qualified, must be a Circuit Steward but a local preacher. The above particulars have been a source of much grief to many of the travelling preachers, and of much contention between them and the Local Preachers.[304]

There was an unwillingness in the Manx-speaking country areas to accept English travelling preachers and in 1818 it was 'resolved that places which have Manks preaching and do not take in the English preaching shall not have

300 Gelling, *Manx Church*, 79, 139.
301 *Mona's Herald*, 8 June 1841.
302 *British Parliamentary Papers: Population 11*, 604–05.
303 W.G. Ward, *Religion and Society in England 1790–1850* (London, 1972), 84.
304 John Rylands University Library, Manchester, Methodist Archives, PLP 74-17-1.

preaching continued unless they make a collection once a month to help the quarterage and other conference collections as required'.[305]

ROMAN CATHOLICISM

Tim Grass

The extent to which Catholic ideas and devotional practices survived has been the subject of varying opinions, as noted above, but here we assess the evidence for the existence of a community of Catholics on the Island. Given its proximity both to Lancashire and to Ireland, we might have expected repeated attempts to win it back to the old faith and to provide sacramental and pastoral ministry to local faithful. But it seems that its potentially strategic location was recognized more by those seeking to counter its possible use as part of an escape route for Catholic priests working in north-west England, than by the priests themselves. In 1590, Bishop Meyrick reported that all the inhabitants conformed to the established church, although some may have been 'church-papists', attending it but retaining Catholic convictions.[306] For all the fears, there are few mentions of Catholic recusants. A John Yong and his wife were presented to the chapter court at Malew on 8 February 1608/9, but I have found no other direct references to Catholic recusancy in presentments.[307] Almost the only priests to evangelize the Island during the seventeenth century were an Irish Jesuit, David Galway (1579–1643), and a Mr Pulton, who was said to have made a few converts.[308] This was probably another Jesuit, Fr Ferdinand Poulton (1605–66), a missioner in Lancashire who came to the Island in 1646 after persecution dispersed many of the county's Jesuits.[309] The same year, the countess of Derby heard from the Island 'that [a] great store of English Papists do live in Douglas town who have licence to go to Mass there'.[310] Doubtless this was an exaggeration, but

305 MNH MD 10097.

306 H. Bird, *An Island that Led: The History of Manx Education* (Port St Mary: the author, n.d.), vol. 1, p.7, following Moore, *Isle of Man*, vol. 1, p.353.

307 J.M. Oates, transcription of Episcopal Wills 1600–18, 211: https://mannincloud.info/Oates/1600-18_ep_0218.pdf.

308 Dempsey, *Catholic Church*, 137. However, I have found no references to Galway in the standard reference work: H. Foley (ed), *Records of the English Province of the Society of Jesus*, vols 1–4 (London, 1877–9).

309 Foley (ed), *Records of the English Province*, vol. 2, 8–9; see William Blundell, letter of 3 June 1661, in M. Blundell (ed), *Cavalier: Letters of William Blundell to his friends, 1620–1698* (London, 1933), 96–97. Blundell claimed that several prominent women held to Catholic opinions but felt constrained to continue attending Anglican services.

310 S. Kmec, *Across the Channel: Noblewomen in Seventeenth-Century France and England. A Study of the Lives of Marie de La Tour, Queen of the Huguenots, and*

it is plausible that there was a Catholic community centred on Douglas and including several in the higher reaches of Island commerce and government.

Such Catholics as remained by the Restoration era were mostly in the employ of the lord of Man, often brought over from other Stanley properties. The Catholic recusant William Blundell's cousin, Anne Hesketh, married Deemster John Cannell (d.1659); as a widow she was imprisoned by Bishop Barrow in 1668 for her Catholic convictions.[311] Blundell also claimed that most of the poorer people continued 'exceedingly tenacious of many old Catholic customs, particularly in that of abstaining from Flesh on Days commanded', although this was probably a matter of conservatism rather than Catholicism.[312]

The smallness of the Catholic community did not assuage fears about what it might become. Bishop Levinz shared to the full in the near-paranoia of much of the English establishment regarding Catholicism. In 1688 he wrote to Archbishop Sancroft of Canterbury that he had received a letter from the governor pressing him to come to the Island because

> as he words it, there are two Jesuits and four priests expected there every tyde, to make converts in yt poor place, in order to wich they have sent a popish Gentleman of quality before ym to view a piece of ground to build a convent on, wich hee says hee hears they have ye King's license to doe, & therefore hee thinks my presence there very necessary to prevent mischiefe.

The threat soon receded, although Levinz seems to have felt bound to justify the credence he had given it.[313] That autumn, he claimed:

> one of ye Jesuits yt is to come heer is a native of this place, of a good family & interest heer, tho hee has been out of his country ever since his youth & bred up in one of ye Jesuits Colleges abroad, this person having our language is ye man I most fear, & w[ha]t keeps him from hence all this while more than gods providence & mercy to this poor people, I know n[o]t.[314]

Charlotte de La Trémoïlle, Countess of Derby (Trier, 2010), 257: Captain Robert Clarke to William Lenthall, 22 August 1646, quoted from HMC *Duke of Portland*, vol. 1, 388.

311 M.A. Everett Green (ed), *Calendar of State Papers Domestic: Charles II, 1668–9* (London, 1894), 219–58: 'Charles II: March1669', *British History Online*, http://www.british-history.ac.uk/cal-state-papers/domestic/chas2/1668-9/pp219-258 [accessed 6 March 2019], 255; Blundell (ed), *Cavalier*, 158–61. She was recalled to prison in 1674, but this may have been because of her failure to produce her late husband's will.

312 Blundell (ed), *Cavalier*, 97.

313 Bodleian, Tanner MS 28, fol. 54, Levinz to Archbishop Sancroft, 3 June 1688.

314 Bodleian, Tanner MS 28, fol. 175, Levinz to Sancroft, 12 September 1688. Since the Cannells mentioned above had five children who entered the religious life, one of them may have been the subject of the rumour.

During the early eighteenth century, the Catholic community appears to have settled down to a clandestine but relatively secure existence. Tradition has it that Lag ny Keeilley continued to be used for occasional Catholic burials, possibly as late as 1800. Waldron reported in 1731 that Catholic priests visited the Island at least annually, celebrating the sacraments in private houses, but that they left the risky business of making converts to the laity.[315] By 1727 a Fr Alessio Dondall had ministered on the Island for twelve years, although there had been no priest for eighteen years before that. More than one congregation was meeting, some of which were 'quite numerous'.[316] In 1757 Fr James Hoy from Connaught came to the notice of the authorities after an Anglican family in Peel resorted to him on account of his reputed ability to perform exorcisms. There was a call for him to be banished, and although Bishop Hildesley refused to get involved, presumably the banishment was enacted, as we read in a court judgment the following year:

> The few papist Strangers who reside & resort to the s[ai]d Isle have generally a priest; but if he discovers himself by any umbrage of offence to Society, he is instantly silenced by the Gov[erno]r, of which there was a late instance (tho' upon a very trivial occasion), and the Gov[erno]r's order still continues in force and the papists have not since had a priest to officiate.[317]

However, the catalyst was not Hoy's exorcisms but the use of the Island as a resort for clandestine marriages: Irish couples who were prohibited from marrying because they did not share the same faith or because they were under age, came over with a Catholic priest or 'some irregular of the establish[ed] Church'.[318] To counter the practice, legislation in 1757 mandated the provision of fuller information for marriage registration and introduced special provisions for non-residents. Those who played up the danger from papists also appear to have been motivated in part by economic jealousy, not religious conviction.

After the Revestment, the English penal code became applicable to the Island, under which informers could receive a reward if their information resulted in the capture of a priest.[319] We know of no instances of attempts to secure such a reward, but the numbers of Catholics declined to their lowest point during this period. If we discount John Wesley's comment in 1777 that there were only

315 G. Waldron, *The History and Description of the Isle of Man*, 2nd edn (London, 1744), 38.

316 M. Gandy (comp), *Catholic Missions and Registers, 1700–1880*, vol. 5: *North West England*, 2nd edn (London, 1998), 15–16, following *Recusant History* 22/1, 60–62.

317 AP, Box 20, folio X69/2, 16, 18; AP, Box 20, folio X/8/1, Governor Cochrane and others, case concerning the naturalization of Papists on the Isle of Man, 17 March 1758.

318 MNH MS 09756, Diocesan archives, fragment of letter, possibly by Rev. Philip Moore of Douglas.

319 Dempsey, *Catholic Church*, 140.

'six Papists and no Dissenters' as exaggeration, we may place more credence in a pastoral letter of 1781 from Bishop Goss of Liverpool, which stated that just twenty-five Catholics remained on the Island.[320]

From this point, Catholic fortunes began to improve. In the wake of the French Revolution of 1789, a Fr Louis Jean Louis came to the Island; like many French priests fleeing persecution, he was sympathetically received by the establishment: he tutored the children of the governor and the bishop and lived at Castle Rushen, but appears to have left the Island before 1794.[321] Following the unrest in Ireland during 1798, several Catholic families sought refuge on the Island, and from this point Irish priests made visits to minister until a resident priest was appointed. The first purpose-built Catholic church was St Bridget's, on the edge of Douglas, opened in 1814. By now the Catholic community had grown to two or three hundred; a school was therefore opened in 1824, and St Mary's church at Castletown in 1826.[322] Its design is reminiscent of a Nonconformist preaching box, although with an altar instead of a central pulpit – a reminder of the need to be as unobtrusive as possible, for Catholics remained a community apart and suspected, as the events attending the opening of St Mary of the Isle in Douglas in 1859 would show.

PROTESTANT DISSENT

Tim Grass

The Isle of Man was a missionary objective not so much for Jesuit priests as for radical Protestants. Blundell claimed that Presbyterianism appeared on the Island at the end of Charles I's reign, and that during the 1640s it was very influential.[323] We might expect that some at least among the Commonwealth soldiers in the garrisons after 1651 would have held Independent views and perhaps belonged to gathered congregations in England, but they have left little mark on the Island. It does not seem that any Presbyterian or Independent congregations were formed here. Moderate puritanism could often be accommodated within the established church on the Island, as elsewhere, although according to Blundell there was some preaching in private houses.[324] Lay agency appears

320 D. Walsh, rev and enlarged by N. Donnelly, *Ireland and the Isle of Man*, Catholic Truth Society of Ireland (Dublin, n.d.), 22. Fr Oswald Johnston visited the Island regularly from Whitehaven after 1779; in 1781 he listed twenty-nine Catholics on the Island: Dempsey, *Catholic Church*, 140 n.8.

321 Gandy, *Catholic Missions*, vol. 5, 16.

322 Dempsey, *Catholic Church*, 141–45.

323 W. Blundell, *A History of the Isle of Man*, William Harrison (ed), 2 vols, Manx Society vols 25, 27 (Douglas, 1876), vol. 2, 166; Blundell (ed), *Cavalier*, 97.

324 Blundell, *History*, Manx Society, vol. 1, xxiii, 91; vol. 2, 166.

to have become a feature of Island church life during the 1650s. Immediately following the Restoration in 1660, the Libri Causarum recorded that lay people had been conducting marriages, baptisms, and churchings in the parishes of Braddan and Malew.[325] This may have been evidence of radical views, or simply a makeshift response to a shortage of effective puritan clergy, probably due in part to the language requirement. If the ministers Fairfax introduced were Presbyterians, then they were ineffective and most of them have left little trace on Manx church records. All the same, 'The success of his preaching methods, though falling short of his hopes, created space for religious independence and – excepting the Quakers – the practice of toleration which permitted a level of religious dissent that even the terrible persecutions of the 1660s were unable to fully break.'[326]

The provisions of the Act of Uniformity (1662), which forced so many English clergy to leave the established church, did not apply to the Island. Whilst this ensured that Manx clergy of puritan convictions could remain at their posts, there do not appear to have been many who fell into this category. The impetus which had fuelled the initial development of Quakerism was no longer so strong, and so any dissent was usually imported from England or Scotland. Sacheverell claimed that in 1689 thousands of Irish Protestants found refuge on the Island,[327] but there is little evidence of any, although on 20 September 1686, 'Wm Dawson son to Tho: Dawson Esquire (a presbyterian) out of Ireland' was buried at Malew.[328] By 1722, Bishop Wilson could claim that 'there has not for many years been one Papist a native in the island; nor indeed are there Dissenters of any denomination, except a family or two of Quakers, unhappily perverted during the late civil wars'[329] There were two attempts to bring a Scotch Presbyterian congregation together in 1763 and 1788, but success had to wait until the rather different religious climate of the nineteenth century. In 1832 a church was opened in Douglas, affiliated to the English Presbytery of Lancashire. Independently, a congregation came into being in Ramsey, which in 1829 petitioned the Wigtown Presbytery of

325 MNH MS 09756, Proctorial documents, extract dated 27 September 1660.

326 J. Callow, '"In so shifting a Scene": Thomas Fairfax as Lord of the Isle of Man, 1651–60', in A. Hopper and P. Major (eds), *England's Fortress: New Perspectives on Thomas, 3rd Lord Fairfax* (Abingdon and New York, 2016), 51.

327 Sacheverell, *Account*, sig.B2v.

328 Lancashire Archives, Kenyon of Peel Hall papers, DDK/HMC/775, 'The Informacon of William: Cooper, of Peeltown taken upon oath before me Jo[n] Rowe, Gent and one of the Justices of Peace in the said Isle', 7 July 1691; 'Notes from the parish registers: Malew', *Manx Note Book*, vol. 3, 138ff.

329 T. Wilson, 'The History of the Isle of Man', in Cruttwell, *Wilson*, vol. 7, 259–60.

the United Secession Church in Scotland for a minister.[330] Slightly earlier, a Scottish student for the Congregational ministry, Samuel Haining, visited the Island in 1804 as a student to see what could be done, and became the first Congregational minister there in 1808; five years later a chapel was opened for him in Douglas. Other groups, such as the Baptists, did not appear until after the period covered by this volume.

QUAKERS[331]

Tim Grass

Analysis of presentments and other records suggests that as many as a hundred and twenty people may have been associated with the movement before 1750, although some doubtless practised occasional conformity. The Island experienced a degree of discontinuity in church life during the 1650s (a key factor in preparing the way for the Quaker message) as Prayer Book worship was formally proscribed and clergy deemed unsuitable by Fairfax's regime were replaced.[332] Such unsettlement means that Quaker missionaries would have found Man a more promising mission field than has hitherto been recognized.

In 1655 two Cumberland Quakers undertook a missionary journey to the Isle of Man.[333] Within a year, according to Joseph Besse, persecution of 'the people called Quakers' in the Island had begun, in line with widespread puritan hostility to the Quakers in England and Wales, who were seen as a dangerous

330 J. Davidson, 'Presbyterianism in the Isle of Man', *Journal of the Presbyterian Historical Society of England* (1918), 187–88; MNH M 17845, F. Coakley, 'The 1851 religious and educational censuses', paper given to the Manx Methodist Historical Society, 7 November 1998, 7–8.

331 For recent research on the Manx Quakers, see MNH MS 09820, C.F. Carswell, 'Man & the Quakers: Quakers in the Isle of Man 1655–1735', (undergraduate dissertation, University of East Anglia, 1997), now published as Carswell, *Man and the Quakers* (Kibworth, 2019).

332 See Oxford, Bodleian Library, MS Fairfax 33, fols 24r–v, 'A funeral sermon preached at Bilbrough Nov.22. 1671, at the interment of Thos. Lord Fairfax, by Richard Stretton. A.M. his domestic Chaplain'. Stretton recalled: 'When he sent over some prudent Men to regulate [the ministry], he first gave orders for displacing of such as through gross ignorance or intolerable debauchery were judged unfit for such a service, still continuing their stipend to them while they lived. Those that were fit to receive encouragement were continued and had augmentations allowed them. And he took care to send over such pious men of competent parts and allowed them considerable stipends to the number of 16 (as I remember I have heard him say) and to one whom he designed as a superintendant or overseer (the true office of a Bishop) he allowed a treble advantage.'

333 T. Hodgkin, 'Ruillick-ny-Quakeryn: notes of the history of Friends in the Isle of Man', *Friends Quarterly Examiner*, vol. 10 (1908), 462; London, Friends House Library, Swarthmore MSS, 3, 552.

threat to spiritual and social stability.[334] In 1658, Governor Chaloner reported: 'They travel up and down the country, especially on the Lord's Day, in numbers, to the great terror and amazement of the people of the country.'[335]

Since the Quakers refused to accept the authority of the established church, they were dealt with by the Island's ecclesiastical courts. The penalties for refusing to conform were fines, imprisonment and, for persistent offenders, exclusion from the Island. One of the first to suffer this fate was the missionary Katharine Evans from Workington, who in 1656 'was taken out of her bed in the night, and banished the Island'.[336] Notable among the earliest Quakers to be brought before the church courts was William Callow (1629–76), a farmer in Maughold, who was 'detained eight weeks in prison for publicly reproving a priest'. Subsequently Callow, with others, was imprisoned for allowing Quaker meetings in his house, refusing to pay tithes and challenging the authority of the church.

Whilst the great majority of those so far identified as Quakers lived in the parish of Maughold (then apparently experiencing a lack of continuity in Anglican ministry), there were others elsewhere. John Callow holds that by the late 1650s 'many' of the company under the command of Lt John Hathorne at Castle Rushen were Quakers.[337] The Malew registers record the baptisms of two children of Quakers in 1656: 'Mary Coward daught: to Rich. & Alice his wife, quaker. Preston daughter to Will: Quaker', and in 1659 one John Preston, a Quaker, was buried there.[338] These may have been connected with the garrison at Castle Rushen, but at the other end of the Island, the parish of Andreas saw the presentment in 1680 of 'The Quakers ffor meeting Contrary to an ord[r] from my Ld Bop published in ye pish church'.[339]

According to the eighteenth-century Quaker historian John Gough, after the restoration to the lordship of Charles Stanley, the Quakers continued to suffer 'persecution in this sequestered island, under the arbitrary rule of the lord of the land', and when Isaac Barrow arrived as bishop in 1663, Callow and other Quakers were again in St German's prison, following a systematic attempt to identify Maughold's Quakers and force them to conform.[340] Barrow urged them

334 J. Besse, *A Collection of the Sufferings of the People called Quakers* (London, 1753), vol. 1, 269.

335 Quoted in J.W. & C.K. Radcliffe, *A History of Kirk Maughold* (Douglas, 1979), 146.

336 Besse, *Sufferings*, vol. 1, 269.

337 J. Callow, '"The Force of Angry Heaven's Flame": Lieutenant John Hathorne and Garrison Government in the Isle of Man, 1651–1660', *Isle of Man Studies* 14 (2016), 96.

338 'Notes from the parish registers: Malew', *Manx Note Book*, 2, 133. See also Callow, '"The Force of Angry Heaven's Flame"', 90–108.

339 MNH MS 10194, diocesan presentments, 1680.

340 J. Gough, *A History of the People called Quakers*, 2 vols (1789), vol. 2, 274.

Fig. 2.35 *Ruillick-ny-Quakeryn, the Quaker graveyard in Maughold. Photo: Charles Guard.*

to return to the Church, but to no avail; in 1664 they were excommunicated.[341] Earl Charles ordered their transportation, but magistrates in Whitehaven and Dublin challenged the legality of the sentence and in June 1666 they were returned to the Island. Besse records a sequence of subsequent attempts to remove them from the Island, culminating in 1669 when Earl Charles seized all the Quakers' property and ordered Callow's transportation to Virginia: 'If the man [Callow] will not conform,' he declared, 'he shall not go to poison my island.'[342] The ship's master refused to take Callow further than Dublin, however, and he was returned to the Island, and thence to England. Eventually Callow and other Quakers were permitted to return home. By 1671 he could report 'our Litle meeting quiet and peaceful after our great and Long sufferings'.[343] He was restored to his tenancy and set aside a portion of his land in Maughold as a burial ground for himself and his friends.[344] Maughold Quakers were still meeting regularly in 1682, when a number were presented for not attending church and 'conventicleinge ymselves on Sundays & Thursdayes'.[345]

341 Hodgkin, 'Ruillick-ny-Quakeryn', vol. 10, 47; Gough, *Quakers*, vol. 2, 278.

342 Gough, *Quakers,* vol. 2, 286; Besse, *Quakers*, vol. 1, 278–88; Hodgkin, 'Ruillick-ny-Quakeryn', 491.

343 Swarthmore MSS, 1, 128, William Callow to Margaret Fell, 23 October 1671.

344 Hodgkin, 'Ruillick-ny-Quakeryn', 492; C. Radcliffe, 'The Maughold Quakers', *PIMNHAS*, 8:2 (1974–76), 126–27.

345 MNH MS 10194, diocesan presentments, Maughold, 1 November 1682.

Nevertheless, some measure of persecution continued until 1685. When Bishop Wilson arrived in 1698, he treated them kindly, allowing them to follow their own form of worship. According to his biographer Clement Cruttwell, 'The few Quakers who resided on the island visited, loved, and respected him'.[346] Wilson's approach succeeded where Barrow's had failed: during the early eighteenth century most remaining Quakers conformed to the established church.

CONCLUSION

Despite its previous isolation, and certain problems caused by this, Manx religious beliefs and practices and the organization of its institutions in the fourteenth and early fifteenth centuries seem to have been closely aligned with those of north-west England. The Reformation brought few changes in the Island's churches until the beginning of the seventeenth century, when influences developing in England and Scotland, and particularly the agendas of the Stanley lords, began to impact church life. Despite its geographical isolation and problems this caused, the Manx church was, for the most part, efficiently administered between the late sixteenth and early nineteenth centuries. Measures of ecclesiastical reform in this period largely replicated the sort of measures that were being taken in other parts of the British Isles, and indeed more widely throughout Europe, so isolation did not mean total separation from what was taking place in the world outside the Isle of Man.

346 Cruttwell, *Wilson*, vol. 1, 227.

3 *Daily Life*

MICHAEL HOY

WITH CONTRIBUTIONS BY KIT GAWNE, NICK JOHNSON, CHRIS PAGE AND JENNIFER PLATTEN †

INTRODUCTION

Although few documents have survived to throw any light on social conditions in the Isle of Man in the fourteenth and fifteenth centuries, there are archaeological and circumstantial clues on which to draw, and since it seems likely that conditions changed very little before the political upheavals of the mid-seventeenth century, there is sufficient evidence to sketch a picture of what daily life was like. In the eighteenth and early nineteenth centuries there is a wealth of documentary evidence to chart the changing conditions across the social strata, not least for the expanding merchant and professional classes, which mirror social changes in north-west England, although the peculiar circumstances of the prosperity brought by the running trade and the challenges of its collapse make the Island's eighteenth-century story distinctive.

Most families, from the most successful quarterland farmers down to the majority poor, had to rely on their own resources in times of individual or collective hardship. There was no secular provision for those in need.[1] It was expected that families would support their own, and where this failed it was the church, through the parishes, which maintained an increasingly effective framework of social care. By contrast, the Stanleys and Atholls used the Island for the most part as a source of income, and only occasionally, as for example during the governorship of the enlightened William Sacheverell, were policies introduced to benefit the majority. Without the help of the church and individual philanthropy, conditions for many would have been desperate. Yet the support of the church came within a framework of moral and social control, designed both to preserve family structures and to promote adherence to a strict moral code, enforced by ecclesiastical legislation and the rule of the church courts.

This chapter first describes evidence about daily life gleaned from artefacts discovered in the Island and listed in probate records. Then various aspects of daily life are explored – family life and the role of women, the lives of children and adolescents, the yearly round of farming and fishing, recreational life, and health and social care. Some areas are underrepresented. For example,

1 *Statutes*, vol. 1, 91, 123–24.

while there is a good picture of the lives of women as evidenced particularly in church court documents, a broader view assessing the role of women and attitudes to gender in Island life, most notably through the eighteenth and early nineteenth centuries, awaits the attention of future scholars. Similarly, the absence of explorations of areas such as the incidence of crime and its impact on community life, social restrictions imposed on a community under military power, particularly in the first half of the seventeenth century, new opportunities brought by the development of a modest consumer society in the later eighteenth century, and changing attitudes to social deference and attempts to reform manners – all of which might be set within the wider context of social change across the British Isles – reflects the selective nature of currently available academic research on which to draw.

THE ARTEFACTS OF DAILY LIFE

Archaeological evidence

Nick Johnson

The lives led by the bulk of the indigenous population are largely invisible in terms of archaeology until the nineteenth century, when there is a tangible increase in the breadth and scope of the available documentary evidence. Before that time, the remains of buildings, waste materials, and domestic and personal objects, such as pottery and clay pipes, either lost or discarded, provide a glimpse of how people lived. The bulk of such evidence may only be obtained through excavation, generally undertaken in advance of development, and where the significance of the location appears likely to justify the cost. Inevitably this tends to focus on existing built-up areas and high-status sites, such as Castle Rushen and Peel Castle, resulting in a bias away from the rural life which was the experience of the majority of the population. However, there have been some useful exceptions to this.

The survival of archaeological remains is more often accidental than deliberate and, in common with all bodies of evidence, it is partial: much of what is handled in our lives is insubstantial and ephemeral, and the meanings and significance of physical objects are mostly subjective. This, too, influences what can be interpreted about past lives.

Good archaeological evidence from urban areas is confined to Peel and Castletown. It is no coincidence that they are also high-status medieval sites, and the locations where the earliest post-medieval material has been found. At both Peel Castle and Castle Rushen, there was continuity of occupation of the sites into the Stanley era and subsequently, with development and modification of the accommodation, and changes in political and strategic role. One hint of the effect of the castles on their locality, beyond their walls, where the nascent settlements developed, is provided by a handful of fifteenth-century finds from the 1992 excavations at Castle Rushen stores, in Castletown, between Malew and Arbory Streets, and the work done on what was once the foreshore at Peel in 2001.[2] At both sites there was no other evidence of this date to suggest that these artefacts were anything more than chance losses and the spreading of night waste on nearby fields.

The work at Kerrowdhoo, a quarterland farm in the parish of Bride, turned up medieval pottery, both locally produced and imported from Cumbria, and eighteenth-century material, while the small scale excavation at Church Farm, Cregneash, found no pottery originating earlier than the eighteenth century.[3] A single fragment of an eighteenth-century plate was found in the ploughsoil downslope from a farm off the Staarvey Road during the installation of a gas pipeline in 2011.[4]

These artefacts tell only a fraction of the story. The field evidence for farms in the Island is confined to the extant sites, and those others where factors such as construction materials, inaccessibility, or marginality have combined to allow the preservation of some remains, which may be more or less obvious to interpretation. It is quite possible that the sites of the poorest farms and the dwellings of crofting, or non-tenant families, who may have laboured on the larger and quarterland farms, are either lost or remain to be confidently identified. While the sites outside the quarterland system are late in development and represent a small proportion of the agricultural economy in any period, they nevertheless fall within the period under review, and the lack of data from and about them makes a proportion of the population invisible. Some of the original farms and crofts beyond the quarterland boundaries may have been built over during boom years in the nineteenth century. Similarly, the quarterland farms themselves, of greater antiquity, have experienced a variety of development during their history, including the levelling up and levelling down of foundation surfaces, and even wholesale clearance and rebuilding. Crucially, no quarterland farm has been comprehensively excavated.

The archaeological work in Castletown and Peel has been able to suggest something about the diets of those using the castles and, in Castletown, in the developing town from the sixteenth century onwards. The evidence is patchy,

2 P.J. Davey, 'Molluscs', in P.J. Davey, D.J. Freke and D.A. Higgins, *Excavations in Castletown, Isle of Man 1989–1992* (Liverpool, 1996), 151–54; N.C. Johnson, 'IRIS Peel, Pumping Station: Trial Trenching' (unpublished report, 2001).

3 P.J. Davey *et al.*, *Kerrowdhoo, Bride, Isle of Man: Field Work and Excavations 1992–1994* (Douglas, 1995); N.C. Johnson, 'The pig-sties and thie veg, Church Farm, Cregneash', in P.J. Davey (ed), *Recent Archaeological Research on the Isle of Man*, BAR Brit Ser, 278 (Oxford, 1999), 280.

4 N.C. Johnson, *pers. comm.*, 6 May 2017.

being dependent on the degree to which bone survives in acidic soil and, as with all other types of archaeological finds, the mixing, redistribution and disturbance of original deposits. The report from Peel on the animal bone has not yet been produced, but the analysis of the Castletown material showed that adult sheep and cattle were the main sources of meat, with pig barely in evidence.[5] In the earlier part of the period, as the animals were generally fully mature before slaughter, it is probable that husbandry was focused on dairying and wool production rather than food. Wool was important economically: it features as one of a few items of export cargo from the Island entering the port of Liverpool in the sixteenth and seventeenth centuries.[6] This balance between the butchery of immature and mature animals shifted slightly in the eighteenth century, when possibly the requirements of a concentrated urban population had a more significant influence on demand. The higher status, and wealth, of the inhabitants of Castle Rushen may be marked by the greater proportion of bones from suckling pigs recovered from that site.

As the military situation changed over the centuries, few of the people who staffed and garrisoned the castles continued to dwell on site, and the construction in the sixteenth century of a boundary, probably a traditional turf hedge, to mark a division between properties fronting on to Malew and Arbory Streets, suggests organization of the land into household plots coincident with expansion of the town.[7] In the eighteenth century, the ground behind 20 Arbory Street was cultivated in rows, probably by hand, and for vegetables or potatoes.[8]

There is, however, a point in the history of the land between Malew and Arbory Streets when the best economic choice for the inhabitants appears to have been to keep livestock. The building to the rear of 17 Malew Street was probably built as a byre, and the organic-rich, well-mixed soils excavated at the rear of 20 Arbory Street may also have resulted from the keeping of animals, at least until the nineteenth century, when the area was sealed by flooring for grocery warehousing. Differences in the level of the ground behind individual properties on the two streets make it possible that the topsoil, enriched with manure, was removed historically. Loss of material and the date of livestock husbandry is certainly also suggested by the comparative absence of eighteenth-century finds from the 1992 excavation, despite a useful closed assemblage found immediately to the south on Malew Street, a group from the excavations

5 M. McCarthy, 'Animal Bone', in Davey, *et al.*, *Excavations in Castletown*, 127–44.

6 J. Kermode, J. Hollinshead and M. Gratton, 'Small Beginnings: Liverpool 1207–1680', in J. Belchem (ed), *Liverpool 800* (Liverpool, 2006), 85.

7 D.A. Higgins, 'The Excavations', in Davey, *et al.*, *Excavations in Castletown*, 58.

8 Higgins, 'Excavations', 57.

Fig. 3.1 *Great auk bone from Castle Rushen Stores: MNH 1989-0159/1521.*

at the grammar school, and a range of household wares from sites further north at The Crofts, the site of Georgian era development.[9]

Chicken and domesticated goose formed a large element in diets at both Peel and Castletown.[10] Wild species were also harvested: both guillemot and shearwater are represented at both sites, especially the juveniles of the latter that were especially vulnerable to capture from their nests which were constructed in burrows. Indeed there was a trade in shearwaters, known locally as puffins, which were salted in barrels, and appear in the cargo listings of ships docking at Liverpool.[11] Along with the harvesting of this species, it is apparent that shags and cormorants were also taken and, remarkably, at Castle Rushen Stores, the bone of a great auk was recovered.[12] This species was extinct from 1844.[13]

As well as birds, people collected molluscs and fished: the material from Castletown and Peel showed that limpets, winkles, oysters and dogwhelks were consumed.[14] Fish were both line-caught and netted, with cod, haddock,

9 P.J. Davey, 'Notes on a collection of post-medieval pottery and glass from 9 Malew Street, Castletown', in P.J. Davey (ed), *Recent Archaeological Research on the Isle of Man*, 267–72, 271.

10 C.T. Fisher, 'Bird Bone', in Davey, *et al.*, *Excavations in Castletown*, 144; C.T. Fisher, 'The Bird Bones', in D.J. Freke, *Excavations on St Patrick's Isle, Peel, Isle of Man 1982–88* (Liverpool, 2002), 252.

11 J. Kermode, *et al.*, 'Small Beginnings', 85.

12 C.T. Fisher, 'Bird Bone', in Davey, *et al.*, *Excavations in Castletown*, 147, 148; C.T. Fisher, 'The Bird Bones', in Freke, *Excavations on St Patrick's Isle*, 253.

13 C.T. Fisher, 'Bird Bone', in Davey, *et al.*, *Excavations in Castletown*, 147.

14 P.J. Davey, 'Molluscs', in Davey, *et al.*, *Excavations in Castletown*, 153; N. McMillan, 'The Molluscs', in Freke, *Excavations on St Patrick's Isle*, 262.

ling and herring the principal species eaten.[15] Fishermen feature strongly in the sixteenth-century list of householders in Castletown, and the fish bones recovered at Peel suggested that processing, such as filleting, was carried out off site.[16]

The excavation at Castle Rushen Stores revealed the use of coal from the sixteenth century, when the nearest sources were Prescot and Whiston.[17] The extent and character of woodland in the Island in previous centuries has often been discussed: certainly timber for construction was in short supply, and it is possible that the availability of firewood was similarly limited.[18] In this early period coal will have been expensive. Not only did it have to be imported to the Island, but there was no infrastructure in England for the transport of goods in bulk, and mining on any significant scale only developed in the eighteenth century.[19] The cost of coal was noted by the earl's comptroller in 1692.[20] Nevertheless, at this time the fuel was in sufficiently widespread use, domestically, to have caused a smoke nuisance, such that the coroners were required to fine householders without adequate chimneys.[21] The rear portion of 17 Malew Street, thought to be seventeenth-century in date, is supplied with fireplaces and chimneys in both gables.[22]

Although bricks were expensive to make, made they were, in quantity. The cost was not such, however, nor the demand sufficient, to warrant importing brick from established manufacturies in e.g. Lancashire. Brick fragments were recovered from both major excavations in Castletown, and brick was used in the construction of Derby House, in the mid-seventeenth century, and Bagnio House, Arbory Street, Castletown.[23] It seems reasonable to assume that construction in brick was beyond the means of most of the population and, given the predominance of masonry in the Island, that brick was used to demonstrate social distinction.

15 A.R. Hutchinson and A.K.G. Jones, 'The Fish Remains', in Freke, *Excavations on St Patrick's Isle*, 258–61.

16 D.A. Higgins, 'The Excavations', in Davey, *et al.*, *Excavations in Castletown*, 49.

17 M. Johnson, *An Archaeology of Capitalism* (Oxford, 1996), 121; Kermode, *et al.*, 'Small Beginnings', in Belchem (ed), *Liverpool 800*, 82.

18 F. Cowin, 'Bricks', in Freke, *Excavations on St Patrick's Isle*, 226.

19 Kermode, *et al.*, 'Small Beginnings', 85.

20 Cowin, 'Bricks', 226.

21 N.C. Johnson, 'Coal, Coke, Cinder and Burnt Stone', in Davey, *et al.*, *Excavations in Castletown*, 122.

22 D.A. Higgins, 'The Excavations', in Davey, *et al.*, *Excavations in Castletown*, 61.

23 Cowin, 'Bricks', 226–27; Johnson, 'Coal, Coke, Cinder and Burnt Stone', 120–22.

By the sixteenth century, glazed windows were 'normal in most houses of pretension'.[24] Diamond-shaped glass, of the type used in latticed windows, was recovered from rubbish pits at the Castle Rushen Stores site, indicating the switch to windows with larger panes when economic circumstances permitted, following the changes in technology which enabled the production of the necessary type and quality of glass. At Peel Castle an early seventeenth-century fragment of a glass dish was recovered, thought to originate from a manufactory near Manchester, and illustrating the effect on trade of the Derby preference.[25]

The majority of the archaeological excavation and fieldwalking which provides the evidence called upon here was carried out in the era before the metal detector was in regular use by archaeologists. This will certainly have negatively biased the evidence for metal artefacts, including coins. However, finds of English coins at Castle Rushen Stores demonstrate that they were in circulation from at least the fourteenth century, while items of dress, such as lace chapes, buttons, cloak fasteners, strap-ends and pins, dating from the sixteenth century onwards, were also recovered at this site and at Castle Rushen.[26] Apart from the end cap of a late seventeenth-century knife at Castle Rushen Stores, no cutlery of the period was recovered from the excavations in Peel and Castletown: unlike pottery, useless once broken, and soon discarded, metal artefacts may easily be repaired and recycled, making their discovery by archaeologists a consequence of either deliberate deposition or chance loss.[27]

It is useful to find that some pottery, likely from the same kilns, is present in the Island in more than one type, and in a variety of different vessels. One example is Cistercian-type ware, probably from South Lancashire, where the manufacture of different types of vessels, in both a fine and a coarse fabric, suggests a distinction between kitchen and table.[28] This ware represents a 'significant element in the table furniture of later fifteenth- and sixteenth-century urban dwellers' in the Island.[29] Similar differences and distinctions in fabric occur in the wares from north Devon, and a considerable range of vessels, including tankards, cups, jugs, pancheons, jars and plates are known

24 R.H. Vose, 'Vessel and Window Glass', in Freke, *Excavations on St Patrick's Isle*, 336.
25 Vose, 'Vessel and Window Glass', 331.
26 M.M. Archibald, 'Coins', in Davey, *et al.*, *Excavations in Castletown*, 118.
27 G. Egan, 'Non-ferrous Metal', in Davey, *et al.*, *Excavations in Castletown*, 113.
28 Recent research has established that Cistercian ware was produced in Rainford in the 16th century. See R. Philpott (ed), *The pottery and clay tobacco pipe industries of Rainford, St Helens: new research* (Liverpool: Merseyside Archaeological Society, 2015), 67–93.
29 P.J. Davey, 'Pottery', in Freke, *Excavations on St Patrick's Isle*, 408.

in eighteenth-century mottled ware.[30] As well as the wares imported from England, post-medieval pottery arrived from northern and south-western France, probably in association with the salt and wine trades.[31] This variety, apparent in both Peel and Castletown, and in rural contexts, points to levels of sophistication and choice, and the ability of some to afford both.

Until the beginning of the seventeenth century, a proportion of the pottery in use across the Island was locally produced. This was hand-made, not wheel-thrown, and probably fired in simple clamp kilns which leave no significant archaeological trace.[32] A range of different wares developed over the four-hundred-year history of this pottery, and included copies of imported continental types.[33] It would appear that the local industry was low-value, perhaps geographically widely dispersed, and did not generate income sufficient for a single trader to invest in substantial infrastructure, such as a stone or brick kiln. Substantial quantities of this type of pottery were recovered from the sixteenth-century contexts at Castle Rushen Stores, and it formed a major proportion of the assemblage from the excavations on the foreshore in Peel. After this date it disappears. The marked contrast in the quantitative proportions of the various types of pottery, Manx, English and continental, between Castle Rushen Stores and the Peel seafront site probably illuminates a difference in standards of living, at the very least in the immediate localities of both excavations.[34]

During the eighteenth century, Douglas became more prominent, superseding Castletown and Peel, confirming a shift in emphasis away from politically strategic considerations to those of trade and commerce.[35] A very small pottery assemblage of this date was recovered from fieldwalking at the site at Ballamona of the new Nobles Hospital in 1996. The considerably greater

30 Davey, 'Notes on a collection of post-medieval pottery and glass from 9 Malew Street, Castletown', 269; P.J. Davey, 'Pottery', in D.J. Freke, *Excavations on St Patrick's Isle*, 412.

31 P.J. Davey, 'Medieval and post-medieval continental imports on the Isle of Man', in Davey (ed), *Recent Archaeological Research on the Isle of Man*, 248; P.J. Davey, 'Les exportations françaises vers l'Isle de Man du XVème au XVIIème siècles', in A. Bocquet-Lienard and B. Fajal (eds), *A propo(t)s de l'usage, de la production et de la circulation des erres cuites dans l'Europe du nord-ouest (xive-xvie siècle)* (Caen: Université de Caen, Centre de recherches archéologiques et historiques médiévales, 2011), 219–27.

32 R. Barton, 'Manx Granite Tempered Ware', in Davey (ed), *Recent Archaeological Research on the Isle of Man*, 221–240.

33 Barton, 'Manx Granite Tempered Ware', 225–26.

34 P.J. Davey, 'The ceramic finds from the Peel IRIS excavations', *Isle of Man Studies*, 14 (2016), 71–79.

35 A. Harrison, 'Sources for the Documentary History of Peel Castle', in Freke, *Excavations on St Patrick's Isle*, 20.

quantity of nineteenth-century finds found during the same work illustrates the expansion of the town, and the consequent spreading of night soil further afield.[36]

Another feature of the pottery used by a population, beyond its economic value and the purchasing power of its owners, is the code of manners it supports. There is an analogy with the changes in cutlery noted by Johnson, where the multiplication in the quantity and type of instrument used at the table indicates the establishment of separate stages to a meal, each with associated manners and expectations.[37] The variety of tablewares recovered from Manx archaeological sites suggests a range of courses, of meals, and of occasions.

The types of pottery, including clay pipes, that have been found in the Island in both urban and rural locations, are such as to suggest that the lifestyle in both was comparable, and similar to that in the Stanley lands in England.[38]

In addition, the similarities between the range and proportions of different post-medieval pottery types found at sites across the Island make it likely that there was a single market, 'with mass-produced wares from England in general circulation'.[39] The pottery also strongly suggests that post-medieval trade to and from the Island was dominated by routes focused on the Dee and the Mersey, for example Chester and Liverpool and, possibly, Meols. Earlier exchange with Cumbria, suggested by the recovery of medieval pottery, appears to stop. Documentary evidence shows that wool, tallow, goose fat, hides, skins, herring and salted seabirds from the Island were entering the developing port of Liverpool, while iron, coal, salt, textiles and hats were the outbound cargoes for Mann.[40] An exception to these routes is the group of wares originating in north Devon, seventeenth-century in date, quite possibly as ballast, which invites consideration of the as yet unknown return export trade.[41]

The artefacts recovered by archaeologists are often used to reveal the routes taken by trade and hence the contacts between people in different locations. They may also be used to demonstrate the functioning of an economy, and deduce relative wealth, or poverty, social position or aspiration. Sometimes trading practices will confirm that a need has developed in a population for specific goods or materials which are locally unobtainable, such as coal or salt; sometimes they will reveal the advantages of acting as an intermediary for another population's needs, such as the Manx running trade; sometimes trade

36 N.C. Johnson, 'Ballamona New Hospital: Recovery of Archaeological Material, Part One: Field Walking' (unpublished report, 1997).

37 M. Johnson, *An Archaeology of Capitalism* (Oxford, 1996), 183, 201.

38 Davey, 'Medieval and post-medieval continental imports', 246.

39 Davey, 'Notes on a collection of post-medieval pottery and glass from 9 Malew Street, Castletown', 272.

40 Kermode, *et al.*, 'Small Beginnings, 85.

41 Davey, 'Medieval and post-medieval continental imports', 247.

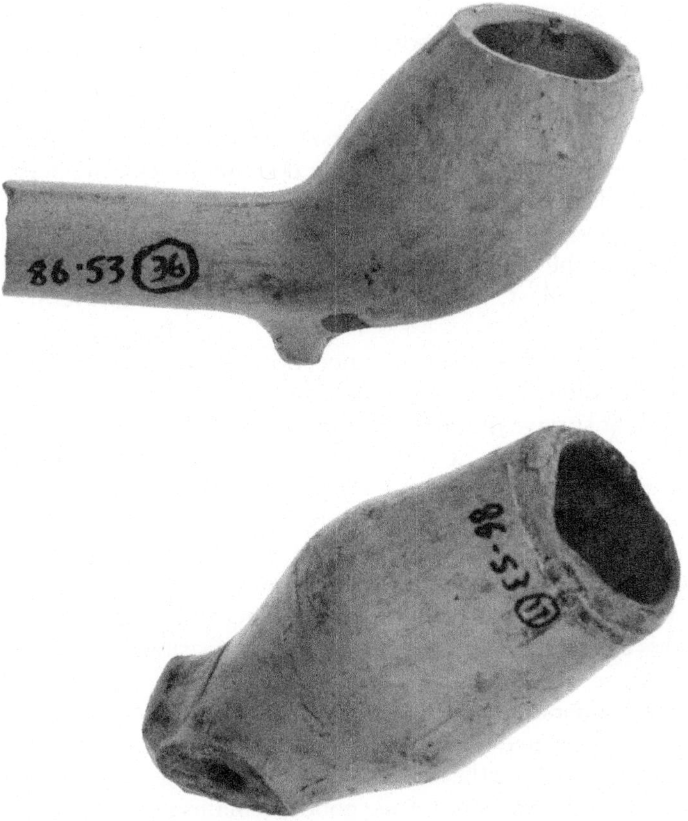

Fig. 3.2 *Clay pipe bowls from Peel: MNH Excavation Report page 430 number 3 and page 432 number 12.*

routes are principally determined by political and strategic considerations or constraints.

Alongside these factors are matters such as availability, prevalence, durability and cost. The extent to which these factors might vary across social, economic and even geographical divides in the Island confirms the need for evidence from different locations and different types of site. All of these are emphasized when trading involves a sea route. Once a particular type of pottery is manufactured in a location from where it is economically and practically viable to ship it to other markets, it will start to appear in the archaeological record. Tin-glazed earthenware, for example, only starts to appear in the Island in the early eighteenth century, even though it was available in England from the sixteenth century. The key change is that from 1710 there is manufacture in

Liverpool.[42] With generic consumable goods, such as coal, interpretation from an excavation depends on the deposit being relatively undisturbed, and dated by other means, and given the value of the material itself, once imported, it will only ever be found in fragments. Another consumable, salt, will necessarily never be recovered by archaeologists, yet it was certainly exported from Liverpool.[43] In the sea trade, cost as a factor does not necessarily operate in an entirely predictable manner. Importing a relatively high-value pottery such as tin-glazed earthenware implies that there was money to be made on this leg of the route (although the market might have been small), whereas the practice of shipping pottery as ballast, suggests that it was the cargo on the return journey which was more valuable.

The potential cultural and social connections between locations may also depend on routes which are only used occasionally, or which are used to trade goods that do not survive in the archaeological record. In the absence of any other evidence, the presence at Peel Castle of seventeenth-century clay pipes from Scotland and, probably, Ireland, is the only confirmation of contact, the absence of which would otherwise seem to be implausible.[44] There are, however, only two such pipes, while at Castletown, the material recovered of this period from both Castle Rushen and Castle Rushen Stores was almost exclusively from south Lancashire. This may illustrate a further factor: the sheer availability of material goods from a single source may occlude the visibility of other connections except where overridden by strong individual preference or enabled by easy portability, in person.

The period presently under review is long, and offers opportunities for change to established practices, and the creation of new ones. The post-medieval trade, however, at least in the visible ceramic goods, remains principally focused on north-west England or, to a lesser extent, directed further south, to north Devon and the Continent. The trade with north Devon may represent a vestige of the importation of a variety of wares from Bristol and Somerset in medieval times, known from finds at both Peel Castle and Castle Rushen, while the pottery imported from the Continent is associated with the salt and wine trades, predetermining a north-south axis.[45] There does not appear to be a link with Ireland, where wheel-thrown pottery is in production in Dublin, nor with Scotland, the formerly nominally dominant power.[46] Yet the development of Liverpool as a port, from the seventeenth century onwards, involved substantial trade with several ports in Ireland, with both luxury items and bulk goods

42 Davey, 'Pottery', in Freke, *Excavations on St Patrick's Isle*, 423.

43 Kermode, *et al.*, 'Small Beginnings', 85.

44 P.J. Davey, 'Claypipes', in Freke, *Excavations on St Patrick's Isle*, 434 (Peel pipes).

45 Davey, 'Medieval and post-medieval continental imports', 247.

46 R. Barton, 'Manx Granite Tempered Ware', in Davey (ed), *Recent Archaeological Research on the Isle of Man*, 232.

listed as export cargoes.[47] The apparent deprecation of trade with Cumbria in favour of Lancashire and Cheshire may, in later years, have been emphasized by developments in industrial capacity and transport infrastructure, especially in Liverpool and its hinterland, but initially, the role of the Stanleys seems likely to have been the significant factor. Cheshire and Lancashire originally formed the principal lands of the family, to which the Isle of Man was added in 1405/6. Stanley rule and administration, and the maintenance of garrisons at Peel and Castletown, meant changes to the Island's culture and population, with settlement from the lord's lands in England, and the apparent creation of new place names analogous with Lancashire examples.[48]

Probate evidence

Michael Hoy

Glimpses of domestic life in quarterland farms and merchants' houses may be found in wills and probate lists, but in contrast to the extensive work done on the archaeology of artefacts in the Isle of Man, there has been no comparable research into or analysis of documentary evidence. This section offers a brief overview of the kind of evidence which may be found in the Island's archives, drawing examples from rural and urban households, and outlines how social, economic and demographic changes in Island life may be charted through the documents.

The earliest extant ecclesiastical court records in the Isle of Man, which date from 1560, include some wills, but although farm stock and crop yields are named, household goods are not listed. In the 1590s more detail was recorded, and from the beginning of the seventeenth century, a clearer picture of what Manx men and women possessed in their homes, together with the artefacts of farming, fishing and mercantile enterprise, emerges. These more comprehensive inventories reflect a modest growth in the Island's economy after 1600, and they are particularly useful in showing not only the cultural, social and utilitarian status of possessions, but also the monetary value of the goods and the competence of those who assessed them.[49] The meagre possessions of the

47 R.A. Gregory, *et al.*, *Archaeology at the Waterfront 1: Investigating Liverpool's Historic Docks* (Lancaster, 2014); Kermode, *et al.*, 'Small Beginnings', 86, 98, 108.

48 J. Roscow, 'Castletown Cottages', in Davey, *et al.*, *Excavations in Castletown*, 157–60; Davey, 'Medieval and post-medieval continental imports', 248; G. Fellows-Jensen, 'The Scandinavian Element in the Place-Names of the Isle of Man', in G. Broderick, *Placenames of the Isle of Man*, vol. 7 (Tübingen, 2005), 357–70.

49 D. Spaeth, '"Orderly made": re-appraising household inventories in seventeenth-century England', *Social History*, 41:4 (2016), 417; T. Arkell, N. Evans and N. Goose (eds), *When death do us part: understanding and interpreting the probate records of early modern England* (Oxford, 2000).

majority poor, however, remain invisible. They are not represented among the wills or probate lists since they had nothing to bequeath.

In June 1601 an inventory was taken of the goods owned by Patricke Kerran of Maughold.[50] This is one of the earliest of the more comprehensive probate lists and comprises 33 items, some composite, including a 'dwelling house, backside [outhouse] and garden', valued in total at £12 13s. 4d. All the items listed are domestic, and most are utilitarian, like a 'dripping pan' and basins, but three valuable items are noted – two silver spoons (6s. 3d.), and a pair of candlesticks and a salt cellar (9s.) – and these, together with a table, suggest a measure of affluence and an aspiration towards social display.[51] The most valuable items, in even the less affluent households, were bedroom furniture and furnishings – Kerran owned a 'bedstocke' [bedstead], two 'fledges' [down-filled coverlets], and a 'side bed' [perhaps a cupboard-bed], with a 'flocke bed' [wool mattress], blankets, bolsters, pillows and 'pillowbeere' [pillowcases], valued together at 34s. 11d.

Two inventories of 1637 give contrasting pictures of rural and urban life. Phillip Corlett of Patrick, a cotler and fisherman, who paid '21d. rent' for 'a cottage house & croft', had few domestic items, but the tools of his livelihood also feature: he owned '1 spade ... a wheele [spinning] and cards [carding combs] ... fishing geares & a pundrell [weighing balance]'.[52] The inventory of Mary Corkill, a Douglas merchant who owned '6 houses & gardens rent 2s 10s price 12 pounds', demonstrates the very different lifestyle and wealth of a few successful Manx entrepreneurs. Among 85 composite entries, valued at £54 9d. in total, are the goods she traded: materials for cooperage (140 assorted barrels, 'barrel boardes' and pitch), fishing (netts, 'lane' [line], oares and 'spinlers') and brewing ('ieasts', 'brewing pann' and 'still'), and cloth and fabrics ('scotch linen', coarse linen, 'woolen cloth made green', board cloth, 'washed wool', felt and 'rough flaxe').[53]

A survey of a random selection of 18 rural and seven urban inventories of moderate size (fewer than 20 entries) from 1701 to 1721 shows that the contents of Manx homes changed very little through the preceding century.[54] Beds and bedding were still generally the most prized of household possessions. By contrast there are very few chairs, stools, benches or tables. More important were items for storage – baskets, chests and barrels of various sizes. Elinor

50 MNH MS 10216 (EW), 1601, Maughold.
51 Nick Johnson, *pers.comm.*, 9 July 2017.
52 MNH MS 10216 (AW), 1637, Patrick: Phillip Corlett.
53 MNH MS 10216 (AW), 1637, Braddan: Mary Vinch (als Corkill).
54 MNH MS 10216 (EW), 1701, Braddan & Onchan; 1702, Malew; 1704, Santon; 1705, Rushen; 1707, Rushen, 1708, Lezayre, 1709, Lonan; 1710, Castletown; 1711, Bride; 1712, Santon; 1715, Michael, Santon; 1716, Bride; 1717, Peel; 1718, Ramsey; 1720, Ayre, Castletown (2), Rushen (2); 1721, Ayre, Douglas, German, Ramsey.

Lace of Castletown (1720) possessed a variety of containers for preparing and storing food, particularly brewing, baking, cheesemaking and dairying.[55] Some of these items are in multiple numbers, including 11 pounds of pewter (at 8d. per pound), which suggests that she may have been a shopkeeper.

Materials and implements for manufacturing cloth and clothing are often listed and many inventories list a wide variety of tools for gardening, milling and general agriculture. Isabel Kelly of Braddan (1701) owned a 'plow, colter & socke [blade and ploughshare], & gears belong to ye plow ... a manks spade, a turfe spade [and] an old woollen wheele [spinning-wheel]' valued at 3s. 4d.[56] Fishing features in five inventories: three men owned a share in a herring boat, and there are multiple listings of nets, lines, sails and 'fishing geares'.

A number of probate inventories in the last quarter of the eighteenth century reflect the Island's changing demography and economy, and this continues in the nineteenth century. There was a demand for specialist skills like those of John Cummings (1780), a Douglas watchmaker, who left watches, components and craft tools valued at £5 19s. 6d. in an estate of £36 16s. 6d. Merchandising on a much larger scale is illustrated by Elizabeth Shaw (1810), a Douglas cloth merchant who left an estate notable not only for the high valuation of her stock and effects (£2,374 6s. 8d.), but also for the variety and quantities of the goods she traded, for which there was a ready market.[57] Yet the modest effects of Thomas Gelling (1811) of Douglas, which included '2 tables & 3 chairs, 2 bedsteads & old bed close [clothes] ... 1 spinning wheel, 3 barrells ... & shoe makers tools' valued in total at just £2 13s. 10d., are more representative.[58] His inventory shows that the contents of most Manx homes in the early nineteenth century were still much the same as they had been two hundred years earlier.

The documentary evidence reviewed here shows that probate records can be an invaluable resource in helping to build a dynamic picture of life in the home and at work.[59] The Island's archives offer real scope for further study and a future programme of research will provide a comprehensive picture of socio-economic diversity and change, and a chance to see this picture in the wider context of north-west England and across the Irish Sea.

55 MNH MS 10216 (EW), 1720, Castletown.

56 MNH MS 10216 (EW), 1701, Braddan: Isable Kelly (als Fargher).

57 MNH MS 10216 (EW), 20 August 1780, Douglas: John Cummings; MNH MS 10216 (EW), 17 September 1810, Douglas: Elizabeth Shaw.

58 MNH MS 10216 (EW), 16 October 1811, Douglas: Thomas Gelling (bound in 1810 box).

59 See T. Arkell, *et al.* (eds), *When Death Do Us Part.*

THE ROLE OF WOMEN IN FAMILY LIFE IN THE HOME

Jennifer Platten †

Records regarding the role of Manx women especially in the domestic environment are elusive in the extant documents. However, information can be gleaned as to their field of influence and the part that they played in everyday life from some of the secular and ecclesiastical records, especially for the period succeeding the seventeenth century.

It is clear from the files of wills and inventories which survive from the 1600s onwards that some women at least held considerable property and would have been regarded as the head of the household. In 1698 Jane Allen of Castletown owned a 'dwelling house, brew house, cellar, backside and Garden'.[60] However, although 41 women were noted as landholders in the church assessment for Malew in 1767, they were only a small proportion of the total.[61] Lack of ownership of land does not automatically imply lack of possessions; women still made formal wills bequeathing lesser items such as a 'blanket, hogshead, barrel, ploughshare'.[62] Indeed up until the passing of the Act for Ascertaining the Interest of a Wife or Widow in the Estate of her Husband in 1777 (which was repealed in 1852), Manx women were given equal rights of property with their husbands. This protection of a Manx woman's property rights was far in advance of the situation in England at that time, where the property rights of a woman passed to her husband upon marriage and they were treated as one person in law with women having no individual control over their assets.[63]

Whilst the few Manx women of property had a reasonable amount of control over their lives this was not the case for the majority of women. In general, very many Manx women were much poorer than their male counterparts, suggesting that they were often limited to a role in the domestic environment. Examination of the level of fines set for ecclesiastical offences in the Commonwealth period, and which were specifically set at a level that each offender was able to pay, show that for sexual offences in 1659 the 21 male offenders were given fines ranging from under 12d. to 5s. and over.[64] Of these 21 individuals only four men received fines of less than 1s, whereas six received fines in excess of 5s. In contrast 16 of the women censured were given fines less than 1s. with only one

60 MNH MS 10194 (Lib.Caus.) 1659–1704, Book 1, (fol. dated 7 July 1698).

61 MNH MS 10194 (Presentments), Malew Assessment, 1767.

62 MNH MS 10216 (EW), 1, Bakie Corsead.

63 *Statutes*, vol. 1, 333. For a fuller discussion of this topic see J.R. Roscow, 'The Development of Women's Rights in the Isle of Man up to 1777', *PIMNHAS*, 10:2 (1994). For the comparable situation in England see William Blackstone, *Commentaries on the Laws of England*, 4 vols (Oxford, 1765), vol. 1, 442–45.

64 MNH MS 10071 (Lib.Scacc.), 1658, fol. 62.

woman receiving a fine greater than 3s.[65] The view that Manx women were in general poorer than men is also supported by figures relating to the distribution of relief. Distributions to the poor of the parish of Lonan in 1659 of between 1s. and 4d. per recipient show that seven women received relief compared to five men. This supposition of the comparative poverty of many women at this time is also further supported by the statutory wage rates set during the seventeenth century. In the early seventeenth century, at a time when a ploughman was entitled to 13s. 4d. a year and a horseman 8s., a woman servant's wages were set 'according as she shall be thought to deserve by the Deemster and Jury', and it was not until 1667 when a ploughman was earning 15s. that a 'maid servant of Ability' could earn 9s. a year.[66]

Whilst some women would have been employed as domestic servants, it is highly probable that many women spent the majority of their time and effort in their own household environment, and from a young age girls would have learned the regular domestic skills of the household. Most important of these were the care and raising of children, providing food, and the staple craft skills of sewing, spinning wool and flax, and weaving.

They would additionally have been involved in farming, (especially in the rural fishing communities when the men were away at sea) or in taking in work. Life for these women, certainly in the seventeenth and eighteenth centuries, involved significant physical labour. The sabbath breaking presentments records show that women, as well as knitting stockings and making cheese, were involved in carrying rawcloth and corn or barley to the mill, winnowing malt, threshing corn, shearing sheep and drawing home turf (which suggests that they were using a hurdle rather than a cart, a process requiring considerable effort), as well as clearing dung from doorsteps.[67] During this period, women were also involved in traditional female roles such as midwives and nurses for the sick, as well as services relating to laying out the bodies of the dead, but such work would most certainly have been on a piece rate as and when required and for many would not have resulted in a regular income outside the domestic environment.[68] Later in the eighteenth century, there is documentary evidence of the sums that women could earn for laundry work or cooking. Invoices from George Moore's records indicate that a washerwoman could earn 15s. 8½d. for washing 18 shirts, 60 stockings and three waistcoats, whilst the considerable

65 MNH MS 10194 (Presentments), 1659.

66 *Statutes*, vol. 1, 70,133.

67 MNH MS 10194 (Presentments), Malew, 1667; Andreas, 1761; Rushen, 1666/67; Lezayre, 1667; unspecified parish, 1640; Rushen, 1666/67; Malew, 1667; Onchan, 166; Ma(lew), 1679; (Lib.Caus.) 1659–1704; (Presentments), Michael, 1702.

68 MNH MS 10194 (Presentments), Rushen, 1667.

Fig. 3.3 *Spinning wheel, late 18th-/early 19th-century: MNH 5956.*

sum of 4s. 3d. was paid to Mary Tracey for providing nine mince pies and three tarts.[69]

Towards the eighteenth century, the possibility of more educated occupations for a few women outside the domestic environment are found in the records. Petty schools were often taught by women although, because they were only permitted to teach young children, the level of education of these teachers

69 MNH MS 04933 C (QBHP: Ballamore Accounts), 1780 receipt for Mary Nell; 1781, fols 9, 10.

is unclear. Evidence from petty schools in Lezayre and Santon, for example, would suggest that women teachers were widespread in the Island.[70] Licensed schools also employed women teachers such as Mrs Flaxney, schoolmistress of Douglas, and Susan Aspinall from Ballasalla, who were granted sums of 10s. and 5s. respectively from the bishops' fund in 1702.[71]

There were, of course, some Manx women who were not obliged to work or perform domestic duties. For them life was less arduous but not necessarily without discomfort. In the early seventeenth century, items could be purchased which were clearly designed for the privileged few; the inventory of the shop of Geffrey Ballamay from Castletown shows a stock of expensive fabrics, lace, velvet, whalebone bodies for women (at 2s. 4d. each), silk buttons, ribbons and hats.[72] The inclusion of such items in the shop's stock suggests that there was a market for such luxuries and that some women were able to have the fineries of life, but the dangers of childbirth and problems of ill health affected wealthy and poor alike. The wife of George Moore, who in 1780 regularly took prescriptions of castor pills, concoctions of bark and laxatives, shows that for the wealthy Manx woman, their less physically demanding life was still no guarantee of health.[73] Indeed, for the elderly woman relying on the shelter of a relative or friend, the life of a Manx woman left much to be desired. Josepha Dalby, who was writing in 1812, was restricted by age and infirmity. She rarely left the house in Kirk Michael in the winter months, first venturing into the garden in late May, and hardly ever left the property from one month to the next; indeed, for external companionship she was wholly reliant upon visitors.[74] Isolation was a part of life for women confined to the domestic environment in rural communities.

Throughout the period, when not actively engaged in paid employment, domestic or agricultural work, the evidence as to how women passed their time is scant. It is clear from the ecclesiastical records, when comparing prosecutions for not attending services, that women were more likely to be present in church than their male counterparts.[75] The ecclesiastical records also show that whilst women danced late on a Saturday night and played cards, they were never presented for physical sports such as archery, swimming or cammag.[76]

70 MNH MS 10194 (Presentments), Lezayre, 1695: Nelly Corrin; Santon, 1736: Susan Arthur and Amy Brew.

71 MNH MS 10194 (Lib.Caus.), 1702.

72 MNH MS 10216 (EW), 1600–18, fol. 2.

73 MNH MS 04932 C (QBHP: Ballamore Accounts), 1780, invoice to Patrick Scott.

74 MNH MS 13603, Diary of Josepha Dalby of Ballacooley, Kirk Michael.

75 J. Platten, 'The Church Court System: Presentments to the Manx Church Courts, 1640–1799' (PhD thesis, University of Liverpool, 2010).

76 MNH MS 10194 (Presentments) Douglas 1799, Castletown 1701, Michael 1731, Marown 1734.

During the period covered by this history, the situation of the Manx woman would have certainly improved as the economy strengthened and the situation of the population in general ameliorated. However, the hard physical conditions for many and the dangers of childbirth meant that life in the domestic environment was forever difficult and unsure.

CHILDHOOD AND ADOLESCENCE

Michael Hoy

In Bishop Hildesley's visitation records of 1757, boys and girls under the age of sixteen are listed separately in every parish, and they make up 37.3% (7,155) of the total population of 19,144.[77] Thirty years later the total population had reached 24,924, of which 37.4% (9,323) were under sixteen.[78] The earliest population figure is given by William Blundell, who estimated that the Island in the 1640s was 'a body of 6 or 7000 ... at this day in a mean populous'; of these no more than about 2,500 would have been children.[79] Although children are not differentiated in the first census in 1821, it can be estimated that there would have been about 15,000 boys and girls under sixteen in a total population of 40,081.

Although some clues may be found in documents like the statutes and court records, the first structured written account of Island life appeared in 1648 when Blundell began to record what he found in the 'little molehill moted about with ye main sea'.[80] But from his observations and later accounts, particularly those of William Sacheverell, George Waldron and John Feltham, together with clues drawn from court records and other sources, it is possible to sketch a picture of the lives of children and young people in the Isle of Man from the fifteenth to the nineteenth centuries.[81]

A very small proportion of Island children would have enjoyed the fortunate conditions of the households of the lord's officers and the 'gentry', numbered

77 MNH MS 00791 C, Parochial visitation records, 1757. In the Customary Laws (1523) and the Spiritual Laws (1577), the 'Yeares of Discretion' are fourteen: see *Statutes*, vol. 1, 28, 41.

78 J. Spranger, *et al.*, *The Report of the Commissioners of Inquiry for the Isle of Man* (1792), appx B, 90 & 91.

79 MNH MS 00049 C, W. Blundell, 'A History of the Isle of Man, 1648–56' (2 vols) (1648–56), vol. 1, 129.

80 Blundell, 'History', vol. 1, 4.

81 W. Sacheverell, *An Account of the Isle of Man* (c.1692) (London, 1702); G. Waldron, *A Description of the Isle of Man*, 2nd edn (London, 1731); J. Feltham, *A Tour through the Island of Mann, in 1797 and 1798* (Bath, 1798). Since apprenticeships usually began at age sixteen, some description of the lives of young people in their late teens is included.

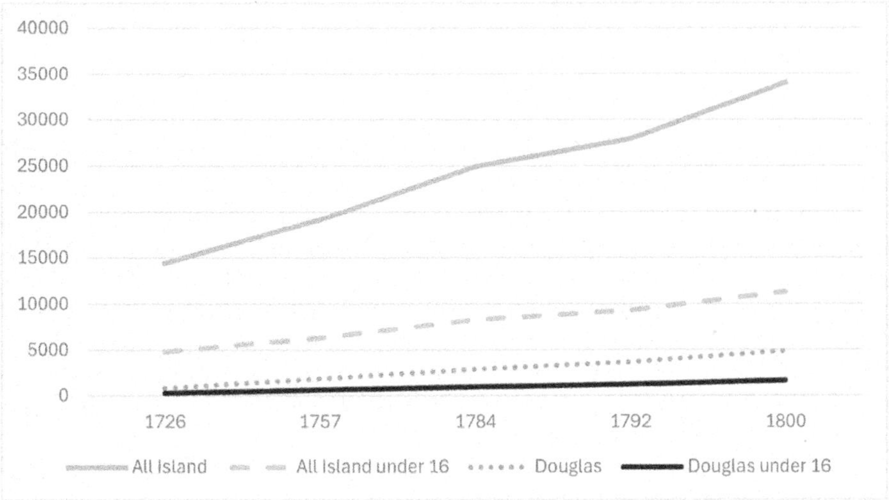

Fig. 3.4 *Isle of Man population 1726–1800: children and adolescents.*

by Blundell as 'not above six families of note in all the Island'.[82] Children in some of the more affluent merchant homes, too, could benefit from 'the commodities wherewith [the merchant] trafficketh ... the barrl'd herrings, and powder'd beef'.[83] In the later years of the eighteenth century, families of the 'middling sort', professional and mercantile, began to enjoy more of the benefits of successful enterprise, especially in Douglas, but from the accession of the Stanleys to the mid-nineteenth century, most children and their parents constituted the majority poor. Blundell's description of the 'habitations' and conditions of most Manxmen gives a glimpse of the life of children: they lived in 'mere hovels ... containing one room only ... yet in this smoking hut ... doth the man, his wife, and children cohabit ...'.[84] These cramped, damp and smoky cottages, which also housed the farm stock, provided little more than the simplest of shelter, but Sacheverell, writing at the end of the seventeenth century, judged that 'as there are few that can be properly said to be rich, so neither are there many that can be said to be miserably poor'.[85] Thomas Quayle, writing in 1811, concluded that 'the condition of the Manx peasantry has for many years been gradually improving, particularly since the year 1765'.[86] As long as the harvests of land and sea did not fail, their frugal fare of 'salt butter,

82 Blundell, 'History', vol. 1, 132, 133.
83 Blundell, 'History', vol. 1, 162.
84 Blundell, 'History', vol. 1, 136.
85 Sacheverell, *Account*, 'Introduction', B2r.
86 T. Quayle, *A General View of the Agriculture of the Isle of Man* (London, 1812), 149.

herrings, and oat cakes … water, or water mixt with milk … or at best butter milk' would have been sufficient for a growing child.[87]

Leaseholders or owners of the larger quarterland farms were relatively few, but their status assured a beneficial lifestyle for their children. During his tour in 1797, John Feltham visited a mixed quarterland farm of 270 acres which sustained seven families comprising forty souls, with a 'house-servant, two men, and three boys, with six labourers, and 25 additional hands in harvest'.[88] In the towns Feltham found that many of the merchant 'middling sort' lived in substantial stone houses of two or three storeys, where the family lived above the warehouse and trading floors.[89] For a favoured few, like George Moore's eldest son Philip, parental money and influence provided entrepreneurial opportunities at a young age; after spending most of his time on amusements while at school in Glasgow, he was just sixteen when he returned in 1753 and set up a factory for tobacco-spinning in Peel.[90]

There was plenty of opportunity for recreation for the children of professional families. Attorney General Wadsworth Busk's son Robert kept a journal during his early teenage years from 1782 to 1784: he went fishing 'in the 2 mile river [and] the White River', swam 'at Neck-Vein [and] Kirk Santan', 'played at Bows and Arrows' and noted one exceptional week when he 'took remarkably violent exercise on several days … running once to ye 2 miles bridge & back again, then round the brown mountain'.[91] For girls in the higher social circles there were gentler pursuits – music, dancing, and skills like drawing and embroidery.

At the opposite end of the social scale, children in the most destitute families were provided for by gifts and church levies. Bishop Wilson explained to his children: 'Church livings were … designed … to maintain our families, to keep up hospitality, to feed the poor'.[92] He recorded many instances when poor children and young people received charitable help: for example, disbursements from his alms fund in 1700/01 included 2s. 10d. to 'Wm Christian, a poor youngman, who lay a long time sick, in great misery', and 10s. 'to Widow Sayle's 4 small Children of [Andreas]'.[93] This charity contrasts markedly with the situation in Ireland, where sectarian bias often obstructed the disbursement

87 Blundell, 'History', vol. 1, 137.
88 Feltham, *Tour*, 51.
89 Feltham, *Tour*, 225.
90 N. Mathieson, 'Sir George Moore and his Sons', *PIMNHAS*, 5:2 (1946–50), 145.
91 MNH MS 07014, Robert Busk's Journal, 1782–84: 25 June 1782; 13 December 1783; 7 February 1784; 15, 18, 19 May 1784. Most of these locations are in Santon parish.
92 Stowell, *Wilson*, 59.
93 MNH MS 10194 (Lib.Caus.), 5 November 1700 & 10 September 1701.

Fig. 3.5 *'Woman and Child in a Garden' – embroidery by Mrs Finigan and her pupils, Catherine Halsall's School, c.1798: MNH 1954-3431.*

of poor relief: in 1714, for example, the affluent residents of Sligo declared that they would not help 'a parcel of beggars' brats'.[94]

The early years of the nineteenth century saw modest improvements in the living conditions of the majority poor, but the daily lives of children changed very little right through to the mid-nineteenth century.[95] Girls had to look after younger siblings and quickly learned staple domestic skills, including sewing, spinning wool and flax, and weaving, which could contribute to a family's income; a child skilled in spinning could earn up to fifty percent of her mother's earnings.[96] Girls' share of outdoor labour included milking; Feltham observed that 'the dairy-maid, in milking, is not accommodated with a seat as in England'.[97] They learned to become expert reapers and, working with

94 E. Nicholson, *A supplement to the method of charity-schools, for Ireland* (Dublin, 1714), 25.

95 J.C. Curwen, *Workington Agricultural Society's Annual Report for the Isle of Man, 1810*, 113.

96 T. Quayle, *Agriculture of the Isle of Man* (1812), 152–54.

97 Feltham, *Tour*, 52.

younger boys, they were indispensable at 'turnip-thinning time', as Bishop Wilson noted in 1703.[98] Throughout the eighteenth century, many older boys shunned the drudgery of farm work and aspired to join a fishing boat: 'The sea is the object of their affection,' John Christian Curwen noted with concern in 1810, when a shortage of labour threatened to hold back agrarian development across the Island. Yet he also commended the initiative and perseverance of at least one Manx youth who developed an efficient method of 'turnip stitching'.[99] In early summer, when many older boys sailed with the herring fleet, Feltham observed that 'girls from nine to thirteen years old, carry the herrings in baskets, from the boats to the houses prepared on purpose' for salting.[100] In the heyday of smuggling in the first half of the eighteenth century, adolescent boys were increasingly caught up in the running trade, if not aboard the boats, then in other associated activities; Malachy Postlethwayt had enterprises like merchant Philip Moore's in mind when he reported in 1755 that 'a number of boys [are] employed in several workhouses [where] tobaccos are … manufactured in the Island into fine pig-tail and coarse roll, and run into Great Britain and Ireland … by the smuggling-boats and night-carriers'.[101]

From the age of about eleven, children would be taken on as husbandmen (farm labourers) and household servants by the leaseholders and landowners on the farms, and in the towns by merchants and professional men. Hiring of 'Men Servants [was] betwixt Allhallowtide and Michaelmas, and [of] Maid servants betwixt Lady Day and May Day'. Wages and hours of labour were regulated by statute; in 1691, for example, the basic daily rate for 'all common Labourers', was set at 4d. or 2d. 'with Meat and Drink'. There is no evidence to show at what age this was applied, but perhaps the greatest bonus for younger servants, most of whom were boarded, was a statutory food allowance, which included barley cake and *sollaghyn* (porridge). Adolescents who were not engaged at the spring hiring were liable to 'yarding', which required them to serve the lord's officers for a fixed wage.[102] Bishop Wilson took steps to ensure that 'yarded' boys were not exploited or engaged to undertake inappropriate or dangerous work: in 1713 he issued an order to the 'Moare of Kk Christ Rushen' that in requisitioning yarded 'Boon men' to supply workers to Richard Reece, the lord's agent for mines, 'all persons [are] not to send boys but able men for that service at their peril'.[103]

98 MNH MS 00802 C, Convocation Papers, 3 February 1703, 4–5.

99 Curwen, *Isle of Man Report*, 107–08, 155.

100 Feltham, *Tour*, 90.

101 MNH M 05329, Malachy Postlethwayt, 'Smuggling in relation to the Isle of Man', extract from *Dictionary of Trade and Commerce* (1755), 3–5.

102 *Statutes*, vol. 1, 50–51, 113, 121, 123, 148–49, 253–54; Waldron, *Description*, 140–41. Yarding was abolished in 1748.

103 MNH MS 10071/3/18 (Lib.Scacc.), 22 October 1713, order to 'Moare of Kk Christ Rushen'.

This is one instance of evidence that there was a duty of care towards children, whose rights were safeguarded in Manx law. As early as 1523, for example, statutory provision was made for children whose father had died to be supported until age fourteen by their mother's second husband; and there are many examples where wills made special provision for children, or required the eldest inheritor to do so.[104] Ill-treatment and excessive punishment of children were liable to censure in the church courts; in 1702 a Bride cotter was presented for cursing children while harrowing, in 1765 two Braddan men were presented for beating children, and in 1794 three Lonan parents were presented for failing to prevent children stoning each other.[105] But there were statutory punishments for children, too; a child guilty of trespass, for example, was liable to be whipped. Parents were reminded in court judgments of their responsibility for their children's behaviour.[106]

The church courts also dealt with wayward adolescents by issuing fines, bonds and penances. In 1734 a gang of Marown youths were presented 'for prophaning the Sabbath by meeting in a wild and disorderly manner on Sunday Evenings – wch they generally spend in Playing, Running, Pitching Stones & Wrestling in wch practices these idle young people have long persisted'; and in 1763 three Lezayre teenagers were presented for 'prophaning the Lord's Day by draining the Mill Race & Dam & catching Trouts therein'. The parish priests guided teenagers' moral upbringing and prepared them for confirmation; in the case of William Karran, who was presented in 1761 'for Playing at Ball in [Santon] Church-yard, on Whitsun Monday, & breaking Three Quarries in one of the Church Windows', the court noted that 'Wm Karran has not yet prepared himself for Confirmation'.[107] Legislation backed up society's duty of care towards adolescents by prescribing statutory punishment for adults who 'intice, inveigle [or] countenance [...] Children [... into] Drinking [and] Gameing' and other immoral or anti-social practices.[108]

In the Isle of Man there was no secular provision for the care of the 'impotent poor' comparable to the Elizabethan Poor Law regulations in England and Wales. Insular customary practice, regulated by the church courts, provided that 'old decrepit and sick Persons shall have the Benefitt of one of their Children, which they like best, to look to and serve themselves [...] and [...] in every Yeare enter the Name of such choice Child'. 'Choice' children were recorded each

104 *Statutes*, vol. 1, 28; A. Ashley, 'The claims and needs of children in traditional Manx law and custom', *PIMNHAS*, 5:4 (1953), 360, 361.

105 MNH MS 10194 (Lib.Caus., Presentments), Bride, 8 March 1701/2; Braddan, November 1765; Lonan, 20 October 1794.

106 *Statutes*, vol. 1, 118–19.

107 MNH MS 10194 (Lib.Caus., Presentments), Marown, 13 October 1734; Santon, June 1761; Lezayre, June 1763.

108 *Statutes*, vol. 1, 118, 132.

year in presentments; in 1717–18, for example, fourteen 'choice' children were entered for exemption from 'yarding' in order to care for a family member at home. The Island's 'choice child' system seems to have no parallel elsewhere in Britain.[109]

The working day for hired boys and girls was from 6am to 8pm in summer and to 6pm in winter. The hours were long, but they found time for games and pastimes. Adolescent boys and girls traditionally played out the songs, dances and rituals of seasonal festivals like Beltaine (May Day), *Hop-tu-Naa* (Hollantide Eve), the play of the White Boys (Christmas Eve) and Hunting the Wren (St Stephen's Day); and from the mid-eighteenth century onwards, resourceful teenagers could exploit the new opportunities of urban life.[110] Any change to the daily routine would have been an opportunity to let off steam. John Wesley's diary of his visit to Douglas in 1781 includes this telling description of some of the youngsters in the crowd: 'At six,' he wrote, 'I preached in the market-place [Douglas], to a large congregation; all of whom, except a few children, and two or three giddy young women, were seriously attentive.'[111]

The provision of elementary schools for all boys and girls and grammar schools for the most able boys is described in the following section on education and literacy. For boys from the age of eleven who did not attend a grammar school, there were opportunities to learn a trade as an apprentice. One of the earliest records of an apprenticed Manx boy dates from 1566, when Robert Davie entered an indenture for six years in the trade of a 'sclater' (roof tiler) to Edward Wilson of Liverpool, who was bound 'to exhibite fynd and gyve unto the sayd Robert Davie meate dryncke and ludgynck holsome and honest, and also vi [shillings] usuall money of England for his apparell and clothing, and to teache the sayd Davie his occupacion'.[112] Island apprenticeships in basic trades must have been available for Manx boys, but no records of indentures in the sixteenth and early seventeenth centuries have survived, with the exception of one indenture of 1503 for a musical apprenticeship in Chester set up by the abbot of Rushen.[113] By the mid-seventeenth century, a critical shortage of skilled

109 *Statutes*, vol. 1, 122, 133; MNH MS 10071/3/11 (Lib.Scacc.), 1665, 64–66; MNH MS 10071/5/14 (Lib.Canc.), 1718, 95–96; Waldron, *Description*, 140–41. There is no reference to a 'choice child' or similar system in Joanna Innes's comprehensive list of institutional and other forms of welfare provision: see J. Innes, 'State, Church and Voluntarism in European Welfare, 1690–1850', in H. Cunningham and J. Innes (eds), *Charity, Philanthropy and Reform* (London, 1998), 23.

110 A.W. Moore, *The Folklore of the Isle of Man* (Isle of Man and London, 1891), 111–13, 122–26, 127–31; Waldron, *Description*, 154–56; H. Bullock, *History of the Isle of Man* (London, 1816), 370–71.

111 MNH MS 12486 (E240/25), John Wesley, *Journals*, May-June 1781, 523.

112 Liverpool Municipal Archives ('Town Books'), MS 1 (c.1550–70), fol. 150v.

113 J.R. Dickinson, *The Lordship of Man under the Stanleys* (Douglas, 1997), 147 n; W. Cubbon, 'Early Schools and Scholarships in Mann', *PIMNHAS*, 3 (1925/6), 114.

labour prompted new legislation in 1765 to address a 'great Scarcity [...] of honest and able Tradesmen in the Isle'.[114] This reform bound an apprentice to his indenture, usually for five years, by a cash bond of ten pounds lodged by his parents, guardian, or sponsor, and in return master craftsmen were required to give proper training. The bond protected a boy from exploitation and encouraged his good conduct and diligence.

It has been estimated that in England fewer than forty percent of apprentices completed their full term.[115] By contrast, in the Isle of Man, apprentice indenture cases rarely feature in eighteenth-century court records, which may indicate that the bond effectively regulated apprentices and employers alike. There does not appear to be any evidence that apprentice boys in the Island were ill-treated, unlike some orphaned boys in Wales who were indentured to unscrupulous masters to avoid the parish's poor law obligations to provide for their maintenance.[116] But it may have been ill-treatment that prompted two Manx boys apprenticed in Liverpool to run away and break their indentures: as a consequence, in 1718 their fathers, William Killey and William Karran of Marown, forfeited their bonds of twenty pounds.[117] By contrast, in a case in 1700 when an orphaned apprentice's indenture bond was at risk through the negligence of his guardian, the ecclesiastical court took action to safeguard the care of the boy and his siblings.[118]

Between apprentices and grammar school boys, there was inevitably ongoing rivalry. In 1761, two apprentices deliberately sat in seats reserved for the grammar school boys in Douglas Chapel (Old St Matthew's). Amid much commotion, they were summarily thrown out and presented to the church court, where the ringleader, Philip Lewn, a shoemaker's apprentice, was bound over for his future conduct by a bond of 20s.; his master, John Crowe, also gave a bond of 20s. for the teenager's conduct.[119]

Running away to sea to make a fortune was not such a ready option for an adventurous Manx teenager as it was for a boy in Whitehaven or Liverpool, since the strict 'watch and ward' regulations prohibited 'Servants or young Persons presuming to transport themselves out of the Isle without [...] Leave or

114 *Statutes*, vol. 1, 119–23, 129.

115 P. Wallis, 'Apprenticeship and Training in Pre-modern England', *Journal of Economic History*, 68:3 (September 2008), 835–41.

116 D.W. Howell, *The Rural Poor in Eighteenth-Century Wales* (Cardiff, 2000), 102; A. Davies, 'Some aspects of the operation of the old poor law in Cardiganshire, 1750–1834', *Ceredigion*, 6 (1968), 26. These children were frequently ill-treated and many failed to complete their indentures.

117 MNH MS 10071/5/14 (Lib.Canc.), 13 October 1718, 20–21.

118 MNH MS 10194 (Lib.Caus.), 22 February 1669/70.

119 MNH MS 10194 (Lib.Caus., Presentments), Douglas, February 1761; Braddan, 9 November 1762.

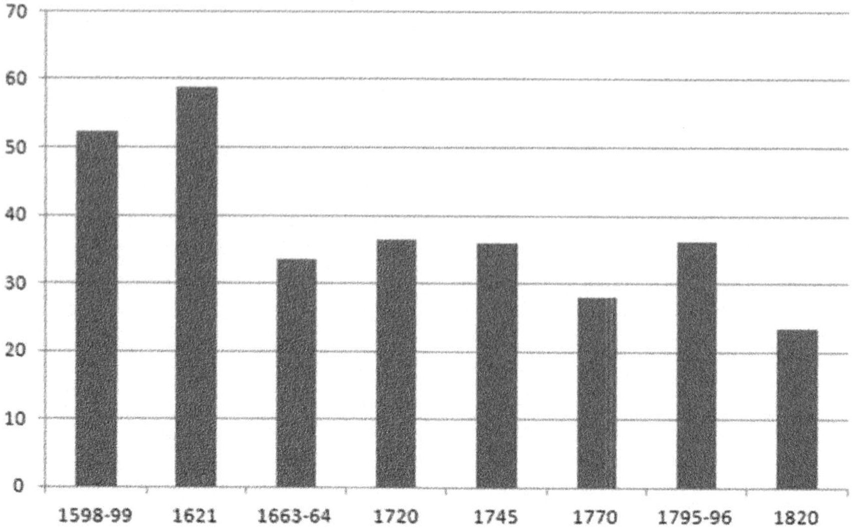

Fig. 3.6 *Child mortality in the Isle of Man 1598–1820. By percentage.*

Lycence'.[120] But by the beginning of the eighteenth century, so many boys and girls aged sixteen or seventeen were being granted licences to emigrate that it became necessary to impose a statutory limitation in order to prevent 'the utter Decay [of the Island], not only of Husbandry and Tillage, but also of all Kind of Trade, being thus drained of its useful Strength and Substance'.[121] Yet many boys went to sea legitimately, as young deckhands and as skilled navigators and marine engineers, and from the second half of the eighteenth century many of these were trained in the mathematical school in Peel or at Peter Fannin's navigation school in Douglas.

Whether they were grammar school boys, apprentices, or young farm workers or servants, every Manx teenage boy was at risk from the scourge of press gang raids. John Gell, who became curate of St Marks in the late eighteenth century, was taught by Philip Moore at Douglas grammar school until the age of fourteen, when his father sent him to Captain Fannin's school to learn navigation. At sixteen he was indentured 'in the seafaring line' to Joseph Bacon, a Douglas merchant. Like other streetwise boys, he evaded press gangs operating in Douglas, only to be pressed by a Liverpool gang in Runcorn. He and his friends made their escape in fine style: 'When we had walked with

120 *Statutes*, vol. 1, 117.

121 *Statutes*, vol. 1, 191–92. Emigration from the Island was particularly high in the late 1760s, 1792 and the early 1820s. See R.E.C. Forster, 'Aspects of Manx Emigration: 1750–1850', *PIMNHAS*, 10:1 (1989–90), 26–31.

them more than a mile,' he wrote in his journal, '... we made a sudden stop, resolved to conquer or die on the spot, and forthwith a desperate engagement took place ... they at last made off, and our bloody engagement ended, leaving us the glory of the field.'[122]

There has been no comprehensive analysis of infant and child mortality in the Isle of Man, but a snapshot of evidence in the parish registers, beginning with the first extant records in Ballaugh in 1598, indicates that from the mid-seventeenth century, Island rates were comparable to those in England, where around thirty percent of children did not survive beyond the age of fifteen.[123]

For those who did survive, the assessments of Blundell, Sacheverell and Quayle suggest that from the seventeenth century to well into the nineteenth century, daily life for most Manx children and adolescents was no harsher than that of their contemporaries in much of England and Wales.

EDUCATION AND LITERACY

Michael Hoy

Introduction

Educational provision in the Isle of Man was haphazard and available to very few children until the late 1660s, when Isaac Barrow, the Island's bishop and governor, established and endowed free English language primary schools, together with grammar and academic schools for the most able. This marked the beginning of a comprehensive system of education which subsequently benefited from the support of bishops like Wilson and Hildesley and continued until Tynwald's Education Act of 1872 made government responsible for education. Other charitable schools at elementary and secondary levels outside the framework of the established church provided additional resources for Island children and played an increasingly prominent role in the early years of the nineteenth century. The provision of schools gave new opportunities to every Manx boy and girl, and, although the poorest in society were slow to take school places, over time the schools fostered the development of literacy in the challenging context of a Manx Gaelic society in which there were no printed vernacular books until the prayer book and bible translations of the mid-eighteenth century.[124]

122 J. Gell, *Journal,* Manx Society, 30 (1880), 5, 9–10.

123 L. Stone, *The Family, Sex and Marriage in England 1600–1800* (London, 1977), 68, 81–82.

124 *The Book of Common Prayer ... translated into Manks, for the Use of the Diocese of Mann* (London, 1765); *Yn Vible Casherick (Manx Gaelic Bible)* (Whitehaven, 1771, 1772, 1773, 1775).

Education before 1663

Although the Cistercian Rushen Abbey was not a teaching house, it was the Island's centre of scholarship, and before the dissolution of the monasteries, it received one third of the tithe revenue 'for education of youth, and relief of the poor'.[125] Educational provision continued after 1540 when the abbey third came into the possession of the Crown, and in 1589 Bishop John Meryck wrote to William Camden: 'The Clergy here ... have had their whole education in the Island. They are not any ways taxed with ignorance'.[126] William Stanley, sixth earl of Derby, dealt the cause of education a blow in 1610, however, when he annexed the abbey tithes. The consequent decline in the provision of education is evidenced in Bishop William Foster's visitation of 1634, which recorded that most of the clergy were 'illiterate men brought up in the island in secular professions'.[127]

Secular schooling was provided in the castle garrisons for the sons of the lord's officers.[128] There was also some educational provision in the four towns, but this was patchy as funds reserved for schooling were often unscrupulously raided.[129] The Royalist exile William Blundell gave a positive assessment, commending Earl James for his 'pious uses [... of] our abbey lands' to provide 'in every one of those 4 towns ... a free school to teach you'.[130] According to A.W. Moore, however, the revenues were a timely windfall which Earl James spent on his household and garrisons.[131] James Chaloner, Fairfax's commissioner and future governor, recorded in 1653 that part of the sequestered diocesan income was being used 'for the maintaining of Free-Schooles *i.e.* at Castletown, Peel, Douglas, and Ramsey'.[132]

125 *Civil and Ecclesiastical Records and Documents of the Isle of Man and Diocese of Sodor and Man*, W.P. Ward (ed) (London, 1837), 37.

126 P.J. Davey and J.R. Roscow, *Rushen Abbey and the Dissolution of the Monasteries in the Isle of Man* (Isle of Man, 2010), 30; W. Camden, *Britain, or a Chorographicall description of ... England, Scotland and Ireland*, E. Gibson (ed), 1st edn (London, 1695), 1070.

127 MNH MS 09756, Diocesan Archives, Bishop Foster's Visitation, 1634; see also *JMM*, 2:28 (1931), 25–27, 28–29 (docs 8, 10), 2:29 (1931), 33–37 (docs 13, 14, 15); 2:30 (1932), 41–42 (doc. 18); 2:31 (1932), 54–57 (docs 21, 22); 2:32 (1932), 67–69 (docs 31, 33, 34).

128 MNH MS 10058 (Ingates and outgates), folders 1578–79 and 1599.

129 *Monumenta*, 225–26; W. Cubbon, 'Early Schools and Scholarship in Mann', *PIMNHAS*, 3:1 (1925–26), 113.

130 J. Stanley (seventh earl of Derby), 'History and Antiquities of the Isle of Man' (Letter to Charles Stanley, 1643), in W. Mackenzie (ed), *Legislation by three of the thirteen Stanleys, Kings of Man*, Manx Society, 3 (1860), 18; MNH MS 00049 C, W. Blundell, 'A History of the Isle of Man (1648–56)', (1), 159.

131 Moore, *Sodor and Man*, 145; Moore, *Isle of Man*, vol. 1, 365 n.

132 J. Chaloner, *A Short Treatise of the Isle of Man* (1653–56), fol. 13.

The provision of primary schools taught by the clergy was left to the initiative of the parishes and for the most part, even on Chaloner's watch, this was at best haphazard. Many parishes were without schools before 1660 and the situation at the Restoration is far from clear.[133] The grammar schools recorded by Chaloner had gone, but a garrison school was still being taught in Castletown and there were some parochial schools.[134]

Bishop Barrow's schools and endowments, 1663 to 1671

William Sacheverell, writing in 1692, praised Isaac Barrow as 'a man of public spirit, and great design'.[135] When Barrow came to the Isle of Man as bishop in the summer of 1663, its church had been without effective leadership for 20 years. He was horrified to find 'the people, for the most part, loose and vicious in their lives, rude and barbarous in their behaviour; and … without any true sense of religion … for they had no means of instruction'. His strategy for reform was 'to acquaint the people with the English tongue … and for this purpose to set up an English school in every parish'.[136] Manx Gaelic-speaking children, boys and girls, would learn English in primary schools accessible to all and free to those who could not afford a fee. To pay for the schools and the clergy who taught them, Barrow used the income of the impropriated abbey tithes, which he bought from Charles Stanley, eighth earl of Derby, together with an annuity from Charles II.[137]

133 MNH MS 09864 GR1/4 (Lib.Irrot., Warrants), petition to Chaloner and reply (n.d. – probably November/December 1658), end page; Chaloner, *Treatise*, fol. 17.

134 In 1663 Isaac Barrow recorded: 'A Grammar School was also wanting.' See W. Butler, *The Memoirs of Mark Hildesley D.D., Lord Bishop of Sodor and Man* (London, 1799), 305.

135 W. Sacheverell, *An Account of the Isle of Man, its Inhabitants, Language, Soil, Remarkable Curiosities, the Succession of its Kings and Bishops, down to the Eighteenth Century,* (c.1694) (London, 1702), 118.

136 MNH MS 09782 (CRP), assorted ecclesiastical documents (Box 2 of 3 at 2014); Butler, *Hildesley*, 304–05. Barrow knew nothing of Bishop Phillips's translation of the Prayer Book (1610), which had existed only in manuscript.

137 A. Wood, *Athenæ Oxonienses. An Exact History of all the Writers and Bishops Who have had their Education in the University of Oxford […] to which are added the Fasti or Annals of the said University* (1691–92), 3rd edn, P. Bliss (ed), 4 vols (London and Oxford, 1813–20), vol. 2, 1141. By 1669 benefactors had contributed £916 8s. 4d. A list compiled in Jurby the following year recorded a total of £1041 8s. 4d.: J. McHutchin and G. Quirk (eds), *The Isle of Man Charities* (Liverpool, 1831), 2, 4, 11. By comparison, according to the Cumbrian traveller Thomas Denton, the total revenue from Island lands received by the Stanleys in 1681 was £1500: T. Denton, 'A Description of the Isle of Man and its Customes' (1681), G.W. Wood (ed), *YLM*, 3 (1898–99), 442; MNH MS 09609, W. Fitzsimmons, 'History of the Isle of Man' (unpublished manuscript, 1805), 173–74. This was the rent reserved by James I when he returned the crown's leases on the former monastic properties to William Stanley, sixth earl of Derby, in 1609/10.

Fig. 3.7 *St Mary's Chapel, Castletown. Grammar school boys were taught here on Bishop Barrow's Impropriate Fund endowment, probably from 1668 until 1931. Photo: Charles Guard.*

In 1666 the first petty (primary) schools were set up, together with a grammar school in Castletown.[138]

Once the arrangements for the petty and grammar schools had been completed, Barrow turned to the education of young men who would in due time become the Island's clergy. To provide a tertiary level of education, he set up two endowments to provide scholarships and to pay the salary of an academic master skilled in 'logick, philosophy, and history'.[139] By 1669 he was

138 *Charities*, 11; MNH MS 09709 (AP) 136/2, 8 February 1667/8; MNH MS 09767/1/2, Malew register, 23, 7 March 1671. In the revised secretarial copy (c.1668) of his 1663 report, Barrow recorded that 'the Grammar Schoole ... is alsoe there allready settled with a stipend of 30*l*. p. annum': MNH MS 09782 (CRP), assorted ecclesiastical documents (Box 2 of 3 at 2014); MNH MS 06575 (Stevensons of Balladoole), box 3, T. Stowell, 'The Free Grammar School of Castletown'. The grammar school students were being taught in St Mary's chapel when Bishop Wilson arrived in 1698; N.V. Crampton, 'Schools in Mann', *PIMNHAS*, 5:5 (1954–56), plates facing 487 & 488.

139 *Charities*, 4, 24–26; MNH MS 01507 C, Academic Master's Fund (1827 compilation), fol. 1r; Wood, *Athenæ*, 4, 809.Barrow signed his Academic Students' Fund trust deed on 7 July 1668. The original deed, transcribed in Charities, 32–34, is lodged in MNH archives but cannot be located. See also Cruttwell, *Wilson*, vol. 1, 369; MNH MS

ready to put this into effect, but in the late summer his health broke down and he left the Island. In one of his last orders he instructed his vicars general to 'Have a speciall Care to see that ye severall schools of this Island bee diligently kept and observed'.[140]

Within a few months Barrow had recovered sufficiently to accept the diocese of St Asaph. He retained Sodor and Man *in commendam* for a further year, and to ensure that the schools were not lost by default in his absence, he enlisted the help of Earl Charles, who ordered all his tenants 'to send their eldest sonnes and all other their children to such pettie schools as they are capable'.[141] But this initiative was short-lived. The schools suffered from the indifference of later bishops, and by the 1690s the grammar school was in a parlous state. Barrow's endeavours to promote tertiary education had also achieved limited success. By 1698 the situation was desperate, prompting Sacheverell to advise the new bishop, Thomas Wilson, that he was coming to a diocese whose 'Church has been sinking into a heap of ruins.'.[142]

Elementary education in the episcopates of Wilson and Hildesley 1698–1772

Wilson acted quickly. Within five years there were schools in every parish again.[143] In 1703 he made primary education compulsory by statute, which required 'all persons ... to send their children ... to some petty school, and to continue them there until the said children can read English distinctly'.[144] He encouraged poor parents to comply by insisting that all who could not afford to pay were 'to be taught gratis'. His Education Act endorsed Barrow's instructions of 1668, and it remained on the statute book until Tynwald's Elementary Education Act of 1872.[145]

All that Wilson had achieved was put at risk by the two defining crises of the eighteenth century: the transfer of the lordship to the Atholls in 1736 and revestment to the British Crown in 1765. One of the first actions of James

---

00482C (QBHP): Richard Wilson's survey of 1768 recorded 'the Gross contents of the sd Estate of Ballagilley & Hango Hill is in English Statute measure 211a. 2r. 29p.' Barrow's acquisition of Hango Hill farm was controversial; there was already a leaseholder, John Lace, and the Keys took his part, but with Charles Stanley's support Barrow used his powers as governor to convene a clandestine abbey court which awarded him the lease; M.J. Hoy, *Isaac Barrow: his Life and Legacy* (Douglas, 2010), 49–50.

140 MNH MS 10194 (Lib.Caus.), 15 July 1669.

141 MNH MS 09756, Diocesan Archives, Impropriate Fund, box 1 of 2, doc. 23, [Charles] Derby to Henry Nowell (Deputy Governor), 2 January 1671/2.

142 Sacheverell, *Account*, letter: Sacheverell to Bishop Wilson, 103.

143 Stowell, *Wilson*, 93.

144 *Statutes*, vol. 1, 158: Ecclesiastical Constitutions, 1703–04, para 9.

145 *Statutes*, vol. 4, 57–94.

Murray, second duke of Atholl, was to annul the tithe agreement Barrow had made with Charles Stanley in 1668. At a stroke, the impropriate fund was lost. The situation remained precarious, notwithstanding a collateral that Barrow had negotiated with Earl Charles, but a generous endowment from Lady Elizabeth Hastings of Ledston in 1739 helped to alleviate the plight of the clergy and schools.[146] Funding was eventually restored in 1758.[147]

The constitutional crisis of 1765 rocked the Island to its core.[148] The Mischief and Revestment Acts had immediate effect. What had been celebrated as 'a place of trade and liberty' was transformed, as Philip Moore lamented to Bishop Mark Hildesley, Wilson's successor, into 'Nothing now but Anarchy & Confusion'.[149] During the decade of political and legislative paralysis that followed, the only instrument of administration that operated with any degree of effectiveness was the church, and so the schools continued, despite the uncertainties of the time.

Hildesley championed education no less than Wilson, but he was sceptical of the value of teaching English to Manx children, who are 'taught to read ... the English Bibles; which numbers can do very roundly, whilst they scarce understand the meaning of a single sentence; nay, I might say, I believe, of some, a *single word!*'[150] He promoted the formal use of Manx Gaelic in church and school and coordinated the completion of Wilson's project to translate the bible and prayer book into Manx Gaelic. It is therefore not surprising that he advocated primary education in Manx Gaelic.[151]

A valuable summary of the state of elementary education in the Island towards the end of Hildesley's episcopate is found in a letter written by Philip Moore in the autumn of 1768, just over 100 years after the establishment of the first of Barrow's schools. Moore confirmed that 'there is an English petty school, with a small endowment, in every parish; where the children are taught to read and write, and instructed in the principles of the Christian Religion'.[152]

146 C.E. Medhurst, *The Life of Lady Elizabeth Hastings* (Leeds, 1914), 223–24; G. Bray (ed), *Records of Convocation 1: Sodor and Man 1229–1877* (Woodbridge, 2005), 200–01; *Charities*, 40–41.

147 MNH MS 06568 MD 436/17/4 (Harrison), 'Tripartite Indenture: Collateral Security', 24 January 1675/6; *Charities*, 11, 13, Orders of Chancery, 7 July 1757 & 11 May 1758.

148 D. Craine, 'A Manx merchant of the eighteenth century', *PIMNHAS*, 4:4 (1942), 655–56.

149 MNH MS 09309, Diocesan records, Philip Moore to Hildesley, 26 June 1765.

150 Butler, *Hildesley*, 42.

151 Butler, *Hildesley*, 41–46.

152 Butler, *Hildesley*, 571.

The grammar and academic schools 1698–1772

Wilson addressed the problems of the grammar and academic schools right at the start of his episcopate. He appointed a well-qualified grammar school master, James Makon, partitioned St Mary's Chapel 'to fit it for two convenient Schooles', built an annex and made 'the Grammar Schooll House ... more commodious ... for the use of the Scholars'.[153] For the academic students he appointed William Ross, a well-qualified Scotsman, and in 1710 he moved the academic school into a new library which he built largely at his own cost.[154]

Makon and Ross served the schools well. A petition of 1763 to the House of Keys noted that 'between forty & fifty Youths at a time' were being taught each year in the grammar school from 1700 to 1736.[155] The academic school also flourished under Ross. In 1757 Thomas Fargher, Thomas Moore and Richard Stevenson, members of the Keys, proudly celebrated the record of the academic school which 'has produced many ingenious scholars who were and still are an honour to this Island'.[156]

Wilson also set up a grammar school in Douglas which he described as 'much the richest, the best market and most populous of any in the whole island'.[157] In 1705 he assigned £250 (Irish) from Barrow's academic endowments to extend the town's petty school in Bond Street 'for the use of a Grammar Schoole in the town of Douglas,' and he also established a library for the scholars.[158] The school's first master was William Walker, an outstanding teacher according to Wilson, of 'a true judicial mind ... [and] sagacity'.[159]

By 1735, however, the Doulgas school was in a wretched state. Philip Moore reported that it was 'kept by ... a dissipated youth, who pawned at the ale-house several of the books belonging to the Chapel'.[160] Wilson acted quickly and appointed Moore to the grammar school. He was a fine teacher, according to Hildesley, 'eminently distinguished as the divine, the gentleman and the scholar'.[161]

153 MNH MS 10194 (Lib.Caus.), 16 June 1698 & 9 August 1704, Articles of Agreement with Thomas Looney; A.M. Cubbon, 'The Mediaeval Chapel of St Mary's, Castletown, later the Castletown Grammar School', *PIMNHAS*, 7:3 (1968), 328–330, 335.

154 MNH MS 00810 C, 88: 'Will: Ross A.M.'; Lib.Canc. 1704, 18 (Malew). Wilson's library occupied the site of the present old House of Keys building.

155 MNH MS 04283.4c (QBHP), Petition to the Keys, 20 August 1763; MNH MD 00436/20, 'Memorial of James Wilks'; Report to the Keys, 1757, *JMM*, 2:33 (1932), 86; R.A. Curphey, 'Bishop Barrow's Trusts' (MNH MS 09562, n.d.), p. 6.

156 Report to the Keys, 1757, *JMM*, 2:33 (1932), 86.

157 Cruttwell, *Wilson*, vol. 1, 356.

158 *Charities*, 27; Cubbon, 'Early Schools', 128.

159 Keble, *Wilson*, vol. 2, 705.

160 MNH MS 09309, Diocesan records, Philip Moore to Bishop Mason, 10 October 1781.

161 Butler, *Hildesley*, 186, 188–89.

Fig. 3.8 *Philip Moore, master of Douglas grammar school, chaplain of St Matthew's, Douglas and Archdeacon of Man: MNH PG/6615.*

Douglas grammar school flourished under Moore, with an average annual roll of eighteen scholars in the 1750s, including the 'Moore Charity boys' who did not pay a fee, and in 1756 an academic tier, endowed by William Murrey, a Douglas merchant, was added.

Ramsey acquired a grammar school before Douglas. In 1687 Bishop Baptista Levinz used £200 of the Barrow funds to provide a school master and by the mid-1690s the northern school was well established.[162]

Peel acquired two secondary schools, independent of the church, during Hildesley's episcopate. Peel grammar school, endowed by Douglas merchant Philip Moore, was established in 1764.[163] The following year his son James gave a separate endowment to establish a mathematical school suited to Peel's maritime trade. Two years later Richard Wilson, an expert in navigation from Whitehaven, was appointed as master. He taught all the mathematical and navigational skills required 'to keep a ship's reckoning', and under his tutelage the school flourished.[164]

The grammar schools were for boys. The first secondary school for girls was 'a Free School … for teaching Girls only, to read, sew, knit and spin,' established in 1764 in Castletown by the will of Catherine Halsall.[165] Other similar initiatives followed: Bishop Hildesley established a girls' school in Michael in 1764, and Thomas Gawne endowed a girls' school in the south in 1777.[166]

Elementary education, 1772–1830

Hildesley's enthusiasm for teaching the elementary schools in Manx Gaelic found no favour with his successors. In 1782 Bishop George Mason's visitation recorded only five schools using the vernacular and four years later there were just two. In the town schools, particularly in Douglas, English was the preferred language for most parents; the 1786 visitation for Onchan reported: 'The schoolmaster does not teach the children Manx, but as much English as he can, agreeable to the request of their parents'.[167]

In some parishes the provision of elementary education in the last quarter of the eighteenth century was less good than it had been in Hildesley's time. By 1788 the proportion of the impropriate fund allocated to pay teachers had fallen from one third to one sixth, and many school buildings were in disrepair. In the towns, by contrast, there were a growing number of elementary schools, many provided by private philanthropy. John and Esther Taubman gave an

162 Levinz to Cholmondeley, 13 October 1687, & Levinz to John Christian, 5 November 1690, cited (without reference) in L.E. Williamson, *A Short History of Ramsey Grammar School* (Ramsey, 1977), 3.

163 R.E.C. Forster, 'The Pioneering Schools of Peel', *PIMNHAS,* 9:3 (1984–87), 275–76.

164 MNH MS 02833 C, 26 February and 26 April 1763; Forster, 'Pioneering Schools', 271–72.

165 *Charities*, 43–44; L.S. Garrad, 'Catherine Halsall's School, Castletown, and the Finigan family', *JMM*, 7:83 (1967), 41–42.

166 MNH MS 00792 C, Visitation, 1766; *Charities,* 132; Bird, *An Island*, vol. 1, 95.

167 MNH MS 00793 C, Visitations, 1786.

endowment in 1799 'for the support of a Free School in Castletown, for the education of twenty five poor boys,' and Jane Qualtrough established a girls' school at Kentraugh in 1798.[168] In Douglas it is likely that at least some of the 'many petty schools' referred to by Philip Moore in 1766 were still operating; Philip Christian's school in Peel was notably well served by Thomas Quine, and from 1762 elementary age children in Ramsey were accommodated with the grammar school boys in College Street.[169]

In the early nineteenth century, influences from England prompted the provision of other schools for primary age children. The first successful Sunday school, founded on the principles of Robert Raikes, an English pioneer of the movement, was established by Hugh Stowell, formerly master of Douglas Grammar School, in 1808. His example was followed in Douglas at St George's church and by the Methodists and dissenters. By 1822 there were 3,280 children attending Sunday schools across the Island. The Sunday School Society provided spelling books, alphabets and sets of lessons, first in English and then, in 1821, in Manx Gaelic, which gave a significant boost to the acquisition of literacy.[170]

The monitorial system of teaching pioneered by Joseph Lancaster reached the Island in 1811 when a 'school for gratuitous instruction of Boys agreeable to Mr Lancaster's plan', funded by public subscription, opened in Douglas.[171] A month later a similar school for girls opened at Mucklesgate (behind south Duke Street). By 1820 more than 2,000 children had passed through these schools, many of whom were among the poorest in the town.[172] In Ramsey, subscriptions were raised to set up similar charity schools in 1812, and by 1829 there were 75 boys and 70 girls on the rolls.[173] In 1822 a similar school based on Lancasterian principles, with books provided by the Society for Promoting Christian Knowledge (SPCK), opened in a warehouse in Castletown under the established church's National schools initiative.[174] By the following year, 132 boys and 101 girls were attending the school.

The success of the charity schools contrasted with the uneven state of the old church schools. In 1814 a letter in the *Manks Advertiser* deplored 'the general condition of the parochial Schoolmasters ... The pittance allotted to their subsistence is insufficient to procure the very necessities of life'.[175] The

168 *Charities*, 125–26, 135; Bird, *An Island*, vol. 1, 95, 103.
169 Williamson, *Ramsey Grammar School*, 4.
170 *Charities*, 133.
171 *Manks Advertiser*, 29 November 1810, 8 June 1811; *Charities*, 116.
172 *Manks Advertiser*, 2 February 1818.
173 C. Radcliffe, *Shining by the Sea: a History of Ramsey, 1800–1914* (Douglas 1989), 137.
174 In 1811 the 'National Society for promoting the Education of the Poor in the Principles of the Established Church throughout England and Wales' was established to support Lancasterian schools based on Anglican, rather than non-conformist, principles.
175 *Manks Advertiser*, 17 December 1814; *Report of the Select Committee of the House of Commons on Education of the Poor* (Brougham Commission), 1822.

quality of teaching varied between parishes, as did the number of children attending school, not least because the principle of free education had largely been abandoned. Hugh Stowell, rector of Ballaugh, reported to the Brougham Commission (which was investigating the provision of education for poor working-class children) that 'The poorer classes have not the means of educating their children'.[176] But the arrival of Bishop William Ward in 1827 saw the beginning of a significant period of improvement when teachers' salaries increased and a number of new church and National schools were built. The *Book of Charities* records a total of just over 1,600 children attending church and other schools in 1827.[177] If the number of children of elementary school age in the 1831 census is estimated at 6,000, then about 25% of the total were attending day schools, and many more were receiving a basic education in the Sunday schools.[178]

The grammar and academic schools, 1772–1830

Thomas Castley served as grammar and academic master in Castletown from 1758 to 1807. A controversial figure, his academic standards were high, but his severe discipline attracted much criticism and he compromised the founding principle of free places for needy students by demanding high entrance fees. In 1781 John Taubman, speaker of the Keys, acclaimed the Castletown school as 'the head school of the Island, both as to Education, and as to number of scholars'.[179]

Philip Moore continued as master of Douglas Grammar School and its academic tier until his death in 1783. In his will he recorded that he had 'been instrumental in the education of several ingenious, sensible and pious young men for the service of the church and other publick stations in life'. From 1801 grammar school masters John Kewley and Joseph Qualtrough took the school in a new direction by appointing professional teachers and levying high fees, but they made no provision for boys who could not afford a fee.[180] The school reverted to its former status in 1817, but Hugh Stowell recorded that the standard of teaching was very poor, and in 1837 the school opened by Wilson in 1704 closed.[181]

176 H. Stowell, observations submitted to the Brougham Commission, *Rising Sun*, 28 Sept 1822.

177 *Charities*, 57–135.

178 Moore, *Isle of Man*, vol. 2, 646.

179 MNH MS 06575 (MD 441–172), Chancery file, Depositions of Witnesses, 19 July 1781.

180 *Manx Advertiser*, 6 June 1804.

181 H. Stowell, *A Memoir of Mr F.P.D. Geneste* (Liverpool, 1822), diary entry, 8 October 1824. In 1858 a second grammar school linked to the St Matthew's endowment was opened in Dalton Street. It closed in 1920. See Hoy, *Isaac Barrow*, 90–93.

As early as 1775, Peter Fannin, a retired naval officer, established a navigation school in Douglas, but it was not until the turn of the century that private enterprises in competition with Douglas grammar school began to appear.[182] Numerous rival establishments were set up by Anglican clergy like Thomas Harrison, dissenting ministers like Samuel Haining, and laymen, and there were similarly a number of schools for girls. New subjects like surveying, engineering and navigation were offered for boys, and modern languages, music and dancing for girls. As the population of Douglas grew there was a ready market for these private schools, and, although many seem to have operated for relatively short periods, the standard of education provided by some was good.[183]

The fortunes of the Ramsey school towards the end of the eighteenth century were less secure.[184] The school was still there in 1797 when the traveller and antiquarian John Feltham visited, but by the end of the century the Barrow funds designated for Ramsey were lost.[185] By 1822 Ramsey's grammar school had gone, its passing lamented in the *Rising Sun*, which asked 'how … a once flourishing institution is permitted to fall into ruins'.[186]

In Peel, the endowed mathematical school flourished for 20 years under Richard Wilson. In 1784 he listed 95 boys as foundation scholars, educated by him on free places since 1768.[187] The school's success attracted additional benefactions to assist poor boys, among them a gift from William Mylrea.[188] The grammar school was less successful, but towards the end of the century, the appointment of John Stowell provided stability and good teaching.

The fortunes of both Peel schools declined rapidly after 1800. James McCrone, the Crown agent, reported that the mathematical school was 'the worst conducted charity school perhaps on the face of the earth – the master is a worthless drunkard [who] has no scholars because in fact from his habits he is unable to teach any'.[189] The condition of the grammar school was no better, and by the time an investigation had been ordered by the Keys in 1824, there had been almost no effective secondary education in Peel for over twenty years. The inspectors discovered that the mathematical school had been converted into an alehouse where 'filth and disorder seemed to reign throughout', and the

182 J. Gell, 'Journal of the Rev. John Gell, 1789', in *Manx Miscellany*, 2, Manx Society, 30 (1880), 7.
183 Bird, *An Island*, vol. 1, 159–60, 162, 178.
184 Radcliffe, *Ramsey*, 94.
185 J. Feltham, *A Tour through the Island of Mann, in 1797 and 1798* (Bath, 1798), 164; Hoy, *Isaac Barrow*, 93–94.
186 *Rising Sun*, 21 May 1825.
187 A. Harrison, 'The Mathematical School, Peel', *JMM*, 7:88 (1976), 212–13, 215–16.
188 MNH MS 04284 (46), deed of gift by William Mylrea, 20 March 1776 (copy).
189 MNH MS 09707 (AP) 124 (2nd) 27, James Crone to Duke of Atholl.

grammar school was being used as a slaughterhouse in a condition of 'most slovenly filth'.[190]

In Castletown, by contrast, Castley's broad, liberal curriculum served the grammar and academic students well and the schools' endowments were secure.[191] Bishop Claudius Crigan judged that 'the fund is in as good a state and the education of the youth as well attended to now, as at any other period.'[192] Robert Brown (T.E. Brown's father) recorded that there were between 20 and 30 grammar and academic students in 1800 and the school was held in high regard when Castley died in 1807.

In 1789 John Feltham recorded that the Island 'afforded a sufficient share of schools for teaching the classics, theology and the arts and sciences'.[193] Thirty years later everything was in ruins; lesser men replaced outstanding teachers, salaries went unpaid, rolls fell and buildings decayed. The crisis came to a head in Castletown when Bishop George Murray persuaded the Barrow trustees to appoint Thomas Thimbleby, chaplain to his uncle, the fourth duke of Atholl, as grammar and academic master.[194] To the consternation of the trustees, Thimbleby promptly abandoned the grammar school boys and set up an exclusive fee-paying academy.

The fate of all five endowed secondary schools now became embroiled in a power struggle between the Keys and the duke of Atholl, and, believing that the schools and the discredited stewardship of their trustees were beyond salvage, the Keys, with the support of Lieutenant Governor Cornelius Smelt, set about planning a new school to serve the whole Island. It would be built on the land of Hango Hill farm using Barrow's academic endowments to finance it. This plan won the support of Bishop Murray's successor, William Ward, and on 1 August 1833 the new school opened as King William's College.[195] Castletown grammar school remained as a feeder to the new school, with scholarships provided for needy students, and it outlasted all the other secondary schools, continuing for another 100 years until its closure in 1931.

190 *Manx Advertiser*, 19 January 1825.

191 Barrow's two academic funds were merged in 1808: see *Charities*, 30–31.

192 MNH MS 09707 (AP) 116 (2nd) 10.

193 Feltham, *Tour*, 270.

194 *Charities*, 38.

195 *Manx Sun*, 27 April 1830; Bishop Barrow's Charity (King William's College): Manx College Account Book.

Fig. 3.9 *King William's College, funded in part by Bishop Barrow's academic school endowments, by A.F. Watts, 1833. Courtesy of the Principal and Council, King William's College.*

The progress of literacy

'How few, how very few are there ... that can exactly read, spell and write true English, or indeed ... but distinctly read a chapter'.[196] Such was the state of literacy across the British Isles as recorded by Thomas Lye in 1677, and its cause was also its consequence – poverty. What Barrow found when he began his episcopate in the Isle of Man in 1663 was the common condition of the poor and disadvantaged, and he planned his schools to give the people basic literacy within a pastoral context as the primary means of moral, spiritual and social improvement.

In England, formal schooling was one resource among many means of acquiring literacy.[197] But in the Isle of Man where, up to the mid-eighteenth century, few could speak or read English and nothing was written in Manx Gaelic, the means and incentive to educate children in the home, other than in an oral capacity, did not exist. Once children had learned to read in school,

196 T. Lye, *A spelling book: or, Reading and spelling made easie, the second edition* (London, 1677), introduction: 'To the reader'.

197 D. Vincent, *Literacy and popular culture, Literacy and popular culture: England, 1750–1994* (Cambridge, 1989), 69; W.L. Sargant, 'On the Progress of Elementary Education', *Journal of the Statistical Society of London*, 30:1 (1867), 82.

however, they brought into the home the opportunity for everyone to benefit from their expertise. Where one or two became literate, they could initiate significant change in the wider community.[198] The part played by the elementary schools and the men and women who taught in them is central to the story of the development of literacy in the Isle of Man.

Sacheverell's assessment of the level of literacy at the end of the seventeenth century would have dismayed Barrow.[199] But Bishop Wilson was confident that literacy would improve, and early in his episcopate he recorded his intention to publish prayers and guidance in Manx Gaelic for the people to read. He also established parochial libraries across the Island.[200] George Waldron, a customs officer who was sent to the Island in 1710, did not share his optimism. What he found during his twenty-year residence led him to conclude that people in general were very poorly educated. 'Why [are] these people so ignorant', Waldron asked; 'why [is] there not better care taken in forming their youth?'.[201]

Competence in reading seems to have been stubbornly elusive, at least during the first two decades of Wilson's episcopate. The Island's exclusively oral culture and a general perception of English as an alien and difficult language continued to present formidable obstacles. Hildesley reflected this in a letter to Archbishop Hay-Drummond in 1762, which repeated the circumstances recorded by Barrow a century before.[202] Yet if they knew little of English, there is compelling evidence that many Islanders were becoming literate in Manx Gaelic. Over the course of fifteen years from 1763, 15,000 prayer books, bibles and devotional books were sent to the Island by the SPCK to be 'disseminated gratis amongst the Manks people, in their native tongue'. These clues point to considerably more progress in general literacy across the Island, even by 1755, than Hildesley's assessment of his diocese suggests.

The advance of literacy in English in the second half of the eighteenth century is further reflected in a growing demand for printed secular material. Tracts and broadsheets were printed at least as early as 1763, and from 1774 the literate public could read Manx news in the imported *Cumberland Pacquet*.[203]

198 R.S. Schofield, 'The measurement of literacy in pre-industrial England', in J. Goody (ed), *Literacy in Traditional Societies* (Cambridge, 1968), 312–14.

199 Sacheverell, *Account*, 7.

200 Cruttwell, *Wilson*, vol. 1, 230; J.P. Ferguson, *The Parochial Libraries of Bishop Wilson* (Douglas, 1975), 61–62; Cubbon, 'Early Schools', 126, 128–29. See chapter 2, 'Religion and the Island Church, 1405–1838'.

201 G. Waldron, 'A Description of the Isle of Man', in T. Waldron (ed), *The Compleat Works, in Verse and Prose, of George Waldron*, 2nd edn (London, 1731), 112–15.

202 Butler, *Hildesley*, 421–22, Hildesley to Hay-Drummond, July 1762; P. Moore, *Address to the Publick*, in Butler, *Hildesley*, 199, 221, 228–29.

203 MNH MS 05298/1C; W. Cubbon (ed), *A bibliographical account of works relating to the Isle of Man*, 2 vols (London and Oxford, 1933/1939), vol. 2, 1134, 1138–39;

In 1824 five booksellers were advertising in Pigot's *Directory*, and in the same year subscription libraries are first recorded in Douglas.[204]

The listing of books in probate inventories can also be a helpful factor in assessing the development of literacy in reading, but for the most part it seems that books, other than the bible and prayer book, were rare in Island households, even among the wealthy, right through the eighteenth century.[205]

It is no surprise that bibles are listed more frequently than any other book in Manx inventories, just as they are in England.[206] Barrow's first aim for his schools was that every child should be able to read the bible, and Wilson and Hildesley made bibles available in homes throughout the diocese through the agency of the SPCK, much as Richard Baxter and others did as gifts to poor families in England and Wales.[207] Whether the recipient could read mattered little. A bible might well be an inducement to learn to read.[208]

The standard method of assessing changes in written literacy is by analysis of signatures and marks in a range of documents.[209] A glimpse of the state of literacy before Barrow's episcopate may be seen in two petitions, in Maughold in 1648 and Arbory in 1660, in which almost all the subscribers made marks.[210] By 1700 some of the children educated during the first ten years of Barrow's primary schools may be expected to feature as participants or witnesses in documents, and it is possible that some parents, too, may have acquired a measure of literacy from their children by this date. But when in the first summer of the eighteenth century all the Island's leaseholders and tenants

---

C. Radcliffe, 'Manx News from Whitehaven, 1774–1794, as read in the *Cumberland Pacquet*', *PIMNHAS*, 10:4 (1996–97), 414–15.

204 *Manks Advertiser*, 13 March 1813; J. Pigot, *Isle of Man Directory* (London & Manchester, 1824), 196, 198–201.

205 MNH MS 10216 (EW), 17 February 1719, 21 February 1726, 26 March 1760, 20 August 1780, 22 May 1724.

206 T. Laqueur, 'The cultural origins of popular literacy in England, 1500–1850', *Oxford Review of Education*, 2:3 (1976), 'History and Education', 1, 265.

207 R. Baxter, *Reliquiæ Baxterianæ: Or, Mr. Richard Baxter's Narrative of the most Memorable Passages of His Life and Times. Faithfully Publish'd from His Own Original Manuscript, by Matthew Sylvester* (London, 1696), 1, 89.

208 Cruttwell, *Wilson*, vol. 1, 56 n.; D. Cressy, *Literacy and the social order: reading and writing in Tudor and Stuart England* (Cambridge, 1980), 51.

209 Stone, 'Literacy and Education', 98–99, 102–03, 107. In the Isle of Man, as in England, marriage contracts, wills and beneficiary receipts, leases, leaseholders' registration or voting lists, jury enrolment and court records all contribute to an effective evaluation of changing literacy from 1668 through to 1830.

210 'Petition', *JMM*, 3:44 (1935), 54: the original document listing 102 parishioners is referenced 'Claghbane Papers', 127; MNH MS X, 14 & 81. (These two documents have obsolete references and cannot be located).

were assembled to appoint representatives to meet the Keys, a gloomy picture emerges: only 6.5% could write.[211]

A more comprehensive longer view, drawn from a wider range of documents over 30 years from 1695, gives evidence of some progress in written literacy.[212] Analysis shows that the percentage of signatures proportional to marks doubled in ten years to an average of 12% by 1705, 35 years after the establishment of Barrow's first schools. This delay before evidence of real progress may be observed accords with a generally accepted estimate that there is a time-lag of 35 years before the results of childhood schooling are reflected in documentary evidence.[213] Over the next ten years, the proportion of signatures rises by another 6% and then gathers pace to reach an average of 29% by 1725 (with more than 35% in three of the years). By far the greater number of signatures proportionate to marks occurs in Chancery and Exchequer Court records, where many of the actions were brought by merchants and retailers, the new 'middling sort' in society, described by Sacheverell as 'men of parts and business'.[214] Most of these men and women have Manx names and had come through the Island schools. The long gap before the first real signs of significant growth in written literacy appear seems at first to suggest that Barrow's strategy had very limited success, but it accords with the 35-year time-lag, and what happened in the Isle of Man is matched by similar outcomes in Scotland and Wales.[215]

The take-up of places at the Island's grammar schools is another indicator that the primary schools, at least in the towns, were providing a significant number of literate boys. James Wilks claimed that 40 to 50 boys were being taught at the grammar school in Castletown from 1700 to 1736, and since a census of 1726 numbered the populations of Castletown and Douglas broadly on a par, it is reasonable to infer that at least a comparable number were attending the grammar school in Douglas, where mercantile enterprise was growing fast.[216] In Peel by 1750 there were sufficient literate boys to provide pupils for the grammar and mathematical schools and if the situation in

211 MNH MS 09782 (CRP), *1703 Act of Settlement: Election of Representatives*, 25 June 1700.

212 See Figs 3.10 and 3.11 below for the range of documents analysed.

213 D. Cressy, 'Education and Literacy in London and East Anglia, 1580–1700' (PhD thesis, University of Cambridge, 1972), 343–44; P.H. Lindert, 'Unequal Living Standards', in Roderick Floud and Deirdre McCloskey (eds), *The Cambridge Economic History of Britain since 1700*, 1 (1700–1860), (Cambridge, 2003–04), 362–63.

214 Sacheverell, *Account*, 7.

215 T. Claydon and I. McBride (eds), *Protestantism and National Identity: Britain and Ireland, c.1650–c.1850* (Cambridge, 1998), 171; M. Clement, 'Gouge, Thomas', in *The Dictionary of Welsh Biography down to 1940* (eds J.E. Lloyd, *et al.*) (London, 1959), 284–85; R.A. Houston, 'The Literacy Myth?: Illiteracy in Scotland 1630–1760', *Past and Present*, 96 (1982), 92–93, 101–02.

216 Report to the Keys, 1757, *JMM*, 2:33 (1932), 86; Curphey, 'Bishop Barrow's Trusts', 6.

Ramsey was similar, it may be estimated that on average 200 boys across the Island were attaining a sufficient standard of literacy to take secondary school places towards the middle of the century.[217]

Although it is not possible to use similar statistics to suggest comparable numbers for girls, since only boys attended the grammar schools, there are clues that some girls attained a measure of literacy. There were notable initiatives by benefactors like Thomas Gawne to provide secondary education specifically for girls, and a range of evidence in wills and inventories suggests that there may have been a greater degree of literacy among Manx women than was the case in parts of rural England, at least in the later eighteenth century.[218]

It would seem that Barrow's schools facilitated a modest growth in literacy, which gathered pace through the eighteenth century and developed rapidly in the early nineteenth century (see Figs 3.10 and 3.11).[219]

In 1663, when Barrow arrived in the Isle of Man, just 3.9% of document authentications across all sets of records were by signature. By 1770, signatures numbered 51.5% and had for the first time overtaken marks. There are two sets of documents in the late eighteenth century which show a remarkable contrast with the sheading representatives' vote of 1700. In a petition of 1780 to the House of Commons, more than 800 'of the Clergy, Landowners, and other Principal Inhabitants of the Isle of Man' subscribed, and nearly all were able to sign their names.[220] Eleven years later, 1,197 (87%) of 1,376 Islanders who subscribed evidence to the 1791 Commission of Inquiry on the duke of Atholl's allegations signed their names.[221]

Conclusion

Statistical analysis of marks and signatures in court records is a blunt instrument and at best can only indicate trends, but it is the only method by which to attempt some conclusions about changes in literacy. The patchy state of court and parish records creates particular difficulties when attempting to apply

217 M.W. Harrison, *South Ramsey and its Churches* (Ramsey, 1923), 9.

218 MNH MS 10216 (EW), 25 June 1680, 24 October 1711, 8 September 1714, 1718 (date below binding), 18 November 1779; D. Cressy, 'Educational opportunity in Tudor and Stuart England', *History of Education Quarterly*, 16:3 (1976), 301–20, 314.

219 The tables are compiled from all archived court records, secular and ecclesiastical, in each year, and from selected probate records and wills in sample years. Signature evidence for the clergy, the Keys and the lord's administrators are not included in the analysis, since all were fully literate.

220 MNH MS 15544, Petition to the Commons of Great Britain by the 'Clergy, Landowners and other principal Inhabitants of the Isle of Man, 1780; transcribed with editorial comment by Cubbon in *JMM*, 3:51 (1937), 195–200. Cubbon commented: 'It is worthy of note that the signatures are remarkably well and neatly written.'

221 MNH MS 09707/10/857–860.

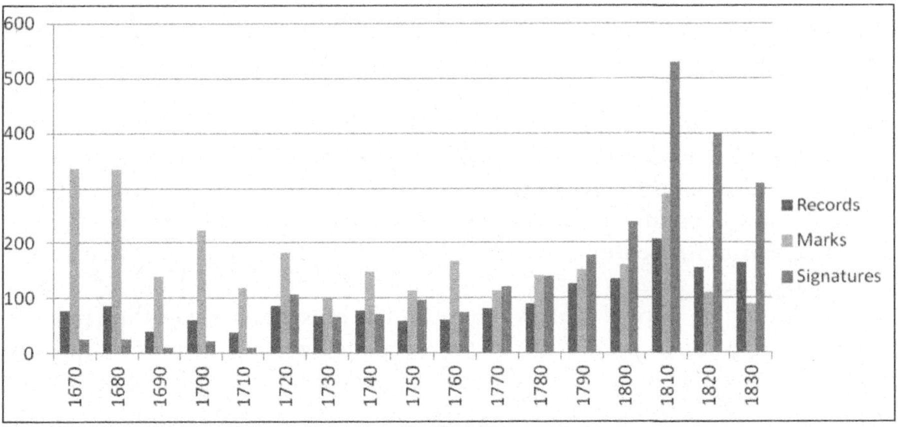

Fig. 3.10 *Signing data in Lib.Canc., Lib.Plit., Lib.Scacc., EW & Lib.Caus. (Presentments), 1670–1830.*

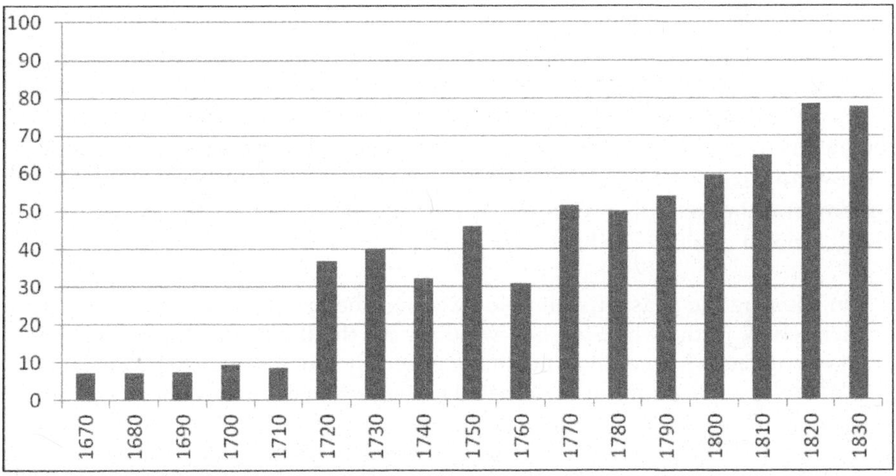

Fig. 3.11 *Percentage of signatures in Lib.Canc., Lib.Plit., Lib.Scacc., EW & Lib. Caus. (Presentments), 1670–1830.*

evaluative criteria. Nevertheless, statistical evidence and glimpses of individual cases and people give some sense of how literacy developed from 1666 to 1830. By 1800 the rate of written literacy was 59.7%. The statistics mask a high rate of continuing illiteracy among the poorest islanders, but the advancing literacy of the 'middling sort' in the towns, who were the most ready to capitalise on educational opportunities, and to a lesser extent, of the old rural tenants and landowners who had at first been slow to take advantage of the schools, is one of the most striking features of socio-economic development in the Isle of Man.

Both Wilson and Hildesley commended the competence and diligence of most of their clergy, the majority of whom had been educated on Barrow's academic foundations. The grammar and academic schools and the scholars they produced made possible the progress of literacy, civil and ecclesiastical reform, and the development of social welfare in the Isle of Man, while the pastoral and social care given by the ministers did much to sustain the poor, not only in the two major socio-political crises of the eighteenth century, but also right through a century marked by desperate need and the indifference of secular agencies.

As late as 1798, Thomas Cubbon wrote: 'The present number of Inhabitants in the Isle of Man … is conjectured to exceed twenty-eight thousand; nearly two thirds of whom are supposed not to understand the English language'.[222] But Cubbon's statistic does not imply that more than 60% were illiterate. There is a good deal of evidence to suggest that many Manx parents came to see the value of schooling for their children, and, if the assumed correlation between oral and written literacy is correct when applied to the Isle of Man, statistical and anecdotal evidence suggests that by 1800 a greater proportion could read than their contemporaries in much of rural England and Wales.[223]

By the early nineteenth century it became the aspiration of the majority to read and learn, using either English or their Manx Gaelic vernacular, and the means to do so were the schools and teachers, not only those endowed by Barrow and run by the established church, but also the growing number of Sunday and day schools promoted and financed independently. So it was that Hugh Stowell could record in 1819:

> On entering the peasant's humble dwelling, the first objects which present themselves, in the white-washed window, are the Bible and Prayer-book in Manx or English, and underneath are generally found some of the Bishop's [Wilson's] publications in both these languages. Such are the contents of the poor man's library in the Isle of Man.[224]

THE DAILY ROUND – MANX FARMING, ARBORICULTURE AND FISHING

Chris Page

Farming and herring fishing were the principal activities of the Isle of Man's economy from 1400 to 1830, although smuggling became the more dominant socio-economic engine in the Island for a hundred years from around 1680.

222 Butler, *Hildesley*, 259, subscript to letter, Cubbon to Butler, 17 March 1798.

223 D. Cressy, 'Levels of illiteracy in England, 1530–1730', *Historical Journal*, 20 (1977), 2; Cressy, 'Educational opportunity', 314; Schofield, 'Dimensions', 440.

224 Stowell, *Wilson*, 108.

There is a good deal of evidence to be found in the statutes and other primary documents, like the 1505 confirmation of church liberties and the dissolution accounts of 1540, on which a general survey of farming and fishing up to the mid-eighteenth century may be based.[225] It is not until the second half of the eighteenth century, however, that sources like the agricultural surveys written by Basil and Thomas Quayle become available. Consequently, although it is possible that conditions in farming and fishing changed little before 1800, this account is largely based on records and descriptions of practice in the Island as it was in the early years of the nineteenth century.

Farming and arboriculture

Agricultural practices were based mainly on hand labour and most farms operated just above subsistence level. In good years there were surpluses, especially of sheep and cattle, but exports remained small until the eighteenth century.[226] By the late seventeenth century estate owners and quarterland farmers had gradually adopted improved agricultural methods. This resulted in changes to the daily farming operations, especially on the wealthier quarterland farms where greater investment was available.

In addition to the quarterland farmers, three categories of rural tenants are listed in the Island statutes of 1691 – cotlers (called cotters in the 1679 statutes), intackholders and cottagers. Many cottagers, together with a fourth category – market town dwellers – farmed small areas of land.[227] By the mid-nineteenth century, all three rural tenants of small landholdings are referred to as crofters, though this term does not imply special tenurial status or carry any legal force. Whereas most quarterland farmers leased productive land, the holdings of many of those who came to be known as crofters were generally on marginal land. The day-to-day duties of the cotler, intackholder and cottager were carried out by family members, whilst on the quarterland farms, much of the work in the house and the farm was undertaken by hired servants.[228] During the winter the farm servants worked from dawn to dusk, but during the summer months they had to be up by 5.30am and work until 10.00pm. On the crofts, the whole family carried out the farming work as well as the domestic tasks

225 1505 confirmation of church liberties: G. Bray (ed), *Records of convocation 1; Sodor and Man, 1229–1877* (Woodbridge, 2005), 60–63; 1540 Dissolution accounts: P.J. Davey & J.R. Roscow, *Rushen Abbey and the dissolution of the monasteries in the Isle of Man* (Douglas, 2010), 144–76. See chapter 5, Introduction.

226 Dickinson, *Lordship of Man*, 81.

227 *Statutes*, vol. 1, 138,145–47. In the 1645 statutes these two categories together are termed 'Tennants Julaynes': *Statutes*, vol. 1, 102.

228 I.M. Killip, 'Crofting in the Isle of Man', *Folk Life*, 9:1 (1971), 61; T. Quayle, *A General View of the Agriculture of the Isle of Man* (1812), 122, 149; *Statutes*, vol. 1, 120.

but during the herring season, between June and October, it was the women who took on the land work.[229]

The farming year began in March with the spreading of manure before cultivation of the fields. Burnt lime and marl and manure were being carted onto the land as early as the 1640s and the practice had become common by the late eighteenth century. Manure, cleaned daily from cow houses and stables, was placed into a midden which was turned by hand in late winter to ensure it had rotted before spreading. In addition, farmers close to the coast filled carts with kelp to put on the land. All such work involved heavy hand labour.[230]

The quarterland farmers cultivated their land by single or double horse plough, made of wood with a straight mould board, as required according to the land type. Since on heavy land ploughs required several horses or oxen to draw them, the task was often shared between neighbours. Crofters farming relatively large areas also used the plough, while the spade was the only practical implement for small areas.[231] By the end of the eighteenth century, lighter iron ploughs with curved mould boards had been introduced. These could be drawn by a pair of horses and produced a better furrow, which resulted in an improved crop yield.[232]

By the 1750s, large Irish and English horses were being imported. The native Manx horse, extinct by 1870, was too small for plough work but was suitable for riding and carrying goods in panniers.[233] With the larger horses, a ploughman and carter could complete their tasks more effectively. The ploughman was an important figure on the farm, as the condition of the horses and the quality of the ploughing determined the success and profitability of the season's crop. The sowing was done by broadcasting the seed over the fields. The main crops were oats and barley, with wheat being grown on some farms with better land.

229 Killip, 'Crofting', 65; T. Quayle, *Agriculture of the Isle of Man* (1812), 123; MNH MS 00970/X42–5, Governor Lindsey to Duke of Athol, 5 February 1747/8.

230 Burnt lime and marl were being spread on the land by c.1650, but they only came into common usage by c.1780. T. Quayle, *Agriculture of the Isle of Man* (1812), 54, 93–97; Curwen, *Isle of Man Report*, 115; John Christian Curwen was president of the Workington Agricultural Society and a member of the Christian family of Mooretown, and as such he was able to hold the position of a member of the Keys and also be a member of the English Parliament.

231 B. Quayle, *Agriculture of the Isle of Man* (1794), 19–20; T. Quayle, *Agriculture of the Isle of Man* (1812), 41.

232 The iron plough left a tight furrow for the seed to rest in so when it was harrowed in it was at the ideal depth. I.M. Kelly, '*Twas Thus and Thus They Lived*' (Douglas, 1987), 147–49.

233 B.R.S. Megaw, 'The Manx Pony', *JMM*, 5:68 (1943), 100–04. The pony was last recorded in 1864.

After sowing the grain, the field was harrowed and rolled.[234] Oats were used for oat cakes, porridge and *couree*.[235] Barley was equally important for producing bread flour and for brewing. Wheat was grown on some of the larger farms to supply the market for wheat bread, which had become fashionable in the towns by 1800.

Crofters and cottagers used the 'lazy bed' method to cultivate their ground for their grain crop. This involved ploughing and, for potato planting, additional spade work to make broad raised beds upon which the crops were sown. Lazy bed ridging was widespread throughout the lowlands and the practice also enabled marginal land with thin soils to be productive. All arable land was laid out in ridges right through to the nineteenth century.[236]

Potatoes, rye and peas were planted in April. The last two were never grown in large amounts and were mainly found on the northern farms.[237] Potatoes were introduced to the Island in around 1706 and by 1730 had become one of its staple foods. In September the women harvested the potato crop, which was stored in a clamp and covered in straw and earth to protect it from frost. By 1790, turnips were being cultivated on quarterland farms and this was the first crop to be sown in a mechanised way by means of a drill.[238] Turnips were important for feeding livestock through the winter. They were lifted at the end of October, topped and tailed, then taken in creels or on a cart to be stored under straw next to the cow house.

By the seventeenth century farms and crofts were growing a small quantity of hemp and a larger area of flax to supply the fishing boats with rope, net and sailcloth. These crops were sown by women in April and harvested in July when they pulled the crop. It was then soaked in a pond, dried, and after separation, the fibres were spun into yarn.[239]

The hay crop was gathered in June. This crop was essential for the survival of the livestock through the long winter months and, supplemented by crushed gorse, it remained the main feed available until the introduction of the turnip. For most farms, the hay harvest was communal work. Gangs of men cut the crop with scythes and after it had been turned and well dried, the women made the hay into small stacks called *rucks*. After drying in the *ruck* the hay was

234 B. Quayle, *Agriculture of the Isle of Man* (1794), 31–34; Kelly, *'Twas Thus and Thus They Lived'*, 128.

235 Kelly, *'Twas Thus and Thus They Lived'*, 133. *Couree* or *courcy* is a Manx dish made from the husks of oats and oatmeal.

236 B. Quayle, *Agriculture of the Isle of Man* (1794), 29; T. Quayle, *Agriculture of the Isle of Man* (1812), 53–54.

237 T. Quayle, *Agriculture of the Isle of Man* (1812), 60, 63.

238 The corn seed drill did not arrive in the Isle of Man until c.1808: Curwen, *Isle of Man Report*, 69, 72–74.

239 T. Quayle, *Agriculture of the Isle of Man* (1812), 76–78; J. Train, *An Historical and Statistical Account of the Isle of Man*, 2 vols (Douglas, 1845), vol. 2, 286.

Fig. 3.12 *Cutting hay and gathering rucks in Warwick Smith's 'East View of Bishops Court', 1795: MNH 1952 7222.*

carried to the *haggard* (stack yard) and rectangular ricks thatched with ling or reed were built.[240]

Between June and October the menfolk went to fish for herring, leaving the women and children to tackle most of the jobs on the farm. Among the most time-consuming tasks were thinning the turnips and pulling thistles from the grain crop. The grain harvest followed in late August and in September on the higher ground. Women worked as a team using sickles to cut the crop whilst children made the straw bands and men who were not fishing made and stooked the sheaves.[241] These sheaves stood for over two weeks before being taken back to the *haggard*, where the grain was built into *thurrans* (round stacks), then thatched. Threshing was done through the winter months with both men and women using flails, after which the crop was winnowed by tossing the grains into the air so that the wind blew away the chaff. In 1793 the first horse-powered

240 B. Quayle, *Agriculture of the Isle of Man* (1794), 14,16; T. Quayle, *Agriculture of the Isle of Man* (1812), 65, 79–80.

241 T. Quayle, *Agriculture of the Isle of Man* (1812), 58, 128; Kelly, *'Twas Thus and Thus They Lived'*, 128.

threshing machine was used in the Island although by 1830 most of the smaller farms were still threshing by hand.[242]

Whilst crop growing was important and required much labour, there were also large areas of meadow, which were more valuable than arable land, while a significant part of the Island's unenclosed land was rough pasture. In the early period, the numbers of sheep and cattle reared locally satisfied the Island's demand for meat. This gradually changed during the eighteenth century when improved husbandry enabled surplus livestock to be produced and exported.[243]

In the fifteenth century the Manx breed of cattle was probably small and hardy, similar to the Kerry, and was found on most farms. They gave good milk for the production of butter and cheese. From the 1750s, the more productive English cattle replaced the Manx breed as the demand from the townsfolk for meat and milk grew. The milking was done by both men and women, but it was the women who produced the butter and cheese and took them to the weekly markets to sell. Cows were milked twice a day, with small herds being milked in the field whilst the quarterland farms had a cow house. Crofters only had one or two cows, which were taken to a larger farm to run with a bull at the appropriate time of the year. Women managed the calves which, once reared, were sold at one of the autumn fairs.[244]

The native Manx sheep are small and hardy, ideal for the wild mountain upland. They were gradually replaced by larger north of England and Scottish breeds. On lowland farms the Cotswolds, Leicesters, Southdowns and even the Merino breeds were tried. The indigenous Manx *loaghtan*, however, with its distinctive mouse-brown fleece, which was described by Basil Quayle in 1794, survives as a designated rare breed.[245] March and April were the main months for lambing. Any orphan or sickly lambs were looked after by the women servants in the farmhouse or by famiies in the croft cottages. The wool was clipped in June and July by the men using hand shears whilst the women rolled and stored the fleeces until they could be sold to the woollen mills at Union Mills, near Douglas. The crofters kept their wool, carding and spinning it into a yarn. This was sent to local weavers and the returned cloth was made into clothes for the family. Any surplus lambs were sold off in the autumn fairs and a ram was put into the flock in November. Until the eighteenth century it was also common for farms and crofts to keep a herd of goats for meat and milk, the animals running with the sheep.[246]

242 T. Quayle, *Agriculture of the Isle of Man* (1812), 38, 59.

243 T. Quayle, *Agriculture of the Isle of Man* (1812), 80, 87–88,

244 T. Quayle, *Agriculture of the Isle of Man* (1812), 106–09.

245 B. Quayle, *Agriculture of the Isle of Man* (1794), 28; T. Quayle, *Agriculture of the Isle of Man* (1812), 111–15. Basil and Thomas Quayle describe the distinctive colour of the indigenous loaghtan sheep, but neither records that the breed has four horns.

246 Killip, 'Crofting'.

The crofters kept one or two pigs as an important source of meat during the winter. These pigs were allowed to run freely around the croft but were housed at night in a small stone shelter.[247] The quarterland farmers kept a larger number of pigs in separate sties, producing meat not only for themselves but for the town market. In the autumn the crofter killed his pig and this was a great occasion for the family. All parts of the pig were salted and preserved for consumption over the winter months.[248]

Poultry was kept on both farms and crofts. Chickens were bred for their eggs, which were collected each morning, cleaned and made ready for market. Geese and ducks were also kept for their eggs and meat. Crofters and cottagers collected seabird eggs, trapping the adult birds for their meat. This practice had largely died out towards the beginning of the nineteenth century.[249] Bees were kept on many farms and crofts to provide honey and beeswax, adding to the range of products that crofters' wives took to market.[250] Markets were held weekly in the main towns, with Douglas being the largest. Produce was very limited in earlier times, but by the end of the eighteenth century, farms and crofts could bring a range of produce before the townsfolk, including vegetables, butter, cheese, honey, field mushrooms, berries, watercress and flowers.[251]

Fairs were important occasions where the crofters' surplus livestock could be sold to the farmers. Even by the early nineteenth century there were 36 fairs for livestock sales. By this date dealers from England and Ireland were buying and selling horses, cattle and sheep, whilst other produce was sold to traders and townsfolk. Fairs were one of the high points of the social calendar where people from around the Island could exchange news and enjoy a variety of entertainment. There were a number of hiring fairs around the Island: the Hollantide Day Fair on the 12 November was when men found a place on a farm, and the Lady Day Fair on the 25 March was when female servants were hired.[252]

An annual task for farmers was to dig turf, the main fuel for the fire. Turf cutting started on 1 May and lasted until 1 July, with each croft or farm having its own turbary. By law, the turf had to be taken off the mountain by 1 October

247 There was a native pig, the Manx *purr*, which roamed freely on the mountain land, but this had become extinct by the seventeenth century: Train, *Historical and Statistical Account*, vol. 1, 16.

248 T. Quayle, *Agriculture of the Isle of Man* (1812), 118–19.

249 J.R. Baldwin, 'Harvesting Seabirds and their Eggs on the Irish Sea Islands', pt 2: Mainland of Man, *Folk Life*, 48:2 (2010), 144, and pt 3: The Calf of Man, 49:1 (2011), 30.

250 MNH MS 10216 (AW), 1637, Braddan: Mary Vinch (als Corkill): '20 quartes of thony 20s … five poundes of bee wax 4s 2d'.

251 Killip, 'Crofting', 63; B. Quayle, *Agriculture of the Isle of Man* (1794), 24.

252 J.J. Kneen, 'Manx fairs and festivals', *PIMNHAS*, 3:1 (1927–32), 59–80.

when the turbaries were closed. The cutting was done by the men who laid the turf on the ground to dry out. The women then carried the dry turf blocks in creels on their backs. A turf rick was made outside each cottage and thatched with ling to keep it dry. However, by the end of the eighteenth century, imported coal was beginning to be used in the farmhouses.[253]

Some farm servants and crofters were skilled at underdraining and making a Manx hedge. To drain a wet field, these men were able to set the levels, dig a deep trench and lay a 'box drain' which was constructed with the sides and top made of flat slate slabs. A Manx hedge was constructed of grass sods with ditches each side and the top planted with gorse. This was a job mainly carried out in the winter months, although smaller temporary turf hedges were made in the summer to protect growing crops. Cattle and sheep were *lanketted* (hobbled) to stop them jumping over hedges and straying.[254] These *lankets* were made from twisted straw rope called *suggane* and fashioned into two loops to be placed around the legs of the animal. *Suggane* was also used in holding down the thatch on cottages, hay and corn stacks and to make creels. Creels were used by the women to take produce to market and to carry turf. Some crofters were skilled in making willow creels which could take heavier loads and were used as panniers on a horse.[255]

The herring fishing was seen by many Manx men as being more important than farming, as it brought food for the winter and money to pay the rent of the farm or croft.[256] Daily life in this occupation is discussed further in the following section of this chapter.

Whilst the daylight hours were filled with cultivating the land and looking after the livestock, there were still many tasks to be done in the evenings. The women would feed the family, spin, knit, make and repair garments, make candles and rush lights whilst the men made or mended nets, wove, repaired tools, made *lankets* and cow skin sandals called *carranes*. By 1830 the estate and large quarterland farms had become a scene of gentility with servants running the homes and the farms. Some of these farms, especially around Douglas, were now occupied by farmers from England and Scotland, a process discernible as early as the 1500s, and these incomers, along with the progressive Manx farmers, gradually developed the Island's agriculture. This had been

253 B.R.S. Megaw, 'The Harvest of the Turbary', *JMM* 4:58 (1939), 95–101; T. Quayle, *Agriculture of the Isle of Man* (1812), 42; MNH MS 11970, 31 January 1784, George Savage (cargo shipmaster) to George Quayle.

254 C.J. Page, 'Manx Farming Communities and Traditions', *Mannin Revisited* (Edinburgh, 2002), 121.

255 C.J. Page & D. Viner, 'Panniers to Stiff Carts: Farm Transport in the Isle of Man', *Folk Life*, 53:2 (2015), 126–27.

256 Blundell, 'History', vol. 1, 125–26.

aided by an improving home market for farm produce and export opportunities.[257] The volume of wheat exported to Liverpool increased significantly after 1815, as did the shipments of cattle.[258] One of the most influential figures in changing Manx agriculture was John Christian Curwen. Through him, a branch of his pioneering Workington Agricultural Society was established in the Island in 1807 and this was an important stimulus for introducing innovative ideas in soil management, crops and livestock, rotations, implements and farm building design.[259] His report on his tour through the Island observing agricultural practice provides a detailed picture of the state of Manx farming at the beginning of the nineteenth century.[260]

Curwen's interest also included the development of the Island's woodland as a crop shelter as well as establishing it as a commercial opportunity. Writers in the seventeenth and eighteenth centuries, when visiting the Island, commented on the lack of large trees. Bishop Wilson began planting trees when he moved to Bishopscourt in 1698. He not only added trees to the gardens but also planted considerable areas on his estate.[261] This influenced some of the Manx gentry, who also began to plant trees in their gardens so that by the mid-eighteenth century a number of plantations had been established around the Island. An example is George Moore, who in 1750 bought Ballamooar and planted woodland around his house and on his estate.[262] Curwen could remember this woodland as a child and he visited it again when he toured the Island in 1810. Curwen's tour took in most of the Isle of Man, where he found examples of new planting such as the woods around Bemahague. These trees were exposed to the wind but were still thriving and it left Curwen with 'no doubt timber may be reared in any part of the Island'.[263]

257 Towards the end of the 18th century the Island's population was augmented by debtors seeking shelter from creditors. After 1815 the Island also became popular for half-pay officers and their families: Moore, *Isle of Man,* vol. 2, 575.

258 Moore, *Isle of Man*, vol. 2, 937, gives a summary of exports. These records are sparse but barley was significant until c.1815 when wheat became more important. The tonnage was somewhat confused by a scam that brought foreign wheat in to be re-exported as Manx grown, but that stopped in 1828. Cattle exports grew, as newspapers record, such as at Whitehaven in June 1824 when four vessels arrived from the Island 'laden with cattle': *Cumberland Pacquet*, Monday 7 January 1824.

259 Curwen recorded agricultural progress in a series of presidential reports for the Manx Agricultural Society, which also gave a review of the many progressive farms in the Island. Although this society only lasted until 1813, farm development carried on and later in the century a new Manx Agricultural Society was formed (1842–45 and 1858–present).

260 Curwen, *Isle of Man Report.*

261 L.S. Garrad, *A History of Manx Gardens*, 1st edn (Douglas 1986), 20.

262 Garrad, *Manx Gardens*, 26; Curwen, *Isle of Man Report*, 115.

263 Curwen, *Isle of Man Report*, 142.

He visited some of the leading agriculturalists and found that many of them were establishing plantations, such as at Ballachurry where around 1780 Thomas Christian had begun his planting. By 1810 Christian had extensive plots of Scotch fir, larch, poplar and ash.[264] Curwen was most impressed with the work of Richard Watson, bishop of Llandaff, who had acquired a large section of mountain land and planted it with 1,200 larch trees to the acre. This was to shelter his sheep, which would be allowed into the plantation once the larch had achieved six years' growth.[265] In 1824 Samuel Haining visited the Island and commented on the new plantations, especially those of John Wade at Injebreck. These later became a popular tourist attraction.[266]

Nurseries were being established in the Island in the early nineteenth century, whereas before that, plants came from Dublin or Liverpool. An 1819 inventory of the nursery at Ballaquinnea included elm, oak, Scotch fir, alder, thorn, ash, birch, sycamore, larch, beech, poplar and Spanish or sweet chestnut.[267]

Much of the woodland being planted was either for ornamental purposes or for providing shelter belts to protect livestock. It would be the second half of the nineteenth century before commercial timber planting would really begin.[268]

The development of the Island's woodland was just one example of the increasing pace of agricultural improvements that were taking place, especially after the second half of the eighteenth century. This was driven by some of the leading Manx farmers and landowners, such as George Moore, John Taubman (The Nunnery), Edward Gawne (Ballagawne, Rushen) and John Crellin (Orrisdale), and also by Scottish and English farmers who had settled in the Island, including Anthony Dunlop (Howstrake), William Faulder (Ronaldsway) and William Coulthard (Braddan and Camlork), and not least by John Christian Curwen.[269]

264 Curwen, *Isle of Man Report*, 165.

265 Curwen, *Isle of Man Report*, 165.

266 S. Haining, *Historical Sketch and Descriptive View of the Isle of Man*, 2nd edn (Liverpool, 1824), 89.

267 Garrad, *Manx Gardens*, 180.

268 G. Davies, 'Agriculture, forestry and fishing', in *The Isle of Man Celebrating a Sense of Place*, V. Robinson & D. McCarroll (eds) (Liverpool, 1990), 217.

269 Moore, *Isle of Man*, vol. 2, 924–28. Anthony Dunlop brought his family's breed of dairy cattle to the Island, the Dunlop breed later becoming known as the Ayrshire. Advertisements for Manx farms were appearing in English newspapers, such as for the 183 acre farm at Balla Kegge, Ballaugh which appeared in the *Cumberland Pacquet*, 11 May 1779, and the *Caledonian Mercury*, 19 May 1779.

Fishing

Herrings and potatoes formed a vital part of the Manx diet, providing a nutritious winter food.[270] 'Herring fever' took hold of the Island each June in preparation for the fishing season, which ran from July to October.[271] In 1804 the herring fleet stood at 384 boats, which employed 3,072 men, some of whom came from the remotest crofts in the Island. Men, women and children were employed in processing the fish on the quayside.[272] All family members were involved in the preparation work, with the women spinning thread for the men to make into nets. Even the boys had to complete a couple of yards before school or risk getting their ears pulled. Each man brought his own section of net to the boat, and these were joined together to form a complete net.[273] The men arrived at the bustling quayside on a Monday morning, each of them with his family and a pony carrying a net, *mollags* (floats made from dog skin) and a *wallad* (a white bag) containing all his food for the week.[274]

As the fleet left port, the men removed their caps and prayed. For the fishermen, religion and superstition played an important part in this dangerous and uncertain occupation. On the outward journey the crew prepared the nets, lines, weights and floats so that they could be easily put over the side without tangling. Once at the fishing grounds, signs such as gulls and gannets diving into the sea indicated where the herring were. Fishing began after sundown, the nets being brought in several times a night so that the decks became awash with herring. At sunrise the fleet returned to port with the catch. In 1821 it was reported that a reasonable catch resulted in 8 to 10 *maize*, but it was not unknown for some boats to return with 40 or 50 *maize* and 100 *maize* (625 herring to the *maize*).[275]

Women and children took the fish to the herring houses for gutting, and then men shovelled them in heaps with salt and left them to cure for several days.[276] The fish were then loaded into large open willow baskets and washed in tubs of water, after which they were packed into barrels and layered with salt. The preparation of red (smoked) herring began about 1780.[277] In this process the herring were gutted and washed, then put onto sticks and placed in rows within tall smokehouses with a wood fire smouldering below. Once smoked,

270 T. Quayle, *Agriculture of the Isle of Man* (1812), 69.

271 Curwen, *Isle of Man Report*, 115, 138; Dickinson, *Lordship of Man*, 109.

272 Curwen, *Isle of Man Report*, 126.

273 S. Morrison (ed), *Wm. Cashen's Manx Folk-lore* (Douglas, 1912), 33–34.

274 From John Seacome, *History of the Stanleys*, 1741, 1821 edn (Manchester 1821), *Journal of a Modern Traveller*, 245; Kelly, *'Twas Thus and Thus They Lived'*, 126.

275 Seacome, *History of the Stanleys: Journal of a Modern Traveller* (1821 edn), 249–50.

276 Seacome, *History of the Stanleys: A Complete History of the Isle of Man* (1821 edn), 149.

277 T. Quayle, *Agriculture of the Isle of Man* (1812), 146.

Fig. 3.13 *Fishing fleet, Port St Mary harbour, c.1882: MNH PG/2359.*

women packed them into barrels with salt for export, providing an important source of income.[278]

Nets were taken onto a hillside to be dried and mended after each sailing. Crew members returned to their allotted lodging house, where they would have a meal and drink ale. Indolence and drunkenness were the two evils of this occupation, a good catch often leading to heavy drinking the following day. Storms also led to prolonged periods of idleness.[279] The danger of storms was exemplified by the loss of about 50 craft and 21 men as the herring fleet (then c.300 vessels) tried to enter Douglas harbour on 21 September 1787.[280] Further

278 'Method of Curing Herring in the Isle of Man', *The Scots Magazine*, 57 (1795: April), 220; T. Callister, *An accurate, interesting, & peculiarly entertaining description of that lucrative branch of business the Herring fishery of the Isle of Man …* (Douglas, 1815), 5, 7.

279 Kelly, *Twas Thus and Thus They Lived*, 126; *History of the Stanleys: Journal of a Modern Traveller*, 258–59.

280 Moore, *Isle of Man*, vol. 2, 626.

dangers to fishermen came with the patrols of the Royal Navy press gangs that plagued Manx ports and coastal waters at the turn of the nineteenth century.[281]

The fishermen returned home each Saturday to spend the Sabbath with their families. While they were at sea, the farm work was carried out by women, boys and old men. Many commentators were impressed by the work of these women, which they described as nearly equal to that of the men. The loss of the men during the herring season was a significant drag on the Island's agricultural development, especially on the larger quarterland farms, with the impact of this loss mainly felt at harvest time.[282]

At the end of the herring harvest, the proceeds of the catch were divided between the crew. A levy by the lord of Man continued until revestment (1765) and a fish tithe continued until the end of the eighteenth century.[283] Part of the catch went to the owner of the boat and to the owners of the nets and the rest to the crew. The herring harvest was not always successful. There were regular periods of failure: 1612, 1648 and 1687 were particularly bad; there was a sequence of poor catches between 1700 and 1710, and a notable failure in 1827 heralded a difficult winter for many rural families.[284]

Longline fishing was also practised in the Island mainly to catch cod, haddock and skate, using small craft called *baulk yawls* (*baulk* means long line).[285] These were used inshore, manned by three to four fishermen, between October and April. In 1774 there were six such craft operating in Ballaugh parish, mainly crewed by older men.[286] Each fisherman brought his own line and when joined together, this became nearly a mile long. To this line, hundreds of hooks on short lines baited with *buckies* (whelks) were attached, and the baited line was then placed into a tray or willow skep in such a way as to not tangle when put over the side. Longline fishing could be hazardous as these were open boats; one came into Liverpool in February 1830 covered in thick ice, the crew nearly dead with cold.[287] Shore lines were also used, being shorter than those used at

281 MNH MS 09707 (AP), Bundle 145 (2nd folder) 2, 1 July 1803: the actions of the press gangs became so serious by 1803 that a memorial signed by 160 fishermen and fish-curers was sent to the duke of Atholl asking for protection.

282 B. Quayle, *Agriculture of the Isle of Man* (1794), 14; T. Quayle, *Agriculture of the Isle of Man* (1812), 148.

283 Moore, *Isle of Man*, vol. 2, 659–60.

284 Moore, *Isle of Man*, vol. 2, 952.

285 A. Cregeen, *A Dictionary of the Manx Language* (Douglas, 1835: 1984 reprint), 10.

286 MNH MS 00197C (A.W. Moore collection), dated 1774: 'Answers to sundry queries proposed by Thos Pennant, returned by the Rector of St Mary's of Ballaugh: Natural History', para 40.

287 *Lancaster Gazette*, 13 February 1830.

sea. These were pegged out at low tide. Crabs and lobsters were also caught in the season, but few other shellfish were taken in this period.[288]

The crofter fisherman gradually disappeared after 1830 as fishing became more professional and agriculture and mining more lucrative.[289] However, the sea and the herring fishing remained strong in many Manxmen's hearts.

Conclusion

Although much of the evidence used in this account – such as Thomas Quayle's 1811 survey for the Island's Board of Agriculture and John Christian Curwen's reports beginning in 1807 – dates from the beginning of the nineteenth century, agricultural practice over the preceding four hundred years had changed relatively little, and this prompted Quayle and Curwen to make their recommendations for practical improvements and more general reform.[290]

Before the late eighteenth century, much of Manx agriculture remained at near subsistence level. There were significant innovations such as the use of marl and lime, and the introduction of new crops such as legumes in the seventeenth century. From the sixteenth century, the circulation of money throughout society suggests that there was a reasonably consistent element of surplus in agricultural production. But agricultural progress was relatively slow until the second half of the eighteenth century when improvements stimulated by some of the larger Manx and incomer landowners began to be seen. Improved livestock replaced native breeds, the use of drainage, better soil cultivation and new varieties of crops improved yields, and the success of their farms gradually filtered down to the smaller farms and crofts. In the nineteenth century the influence of fishing upon the farming community, so long a feature of rural life, began to diminish, while at the same time cured herring exports increased. There were also improving opportunities for exporting agricultural produce, which increased the returns to many quarterland farms. This resulted in a dramatic change of lifestyle for farmers' and crofters' families as they were able to turn away from the traditional daily round. The depression which followed the end of the Napoleonic wars hit the rural community hard, but nevertheless by 1830 the groundwork towards an invigorated agricultural industry had been laid.

288 H.A. Bullock, *History of the Isle of Man* (London, 1816), 377: 'none of the shellfish are very plentiful accept crab, scollops and lobster are met in season'.

289 C. Radcliffe, *Shining by the Sea: A History of Ramsey, 1800–1914* (Douglas, 1989), 168–69.

290 Quayle, *Agriculture of the Isle of Man* (1810), 166–69.

SPORTS AND GAMES

Kit Gawne

Traditional sports and games changed from season to season and were rooted in the agrarian and rural lifestyles of the various classes of society during a period when people generally made their own amusement. With the arrival of newcomers to the Isle of Man who were used to different ways of life and the gradual movement of local people from the countryside to the towns, the variety of activities increased. But the basis of them all remained the same and ranged from the various elements of long-established country sports, through to formal and informal team sports and on to rule-based outdoor and indoor games.

Hunting, shooting and fishing sports

Whether hunting for food or sport, the Isle of Man under the lordship of the Stanleys and the Athölls offered the residents a wide range of wildlife and game. But there were restrictions on what could be legally hunted and by whom. William Cottingham, who 'commonly hunts at dawn and at dusk the forest destroying the beasts', was caught doing so in 1418 by John Bogington, one of Sir John Stanley II's foresters.[291] In the same year, John Merton and six soldiers arrested Alaun McJohn Andrew and others who were fishing in the river at Peel without the lord of Man's permission. Various laws made from 1422 onwards forbade the poaching of hawks, herons, pigeons, partridges, grouse, deer and hares, and anyone found hunting without a licence could be fined from £1 to £3.[292] The lord's land was particularly protected:

> Whosoever shall be found to kill or destroy any hares, with greyhound, mungrell or handgun within any part of the Lord's warren, that is to say from Kirk Santon River until Kentraugh River and from there upwards to the mountains, such person or persons shall be fined in iiiL [£3] and shall endure half a year's imprisonment besides the hanging of his greyhound or mungrell and forfeiting his handgun.[293]

In 1511 Robert Calcote, who served Thomas Stanley, the second earl of Derby, as receiver general in the Island, was recorded in the manorial roll as having

291 MNH MS 00510 C, J. Quayle (comp.), *A Book of Precedents* (comp. late 18th century), 4: *anno* 1418, no 43.

292 *Statutes*, vol. 1, 'Customary Laws' (1422), 8, and (1577), 52; 'Exchequer Book 7' (1586), 61; 'More effectual preservation of the Lord's game' (1748), 255.

293 *Statutes*, vol. 1, 'Exchequer Book 62' (1687), 144.

'a hawkshouse with garden at Castletown, rent xiid [12 pence]'.[294] William Blundell was living in the Island in 1648. He noted that:

> I cordially could wish their hares were much more numerous in this island; not that more here were desired for the pleasure and recreation in hunting 'em. You may there find a few ayries of excellent hawks. Her[o]ns also for your sport with the Lord's leave, otherwise you are to pay the fine foresaid, but you are to take any other fowls, either wild ducks, cranes, bittern, widgeans, or teal, etc.[295]

Charles Stanley, the eighth earl of Derby, ordered Receiver General Richard Stevenson in 1668 to 'allow out of my revenue unto Major Henry Stanley the sum of forty shillings towards the keeping of my hounds in my Isle of Man and this to continue till my furthermost order'.[296] It was recorded by William Sacheverell when he was deputy governor and then governor during the period from 1692 to 1696 that 'There are some small quantities of red deer in the mountains, and the Earl of Derby has lately sent over some fallow deer into the Calf [of Man]. We have yet no pheasant or heath game'.[297] Caesar Brew was paid £1 2s. 0d. in 1706 'for looking to our Hon'ble Lord's hawks and feeding 'em at 6d. a week' and 11s. 0d. the following year 'for feeding and looking to our Hon'ble Lord's eagel, 22 weeks at 6d. per week'.[298] George Waldron recorded in 1731 that 'Angling and shooting would be agreeable diversions for gentlemen here, were not the air so extremely cold and aguish. Tis certain that there is not a place in the known world which affords finer fish; I have seen eels of six foot long, and salmon of between four and five foot'.[299] In 1782 Thomas Quayle wrote in a letter to his father that 'a dearth of grouse will not be important but the conduct of the Compting House gentry amounts to poaching, these gentry will make an excursion to the Calf before they return'.[300] Thomas hoped that his brother, George, would find some way or other to spoil the gentlemen poachers' sport. Robert Busk, the young teenage son of Attorney General Wadsworth Busk, wrote in his 1783–84 journal about his many countryside pursuits:

> 26 January 1784 – Went out coursing and met with P[aul] Q[uirk] in the Couragh [marsh] of whose hedge we killed a hare.

294 W. Cubbon (ed), 'The Peregrine Falcon in Man', *JMM*, 3:45 (December 1935), 66.
295 Blundell, 'History', vol. 1, 111, 112, 113.
296 MNH MS 09782, CA1, iii, box 8, folder 17 (CRP), Derby papers, 20 July 1668.
297 Sacheverell, *Account*, 4–5.
298 MNH MS 09782, CA2 (CRP), Castle Accounts, vouchers of Petty Disbursements, March 1706 and April 1707.
299 Waldron, *Description*, 158.
300 MNH MS 00907/40 (QBHP), Thomas Quayle to John Quayle, 31 August 1782.

> 15 May 1784 – After dinner, I and Billy went to the White river to fish, caught 3 dozen betwixt us.[301]

On 6 November 1799, Caesar John Wattleworth touched on one of the risks that hunting could hold, writing that 'There was the men out shooting from Douglas in Kirk Maroon, and one of them shot the other through the body that he died in a few minutes afterwards'.[302] The *Rising Sun* newspaper gave an account of a hare hunt in 1823:

> The Southern Hunt hounds were cast off on Friday (St Stephen's Day) at Ballakilley, before a great field of members, in full uniform, and other gentlemen, and, notwithstanding the severity of the weather, killed four hare in gallant style; after which the gentlemen retired to the George Inn, where a most excellent dinner was provided for them by Mrs Kneen, in the style of old Downs in the old George; after which the bottle circulated freely, many loyal toasts were drank, and excellent songs sung and harmony prevailed – the pun, the joke and the wit flashed from every side, and the merry glee was kept up until an early hour.[303]

Team sports

No doubt many of the troops garrisoned at Castle Rushen, Peel Castle and the various forts and batteries kept their eye in at archery by competing in teams against each other. The earls of Derby ensured that all members of their militia in the Isle of Man were well trained, able-bodied and kitted out. In 1422 a statute required every officer and soldier to have 'Bowe and Arrows, sufficient Dublet and Habergion, a Sword and a Buckler, Spurrs and Saddle upon Paine of Forfeiture of their Wages'.[304] Archery skills were considered very important in England as well, and its practice was included in parliamentary statutes. In 1511 Henry VIII required that 'All Sorts of Men under the Age of Forty Years shall have Bows and Arrows'.[305] In 1731 Waldron wrote that 'The young men here are great shooters with bows and arrows. There are shooting matches frequently, parish against parish, and wagers were laid which side would have the better'.[306] In midsummer in 1793 a competition was to take place between teams of archers from Douglas and Castletown.[307] 'An excellent dinner had

301 MNH MS 05401B, Robert Busk, journal, 1783/84.
302 MNH MS 06193, Caesar John Wattleworth, diary, 1799.
303 *Rising Sun*, 6 January 1824.
304 *Statutes*, vol. 1, 'Customary Laws' (1422), 12.
305 *Acts*, 3 Hen. 8, c.3 (1511).
306 Waldron, *Description*, 156.
307 *Manks Mercury*, 25 June 1793.

been sent up for the occasion by the Douglas party', and spectators from all around the Island gathered in anticipation of an enjoyable sporting occasion. But the Castletown team failed to turn up. 'We don't want to say the superiority of our Douglas archers frightened them into the measure – we rather suppose the gentlemen o'erslept themselves that morning'. In 1825 a challenge match between archers from Douglas and those from Peel took place at Dixon's large meadow.[308] With the Douglas team trailing seven points to Peel's eleven:

> The Peel archers had now the choice of a mark, and they took their favourite butt-mark at 60 yards, from which they played the whole day. The play on both sides was on this occasion excellent, the Douglas, however keeping the lead, until the best archers on both sides had played, Douglas having six arrows close to the mark, when a veteran, not in archery but in war, shot an arrow so true, that it took ground touching the stick on which the mark was fixed, and cutting out the Douglas arrows by less than an inch. The game was now 7 to 12. The next mark settled the game in favour of the Peel archers. The game lasted from half-past ten in the morning, till half-past five in the evening, when the parties sat down to an excellent dinner; the feats of the day were amply discussed over the bottle, and harmony and good humour prevailed.

An early version of hockey is the Manx sport of cammag.[309] The word 'cammag' comes from the same derivation as *camanachd*, the name of the Scottish Gaelic stick and ball game. Both words incorporate *cam*, the Gaelic for 'crooked' (as in the head of the stick). Any hooked piece of wood was used as a stick, from a rough root of gorse to a carefully hewn ash or elm branch. The stick is known in Manx as the *maidjey*. The ball, the *crig*, was made of cork or wood, varied from circular to egg-shaped, with a diameter from two inches to the size of a fist, and was occasionally wrapped in a rag.

Matches were played amongst local teams, as travel outside walking distance was rare. Consequently, rules varied from district to district. Cammag was mainly a winter sport with special matches being played on St Stephen's Day. In March 1760, the Isle of Man ecclesiastical court presentments (the system by which the Anglican Church controlled moral discipline) examined the case of three men and a boy who were reported for playing cammag on a Sunday in Kirk Michael:

> They also present John, son of William (Willy) Cannell, Thomas Kneen, said Cannell's servant, and John, son of John Cannell, of Kerrooglass for prophanation of the Lord's day, by playing at what is called the cammag. They also present there William Cannell for suffering John Caine, his ward, a child under age, to prophane the Lord's Day in manner above mentioned.

308 *Manks Mercury*, 29 September 1825.
309 C.W. Gawne, *Isle of Man Hockey* (Douglas, 2010), 1–2.

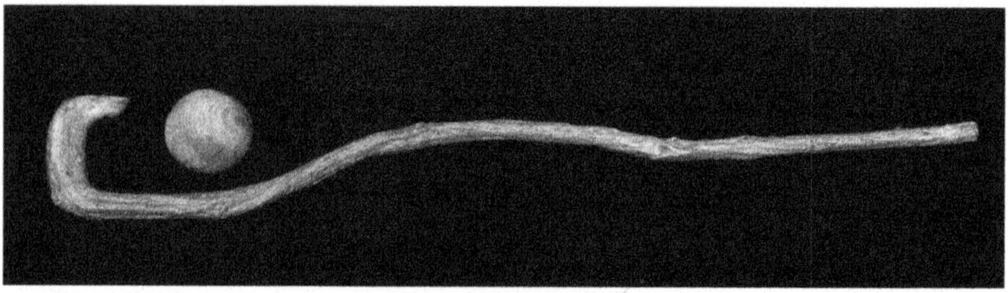

Fig. 3.14 *Cammag stick and ball: MNH 1954-6441/ 1 & 2.*

As in the case of cammag, there would be various other team sports, such as early versions of football, tennis and cricket, which needed some form of suitable ball for kicking, throwing, hitting or catching. There was the choice of a soft one made out of an animal bladder filled with air or a harder one made out of sewn leather stuffed with feathers or hair.

Competitive outdoor games

During his time as lord of Man (1627–51), James Stanley, the seventh earl of Derby, pursued his family's interest in the turf by instituting a horserace on a piece of land extending rather more than a mile across the sandy peninsula of Langness. A 1668 document signed by the earl's son, Charles Stanley, stated that 'It is my good will and pleasure that the 2 prizes, formerly granted for hors[e] running and shooting shall continue as they did be run and shot for and so to continue dureing my good will and pleasure'.[310] Whilst the funding of the £5 first prize was to come out of his Manx revenues, all entrants had to pay nine shillings each 'toward ye enlaying of a plate, which the winner shall oblige himself to buy within a year'. The rules of the race described the course:

> Every rider shall leave the first two powles in Macbrae's close, one on his right hand, the other on his left; the two powles by the rocks on his left hand, the fifth powle in the coney warren also on his left hand and so turning next to Wm Looyre's ho[u]se on his left, the next two powles, one on either hand and the distant powle on either hand.

Over the centuries, members of the Derby family have been renowned for their interest in horseracing. It has been suggested that the 'Manx Derby' may possibly be the original precursor of the famous 'English Derby' which was first

310 MNH MS 09782, CA1 (CRP), Derby papers, box 8, folder 23, 11 October 1670; Stenning, *Portrait of the Isle of Man* (London, 1978), 147–48.

run in 1780. A newspaper advertisement declared that there would be a series of horseraces held in Peel on Easter Monday 1811:

> A given prize of two saddles, value five guineas, will be given for the first horse, mare or gelding, the best of two 3-mile heats. Entrance, one shilling to the pound, for any horse, mare or gelding that never was known to win the sum of ten pounds, catch weight. Any gentleman who wishes to enter a horse, mare or gelding must apply before eleven-o'clock; if not, double entrance at the post.[311]

Two masons, John Quayle and John Aspinall, were paid four shillings in 1705 for 'mending the walls of ye Long Bowling Green' at Castle Rushen.[312] In 1753 three members of the Bridson family of Malew were temporarily put into Peel Castle gaol 'for being guilty of the heinous sin of prophaning the Lord's day by playing at bowls thereon'.[313] Thomas Whowell opened a new hotel in Douglas in 1810, appropriately naming it the Bowling Green, as he had arranged for a bowling green to be laid there 'for the accommodation of gentlemen and others who may patronize the undertaking'.[314]

Quoits was a favourite summer sport which was played by throwing rope rings, metal rings, horseshoes or stones at pegs. Four men, Nicholas Woods, William Quiney, John Cain and Robert Cowle, were discovered playing quoits in Santon one Sunday in 1737.[315] Their punishment by the Church court was simply to acknowledge their wrongdoing and promise not to offend again.

George Moore had a cock-fighting pit, arena and gaming house built at his Ballamoore estate in Patrick some time after he bought the property in 1750.[316] By 1829 this bloody pastime was banned, but there were occasions when it was still illegally going on:

> The scandalous practice of cock-fighting, which has been disused for years, has revived within a short time. The commencement of this diabolic pleasure was on the Sabbath-day in our market place, and has been continued ever since at different public houses in and about the town. We hope that the mention of this shameful amusement, will put the officers of such a police as we have on the alert, to prevent the ruinous and cruel practice.[317]

311 *Manks Advertiser*, 30 March 1811.
312 MNH MS 09782, CA2 (CRP), Castle Accounts, vouchers of Petty Disbursements, May 1705.
313 MNH MS 10194 (Presentments), Malew, 1753.
314 *Manks Advertiser*, 19 May 1810.
315 MNH MS 10194 (Presentments), Santon, 1737.
316 MNH MS 09494 (Mortgage and Deeds series), Northside sales, 1750 deeds; *Isle of Man Examiner*, 16 October 1953.
317 *Manks Advertiser*, 28 April 1829.

Competitive indoor games

Archaeological excavations have found stone gaming boards at Cronk yn Howe and Braddan vicarage, gaming pieces made out of tope shark vertebrae at Castle Rushen and bone dice at Rushen Abbey.[318]

All these pieces date up to about 1400. The scratched markings on the boards indicate that they were used for the game of merels or one of its variations, such as mill, nine men's morris and nine holes. The basis of the game, a seemingly simple pastime but one which really calls for great strategy, requires two players to try to get three of their own counters in a line on a multi-pointed square board. In 1702 John Gill and William Wattleworth of Lezayre played nine holes on a Sunday, and when confronted with their misdemeanour, they both publicly acknowledged that they were at fault and promised to reform their ways.[319]

Playing card games was a popular pastime, but when John Ellison and John Corlett were reported to the churchwardens of Andreas for doing this on a Sunday in 1659, they were found guilty and sentenced to the choice of one hour in the stocks or a fine of one shilling.[320] Cards and other such games provided all classes of society with amusement. In 1794 David Robertson commented on how, in his experience and opinion, they affected the upper class differently from the lower:

> Convivial societies, assemblies, and card-parties, are now frequent among the higher circles of Douglas. Whist is their favourite game; and they seldom play high. Cards are however introduced on every occasion, and generally accompanied with a plenitude of excellent wines. Among the inferior classes gaming is far more pernicious. Inebriation is here its constant attendant. The taverns are nightly filled with tradesmen; who, on the chance of a card, a die, or a billiard-ball, will hazard their last farthing.[321]

An infamous Church court case of 1799 was taken against Richard Daley, his daughters and his friends, including Lady Barrymore.[322] 'Lady Barrymore' could have been Mary Anne Pierce (the 'Boxing Baroness' who had been the mistress of Richard Barry, the rakish seventh earl of Barrymore) or Charlotte Goulding who had married the earl in 1792 only to be widowed a year later. The defendants were all accused of playing cards and dancing one Saturday evening

318 Information from Allison Fox, Curator of Archaeology, MM, 8 November 2016, accession numbers 1959-0346, 1966-0309, 1980-0519/0001a, 2006-0228/0086 and 0087.

319 MNH MS 10194 (Presentments), Lezayre, 1702.

320 MNH MS 10194 (Presentments), Andreas, 1659.

321 D. Robertson, *A Tour through the Isle of Man: to which is subjoined A Review of the Manx History*, 1st edn (unexpurgated) (London, 1794), 22–23.

322 MNH MS 10194 (Presentments), Douglas, 1799; National Library of Scotland, MS EB.1488, Crawford Collections.

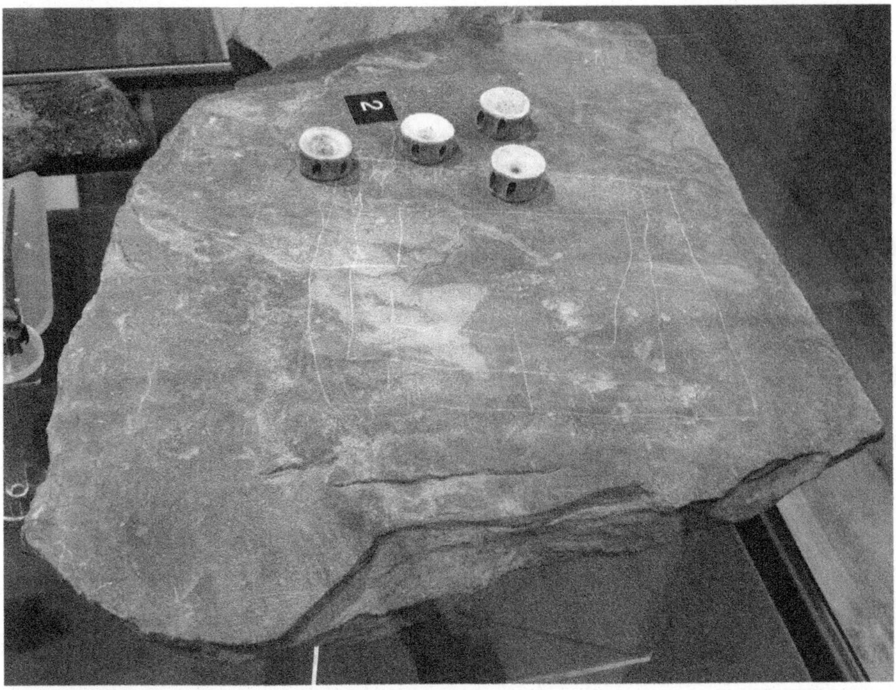

Fig. 3.15 Gaming board and dice, c.1400: MNH 1966-0309 & 1989-0159/0001a.

and on into Sunday morning. But when Bishop Claudius Crigan headed the hearing which considered the case, he concluded that the curate and wardens of St George's chapel in Douglas had failed in substantiating the charges against any of the defendants.

Richard Daley evidently did not learn from his card playing experience in 1799. A few months later he was once again before the Church courts, this time accused of playing billiards on a Sunday.[323] He was imprisoned for a few days whilst he raised the money for his £10 bond and the £3 10s. 0d. costs. A billiards table was 'put up by a gentleman who is fond of the amusement' at the house of Mrs Riggs in Moore's Place in Douglas in February 1817 for the use of anyone interested in playing the game.[324] The advertisement in the *Isle of Man Weekly Gazette* for this facility also informed the public that 'the profits will be given to the poor of Douglas' and that 'an active, steady youth, as marker', was required.

323 MNH MS 10194 (Presentments), Douglas, 1799.
324 *Isle of Man Gazette*, 27 February 1817.

Chess and backgammon sets were often included in the sale of house contents. The *Manks Advertiser* listed 'two chess boards with handsome set of ivory chess men; backgammon board, men, boxes and dice, complete' in an advertisement in its edition of 25 August 1825.[325]

Children's outdoor games

Children's physical games were generally based outdoors, and the rules were passed on from child to child and generation to generation. Such activities needed minimal equipment and included features such as physical skills, strategy, repetition, creativity and imagination. Children of all ages would have played a wide selection of games, including the following popular ones: ducks and drakes, swimming, running races, skipping, hopscotch, tip, jacks, hoops and conkers. Clay marbles, dating to about 1700, were discovered when archaeological excavations were carried out at the old grammar school in Castletown.[326]

J.J. Joughin recalled a number of historical street games which were still being played in Peel in the middle part of the nineteenth century.[327] They included the following examples:

> Hares and Hounds – This was a kind of hide-and-seek, played in the streets at night when it was dark. The hares started off from the den, and when about a hundred yards away, one of them cried 'Ahernt!', the hounds immediately giving chase. The hares sought cover in doorways, blind alleys, dark passages, or anywhere where they could hide. When a hound caught a hare he immediately yelled, 'Ahernt, you're caught'. All the players then returned to den, the game proceeding as before, the former hounds in turn becoming the hares. When one hare was caught they were deemed to be all caught, the cry 'Ahernt, you're caught!' being an intimation to the other hares that they were discovered.

> Hop the Hat – The players placed their caps in a row on the ground about two yards apart. Each boy hopped over the caps three times, and in and out among them about three times; this brought him back to his own cap, which he had to pick up with his teeth, with his hands behind his back, still keeping on one foot, and throw it backwards over his head, taking care that none of

325 *Manks Advertiser*, 25 August 1825.

326 Information from Allison Fox, curator of archaeology, MM, 8 November 2016, accession numbers 1960-0396 and 0397.

327 J.J. Joughin, 'Folk-lore Notes', in S. Morrison (ed), *Mannin: A Journal of Matters Past and Present relating to Mann*, vol. 8 (Douglas 1916), 486–88, and vol. 9 (Douglas 1917), 530–33.

> the other players caught it before it reached the ground. If he failed to do this, or touched a cap whilst he hopped, or put the foot held up to the ground, he had to go through 'fire and water' (i.e. the successful players stood in a line, one behind the other, about a yard apart, with their legs spread), and the unsuccessful one had then to creep on hands and knees three times through the arches thus formed, being well pelted by the others with their caps.

Conclusion

Sports and games flourished in Tudor times, albeit attempts were made to ban mob football. But the age of puritanism certainly frowned upon what was seen as pointless enjoyment and pleasure. The restoration of the monarchy after the English Civil War led to these diversions being revived, and people were once again able to enjoy their active leisure time. Parish festivals, fairs and market days featured and encouraged traditional physical pursuits. But the Church of England was against anything which might lead to idleness, drunkenness and low morals, and it ensured that any recreational activities which took place on the Sabbath were punished by ecclesiastical law. Whilst the spiritual and temporal authorities worked closely together, the imposition of control was solely that of the Church.[328]

All these influences would have made their way to the Isle of Man and touched the lives of the local people. The attitudes, mores and conventions of the Church, the lords of Man, their retinues, new residents and visitors would have undoubtedly influenced the ways in which folk of all social classes and ages kept themselves amused.

HEALTH AND WELFARE

Jennifer Platten †

Three key aspects of health and welfare in the Island's history from the beginning of the fifteenth century are described in this section – welfare support and poor relief, public and family health, and medical provision. Other topics, such as the incidence of famine and diseases such as cholera and the challenges and opportunities in public health brought by the development of a modest consumer society in the later period are not included in this section and await the attention of future academic researchers.

Social welfare and support for those such as the poor, infirm and orphans was primarily under the control of the Manx church for the majority of the period between 1405 and 1830. Although there was no compulsory poor rate levied during the period, this situation was not unique to the Island for in

328 John Gelling, *A History of the Manx* Church (Douglas 1998), 6.

parts of Wales and other areas of the British Isles a voluntary system of poor relief contributions also functioned. The system of poor relief employed by the Isle of Man was in many respects the best that its economy could sustain given the general poverty of the Island. James Chaloner (governor of the Island from 1658–1660) noted that 'the poverty of this island is its greatest security', a view in some way supported by Thomas Denton writing 20 years later, who likewise confirmed the poverty of the Manx, although he remarked that there was no door to door begging at that time.[329] Similarly, William Sacheverell noted that whilst there was a general poverty in the Island there were 'fewer beggars in proportion than in any nation'.[330] The situation at the close of the seventeenth century, however, was an improvement over the situation in 1658 when roaming paupers were giving cause for concern; in the statutes of that year, orders enforcing the retention of the poor in their own parishes were made with the aim of preventing 'filchinge and stealinge' by beggars.[331] Apart from a brief period during the Commonwealth period, voluntary provision for the poor was funded in part by testamentary bequests in the form of either fixed monetary sums or consumables. However, the inclusion of bequests for the poor was always concomitant with the economic situation of the Island in general, and whilst the majority of unpaid bequests were small, some such as the £150 bequeathed by Mrs Watkins of Castletown remained unpaid by the executors several years later.[332]

During the Commonwealth period, the monies raised by the fines levied upon those who contravened ecclesiastical laws (such laws falling under the secular authorities at this time) were used to provide a form of poor relief. In the early months of this system, the overall poverty of the Island is affirmed, for the first fines levied under this system were returned for reassessment as they had been set at an excessive level that was not attainable by the offenders.[333] A couple of years later, however, records indicate not only that the funds available for distribution were often limited but that the needs of the Island's parishes were variable. Commutation monies of 3s. 6d. raised from the parish of Patrick in 1658 were distributed between four individuals, whereas the neighbouring parish of German distributed £2 14s. 0d. between 15 recipients. Interestingly, on the other side of the Island, fines levied by Lonan had amounted to £1 6s. 0d., but the chief offender (20s. fine) had absconded to Ireland, leaving the parish with only 6s. 0d. to distribute amongst 12 needy individuals. The status of those requiring relief shows that over half were women and that two were

329 Chaloner, 'Treatise', fol. 44; T. Denton, 'Description of the Isle of Man and its Customs, 1681', n.p.

330 Sacheverell, *Account*, Introduction, B2r.

331 Moore, *Isle of Man*, vol. 1, 282–83.

332 MNH MS 10194 (Lib.Caus., Presentments), Malew, 1764.

333 MNH MS 10071 (Lib.Scacc.), 1658, fol. 62.

blind.[334] The church also received specific requests for relief, such as noted in the petition of William Corrin in 1760, wherein he stated that his wife, who had been wet nursing an infant, was left with sole care of the child when the mother abandoned it and left the Island.[335]

In the early eighteenth century, under the guidance of Bishop Wilson, the Manx clergy, experiencing their parishioners' poverty first hand, decided at their monthly meetings to give whatever they could afford 'considering the poverty of the place and circumstances of the clergy' in order to alleviate suffering for a variety of causes. The sum raised at meetings varied from £3 15s. 10d. in May 1701 to only 17s. 0d. in July of the same year. However, the bishop and the earl of Derby added to the benefaction in 1700 and indeed Bishop Wilson frequently added 10s. to the total raised. Their list of possible recipients was ordered as:

> First for the encouragement of … poor schoolmasters. 2. For relieving of distress'd strangers w[hi]ch shu'd be cast upon and detained in the island by bad weather. 3. For supporting of such poor housekeepers … in danger of falling into decay or misery.

This presupposes that relief for the generality of the poor was at that time already provided by other contributions. Nevertheless, for a ten-month period in 1700 to 1701, these benefactions from the clergy amounted to over £17. Accordingly, the amounts distributed varied from £1 to William Goldsmith who 'suffer'd by fire', 2s. 6d. to Jane Kerk … 'a poor stranger who was left here having lost her passage', 4s. to a 'poor sickly man who has … 5 small children', 1s. 9d. for the 'lodging and dyet of a poor strange boy', and 6s. to Edmund Cain … 'a poor boy afflicted with the King's evil [scrofula]', which was indicative of a poor diet.[336]

In the later years of the period, donations for the poor had increased due primarily to the influx of wealth associated with the running trade. For apart from the clergy, who without fail left bequests to the poor, the trading and mercantile classes were often those who were more likely to provide some form of social welfare upon their death. William Moore, who died in 1757, left a substantial property portfolio, the income from which was to provide an annual bequest to the poor of Douglas. When the Manx economy collapsed in 1765 and the demand for relief rose, however, the revenue from this bequest was insufficient to meet its obligations, falling from £103 in 1757 to £84 11s. 9½d. in 1768.[337] Similar conditions were found in other areas of the Island:

334 MNH MS 10194 (Lib.Caus., Presentments), Patrick 1659, German 1659, Lonan 1659.

335 MNH MS 10194 (Lib.Caus.), 1760, vol. 1.

336 MNH MS 10194 (Lib.Caus.), November 1702.

337 MNH MS 10194 (Lib.Caus., Presentments), Douglas 1769: documents 16 November 1769 (filed post Douglas).

at the height of the running trade, grants to the poor of Marown amounted to £4 10s. in the 1740s, £27 in the 1750s and £27 10s. in the period 1760–64; subsequently, however, there were no other significant bequests until 1789.[338] Provision for the poor, whether it was reliant upon voluntary or compulsory contributions, reflected the health of the Manx economy. By the close of the eighteenth century, this provision varied. By 1794 Douglas was to resort to extra provisions for the destitute with the creation of the Douglas Benevolent Society, for 'the Relief of the Sick and Distressed of every Denomination', a venture that was to be eventually replaced by a House of Industry, which also provided a housekeeper/cook and superintendant/overseer for the poor.[339] That the committee noted that 'the present system of giving Alms to Mendicants ... is not the most effectual ...' enforces the view that poverty in Douglas was a major problem by the early nineteenth century.[340] However, in the rural areas of the Island, the situation was very different. In 1790 the parishes of Santon and Malew were holding poor funds amounting to £15 and £20 respectively, whereas Arbory was sitting atop a poor fund of £300.[341] In general throughout much of the period, provision for the destitute and infirm was often supplied by family members and the Manx church actively enforced the care of the elderly and infirm upon those of their relatives who had means to provide support.[342] Similar provision was enforced upon the fathers of illegitimate children for the maintenance and welfare of their offspring throughout their childhood, no doubt lifting some of the burden from the poor funds available.[343]

The day-to-day health of the Manx was possibly remarkable given the severe conditions under which many of them lived out their lives. Although James Chaloner had noted the 'Incontinence of body' of the population which he believed was caused by their diet of 'flatuous' fish, other observers such as Waldron noted 'the people generally live to a very great age'.[344] Be that as it may, the population was ravaged at regular intervals by outbreaks of smallpox and less specified diseases such as sweating sickness, although as Waldron noted there was no evidence of plague being recorded in the Island.[345]

Examination of the parish registers, however, does show a significant mortality rate associated with outbreaks of smallpox. Cutting swathes through the population at regular intervals, its impact was traumatic and wide reaching, affecting all sectors of the population. Evidence from the presentments to the

338 Evidence from plaque situated on the interior of St Runius old church, Marown.

339 *Manx Advertiser*, 30 December 1819, 30 April 1814; Moore, *Isle of Man*, vol. 2, 556.

340 *Manx Advertiser*, 30 April 1814.

341 Feltham, *Tour*, 252, 259, 261.

342 MNH MS 10194 (Lib.Caus.), 17 May 1760: case of Christopher Corlet.

343 MNH MS 10194 (Lib.Caus.), 1762, fol. 4, 1: child of John Clague and Elinor Corrin.

344 Chaloner, 'Treatise', fol. 7.

345 Waldron, *Description*, 3.

church courts suggests that many types of social interaction were curtailed during these outbreaks.[346] The high smallpox mortality rate was further exacerbated by ineffectual attempts at inoculation which only served to infect and kill more of the population, and indeed sometimes seems to have caused further outbreaks of the disease, as was noted in the register for the parish of German in 1794, when one outbreak of the disease was preceded by two deaths that were due to an attempted inoculation.[347] Major outbreaks of smallpox were not always specifically documented, although towards the close of the eighteenth century, the parish of German clearly illustrates the mortality associated with the virus. During the outbreak of 1764/5 in German (covering the majority of the town of Peel) there were 17 natural deaths between November 1764 and December 1765 compared to 88 from smallpox. Some 20 to 30 years later, the figures were much the same: between September and December 1785 there were five natural deaths and 37 resulting from smallpox, between June and September 1789 there were three natural deaths and a further 26 from smallpox, between June and December 1794 there were six natural deaths and 24 from smallpox and finally, between January and May 1799 there were 15 natural deaths and 14 from smallpox.[348] The majority of the deaths were those of children, for the remainder of the population had already been exposed to the virus in previous outbreaks. Additionally, apart from the well-documented large outbreaks, the smallpox virus also surfaced in isolated incidences throughout the period. Years untouched by major deaths still involved a small number of cases; George Moore's son caught the disease in 1755, and the fear and concern underlying the simple phrase 'George is this day take ill and we think it is the small pox ...' must have been experienced by many Manx parents.[349]

Until the nineteenth century, medical provision for the Manx was dependent entirely upon wealth and availability. Whilst the lord of Man employed a 'surgeon to the household' it was not until the eighteenth century that there were a few 'educated doctors who tended to service the needs of Incomers and the small set of wealthy Manx', and their presence in the population is noted in their minor transgressions being noted in the church court records.[350] In the later eighteenth century, George Moore paid an annual subscription of

346 MNH MS 10194 (Presentments), German, 1738.

347 MNH MS 10974, German parish register, 3.

348 MNH MS 10974, German parish registers, 1, 2, 3.

349 MNH MS 10194 (Presentments), Ballaugh, 1704: Wm Quayle; quoted in F. Wilkins, *George Moore and Friends, Letters from a Manx Merchant (1750–1760)* (Wyre, 1994), 239.

350 A. Standring, 'An Introduction to Manx Folk Medicine, the Informal Provision of Community Healthcare in the Isle of Man Before 1899', *PIMNHAS*, 12:3 (2012), 435; MNH MS 10194 (Presentments), Malew, 1737: Dr Thomas Archer; Malew, 1794: Dr William Quillin; Douglas, 1798: Dr. T. Causey.

£1 1s. to Patrick Scott, who visited Mrs Moore when required and provided ointments, laxatives and 'throat gargle'. Interestingly, Patrick Scott also charged George Moore 10s. 6d. for 'stating a case to Doctor Hunter', suggesting that his abilities were limited to providing medicines and treating minor ailments.[351] Indeed, the services of a doctor were far too expensive for the majority of the population; the lying in expenses for Cath Corkill who gave birth to a stillborn illegitimate child in 1762, amounted to 1s. per day for the nurse and a further £3. 3s. for the services and medicines provided by Doctor Gillespie.[352] However, by the early nineteenth century there was provision for sick paupers in Douglas who could receive 'medical or surgical assistance' one morning a week at a dispensary opposite Cosnahan's Brewery, or in the case of 'acute or contagious Disorders' visited in their own homes.[353] Increased circulation of local newspapers in the early nineteenth century provided ample opportunity for the surgeon, apothecary and 'Man Midwife' to advertise their services to the population of Douglas, although those such as Philip Garrett of Duke Street made no mention of any qualifications, whereas Mr. Simon Little of Lord Street described himself as 'late Student at the Medical College of Edinburgh'.[354]

Throughout the period, however, the practices and services of a charmer were also an alternative that was used by many of the population for assistance in healing the sick.[355] Much to the consternation of the Manx church, the services of a charmer were frequently sought during outbreaks of disease, and some of these charmers, such as the Teare family from Andreas, held an Island-wide reputation.[356] In addition to charmers, there were others who provided medical services to the community, such as 'bone setters' noted in the Clucas family, whose skill was passed down from father to son, and midwives who from the seventeenth century were licensed by the church.[357] By 1830 the Isle of Man was able to offer to those of its inhabitants who were able to pay a greater variety of medical services, but the traditional services of those such as charmers were still used by many well into the nineteenth century.[358]

It is evident that during the period under review, as in similar areas throughout the British Isles, the medical services available to the Manx improved dramatically. Medical expertise was far more readily available in the early nineteenth century than had been the case in previous centuries. Nevertheless, the continued practice of charmers well into the Victorian period indicates that some, at least,

351 MNH MS 04932 (Ballamore Accounts), 10 April 1777, fol. 4.
352 MNH MS 10194 (Lib.Caus.), 1762, fol. 14.
353 *Manx Advertiser*, 3 February 1810. See chapter 4, Associational Culture.
354 *Manx Advertiser*, 6 August 1808; *The Rising Sun*, 26 October 1822.
355 MNH MS 10194 (Presentments), Onchan, 1732: Thos Quay.
356 Moore, *Folklore*, 79; MNH MS 10194 (Presentments), Andreas, 1738.
357 Standring, 'Manx Folk Medicine', 441; MNH MS 10194 (Presentments), Malew, 1667.
358 Moore, *Folklore*, 79.

of the Manx population were still inclined to seek assistance from traditional methods under certain circumstances. The improvement in medical provision in the Island, however, was not mirrored in welfare provision for the poor. The expanding and increasingly mobile population placed a strain on the voluntary poor relief system that had adequately served the Island during the majority of the preceding centuries. As a result, when faced with periods of economic hardship, the demand for relief outstripped the provision available. By the early nineteenth century, the social provision in many rural areas of the Island was adequate for the population's needs, but in the large urban area of Douglas, there was significant need for additional relief. Here the voluntary system that had served the Island well for the preceding centuries was insufficient for the numbers of paupers and needy that required support. In some areas at least, the close-knit Manx community that had provided for its neighbour had been replaced by a society which would require a more concerted effort on the part of social reformers and benevolent societies to improve the lot of the poorer members of society.

CONCLUSION

From 1405 to the second half of the seventeenth century, the pattern of daily life in the Isle of Man, whether for the richest or poorest in Manx society, changed little. During the eighteenth century, however, the picture that emerges is very different. Land tenure reform, the widening benefits of education, improvements in the quality, diligence and effectiveness of the clergy, new agricultural practices, and the growing influence of changes and trends in north-west England and around the wider Irish Sea – all played a significant role in developing the Island's society and economy. The pace of change was not uniform: in the period from 1765 to the 1780s, for example, the adverse consequences of the Mischief Act affected much more than mercantile enterprise. But in the last years of the eighteenth century, everything was on the move again and by 1830 the foundations of Island society described by A.W. Moore at the conclusion of his history were in place.[359]

359 Moore, *Isle of Man*, vol. 2, 685.

4 *Arts and Culture*

FENELLA BAZIN

WITH CONTRIBUTIONS BY MIKE CLAGUE, ULLA CORKILL †, YVONNE CRESSWELL, COLETTE DAVIES, MICHAEL HOY, SUE KING, CHRISTOPHER LEWIN, CATRIONA MACKIE, STEPHEN MILLER AND TIM THORNTON

INTRODUCTION

It is inevitable that this chapter can only give an overview of the cultural life of the Isle of Man during the period. Reflecting economic and political changes, and through language, literature, the arts and entertainment, it offers glimpses into the developing ideas and beliefs of both the Manx and the incomers, and the growing awareness of the Island's history and unique identity. While the early part of the period draws mainly on primary documents such as the presentments, later histories and commentaries, mainly by visitors to the Island such as Waldron, Feltham and Robertson, provide interesting insights. Newspaper reports, diaries and other manuscripts are important sources and contributors to this chapter have also made good use of up-to-date research by scholars in a wide number of disciplines.

The evidence for Manx cultural activities during this period is uneven. Apart from accounts in diaries and journals, the early centuries reveal little factual information outside of the Stanley/Derby household. During the late 1700s, newspaper reports detail some of the more formal events or give occasional descriptions of the more unusual happenings, such as the circuses that visited the Island. Artworks that survive are those of personal, social and political value to the owners. The output of the bulk of the population seems to be invisible.

Each of the following sections provides an introduction to the subject and will hopefully stimulate new research.

MANX LANGUAGE AND LITERATURE

Christopher Lewin

Historiography of Manx language studies

For most of the period covered by this volume, the great majority of the Island's population were Manx-speaking, often exclusively so. Despite this, the Gaelic language of Man has rarely played a prominent role in the historiography of the Island, and few scholars of Manx history have been proficient in it. And other than for personal interest, why should they take the trouble to learn it, one might retort, given that so few documents of historical interest have been written in Manx? Proficiency in the language can hardly be deemed essential for any sphere of Manx historical enquiry except those pertaining directly to the language and its literature – one small exception might be the value for social history of the curses and slanders recorded in Manx in the ecclesiastical court records;[1] another might be the study of place-names and the light they shed on settlement and land use.[2] Nonetheless, the story of the language and its literature is of significance for our understanding both of the cultural and social history of the Manx people and the development of Manx national identity, and of the Island's religious and ecclesiastical history.

The language has not always been marginal in Manx historical scholarship. Several of the volumes of the nineteenth-century Manx Society pertained to the language, including John Kelly's grammar and dictionary and Phillips' Prayer Book,[3] and A.W. Moore, the author of the standard general history of the Island prior to the present series, was also a founding member of the Manx Language Society in 1901 and a prominent scholar of the language.[4] After the enthusiasm for cultural revival of the *fin de siècle* period waned, however, a degree of bifurcation is evident between the broad, mainstream movement of patriotic, cultural and antiquarian pursuits, which includes the Island's various historical societies on the one hand, and the language movement on the other, which for most of the twentieth century was associated with fringe political sentiments of nationalism and pan-Celticism largely alien to the Island's now solidly anglophone population.[5] Many publications from within the Manx language movement are influenced by revivalist aspirations as well as romantic and purist interest in the other Gaelic tongues, rather than being objective academic treatments of the historical language and its literature.[6]

1 D. Craine, *Manannan's Isle* (Douglas, 1955), 22–25.

2 See especially G. Broderick, *Place-names of the Isle of Man*, 7 vols (Tübingen, 1994–2005).

3 W. Gill (ed), *Fockleyr Manninagh as Baarlagh* (Douglas, 1866); W. Gill (ed), *A Practical Grammar of the Antient Gaelic … usually called Manks* (Douglas, 1870); A.W. Moore and J. Rhŷs, *The Book of Common Prayer in Manx Gaelic*, 2 vols (Oxford, 1895).

4 A.W. Moore, *A History of the Isle of Man*, 2 vols (London, 1900); A.W. Moore (ed) *Carvalyn Gailckagh chyndaait ayns Baarle, marish goan-foshlee giare (Manx Carols, Translated into English, with a short preface)* (Isle of Man, 1891); A.W. Moore, *Manx Ballads and Music* (Douglas, 1896); Moore and Rhŷs, *Common Prayer*.

5 Cf. G. Broderick, 'The Revival of Traditional Songs and Music in the Isle of Man', *Isle of Man Studies*, 18 (2023),77.

6 E.g. J.J. Kneen, *A Grammar of the Manx Language* (Oxford, 1931), D. Fargher, *Fargher's English–Manx Dictionary* (Onchan, 1979). For assessments of these works, see R.L. Thomson, 'The Study of Manx Gaelic: Sir John Rhys Memorial Lecture', *Proceedings*

In the professional academic sphere, study of the language has been the preserve of a small number of scholars within the philological discipline of Celtic Studies. Even here the language has suffered widespread neglect as a 'Cinderella' topic, which has been attributed to factors such as the lack of medieval literature in Manx[7] and negative perceptions of the allegedly anglicized nature of the language and its English-based orthography.[8] Until the middle of the twentieth century, most published studies of the language were strictly linguistic (mostly phonological).[9] In the second half of the century, there was greater consideration of the surviving literature in its broader sociohistorical context, the bulk of it by the first two professional Celticists to specialize in Manx, Robert L. Thomson and George Broderick. Thomson's main interests lay in the translated religious literature of the seventeenth and eighteenth centuries,[10] as well as other important texts including the Traditionary Ballad and the Manx *Paradise Lost*,[11] while Broderick's main focus in our period has been on folksong literature;[12] his work on the sociolinguistic decline of

of the British Academy, 55 (1969), 189–90, and C. Lewin, 'Scholarship and Language Revival: Language Ideologies in Corpus Development for Revived Manx', *Studia Celtica Posnaniensia*, 2 (2017), 97–118, respectively.

7 T.F. O'Rahilly, *Irish Dialects Past and Present with chapters on Scottish and Manx* (Dublin, 1932), ix; Thomson, 'The Study of Manx Gaelic', 177.

8 C. Lewin, '"Manx hardly deserved to live": perspectives on language contact and language shift', *Zeitschrift für celtische Philologie* 64 (2017), 141–205.

9 E.g. O'Rahilly, *Irish Dialects*; C.J.S. Marstrander, 'Det Norske Landnåm på Man', *Norsk Tidsskrift for Sprogvidenskap*, 6 (1932), 40–386; K. Jackson, *Contributions to the Study of Manx Phonology* (Edinburgh, 1955).

10 R.L. Thomson, 'Early Manx. A Contribution to the Historical Study of Manx Gaelic arranged as a supplementary volume to the Moore-Rhys edition of the Phillips Prayer Book (1610)' (BLitt thesis, University of Glasgow, 1953); R.L. Thomson, 'A Glossary of Early Manx', *Zeitschrift für celtische Philologie* 24 (1954), 272–307; 25 (1956), 100–40, 264–308; 27 (1959), 79–160; Thomson, 'The Study of Manx Gaelic'; R.L. Thomson, 'Introduction' in *Bible Chasherick yn Lught Thie* (Onchan: 1979); R.L. Thomson, *Lessoonyn Sodjey 'sy Ghailck Vanninagh* (Douglas, 1981); R.L. Thomson, 'Manx language and literature', in G. Price (ed) *The Celtic connection* (Gerrards Cross, 1992); R.L. Thomson, *Yn Fer-raauee Creestee (1763) The Christian Monitor (1686) A Bilingual Edition with Notes and Introduction* (Douglas, 1998); R.L. Thomson and A. Pilgrim, *An Outline of Manx Language and Literature* (Douglas, 1988).

11 R.L. Thomson, 'The Manx Traditionary Ballad', *Études Celtiques* 9 (1960) 521–48, 10 (1962), 60–87; R.L. Thomson, *Pargys Caillit. An abridgement of John Milton's* Paradise Lost *By Thomas Christian with the anonymous translation of Thomas Parnell's* The Hermit (Douglas, 1995).

12 G. Broderick, 'Baase Illiam Dhone', *Celtica*, 14 (1981), 105–23; G. Broderick,'Ny Kirree fo Niaghtey', *Celtica* 16 (1984): 157–68; G. Broderick, 'Berrey Dhone: A Manx Caillech Bérri?', *Zeitschrift für celtische Philologie*, 40 (1984), 193–210; G. Broderick, 'Ec ny Fiddleryn', *Zeitschrift für celtische Philologie*, 40 (1984), 211–27; G. Broderick, 'Fin as Oshin', *Celtica*, 21 (1990), 51–60; G. Broderick, 'Fin as Oshin: A reappraisal', *Zeitschrift*

Manx should also be mentioned.[13] More recently, a new generation of scholars have turned their attention to previously neglected topics such as the Manx sermon[14] and the origin and evolution of Manx orthography,[15] and certain areas have been revisited, including fresh examinations of the seventeenth-century Phillips Prayer Book translation[16] and the Manx retelling of *Paradise Lost*,[17] the editorial and publication history of eighteenth-century Prayer Book and Bible translations,[18] and connections between the Manx intellectual elite and the wider Gaelic world with regard to the collection and dissemination of oral literature in the mid-eighteenth century.[19] The study of Manx texts has been greatly facilitated by the growth of digital resources in the last twenty years, including online searchable versions of the Manx Bible, and more recently in the form of the Manx Corpus website.[20]

Despite these advances, much remains to be done, especially in respect of manuscript material. Notably, very little work has been done on the vast corpus of 325 carvals, many in multiple copies, dating from the eighteenth

---

für celtische Philologie, 65 (2018), 7–25; G. Broderick, 'Mylecharaine: A Manx traditional song collected from Manx oral tradition', *Béaloideas*, 90 (2022), 26–49.

13 G. Broderick, *Language Death in the Isle of Man* (Tübingen, 1999).

14 C. Lewin, 'A sermon in Manx translated from the work of Thomas Wilson: Text and Commentary', *Scottish Gaelic Studies*, 28 (2011), 175–210; C. Lewin, 'A Manx sermon from 1696', *Zeitschrift für celtische Philologie*, 62 (2015), 45–96; C. Lewin and P. Ó Muircheartaigh, 'Manx manuscript sermons, 1696–1863: language and historical context', *Celtica*, 34 (2022), 126–78.

15 Lewin, 'A Manx sermon'; C. Lewin, 'Aspects of the historical phonology of Manx' (PhD dissertation, University of Edinburgh, 2020); C. Lewin, '"An English monstrosity"? Evolution and reception of Manx orthography', *Studia Celtica Posnaniensia*, 5 (2022), 35–59; Lewin and Ó Muircheartaigh, 'Manx manuscript sermons', 134–51; M.W. Wheeler, *Phillips' Manx translation of the Psalms (MNH MS 00003) Diplomatic edition* (2019), https://www.academia.edu/41457167/ (accessed 27 August 2023), 3–8.

16 Wheeler, *Phillips' Psalms*; M.W. Wheeler, *Psalmyn Ghavid. A critical parallel text edition of the two Manx translations of the Psalms, alongside the English* (2020), https://www.academia.edu/41917797/ (accessed 27 August 2023); C. Lewin, T. Grass and M.W. Wheeler, 'A newly discovered fragment of the Phillips Manx Prayer Book' (in preparation). M.W. Wheeler, *Phillips' Manx Translation of the Prayer Book (1610), a new edition with translation and notes* (in preparation).

17 M.W. Wheeler, *Pargeiys Caillit* (forthcoming); P. Ó Muircheartaigh, 'Pargys Caillit and John Kelly's Manx dictionary', *Celtica*, 32 (2020), 261–63.

18 M.W. Wheeler, *The Book of Common Prayer in Manx Gaelic, 1765/1777* (2021), https://www.academia.edu/49187655/ (accessed 27 August 2023).

19 P. Ó Muircheartaigh, 'Fin as Ossian revisited: A Manx ballad in Belanagare and its significance', *Zeitschrift für celtische Philologie*, 63 (2016), 95–128; C. Lewin, 'Lexical influence of the 1767 Scottish Gaelic New Testament on the Manx Bible translation', *Studia Celtica Fennica*, 19 (2023), 5–13.

20 https://corpus.gaelg.im/ (accessed 27 August 2023). This volunteer-run project is overseen by Yn Cheshaght Ghailckagh's Manx Language Research Group.

and nineteenth centuries.[21] These are lengthy religious ballads in Manx traditionally performed after the church service on Christmas Eve; they have been catalogued, but no modern academic editions or studies have yet been published.[22] In contrast to the clerical provenance of most other Manx genres, there was a considerable tradition among the laity of copying and transmitting these texts, which adds to their linguistic and historical value. Beside the carvals, a recent project to transcribe and analyse 90 manuscript sermons has only scratched the surface of the over 650 extant texts dating from the late seventeenth to the mid-nineteenth century.[23]

Manx and the Gaelic world

Until the early modern period, Gaelic Ireland and Highland Scotland developed largely in tandem, with a closely related linguistic and literary culture. At least among the elites, a strong sense of common ethnolinguistic identity as Gaels prevailed, although it interacted in complex ways both with more local loyalties and emerging national identities.[24] A codified register of literary Classical Irish was employed for strict metre *dán díreach* poetry of praise and satire, composed by the itinerant master poets who ranged freely across the North Channel. Gaelic literary registers were also widely employed for narrative, legal, medical and historical prose. Despite increasing political and religious separation between Scotland and Ireland since the Reformation, this perceived linguistic unity was sufficient to delay the completion of a distinct Scottish Gaelic Bible until 1801, three decades after its Manx equivalent.[25] Earlier generations of Scottish Gaels had had to make do with versions of Bedell's Bible in literary Irish, and their vernacular was routinely labelled '(Highland) Irish' into the nineteenth century.[26] Moreover, the emergent Scottish Gaelic standard long retained a strong Classical Irish lexical and grammatical influence.

In contrast, it never seems to have occurred to anyone to try to use Irish translations in the Isle of Man, and while Irish and Scottish versions of the

21 For the Carval tradition, see this chapter, F. Bazin, 'Music'; Clague, Marie P., 2005, 'The carval tradition: report on project', MNH MS 13144; and A.G. Gilchrist, 'Introduction to the Carvals', *Journal of the Folk-Song Society*, 29 (1925), 225–30.

22 The only published collections are Moore, *Carvalyn Gailckagh* and A.G. Gilchrist, 'Sixteen Carvals', *Journal of the Folk-Song Society*, 29 (1925), 231–73.

23 Lewin and Ó Muircheartaigh, 'Manx manuscript sermons'.

24 W. McLeod, *Divided Gaels: Gaelic Cultural Identities in Scotland and Ireland 1200–1650* (Oxford, 2004); R. Ó hUiginn, 'Éireannaigh, Fir Éireann, Gaeil agus Gaill', in C. Breatnach and M. Ní Úrdail (eds), *Aon don éigse. Essays marking Osborn Bergin's centenary lecture on bardic poetry (1912)* (Dublin, 2015), 17–50.

25 Thomson, 'Introduction'.

26 *Oxford English Dictionary*, s.v. 'Irish', adjective, sense 3b, https://doi.org/10.1093/OED/5342469694 (accessed 28 August 2022).

Scriptures were occasionally consulted during the Manx translation project, the Manx clergy's comprehension of them was limited.[27] While all three Gaelic languages remain closely related and, with effort, partly mutually intelligible, Manx is in practice the most divergent owing to 'an impoverishment of the vocabulary in comparison with that of Irish or Scottish Gaelic, by the loss of those elements that might be vaguely termed "literary"',[28] as well as a somewhat greater prominence of English loanwords, and both innovations and archaisms in the grammar and semantics. There was some passing awareness of linguistic affinity with Irish and Scottish Gaelic among both educated commentators[29] and Manxmen who came into occasional contact with other Gaelic speakers.[30] However, right from the earliest explicit mentions of it in the seventeenth century, there appears to have been no perception of Manx as other than a distinct language in its own. The earliest reference to 'the Manks language' given by the Oxford English Dictionary is from 1630,[31] and Bishop Phillips in 1610–11 refers to 'the Mannish Book of Common Prayer by me translated'.[32]

In Manx itself, the name of the language is *Gailck* (spelled variously), the Manx form corresponding to Irish *Gaeilge*, Scottish *Gàidhlig* 'Gaelic', but there is no record of this being used for non-Manx varieties of Gaelic before the revival period. Moreover, the ethnonym *Gaoidheal* 'Gael', which is ubiquitous elsewhere in the Gaelic world, appears to have been absent from vernacular use among the Manx in the historical period; there is an adjective *Gailckagh*, meaning 'Manx-speaking' or 'pertaining to the Manx language' (and *Baarlagh* from *Baarle* 'English'), terms which are not usual in the other Gaelic languages. The term *Manninagh* 'Manxman' is already established as an ethnic label in the Traditionary Ballad, the earliest text in the Manx language, which dates from the fifteenth or sixteenth century.[33] In contrast, the Irish equivalent *Éireannach*

27 W. Butler, *The Memoirs of Mark Hildesley, DD, Lord Bishop of Sodor and Man* (London, 1799), 477; Gill, *Fockleyr*, 89, 136; Lewin, 'Lexical influence'.

28 Thomson, 'The Study of Manx Gaelic', 180.

29 Hence Speed's (1611) comment that the 'the common sort of people, both in their language and manners, come nighest vnto the Irish' (W. Harrison, *The Old Historians of the Isle of Man* (Douglas, 1871), 37–38), while Chaloner (1653) states that the Manx language 'is the very same with that of the Scottish-Irish' (J.G. Cumming, *A Short Treatise of the Isle of Man* (Douglas, 1864), 9). Similarly Bishop Wilson acknowledges that the Manx 'language is the Erse, or a dialect of that spoken in the Highlands of Scotland' (Harrison, *Old Historians*, 99).

30 Broderick, *Language Death*, 34–35; G. Broderick, *Handbook of Late Spoken Manx*, 3 vols (Tübingen, 1984–86), vol. 1, 348–52, 464–65.

31 *Oxford English Dictionary*, s.v. 'Manx', adjective, https://doi.org/10.1093/OED/5562666957 (accessed 28 August 2023).

32 Moore and Rhŷs, *Common Prayer*, xi.

33 Thomson, 'Traditionary Ballad' [part 1], 546.

'Irish(man)' remains contested much later and to some extent competes with *Gael* until the present day.[34]

The Ballad emphasizes Manx separateness and resilience in the face of a range of larger geopolitical powers, especially England, Scotland and Norway,[35] with only a passing reference to Ireland; it is striking that the country is not even mentioned as the place of origin of the list of Gaelic saints such as Patrick, although the association of the latter with Ireland can hardly have been unknown to the author. Similarly, the small amount of extant Manx Fenian material (literature pertaining to the pan-Gaelic hero Fionn mac Cumhail), while obviously deriving from an older pan-Gaelic tradition, is localized to the Isle of Man and most of it makes no mention of Ireland.[36] Moreover, in wider Manx folklore, Irish characters tend to be portrayed with the negative tropes (drunkenness, violence, boorishness, stupidity) characteristic of wider British popular culture.[37] The evidence of the Ballad would suggest that the apparent alienation of the Manx from wider Gaeldom predates the Reformation, and likely reflects the growing importance of the English and Scottish polities as early as the Norse period.

The Island was not always so isolated from the wider Gaelic world, however. One of the earliest *dán díreach* poems is a thirteenth-century work in praise of Raghnall mac Gofraidh (Rǫgnvaldr Guðrøðarson) (d. 1229), Norse-Gaelic King of Man.[38] This was presumably composed for and performed in Raghnall's court in the Island. It is unclear to what degree the Gaelic learned tradition was established in Man, but it is unlikely to have survived long beyond the fall of the Crovan dynasty in 1265 and the subsequent Scottish and English

34 Ó hUiginn, 'Éireannaigh'.

35 See chapter 2, 'Religion and the Island Church 1542–1838' and J. Kewley Draskau, *Account of the Isle of Man in Song* (Douglas, 2006).

36 See G. Broderick, 'Fíanaigecht in Manx tradition', *Scottish Gaelic Studies*, 30 (2016), 191–241. The material consists of the *Fin as Oshin* ballad, where the Fenian character *Garadh* is conflated with *Gorree* (*Gofraidh*, i.e. the Norse Manx king Godred Crovan), a children's rhyme, and two folktales, including versions of the tale of 'Fionn in the cradle', where Finn's adversary the giant or *buggane* lives on Barrule. Only in one version of this tale (collected by Sophia Morrison in English) is Finn referred to as an Irish giant who moves to Cregneash, whereas in Edward Faragher's versions (in Manx and English) Finn is described as living at the Sound and there is no mention of Ireland.

37 E.g. G. Broderick, 'Manx Stories and Reminiscences of Ned Beg Hom Ruy', *Zeitschrift für celtische Philologie*, 38 (1981), 113–78, 39 (1982), 117–94.

38 B. Ó Cuív, 'A poem in praise of Raghnall, king of Man', *Éigse*, 8 (1957), 283–301; C. Etchingham, J.V. Sigurðsson, M. Ní Mhaonaigh and E.A. Rowe, *Norse-Gaelic contacts in a Viking world* (Turnhout, 2019), 123–96; C.W. Macquarrie, 'The Isle of Man in medieval Gaelic literature', in S. Duffy and H. Mytum (eds), *A New History of the Isle of Man*, vol. 3: *The medieval period 1000–1406* (Liverpool, 2015), 281–304.

administrations.[39] Nevertheless, a number of vocabulary items survive in Manx which appear to originate as technical terms relating to law or poetry. A few such terms survive in legal use to modern times,[40] but others have undergone semantic broadening in Manx, suggesting a considerable period of dislocation from their original context. For example, Manx *oltooan* 'reproach' appears to be cognate with Irish *ail tsuthain*, 'perpetual disgrace', 'lasting reproach'. This is a type of satire mentioned in Old Irish legal material regulating the activities of professional poets, but the Manx word has a much more general application.[41]

Manx verse and song

A further sign of the early separation of the Isle of Man from Gaelic literary culture is the apparent lack of affinity between Manx and other Gaelic verse traditions, both learned and vernacular, in both structure and content. There is relatively little trace even in the oldest Manx verse of the complex patterns of end and internal rhyme and alliteration, or of the sophisticated imagery of praise and satire, characteristic of the Irish and Scottish Gaelic poetic and song traditions down to the twentieth century. The divergence in rhyming patterns is especially striking. In general, Irish and Scottish Gaelic verse of all genres, periods and registers requires strict correspondence in quality and length between vowels in rhyming positions. Consonants are less important; in vernacular tradition they may be ignored entirely, while in the classical strict metres, members of phonological classes (voiceless stops, tense sonorants, etc.) of consonants rhyme among themselves, though the specific consonants may differ.[42] In contrast, Manx verse tends to reverse this pattern. In the eighteenth-century retelling of *Paradise Lost*, for example, consonants in most cases must match (ignoring the broad and slender contrast, and the presence or absence of /r/ and sometimes /l/ in clusters), and vowels in final open syllables, but otherwise vowels may be different in quality, and short may rhyme with long, and stressed with unstressed or lightly stressed.[43] In the following passage, for example, we

39 R.L. Thomson, 'The Continuity of Manx', in C. Fel, P. Foote, J. Graham-Campbell and R.L. Thomson (eds), *The Viking Age in the Isle of Man* (London, 1983), 173.

40 R.L. Thomson, 'Manx-Latin *gilbogus* again', *Celtica* 20 (1988), 141–44.

41 R. McLaughlin, *Early Irish satire* (Dublin: 2008), 88; *Electronic Dictionary of the Irish Language*, s.v. 2 *ail* https://dil.ie/955 and *suthain* https://dil.ie/39343 (accessed 28 August 2023); C. Lewin, 'Manx lexicology and etymology: four case studies', *Éigse* 42 (in press).

42 E. Knott, *An Introduction to Irish Syllabic Poetry of the period 1200–1600, with selections, notes and glossary* (Cork, 1957).

43 Wheeler, *Pargeiys Caillit*, introduction.

have secondary-stressed short /a/ in *firrinagh* rhyming with stressed long /ɛː/ in *bragh*; /əː/ in *deyr* with /ɛː/ (>/eː/) in *airh*, and /-eːn/ *soilshean* with /aːrn/ *ayrn*.

'Sy reeriaght shen ta'n eunys firrinagh,
mieys 'skyn smooinaght, farraght son dy bragh.
Ayns shoh gyn laue ny saase, agh pooar e Ghoo,
ard-valley aalin, niartal, ren eh 'chroo.
Yn voalley ard ta jeant jeh claghyn deyr,
ny straidyn rea ta peamadit lesh airh.
Daa ghorrys jeig t'er, as ad shoh leeideil
gys whoilleen straid, ayns y chesh-vean meeiteil;
ec plaase reeoil, y Jee mooar ard soilshean,
cur sollys gennal 's gerjagh gys dagh ayrn.

In that kingdom is true pleasure,
goodness beyond imagination, everlasting.
Here without hand or implement, but [with] the power of his Word
he created a mighty, beautiful city.
The high wall is made of precious stones,
the level streets are paved with gold.
There are twelve doors, and these leading
to as many streets, meeting in the very centre;
at the royal palace, great God, high shining,
giving cheering light and comfort to every part.[44]

In his introduction to this text, Wheeler notes that '[w]hat counts as rhyme in a particular poetic tradition is a matter of convention', arguing against the practice in earlier scholarship[45] of suggesting emendations for 'faulty' rhymes.[46] The whole matter of Manx rhyme deserves much more study,[47] but it appears to owe little to inherited Gaelic models. We may suspect the influence of English tradition – it should be borne in mind that inexact rhyme was common in much Middle English verse.[48] Similarly, non-lexical vocables of an English type, unattested in the wider Gaelic tradition, are found in some of the oldest Manx

44 Wheeler, *Pargeiys Caillit*.
45 Notably Thomson, 'Traditionary Ballad'.
46 Wheeler, *Pargeiys Caillit*.
47 C. Lewin and M.W. Wheeler, *Lioar dy Hymnyn: A critical edition of the four Manx Gaelic hymn books printed 1795–1846*, https://www.academia.edu/38262104/ (accessed 28 August 2023), 3.
48 E.G. Stanley, 'Rhymes in English Medieval Verse: From Old English to Middle English', in E.D. Kennedy, R. Waldron and J.S. Wittig (eds), *Medieval English Studies Presented to George Kane* (Cambridge, 1988), 115–38.

folk songs, including *Fin as Oshin* and *Mylecharaine*,[49] and many of the tunes originate in anglophone traditions.[50] No doubt more could be said about the possible affinity of the Manx with wider Gaelic song traditions if more was known about performance styles beyond tantalizingly vague descriptions; while there are recordings of native speakers reciting the lyrics of traditional songs, there are virtually no recordings of actual singing in Manx.[51]

Critics have tended to be dismissive of the literary quality of the Manx tradition. A.W. Moore, in his *Manx Ballads and Music* considers the Manx verse collected within it as 'for the most part, of a very low order', significant mostly for linguistic, historical and cultural reasons.[52] In his preface to the same volume, T.E. Brown described the folk songs in the collection as 'in quality, so trifling, so unromantic, so unpoetical, and so modern', despite nonetheless being 'not without traces of a struggling utterance, and a real, if depressed, national genius'.[53] We might avoid such scathing assessments today – the author of the next section below prefers 'unpolished simplicity'[54] – but we cannot claim any of the Manx folksongs as works of artistic genius. Some of them were no doubt effective in performance when combining a stirring air with poignant subject matter, as in the *Illiam Dhone* elegy for William Christian, the leader of the Manx rebellion executed in 1663. This is one of the few cases where an echo of older Gaelic praise imagery may perhaps be discerned in the descriptions of Christian's gentility, wisdom, his popularity with lord and people, and in the string of adjectives praising the beauty of his residence:

> V'ou dty Resour Vannin, ard-ghooinney ny cheerey
> V'ou goit son dooinney seyr as dooinney creeney
> As she jeh dty ghellal vie cha row shin skee
> Agh ta dty vaase Illiam Mooar brishey nyn gree
>
> V'ou laue yesh yn Eearley as sooill yesh y theay
> Shen hug da dty noidyn gatt wheesh dt'oi ayns feoh
> […]
>
> B'aalin dty state thallooin ec Runnysvie
> B'eunyssagh dty gharaghyn, b'ooasle dty hie
>
> *You were Receiver of Man, the leading man of the country; you were taken as a gentleman and a wise man. And yea, we were not*

49 G. Broderick, 'Mylecharaine: A Manx traditional song collected from Manx oral tradition', *Béaloideas*, 90 (2022), 30; G. Broderick, 'Fíanaigecht', 197.
50 See this chapter, F. Bazin, 'Music'.
51 Broderick, 'Revival'.
52 Moore, *Manx Ballads*, xiv.
53 Moore, *Manx Ballads*, x, xii.
54 See this chapter, U. Corkill, 'In the language of strangers'.

> *tired of your good dealing, but your death, Illiam Mooar, breaks our hearts.*
>
> *You were the right hand of the earl and the right eye of the people; that was what made your enemies rise so much against you in abhorrence. [...]*
>
> *Fair was your estate at Ronaldsway, pleasant your gardens, and noble your house.*[55]

If Broderick is correct in his suggestion that the song was composed by Christian's widow or a close female relative,[56] this may be also the earliest, and one of very few, identifiable female voices in Manx Gaelic literature. The elegy composed by the mother of William Walker (1679–1729), the translator of the Gospels and Acts, to her sons should also be mentioned in this connection.

> Bannaght ny moght, scaa ny mraane treoghe,
> Fendeilagh cloan gyn ayr;
> Da ny hannooinee dreeym, nagh goghe
> Veih treanee ghewil aggair.
>
> *The poor's blessing, the widow's help,*
> *Guard of the fatherless*
> *Supporter of the weak, he'd not*
> *Bear from tyrants a wrong.*[57]

According to Stowell,[58] this 'has been sung and sung again in unison not with the harp of former days, but with the less melodious notes of the spinning-wheel', hinting at an important role for women as bearers of oral tradition. There is also evidence of women as performers of Fenian material in Man, in contrast to Ireland, where this genre was generally considered the preserve of men.[59]

Phillips' Prayer Book and the origins of Manx writing

Apart from differences in literary genre and style separating Manx from the wider Gaelic tradition, the most striking characteristic of Manx writing is that it uses an orthography based on modified English conventions (for example

55 After Broderick, 'Baase Illiam Dhone', 112–13, with minor adjustments.
56 Broderick, 'Baase Illiam Dhone', 111.
57 After Moore, *Manx Ballads*, 202–07.
58 Stowell, *Wilson*, 419.
59 Ó Muircheartaigh, 'Fin as Ossian revisited', 120.

<ee>, <oo>, <ch> and <j> have their English values), rather than the conventional Gaelic system used in Ireland and Scotland. This system reached a high degree of standardization by the time of the completion of the printed Manx Bible in the 1770s, in that most words had only one spelling. The sound-symbol correspondences of the eighteenth-century 'Classical Manx' orthography are complex and far from entirely consistent, but they show a degree of systematization and internal evolution which differentiate it from some of the more rudimentary attempts to write Gaelic in English orthography in other parts of the Gaelic world.[60] This is not merely Gaelic in English dress, but a sophisticated attempt to represent Gaelic phonology and lexis in an autonomous orthographic system with its own internal logic.

The earliest extant extended text in any version of Manx orthography is the Anglican Prayer Book and Psalter, translated between 1604 and 1610 under the auspices of Bishop John Phillips (c.1555–1633).[61] This survives in a single almost complete copy as MNH MS 00003–4 which has been dated to between 1625 and 1628;[62] a further single page fragment has recently come to light (MNH MS 15274).[63] Phillips, a Welshman, is reported to have mastered Manx well enough to preach in the language, and he seems to have had an active role in the translation itself, probably with assistance from native Manx clergy.[64] Phillips' orthography appears not to have found favour with some of the Island's clergy, 'for that it is spelled with vowells wherewith none of them are acquainted', in the words of William Crowe, one of the vicars general asked to inspect the work in 1611.[65] Indeed, Phillips' vowels are the area where his orthography diverges most sharply from the later one, generally following what Thomson refers to as 'continental' values; compare e.g. Phillips *bii* for later *bee* 'food' /biː/.

Thomson was inclined to think there was little connection between Phillips and the later orthography:

> The two systems seem to be quite distinct [...]. Neither does the old orthography survive as a competitor to the new. In short, one might suppose that we have two different attempts to write down Manx, which largely coincide in

60 Lewin, '"An English monstrosity"?'; Lewin and Ó Muircheartaigh, 'Manx manuscript sermons', 134–51.

61 Moore and Rhŷs, *Common Prayer*, vol. 1; Thomson, *Early Manx*.

62 Thomson, *Early Manx*, 4, gives a range of 1625–30; Max W. Wheeler (personal communication, 10 October 2023), points out that the manuscript (f. 21r) includes among the royal family to be prayed for Henry Frederick, Hereditary Prince of the Palatinate, who died 7 January 1629.

63 Lewin *et al.*, 'A newly discovered fragment'.

64 J.G. Cumming, *A Short Treatise of the Isle of Man* (Douglas, 1866), 9; Moore and Rhŷs, *Common Prayer*, vol. 1: xxii.

65 Moore and Rhŷs, *Common Prayer*, vol. 1: xii.

consonantism, having taken the same model, but diverge in vocalism, having chosen different standards.[66]

However, the situation may be less clear-cut. In his recent new edition of the Phillips psalter, Wheeler points to certain fixed spellings of common words which are idiosyncratic within Phillips' orthographic system as a whole, raising the possibility that these indicate 'that certain words already had, for him, a "standard" spelling from which he was unwilling to deviate'.[67] One feature common to both Phillips and the Classical Manx orthography is the use of <y> and <i> to mark vowel length, e.g. <ay> /aː/, <oy, oi> /oː/. The appearance of these in both systems may suggest a degree of continuity between Phillips and the later system, or else that Phillips took them from an existing Manx orthographic tradition which was also ancestral to later usage. They also may suggest that this putative existing Manx tradition was of some antiquity, since spellings such as <oy, oi> for /oː/ are characteristic of northern English spelling, especially of the late fifteenth and early sixteenth centuries.[68] Phillips has generally been taken to be the inventor of his spelling system, and there are elements of Welsh influence which can only have come via him,[69] but it is possible that he modified, or revived, an orthography previously in use; either of these scenarios could explain Crowe's comments.

One distinctive spelling common to both Phillips and the Classical orthography is the spelling *ayn* in forms of the preposition 'in' (G. *ann*), and this may in fact be one of the oldest elements of the orthography surviving into the eighteenth-century standard. In the Classical Manx orthography, <ay> usually represents long vowels /eː/ or /ɛː/, but *ayn* was pronounced /oːn/ in the south and /uːn/ in the north, while short vowels are attested in derived forms such as *aynym* 'in me' and in destressed position.[70] The spelling *ayn* makes more sense in the Phillips orthography if we assume that *ann* was pronounced /aN/ or /aːN/ at this period (cf. Ph. *kian* 'head', CM *kione*, G. *ceann*), or earlier if Phillips himself had inherited the spelling from an existing tradition. The spelling *ayn* may have been retained in the later orthography to provide a common representation for the variety of positional and dialectal realizations of the morpheme.[71]

There are some hints in his orthography itself, then, that Manx writing may not have originated with Phillips. In what contexts might it then have come

66 Thomson, *Early Manx*, 8.

67 Wheeler, *Phillips' Psalms*, 8.

68 A. Roig-Marín, 'Northern Middle English spelling evidence in the Durham Account Rolls', *Lingua* (253: 2021), 1–19.

69 Wheeler, *Phillips' Psalms*, 3–8.

70 Broderick, *Handbook*, vol. 2, 16.

71 Lewin and Ó Muircheartaigh, 'Manx manuscript sermons', 147.

into being? As early as the 1350s, Manx bishop William Russell had instructed his clergy to

> instruct their subjects diligently in the articles of the faith, and admonish and persuade them to learn the Apostle's Creed in their mother-tongue and to expound the faith to their children and teach them the articles[72]

While items such as the creed may have been translated extemporaneously into the 'mother-tongue', or had established but orally transmitted vernacular forms, it is hardly unlikely that at some point in the ensuing centuries it occurred to some of the Manx clergy to commit some material such as prayers and homilies to writing; this would have been just as useful in the 1400s or 1500s as in the 1700s. It does not seem fanciful to imagine the pre-Reformation monastic establishments in Man playing a role analogous to Glasney College in medieval Cornwall in producing vernacular material (if no doubt on a modest scale),[73] although this must remain speculation unless further evidence comes to light. Thomson suggests that any pre-Phillips writing tradition is unlikely to predate the fifteenth century, and may be associated with the beginning of the Stanley lordship in 1405 and the importation of an English-speaking administration.[74] On a more limited scale, English-based orthography was used for Manx place and personal names in administrative documents during this period,[75] and as mentioned above, for verbatim recording of curses and slanders in church court records. Possible relationships between the spellings used in these contexts and the orthography found in the extended religious texts have yet to be investigated.

It has often been said that, as well as being an orthographic dead-end, Phillips' text itself made little impact. Bishop Barrow in 1663 notes the practice of oral instruction and extemporary translation by clergy illiterate in Manx, 'for there is nothing either written or printed in their language, which is peculiar to themselves; neither can they who speak it best write one to another in it, having no character or letter of it among them'.[76] How could this be the case, only thirty-odd years after the surviving copy of Phillips' Prayer Book was written? We know that Phillips initially intended to have the work printed, and there is a surviving letter of his to the Lord High Treasurer of England with an appeal for

72 C.R. Cheney, 'Manx synodal statutes: A.D. 1230(?)–1351 part 2: translation of Latin texts', *Cambridge Medieval Celtic Studies* 8 (1984), 61.

73 Compare the known but poorly understood educational role of Rushen Abbey.

74 Thomson, 'The Study of Manx Gaelic', 182.

75 G. Broderick, 'Manx', in M.J. Ball and N. Müller (eds) *The Celtic Languages* (London, 2009), 306; Broderick, *Place-names* [vol. 1], xvii–xviii. R.L. Thomson, 'Manx language and literature', in G. Price (ed) *The Celtic connection* (Gerrards Cross, 1992).

76 MNH MS 09782 (CRP), assorted ecclesiastical documents (Box 2 of 3 at 2014).

funds, which was evidently unsuccessful.[77] Phillips was 'a determined supporter of Church discipline';[78] he fought and won significant legal and political battles with the secular authorities;[79] and in 1610 he introduced strict decrees regarding clerical responsibilities, such as a duty to catechize parishioners 'in the vulgar tongue'.[80] It is implausible that such a conscientious, strong-willed and politically significant individual would have allowed either the opinions of the vicars general, or the failure of his printing plans, to frustrate his intention for his translation to be used throughout the Island's parishes.

Nor is it plausible that, having expended so much effort on the translation, Phillips would merely sit on the translation for the remaining twenty-three years of his episcopate. Thomson believed that the extant copy MS 00003–4 was a fair copy for the press 'in view of its varied scripts and sizes of writing, running titles, and so forth', with this aim being frustrated by the bishop's death in 1633, although he also notes the possibility that it was 'a copy for use, one of a score or so to be supplied to the parishes (like the Synod of Argyll's *Shorter Catechism*)'.[81] The second possibility is rather more likely; the presentational features Thomson mentions are also consistent with a neat copy for use – running titles are just as functional in a manuscript as in a printed book – and in point of comparison, such features are found in the later manuscript of parts of a new Prayer Book translation (MNH MS 13221/1/1) from the 1730s.[82] By the time the extant copy was made in 1625–1628, Phillips was likely resigned to the fact that the resources of the diocese could not support the printing of the work. Even a century and a half later, Manx publications were only achieved through subsidies from the Society for Promoting Christian Knowledge, founded in 1698, many decades after Phillips' time. It is possible that the date of production of MS 00003–4 is explained by the fact that there had been an expectation for some years after the translation was completed that it would be printed. When in time it became clear this would not be the case, the bishop may then have ordered full manuscript copies to be made for the parishes instead. Why then has only one copy plus one fragment survived? One probable factor which has been overlooked is the impact of the Cromwellian occupation of the Island between 1651 and 1660.[83] The new regime had strong Puritan leanings, which led to a ban on the use of the Book of Common Prayer as well as the abolition of episcopacy. It is likely that other copies of Phillips' work

77 Moore and Rhŷs, *Common Prayer*, x-xi.
78 Moore and Rhŷs, *Common Prayer*, ix.
79 Moore and Rhŷs, *Common Prayer*, xvi.
80 Moore and Rhŷs, *Common Prayer*, x.
81 Thomson, 'The Study of Manx Gaelic', 182.
82 Wheeler, *Common Prayer*.
83 A.W. Moore, *SPCK Diocesan Histories: Sodor and Man* (London, 1893), 146.

were destroyed at this time, or at least neglected and later lost.[84] Furthermore, the Phillips' text may have been considered obsolete following the 1662 revision of the English Prayer Book.

Manuscript culture 1690s–1760s

Thomson's comment that 'the old orthography [does not] survive as a competitor to the new' is in need of qualification in light of a manuscript sermon in Manx, first preached in March 1696/7 (MNH MS 13221/2/1), by John Woods (Vicar of Malew 1696–1739, also chaplain and schoolmaster of Castletown 1695–1700). The Phillips manuscript is known to have been in the hands of Woods, who made extensive emendations to the text.[85] Woods' sermon shows substantial influence from the Phillips orthography but does not appear to be an organic continuation or evolution of it. Rather, Woods combines a version of the later orthography, which presumably was already in use among his contemporaries, with Phillips-derived spellings of individual frequently-occurring words.[86] Woods' interpolations in the Phillips manuscript show that he held the text in high esteem and studied it carefully. In 1707, Bishop Wilson had a bilingual edition of his catechism *Coyrle Sodjeh* ('Further Advice')[87] printed, the first published work in Manx. The preface contains a tantalizing reference to variation in ways of writing – presumably meaning spelling – and the potential for conflict over this, which Wilson is eager to pacify:

> They that have had the Trouble of Translating it, are very Sensible that the Liberty which every Man takes of Writing after his own Way, will expose them to some Censure: But then he must be a very ill Man, who, for so little Reason, will go about to hinder so much Good as is intended by this Book, since this would have been the Case, whoever should have undertaken it.[88]

It seems plausible that Woods, as a champion of the Phillips text and orthography, was a participant, and on the losing side, in the debates alluded to by Wilson.

In any case, there is reason to suppose that more writing must have been going on in Manx in the seventeenth and early eighteenth centuries than now survives. The orthography of *Coyrle Sodjeh* already has the appearance of a mature, developed system, rather than an *ab initio* attempt to write Manx based

84 Lewin *et al.*, 'A newly discovered fragment'.
85 Lewin, 'A Manx sermon'.
86 Lewin, 'A Manx sermon', 49–51.
87 T. Wilson, *The Principles and Duties of Christianity … in English and Manks* (London, 1707), generally referred to by an abbreviation of its Manx subtitle.
88 T. Wilson, *Principles and Duties*, letter to the clergy.

directly on English conventions, and both it and Woods' sermon of a decade earlier would appear to belong to a milieu in which writing in Manx was an established practice among the clergy, even if on a limited basis. Moreover, it is implausible that Woods' extant Manx sermon from 1697 was his only venture of the kind in the course of his career, given his undoubted diligence and initiative in engaging with the Phillips manuscript. Likewise, it seems implausible that William Walker, translator of the Gospels and Acts and possibly *Coyrle Sodjeh*, never wrote a Manx sermon, although none have survived. A good number of the surviving eighteenth-century manuscript sermons in Manx date from their authors' youth, in some cases from their teens and well prior to ordination, suggesting that composition or translation of sermons formed part of the prospective clergy's training. Indeed, we have an explicit account from William Crebbin (chaplain and then vicar of Jurby 1743–1803) that during his stay in Bishop Wilson's household for twelve months for training prior to ordination, he was lent Walker's manuscript translations 'in order the better to qualify him also for translating'.[89]

Between the 1740s and 1760s, there are references to officially mandated manuscript translations of parts of the liturgy and psalms, which the clergy were required to copy for their own use,[90] and a neatly copied section of the Prayer Book Communion service has recently come to light dating from between 1729 and 1736.[91] It is also in this milieu of increasing Manx literate activity that the most significant original literary text, *Pargys Caillit* ('Paradise Lost', excerpted above), may have been composed.[92] In his new edition of the poem, Wheeler argues persuasively on a number of linguistic, literary and historical grounds that it was composed not by the scandalous figure of Thomas Christian (1754–1828), as supposed by previous editors and commentators, but by his grandfather, also Thomas Christian (Vicar of Marown 1734–52).[93] Wheeler also makes a strong case that the Manx poem should be viewed as an ambitious and skilful original composition, retelling for a Manx vernacular audience the narrative of the fall of Satan and the temptation of Adam and Eve, with only a minority of passages which draw more directly on Milton. The text appears

89 Butler, *Hildesley*, 254.

90 G. Bray, *Records of Convocation I: Sodor and Man, 1229–1877* (Woodbridge, 2005), 209–277.

91 MNH MS 13221/1/1, edited in M.W. Wheeler, *The Book of Common Prayer in Manx Gaelic, 1765/1777*. https://www.academia.edu/49187655/ (accessed 1 August 2021).

92 I have used the spelling *pargys* in the title of the poem (cf. 1796 running title *Phargys Callyt*), as the form hitherto most widely known to scholarship, but in his forthcoming edition Wheeler prefers *Pargeiys Caillit*, reflecting the variant form of the word with final stress found in the body of the poem itself; Lewin, 'Manx lexicology and etymology'.

93 For details of Thomas Christian Jr's misdemeanours, see Thomson, *Pargys Caillit*, 11–16.

to have circulated among the clergy in manuscript for several decades prior to its first appearance in print in 1796,[94] and also entered oral tradition among the wider Manx-speaking population.[95] The tradition of the manuscript carval book likely also goes back to an earlier period, although most of the surviving copies date from the second half of the eighteenth century or later.[96] All in all, it appears that there was a more vibrant and self-confident Manx-medium literary and manuscript culture in the late seventeenth and early eighteenth century than has hitherto been appreciated.

The Manx Bible and related projects

If *Pargys Caillit* is to be considered the greatest masterpiece of (more or less) original composition in Manx, then the Manx Bible is undoubtedly the most important monument of translated literature. Bishop Wilson is remembered as a friend of the language,[97] and deserves credit for initiating the project of translating the Scriptures. However, only two Manx books were published during his long episcopate (1697–1755), with a gap of four decades between *Coyrle Sodjeh* (1707) and Matthew's Gospel (1748), which was published at Wilson's own expense.[98] The latter, along with the rest of the Gospels and Acts of the Apostles, had been translated by William Walker in the 1720s. The project was planned while Wilson and Walker were imprisoned in 1722.[99] Wilson's publication plans were likely truncated for the same financial reasons which had frustrated Phillips a century earlier, as well as the many other initiatives and challenges which required his attention and expenditure.

Although always in his illustrious predecessor's shadow in public memory, Bishop Mark Hildesley is perhaps the most consequential figure in the history of Manx literature and for our knowledge of the language today, even though he took no direct part in the translation work. Upon receiving representations from Hildesley, in 1763 the Society for Promoting Christian Knowledge (SPCK) produced a proposal for remedying the fact that 'the ancient church of the diocese of Mann [...] is probably the only Christian church in the world, which

94 Wheeler, *Pargeiys Caillit*; Ó Muircheartaigh, 'Pargys Caillit'.

95 S. Morrison, 'Introduction', in W. Cashen, *Manx Folk-Lore* (Douglas, 1912), ix. Once again it is noteworthy that the poem is described as being recited by a woman, as with other items of Manx oral tradition mentioned above.

96 In an unpublished edition of *Carval er Maynrys Niau* 'A carol on the happiness of heaven' (Moore, *Carvalyn Gailckagh*, 66), M.W. Wheeler suggests that the handwriting in the oldest witness, MNH MS 01405A, dates from the first half of the eighteenth century, although dated to 1772–84 in the MNH carval catalogue. The date of composition is given as 1721 in *Mona's Herald*, 17 November 1886.

97 Stowell, *Wilson*, 104–106.

98 Stowell, *Wilson*, 106.

99 Butler, *Hildesley*, 41–43, 254.

is absolutely destitute of a printed copy of the Holy Scriptures, in the vulgar tongue'.[100] In an era of fervent evangelism on distant shores, it was considered increasingly anomalous and offensive to Protestant sensibilities that the light of the Scriptures was 'extended even to the distant parts of India and Arabia', while being obscured by a language barrier in the heart of the British Isles. Furthermore, there had long been dissatisfaction with the practice of extemporary translation of church services by the Manx clergy,[101] 'according to the different sense, attention, and ability, of the officiating minister'.[102] Archbishop Yardley of York, one of the project's most avid supporters, drew attention to '[t]he numberless inconveniences, both to the minister and people, and more particularly the danger of injury to the tenor of the sacred writings, and of our excellent Liturgy, by such vague translations'.[103]

Walker's manuscript of the Gospels and Acts had been preserved among Bishop Wilson's papers and was borrowed from his son, now resident in England, and prepared for the press in London with the SPCK's support in winter 1763–4.[104] A new translation of the Book of Common Prayer followed in 1765, the rest of the New Testament in 1767, and a second edition of the Prayer Book in 1769 – the latter being the first book printed in the Island, at Ramsey. Two other religious works, Manx translations of John Rawlet's *The Christian Monitor* (1763)[105] and John Lewis's *The Church Catechism Explained* (1769)[106] also appeared as part of the same scheme, as well as a second edition of *Coyrle Sodjeh* (1761). Several thousand copies of these works were distributed free of charge in the Island.[107] Their enthusiastic reception by the Manx public, and the success of Hildesley and his allies in raising the necessary funds, made feasible an extension of the project into the Old Testament. This appeared in two volumes in 1771 and 1772, with the final part coming into Hildesley's hands in November 1772, only a few days before his final illness and death.[108]

100 Butler, *Hildesley*, 214.
101 Moore, *Sodor and Man*, 157–58.
102 Butler, *Hildesley*, 214.
103 Butler, *Hildesley*, 425.
104 The manuscript is now presumed lost, but much of Walker's conservative language and spelling is evident in the 1748 and 1763 printed texts. Details of the rediscovery of the manuscript and its preparation for the press are given in correspondence from Hildesley to Wilson junior (MNH MS 10537).
105 Thomson, *Yn Fer-raauee Creestee*; C. Lewin and M.W. Wheeler, *Yn Fer-raauee Creestee çhyndait dys Gaelg liorish Paul Crebbin as prentit 'sy vleïn 1763*, https://www.academia.edu/49260468/ (accessed 2 October 2023).
106 C. Lewin and M.W. Wheeler, *Lewis's Catechism in Manx Gaelic, 1769*, https://www.academia.edu/49133139/ (accessed 2 October 2023).
107 Butler, *Hildesley*, 230.
108 Butler, *Hildesley*, 51–52.

A substantially revised New Testament, as well as a complete Bible, were published in 1775.

Further details of the various editions, and the practical and financial arrangements for their publication, are available in the accounts by Butler and Cubbon, and in the Convocation records.[109] More interesting for our purposes will be to turn our attention to the literary and linguistic aspects of the translation project and its social context. Unlike the Irish and Welsh Bibles, which are primarily the work of a small number of key figures, the project of translating the Bible and Prayer Book into Manx was very much a team effort, eventually coming to encompass virtually all of the Island's clergy.[110] This was a major organizational undertaking, and a substantial demand on the translators' time, not all of whom appeared equally keen; Hildesley was obliged by turns to encourage, cajole, guilt-trip and obtain written commitments from the clergy to complete the various stages of the task.[111] Privately he even considered financial inducements in the form of 'premiums', but feared the clergy might not want to be regarded as 'mercenary'.[112] The project was overseen by a small number of the more senior and experienced clergy, led by Philip Moore (1705–83), Rector of Bride and master of Douglas Grammar School. For the later stages of the Bible translation, the corrected drafts were copied for the press by the young John Kelly (1750–1808). Encouraged by Hildesley, Kelly also turned his hand to lexicography, which later resulted in two important Manx dictionaries, which, however, did not see publication during his lifetime.[113]

Substantial sections of the translators' manuscript drafts[114] for the first half of the Old Testament and the second half of the New survive, containing significant editorial revisions which provide a valuable insight into the evolution of the text. It was recognized at the time that the individual translators varied in skill; for example, Philip Moore complains of 'the poor miserable translation' of the Book of Ezekiel 'furnished by the Rabbi of Rushen' (Nicholas Christian, Vicar of Rushen 1748–82).[115] As a result, some sections required

109 Butler, *Hildesley*, 233–260; W. Cubbon, *A Bibliographical Account of Works Relating to the Isle of Man*, vol. 2 (London, 1939), 760–775; Bray, *Concovation.*

110 Butler, *Hildelsey*, 252–256; G. Broderick, 'The Manx Bible and the date and authorship of *Pargys Caillt*', *Celtica* (2023: 34), 179–191.

111 Bray, *Convocation*, 251–305.

112 Hildesley to Thomas Wilson, 18 January 1764, MNH MS 10537. Some of the clergy were recompensed by the SPCK for their contributions in due course, as detailed in Butler, *Hildesley*, 237–40.

113 R.L. Thomson, 'The Revd Dr John Kelly as a Lexicographer', *PIMNHAS, 9* (1990), 443–458.

114 MNH MS 05690 C; Broderick, 'The Manx Bible', 182–188.

115 Philip Moore, 'The Manx Bible' (1771), in 'Letters of Rev Philip Moore', *Ramsey Church Magazine* (1897: 2.24). The draft of Ezekiel is not extant but Christian's manuscripts of Leviticus and 2 Corinthians survive.

significant rephrasing by the editors, whereas in the more skilfully translated portions the emendations are mostly restricted to standardization of spelling and terminology. In the more heavily edited passages, many of the revisions consist of substituting more idiomatic phraseology for overly slavish renderings of the English or original languages.[116] Indeed, this is perhaps the most striking feature of the Manx translation. The English and the other authorized Celtic translations of the post-Reformation period provide a generally close, literal rendering of the original. In contrast, the Manx version is in general much looser, and more in line with vernacular Gaelic idiom, and hence more easily comprehensible and 'modern' in appearance. In the following example from the book of Leviticus 4. 23, the AV and other Gaelic translations, and Nicholas Christian's Manx manuscript version, all give some variant of the repetitious Hebrew 'his sin, wherein he hath sinned', while the Manx editors modify to the more natural 'the sin which he has done'.

English (AV):	'his sin, wherein he hath sinned'
Manx manuscript draft:	y pheccah, ayn te er ve peccoil *(the sin in which he has been sinful)*
Manx print (1771):	y peccah t'eh er n'yannoo *(the sin he has done)*
Irish (1685):[117]	an phecaidh ionar phecaidh sé *(the sin in which he sinned)*
Scottish Gaelic (1783):[118]	a pheacadh, a pheacaich e *(his sin, which he sinned)*

In part, these more idiomatic renderings are induced by the structure of the language itself, with its absence of abstract literary vocabulary and the prominence of phrasal verbs such as *jean peccah* 'do sin'; there is no single-word verb 'to sin'. As Bishop Wilson observes, 'many things which, in the English language, are derived from the Latin and Greek, and little understood by those that know nothing of those languages, in Manks are expressed by a periphrasis easily understood by the common people'.[119] There was also a deliberate policy to pursue more interpretative translations, following the spirit of Enlightenment scholarship, as Philip Moore explains:

116 It is evident that the Manx translators worked primarily from the English Authorized Version rather than the original languages, especially in the Old Testament (Thomson, 'Introduction', vi).

117 U. Bedel, *Leabhuir na Seintiomna* (London, 1685).

118 *Leabhraiche an t-Seann Tiomnaidh [...] Earrann I* (Dun-Eidin, 1783).

119 Harrison, *Old Historians*, 99.

> [T]he rule we laid down to ourselves was, to consider and treat the Scriptures, as we would any other classical author, of whom a new translation was to be made. In consequence of this method, I found we were under the necessity of making many variations from the present English Version; and of venturing at some bold strokes, where we found good authority for such deviation.[120]

Especially in the more obscure figurative passages of the Old Testament, use was made of the latest textual scholarship, and Moore was in correspondence with some of the leading scholars of the time, such as Robert Lowth.[121] The support of figures such as Lowth and Yardley seems to have boosted the senior Manx clergy's confidence both in their work and in the legitimacy of their language as a literary and religious medium. Thus Moore is keen to recount that

> [o]n mentioning these and other Variorums [variant readings] to a very learned prelate, he was pleased to say, that our Manks version, as it was the last, so would it be the best translation of the Scriptures this day extant.[122]

Indeed, there seems to have been a perception, in tune with the emerging Romantic tendencies of the period, that the 'ancient simplicity of living and speaking'[123] of the Manx peasantry made their language especially well suited for rendering the Word of God. Another of Moore's correspondents, the Dublin-based English antiquarian Charles Vallancey, waxes lyrical about 'the simplicity and force of the language, and the beauty of the version, where many vulgarisms have crept into the Irish translation'.[124] Similarly, Wilson's biographer Hugh Stowell claims that, despite being 'overspread with corruptions and barbarisms', the Manx language 'possesses considerable spirit and energy, and is peculiarly adapted to convey sentiments of fervent devotion'.[125]

As well as their connections to the latest classical and biblical scholarship, Moore, Kelly and others were in touch with a pan-Gaelic network of scholars and antiquarians, including Vallancey and the Scottish clergyman and folklore collector James McLagan. Against the backdrop of international enthusiasm for James Macpherson's *Ossian* in 1761–63 and the emerging Romantic movement, these connections saw a modest upsurge in interest in Manx oral literature. McLagan appears to be responsible for the collection of the *Fin as Oshin* ballad, manuscripts of which survive in the hands of both Moore and

120 Philip Moore to 'Rev. J[ohn] Stuart of Luss, North-Britain' (translator of much of the Old Testament into Scottish Gaelic), 6 June 1780, in Butler, *Hildesley*, 668.

121 Butler, *Hildesley*, 667–68.

122 Moore to J. Stuart, 6 June 1780, in Butler, *Hildesley*, 669.

123 Bishop Wilson in Harrison, *Old Historians*, 99.

124 Vallancey to Moore, 26 December 1780, in Butler 1799: 670–71.

125 Stowell, *Wilson*, 104–05.

Kelly,[126] as well as for the limited lexical influence of the other Gaelic translations on the Manx Bible.[127]

The Bible editors achieved a high degree of standardization of spelling, technical terminology, and word forms, but considerably more variation is permitted in the syntax and initial mutations.[128] The eighteenth century was a period of rapid ongoing change in Manx grammar, especially in the verbal system, with conservative and innovating forms existing side by side.[129] At times such variation appears to be exploited deliberately for stylistic effect,[130] notably in rendering the characteristic parallelisms of Hebrew poetry, a literary device which Moore's correspondent Lowth is known for having brought to scholarly attention.[131]

1. Shey laa nee oo gobbraghey, agh er y chiaghtoo laa **gowee oo fea**. Ayns yn niarragh, as 'syn ouyr, **nee oo fea y ghoaill**.
   Six days thou shalt work, but on the seventh day thou shalt rest: in earing time and in harvest thou shalt rest.[132]

2. Ta'n Chiarn yn Ree, foddee'n seihll **goaill boggey** jeh: dy jarroo foddee ny ymmodee ellanyn **boggey 'ghoaill** jeh.
   The Lord is King, the earth may be glad thereof: yea, the multitude of the isles may be glad thereof.[133]

While the wording in the highlighted verbal phrases in the English versions is the same in both halves of the verse, the Manx versions show variation (1) between inflected and periphrastic verb forms and (2) in placement of the direct object.

Later literature and language shift

The later eighteenth century saw a consolidation of Manx literacy among the populace, while at the same time, various socio-economic pressures began to weaken the language's social base, as English spread first in the towns and the higher social classes, and the island was increasingly exposed to the

126 Ó Muircheartaigh, 'Fin as Ossian revisited'.
127 Lewin, 'Lexical influence'.
128 Thomson, 'Introduction', vi.
129 C. Lewin, 'The syntax of the verbal noun in Manx Gaelic', *Journal of Celtic Linguistics*, 17 (2016), 147–239.
130 R.L. Thomson, 'Manx', in P. Trudgill (ed) *Language in the British Isles* (Cambridge, 1984), 306.
131 R. Lowth, *De sacra poesi Hebræorum* (Oxford, 1753).
132 Exodus 34. 21.
133 Psalm 97. 1.

outside world.[134] After completion of the Bible in 1775, two further substantial devotional works associated with the established church saw print: a bilingual edition of Bishop Wilson's *Short and plain instruction for the better understanding of The Lord's Supper* (1777), funded again by the SPCK, and a volume of translation of twenty-two of Wilson's sermons (1783), printed in Bath at the expense of Wilson's son. Although somewhat more intellectual and involved than most manuscript parish sermons, the translation is a skilful one, and was reportedly well received by Manx congregations to whom it was read, partly as a result of their abiding respect for the late bishop.[135] The growth of Methodism in the last quarter of the eighteenth century led to the emergence of a new genre for the language, the hymn book, with four editions of translations of hymns by Wesley and Watts printed between 1795 and 1846. These evidently made a great impression on the Manx public, and some of the last native speakers recorded in 1948 were able to recite hymn lyrics.[136] As Thomson and Pilgrim note, '[t]he end of the eighteenth and the beginning of the nineteenth saw an increase in the number but a diminution in the scale of Manx publications'.[137] These included the hymn books, and also numerous temperance and other religious tracts,[138] for whom the masses newly literate in the vernacular provided a ready audience. *Pargys Caillit* was printed in c.1796, and the Traditionary Ballad in 1778 and 1802.[139] From the 1820s to the 1850s, occasional articles, letters and verse in Manx appeared in the Island's newspapers, with topics including debate on the usefulness or otherwise of maintaining the language, and the movements for political reform which were gathering steam at the time.[140] There is also extensive manuscript material, most notably in the form of sermons and carvals, the bulk of which date from the 1770s to the mid-nineteenth century.

While these uses of the language reflect increased literacy in Manx, for most, this would have remained a distinctly passive ability, with few having cause to write the language. Even those who could write in Manx only did so when necessary, and with a presumed monolingual audience in mind; it is noteworthy that private notes and editorial comments in Manx language manuscripts are

134 R. Hindley, 'The decline of the Manx language: a study in linguistic geography', *Bradford Occasional Papers*, 6 (1984), 16–20.

135 Keble, *Wilson*, 969.

136 Manx National Heritage, *Skeealyn Vannin* (Douglas, 2003).

137 Thomson and Pilgrim, *Outline*, 16.

138 Cubbon, *Bibliographical Account*, 782–88.

139 No copies of the 1778 edition are extant; see Thomson, 'Traditionary Ballad' [part 1], 521.

140 Broderick, *Language Death*, 254; C. Lewin, *Lioar-lhaih Ghaelgagh: Original Manx Gaelic Prose 1821–1907* (Douglas, 2014).

invariably in English, and there is no private correspondence in Manx,[141] until the letters of Edward Fargher (1831–1908) to Archdeacon Kewley and Charles Roeder, written in Manx at their request and with evident unfamiliarity on Fargher's part.[142]

Manx was used in the courts well into the nineteenth century, some official proclamations and notices were translated into Manx until the 1860s, and new laws were promulgated in both Manx and English at the Tynwald ceremony, as they still are. Nevertheless, the growth in publishing and literacy, the limited official uses of Manx, and the occasional voices raised in explicit defence of the language in the press,[143] proved insufficient to instigate a wider revival in the language's fortunes. The use of Manx in the courts, as in the churches, was never suppressed or abolished *per se*, but simply fell into abeyance as the population gradually became bilingual and then predominantly English-speaking, and as professionals with Manx language skills became scarcer. The language faded from public view more by apathy, and gradually increasing stigma internalized by Manx speakers themselves, than outward persecution by official institutions. As Hindley notes, the churches and schools 'were not so much anti-Manx as pro-English'.[144] Nor can any specific societal trauma explain the decline of the language:

> The island suffered no Plantations, no Highland 'pacification', no Penal Laws, no Clearances or Evictions, and after 1704 lacked tenurial problems to compare with the other Gaelic lands. Its experience of the potato famine of the eighteen-forties was severe but by then the economy had a broad enough base to absorb the shock. In contrast, therefore, to Irish and Scottish Gaelic, Manx escaped major disasters or sufferings to explain its collapse.[145]

Rather, the more insidious forces of anglicization which had long been incipient in Manx society – class structure, education, trade, immigration, emigration, the Island's small size and geographical position, 'the utilitarian spirit of modern times'[146] – while less dramatic or emotionally compelling, must suffice to explain the 'sociolinguistic revolution'[147] of the nineteenth century, a watershed in Manx history as significant and far-reaching as any of the more material transformations recounted in this series.

141 Although English correspondence occasionally includes quotation, proverbs in Manx, etc.
142 Lewin, *Lioar-lhaih*, 87–92.
143 Broderick, *Language Death*, 27–30.
144 Hindley, 'Decline', 17.
145 Hindley, 'Decline', 26.
146 S. Walpole, 'The Manx Note Book, January 1885', *The Manx Note Book*, 1 (1885), 1.
147 Hindley, 'Decline', 26.

IN THE LANGUAGE OF STRANGERS: LITERATURE IN ENGLISH RELATING TO THE ISLE OF MAN 1405–1830

Ulla Corkill †

The literature reviewed in this chapter has been selected either because it was written in the Isle of Man or because its subject matter directly concerns people or events related to the history of the Island. English was the language of *joarreeyn* ('strangers'), of the lord of Man and his entourage, of officials and soldiers, priests and traders, and these, together with occasional visitors and travellers, are the authors of almost all writing relating to the Isle of Man during the above period. Although elementary English was taught in the Island's parochial schools from 1670, the language was not generally accessible to the majority of Manx Gaelic-speaking Islanders until the second half of the eighteenth century. It is therefore not surprising that we have little in writing to reflect the views of those who lived here. What the Manx had was a strong oral tradition, which preserved the breast laws, while songs and stories were passed on from one generation to the next. This cultural memory bank would be explored in the nineteenth century, when the movement referred to as Romanticism made such finds valuable.

The literature reviewed has generally been organized according to the chronology of its composition or publication, and not according to the subject matter.

In 1417 John Stanley, the second lord of Man, came to the Isle of Man to quell a rebellion against his lieutenant-governor, John Letherland. The ringleaders were brutally executed, but in order to deal with the general unrest in the Island, Stanley thought it would be a sensible move to request his officials to set down in English the Island's constitution and old laws. This was completed in 1422 and forms the first extensive piece of writing in English in the Isle of Man in the late medieval period. The record of the court begins:

> Our doughtful Lord, and gratious, this is the constitucons of the ould tyme, the which we have seene in our dayes, how you shalle be governed upon your Tynwald dayes. First, you shall come thither Royally and in your Royall arraye as a Kinge ought to doe by the prerogatives and Royalties of the land of Man: upon the Tynwold sitt in a Chaire covered with a Royall Cloth and Quishine [cushion], and your visage unto ye east, your swoard before you, houlden with the pointe upwards, your Barones sitting in their degree beside you, and your Benificed men and your Demesters sitting before you, and your clarkes and your own knightes, esquires, and yeomen in wynge about you in their degree, and the worthiest men in your Lande to be called in before your Demesters, if they will aske any thinge of them, and to heare the governance of your Land ...[148]

148 J. Gill (ed), *The Statutes of the Isle of Man, 1417–1824*, 1(Douglas, 1883), 3–4.

This concise account shows the Manx pride in its ancient Tynwald ceremony.

After 1422 the main English work of substance relating to the Island throughout the fifteenth century and into the sixteenth is the continuing written record of the business of the Keys and the statutes.[149]

However, the Isle of Man is mentioned in a range of other literary works, including various histories and ballads, mostly written elsewhere. Notable among these is a description of Thomas Stanley's role at the battle of Bosworth, part of the developing account of the dynastic history of the Stanleys written by Bishop Thomas Stanley, although it has also been suggested that the likely author of the ballad itself was Richard Sheale, a minstrel-retainer of the earl of Derby in the mid-sixteenth century. Another ballad involving the Stanleys is Richard Johnson's mid-seventeenth-century ballad 'The Lamentable Fall of the Great Duchess of Gloucester', who was imprisoned in Peel Castle in 1446. It was popular and strengthened the Manx notion that the duchess died in Peel Castle, which she haunts.[150]

The Isle of Man itself features more substantially in Michael Drayton's *Poly-Olbion,* an ambitious verse composition of 30 songs in alexandrine couplets, conceived in the late 1590s, which describe scenes of topographical or antiquarian interest in the British Isles. Song 27 in Drayton's second set, published in 1622, is the first poetical description of the Isle of Man in English:

> The Sea-Nymphs with their Song, so great a coyle doe keepe,
> They cease not to resound it over all the Deepe,
> And acted it each day before the Isle of *Man*,
> Who like an Empresse sits in the *Virgivian*,
> By her that hath the *Calfe*, long *Walney*, and the *Pyle*,
> As Hand-mayds to attend on her their Soveraigne Isle …
> With Corne and Cattell stor'd, and what for hers is good,
> (That we, nor *Ireland*, need not scorne her neighbourhood).[151]

149 Gill (ed), *Statutes*, 1, 1–69.

150 Stanley's poem (from MSS including Bodl Rawl Poet 143.II) is published in J.O. Halliwell Phillips (ed), *Palatine Anthology: A Collection of Poems and Ancient Ballads Relating to Lancashire and Cheshire* (London, 1850); A. Taylor, *The Songs and Travels of a Tudor Minstrel: Richard Sheale of Tamworth* (York, 2012). Sheale was a minstrel-retainer to Edward Stanley, 3rd earl of Derby: F. Aydelotte, *Elizabethan Rogues and Vagabonds* (Oxford, 1913), 46; R. Johnson, *The Crown Garland of Golden Roses* (London, 1659. There is a tenuous link, too, with William Shakespeare, who was on the payroll of Ferdinando Stanley at Lathom in 1592: Eleanor Cobham's exile is dramatised in *Henry VI, pt* 2, act 2, scenes 3 & 4.

151 M. Drayton, *Poly-Olbion*, 2nd edn (London, 1622), song 27, lines 261–70; reprinted in *JMM*, 6:79 (1962–63), 169, plate 262 (facing 169). 'Virgivian': Irish Sea, 'Pyle': St Patrick's Isle. A new re-print of Drayton's *Poly-Olbion* is in preparation at the University of Exeter for Oxford University Press: see http://poly-olbion.exeter.ac.uk/the-text/scholarly-edition/ (accessed 7 October 2017).

Drayton was particularly keen to link his county portraits with ancient tales from the old bardic traditions, while at the same time recording contemporary factual details. His description of the Island's 'bituminous Turfe, squar'd from her Mossy ground,/ And trees farre under earth, by daily digging found' suggests that he received eye-witness evidence from someone who knew the Island well. It is significantly more accurate than William Hole's accompanying map.

There are accounts of the Isle of Man by William Camden, but written in Latin, and a record in English of a topographical survey conducted by Thomas Durham in 1595, in which:

> The Isle of Man [is] exactly described and into several Parishes divided, with every Towne, Village, Baye, Creke, and River therein conteyned. The boardringe Coasts where with it is circulated in their situations sett and by the Compasse accordingly shewed …

John Speed drew on Durham's work and used his map in his own history of the Isle of Man.[152]

The descriptions by Camden, Durham and Speed are chorographical, but as the historiography of Britain and the Isle of Man changed in the first half of the seventeenth century, different types of topographical writing emerged, and the events of the civil wars and the constitutional upheaval of the Commonwealth prompted more direct personal reflections in writing about the Isle of Man. This is most obviously represented in William Blundell's history. Blundell was a Lancashire recusant who came to the Isle of Man in 1648 to escape Parliamentarian persecution. He gave his reason for choosing the Island as his place of refuge in his preface:

> For first, ye Island being but as a little molehill moted about with ye main sea, and removed from England, I fancied it a place freed from our Island, so likewise freed from our fears and troubles, and therefore probably I cou'd not meet with any nightmares in Man to molest me.[153]

Blundell stayed for almost a year and used his time to make a perceptive and authoritative assessment of the nature of the Isle of Man and its people. He

152 W. Camden, *Britannia sive Florentissimorum regnorum, Angliæ, Scotiæ, Hiberniæ, et insularum adjacentium ex intima antiquitate chorographica* (London, 1586), 528–42; J. Speed, *The Theatre of the Empire of Greate Britaine Presenting an Exact Geography of the Kingdomes of England, Scotland, Ireland, and the Iles Adioyning: With the Shires, Hundreds, Cities and Shire-Townes, Within ye Kingdome of England* (London, 1611), 91–92. Durham's survey, commissioned by Thomas Gerrard, Elizabeth I's governor of the Isle of Man, was printed by John Speed.

153 MNH MS 00049 C, W. Blundell, 'A History of the Isle of Man', 2 vols (1648–56), vol. 1, 4: 'The Author to the Reader'.

was scathing about Camden and Speed, as neither had actually visited the Isle of Man, and he was even more scornful towards John Merrick, the Island's bishop from 1577 to 1599, who had supplied Camden with information about the Island, which Blundell regarded as mainly nonsense.

Blundell's work was ground-breaking. His knowledge is comprehensive, his comments are discerning and his written style is lively. He spent many years working on his history and intended to have it printed, but by the time he had finished, he did not have the finances to do so. Careful and not so careful copies of his manuscript were made and used in later descriptions of the Isle of Man.[154]

An early sketch of the history of the Isle of Man opens with a sequence of letters written from Castle Rushen in 1643 by James Stanley, seventh earl of Derby, to his son Charles. The forthright perspectives and confident tone of the letters reflect the authority of the Stanley lordship, but this is moderated by a careful reflection on the nature of that authority: 'I conceive,' the earl wrote, 'that to be a great lord is a more honourable title than a petty king. Besides: it is not for a king to be subject, but to the King of kings.' He makes much of his skill in dealing with the Islanders' grievances in the rebellion of 1643, and gives his son perceptive advice, both on how to live honourably and how to get the better of his Manx subjects.[155]

These letters show his hands-on knowledge of the Island and its people and his determination to exploit it, as much for his own benefit as for the Island's future prosperity. James Stanley's letter-writing gives striking illustrations of both his character and the distinctiveness of his epistolary style. His acid letter in 1649 to Commissary General Ireton, who offered him full restitution of his English estates if he would make over the Isle of Man to the Parliamentarians, combines rhetorical devices with personal engagement:

> I received your letter with indignation, and with scorn I return you this answer: . . I scorn your proffers; I disdain your favours; I abhor your treasons; and am so far from delivering this island to your advantage, that I will keep it to the utmost of my power to your destruction. Take this final answer, and forbear any further solicitations; for if you trouble me with any more messages upon this occasion, I will burn the paper and hang the bearer.[156]

154 Sacheverell and Seacome used Blundell. See W. Sacheverell, *An Account of the Isle of Man* (London, 1702); J. Seacome, *Memoirs; containing a genealogical and historical account of the ancient and honourable house of Stanley, from the Conquest to the death of James, Earl of Derby in the year 1735; as also a full description of the Isle of Man* (Liverpool, 1741).

155 W. Mackenzie (ed), *Legislation by three of the thirteen Stanleys*, Manx Society, 3 (1860), 1–53.

156 Seacome, *Memoirs*, 92–93.

By contrast, his last letters to his wife and children, written from Bolton as he awaited his execution in 1651, are expressed in a very different tone and are a moving read.[157]

The Isle of Man was given to Fairfax by the Rump Parliament in 1649, but it was not until 1651 that he sent three commissioners, James Chaloner, Robert Dynely and Joshua Witton, to survey his new domain. Chaloner's report was later included in *The Vale Royal of England; or, the County Palatine of Chester*, published by Daniel King in 1656 as an appendix with its own title page, *A Short Treatise of the Isle of Man*. It consists of six chapters dealing with the Island's geography, inhabitants, civil and church government, trade and fortifications. As to the Manx people, he gives the following description:

> The Inhabitants ... are at this day a very civill People, laborious, contented with simple Diet and lodging; their Drink, water; their Meat, Fish; their bedding, Hay or Straw, generally; much addicted to the Music of the Violyne.[158]

Chaloner's treatise is the oldest printed history of the Isle of Man in English.[159] It is enlivened by his antiquarian interests and the writing reflects his skill as a commentator and his even-handed approach to the events he describes.

One of the most significant events in the development of writing in English in the Isle of Man was the establishment, by order of Bishop Barrow, of primary schools to teach Manx children to read and write English. Barrow had been appointed bishop of Sodor and Man in 1663. His initiatives to promote education and literacy were commended by William Sacheverell, the Island's governor, at the end of the seventeenth century.

In 1702 Sacheverell published a history of the Isle of Man written in the form of letters or 'essays' to various people. His style is elegant, often with an undertone of irony which begins in his preface, where he claims that his book:

> ... is the effect of mere idleness, so if it chance to amuse any person as idle as myself, I have all I dare pretend to, and yet even in this I almost despair of success; for the place is so obscure, and the matter so narrow, that it is incapable of those curious transitions, those admirable reflexions, and all those refined characters which at once serve to adorn and to instruct; though

157 Seacome, *Memoirs*, 133–34, 147- 48.

158 J. Chaloner, *A Short Treatise of the Isle of Man [...] Illustrated with Severall Prospects of the Island, by Daniel King* (London, 1656).

159 John Speed's *Theatre of Empire*, first printed in 1611, contains a short description of the Isle of Man, but Chaloner's *Treatise* is the first extended history of the Island.

> by taking the looser way of essay, I have endeavoured to render the whole as diverting as I could.[160]

Sacheverell offers more than a standard history. His work reflects a practical agenda for the development of the Island, and it is no surprise that he expresses strongly his sense of the primacy of English as the Island's language of communication. In addition to his focus on the Island's economy and welfare, he also shows a lively antiquarian interest in the character of the Manx, as for example in his accounts of Fairy Hill.[161]

Thomas Wilson, the Island's much-loved bishop, who held the see from 1698–1755, was urged to write a history of the Isle of Man by Edmund Gibson, bishop of London, an earnest antiquarian. He duly did so, and although it seems that his history was never printed separately, Gibson included it in his 1722 edition of Camden's *Britannia*, and it was included in Clement Cruttwell's eight-volume collection of Wilson's works, first published in 1784.[162] Wilson's history, like Sacheverell's, reflects more than just an antiquarian interest, and includes comments on moral and social issues, such as ecclesiastical discipline and the rights of women.[163]

One of the most influential of Wilson's didactic works is *A Short and Plain Instruction for the Better Understanding of the Lord's Supper*, first published in 1734. This treatise demonstrates particularly well Wilson's accessible and compelling style of language which enabled him to communicate effectively with ordinary people: 'Stop here a-while,' he exhorts the reader, 'and adore the infinite goodness of God, who did not overlook mankind, but sent his Son to redeem us.'[164]

The Reverend Hugh Stowell's biography of Bishop Wilson, published in 1819, was widely read by the Manx.[165] He was a Manxman and reflected his fellow Islanders' opinions and stories about Bishop Wilson. When Robert Brown in 1826 published a collection of poems, he dedicated the book to Stowell in appreciation not only of the edifying example he set by his life but also because

160 Sacheverell, *Account*, 'Preface to the Reader', n.p. Sacheverell had been made deputy-governor of the Island in 1692 and served as governor from 1694 to 1696.

161 Sacheverell, *Account*, 14–17.

162 E. Gibson (ed), *Britain, or a Chorographicall description of … England, Scotland and Ireland* [Camden's *Britannia*], 2nd edn (London, 1722); Cruttwell, *Wilson*, 1, 299–342.

163 Cruttwell, *Wilson*, 1, 329–32.

164 T. Wilson, A Short and Plain Instruction for the Better Understanding of the Lord's Supper, with the necessary Preparation requir'd: for the Benefit of Young Communicants and of such as have not well Consider'd this Holy Ordinance (London and Dublin, 1734): in Cruttwell, *Wilson*, 2, 5–140. The book became a theological bestseller.

165 H. Stowell, *The Life of the Right Reverend Father in God Thomas Wilson, D.D., Lord Bishop of Sodor and Man* (London, 1819).

of his 'inestimable memoirs of Bishop Wilson'. Another attraction to Manx readers was its single-volume price.

The Rev. Clement Cruttwell on the other hand had what can only be called an obsession with Bishop Wilson. He not only published a biography of him, he collected everything Wilson had preached or written or said or even thought in his *Sacra Privata* (his private diaries) until Cruttwell had his eight volumes presentation ready in 1784. This collection was reprinted in many editions throughout the nineteenth century.

In the appendix to volume 1, Cruttwell includes three poems to Wilson's memory, of which the first is an elegy, written by '*a Gentlewoman of the Isle of Man*' in an ornate style that shows her familiarity with poetic conventions in the mid-eighteenth century:

> A Chilling damp invades my trembling heart,
> Steals through each vein, and sickens every part!
> The morning weeps and wears a sullen face;
> Serene Nature feels some sudden sad distress.
> ... Ah! Hold, my boding heart – is SODOR dead?
> Is Mona's Guardian Angel from her fled?[166]

Cruttwell's collection of Wilson's works was reprinted in many editions throughout the nineteenth century.

In 1711 the British Government sent customs officers to the Isle of Man to report on what cargoes were being unloaded or shipped out – in other words, to keep an eye on the smuggling trade. George Waldron held such a brief.[167] During his stay he became interested in Manx folklore and his collection was supposedly published in 1726, although no copy has been found.[168] He died in London in 1730 and in the following year his widow, Theodosia, had his collected oeuvre printed by subscription in a handsome folio edition.[169] *A Description of the Isle of Man: with some Useful and Entertaining Reflections on the Laws, Customs, and Manners of its Inhabitants* was the result – in Waldron's own words – of almost twenty years on the Isle of Man. Did he understand or speak Manx? As there are no written sources for the stories before his collection, were all of them genuinely old or told for the price of a *jough* (beer) and a smoke in the company of a gullible Englishman? Evidence from some of Waldron's other

166 Cruttwell, *Wilson*, 1, 282.

167 See E. Baigent, 'Waldron, George (1689/90–1726)', in *ODNB* (Oxford, 2004).

168 Cubbon has no record of a folklore collection published by Waldron. See Cubbon, *Bibliographical Account*, vol. 1, 463–64.

169 Waldron also wrote poetic eulogies about important persons in the hope of gaining favours. He seems to have been in financial difficulties, which may account for the apparent failure to publish in 1726; he had been forced to sell off family heirlooms, as a letter to Sir Hans Sloane dated 13 December 1722, shows: BL, Sloane 4061, f.316.

writing, for example his *Perswasive Oration to the People of Great Britain to stand up in defence of their Religion and Liberty*, published in 1716, suggests that Waldron was more discerning than he seems to be here. Whatever the truth, these stories have ever since been regarded as genuine and used repeatedly in literary contexts. Waldron's less fanciful descriptions of how the Manx lived are invaluable to the social historian.

It is understandable that not everyone living on the Isle of Man found it agreeable and to their liking, but one can only guess at what had happened to the miserable stranger who in 1733 left behind an almost hysterical tirade called 'Mona Farewell':

> With thy three monstrous emblematic legs,
> With all thy brandy, and with all thy kegs,
> Mona! where none but fools and madmen come,
> To drench their care in brandy and in rum;
> Mona! where strangers are most strangely treated,
> And all combine to cheat, or to be cheated;
> ... Mona! thou territory of the devil; –
> Blessed be this day that thou and I do sever.[170]

In John Seacome, steward to the ninth earl, the Stanley family had their own chronicler. He had access to the family's manuscripts, documents and letters, and he had also read the manuscript of Blundell's history of the Isle of Man (kept at Knowsley), although he seems to have mostly used Chaloner's *Treatise* in his own history, which he published in Liverpool in 1741 and called *A Compleat History of the Isle of Man* as part of his *Memoirs of the Ancient and Honourable House of Stanley*. It proved popular and several editions were printed with additions. The Manx content is largely derivative as Seacome's introduction shows:

> This Island appears but little, or but darkly known to the Ancients; and amongst all our modern Historians and Geographers there is not one has given any tolerable Account of it before Mr. James Challoner [*sic*], Governor for the Lord Fairfax, and the great and learned Mr. Blundell of Crosby.[171]

Commemorative ballads always found a ready readership. They were printed and sold for a penny a sheet, which was affordable to many. Several ballads in Manx or English recorded the death of François Thurot in 1760. He had been

170 *Mona Miscellany*, 1st ser., Manx Society, 16 (1869), 240. W. Harrison (ed) calls the author 'an odd-tempered gentleman', but gives no other information about the provenance of this poem.

171 J. Seacome, *A Compleat History of the Isle of Man*, published with *Memoirs of the Ancient and Honourable House of Stanley* (Liverpool, 1741), 1.

a successful privateer, who during the Seven Years War became engaged as a respectable naval captain by the French government for his superior navigational skills and knowledge of the British and Manx coastlines. He was killed during a sea battle off the coast of Bishopscourt, when Captain John Elliott RN took on and defeated Thurot's squadron. John Quirk's translation from the Manx of 'Thurot and Elliott' has an unpolished simplicity typical of many of the Island's ballads:

> The people who dwelt on the west side of Mona,
> E'en Bishop Mark Hildersley with all of his train,
> Could hear the tough music of cannons were booming,
> And much of their doings could plainly be seen.
>
> They saw the Bellisle was deprived of her bowsprit,
> A log which soon reached the Bishop's domain,
> To stand on an eminence commemorating
> The day and its deeds, with all things that came.
>
> Then round Point of Ayre most gallantly leading,
> They brought up their captives towards Ramsey Bay;
> At day-light's returning poor Frenchmen were mourning,
> To know their great Thurot was lifeless as clay ...[172]

Unpolished simplicity was hardly an expression startled readers of the *Town and Country Magazine* in 1769 would have used when coming across a poetic account of Godred Crovan's third attempt to conquer the Isle of Man. It was a wild and furious poem with amazing word-paintings, supposedly written by 'Dopnal Syrric, Scheld of Godred Crovan, King of the Isle of Man'. But like the Ossian-poems that had inspired it, it was a forgery by the troubled seventeen-year-old poetic genius Thomas Chatterton, who took his own life in desperation over lack of income.

One of the most notable Manx ballads describes the wreck of the herring fleet in Douglas harbour in the storm on the night of 21 September 1787. It was translated into English in a number of versions. John Quirk rendered it as *The Fishermen's Ballad*.[173] Quirk's education was rudimentary, but he had a great talent for writing ballads and *carvals* and translated many old Manx ballads into English.[174] A second ballad dealing with the disaster, called *A Doleful Ditty*, was composed by 'a native poet', sung to the now forgotten *Boreas* tune. In

172 *Mona Miscellany*, 2nd ser., Manx Society, 21 (1873), 83–86.
173 *Mona Miscellany*, 1st ser., Manx Society, 16 (1869), 90–95.
174 See this chapter, F. Bazin, 'Music'.

contrast to Quirk's lively style it is a pedestrian attempt, but strophe six, which puts the blame squarely on the government, is unexpected.[175]

> Had the pier of Douglas been rebuilt,
> The misfortune had not been,
> And it really is most scandalous
> That the ruins are still seen.
> Ships and boats pay certain duties,
> The harbour to keep in repair;
> Pray then why not repair our harbour,
> And rebuild our quay and pier?

There was also an eyewitness to the tragedy, David Robertson, a customs officer whose description written seven years later and published in his *Tour through the Isle of Man* became a classic account.[176] He spent the summer of 1791 visiting old friends and walked his way around the Island, describing buildings and landscapes to future visitors. He was a true son of the Romantic movement, and there is hardly a page without the words 'romantic', 'serene' or 'awe-inspiring'. But he had also been shaped by the Enlightenment, and his book ends with an attack on the duke of Atholl, together with a clarion call to overthrow the ruling classes:

> The tyrant shall be hurled from his throne; the traitor of Liberty sacrificed at her altar, on the firm basis of Justice shall be established the Rights of Mankind: the wreath of Honour alone deck the brow of Virtue and Genius: and 'throughout the whole earth', every knee shall bow to the MAJESTY OF THE PEOPLE!'[177]

Perhaps the rugged coastline of the Island and the independent character of its people struck a chord with his revolutionary ideas and, echoing popular sentiment at the end of the eighteenth century, the Atholls were an obvious target. Not surprisingly, his tirade landed Robertson in jail. Nonetheless, his *Tour* became very popular and was reprinted in a number of editions but without pages 233–35. That the book was in tune with the time is shown by its translations into French and German, a treatment not given to any other book about the Isle of Man at this point.

Adventures at sea far away from the Isle of Man are recounted by John Gell, a Manxman, who in 1789 wrote an account of the horrors of the Seven Years Wars that he met with while he was apprenticed to Joseph Bacon, a Douglas

175 *Mona Miscellany*, 1st ser., 96–97.

176 D. Robertson, *A Tour through the Isle of Man: to which is subjoined A Review of the Manx History*, 1st edn (London, 1794).

177 Robertson, *Tour*, 1st edn, 235.

merchant. During his first voyage aboard one of Bacon's ships, the vessel was captured by a French privateer, and the trials of Gell's second voyage were even worse:

> Some few weeks afterwards I again sailed from Douglas in a large cutter, the property of the said merchant, Mr Bacon, and bound to South Carolina, and within three leagues of that place we met with three American ships well armed, bound to France, and were by them taken prisoners and landed in Lorion, in France, and from thence marched to Donan prison, a distance of scores of miles, and there closely confined with hundreds of prisoners of different nations, nearly in a way of starvation, having very little to eat, and no beds, but merely a trifle of straw, without any covering but our own clothes, some of the prisoners dying daily, from eight to ten in number.[178]

That the Isle of Man had started to interest the outside world can also be judged by the fact that Colonel Richard Townley could in 1791 publish *A Journal kept in the Isle of Man* and find people willing to pay to read it. His diary starts in Whitehaven on 30 April 1789 and ends on 20 April 1790, when he left the Island at 3 o'clock in the morning. Townley took lodgings at the Liverpool Coffee House in Douglas. His entries describe the circumspect life of a solitary retired gentleman of modest means. His favourite pastime is walking, he is fond of birds and often refers to them in his diary, and each day he carefully notes down wind and weather. A typical entry reads:

> 23d. [January, 1790] A very mild looking morning tempted me to break my confinement, a little after eleven, and take a few turns upon the pier head. - Numbers were entertained, as well as myself, with the melody of my sweet thrush, perched on his beloved thorn, and warbling with as much spirit as if it had been an April morning; not one of those that are clad in a wintry cloud, but one of these rare ones, when mildness and serenity equally prevails.[179]

When the weather was inclement, he sat by the fire and copied passages from a history of the Island, which he thought was written by a Welshman. He scarcely conceals his low opinion of the author, but what he was reading was a manuscript copy of Blundell's *History*.[180]

178 *Manx Miscellanies*, vol. 2, Manx Society, 30 (1880), no. 5, 'Journal of the Rev. John Gell', 8.

179 R. Townley, *A Journal kept in the Isle of Man*, 2 vols (Whitehaven, 1791), vol. 1, 152–53.

180 Townley's copy of Blundell's manuscript was lent to him by a Manx acquaintance, James Oates. See P.W. Caine, 'William Blundell and his Manx History', *PIMNHAS*, 5:2, 128–35.

David Robertson was equally critical of Townley's book, which he described as his 'voluminous Journal of Trifles'.[181] John Stowell, who wrote for the Island's first newspaper, *The Manx Mercury and Briscoe's Douglas Advertiser*, and was well known for his satirical poems under various pseudonyms, also found Townley pompous and dull.[182] His verse satire of Townley's *Journal*, 'A Literary Quixote; or, The Beauties of Townley Versified', is sharp and well-observed, as in this parody of Townley's discovery of a grey-goose pinion in the sand:

> Douglas, May 14, 1789 …
>
> For know ye natives of this happy land,
> 'Tis that same quill I now hold in my hand:
> … 'Tis that same quill that lifts my fame like stilts on,
> And safely conducts me to my landlord Wilson.
> By that same quill is Mona's greatness known;
> By that same quill the world finds out my own:
> But for this very quill what had I been?
> A sweet neglected flow'r to blush unseen.[183]

It is not known whether Townley read it.

In 1797 John Feltham arrived in the Isle of Man on the first of two walking tours. He kept a journal and published it, in letter form, as *A Tour Through the Island of Mann, In 1797 and 1798*.[184] In marked contrast to Robertson and Townley, Feltham's voice does not intrude into his narrative, and the *Tour* reveals a man fascinated by facts and statistics, as in his description of fishing and the herring:

> The fresh herrings of the Island are peculiarly good, and larger than those of Yarmouth. When the season arrives, the fish are looked for, and their appearance is indicated by the quantity of gulls that hover around them, no less eager than the Manksman to feast on the delicious fare. At this period, therefore, the gull is considered sacred. The first maize that are caught are entitled to a bounty.

He links his account with the deemster's oath, with its promise to execute the laws 'as indifferently as the herring's backbone does lie in the midst of the fish',

181 Robertson, *Tour*, 1st edn, 34.

182 John Stowell, master of Peel grammar school, is the Island's 'solitary poet' referred to in Samuel Burdy's reminiscences of a Manx holiday, *Ardglass, or The Ruined Castles* (Dublin, 1802), 23.

183 J. Stowell, *The Literary Quixote: or, the beauties of Townley versified* (Douglas, 1791), 9.

184 J. Feltham, *A Tour through the Island of Mann, in 1797 and 1798* (Bath, 1798).

and copies for the reader a long poem entitled 'The Herring Fishery', written by 'A Manks Lady'.[185] It is also Feltham who in his book mentions the first novel written in the Island. It was called 'Literary Lovers', printed by Briscoe, but there is no record that a copy has ever been seen.[186]

There is better luck with the second novel, also printed by Briscoe, in 1792. It is called 'The Manks Monastery: or, Loves of BELVILLE & JULIA' and was written by Thomas Ashe, a talented writer of somewhat dubious reputation.[187] The Manx Museum Library has the only known copy.[188] It is a story about a young couple in medieval times in the Isle of Man. The father does not approve of his daughter's admirer and puts her in the Nunnery, but Belville gains entry late one night and with a lot of weeping on both sides the couple spend a night of passionate love. The young man leaves in the morning but cannot gain entry again. He stands day after day at the Nunnery's gate, pleading, and neglects his health until he finally falls down dead. When Julia learns about it, she suffers the same fate. It would have been interesting to ascertain what Manx readers at the time thought of the book, as they had in general a strong dislike of fiction.

Feltham's eclectic interests and new perspectives on the Island marked a distinctive shift away from earlier voices like Blundell and Seacome, and something similar was heard again in 1811, when George Woods published his *Account of the Past and Present State of the Isle of Man*, a handsome book, richly illustrated, with a new map, and chapters on the Island's mineralogy and agriculture.[189] Five years later, Hannah Bullock, who came to the Island in 1809, published her *History of the Isle of Man*.[190] This is a lengthy and detailed study running to 382 pages, and although the historical chapters are largely derivative, based on Seacome, her careful observations of the state of the Island in the beginning of the nineteenth century follow Feltham's lead. Her opinions and style are forthright. She found little to commend in the Island's landscape, finding 'no great beauties, nothing to elevate or astonish, and not much to admire: the mountains are of too tame a character, and too frequently covered with fog'. She is no less scornful of newly resident ladies, who 'exhibit a sovereign contempt for those they came to live amongst, a prodigious flippancy… and pretensions to a rank in their own country not always borne

185 Feltham, *Tour*, 88 (maize – a measure of 625 herring), 93–98.
186 Cubbon, W. (ed), 1933 & 1939, *A Bibliographical Account of Works relating to the Isle of Man*, 2 vols (Douglas), vol. 2, 1138.
187 See U. Corkill, 'Nineteenth-century literature in English relating to the Isle of Man', in J. Belchem (ed), *A New History of the Isle of Man*, vol. 5, *the modern period 1830–1999* (Liverpool, 2000), 329.
188 Cubbon, *Bibliographical Account*, vol. 2, 1100–01.
189 G. Woods, *An Account of the Past and Present State of the Isle of Man* (London and Edinburgh, 1811).
190 H. Bullock, *History of the Isle of Man* (London, 1816).

out by facts', whereas the homely virtues of Manx women are commended as 'most favourable to feminine virtues'.[191]

In many ways, Feltham, Woods and Hannah Bullock were writing early guidebooks. The first publication designed as a guidebook was Samuel Haining's *A Historical Sketch and Descriptive View of the Isle of Man; Designed as A Companion to Those Who Visit and Make The Tour of It*, printed in Douglas in 1822.[192] It contained a map with roads marked out, details of distances from various geographical points, a brief account of the Island's civil and ecclesiastical history, and a description of places to visit. Two years later, Haining produced a second edition, reflecting his readers' comments, 'carefully corrected and greatly improved'.[193]

It is hardly likely that Dorothy Wordsworth would have bought a copy. She came in 1828 to visit her brother-in-law Henry Hutchinson and his sister Johanna, stayed for three weeks and, as always, she wrote a lively and observant diary. On 27 June she described her first impressions of Douglas Bay:

> Very fine walk after tea on the cliffs; sea calm, and as if enclosed by hazy dark steps; fishes sporting near the rocks, a few sea-birds chatter and wail, but mostly silent rocks; two very grand masses in a little bay, a pellucid rivulet of sea-water between them. The hills mostly covered with cropped gorse, a very rich dark green. This gorse cropped in winter, and bruised for cattle fodder. The moon rose large and dull, like an ill-cleaned brass plate, slowly surmounts the haze, and sends over the calm sea a faint bright pillar. In the opposite quarter Douglas harbour illuminated; boats in motion, dark masts and elegant ropes; noises from the town ascend to the commanding airy steps where we rested.[194]

Her descriptions of sights and sounds have an imaginative charm. She has a painter's eye, yet at the same time she shows, in the 'gorse … bruised for cattle fodder', that she is well acquainted with farming methods. The Manx had to wait another five years before her famous brother William would visit the Isle of Man and would write a series of simple poems about the Island.[195]

191 Bullock, *History*, 201, 343, 344.

192 S. Haining, *A Historical Sketch and Descriptive View of the Isle of Man; Designed as A Companion to Those Who Visit and Make The Tour of It*, 1st edn (Douglas, 1822). Haining (1778–1846), who originally came from Kirkcudbright, was minister of the Independent Chapel in Athol Street and a teacher at the Lancastrian School in Douglas.

193 Haining, *Historical Sketch*, 2nd edn (Douglas, 1824), 'Prefatory Remarks'.

194 E. de Selincourt (ed), *Journals of Dorothy Wordsworth* (London, 1939), 2, 402.

195 T. Hutchinson and E. de Selincourt (eds), *The Poetical Works of William Wordsworth* (London and Oxford, 1936): 'Itinerary Poems of 1833', 365–69. Wordsworth's elegy 'Peele Castle', in his Poems of 1807, long cherished by Manx readers, is a reflection on George Beaumont's painting of Peele castle at Foudrey, near Barrow.

The literature related to the Isle of Man and created up to the end of the eighteenth century is almost entirely of an informative nature, although enlivened in a number of instances by personal and sometimes patronising comments. The authors are almost always English. Manx writers like John Gell and Hugh Stowell are few and far between. Most of the poetry, whether original or translations of Manx ballads, is unsophisticated but often has a simple charm. Visitors like Robertson and the Wordsworths brought a glimpse of the flowering of Romanticism into English writing about the Isle of Man before 1830. However, the educated Manx, able to get newspapers and books and to travel, were now well acquainted with cultural fashions. Robert Brown, T.E. Brown's father, showed in his collection *Poems, principally on Sacred Subjects*, published in London in 1826, his deep love of homeland, in itself a result of the Napoleonic wars, in his poem 'My Native Land', while in 'Lines on Viewing Peel Castle by Moonlight' he refers to the Isle of Man as 'yonder small romantic isle'. The very fact that Peel Castle is now viewed in moonlight is a romantic trait. The same sentiment is present in the poem 'Lines on viewing The Nunnery near Douglas':

> How sweet at this still hour to rove,
> And by the moon's soft light to view
> The foliage of that dusky grove,
> The water of that streamlet blue,
> The ivy robe which age has thrown
> On yonder chapel's mouldering stone.

From now on and during the entire nineteenth century Manx-born writers and poets would appear who could compete with British writers in their own language.

MUSIC

Fenella Bazin

Documentary evidence only offers occasional glimpses into the musical life of the period. Diaries, wills, presentments, newspapers and music manuscripts are just some of the sources that allow us to see something of the Island's music making. It is inevitable that most of the singers, dancers and instrumentalists will remain anonymous and we will never know the songs, dances and melodies in their repertoires. The records that do survive, however, give a lively and often vivid insight into the musical life of a musical nation.

Popular music and dance

The Church authorities were strict when it came to the Sabbath. In 1635, the parish of Arborie [*sic*] gave assurances that 'Many have used dancing on ye Sabbath after ye services; but have given it ovr nowe', and in 1762 John Cannell of Douglas was presented for playing the fiddle late on Saturday night. He was confined in St German's prison but released on payment of £3.[196] The presentments are probably only the tip of the iceberg, suggesting that music and dance were popular pastimes. Chaloner, writing in around 1650, commented that 'the Manks… are much addicted to the Musick of the Violynes' but commented that 'as they are all ill composers, so are they bad players'.[197] The fiddle was the most common instrument as it was portable and a simple violin could be made cheaply by a good craftsman.

Popular music arrived by a number of means, through the oral tradition as well as printed sources. The *Fitzwilliam Virginal Book* includes 'Quodling's Delight', a tune attributed to Giles Farnaby. By whatever means it was popularized among the Manx population, there are at least nine variations in the Manx repertoire, appearing with both Manx and English titles and in major and minor keys. In 1677, Grace Quaile died, leaving instructions that if her daughter Ann decided to stay with her step-father in Ramsey, he was 'to send for a woman of skille and knowledge to keep his house and to teach my daughter her book and needle and to learn the virginals [*sic*] (which virginals are now in my house)'.[198]

Press advertisements with lists of new songs and dance tunes show that the gentry kept up with wider fashions.[199] By the early 1800s there were many established music teachers and other professional musicians, mainly from Ireland and England and based in Douglas. Social life centred on musical events. There were concerts of sacred music, as well as theatres and formal dinners, and local bands took part in the annual ceremonies and celebrations of the numerous benevolent societies. The folksong collectors of the nineteenth century discovered that many of the popular tunes of the seventeenth and eighteenth centuries found their way from the surrounding countries into the oral tradition.[200]

196 *JMM*, 2:29 (December 1931), 37, doc. 16.

197 J. Chaloner, *A Short Treatise of the Isle of Man […] Illustrated with Severall Prospects of the Island, by Daniel King* (London, 1656), 5.

198 MNH MS 10216 (EW), 1677.

199 *Manks Advertiser*, 1 February 1830.

200 F.C. Bazin, 'Music in the Isle of Man up to 1896' (PhD thesis, University of Liverpool, 1995), 239–42, 225–26, 297- 400. *Manks Advertiser*, 1 February 1831: a 'Concert of Sacred Music'; *Manks Advertiser*, 13 December 1831: a 'Charity Concert for the poor of this town'.

Sacred music

No records have yet emerged of the music sung by the monks of Rushen Abbey or the earls of Derby's private chapel. For six years from 1503, John Darse was sponsored by the abbot of Rushen to study music with William Parke of Chester. The indenture specified writing in five parts, composing 'in every mesur', organ-playing and teaching skills, so that Darse would return to the abbey to impart his knowledge. In the absence of evidence, there is no indication of the quality or repertoire, or whether the music was influenced by any neighbouring foundations in Cumbria, Scotland or Ireland, or if echoes survived from historic Nidaros.[201] Sacred and secular music for the earls of Derby would certainly have kept pace with contemporary fashions, but there is a question mark as to whether this influence fed into the small community at the Abbey.[202] The Reformation seemed to have little effect on the Manx Church, so it would be reasonable to assume that any music in parish churches owed much to that of the early Celtic church, a style that was prevalent in urban Edinburgh and Aberdeen as late as 1756 and that still survives in the remarkable Gaelic psalms of the Isle of Lewis.[203] Hall Caine hints that some remnants still existed in Man: 'the wild discord of their voices ... When they had finished the hymn, they began on it again ... sweeping the dying note of the last word into the rising pitch of the first one'.[204]

In 1683 Samsburie Radcliffe, then aged 66, reported that there had been quire stalls in St German's Cathedral and there had also been 'a rood loft for organ over ye entrance into ye Chancel which was also curiously carved on ye east and west end', including the eagle and child, the Derby family crest.[205]

The first organ in a parish church was installed in the stylish newly-built town church of St George's in 1778, but this was felt to have caused a decline in the quality of the congregational singing.[206] The trustees had bought the second-hand instrument for £100 (Irish) and, contrary to popular belief, it was not the instrument that Handel had played for the first performance in Dublin of the *Messiah*.[207] Castletown residents petitioned Governor Cornelius Smelt

201 There is a hint of the old Norwegian connection in 'Arrane ny Ghelby', one of the folk tunes collected by Sophia Morrison, which bears an uncanny resemblance to a wedding song performed at the marriage in Bergen of Margaret of Scotland and King Eric II of Norway in 1281: J. Purser, *Scotland's music: a history of the traditional and classical music of Scotland from earliest times to the present day* (Edinburgh, 1992), 60–61; Bazin, 'Music in the Isle of Man', 39.

202 Bazin, 'Music in the Isle of Man', 37.

203 Purser, *Scotland's music*, 146.

204 H. Caine, *The Manxman* (London, 1897), 164.

205 R.A. Curphey, 'Peel Castle', *PIMNHAS*, 9:1 (1982), 86.

206 F.C. Bazin, *The Everlasting Hills: Hymns from the Isle of Man* (Isle of Man, 2006).

207 Bazin, 'Music in the Isle of Man', 201.

in 1806 for money to purchase an organ for St Mary's. Couched in flowery language, the document emphasized the power of music to strengthen devotion and advance 'Praise into Rapture', promising to exclude the 'effeminate and frittered music of modern Italy'.[208] The first recital was in 1811, but in 1826 the congregation was disturbed to see that the Manx coat of arms had been removed from the front of the organ gallery to be replaced by the royal arms.[209] Generally, the installation of organs was slow, partly due to resistance to change but mainly because of cost.

There seems to have been a long tradition of more familiar forms of sacred singing in the Isle of Man. John Wesley compared Manx singers favourably with standards in centres such as Bristol and Lincoln. 'Both men and women', he wrote, 'have admirable voices and they sing with good judgement. Who would have expected this in the Isle of Man?'[210] This suggests a mainstream tradition, probably brought about because of the parochial system of schooling and through the efforts of late eighteenth-century figures such as Bishop Hildesley in 1763 to encourage the work of travelling choir masters. His actions seem to have borne fruit as, just two years later, Wilfred Richardson, teacher of psalmody, was witness to the marriage between Patrick Kewley and Ann Shimmin of the parish of German.[211]

Itinerant singing masters from Cumberland trained Manx church choirs from the late 1700s, bringing with them settings of metrical psalms. William Shepherd from Cockermouth in Cumberland is known to have spent many years, particularly in the south of the Island, active between 1809 and 1820, training at least three separate church choirs and leaving behind him documentary evidence in the form of handwritten choir parts and books.[212] There was also a less tangible heritage as melodies, sometimes memorable for the wrong reasons, filtered their way into the oral tradition.

Music in the parish churches seems to have gone into a decline as many of the singers and musicians chose the Methodist route. By 1828 there was a formal move to raise musical standards in at least one parish church: a supper meeting was held in Malew with the sole purpose of restoring 'the most interesting and

208 *JMM*, 2:32 (September 1932), 72, doc. 37.

209 *Manx Sun*, 24 June 1826.

210 Bazin, *Everlasting Hills*, 1.

211 MNH MS 09309 (Diocesan Records: correspondence of Hildesley), Hildesley to Philip Moore, 13 January 1763. In Hildesley's letter of 13 January 1763 he commented that he saw and heard 'nothing of the Teaching Psalmodist', perhaps a reference to Wilfred Richardson.

212 F. Roads (ed), *Ye Boundless Realms of Joy: Forty West Gallery psalms, hymns and anthems from the Colby Manuscripts, collected and used by William Shepherd in the Isle of Man in the early decades of the 19th Century, with 32 added Manx texts* (Isle of Man, 2006).

ancient mode of Divine Service, Psalmody, which is usually so neglected in our Church ... and in which sacred duty the Dissenters so successfully rival us.'[213]

On special occasions, congregations were accompanied by makeshift bands. Standards of playing would have swung from very basic to competent or, on occasion, inspired. One trumpet descant to Luther's hymn was said to have been so overwhelmingly powerful that every member of the congregation vowed to lead impeccable lives henceforth![214]

Otherwise, as in other areas in the British Isles, the story is a familiar one. Until the installation of organs in churches and chapels in the late eighteenth and early nineteenth centuries, singing was usually unaccompanied. Advertisements for parish clerks called not only for literacy, both in Manx Gaelic and English, but also for candidates who could sing well. The appointment in 1698–99 of Edmond Corlett to the role of parish clerk in Lezayre notes 'his sufficiency for reading and writing and also of his competent skill in singing, which qualifies him for the capacity of a parish clerk's office.'[215] They were expected to 'raise' the hymns, singing them out line by line, to be echoed by congregations. So in theory every hymn would last twice as long as it would otherwise. Remnants of this tradition can be heard still. In some Methodist churches the whole of the first verse is read out when the hymn is announced. A more unusual survival is that of hymn-raising competitions in rural festivals in the Isle of Man (*cruinnaghts*) and Wales (*eisteddfodau*).

At Bishop Hildesley's suggestion, the 1768 edition of the *Book of Common Prayer* included a selection of metrical versions of the Psalms of David in Manx, many based on those of Tate and Brady for use in parish churches.[216] Although Daniel Cowley had published some of Wesley's hymns in Manx in 1778, it was not until 1799 that the first printed hymn book in Manx of any significance appeared.[217] Both were produced for use by Methodists, as the singing of hymns in the Anglican Church was technically illegal until the nineteenth century.[218]

213 *Manx Sun*, 15 January 1828.

214 J. Cowin, *Reminiscences of notable Douglas Citizens and a Review of Manx Men and Manners fifty years ago* (Douglas, 1902).

215 R.D. Kermode, *The Annals of Kirk Christ Lezayre* (Douglas, 1954).

216 The Book of Common Prayer [...] translated into Manks, For the Use of the Diocese of Mann (the 'Ramsey' Book of Common Prayer, Ramsey, 1769). See chapter 2 'Religion and the Island Church 1405–1838'.

217 G. Killey (ed), *Lioar dy Hymnyn as Arraneyn Spyrrydoil chyndait gys Gaick veih lioaryn Wesley, Watts as Scriudeyryn Elley* (Doolish [Douglas], 1799). [*Book of Hymns and Spiritual Songs translated into Manx from the books of Wesley, Watts and Other Writers*].

218 Hymns had first been popularized at informal Methodist meetings, gradually creeping into parish churches, where only metrical psalms had been permitted. N. Temperley, *The Music of the English Parish Church*, vol. 1 (Cambridge, 1979), 208–09.

West Gallery music

By the late 1700s and early 1800s, professional singing masters like Shepherd were employed in churches, mainly in the Colby area. He supplemented his income by producing part-books, which he sold to his choir members, leaving them to complete the words in English opposite his hand-written music.[219] Many of these part-books contain non-sacred material, including one from the Kneen manuscript that includes a page of Latin text and instructions such as 'Benevolence is commendable'.[220]

A wide variety of examples of this popular church style, known as West Gallery music, occurs in Manx manuscripts, and through contemporary accounts, service sheets and newspaper reports, we know that these were performed as part of the standard repertoire of Manx church and chapel choirs.[221] They range from straightforward unaccompanied settings of metrical psalms to sophisticated set pieces with soloists, choir and orchestra.

Carvals

Carvals, locally composed religious ballads, are one of the more distinctive forms found in Manx music. Usually performed at events known as *Oiell Verreys* (the festivals of Christmas Eve or the feast of Mary), they were sung by male soloists after the Christmas Eve service and the departure of the vicar, and were lengthy texts sung to familiar tunes. It is not uncommon for a carval to contain upwards of 250 lines.[222] The authors of the earliest-known carvals were often clergymen such as Thomas Allen, vicar of Maughold from 1772–1745. At least two of his texts survive: '*Traa ta mish geeaghyn*' ('A hymn on Man's shameful downfall') (1726) and '*Trog seose, my chree*' ('Rise up, my heart') (1739).[223] Patrick Caley was a well known Wesleyan preacher in Manx and English and one of many authors who chose the topic of the Prodigal Son: many

219 The work of Francis Roads has breathed life into these dusty manuscripts, publishing, as a performing edition, a collection of those that are specific to the Isle of Man.

220 Bazin, 'Music in the Isle of Man', 461.

221 For examples and more details of this style of music, see F. Bazin (ed), *The Promised Land: thirty-two country anthems from the collection of Edward Quayle* (Douglas, 2000) and Roads (ed), *Ye Boundless Realms*.

222 An anonymous carval, published in A.W. Moore (ed) *Carvalyn Gailckagh chyndaait ayns Baarle, marish goan-foshlee giare* (*Manx Carols, Translated into English, with a short preface*) (Isle of Man, 1891), composed in 1720, runs to 368 lines and consists of verses of eight lines, alternating between questions and answers. The singer started at the west end of the building, taking a step forward at the beginning of the verse until he had reached the altar, when he was supposed to stop.

223 Moore (ed), *Carvalyn Gailckagh*, 2 and 6.

writers dealt with topics such as salvation, Christian duty and judgement.[224] Later carvals were written by less-educated, sometimes illiterate singers, and only occasionally refer to Christmas.[225] John Moore, a crew member of the privateer *Tiger* who was known as 'Moore the Tiger', took the subject of St Paul.[226]

Music as a political tool

In 1643, invitations were sent out by Earl James to 'all the Officeres, temporall and spirituall, the clergie, the 24 Keys of the Isle, the Coroners, and all their wives, and likewise the best sort of inhabitants of the Isle, to a great masque.' Although the Derbys had been enthusiastic about the performance of masques at Knowsley 'to beguile the tedium of winter', by the mid-1600s masques were old-fashioned and rarely seen. It is surprising, then, that the Derbys continued with them, especially during the Civil War. *Cloridia* was the last of Ben Jonson's masques, in which Lady Strange had perhaps performed at Queen Henrietta Maria's English court at Shrovetide, 1630.[227] Masques were often used in a political context and the Stuart court was particularly adept at the genre. It is more than likely that this 1643 performance at the beginning of December in the presence of 'all the Officers, etc' emphasized the power exercised by the earl in the light of Edward Christian's trial and subsequent incarceration.[228]

Following the Act of Revestment in 1765, there was a growing sense of a Manx identity. The earliest reference to '*Mylecharaine*' dates from 1770, when the text is described as 'an ancient Manx song'.[229] By 1790, it is described as 'an old Manks madrigal', suggesting that it was sung.[230] The first written melody emerges in a manuscript of 1810 as a two-part hymn tune in C minor, under the inscription 'an original Manks tune'.[231] It was first published as 'Air. Molly Charrane', a showy set of variations in *The Mona Melodies* in 1820 and twenty years later it was described as 'the Manx National Air'.[232] '*Mylecharaine*', 'the

224 Moore (ed), *Carvalyn Gailckagh*, 99.
225 Bazin, 'Music in the Isle of Man', 99–130.
226 Moore (ed), *Carvalyn Gailckagh*, 166.
227 W. Harrison (ed), *Mona Miscellany a selection of Proverbs, Sayings, Ballads, Customs, Superstitions and Legends peculiar to the Isle of Man*, 2nd ser., Manx Society, 21 (1873), 258–59.
228 Bazin, 'Music in the Isle of Man', 61–63.
229 University of Glasgow Special Collections: McLagan MS Gen, 1042/180.
230 BL Add MS 11215, Collections relating to Gaelic antiquities and language: with an original letter from John Buchanan to Professor Thorkelin, dat. Harris, 3 Sept. 1787: collection of songs in the Manks language, with English version, etc.
231 MNH MS 00437 A, 'Shepherd's Music', E (1810).
232 S. Miller, 'The Mona Melodies are now published and ready for delivery' – a bibliographical note on *The Mona Melodies* (1820), *PIMNHAS*, 11:4 (2007), 565–70.

Fig. 4.1 *'Molly Charrane' first appeared in manuscript in 1810. It was published as 'Air. Molly Charrane' in J[ohn] Barrow, The Mona Melodies, (London: Mitchell's Musical Library & Instrument Warehouses, [1820]): MNH M 02593.* F. Bazin, '"Mylecharaine": a forgotten call to nationhood', in I. Russell and D. Atkinson (eds), *Folk Song: Tradition, Revival and Re-Creation* (Aberdeen, 2004), 336–48.

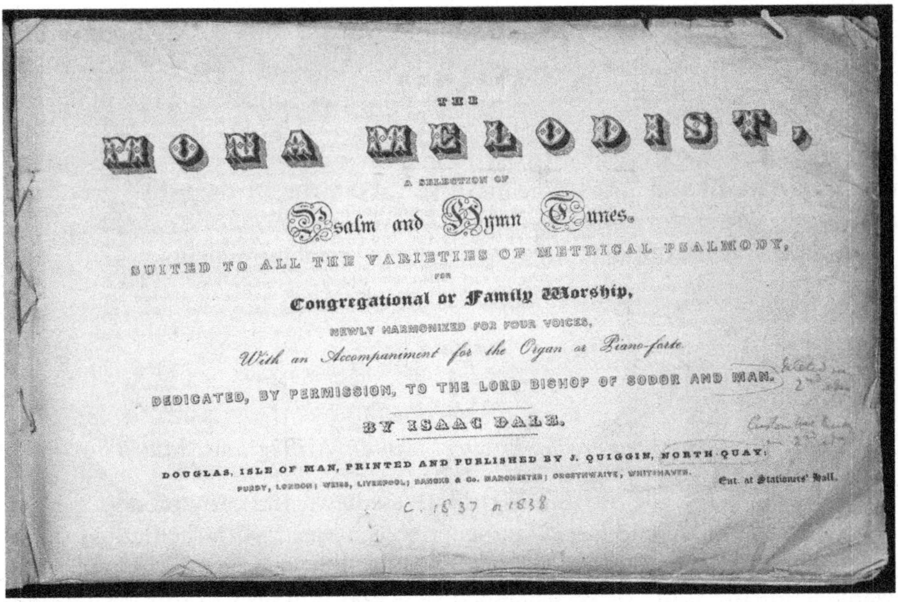

Fig. 4.2 *Isaac Dale, The Mona Melodist: MNH M08705.*

chief favourite of the Manx people', became a secret call for more independence, appearing in a number of guises: as a minor ballad, a hymn, a dance tune, and a march. Once it was adopted as the Manx National Anthem in 1907, and was no longer a 'secret' musical code, it was only performed in its official version.

Conclusion

Given the Island's trading role and its links with its neighbours and further afield, the variety of music-making comes as no surprise. In spite of the lack of documentary evidence, it seems likely that there was 'court' music in the Derby household and an active tradition of music at Rushen Abbey. Choral music was certainly thriving in the eighteenth century and by the early 1800s there was a growing interest in vernacular church music. From the late 1600s, the gentry had time and money to spend on instruments and printed music; their musical world was similar to that of other parts of the British Isles, although the majority of music teachers came from England. Whether intentionally – as with the earl of Derby – or incidentally, music was able to influence events and was becoming particularly important in the awareness of a Manx identity. The introduction of Wesley's hymns led to greater freedom of thought, which was to become important in later decades of the nineteenth century, but Wesley's advice to use English in worship was to be a key moment in the decline of the

Manx language. However, Manx men and women took to Methodism like ducks to water. It gave them freedom to take charge of their worship and to break away from the established church. It was Wesleyanism that prompted the publication of the first Manx hymn-book in 1799. Hymns and secular songs could also be used politically: to encourage emigration, to promote a sense of emerging nationhood, or as a means of social reform. By the early part of the nineteenth century, revivalist meetings were a vehicle for orators, many of whom went on to become important figures in the political movements.

FOLKLORE

Catriona Mackie

With contributions by Fenella Bazin, Stephen Miller and Tim Thornton

The folklore of the Isle of Man in the late medieval and early modern period is a potentially huge and largely impenetrable subject. With the limited space available here it is possible to sketch out only limited aspects of the material available for the study of vernacular beliefs and practices in this period, but it is nonetheless important to do so in a chapter considering the culture of the Island. Furthermore, the case studies of witchcraft and fairy lore noted here indicate that much Manx material lies within the contexts of Celtic and Scandinavian traditions, while some customs and beliefs appear to belong more exclusively to the Island's story.[233]

The earliest reference to folk belief in the Isle of Man comes from the late medieval period. Ranulf Higden, a fourteenth-century monk at St Werburgh's monastery in Chester, mentions the Island in Book 1 of his *Polychronicon*, noting that

> In the Isle of Man is sorcery and witchcraft used; for women there sell to shipmen wind, as it were closed under three knots of thread, so that the more wind he would have, the more knots he must undo. There often by daytime, men of that Island see men that have died beforehand, beheaded or whole and what death they died. Aliens set their feet upon the feet of the men of that land, for to see such sights as the men of that Island do.[234]

Writing in the 1690s, William Sacheverell also suggests that witchcraft was prevalent in the Island during the medieval period, noting that the Island's

233 See K. Danaher and P. Lysaght, 'Supplement to a Bibliography of Irish Ethnology and Folklore', *Béaloideas*, 48/49 (1980–81), 206–27; L. Henderson and E.J. Cowan, *Scottish fairy belief: a history* (East Linton, 2001).

234 Ranulph Higden, *Polychronicon*, Churchill Babington and Joseph Rawson Lumby (eds) (9 vols, Rolls Ser, 41, 1865–86), vol. 1. 41–43.

Governor in 1338, Martholine, 'wrote against witchcraft (a practice too frequent in those days).'[235] It is unclear what writing this refers to. The Isle of Man's reputation for witchcraft appears to have continued into the early modern era, with a number of sixteenth-century works also referring to the practice of selling wind to sailors, presumably after Higden.[236]

The most significant body of evidence about witchcraft and folk belief in the Isle of Man during the early modern period is that of the ecclesiastical court records. A full set of records exist from 1659–1874. Before this, the records are sporadic.[237] A selection of court records has been studied by Craine, Hutton, Miller, Platten and Sharpe but a full analysis has yet to be completed.[238]

Suspected cases of witchcraft were initially presented to the parish chapter quest. If the jury found that there was a case to be answered, the bishop could choose to transfer it to the secular courts.[239] In the second half of the sixteenth century, two women were brought before the Court of General Gaol Delivery, charged with witchcraft. In 1569, Alice Ine Gilbay was found guilty, but avoided execution because she was pregnant. In 1598 another woman accused of witchcraft avoided trial due to a legal technicality.[240]

Only one case of witchcraft on the Isle of Man resulted in a sentence of death, handed down by the secular court. In 1617, Margaret Ine Quayne and her son John Cubon were burned at the stake in Castletown. Unfortunately, there are no extant records of the exact charges against them. The impact of this execution appears to have had far-reaching consequences for the persecution of witches in the Island. Thereafter, cases were almost exclusively dealt with by the ecclesiastical courts, where the most severe penalty was a very short term of imprisonment.[241]

The most common types of witchcraft-related misdeeds that were brought before the church courts were charming and cursing.[242] In 1713, Alice Cowley

235 Sacheverell, *Account*, 72.

236 R. Holinshed, *Chronicles of England, Scotlande, and Irelande* (London, 1577), vol. 1, 66; J. Rhys, *Celtic Folklore* (Oxford, 1901), 1, 330.

237 J. Platten, 'The Church Court System: Presentments to the Manx Church Courts, 1640–1799' (PhD thesis, University of Liverpool, 2010), 7.

238 D. Craine, *Manannan's Isle* (Douglas, 1955); R. Hutton, 'The Changing Faces of Manx Witchcraft', *Cultural and Social History*, 7:2 (2010), 153–69; S. Miller, 'Episcopacy of Bishop Wilson: Presentments for Ballaugh (for Magical Practices)', and '"For giving charm for the ague". Alice Cowley before the Church Courts (1709–13)', *Ballaugh Heritage Trust Newsletter (BHTN)*, 13, (2015), 13–17, 18–27; Platten, 'Presentments' (2010); J. Sharpe, 'Witchcraft in the Early Modern Isle of Man', *Cultural and Social History*, 4:1 (2007), 11–28.

239 Gill (ed), *Statutes*, vol. 1, 46.

240 Sharpe, 'Witchcraft', 13.

241 Craine, *Manannan's Isle*, 14; Sharpe, 'Witchcraft', 13; Hutton, 'Changing Faces', 155.

242 Sharpe, 'Witchcraft', 17; Platten, 'Presentments', 155.

was found guilty of 'many wicked and Evil practices in Charms & Sorcery and has been Guilty of Drawing or leading several people to believe in her; by her wicked devices, which is a great Scandel to the Christian Religion'. Her practices included giving or removing fertility from women and cattle and the *tarrey* (yield) from stock and crops, causing or curing illness, and creating charms to induce love. She was also charged, along with Isobel Gawne, with taking earth from the threshold of a house where a wedding was being held and putting it under the bride's chair. As a result, the bride was unable to conceive until she sought out the witches and drew their blood, thus breaking their charm.[243] Drawing blood from the perpetrator was seen as an effective way to end a curse.[244]

Belief in the magical potency of earth and dust is a peculiarly Manx phenomenon. Sharpe notes a number of examples, including the use of dust from under a witch's foot to counteract an illness believed to be the result of witchcraft, the use of earth to protect cattle from the evil eye, and the use of earth as a means of removing or transferring the *tarrey* from crops and stock. Henry Kelly of Marown was charged in 1697 with sending his son to remove some earth from a neighbour's recently sown field to put on his own.[245]

The power of the 'charmer' was believed to run through certain families, such as the Tear family of Andreas. John Tear was accused of charming in the 1730s, and some family members were still known throughout the Island as charmers in the late nineteenth century.[246] Craine notes that the family was renowned for making healing charms, charms to bestow good fortune, and for the ability to foretell the future, citing the 1741 example of a man from Kirk Braddan who walked to Andreas to find out if his wife would recover from her illness.[247]

Cursing features prominently in the ecclesiastical presentments until well into the eighteenth century. The form of words used is rarely given, with references made simply to 'the curse of God'. However, in 1659, Catherine Cottier was presented for having cursed John Casement that 'he might have neither son or daughter about his fire or hearth to the third or fourth generation and that his house might be ruinated.'[248]

243 Miller, 'Charm for the Ague', 18–27; Keble, *Wilson*, vol. 1, 301.

244 Craine, *Manannan's Isle*, 25.

245 Sharpe, 'Witchcraft', 15–16.

246 Platten, 'Presentments', 170–71; J. Platten, 'Church Court System', 170–71; A.W. Moore, *The Folk Lore of the Isle of Man* (Isle of Man and London, 1891), 79.

247 Craine, *Manannan's Isle*, 28.

248 Sharpe, 'Witchcraft. 20.

The most formidable curse was that of the *skeab loam*, the 'naked besom'. This curse was performed while making sweeping gestures facing the house to be cursed and uttering the words of the curse.[249] The full curse is usually not recorded, but there are some examples, such as this one from Rushen in 1744: 'May the besom of destruction come upon thee thyself, upon thy heart, upon thy health, upon thy possessions and upon thy children'.[250] Platten notes that, by the 1730s, there was an increase in the number of men who were accused of cursing while the severity of the *skeab loam* curse appears to have declined, often being used more as a profanity.[251]

During the early eighteenth century, when concern with witchcraft was declining in Britain, a renewed effort was made under the episcopacy of Bishop Thomas Wilson to identify and stamp out witchcraft on the Isle of Man. It is clear from the writings of Bishop Wilson and from the church presentments that the Islanders' belief in the efficacy of witchcraft was rooted in superstition and ignorance, rather than in anything more sinister. However, Wilson was keen to ensure that the seriousness of charming and cursing was understood by the people of the Island. By 1712, Wilson was issuing missives urging his clergy to make their congregations 'sensible that all charms, let the words be good or bad, intelligible, or meer jargon, are of the devil, with whom there is a compact implied by the very practice ... Let not your people fancy that these practices are rather foolish than wicked. ... Besides, these beginnings may, if not timely discouraged, end in downright witchcraft.'[252]

Despite this, the penalties awarded by the ecclesiastical courts for cursing and charming were generally not severe. These usually involved the guilty party denouncing their crimes in church, or in the market square, with the added possibility of a fine and/or a short stay in the bishop's prison in Peel. Hutton notes that the harshest penalties were given to those who practised charming for a fee, with cases peaking in the 1710s due to the efforts of Bishop Wilson to encourage prosecution and declining from the 1720s onwards.[253]

In 1713, Alice Cowley, who was accused of soliciting money for charms, was given a harsher sentence than most. She was ordered to be imprisoned for thirty days in the bishop's prison and, on her release, to stand in a white sheet, holding a white wand, with 'these words, "for charming and sorcery," in capital letters on her breast' for two hours at the market cross in each of the Island's towns, 'in the height of the market'. She also had to renounce her practices publicly in

249 MNH MS 10194 (Presentments), Ballaugh, 2 April 1732; (Presentments), Patrick, 14 October 1717; (Presentments), Patrick, May 1740.

250 Craine, *Manannan's Isle*, 24.

251 Platten, 'Presentments', 160.

252 Keble, *Wilson*, vol. 1, 303–04.

253 Hutton, 'Changing Faces', 155.

Ballaugh church. In addition, she was fined 10 shillings. In the event, she was released from prison after two weeks.[254]

People could be accused of charming or engaging the help of a charmer. Sharpe gives the example of Bahy Quayle who was presented for charming in 1706, alongside John Cubon, who was presented for having used her services.[255] Penalties for seeking the assistance of a charmer could be as severe as those handed to the charmer. Platten describes a number of cases from 1703 where four men were censured: two for making charms and two for consulting a charmer. Each were given the same penance, suggesting that seeking the assistance of a charmer was seen as an equal offence to charming itself.[256]

It was not uncommon for the tables to turn during a trial, and the accusers find themselves charged with defamation.[257] When Jane Cesar was charged with witchcraft in 1658, the case was dismissed and her accusers were reprimanded for having slandered her. Unusually, despite this, she was told to denounce witchcraft in church.[258] Anyone else found to be slandering her or her descendants in this manner would be liable for a £10 fine and would have to make reparation to the accused. In 1693, Alice Cowle of Castletown was found guilty of slandering the same Jane Cesar (now deceased) and was ordered to do penance in several parish churches for seven Sundays, asking Cesar's family for forgiveness. In addition, she had to pay all legal costs and spent fourteen days in prison.[259]

Sharpe has noted that the evidence points to a 'rich and distinctive set of witchcraft beliefs' in the Island during the early modern period, including a strong belief in charming and healing, and in the power of the curse.[260] Some of these beliefs were common in Britain, such as the use of the sieve and shears for divination, but others appear peculiarly Manx, such as the belief in the power of earth and dust and the ability of witches to transform themselves into a hare.[261]

The societal concerns that emerge through the church presentments were common to rural areas and typically related to fertility and yield, love and health, and general neighbourhood tensions. Hutton notes that the ecclesiastical courts treated many accusations of witchcraft as 'ill wishing between

254 Keble, *Wilson*, vol. 1, 302.
255 Sharpe, 'Witchcraft', 17.
256 Platten, 'Presentments', 170.
257 Sharpe, 'Witchcraft', 14–15.
258 Sharpe, 'Witchcraft', 14.
259 Sharpe, 'Witchcraft', 15.
260 Sharpe, 'Witchcraft', 13.
261 Sharpe, 'Witchcraft', 17; Platten, 'Presentments', 165,166.

neighbours' that was better handled through the issue of apologies, rather than more serious sanctions.[262]

The Isle of Man appears to have followed Ireland, Wales, and the Gaelic-speaking areas of Scotland in the reluctance of the courts to prosecute witchcraft in the early modern period. A number of studies have suggested that this may be because Celtic regions had a very strong fairy tradition, and a firm belief in the power of malignant fairies.[263] Hutton has suggested that the belief in dangerous supernatural creatures may have made it less likely that malevolent attacks were seen as the work of malignant witchcraft. While witchcraft might be used to steal the milk from someone's cattle, fairies could steal human babies or mothers and permanently injure otherwise healthy men. Large-scale witch-hunts were not a feature of the Celtic nations because there was no real fear of witchcraft.[264]

Written accounts of the Isle of Man begin to emerge in the seventeenth century and some of these contain information about the beliefs and customs of the Island's population, including its fairy beliefs. Such accounts increase from the 1790s onwards as the Island emerged as a key tourist destination.

The most important and also the most problematic source of information on Manx fairy beliefs is George Waldron's *Description of the Isle of Man*, written in 1726. Waldron spent nearly twenty years in the Island (c.1710–c.1730) working as a customs officer for the British government.[265] The earliest extant edition (1731) was published in London a year after his death.[266] It contains information about the Island's history, laws, and religion, and devotes significant space to describing the customs and superstitions of the inhabitants. He includes tales of people's encounters with fairies, changelings, apparitions, and supernatural creatures, such as the water bull. His volume also contains the earliest published sources for many of the Island's folktales, including the *Moddey Dhoo* of Peel Castle and the fairy cup of Kirk Malew. There is no mention of witchcraft or charming in the text, but it is possible that such information was contained in papers that were lost after his death.[267]

Waldron's accounts are problematic because it is unclear how he collected this information, how faithfully he represented what he was told, and whether the tales that were told to him were exaggerated in any way. The tales are

262 Hutton, 'Changing Faces', 155; Sharpe, 'Witchcraft', 18.

263 R. Hutton, *The Witch: A History of Fear, from Ancient Times to the Present* (New Haven and London, 2017), 244–52; Sharpe, 'Witchcraft', 19–20.

264 Hutton, *The Witch*, 244–52.

265 W. Harrison, (ed), *A Description of the Isle of Man by George Waldron*, Manx Society, 11 (Douglas, 1865), vii-viii.

266 *A Description of the Isle of Man*, by George Waldron, 1731, in T. Waldron (ed), *The Compleat Works, in Verse and Prose, of George Waldron*, 1731, 2nd edn (London).

267 Hutton, 'Changing Faces', 156.

recounted in English without any Manx idiom, and Moore suggests that they may contain 'additions suggested by his own fancy', presumably for the entertainment of his readership.[268] Miller has shown, however, that much of the Manx fairy lore Waldron recounts may also be found extensively in tales and motifs in Celtic and Scandinavian fairy lore.[269] Generally, Waldron portrays the Manx as ignorant, superstitious, and uncivilised, including men who 'passed for persons of sound judgement'.[270] Platten has exposed the inaccuracies in his comments about the preponderance of sexual offences in the Island in the early eighteenth century, and it might be assumed that his text contains other inaccuracies.[271] Indeed, Harrison could find no evidence of a case Waldron described of a woman charged with murdering her three children.[272]

A political agenda might also have influenced Waldron's depiction of the Island's inhabitants. At this time, the Isle of Man was a hotbed of smuggling activity and the British government was in discussions with the earl of Derby to purchase the Island's customs revenue. Waldron's depiction of the Manx and their clergy could only have contributed to the notion that the Island was somewhat of a cultural backwater that would benefit from the civilising processes of the British crown.

Whatever the truth of it, Waldron's publication was to have significant impact, with many later writers quoting Waldron or recounting his tales. While some of the practices Waldron discusses are attested in other sources, others are only known from Waldron's text, such as 'Cutting off the Fiddler's Head' whereby on the twelfth day of Christmas a fiddler lays his head in a woman's lap and is asked to pronounce on which men particular girls will marry: 'whatever he says is as absolutely depended on as an oracle'.[273]

In addition to Higden's earlier statement on the second sight, portents of death and prophecies of forthcoming events are mentioned by Sacheverell in the late seventeenth century, and by Waldron in the early eighteenth century.

268 Moore, *Folk Lore*, 1.

269 S. Miller, 'Norwegian Dead-Child Legends in Mann (ML 4025)', *Béaloideas*, 69 (2001), 107–14. See also S. Miller, 'George Waldron and the Good People', in S. Young and C. Houlbrook (eds), *Magical Folk: British & Irish Fairies 500 AD to the Present*, 165–80 (London, 2018); S. Thompson, *Motif-Index of Folk-Literature: A Classification of Narrative Elements in Folk-Tales, Ballads, Myths, Fables, Mediæval Romances, Exempla Fabliaux, Jest-Books and Local Legends*, revised & enlarged edn, 6 vols (Copenhagen, 1955–58), and T.P. Cross, *Motif-Index of Early Irish Literature*, Indiana University Folklore Series, vol. 7 (Bloomington, Indiana, 1952).

270 Waldron, *Description* (1731), 66.

271 Platten, 'Presentments', 64–65.

272 Harrison (ed), *Description* (Waldron) 100.

273 Waldron, *Description*, 98; C.I. Paton, 'Manx Calendar Customs', *Folklore*, 51:1 (1940), 44.

Sacheverell describes the appearance of lights when someone dies and Waldron describes sightings of fairy funerals as portents of death.[274]

Fire was also seen as an important resource in the folk belief of the Isle of Man. There are instances in the church records of calves being burned in order to overcome the evil eye or to restore health to a failing herd.[275] Writing in the late eighteenth century, Townley describes a similar practice as 'burning the witch' out of fishermen's boats, by passing over the boat with a lighted piece of heather.[276]

Much of the evidence for Manx fairy belief comes from the later nineteenth and early twentieth centuries. With the exception of Waldron, sources for the period prior to 1830 are scarce. David Robertson touches on the subject in his 1794 *Tour*, noting that there were two kinds of Manx 'fairies': those that were 'playful and benignant spirits' and those that were 'sullen and vindictive'.[277] Hannah Bullock's *History*, published in 1816, relies heavily on earlier texts for her discussion of superstition, though she notes that, at that time, the lower and middle classes 'have the fullest belief in fairies and witchcraft, and to the supernatural influence of one of these imaginary powers nearly all the good or ill that befalls them is ascribed'.[278] More detailed accounts of Manx fairy lore do not emerge until Joseph Train's *History*, published in 1845.[279]

Levels of elite scepticism and hostility to Manx fairy lore had reached a peak towards the end of the period of this volume, as evidenced by Robertson, who is scathing about the 'superstitious delusions of the natives', ascribing this to 'an inert disposition', which 'by enervating the mind, renders it a slave to every superstition'.[280] His view might have been coloured by contemporary attitudes, when little-known areas of the British Isles were being explored by tourists in search of the 'Picturesque'.[281] By contrast, when in 1869 William Harrison published a *Miscellany* which aimed to bring together 'everything that would in any way illustrate the history of this little Island, he did so with an antiquarian's interest, replacing Robertson's overt scepticism with a more objectively engaged disbelief and little personal comment.[282]

274 Sacheverell, *Account*, 14–15; Waldron, *Description*, 74–75.
275 Craine, *Manannan's Isle*, 26–27.
276 Townley, *Journal*, 1, 197, 207.
277 D. Robertson, *A Tour through the Isle of Man: to which is subjoined A Review of the Manx History*, 1st edn (unexpurgated), (London, 1794), 76.
278 H.A. Bullock, *History of the Isle of Man* (London, 1816), 363.
279 J. Train, *An historical and statistical Account of the Isle of Man, from the earliest times to the present date*, 2 vols, 2 (Liverpool, 1845).
280 Robertson, *Tour*, 1st edn, 154.
281 Robertson, *Tour*, 1970 edn, W. Rollinson (ed), Introduction, n.p.
282 W. Harrison, *Mona Miscellany: a Selection of Proverbs, Sayings, Ballads, customs, Superstitions, and Legends, Peculiar to the Isle of Man*, 1st ser (Douglas, 1869), Preface.

Although published outside the period of this volume, Harrison's account is largely from his own observation, and it is likely that the superstitions and beliefs that he describes had been followed in previous centuries.[283] One significant feature of his *Miscellany* is that it allows access to material from which themes in vernacular belief and practice around the calendar can be identified.

The Isle of Man is rich in calendar customs and traditions. May Day and Christmas traditions are described by Waldron and the church presentments indicate that May Eve and May Day were important dates and had associated customs, from at least the seventeenth century.[284] Many of these customs have parallels in other Celtic countries as well as in European tradition, and it is therefore likely that Waldron's and Harrison's descriptions can be relied upon in these cases. Harrison recounts, for example, that it was (and still is) important to have a visit from the *qualtagh* on New Year's Day, and that the floor had to be swept towards the hearth to avoid sweeping the household's good fortune out of the house; on Good Friday no metal was to be put into the fire; and there were customs associated with saints' days, such as passing smoke over the corn on St John the Baptist's eve, and driving cattle through smoke 'as an antidote to the murrain' on May Day.[285]

Evidence of these beliefs, and much else recorded by Harrison, may be traced back in earlier primary sources, most notably in court presentments. The repeal in 1736 of the 1542 Witchcraft Act in Britain did not have any immediate effect on the types of cases prosecuted in the Isle of Man. Instead, it effectively aligned British attitudes to witchcraft with those which had been prevalent in the Isle of Man for over a century.[286] Cases continued to appear before the Manx ecclesiastical courts, such as the 1744 curse noted above. However, Platten's research suggests that the number of presentments for charming declined between the 1730s and the 1760s and that this trend continued until the end of the eighteenth century.[287] By 1756, Bishop Wilson had been replaced by Bishop Hildesley, and it is likely that Hildesley, and the church in general, no longer saw charming as a religious priority. By the end of the eighteenth century, references to witchcraft tend to be those referring to the use of physical charms to ward off malevolent spirits.[288] Despite this, the role of the charmer remained strong in Manx society, surviving down to the late nineteenth century in some areas.[289]

In presenting these examples of witchcraft, folklore and customs in the Isle of Man, this section has aimed to provide an overview of some of the most

283 Harrison, *Miscellany*, Preface.
284 Sharpe, 'Witchcraft', 16.
285 Harrison, *Miscellany*, 136, 138, 143. *Qualtagh* – 'first foot'.
286 Hutton, 'Changing Faces', 156.
287 Platten, 'Presentments', 172.
288 Platten, 'Presentments', 166–67.
289 Moore, *Folk Lore*, 79.

important sources of research in these areas. Much work remains to be done. For example, while there has been significant investigation into the Island's folklore, beliefs and customs, few studies have sought to situate this within a broader British and international context. Such work would help highlight those beliefs that have Celtic or Norse counterparts, and those that are part of a wider European tradition, as well as drawing attention to customs with peculiarly Manx attributes. In addition, further analysis of the ecclesiastical court records would help clarify the rise and fall of particular beliefs and practices, changing attitudes towards them, and any gender or class differences that emerge. It will also enhance more generally our understanding of the Isle of Man during this period, and the social, cultural and economic conditions in which these beliefs and practices were situated.

POPULAR ENTERTAINMENT

Fenella Bazin

Additional Contributions on Circuses snd Novelty Entertainment by Sue King and Mike Clague

It was only with the advent of newspapers that there were more than occasional accounts of popular entertainment. Eighteenth-century observers such as David Robertson suggest that the social life of Douglas in particular was very similar to that across the water in England, with the English giving 'life and gaiety to the town; and [they] have contributed to polish the manners of the natives'.[290] Card parties were popular, often accompanied with 'a plenitude of excellent wines'. He had few good words to say regarding 'the inferior classes', whom he saw as gamblers and drunkards.

The story of popular entertainment in the Isle of Man tends to be elusive, with brief glimpses of occasions sufficiently special to justify a newspaper report, or a diary entry. Robertson's observations as well as other accounts suggest that there was a marked difference not only between the English incomers and the native Manx but also between town and country.

Dancing

In his *Manx Reminiscences*, John Clague recalled that on May Day a great feast would be held in Castletown, attended by people 'from every part of the island' dressed in their holiday clothes. There would be a sham fight between two groups, representing the battle between summer and winter, led by the Queen of Summer and the King of Winter. The fight continued until the group

290 Robertson, *Tour*, 1st edn, 22.

reached Scarlett, and fighting was over and the sun had set. After supper, 'there was dancing and games of every kind'.[291] The seventh earl of Derby described something similar: a Manx fair was held in the market place in Castletown where 'dancers did dance through the streets, winding hither and thither among the townsfolk'.[292]

If the Arbory church presentments of 1635 are to be believed, dancing seems to have been popular. In 1635, dancing after Sunday services had generally disappeared, although there were 'Dances used on Sunday afternoons'.[293] By 1822, dancing seems to have been as popular as ever, with George Quayle Snr. writing to his 'Dear Cousin' that he had heard of the 'gaiety of Castletown', where a dancing master had been busily giving lessons. The fact that he came from Brighton was 'alone enough to stamp him as the acme of fashion'.[294] Reminiscent of Jane Austen is the description given by Dorothy Wordsworth in 1828, when she wrote that Castletown had 'a drawbridge, handsome strong fortress, soldiers, prancing sentinels, officers, and music, and groups of women in white caps listening, very like a town in French Flanders'.[295]

Theatre

An early record of travelling players appears in the Book of Charge, Castle Rushen, when a payment was made to 'my Lord Vause's Players in reward for a Plaie acted by them xxs'.[296] The group is on record as performing in Leicester, Coventry and Skipton Castle between 1601 and 1609. We know of the existence of a theatre in Douglas from at least 1759, for it was 'as he was coming from the playhouse' that a pilot of a cutter was allegedly attacked.[297] In 1772, the *Cumberland Pacquet* reported that 'strolling players from Ireland were off to the Isle of Man for a winter season', and fifteen years later the same newspaper indicated that a 'theatrical corps' had been formed by Captain Tennison in Douglas. Tennison also built a playhouse, described by Robertson as 'a neat theatre ... erected ... with the benevolent idea of contributing to the relief of the poor'.[298] Whether 'neat' referred to its size or condition, Robertson does not say. Tennison's venture did not last long. Robertson indicated that 'the

291 J. Clague, *Cooinaghtyn Manninagh [Manx Reminiscences]* (Castletown, 1911), 53.

292 P.L. Stowell and B. Osborne (eds and arrs), *The Leighton Stowell Book of Manx Dances* (Isle of Man, 1981), 9.

293 *JMM*, 2:29 (December 1931), 37, doc. 16.

294 MNH MS 02568 C, 28 May 1822, George Quayle to his cousin Mark H. Quayle.

295 T. Roscoe, 'Dorothy Wordsworth visits the Island, 1828', *JMM*, 5:69 (1943), 114.

296 MNH MS 09782 (CRP), Castle Accounts, box 4, doc. 28 (1587?).

297 MNH MS 10071/3/25 (Lib.Scacc.), fol. 7 (unnumbered), 21 August 1759, letter of John Shortland.

298 *Cumberland Pacquet*, 20 October 1772, 21 March 1787; Robertson, *Tour*, 1st edn, 23.

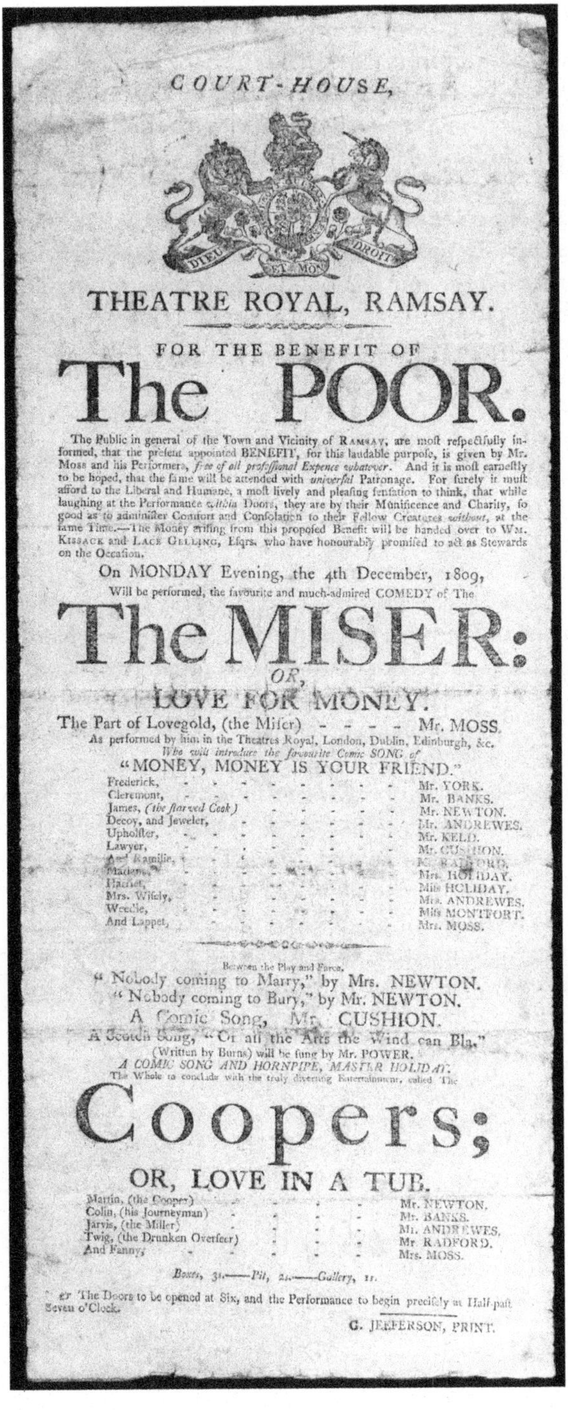

Fig. 4.3 *Poster advertising a benefit concert at the Theatre Royal, Ramsey, 4 December 1809: MNH P.6588/3.*

liberal arts have few votaries here' and, only seven years after the project had been launched, he stated that 'the admirers of the Drama are too inconsiderable to support, even for a few weeks, a regular company'.[299] Few of the many eighteenth-century guides published about the Island, including Waldron (1726), Feltham (1797–98), and Haining (1822), contain any references to theatres.

By the early 1800s, Douglas had become the centre of social life with dinners and dances, theatres and concerts. Tennison's charitable efforts are mirrored in the number of events where amateur musicians helped to raise money for worthy charities by giving concerts in the Assembly Rooms and other meeting places, probably to accompany dancing.[300]

Rural entertainments

From the hymns, dance tunes and marches in music manuscripts dating from the end of the period, it is clear that local entertainment was important. These were events that were seldom reported in the press and only occasionally in diaries. Harvest celebrations marked an important point in the year and varied from area to area, but the one given by Mr Mitford in 1812 seems to have been very special. There was a dinner and supper for a hundred workmen held at his estate at Airey [*sic*] Kelly, with a rich Manx broth, a whole mutton and a side of beef. Recording the event, Josepha Dalby comments that 'this broth the Manks are particularly fond of', noting that Mr Mitford's Mhellia was 'the best throughout the whole Island and for this he never wants for workmen'.[301] For those who could still manage it, the supper was followed by a dance that continued until 5am.

John Moore's Music Book (1804) and the *Andreas Flute Book* (1825), which exists only in manuscript, show how varied the repertoire of these largely amateur musicians was, covering a variety of genres from popular songs, traditional ballads, marches, and the fashionable dance tunes of the day.[302] It was these musicians who were to become the mainstay of the entertainment needs of burgeoning tourism.

299 Robertson, *Tour*, 1st edn, 24.

300 Bazin, 'Music in the Isle of Man', 226. See this chapter, M. Hoy, 'Associational Culture'.

301 MNH MS 05583 A, 'The diary of Josepha Dalby of Ballacooley Lodge, Kirk Michael, 1812'.

302 J. Moore (comp), John Moore's Music Book (1804): in private hands. See also F.C. Bazin, *John Moore's Music Book* (Douglas, 2009); MNH MS 11195, Andreas Flute Book (1825).

Entertainment and the church

Feasting was a feature of the archdeacons' annual visits to churches. According to detailed instructions carefully noted down in 1677, 'the parson or vicar should entertain according to means'. The writer continued, 'Churches of greater value should have sumptuous banquets and brought with them hounds and hawks'. Archdeacons were instructed to bring no more than five or seven horsemen with them to wealthy churches, and fewer to those churches less well endowed. There is no indication as to the author, who comments that 'this composition seems to have a special care for the belly; especially enjoyning a breakfast to be provided for the Archdeacon and his company'. However, he adds that 'Archbishop Stratford in his constitution ... was content with dinner and supper'. The author's feelings about the paper erupt on the final page. Whether he was tired of the task or felt the business of entertainment was too lavish is not clear, but his outburst is clearly a man at the end of his tether: 'But what do I, raking in the dunghill of this composition. I hate it. I leave it.'[303]

Circuses and novelty entertainment

Sue King and Mike Clague

In the first year or so of the nineteenth century, the residents of Douglas, promenading during summer evenings on the newly constructed Red Pier, were able to enjoy simple entertainments provided by a colourful array of individual performers – jugglers, musicians and contortionists. But in late July 1802 a group of performers of a far more audacious nature arrived in town, marking the first recorded visit to the Isle of Man by an English circus. Ireland & Woolford set up their circus in a rope yard belonging to Mr Lewin on Douglas quay and, with the permission of the lieutenant governor, performed for six nights over a period of two weeks, before moving on to Castletown and Peel for single performances. According to the *Manks Advertiser*, the Douglas venue was crowded with 'ladies and gentlemen of the first respectability', who came to see a variety of acrobatic feats including tumbling, slack rope walking, tightrope walking and 'leaping' (jumping over obstacles without the aid of a springboard).[304]

It was to be more than twenty years before the Island was visited by a similar concern. In September 1826 a highly organized, professional troupe managed by Mr Kinloch arrived from Liverpool. The local newspapers reported that 'We have this week the pleasure of announcing a fresh treat, which all amateurs of

303 MNH MS 00213 A, paper of Archdeacon's Procurations and entertainment by Rural Deans, c.1677.

304 *Manks Advertiser*, 31 July 1802.

equestrian science will be delighted to witness; … the performers are choice spirits from the Liverpool Circus … a constellation of luminaries of the first magnitude.' Kinloch's troupe were specialists in equestrian performance, as was the norm in circuses at the time, and their programme contained a variety of individual and group acts designed, as one newspaper put it, 'to witch the world with noble horsemanship'.[305] These were well-regarded entertainers. In Liverpool the salaries paid at Kinloch's Olympic Circus ranged from £1 10s. to £3 per week.

Douglas had also visibly developed by this time with many new houses, streets and shops, and the circus was able to set up in one of the more 'genteel' parts of town – in a livery stable just off the Parade, close to the Court House and the harbour. The stable was owned by Thomas Dixon of the British Hotel, a man with an eye for a business opportunity. The stable not only offered accommodation for the horses, tack rooms and workshops but presumably also a large, spacious yard in which the performances could take place.

The most basic of the acts on the Douglas programme was known as 'still vaulting', in which the performer leaps on and off a moving horse. This was an act inspired by training for the battlefield when a soldier might be required to mount his horse from the ground while the horse was already moving. Individual cast members included Pablo Paddington and an 'Italian' strongman named Signor Spelterini whose act included his 'unparalleled leap over eight horses'. Other features of the programme included a thrilling and daring performance on the 'flying rope' or *corde volante*, a slack wire suspended high in the air on which the performer would balance, spin and turn somersaults. There were also 'antipodean performances' (in which the artiste performs upside down), stilt dancing, and comic interludes by Mr James, a well known clown.

The circus performed in Douglas for a fortnight before moving on to Castletown at the end of September and it appears that it went down well with Manx audiences. According to the *Manx Sun* 'the public have derived much amusement from the performances of Mr Kinloch's troop of horsemen from Liverpool. We believe it to be a most excellent treat of the kind and very well deserving of the public patronage'.[306]

Entertainment by magicians was also popular. Over eighty magicians performed on the Isle of Man during the nineteenth century, although only a small number are known to have visited before 1830. Itinerant magician Thomas Ingleby arrived from Whitehaven and performed in Castletown and Douglas during October 1805, advertising himself as the 'King's Conjuror'. His performances were said to 'evince more of miracle than deception'.[307] Ingleby returned in 1812, arriving from Dublin aboard the new packet ship *Stag*. In

305 *Manks Advertiser*, 14 September 1826.
306 *Manx Sun*, 16 September 1826.
307 *Manks Advertiser*, 19 October 1805.

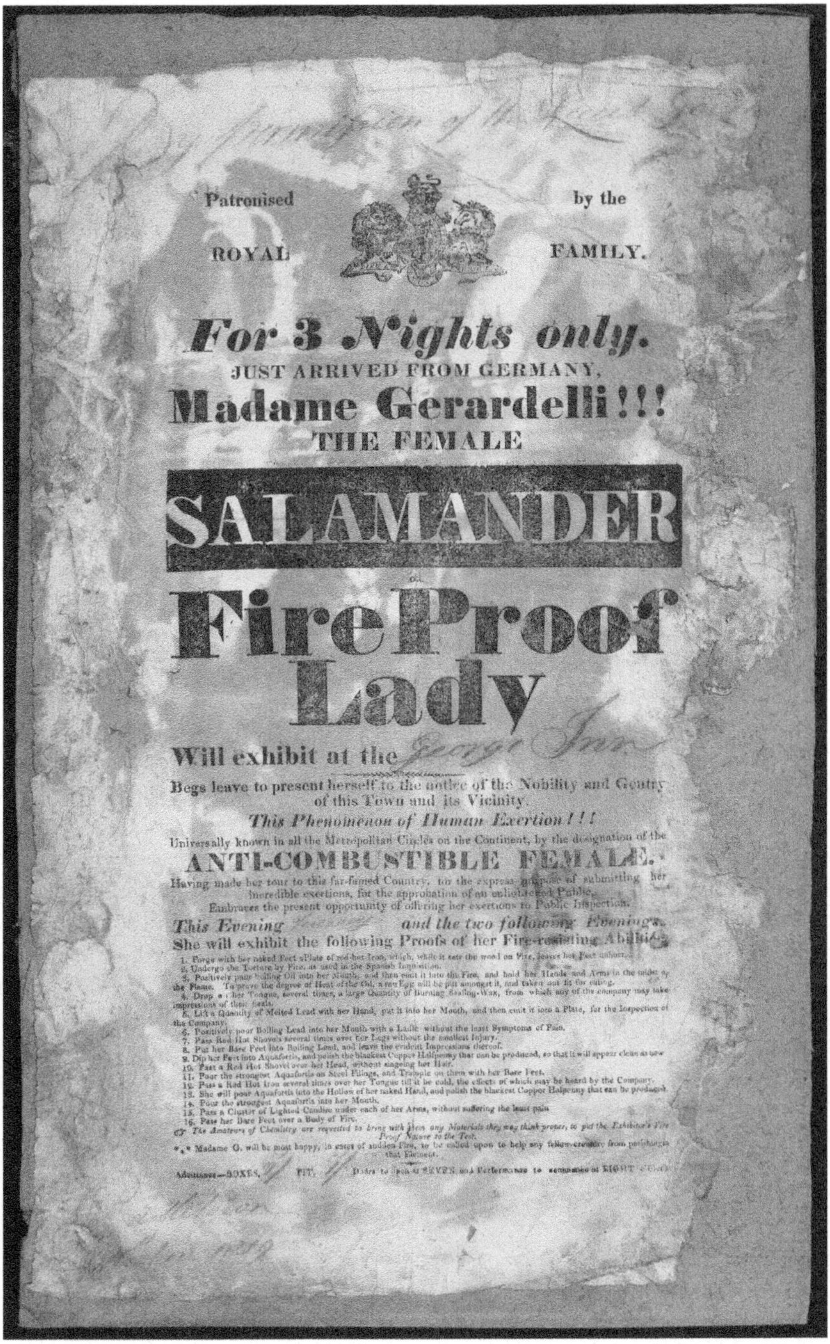

Fig. 4.4 *'The Fire Proof Lady'*, *Mme Girardelli poster 1819: MNH P.6531.*

addition to his shows in Mr Downward's large room on the Quay in Douglas and the new Assembly Room in Castletown, Ingleby offered to perform at gentlemen's houses for a fee of ten guineas. *The Isle of Man Weekly Gazette* reported that a trick involving 'his deception of the Rose Tree seems to be effected by supernatural agency'.[308]

An unusual act was that of Josephine Girardelli from Italy, who advertised herself as the anti-combustible lady in 1819.[309] Her stage setting included burning braziers, used to melt lead and sealing wax. The molten metal was lifted with her hand and poured into her mouth with a ladle. Other effects included walking on a plate of red-hot iron, dropping molten wax onto her tongue and pouring nitric acid into her mouth. Girardelli returned in 1827 with her husband, who advertised shows at Mr Dixon's Assembly Room in June.[310] Girardelli's performances included 'French Mechanical Transformations' and other exhibits, as well as conjuring tricks.

The French magician Mr L. Charles, 'Ventriloquist and Professor of Recreative Philosophy', appeared at the Theatre Royal in Douglas on 28 and 29 October 1829. 'Pleasing Magical Illusions, Chemical Experiments, Ventriloquism and ... Intricate Pieces of Mechanism' all formed part of his varied entertainment, and he was able to command high ticket prices – 'Boxes, 3s. – Pit, 2s. – Gallery, 1s.'.[311] Further performances were advertised as taking place at the George Inn in Castletown and in Ramsey.

Conclusion

It was inevitable that novel entertainment such as circuses and magicians would be chronicled. Many of the other events that were reported centre on food: dinners and dances, harvest celebrations and ecclesiastical visitations. It is a pattern that continues today, particularly in the countryside, when no occasion can take place without ample refreshments. It was these happenings that brought communities together, whether through church or chapel, theatre or local gathering, private party or public banquet. Events such as these, many with charitable aim, were, and still are, the very fabric of society.

308 *Manks Advertiser*, 13 June 1812; *Isle of Man Weekly Gazette*, 25 June 1812.
309 *Manks Advertiser*, 25 November 1819, 6.
310 *Manks Advertiser*, 21 June 1827.
311 *Manx Sun*, 27 October 1829.

THE PRESS AND PUBLISHING

Michael Hoy

In about 1760, Henry Pepyat, a Dublin printer, issued a prospectus offering to bring 'a compleat Printing-House' to the Isle of Man, take on 'an Apprentice … on easy Terms' and publish a newspaper.[312] This failed to attract financial support, but Pepyat's initiative suggests that in the second half of the eighteenth century there were a number of literate Islanders who might be expected to take advantage of an Island-based press and subscribe to a newspaper.[313]

Although it is likely that printed tracts and broadsheets circulated in the Island before the eighteenth century, the earliest extant temperance tract lodged in the Manx Museum dates from 1763.[314] An unattributed article on early Manx printers in the *Journal of the Manx Museum*, almost certainly written by William Cubbon, states that all books, pamphlets and broadsides written before 1790 were printed in Dublin, Liverpool, London or Whitehaven, but some may have been printed locally.[315] There was a 'Tuck Mill or Paper Mill' at Ballawhetstone, Malew, before 1696, and in the 1760s a printing press was set up in Ramsey by W. Shepherd; part of the Manx Gaelic *New Testament*, dated 1767, was produced on this press.[316]

Pepyat's initiative was not followed by any other proposals for an Island newspaper, and the literate public had to read the news in the *Cumberland Pacquet*, a four-page weekly which began publication in 1774. The *Pacquet* was produced in Whitehaven by John Ware, printer of large sections of the Manx Gaelic Bible, and copies were carried on the mail packet between Whitehaven and Douglas.[317] Its style and content matched that of other contemporary newspapers; advertisements and information about shipping movements made up more than half the content, and international and national news was reported without editorial comment. The *Pacquet* included in most editions at least one item from, or about, the Isle of Man, many supplied by William Callow, Ware's Douglas agent. In her survey of the part played by the *Pacquet* in Island life in the last quarter of the eighteenth century, Constance Radcliffe notes its engagement with the Island's political affairs and its frequent support

312 W. Cubbon, 'The Early Manx Printers', *JMM*, 3, 53 (December 1937), 239: facsimile of Henry Pepyat's 'Proposals for establishing a Printing-House in the Isle of Man'.

313 For an assessment of levels of literacy in the second half of the eighteenth century see chapter 3, M. Hoy, 'Education and Literacy'.

314 MNH MS 05298/1.

315 *JMM*, 3, 53 (December 1937), 238.

316 MNH MS 00511C (QBHP), extracts from 'Liber Cur. Monaster', 1696–1705: preface note in John Quayle's handwriting, n.p.; William Cubbon (ed), *A Bibliographical Account of Works relating to the Isle of Man*, 2 vols (Oxford and London 1939), vol. 2, 1467.

317 The Whitehaven packet was established by statute in 1767.

for the Keys in their long campaign against the fourth duke of Atholl; in its reports of John Christian Curwen's speeches in parliament in defence of the Islanders' ancient rights, for example, the *Pacquet* claimed to be giving a more authentic account than was carried in the London papers.[318]

Paper manufacture as a successful enterprise in the Isle of Man is first recorded in 1784.[319] Five years later, when Alexander Lewthwaite set up a factory at Tromode, more than two thousand reams were exported.[320] The efficient production of paper enabled Christopher Briscoe to publish on 27 November 1792 the Island's first weekly newspaper, the *Manks Mercury and Briscoe's Douglas Advertiser*, which, like the *Pacquet*, reported news without editorial comment.

It was a pioneering publication, and not only in the Isle of Man. Although Dublin's first newspaper, the *Dublin Intelligence*, was published as early as 1710, in north-west England only Chester, Manchester and Whitehaven had newspapers before 1792.[321] Liverpool had to wait three more years before the first issue of *Gore's Liverpool General Advertiser* appeared.[322] Circulation of the *Mercury* was modest, but it was popular, and at a cost of 2d. (British) it was far cheaper than imported English papers, which were subject to stamp duty and taxes on newsprint and advertising. Publication of the *Mercury* may have been relatively short-lived; the Manx Museum holds no copies after 16 August 1794, but John Feltham found copies during his visit in 1797 and 98, and according to A.W. Moore, publication continued until 1801.[323] There was clearly a market for an Island newspaper and the gap was filled on 8 August 1801 by the first issue of the *Manks Advertiser and Weekly Intelligencer*, published by George Jefferson, a Liverpool journalist.[324] Jefferson had little interest in Manx affairs and aimed his publication exclusively at English residents. His paper

318 Constance Radcliffe, 'Manx news from Whitehaven 1774–1794 as Read in the *Cumberland Pacquet*', *PIMNHAS*, 10, 4 (1995–97), 428; *Cumberland Pacquet, and Ware's Whitehaven Advertiser*, 5 May 1790.

319 No evidence has survived to indicate the level of paper production at Ballwhetstone in the late seventeenth century: see Cubbon (ed), *Bibliographical Account*, 2, 1467–68.

320 *Report of the Commissioners of Inquiry for the Isle of Man* (1792), appx B, 24: products created in the Isle of Man and exported in the years 1781 to 1790, compiled by Senhouse Wilson, Deputy Receiver General; Kenneth Williamson, 'Paper Making in Man: the Story of a Lost Industry', *JMM*, 4, 59 (1939), 126.

321 *Dublin Intelligence*, 18 July 1702; *Manchester Mercury*, 3 March 1752; *Chester Chronicle*, 2 May 1775; *The Whitehaven Weekly Courant*, December 1736 (facsimile in *Cumberland Pacquet*, 21 November 1848).

322 *Gore's Liverpool General Advertiser*, 23 April 1795.

323 J. Feltham, *A Tour through the Island of Mann, in 1797 and 1798* (Bath, 1798), 59; A.W. Moore, *A History of the Isle of Man*, 2 vols (London 1900), vol. 2, 596.

324 N. Mathieson, 'Early Newspapers in the Isle of Man', *PIMNHAS*, 6, 2 (1958–60), 209, 214.

Manks Mercury

AND BRISCOE'S DOUGLAS ADVERTISER.

Vol. I. MUMB. 31. *TUESDAY, June 25. 17-3.* [Price Two-Pence, British

Pro Rege, Lege, Grege.

G. R. III.

By the King's Patent.

HORIZONTAL

SCREW SADDLES.

On a Peculiar, New, and Useful Construction, so as to fit every Horses' back.

Manufactured and sold by Milroy *of London, Mr.* Thomas Clarke, *of Liverpool, and* Peter Johnson, *of Douglas.*

WHICH His Majesty has been graciously pleased to Inspect, and give his Royal Approbation of, and to grant his Letters Patent for this unparrelled invention which Royal Sanction has induced the Manufacturers to offer them to the Public, being upon a principle entirely new, and of such utility, that any person, by the turning of a screw, in the fore and hind parts, which contracts or expands the Saddle, may fit from the largest Coach-Horse, to the finest weathered Racer.

The Advantage of Saddles, upon this construction is, that Gentlemen may change Horses every day throughout the year, and fit the same saddle to the back of every Horse without any expence.

For Gentlemen in the army, or who trade to foreign countries, hunt, or change horses often, this invention is far pre-eminent to any other that has been hitherto discovered.—Ladies Saddles upon the same construction.

PETER JOHNSON deeply impressed with gratitude to his friends for their liberal encouragement since his commencement in business, begs leave to return his most sincere thanks, and humbly solicits for a continuance which will be ever his study to merit.

He humbly informs his friends in particular, and the public in general that he has just arrived from England with a large assortment of Saddleary goods, together with a variety of Ladie's and Gentleman's whips, which will be sold upon the most reasonable terms, as they are purchased from the best market in England.

☞ An Apprentice wanted immediately.

FOREIGN INTELLIGENCE.

From the Head Quarters of the Prince de Cobourg, *June 4.*

"On the 2d, at four o'clock in the morning, the garrison of Conde attempted a sortie, or rather, to reconnoitre, for it advanced little beyond the glacis, although protected by a very brisk fire from the fortress. A squadron of the regiment Royal Allemand, endeavouring to turn its left flank, lost two horses by cannon balls. The garrison re-entered the fortress at ten o'clock. At noon it fired seven guns, but at equal intervals, which proves that they were signals. The Commandant has been permitted to send an Officer to the camp of Famars, and convince himself that it is really evacuated.

"Three deserters arrived from Valenciennes, assure us that there are not more than 9000 men in the place.

"A bridge is constructing over the Scheldt, near Fontenelle, in order to establish a certain communication between the two armies. Ten thousand workmen are employed at it, and it is erected upon piles. It is obliged to be made very long, on account of the inundation, which daily encreases; and as soon as it is finished, we shall endeavour to push the trenches forward.

"The fortress fires but seldom. Part of our heavy artillery is arrived, and is placed near Onnaing. M. de Frecheville, an emigrant French engineer, directs the siege.

"After the defeat at Famars, the patriots retired in one march to Arras; and fatigue surmounting fear, they stopped there. They are now encamped between Bouchain and Cambrai, having the high way in front, and the Scheldt at their left. Numbers arrive to them, but destitute of clothes and arms.

"Our advanced posts, commanded by General Otto, are always in advance. They are near Bouchain. If Custine would make the siege of Valenciennes to be raised, he must attack the Prince de Cobourg in the plain; where our cavalry can act, but we do not think he will venture."

From the Camp at Denain, *June 2.*

"We are forming here an army of observation to cover the siege of Valenciennes. It is [illegible] men strong, and occupies the same position that Prince Eugene did in 1712, when he was beaten by Marshal Villars. We are not afraid of suffering the same fate, although we expect to be attacked by Custine, who is supposed to be projecting a last effort to make the combined armies raise the siege of Valenciennes.

"The works before the place are so far advanced, that the batteries will certainly be finished by the 4th. Two hundred pieces of cannon and 50 mortars will be placed upon them.

"It is astonishing how troops, so badly organized and exercised as the patriotic armies are at present, can hold out so long, notwithstanding their frequent defeats, fanaticism is still so high among them, that many women of Valenciennes have taken up arms to defend the place.

"According to an exact return of the loss of the combined armies on the 23d, it appears that there were 1216 men killed and wounded. The Prince de Cobourg had calculated that the success of the day would cost an infinitely greater number."

LONDON, *June 11.*

The Letters received yesterday from Flanders add nothing very material to the accounts brought by express from the army.

So little alarm has been excited at Mentz by the approach of the Prussian army, that the streets were not unpaved on the 29th of May. The Prussians had not then got near enough to be able to throw a single shell into the place.

Valenciennes was summoned to surrender. The answer of the Commandant was manly. "It gives me great pleasure, that the city is invested by the best troops, and the greatest generals in the world.—I trust, that my behaviour in the eyes of these generals and armies will be such, as not only to deserve their commendation, but that of the universe, who are to be our spectators."

The number of the garrison of Valenciennes is reckoned to be about 9000 men; a great number of dead horses have been observed round the glacis of the town. This, though it go to prove that they are deficient in forage, does not imply that they are driven to the hard necessity of converting their horse-flesh into beef.

The besiegers labour to advance with their works as near as possible; in this, however, they do not proceed without interruption—the enemy keep up an incessant fire.

Conde, by every account, appears capable of holding out for a long period, if provisions do not fail, as it is entirely surrounded with inundations, for the distance of several miles from the walls. This, as we have before hinted, is one of the best fortified places in France, Lisle excepted.

Bouchain, as well as Quesnoy, is invested. The principal French force is stationed between Cambrai and Douay. Custine, it is said, has there taken the command.

The general attack to be made on Valenciennes is to be by a train of artillery, of not less than one hundred and twenty pieces of heavy cannon, and eighty mortars and howitzers.

General Custine is said to be at Lisle, and the Prince of Orange, who is near Turcoin, apprehending every thing from his enterprising spirit, has sent for a re-inforcement. He intimates that an attempt to break the cordon of the allies may be expected from that quarter.

According to recent advices from Petersburgh the Empress of Russia does not approve of that order which was prepared by her Council, which prohibits the importation of certain articles of merchandize into that country, the stoppage of which would have materially affected the commerce of England. It was therefore the opinion that no part would be carried into effect but what regarded the French articles.

PARTNERSHIP DISSOLVED.

NOTICE is hereby given, That the Copartnership between EDWARD CALLOW and WILLIAM CAIN, of Douglas, was in April 1792, by mutual consent, dissolved. All persons therefore, having any demands on the said partnership, are desired to send in their accounts to the said Edward Callow, that the same may be liquidated; and all persons indebted to the said partnership are requested to pay the same on or before the 12th day of July next, to the said Edward Callow, who is authorized to receive and settle the same.

Douglas, June 10.

AN advertisement having appeared in this paper dated the 10th inst publishing that the copartnership between Edward Callow and William Cain, of Douglas, ship-carpenters, was dissolved in April 17[illegible], by mutual consent, and calling upon all persons having any demands thereon to send in their accounts to the said Edward Callow, that the same might be liquidated, and also desiring all persons indebted to the said partnership, to pay the same on or before the 12th day of July next, to the said Edward Callow, as being authorised to receive and settle the same:— I, Sarah Cain, wife of the said William Cain, in the absence of my husband, (who at present is engaged in repairing the Hero, at———— about 8 miles from Ramsay) think it my duty to inform the public, that I do not know, nor ever heard of any authority that my husband gave to the said Edward Callow, impowering him to receive and settle the accounts of the said partnership, separate and distinct from himself; and I therefore think it proper to caution all persons concerned thereto from so doing, until my said husband shall return to this town, or otherwise grant a sufficient power to the said Edward Callow for that purpose.

Dated at Douglas June 15.

Extract of a Letter from Portsmouth, June [illegible]

"This morning arrived his Majesty's frigate Perserverance, Capt. Smith, from the East Indies, with the nine following homeward-bound East Indiamen under convoy:

Walpole, Churchill; Airy Castle, Stewart; Lord Macartney, Hay; Rockingham, Blanchard; Sir E. Hughes, Anderson; Nottingham, Barlow; Thetis, Nutt; Duke of Montrose, Dorin; Middlesex, Rogers; and Kaunitz, a Genoese [illegible], Capt. Giovanni [illegible], from Bengal, bound to Ostend."

Fig. 4.5 *The Manks Mercury and Briscoe's Douglas Advertiser, 25 June 1793.*

represented officialdom and the Church of England, which made it an uneasy training ground for the radical young Robert Fargher, Jefferson's nephew, who was apprenticed at the *Advertiser* before he branched out in 1833 to partner William Walls in publishing the *Mona's Herald* as the mouthpiece of reform.[325]

In 1812 George Beatson broke Jefferson's monopoly with the publication of the *Isle of Man Weekly Gazette*.[326] Three years later the *Gazette* was purchased by Mark Anthony Mills, a combative young Irish lawyer. He used Beatson's Phoenix Press to campaign in support of Manx residents against English incomers who claimed exclusive ownership of the Island's new-found prosperity. Mills and Jefferson were not only business rivals. Their political confrontation led to increasingly acerbic attacks on each other through the pages of the *Advertiser* and *Gazette*. Hannah Bullock was 'both astonished and alarmed at the enmity existing between them. The weekly paper was an instrument of war, and the anger of both sides was vented in repartee and innuendo ...'[327] These excesses prompted Tynwald to enact new legislation in 1817, which made 'the spreading of false News [and] malicious ... libellous Printing' criminal offences.[328]

Opposition to the Atholl faction was taken up in the Island press in 1821 when Samuel Colquitt established the *Rising Sun*. This was printed on larger newsprint than the earlier papers and carried more insular matter, much of it in the form of letters. Colquitt supported the lieutenant governor and the Keys, and he proved a match for Mills and Jefferson; he attacked Mills as 'a chattering Jackdaw in borrowed plumage ... a dead body hung in chains, who was always wanting to be hung somewhere else,' and dismissed Jefferson as 'an uneducated, silly, insignificant being, unworthy of our notice.'[329]

The *Advertiser*, *Gazette* and *Sun* all relied for their international and national news on English newspapers brought over from Whitehaven. When this route became increasingly unreliable, they lobbied together successfully in 1821 for the mail packet to be relocated to Liverpool. Subsequently in the 1820s, as steam power further improved the timing and reliability of crossings, all three papers played a major role in promoting the advantages of Island life to attract visitors and new residents. This cooperation was superficial, however, and the political rivalry between the newspapers continued unabated.

A libel action in the courts eventually bankrupted Mills and forced the closure of the *Gazette* in 1824.[330] Jefferson emerged unscathed from this case

325 W.T. Kneale, 'The Trials of a Manx Radical: the Life and Times of Robert Fargher, 1803–1863', *JMM*, 6, 76 (1957), 89.

326 Mathieson, 'Early Newspapers', 208–10, 219.

327 H.A. Bullock, *History of the Isle of Man* (London 1816), 208, 358.

328 Gill (ed), *Statutes*, Criminal Code Act, 1817 (sections 41 and 45), vol. 1, 388–89.

329 *Rising Sun*, 5 May, 9 September and 1 December 1821.

330 D. Craine, 'Mark Anthony Mills: a Tragedy', *JMM*, 4, 54 (1938), 10.

and the *Advertiser* continued publication until 1842. In 1824 the *Rising Sun* was acquired by James Grellier, who was no less adept in trading insults than Colquitt had been, but he advocated a less confrontational tone in political campaigning.[331] In its support for the Keys, however, the *Sun* was just as conservative as the *Advertiser*, and from 1833 both were targeted by the new voice of radical reform – Fargher's *Mona's Herald*.[332]

In addition to the newspapers, two magazines were published in the early nineteenth century – the *Manx Repository* in 1815 and the *Reflector* in 1821. Two years later a new illustrated magazine was advertised by Trevor Ashe, who had briefly owned the *Sun* in 1824; this venture came to nothing, although in 1825 Jefferson published Ashe's plates independently.[333]

The rise of the Manx newspapers and magazines would not have been possible without the establishment of Island printing presses and paper manufacture. Newspaper production was the main impetus for the development of the printing enterprises, but the presses were also used for book and broadsheet production. William Cubbon lists five broadsheets printed in Douglas from 1821 to 1823; on a grander scale, David Craine describes Mills's *Ancient Ordinances and Statute Laws of the Isle of Man*, published in 1821, as 'perhaps the noblest piece of typographical work ever done by a Manx press.'[334] John and Mary Quiggin took over the press and ownership of the *Manx Sun* in 1828 and their printing business flourished until the 1860s. No less important in the development of newspaper and book production was Island paper manufacture by entrepreneurs like William Banks (Braddan), Lewthwaite's son Alexander (Ballamillaghyn), William Walker and Thomas Topliss (Laxey).[335]

'This is the era of newspapers,' Jefferson wrote in 1826, 'and the mania for scribbling seems to obtain to a wide extent ... We have had a number of weekly papers in this enlightened country this century.'[336] The development of a medium which promoted vigorous political and social debate, enlivened by the vituperative wit of the journalists and publishers, is a notable feature of the closing years of the eighteenth and the first three decades of the nineteenth centuries.

331 Mathieson, 'Early Newspapers', 225–26. Grellier changed the title to the *Manx Sun* in 1826.

332 Kneale, 'Trials of a Manx Radical', 89.

333 T. Ashe (comp), *The Manx Sketch Book or Beauties of the Isle of Man in a series of Lithographic Engravings* (Douglas 1825). http://www.isle-of-man.com/manxnotebook/views/as1825/index.htm

334 Cubbon (ed), *Bibliographical Account*, 2, 782; Craine, 'Mark Anthony Mills', 7.

335 See Cubbon (ed), *Bibliographical Account*, 2, 1470–75 and 1481–91; Williamson, 'Paper Making', *JMM*, 4, 59 (1939), 126–28 and *JMM*, 4, 60 (1939), 147–50.

336 Quoted by George Goodwin, 'Manx Annals of Eighty Years Ago: Newspapers', in *Peel City Guardian*, 28 December 1901.

ASSOCIATIONAL CULTURE

Michael Hoy

An account compiled in part from the research papers of Ann Harrison †[337]

In the summer of 1749, George Shemeld, tenant of the White Lion in Parade Street, Douglas, and Ulsterman Robert Black, a wine merchant who built the Douglas Hotel on North Quay, were presented with medals recording their services as ceremonial officers of the earliest known Manx association, the Knights of Laxey.[338]

The society was active in the 1740s and 50s, but there are no records of its meetings and the medals provide the only clues about the interests of its members. Of six known recipients, three were Islanders, associates of the successful entrepreneur William Fine, of Ballahott (Malew), and three came from North Wales. The inscriptions 'We stand firm to each other' and 'In love and friendship' indicate that it was an exclusive social club, while the maritime connection represented in the medal given to William Vaughan, with its engraving of a merchant ship, suggests that the common interest of the Knights of Laxey may well have been the running trade.

The first associations in the Isle of Man for which records survive are the Society of Bucks and the Manx Society. The Douglas Lodge of the Society of Bucks, a Masonic-style group of associations founded in London in the early 1700s, was established on 6 March 1764, probably as an affiliate of the Liverpool Lodge.[339] Members met regularly at the Anchor Inn in Buck's Row (Fairy Ground), Douglas, where they combined elaborate ceremonies and social conviviality with a serious agenda 'to promote the welfare and happiness of the Island', through the protection of trade, without espousing any political stance.[340] Peter Heywood of the Nunnery was the Lodge's first secretary, and from 1764 to 1767 there were fifty-six members, of whom thirty-six were incomers and twenty-four were merchants.[341] Annual sermons by the Lodge Chaplain in St Matthew's Church frequently addressed issues of trade and prosperity; in 1788, for example, Henry Corlett, vicar of German, preached on the virtues of manufacture and employment, and the advantages of wealth

337 MNH MS 10933, Ann Harrison, 'Associational History of the Isle of Man, 1764–1916' (University of Liverpool, Ph.D. thesis, 1988).

338 A.W. Moore, *The Manx Note Book* (Douglas), 1 (January 1885), 36 and 6 (April 1886) 91; Neil Mathieson, 'Old Inns and Coffee-Houses of the Isle of Man', *PIMNHAS*, 5:4 (1953–54), 419, 422.

339 Peter Dickenson, *Society of Bucks: A Candid Enquiry into the Principles and Practices of the most Ancient and Honourable Society of Bucks* (London 1770).

340 *Manks Mercury*, 2 August 1793.

341 MNH MS 00876 B, Constitution Book of the Manx Society of Bucks, 1763.

Fig. 4.6 *Silver gilt medal: inscribed 'IN LOVE AND FRIENDSHIP – Sir Rbt. Black L. Privy Seal to the Knights of Laxey, August 14th 1749': MNH 1954-5913.*

and plenty.[342] The last meeting of the Manx Lodge of the Society of Bucks was in 1818.

The Manx Society was established in July 1764. It was modelled on the Royal Society for the Encouragement of Arts, Commerce and Manufactures in Great Britain, founded ten years earlier in London. Its agenda was 'to promote or protect the public good of this Isle.'[343] None of the Society's records have survived, but some evidence of its members and activities may be found in the Atholl Papers. Among the founding members were leading figures of the establishment, including the third duke of Atholl, John Wood (Governor 1761 to 1777), John Quayle of Bridge House, Castletown, and Vicar General James

342 MNH MS 00268 A, Manx Sermons, 2, 165–77; Harrison, 'Associational History', 23.

343 MNH MS 01147 C, Proposal to establish 'an amicable Society to be Stiled and intituled "The Manx Society"' (n.d.).

Wilks.[344] Merchant entrepreneurs of the 'middling sort', Manx and incomers, also joined the association. Although the Society's activities were not limited to the promotion of trade, the members worked effectively to counter the Island's depressed state following the Revestment and Mischief Acts, and among its most notable successes was the development of linen weaving to broaden manufacturing capacity. In a minute of 3 February 1768, Wilks recorded this achievement and offered the Society's thanks to the duke of Atholl 'for his generous and liberal benefactions towards promoting manufactures, industry and agriculture in the Isle of Man.'[345] This is the last record of the Manx Society's activities; the duke of Atholl paid his annual subscription of one guinea in 1770, but at some time after this date, probably in the late 1780s, the Society was disbanded, its demise much regretted in the Society of Bucks' records.[346]

Ann Harrison argues convincingly that membership of the Society of Bucks and the Manx Society boosted the confidence and self-esteem of the Island's leading citizens, lay and clerical, professional and mercantile, and empowered them to turn to advantage the socio-political challenges which followed the Revestment and Mischief Acts and the demise of the running trade.[347]

On 6 June 1790 the Isle of Man Friendly Society, the first of the Island's mutual associations, was formed in Douglas, three years before the Rose Act gave statutory encouragement to the establishment of mutual societies in England and Wales.[348] The association was not required to register or document its activities and no records have survived, but a picture of its activities may be traced in the press. Membership was open to tradesmen aged twenty-one to thirty-five, resident within two miles of Douglas. They paid an annual subscription of one guinea and monthly payments of 1s., which entitled them to welfare relief, including sickness benefit and the services of a visiting surgeon, and gave them access to a loan fund. For the first time, help in time of need, which had previously only been provided by the church in the parishes, was available to subscribing members and their families. The society also owned and leased properties and built new housing in Douglas.[349] Since it was concerned solely with issues of mutual self-help, the Island authorities saw no threat of subversive politics in the society's activities, and Ann Harrison suggests that

344 MNH MS 04952 A (b), John Quayle's Note Book (1765).

345 MNH MS 09707 (AP), 36/38 (2nd) - 18.

346 Harrison, 'Associational History', 25, 27; MNH MS 00876 B, Constitution Book, amended toast: *'Revival of The Manx Society'*.

347 Harrison, 'Associational History', 27, 31.

348 1248The Friendly Societies Act (Sir George Rose's Act): Ch.54, 1793; *Manks Advertiser*, 12 June 1813; Harrison, 'Associational History', 37–38.

349 *Manks Advertiser*, 9 June 1829: The Isle of Man Friendly Society laid 'the foundation-stones of six new cottages [with] the title of the "Taubman Terrace"'.

members of the Keys, notably John Christian Curwen, may well have actively supported its work.[350]

In 1795 a second association, the Ramsey Philanthropic Society, was formed to provide similar welfare, and other mutual associations followed early in the nineteenth century.[351] At first, most were located in the Island's growing urban communities, and many of these had a restricted membership. The Methodist Friendly Society of Douglas, founded in 1798, was the first church affiliation; the Artificers' Friendly Society of Douglas, the Douglas Labourers' Friendly Society, both founded in 1811, and the Castletown Artificers' Friendly Society, founded in 1813 with the motto 'Unanimity, Concord and Peace', represented the welfare of working men; the Strangford Union Society was formed in 1822 to serve manufacturing workers in Union Mills; and in 1825 the Laxey Patriotic Society was set up for the benefit of the growing number of men employed in the mining industry.[352] The interests of gentlemen farmers were fostered by the Isle of Man Agricultural Association, established in 1807, of which the reforming agriculturist John Christian Curwen was president.[353]

The success of mutual associations depended on their members having some measure of independent financial security in order that they could contribute regular subscriptions, and consequently in the relatively poor rural areas such societies were slower to develop. Onchan, perhaps with the advantage of its closeness to the burgeoning economy of Douglas, was the first village to have a Friendly Society. It was founded in May 1810 'to promote the advantage and happiness of each member … by relieving such as by some unhappy accident stand in need'; members paid an annual subscription of 12*s*, and its aims in addressing social welfare needs through mutual self-help were similar to those of the 1790 society. Although its membership was relatively small, the Onchan Society was reputed to be the wealthiest of the Island's mutual associations.[354] John Christian Curwen noted the popularity of the new rural societies, and

350 Harrison, 'Associational History', 35–36.

351 MNH D126/3, *Code of Articles of the Ramsey Philanthropic Society instituted in the year 1796* (Douglas 1831).

352 *Manks Advertiser*, 26 January 1811, 13 August 1812, 13 August 1814; MNH MS 09707, AP, 102 (2nd) – 30; *Manks Advertiser*, 31 December 1814; R.A. Curphey, 'The Castletown Artificers' Friendly Society', *PIMNHAS*, 7:2 (1966–68), 164, 169; *Manx Sun*, 23 May 1823; P.M. Lewthwaite, *Fleece and Flail United: the History of Union Mills Isle of Man* (Braddan 1986), 75–76; MNH F78/RUL, *Rules and Orders to be observed by the Members of the Laxey Patriotic Society, instituted May 23, 1825* (Douglas 1847).

353 J.C. Curwen, *Workington Agricultural Society's Annual Report for the Isle of Man, 1810* (Cumbria Archive Centre, Carlisle DCU/Additional/261), 133.

354 MNH MS 05179 C, Onchan Friendly Society Cash Book, 1810–46.

in 1812 Thomas Quayle recorded: 'In the towns of the Island, box-clubs have existed for several years, and are now spreading in the country-parishes.'[355]

The highlight of the year for the Friendly Societies, especially in the villages, was the Club Day, 'a Red Letter day,' according to John Kneen, when all the men and boys in the parish processed to the church, and then played music outside the homes of all the 'benefit-free members' who had paid their club fees without drawing any benefit. In the evening, members returned to the society's hall for 'boiled beef and a good tea … children gathered to get a good feed, whilst the young men and women danced to the music of the band … Thus the club day was a day to be remembered by all.'[356] The associations and their members had much to celebrate. By 1830 there were Friendly Societies in the four towns and in fourteen parishes and villages. All were island initiatives set up to address the challenges of local community life which encouraged prudence and assiduity; they fostered a growing sense of social cohesion and confidence, and they were commended in the *Mona's Herald* as 'a formidable barrier against pauperism and other social evils.'[357]

In 1828 the Fourth Annual Conference of the Manchester Unity of Oddfellows was held in the Isle of Man. Two years later, two Englishmen, J. Foster, who worked at Union Mills, and Jeremiah Lee, of Leeds, founded the Loyal Mona Lodge of Oddfellows.[358] It was affiliated to the Yorkshire Unity and opened in Douglas at the Saddle Inn, Queen Street (North Quay), with twenty members, nearly all of whom were incomers. Similar affiliated associations like the Rechabites and Foresters followed in the 1830s and 40s.[359] The three groups had distinctive traditions and styles, but they worked together to address new problems, such as the growing movement of workers, and they brought a new impetus to associational culture in the Island, not least with their flourishing juvenile sections, at a time when the older Friendly Societies, with an ageing membership, were struggling to adapt their finances and administration. The Oddfellows, Rechabites and Foresters gave their members opportunities for convivial fellowship and financial security within a moral framework of Christian values, and they addressed local causes and social issues with notable success.[360]

355 Curwen, *Annual Report for the Isle of Man*, 130; Thomas Quayle, *General View of the Agriculture of the Isle of Man* (London 1812), 150; Harrison, 'Associational History', 32.

356 MNH FLS, Notebook of John Kneen, Ballamona, Ballaugh (collected 1950s); Harrison. 'Associational History', 39, 47–48.

357 *Mona's Herald*, 28 December 1850.

358 Harrison, 'Associational History', 42.

359 Harrison, 'Associational History', 44–47.

360 See *Mona's Herald*, 28 December 1850.

When John Feltham visited the Isle of Man in 1797 and 1798, he observed: 'At Douglas and Ramsey there are clubs for mutual benefit ... [although] the females have no society of this kind.'[361] This changed in 1816 when the Isle of Man Sisterly Society, a Friendly Society for Working Women, was formed in Douglas.[362] It is possible that this was modelled on the Workington Sisterly Society, founded in 1793 with Isabella Curwen, wife of John Christian Curwen, as patron, although Ann Harrison suggests that a connection with similar female societies linked with the textile industry in North West England is more likely. Membership was open to women aged fifteen to thirty of good character and 'free from any infirmity of body', residing within two miles of Douglas. A joining fee of 5s., followed by monthly payments of 9d., entitled a member, after two years of paid contributions, to weekly financial support, if 'rendered incapable of following her calling by sickness or accidental misfortune ... till her health be restored.' The Society employed two wardens and a surgeon, whose duties were 'to visit sick members ... free of any expense to such members.'[363] It was administered by women and did much to foster women's health and welfare. Eight years later its work was complemented by the Society for Lying-in Women.[364]

More general welfare associations were also set up and administered by women. The Society for the Relief of the Poor of Douglas began in 1814 by supporting twenty-five destitute people in Sand (now Strand) Street, Douglas; in the same year the Female Association for Clothing and Educating Girls for Work was set up, followed by the Douglas Ladies' Soup Dispensary in 1818.[365] A.W. Moore characterises the first two decades of the nineteenth century as a period of growing poverty and hardship for many Manx families, and the voluntary welfare relief provided by women played a significant role in relieving the condition of those who had no means of contributing to mutual associations.[366]

One further welfare society of special significance in the Island's maritime story is the Isle of Man District Association of the Royal National Institution

361 J. Feltham, *A Tour through the Island of Mann, in 1797 and 1798* (Bath 1798), 200.

362 *Manks Advertiser*, 6 June 1816; Harrison, 'Associational History', 50.

363 Harrison, 'Associational History', 120; MNH D126/3 (b), *Rules and Orders to be observed by the Isle of Man Sisterly Society, instituted First day of May, 1816* (Douglas 1830).

364 W. Cubbon, *A Bibliographical Account of Works relating to the Isle of Man*, 2 vols (London and Oxford 1933), vol. 1, 182–83.

365 Harrison, 'Associational History', 115–16; *Manks Advertiser*, 30 April 1814, 9 November 1815, 2 January 1823; Rising Sun 21 January 1823.

366 Moore, *Isle of Man*, vol. 2, 550–53.

for the Preservation of Life from Ship-wreck, founded in 1826 two years after William Hillary's National Association was established.[367]

The Court of Apollo had a very different provenance and purpose from the welfare societies. Founded in May 1794 by a group of expatriate Englishmen drawn to the Isle of Man by the prospect of cheap living, the *Manks Mercury* reported that its first meeting 'was spent in the greatest harmony and social mirth.'[368] It was the first of a number of convivial clubs intended to attract incomers, like the Mona Service Club (1822), which grew out of an 1819 informal social gathering of retired half-pay officers. The Finish Club, founded in 1821 with John Tallan, a founder member of the Mona Service Club, as its president, was for Manxmen.[369]

There were active military associations, too, following a tradition established much earlier in the eighteenth century, which attracted ready volunteers, notably during the period of European wars from the 1790s to 1815. Four cavalry volunteer companies and one of foot were raised, the first, the Troop of Constitutional Dragoons organized by George Quayle of Bridge House (Castletown), in 1793. None saw active service, and after 1816 only one volunteer company, the Manx Yeomanry Cavalry, was still assembled. Its activities were largely ceremonial; in 1813 and 1822 the cavalry, described as 'a very respectable, well-dressed body of men,' escorted the duke of Atholl at the Tynwald ceremonies.[370]

Notable among popular cultural societies were the Literary and Philosophical Society of the Isle of Man, founded in 1817, the Gentlemen Amateurs, who gave theatrical performances in the New Theatre, Athol Street, over nearly thirty years from 1823, and the Douglas Harmonic Club, founded in 1827, which gave concerts for charitable causes.[371] The first of a number of societies associated with the revival and preservation of Manx Gaelic was formed in 1821.[372] Rooms of public assembly, too, offering dancing, card playing and other recreational activities, were provided in the British and Hanby's Hotels in Douglas in the 1820s.[373]

367 *Manks Advertiser*, 12 January 1826; MNH B.162/HIL (3), *First Annual Report of the Isle of Man District Association of the Royal National institution for the Preservation of Life from Shipwreck* (Douglas 1827).

368 Harrison, 'Associational History', 57.

369 *Manks Mercury*, 20 May 1794; MNH MS 14103, *Standing Rules for the Government of the Mona United Service Club, established 13th October, 1828* (Douglas 1832); *Rising Sun*, 5 October 1922.

370 Moore, *Isle of Man*, vol. 2, 639.

371 Harrison, 'Associational History', 120, 130, 134.

372 Cubbon, *Bibliographical Account*, 2, 1014; *Manx Sun*, 1 December 1829; *Manks Advertiser*, 6, 13, 20, 27 June and 4 July 1822; 2 June 1825.

373 G. Jefferson, *The Geographical and Topographical Guide of the Isle of Man* (Douglas, 1824), 55.

Libraries played an important role in the development of associations. When John Feltham visited the Island in 1797–98, he noted as 'an instance of its progress in refinement' the existence of 'a circulating library' in Douglas.[374] This was probably Briscoe's library, which was run by Joseph Briscoe, printer and publisher, from the late 1780s to the beginning of the nineteenth century, when it seems to have been superseded by George Jefferson, who advertised in his *Manx Advertiser* his intention to start a circulating library.[375] At least three more circulating libraries were opened in Douglas over the next twenty years.[376] Members of the Douglas Mechanics Institute, which was founded in 1825, just two years after the first Institute in England was established in Liverpool, paid 3d. per week to attend evening meetings and towards the formation of a library, which was duly opened in 1831.[377]

In addition to these private enterprises, a public subscription library and reading room were established in Douglas in 1810, 'a great acquisition to the town', according to George Woods.[378] By 1824 the library contained nearly 1,200 books, and despite some vigorous criticism of its management and acquisitions policy, notably by Hannah Bullock, Samuel Haining and Kermotte Stowell, records in the press and directories suggest that it provided a valued service.[379] John Welch noted dismissively in 1836 that there were 'two or three indifferent libraries' in Douglas, but George Jefferson's circulating library continued into the 1840s; according to Cannell's Guide of 1843 'it is the oldest and best in the Island, for choice selection and variety.'[380]

In 1698 an entry in the Receiver's accounts lists a payment of five shillings 'towards a Coffy House signe to be set up in Castletowne'.[381] In Dublin in the same year, John Dunton held a book auction in Dick's Coffee House, one of a number which were popular in Dublin in the late seventeenth century.[382]

374 Feltham, *Tour*, 200.

375 *Manx Advertiser*, 4 November 1801.

376 *Manx Advertiser*, 22 February 1812 (R. Stubbs' Circulating Library at Heywood House); 22 January 1813 (Sarah Sharp's library); 7 September 1820 and 3 November 1825 (Luke Lane's Wellington News Room and library).

377 *Manks Advertiser*, 2 June 1825.

378 G. Woods, *An Account of the Past and Present State of the Isle of Man* (London and Edinburgh, 1811), 108.

379 H. Bullock, *A History of the Isle of Man* (London, 1816), 207–08; Jefferson, *Guide* (Douglas, 1823), 39; W. Harrison, *Bibliotheca Monensis*, Manx Society, 8 (1861), 122; Kermotte Stowell, letter (Douglas, 1813), 16–17, 20; S. Haining, *Isle of Man Guide* (Douglas, 1822), 157.

380 J. Welch, *A Six Days' Tour through the Isle of Man* (Douglas, 1836), 66; W. Cannell, *A New Guide, and Visitor's Companion, through the Isle of Man* (Douglas, 1843), 70.

381 MNH MS 10192 (Receiver's Accounts: Petty Disbursements, 1698), 7; Mathieson, 'Old Inns', 430.

382 J. Dunton, *The Dublin Scuffle* (London 1699).

Whitehaven had a coffee house in 1774, and in Liverpool six coffee houses are recorded between 1756 and 1758.[383] Whether the Castletown coffee house flourished is not known, but the Receiver's substantial outlay suggests that it must have been a significant enterprise. In the early 1780s the opening of the Liverpool Coffee House near old St Matthew's in Douglas provided the Island with another convivial venue for informal association, where incoming visitors in particular found surroundings similar to those which had existed in London and other cities for more than a century. By 1830 there were eight more coffee houses in Douglas, one, Fargher's 'Coffee Room', offering its clientele readership of newspapers for an annual subscription, and Peel, too, had a coffee house in the Caledonian and Liverpool Inn.[384] The popularity of these coffee houses reflects the same changes in demography and economic and social confidence as may be seen in the development of associational culture more generally in the Isle of Man.

By 1830, associational culture was woven into the fabric of Manx society. Ann Harrison lists fifty-five societies established since the 1740s, of which twenty-seven were Friendly or Affiliated subscription societies and nine were independent philanthropic associations set up to help the poor and needy. These associations gave the island community of nearly forty-two thousand people a framework of support which the limited resources of the Church could no longer provide.[385] Other societies reflect the diverse interests and concerns of many Islanders, some, like the Mechanics Institute, representing a growing confidence and determination among working men and women. From the earliest foundations of 1764, when the first members of Douglas Lodge of the Society of Bucks aspired 'to promote the welfare and happiness of the Island,' associations played a significant role in supporting the disadvantaged and forming the distinct character and way of life of the Isle of Man.[386]

ART IN THE ISLE OF MAN

Yvonne Cresswell and Colette Davies

What is Manx art? It has been defined for the purposes of the National Art Collection (Manx National Heritage) as work by a Manx-born artist and/or of a Manx-related subject. As few works by Manx-born artists from this period have survived, it is this latter definition that encompasses most work produced

383 *Universal Magazine* (London, 1785) January, 23; S. Inwood, 'Coffee Shop Society in Seventeenth Century London' (lecture transcript, Gresham College, London 2004); *Cumberland Pacquet*, 1774; *Manchester Courier*, 25 November 1912.

384 Jefferson, *Guide* (1823), 70; Mathieson, 'Old Inns', 428–31.

385 A.W. Moore, *Sodor and Man* (London 1893), 253.

386 *Manks Mercury*, 2 April 1793.

between 1405 and 1830.[387] The main types of artwork considered are maps, topographical views and portraits. However, these do not represent the wide variety that would have been produced. The very small proportion of surviving material includes a disproportionate amount of art which may be considered as works of both high quality and status. Sadly, most examples of vernacular 'folk art' have been lost.

Cartography and maps

A consistent example that can be found throughout the period is the 'art' of cartography. Maps can be purely functional but could also be used to illustrate written accounts and histories. They may be displayed as symbols of wealth, learning and cultural aspirations. Technological advances in surveying techniques and printing can be seen in the growth of popularity of 'county histories' by antiquarians, of which William Camden's encyclopaedic publication *Britannia* is a distinctive early example.[388]

Probably the most significant map of the Isle of Man is by John Speed (1552–1629) for his work *The Theatre of the Empire of Great Britain* (1611–12).[389] Now best known as a cartographer, his major work was the *Historie of Great Britain* (1611), now valued for its county and town maps. Speed principally corrected and updated existing maps and surveys. His map of the Isle of Man was based on Thomas Durham's 1595 survey and was significant for a variety of reasons. Previously, the Island was shown as part of the British Isles. Maps were not based on surveys, so were inaccurate and had little detail. Even Saxton's version (1583), which is the first to show inland details, was based on earlier versions by Mercator (1564), Ortelius (1570) and Lhuyd (1573).[390] Distorted representations continued to be seen in the late eighteenth century as earlier map plates were still being used. By contrast, Durham's survey was based on personal observation, possibly undertaken for military purposes as the Island came under direct control of the English Crown. Military surveys had already been undertaken in Ulster (1590).[391] Speed's map was a single sheet centred on the Island and bordered by the surrounding countries (1605). A written

387 This is in stark contrast to the significantly large proportion of Manx artwork produced post-1830 by Manx-born artists or long-term residents of the Island.

388 Camden's *Britannia* was first published in Latin in 1586, with an expanded 6th edition by1607 and an English translation by 1610.

389 J. Speed, *The Theatre of the Empire of Great Britain: Presenting an exact geography of England, Scotland, and Ireland* (London, 1611–12); MNH P.1919 (c.1611 edn).

390 C. Saxton, *Britannia Insularum* (1583): Birmingham Central Library; BL, Maps C.7.d.7. Saxton's map is the first to display the Isle of Man as a separate plate.

391 A.M. Cubbon, *Early Maps of the Isle of Man: a guide to the collection in the Manx Museum* (MNH: Douglas, 1954), 8–10.

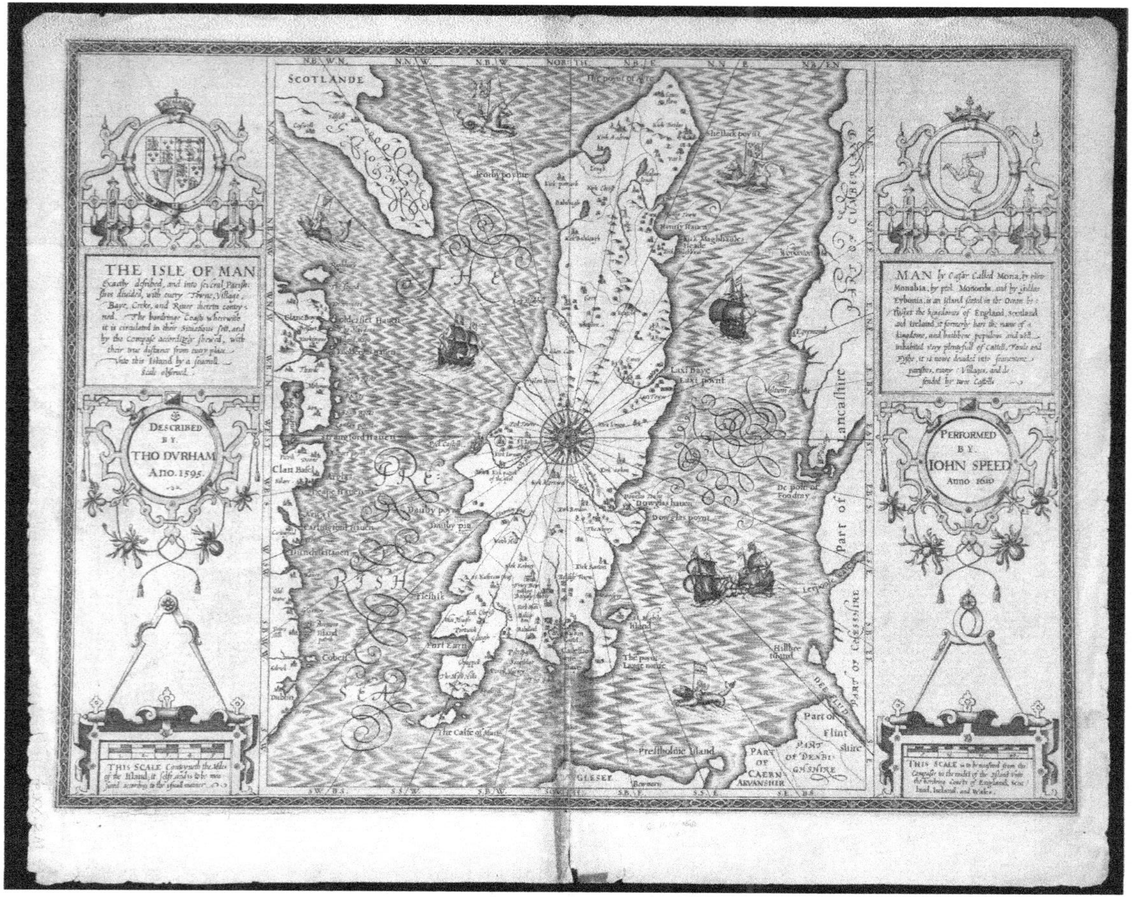

Fig. 4.7 *Thomas Durham's survey of the Isle of Man (1595) 'performed by John Speed Anno 1605 [1610]': MNH P.XX.2M.*

description of the Island was added in 1610. Either Speed or Durham decided to use two scales on the map; one scale shows the adjacent countries in relation to the Isle of Man, whilst the second is large enough to show the Island's principal towns and settlements, the two castles and the parish boundaries. Inaccuracies in spellings, boundaries and number of parishes are thought to have been introduced at the engraving stage.[392]

Speed's improved accuracy and detail illustrate the importance of the map as 'both a scientific document and a work of art', but the decoration is more than merely aesthetic. The patterning of the sea is typically Dutch; the four sea monsters each carry a figure and banner symbolising England, Scotland, Ireland and Wales. England and Scotland appear to be taking hostile stances against each other whilst the two ships engaged in a sea battle fly the English and Scottish flags. This may represent the strained relations between the two countries when the survey was first conducted (1595). By the time of publication, relations were far better: the crowns are united and a combined royal coat of arms is shown together with the 'Three Legs of Man' (1605).[393]

Speed's map was superseded in terms of accuracy, if not initially in quality, by Collins (1693) and Mackenzie (1775), whose maps were based on marine charts.[394] While the Island's coastline was more recognizable, inland detail was still limited and the misspelling of place names was perpetuated. In 1789, Peter Fannin published a map of the Island, which contained several new and major additions, including the most accurate depiction to date of the Island's hills, the inclusion for the first time of roads, details of harbours, the first map of Douglas and a view of the buildings on the south side of Douglas harbour.[395]

The nineteenth century saw the need for a new type of map to illustrate the growing number of guides and directories being published for visitors and residents alike. The maps were small to fit the books, but they still had to contain useful information. While some followed Fannin's map, many drew on John Drinkwater of Liverpool's map (1826) which in turn was based on a trigonometrical survey by Benjamin Smythe.[396] As a result, highly stylised representations of the island's topography, towns and villages were now replaced by

392 Cubbon, *Early Maps*, 10–12: Speed's map was engraved by Jodocus Hondius of Amsterdam, as Dutch cartographers and engravers were regarded as producing the most accurate and richly-decorated maps of the period.

393 Cubbon, *Early Maps*, 3, 11–12.

394 G. Collins, *Great Britain's Coasting Pilot. The Second Part* (London, 1693): Collins conducted his maritime survey of the Irish Sea in 1687. M. Mackenzie, *A Maritime Survey of Ireland and the West of Great Britain. Vol. II* (London, 1775).

395 Cubbon, *Early Maps*, 16. Peter Fannin, a 'Master in His Majesty's Royal Navy' and a naval officer who accompanied Captain Cook on his second voyage circumnavigating the globe (1772–75), retired to Douglas in 1775 and founded a navigation school.

396 J. Drinkwater and B. Smythe, *To the Rt. Hon.ble George Canning … this map of the Isle of Man* (Douglas, 1826); Cubbon, *Early Maps*, 17–18.

more accurate and detailed maps, reflecting improved surveying and engraving. Hills, no longer small rounded humps scattered across the map, were carefully delineated to show the orientation of mountains and valleys, and roads shown within towns and across the island. The era of the modern map was beginning to dawn.

Landscapes and topographic views

The first known visual depictions of the island are found in an album of prints and pen-and-ink drawings traditionally ascribed to Daniel King (c.1616–c.1661), printmaker and pupil of Wenceslaus Hollar, who is thought to have engraved the drawings for publication.[397] A collection of fourteen views illustrated *A Short Treatise of the Isle of Man*, published as a supplement to Daniel King's *Vale Royall* (1656).[398] Eight of the drawings flanked a modified version of Speed's map, with the sea monsters and sailing ships removed but with the addition of Lord Fairfax's coat of arms. The names of four sheadings and their boundaries create a rather confused representation of the Island.[399] The vignettes concentrate on coastal views of the island, whilst the remaining six larger views are of Castle Rushen, Peel Castle, Douglas, Bishopscourt, Rushen Abbey and the Nunnery, the Island's main administrative, historic and religious sites. Although several of the views contain figures, these simply provide a sense of scale. The map seems to be as important, or potentially even more so, than the illustrations.

The album also holds eighteen sepia pen-and-ink drawings annotated with descriptive notes, providing more detail of the principal settlements and contemporary life. The single illustration of Castle Rushen in the *Treatise* can be compared with seven detailed views of the castle and its surroundings, annotated to identify areas of the castle. They include detailed illustrations of daily life: vehicles, livestock, costume, people at work and at 'play' and numerous dogs. Described as 'almost painfully naïve' by a former keeper of prints and drawings in the British Museum, their importance and significance is mainly as a primary source for historic research.[400] Although the provenance of the album is well documented, the proliferation of facsimile copies of the drawings in the late nineteenth and early twentieth century has meant that people have made assumptions based on the copies rather than the originals.

397 BL Add MS 27362, *A collection of views of the Isle of Man, formerly belonging to Ralph Thoresby, Esq. Leeds [1650].*

398 J. Chaloner, *A Short Treatise of the Isle of Man [...] Illustrated with Severall Prospects of the Island, by Daniel King* (London, 1656).

399 Cubbon, *Early Maps*, 13.

400 E. Wilson, *A Book of Prospects: Seventeenth-century prints and drawings of the Isle of Man* (Castletown, 2014), 9.

Fig. 4.8 *'Peel Castle, Isle of Man', unknown artist, English School, c.1700: Derby Collection K239. Image reproduced courtesy of the right hon. the earl of Derby, 2019.*

There has also been a conflation of the prints illustrating the *Treatise* with the original drawings and with all of them being described as 'Daniel King's'. A current view is that Daniel King made an original set of topographical drawings, which served as under-drawings for Hollar's prints, and source material for pen-and-ink drawings by an 'amateur hand' thought to be James Chaloner. Although attributions may be subject to debate, the work is undoubtedly of historic importance.[401] A landscape painting of St Patrick's Isle (similar to King's fol. 28r – 'Peel Castle as it doth appeare from the east') by an unknown artist, entitled 'Peel Castle', dating from around 1700, is held in the Derby Collection at Knowsley.

401 For current debate see Wilson, *Book of Prospects*.

The next major collection of Manx topographical views is by the Welsh artist and engraver, Moses Griffith (1749–1819), who was employed to accompany Thomas Pennant (1726–1798), the Welsh naturalist and antiquarian, on his tours to produce drawings to illustrate Pennant's publications.[402] Between 1769 and 1783, a group of artists, including Pennant and the English antiquarian Francis Grose (1731–1791), travelled the British Isles and visited the Island in 1774 as part of their 'Grand Tour'. These illustrations are more accurate impressions of the Island's principal buildings, particularly in regard to perspective and the use of colour. Griffith also drew places unrecorded in earlier seventeenth-century collections. Their antiquarian interests can be seen in the choice of the Meayll Circle, carved Manx crosses at Kirk Braddan, and an abbot's tomb at Rushen Abbey. People going about their daily work are conspicuously absent in Griffith's record.

Seventeenth-century views became relatively well known through the reprinting of Chaloner's *Treatise* by the Manx Society in the nineteenth century and the copying of the originals at the British Museum. In contrast, the Griffith paintings apparently remained unpublished and some only came to the Isle of Man in 1938 when the Pennant library was auctioned at Christies. A comparison with the Manx illustrations in Grose's *The Antiquities of England and Wales* shows that the engravings are based on Griffith's earlier watercolours, but without the quality found in the originals.[403] The engravings in turn then appear to have been used as the foundation for the illustrations in David Robertson's *A Tour Through the Isle of Man*.[404] Although the eight aquatints are attributed to G.I. Parkyns, the views are based on the earlier works, with a degree of detail being lost at each stage of repetition.

By the late 1700s and early 1800s, the growing number of guidebooks meant an increasing need both for maps and views of the Island; these often included a brief history of the Island, helping to establish a sense of a Manx cultural identity. Some illustrations for guidebooks and 'tours' were drawn and painted by professional artists. Where the European 'Grand Tour' had been the sole preserve of a wealthy elite, travel was now available to greater numbers of the educated, curious and culturally aware middle class. Travel in mainland Europe was curtailed due to revolution and war, but a desire to explore the recently (re)discovered 'margins' of the British Isles meant greater numbers travelling to the edges to discover sublime landscapes and antiquities and a sense of 'other' in one's own home countries.

Perhaps the most important of all the Manx landscape views is the 1795 collection of twenty-six watercolour paintings by John 'Warwick' Smith

402 *Moses Griffith, 1747–1819, artist and illustrator in the service of Thomas Pennant*, (Exhibition catalogue: Welsh Arts Council, 1979).

403 F. Grose, *The Antiquities of England and Wales*, vol. 6 (London, 1783).

404 Robertson, *Tour*, 1st edn.

Fig. 4.9 *'Douglas Bay', c.1810, unknown artist: MNH 1959-0119.*

(1749–1831) (Fig. 4.10).They provide a relatively comprehensive record of the Island's principal towns and settlements, including a watercolour of Castle Rushen, providing a unique record of the Isle of Man just before the urbanisation, tourism, commercialisation of fishing, farming and mining and population growth of the nineteenth century.

Griffith, and even King, would have recognized these scenes and the people who inhabited them. But within decades, all these views would change as towns expanded and harbours grew. Discovered in 1950 by Basil Megaw, director of the Manx Museum, whilst visiting Blair Castle, Scotland, it is thought that the paintings were commissioned by the fourth duke of Atholl, who is known to have been on the Island in 1795. He had previously commissioned Smith to produce a series of Perthshire views (1786).

The *'Promulgation of the laws on the Tynwald Hill, 1795'* is the earliest-known picture of the Manx day of ceremonial legislature, although it is questioned whether it is by Smith or his occasional painting companion Julius Caesar Ibbetson (1759–1817), who may also have supplied the figures in the other paintings (Fig. 4.11).[405]

405 A.M. Cubbon, *Views of the Isle of Man of 1795 by John 'Warwick' Smith* (Reproduction of six watercolours: MNH 1982), 4.

Fig. 4.10 *'Castle Rushen', by John Warwick Smith: MNH 1954-7203.*

Fig. 4.11 *'Promulgation of the laws on the Tynwald Hill, 1795', by John Warwick Smith: MNH 1954-7220.*

As the fourth duke was present at this Tynwald, guns are being fired from the hill in his honour. To the right there is the carriage in which he arrived. Smith (or possibly Ibbetson) is here being both caricaturist and critical commentator. The horses in the foreground are wildly agitated and the riotous nature seems to represent the crowd's emotions. The fascinating detail and the wealth of information are invaluable to historians.

Portraits

During the seventeenth century, women as well as men began enthusiastically to embrace progressive roles as both 'consumers' and connoisseurs.[406] Commissioning and purchasing works of art was no longer the preserve of the aristocracy or the Church. James Stanley, the seventh earl of Derby, and his wife, Countess Charlotte, displayed their wealth through their surroundings and following royal examples. A contemporary statement that 'the pictures I desire to have ... must be exquisitely done and by the best masters' was certainly followed by the earl and his wife when they commissioned a family portrait from the leading and most fashionable portrait painter of the period, Sir Anthony van Dyck (Fig. 4.12).[407]

Worked between 1632 and 1641, the Isle of Man is in the background of the painting, indicating the earl's position as lord of Man. It is gently bathed in overtones of orange, demonstrating the familial connection of Charlotte with the house of Orange; her features show her 'sagacity, prudence, loyalty, grandeur of spirit, and active heroism.'[408] As it was painted before the countess of Derby's defence of the family seat of Latham during the Civil War, this could have the advantage of hindsight and be interpreted as a Victorian reading, identifying the countess with the attributes of the ideal Victorian wife.

In contrast, William Christian may be viewed as traitor or patriot, or both, depending on one's view of his actions during the 'Manx Rebellion' of 1651. His portrait equally raises more questions than it can currently answer (Fig. 4.13). There is no known early provenance for the portrait and the painting appears to date from two different time periods and with varying quality of execution. The original is thought to comprise only the head and shoulders. Later, probably in the late eighteenth or early nineteenth century, it was incorporated into a larger canvas to create the full-length imposing portrait we see today. Strong suggests that the extension 'accounts for the inaccurate and

406 L.L. Peck, *Consuming Splendour, Society and Culture in Seventeenth-Century England* (Cambridge, 2005), 68–70.

407 J.P. Ferris, 'A Connoisseur's Shopping-List, 1647', *Journal of the Warburg and Courtauld Institutes*, 38 (1975), 339–41.

408 P. Draper, *The House of Stanley* (Ormskirk 1864), 245.

Fig. 4.12 *James Stanley, Lord Strange, later seventh earl of Derby, with his wife, Charlotte, and their daughter, after van Dyck, 1636: New York: Copyright The Frick Collection.*

somewhat comic costume' and the appearance of retouching on the original section of the painting.[409]

409 A.M. Cubbon, 'The Cap of Illiam Dhone', *JMM*, 6:80 (1964), 218: letter, J.N. Strong (National Portrait Gallery) to A.M. Cubbon (Director, Manx-Museum), 20 August 1963. In 1951 Curwen Estates presented the portrait of Illiam Dhone to the Manx Museum.

Fig. 4.13 *William Christian (Illiam Dhone), unknown artist: MNH 1954-6561.*

Fig. 4.14 *James Stanley, seventh earl of Derby, follower of Anthony van Dyck, mid-late 17th century: MNH 1954-7272.*

Another ambiguous and challenging portrait is that of James Stanley, seventh earl of Derby, attributed to the studio or follower of van Dyck (Fig. 4.14).

As with the previous work, the quality of painting is varied, particularly when comparing the face and the armour with that of the hands and background landscape. The portrait shows Stanley in a similar pose and at a similar age as in the van Dyck family portrait (1636), aged about twenty-nine, but shows him holding a baton, signifying his rank as a commanding officer. To add to the ambiguity of the portrait, the 'KG' in the inscription identifies him as a Knight of the Garter, indicating his support for the Royalist cause, an order to which he was admitted in 1650 but never installed.

There is a rocky outcrop in the background, with an encampment of cavalry troops, all apparently wearing similar armour to Stanley. The flags have been identified as the royal standard and the Stanley emblem of the eagle and child. An inscription lists Stanley's titles, military career and execution which, dating it to after 1651, suggests that it was commissioned as a memorial by his family. However, the inscription could have been added posthumously. Regardless of when the portrait was painted, it is apparent that his family wanted to depict the seventh earl as a noble, dignified soldier, loyal to his king and in their eyes, a martyr to the Royalist cause.

By the eighteenth century, members of the growing merchant class on the Island are commissioning portraits. Although the artist is unknown, a compelling pair of paintings of husband and wife Ann and Thomas Durie follow the fashion promoted by Gainsborough and Reynolds, demonstrating the Duries' prosperity and position (Figs 4.15 and 4.16). They owned a large house in 'the town of Douglas', but were mainly resident at the Nunnery. Ann is portrayed as a shepherdess according to the romantic notions of the time.[410] The pale blue suggests aristocracy and the fabric, luxury. In the background a merchant ship is anchored alongside a stylised representation of the old fort of Douglas, illustrating the origins of their wealth.

The surviving art of the period may be limited in volume and fragmentary in coverage for the period, but it provides fascinating glimpses of what the Island and its people looked like. Whether a map, a topographical view, or a portrait, it may not always be possible to distinguish what is 'true' or 'false'. The art of the period, in its many forms, shows how people in the past saw the world around them and how they wanted to record it. For the historian, this wealth of material is invaluable to illuminate individuals, places and events.

A disproportionate amount of high quality and high status artwork has survived, unlike the more vernacular examples of 'folk art' which have either not survived or are not known about due to lack of provenance and documentation. Therefore any surviving 'folk art' will not equate to the wide variety

410 A.M. Cubbon, 'Thomas and Ann Durie, An Eighteenth Century Douglas Merchant and His Wife: Two handsome portraits presented by the Friends of the Manx Museum'. *JMM*, 6:75 (1958), 41–42; J. Woodall, *Portraiture: facing the subject* (Manchester, 1997), 3.

Fig. 4.15 *Thomas Durie of the Nunnery House and Durie House, Old Douglas, Merchant, unknown artist: MNH 1956-0403.*

Fig. 4.16 *Ann Fine, wife of Thomas Durie, dressed as a shepherdess, with the old fort of Douglas in the background, unknown artist: MNH 1956-0404.*

of work, in terms of both volume and medium, which would have originally been produced during the period 1405 to 1830. As a result, little is now known about the artistic and creative expressions of the vast majority of the Island's population at all levels of society. Often only the highest echelons of society had the political or social reasons for the commissioning of works of art and then the financial wherewithal and stability to retain and preserve these works for posterity. The intrinsic financial value and aesthetic appreciation of higher status artwork (in various forms) would then have ensured its survival, whilst other more 'vernacular' artwork would not have been considered worthy of preservation. The issue of history traditionally being the 'stories' of the 'good and the great' is as relevant to the study of a society's material culture as to its documentary sources in terms of both the survival and recognition of a wider cultural history.

THE BEGINNINGS OF ANTIQUARIANISM IN THE ISLE OF MAN

Fenella Bazin

When Bishop Hildesley arrived in the Isle of Man in 1755 after a stormy ten-day journey from Whitehaven, he could hardly have envisaged that his plans to translate the Bible into Manx would have such far-reaching consequences. His intention was to make the Scriptures available in their own language to the many Manx-speaking men and women, particularly those who lived in rural areas. Sections of the Bible were allocated to most of the clergy, with the result that the quality of the translations was uneven. As well as translating part of the Psalms and Acts, the Rev. Philip Moore (1705–1783), then Rector of Ballaugh, was responsible for the revision of the whole of the Old Testament and the second edition of the New Testament. During his earlier career he had been Master of Douglas Grammar School and was clearly a gifted teacher, who, by 1783 had taught all but four of the Manx clergy.[411] One of his pupils was John Kelly, who, aged sixteen, worked alongside Moore on the revision, correction and preparation of the Old Testament. Entrusted with the safe delivery to the Whitehaven printers of the first section of the translation, he was shipwrecked, managing to save the manuscript by holding it above his head until he was rescued. The translation work stimulated his interest in the Manx language and he began 'to collect and form the rules' of the first Manx grammar.[412] Completed in 1780, it was not published until 1804. Between 1779 and 1790, he

411 A.W. Moore, *Manx Worthies* (Douglas, 1901), 25.

412 J. Kelly, *A Practical Grammar of the Antient Gaelic, or Language of the Isle of Man, usually called Manks*, Manx Society, vol. 2 (1859).

produced the *Triglot Dictionary of the Gaelic Languages of Scotland, Ireland and Man, with an English translation*.[413]

Kelly's *Manx Grammar* is one of the earliest examples of antiquarianism in the Isle of Man. Part of a much wider movement, it was to grow and reach its greatest flowering towards the end of the nineteenth century and the foundation of the *Isle of Man Natural History and Antiquarian Society*. The antiquaries were bent on the collection rather than the interpretation of historical objects or landscapes, and this pattern was generally reflected in the Isle of Man.[414] The wider movement was often closely associated with local history and the clergy.

Many Manx clergy had studied off the Island, where they must have been aware of the growing movement. It is unsurprising, then, that the first stirrings of antiquarianism were from individual clergymen such as Philip Moore, John Kelly and Joseph Stowell. Stowell was reputedly 'a scholar of no ordinary attainments'; he studied insular records and drew up a prospectus for a history of the Isle of Man which, unfortunately, he did not develop.[415]

Just five years after the Act of Revestment, the text of the ballad 'Mylecharaine' was described as an ancient Manx song and twenty years later as 'an old Manks madrigal'.[416] Unfortunately, there is no record of where the tune was first noted down. Philip Moore is believed to have given the earliest known text to James McLagan, an avid collector of Gaelic literature, who was on the Island in his role as chaplain to the Black Watch.[417]

The text is a dialogue between a farmer and his unmarried daughter, who, because of her father's frugal lifestyle, finds herself still single at an age she could have expected to be married. She accuses her father of meanness. His response is that his wealth lies '*dowin, dowin dy-liooar*' ('deep, deep enough'), implying that it lies in the farmland. The song ends with a powerful seven-fold curse on Mylecharaine, as he had had to give a dowry with his daughter, the first man on the Island to do so. The song is also closely associated with the fifteenth-century pectoral Mylecharaine's cross, now in the Manx Museum. Many believe that the cross was found by the farmer and kept locked safely away. The first time the song appears on paper in the Isle of Man is in a manuscript dated 1810 under the inscription of 'an original Manks tune'.[418] Ten years later

413 Moore, *Manx Worthies*, 94. The printing of Kelly's Dictionary was not begun till 1807, and in February 1808, when it had reached as far as 'L,' a fire in the printing-office destroyed the whole impression except two copies.

414 The strategy of recording antiquities was the basis of the work of the first English antiquary, John Leland (1503–53).

415 Moore, *Manx Worthies*, 31.

416 BL Add MS 11215.

417 University of Glasgow Special Collections: McLagan MS Gen, 1042/180. McLagan later became the minister at Blair Atholl and Strowan, Perthshire.

418 MNH MS 00437 A, 'Shepherd's Music', E (1810).

it was printed in a collection of Manx tunes under the title *Mona Melodies*, implying that it was already an established part of an oral tradition, borne out by the numerous variants of the melody.[419] At this point it moved from being the subject of antiquarian interest and began to acquire political overtones.

A hundred years earlier, Governor Chaloner had 'caused a mound to be opened and found fourteen urns'.[420] They were 'so ill burnt ... that it is scarce possible to take them out without breaking them. They are full of burnt bones, white and fresh as when first interred'.[421] In spite of Samuel Haining's dismissive comment that 'it can not be expected to find many things to arrest the antiquarian', he did include descriptions of some of the sites and noted that there were barrows 'that contain nothing but clay urns filled with ashes'.[422] Bishop Wilson was interested in the Runic inscriptions on the Manx crosses, suggesting that 'Here are more Runic inscriptions ... in this island, than, perhaps, in any other nation'.[423] This strongly shows not only his interest in local knowledge but also his awareness of studies further afield.

Several similar guides and histories were published at the end of the eighteenth and the beginning of the nineteenth century, many containing references to archaeological sites and, although not ostensibly antiquarian, certainly there is a nod in that direction. Although outside the period of this volume, in 1845 Train went as far as classifying the ancient monuments.[424]

With the growing enthusiasm for the study of natural sciences, perhaps the most exciting find was the great elk, discovered by Thomas Kewish, blacksmith and owner of the field in Ballaugh. Initially, this was a welcome source of income for Kewish, and James Taubman, local brewer and innkeeper, who rented the field and employed Kewish to dig for marl. Kewish assembled the bones to create the first complete skeleton of the species seen anywhere in the British Isles, replacing missing bones with some taken from a dead horse. Together, Kewish and Taubman charged 'Ladies and Gentlemen 1 shilling, and tradesmen and children half price' to view this marvel.[425] 'Amateurs from Oxford and Cambridge' were soon offering 'hundreds of pounds' to buy the enormous skeleton, the first ever to be found in the British Isles.[426] It was not long before Bishop Murray wrote to his uncle the duke of Atholl, suggesting

419 J. Barrow, *Mona Melodies* (London, 1820), 9: Air 'Molly Charrane'.

420 G. Woods, *An account of the past and present state of the Isle of Man* (London and Edinburgh, 1811), 156.

421 D. Robertson, *A Tour through the Isle of Man* (London and Edinburgh, 1794), 98.

422 S. Haining, *A Historical Sketch and Descriptive View of the Isle of Man* (Douglas and Ramsey, 1822), 126, 135.

423 Robertson, *Tour*, 98.

424 J. Train, *An historical and statistical account of the Isle of Man* (Isle of Man, 1845).

425 J. Ling, *The Ballaugh Elk of 1819* (Isle of Man, 2008), 10.

426 Ling, *Ballaugh Elk*, 9.

that the duke had a better claim than either of the men who had found and rebuilt it. Rumours were rife that Kewish was to put the skeleton on display in Whitehaven. A letter was sent to the two men forbidding them to take the elk off the island. A clandestine operation, involving a cart loaded with bones and antlers on view left Ballaugh, hotly pursued by the duke's men. This was a decoy. An hour later, two more carts went quietly through Ramsey to be loaded on a ship sailing for Whitehaven. This enterprise was a failure, as the duke had influence in the town and the skeleton was duly returned to Ballaugh. After

Fig. 4.17 *The Great Elk: National Museum of Scotland. Photo: Fenella Bazin.*

threats of lawsuits, and considerable negotiation, an agreement was signed by the duke, agreeing to pay Kewish and Taubman £70 and an extra ten guineas to Kewish for his work in assembling the bones and the promise of delivery to Edinburgh University. The Ballaugh Great Deer is now in pride of place in the National Museum in Edinburgh.

Antiquarianism seems to have permeated the Island from many different sources. Apart from the incident of the great elk, the duke of Atholl seems to have had more than a passing interest in antiquaries, which is hardly surprising since the Scottish Enlightenment was at its peak. Many Manx clergy were trained in Dublin, others studied at Oxford or Cambridge, and this created useful and stimulating networks. A common denominator for them seems to have been their early education at Douglas and Castletown Grammar Schools and, particularly, the Castletown Academic School. A similar link took place in the later part of the nineteenth century, when an enthusiastic interest in folklore and music was nurtured at King William's College by John Clague and the Gill brothers.

CONCLUSION

This chapter offers a brief picture of the cultural life of the Isle of Man during the period. However, it is inevitable that it was generally the unusual events that were recorded, and these mainly in Castletown and Douglas. There are occasional tantalising glimpses of rural life but, sadly, these are few and far between. They would probably have centred on church, chapel and smithy, and would have been a vital part of life for those who lived and worked in the scattered communities of the countryside.

5 *Landscape and the Built Environment*

CATRIONA MACKIE

WITH CONTRIBUTIONS BY NIGEL G. CROWE †, PETER DAVEY, ANDREW JOHNSON, EDMUND SOUTHWORTH AND PATRICIA A. TUTT

INTRODUCTION

The Manx landscape today presents a wide range of physical evidence for its history. The presence of long-standing habitat types within the 'natural' vegetation demonstrates a varied response to human agricultural activity. The field boundaries shown first in full on the first edition of the Ordnance Survey (1867–70) can mostly still be explored. From their form and composition, from earthen banks to stone walls, they represent an evolving, organic system. The same applies to the routes between farms and settlements. Mining, quarrying, peat and marl digging also represent major human impacts on the wider landscape that remain visible today.

Apart from the castles and abbey, there is little within the modern landscape that can be securely dated to the fifteenth and early sixteenth centuries. Nevertheless, using the evidence of field archaeology and surviving architecture together with what few documentary sources are available, a broad overview of what is both likely and possible can be offered. The main documentary sources are the thirteenth-century *limites*, the rent books, the 1417 Sheading Roll, the 1428 Garrison Roll, the statutes, especially the 1422 code, the 1505 confirmation of church liberties and the 1540 Dissolution accounts.[1] For the later sixteenth and seventeenth centuries, the statutes continue to be a vital written source, augmented by informed observers like Chaloner and Blundell.[2]

1 G. Broderick & B. Stowell, *Chronicle of the Kings of Man and the Isles* (Edinburgh, 1973): *Limites Terrarum Monachorum*, fol. 52v to fol. 54v (86–87); rent books: T. Talbot, *The manorial roll of the Isle of Man 1511–1515* (London, 1924); 1428 Garrison Roll: MNH MS 09241, transcribed by M. Crellin, '1428 Garrison Roll', transcription; statutes: J.F. Gill (ed), *The Statutes of the Isle of Man*, vol. 1, 1417–1824 (London, 1883), 1–22; 1505 confirmation of church liberties: G. Bray (ed), *Records of convocation 1; Sodor and Man, 1229–1877* (Woodbridge, 2005), 60–63; 1540 Dissolution accounts: P.J. Davey & J.R. Roscow, *Rushen Abbey and the dissolution of the monasteries in the Isle of Man* (Douglas, 2010), 144–76.

2 J. Chaloner, 'A Short Treatise of the Isle of Man' (1653/56): MNH MS 12587; W. Blundell, 'A History of the Isle of Man, 1648–56', 2 vols: MNH MS 00049 C & MNH MS 00050 C.

THE DEVELOPMENT OF THE MANX LANDSCAPE

Boundaries in the landscape

The Manx landscape includes a wide range of existing field systems and some evidence of earlier ones. The main impediment to their understanding is a lack of absolute chronology. Whilst relative dating between systems is often possible through analytic mensuration, typological analysis is almost the only tool available for their study. In places, coaxial patterns survive which, together with reeve-like systems (e.g. Meayll Hill), may well be prehistoric in origin. In contrast, the very regular, rectangular fields that can be found in many lowland areas and just above the mountain hedge can be associated with intaking almost certainly of post-medieval date. Within existing fields there are occasional relics of cultivation strips, often in parts of fields inconvenient for modern ploughs. These slight earthworks are normally straight, parallel and narrow. Where they occur in England or Scotland they would be considered post-medieval in date. On Man they are variously described as 'run-rig', 'lazy-beds' or 'ridge and furrow'. No systematic survey or analysis of them has been carried out.

Archaeological evidence suggests that well before 1400 there were some physical divisions within the landscape, some of which partly survive to the present. Excavation on Dreem Geeil located a major enclosure phase dating to the medieval period.[3] Examination of field boundaries cut by a gas pipeline in 2002 suggested that some of these were late medieval in date.[4] It is clear from the *limites* that, whilst the boundaries of the monastic and secular estates were normally natural features, some man-made structures were present. For example, in the Malew lands there is repeated mention of a 'wall and ditch' (*murum et foueam*) dividing the monks' lands from other estates, and in Laxey it is an 'old wall' (*ueterum murum*).[5] The successors of some of these features can still be seen.[6]

The way in which agricultural land was organized in the later Middle Ages and how far any such system can be identified as surviving into the Early Modern period remains a subject of debate. Crowe has suggested that the remnants of open field cultivation such as is known in medieval Cumbria and Lancashire can be discerned both in the documents and the field. Moore has

3 P.J. Davey, *After the Vikings* (Douglas, 2013), 140, fig. 105.

4 Davey, *Vikings*, 140–43, fig. 106.

5 Broderick & Stowell (eds), *Chronicle*, fols 53r, 54v.

6 For Laxey see L.A.S. Butler, 'The Cistercian landscape on the Isle of Man' in L. Pressouyre (ed), *Espace Cistercien* (Paris, 1994) 185–89; Davey and Roscow, *Rushen Abbey*, 81, in particular, area G of the abbey demesne farm in Malew.

proposed a multiple estate structure such as can be seen in Wales, Northumbria and elsewhere.[7]

There is evidence for new enclosures from as early as the thirteenth century and in the earliest rent books, the process of enclosing parcels of common land, later described as intack, is well documented.[8] In 1422, there is statutory encouragement for individuals to enclose their 'farme land', and subsequent repeated statutory references to enclosure (initially permitting, then enjoining enclosure, and ultimately making it obligatory).[9]

Further laws in 1577 required tenants to maintain stock-proof boundary ditches with their neighbours throughout spring and summer, and the boundary between farm and hill land is described as the 'fell ditch'. In 1582, half a dozen laws, all relating to land management, were restated and strengthened in response to popular concern at their neglect and abuse. The first of these made it a legal requirement for boundary ditches to be maintained throughout the year, while the others dealt with the control of trespassing stock and outlawed the sale of land and property without the lord's approval. Implicit in all these provisions is the intended physical partition of the landscape, and probably its subdivision as well.

Just over 80 years later, in 1665, it is apparent that such intentions were not adequately being met, resulting in the enacting of six further provisions designed to create effective, stock-proof boundaries. These mention, for the first time, hedges as well as fences and ditches to deal with wandering stock. Nevertheless, the Island's lawmakers were forced to return to the issue again in 1691 and set down explicit physical requirements for stock-proof boundaries between landholdings.

Whether these new physical boundaries represent a change from communal to individual 'ownership' or simply a modification of internal organization within each holding is debatable. It would seem wise, with Dodgshon, to distinguish between the study of fiscal or territorial systems and patterns of settlement and field boundaries.[10] On Man, both these subjects deserve a good deal more of academic attention.

7 R. Moore, 'The origins of the Manx land system debate', in P.J. Davey (ed), *Recent Archaeological Research on the Isle of Man*, Oxford: British Archaeological Reports: British Series 278 (Oxford, 1999), 171–82; J.G.R. Jones, 'Multiple estate and early settlement', in P. Sawyer (ed) *Early Medieval Settlement* (London, 1976), 15–46.

8 E.g. in the first entry for Rushen in 1511 (Talbot, *Manorial roll*, 1).

9 *Statutes*, vol. 1 (1422), 20 (section 98).

10 R.A. Dodgshon, 'Human and historical geography', in F.C. Bazin *et al.*, *Research Review*, Douglas: Centre for Manx Studies, Research Report 1 (Douglas, 1995), 17–21.

Rights of way

Although it seems likely that the sea provided the most used route system in this period (and may possibly be reflected in the large number of rights of way leading down to even the most secluded of beaches around the coast), there are linear earthworks in the uplands which appear to represent earlier long-distance routes. The Malew section of the *limites* shows that the concept of a public road in the Isle of Man existed as early as the thirteenth century.[11] The Myerscough section of the *limites* lists the *Via Regia* (or Royal Way) as one element of the monastic boundary.[12] Whilst excavation across this road in 2007 only managed to document recent erosional features and the effects of Chernobyl, a cross-section across a neighbouring linear feature – the upland extension of the road through Narradale – did produce late medieval carbon dates.[13] Although the King's Highway is mentioned in the 1422 statute (sec. 7), it is not clear to which route this refers. However, by 1577 (sec. 32), each of the lord's tenant farmers had a legal right to a way from his farmstead to the highway, implying that the latter extended throughout the Island.[14] The route had to take the shortest line across a neighbour's land, the farmer having first got as near as possible on his own ground, even if this was not the most convenient way. In addition to confirming the continued existence at this time of what were effectively public high roads, the 1577 law also demonstrated the principles of rights of way as a means of crossing another's land, specifying that these were to be 18' (5.5m) wide. Other public routeways also existed, providing access to hill land for grazing, peat and heather. Their users were required to pay a duty (apparently to those whose lands these routes traverse), and they were to be kept secure – presumably with gates or hurdles – to avoid wandering stock (sec. 13).[15]

Quarterland roads form another distinctive class, often surviving as private accommodation roads, or green lanes. Each was sited within a single, often fragmented, quarterland. Classically, the lowest section gives access from the farmsteads to the coastline or valley bottom, while the upper section leads out onto the former common grazing land above the farms. The road may well have played a role in the sub-division of the holding, serving to link the various settlement sites sharing the same name, and the fields belonging to each.[16]

11 Broderick & Stowell (eds), *Chronicle*, fol. 53v: '... usque vadum per quod transitur puplica uia inter ...' is recorded in the Malew section.
12 Broderick & Stowell (eds), *Chronicle*, fol. 54r; Davey, *Vikings*, 164–65, fig. 120.
13 Davey, *Vikings*, 165; Cal AD 1300–1430 at 1 sigma; Beta-247378.
14 *Statutes*, vol. 1, (1422), 9 & (1577), 52.
15 *Statutes*, vol. 1, (1577), 49.
16 Such roads, where now in public use, may frequently bear the quarterland name: e.g. Ballakilloweу Road, Rushen, and Ballavitchell Road, Marown, although according to Walter Gill these were 'not strictly road-names'. Gill also provides a colourful discussion

Driving ways allowed for the safe passage of herds or flocks from one area of grazing to another. They were usually of significant width, secured on both sides by Manx hedges, and generally known by the ubiquitous name-element *bayr*.[17] In-filling of the original, generous road width by encroachments is sometimes detectable on maps.[18] The statutes refer to 'Inlaynes', an otherwise landless class whose roadside settlement sites were of this origin, and which the Act of Settlement did its best to eliminate.[19] A clear distinction existed between driving ways and leading ways, which often originated as poorly defined pathways or bridleways through incompletely-enclosed arable land, along which a horse might be ridden, or pack ponies led. Sometimes these origins are fossilised in modern place names, for example Pack Horse Lane in Baldrine. This right might be limited to certain neighbours, at certain seasons, or for particular purposes; not only to church, mill and market, but also to access water or fuel.[20] Where disputes arose, evidence was sought as to whether passage was enjoyed by right, or only with permission, or even for a payment.[21] Customs linked to the use of burial ways lingered long in the collective memory, along with more modern traditions insisting that what became public footpaths originated as time-saving routes for miners or school children.[22] Safe fording-points must have been tenacious landscape features, and the name of Mullen e Cleigh, Patrick, may refer to 'stepping stones across a stream' at the adjacent ford.[23]

---

of superseded roads generally: see W.W. Gill, *A Manx Scrapbook* (London & Bristol, 1929), 121–66.

17 Literal derivation of this term from Old Irish bóthar - cow way: G. Broderick, *Place names of the Isle of Man*, 7 vols (Tübingen, 1994–2005), vol. 7 (2005), 199–200; F. Kelly, *Early Irish Farming* (Dublin, 2000), 609.

18 A classic example may be found on Upper Packhorse Lane, Baldrine OS SC 427813. The road leading north from St. Luke's Church, Baldwin (OS SC 360823) was narrowed between 1840 & 1869, thus losing the old Tynwald site marker; IOMPRO, Braddan tithe map, 58.

19 *Statutes*, vol. 1 (1504), section 6, 25; Act of Settlement (1704), section 8, 164–65, & section 3, 173.

20 J.W. & C.K. Radcliffe, *A History of Kirk Maughold* (1979), 198–203; J.W. & C.K. Radcliffe, *Kirk Bride: a miscellany* (1982), 40, *sub Bayr ny Lhaggey.*

21 In 1711 the landholder at Creg y Cowin, Braddan, sued to establish a right of way from his holding 'through Glanbolding' to Mullen y Corran: MNH MS 10071/2/ (Enquest Files), 1711.

22 Notably in Bride and leading from the Kerrowkeil district of Malew (which lay in Arbory for ecclesiastical purposes) towards Ballabeg.

23 J.J. Kneen, *The placenames of the Isle of Man* (Douglas, 1925, republished 1979), 359.

Highways

Until the Act of Settlement, because much of the land was within the control of the lord of Man, the governor could direct the making of new roads, or less momentous changes. Some highways started off as private ways, and these began to multiply under the ministrations of sheading juries, the great enquests, exercising common law powers.[24]

The Act of Settlement changed matters. In strengthening the position of landholders, no steps were taken to preserve public rights of entry onto land to carry out highway works. New enactments were then needed to allow bridges and new roads to be built or improvements made. Lacking obvious precedent in the Westminster statute books, highway legislation accumulated by trial and error. The first attempt in 1713 sought to adapt the English model – the result of some centuries of evolution – to Manx circumstances. An overseer of highways was to be appointed for each parish by the setting quest, rather than the wardens. Frontagers had to set about immediate repairs, and statute labour was introduced for future repairs.[25]

The next attempt was made in 1739, when an annual poll tax of 1d. per head was established, for the construction of new bridges and repair of old ones.[26] Arrangements were made for approach roads to the new bridges and the substitution of new roads for old. The 1753 Highway Act instituted a new body, a committee of the Keys with overall highway responsibility. Its power to make ordinances 'for the altering, cutting or striking of any Highway ... through the lands of any person or persons' was subject to a drastic proviso which forbade the authority from routing a new highway 'through any dwelling-house, yard, haggard or garden.'[27] The appointment, in 1753, of James Hamilton as surveyor-general of highways was the catalyst which turned good intentions into concrete progress.[28] He oversaw the construction of bridges where there

24 Radcliffe, *Maughold*, 199, illustrates proceedings concerned with the establishment of private rights of way in Maughold.

25 Not to be confused with the Manx landholders existing tenurial obligation to perform carriages and boon-days: J. Spranger *et al.* (Commissioners of Enquiry into allegations by the John Murray, 4th duke of Atholl), *Report of Commission of Enquiry* (1792), 17; Moore, *Isle of Man*, vol. 1, 318–19, 322; vol. 2, 534, 537.

26 *Statutes*, vol. 1 (1739), 239–41.

27 The antecedent of this proviso may be found in the 1713 Act, where the right of entering on land to quarry materials for roadmaking could not be exercised 'in any house, yard, garden or meadow': *Statutes*, 1 (1713), 194. At this point the possibility of land being surrendered into the lord's hand (*in manu domini*) by order of the governor and payment of compensation appears to have survived; J.R. Roscow, 'The Development of Castletown 1601–1703', *PIMNHAS*, 11:1 (2000), 15.

28 R.M. Stott, 'Highways Legislation in the Isle of Man 1736–63: Elements of a New Political Landscape', *PIMNHAS*, 11:1 (2000), 85. Stott details the administrative arrangements made for the highway building programme.

had been fords, and the building or improvement of roads to at least 18-foot width, where there had previously been 'mere bridle tracks.'[29]

The separation of sovereignty from the territorial rights of the Murray family in 1765 left the highways committee (lacking status as a body corporate) without the power of acquiring ownership of, or dealing in land required for, bridge or roadmaking. No legal means existed of protecting new lines of road from encroachments, and once a road was fronted by dwellings, it became impossible to widen the route.

Working the land

There is evidence of enclosure and ploughing in areas that now lie beyond the late medieval and early modern limit of cultivation. Some, such as those excavated on Dreeim Geeil, are certainly prehistoric, others, such as those on Slieu Curn are medieval. Field survey in the Sulby valley, the Glendhoo catchment and the Lezayre hills has identified what appear to be the earthwork remains of farm buildings and enclosures well above the upper limit of arable land defined in the earliest rent books.[30] Excavation of one structure on the slopes of Slieu Curn showed it was occupied between the twelfth and fourteenth centuries and surrounded by a developed plough soil.[31] This seems to reflect an extension of agriculture upslope during a period of more benign climatic conditions, followed by a retreat to the upper boundaries of the quarterland farms as defined in the rent books in response to climatic decline. At Slieu Curn, more recent intaking has not quite reached the earlier medieval limits, but in other places it has overtaken it. A further example may also be seen to good effect in Sulby, where an extensive system of one- and two-acre fields on the south side of Mount Karrin is partially overlain by larger, later fields belonging to Killabrega farm.

Downslope, the intaking of low-lying land and its subsequent drainage and improvement would similarly increase the extent of agricultural land, but even as late as the mid-seventeenth century, such marshy ground could be expected to provide a measure of protection to the southerly flank of the Civil War fort at Kerroogarrow and force the enemy to the north where they would

29 Moore, *Isle of Man*, vol. 2, 633.

30 A.C.C. Johnson, 'A preliminary gazetteer of early archaeological remains in the upper Sulby valley', in Davey, *Recent archaeological research*, 153–170; J.J. Woodcock, 'The archaeology of the hills and slopes above Glendhoo' in P.J. Davey *et al.*, *Upper Glendhoo, Ballaugh, Isle of Man: filed survey, September 1996* (Douglas, 1997), 5–26; C. Corkill, 'An archaeological survey of Lezayre' (MA thesis, University of Liverpool, 2005).

31 Woodcock, 'Glendhoo', 10–11, 21, fig. 4, nos 10B and 15; Davey, *Recent research*, 138–39, fig. 104.

be vulnerable to the fort's guns. The same conflict drew comment from the invading Parliamentary forces upon the Island's open countryside, 'for they have no trees to hide them', and less than twenty years later Charles Stanley intervened to propose laws encouraging the creation of woodland and the preservation of hedgerow trees.[32]

The existence of pinfolds is noted as early as 1422, implying that the gathering and controlling of stray animals was already an established practice.[33] The need for pinfolds hints at the inadequacy of physical boundaries for controlling livestock, even though the same record of customary laws states that land may be enclosed at all times of the year.[34] Provision for impounding loose animals is made in the laws for 1577 and 1582 and, by 1665, a second pinfold could be erected in a parish to reflect the practical and geographical implications of incarcerating wandering stock throughout the year rather than in the summer. As late as the mid-twentieth century, most of the Island's parochial pinfolds survived recognizably. Lezayre, as befitted the largest parish, was indeed in possession of two.

In the early eighteenth century, there is evidence of cattle and sheep being penned on arable land by temporary miniature sod hedges, as a means of enriching the soil ready for planting grain.[35] A registered deed of 1712 refers to the sale of various rights by the holders of Rowany quarterland, Rushen, to subtenants.[36] These rights included 'the mucking of four sheep', evoking Bishop Wilson's description. In the south of the Island, seaweed was also used as fertiliser. In the north, clay marl could be found a few feet below the surface and, by the late eighteenth century, it was commonly used for manuring the land. Since this time, the remains of a number of prehistoric deer have been discovered, preserved in marl pits.[37]

Governor Greenhalgh was reputed to have introduced the liming of land in the 1640s, and it had become common by the early nineteenth century.[38] Limestone is widely available in the south of the Island and, from there, it could be transported by boat or by cart, either as limestone or as burnt lime, to where it was needed. Thomas Quayle notes that 'From the beginning of April, 'till the fall of autumnal rains impedes the carriage of lime, the kilns

32 W. Harrison (ed), *Illiam Dhone and the Manx Rebellion 1651, Records and Proceedings*, Manx Society, 26 (1877), doc. 29: Extract from *Mercurius Politicus*, no. 75, 65; *Statutes*, vol. 1 (1667), 133.

33 *Statutes*, vol. 1 (1422), 13 (Section 43).

34 *Statutes*, vol. 1 (1422), 20 (Section 98).

35 Cruttwell, *Wilson*, vol. 1, 313–14.

36 MNH MS 09494, (Registered deeds), Rushen, 1712.

37 G.W. Lamplugh, *Geology of the Isle of Man* (London, 1903), 376–77.

38 W. Sacheverell, *An Account of the Isle of Man* (c.1692) (London, 1702), 3.

draw daily'.[39] The remains of lime kilns can still be seen in many parts of the Island, although the antiquity of lime kiln construction is also unclear and only one site in Ballaugh Glen has been subject to summary archaeological investigation.[40]

Quarrying was a constant requirement. Stone was picked from the fields and incorporated in boundaries; it could be won with little effort from outcrops on farmland and common, and from the rockier stretches of coast and shoreline. When building stone was required in quantity and quality, as in the construction of fortifications and larger public buildings, red sandstone was available at Peel, and limestone around Castletown; neither are true freestones. The extensive quarry just outside the curtain wall on the north side of St Patrick's Isle, where Manx series rock has been removed, is one of the few examples where the use to which it was put, and hence its late medieval date, can be inferred with some certainty. The limestone in the south-east of the Island was also crucial to the local manufacture of the mortar needed to construct the major stone buildings of the period.

The Island began to produce linen in the late seventeenth and eighteenth centuries and the growth of flax was promoted by both James, second duke of Athol, and the Manx Society.[41] Feltham noted in 1798 that most farmers and cottagers grew it, both for home use and for export.[42] Farmers would have their own, or have access to, a retting pond, to soak the flax, prior to processing. Many of these can be seen on the 1860s Ordnance Survey maps, although they are more difficult to distinguish today.

Lack of coal on the Island meant that the use of turf as fuel was ubiquitous. The 1417 requirement for all tenants of the six sheadings to provide turves for the lord confirms the widespread availability of turbaries for peat-cutting.[43] References to the cutting and protection from fire of peat in the King's Forest continue in the statutes for 1577 and 1610. Supply to the castles is referred to in 1593, and penalties for stealing turves already cut by other tenants were set down in 1629. Chaloner rightly drew attention to the importance of peat as the only widely available fuel in an island without coal or woodland.[44]

39 T. Quayle, *Agriculture of the Isle of Man* (Douglas, 1812), 95.

40 N.C. Johnson, 'The built structures in the valley floor', 39–48, in Davey, *Upper Glendhoo*, 43: fig. 14, 48; P.J. Davey & D. Allwood, 'Archaeological Fieldwork and Research Summaries', *Isle of Man Studies*, 15 (2017), 183.

41 P.T. McClure, 'The Archaeology of Manx Church Interiors: contents and contexts 1634–1925' (PhD thesis, University of Liverpool, 2013), 183–85; Moore, *Isle of Man*, vol. 1, 394–95; B. Quayle, *General view of the agriculture of the Isle of Man* (Douglas, 1794), 31.

42 J. Feltham, *A Tour through the Island of Mann, in 1797 and 1798* (Bath, 1798), 51.

43 *Statutes*, vol. 1 (1417), 5 (section 9).

44 Chaloner, 'Treatise', 3.

Evidence of recent peat digging can still be seen on Beinn-y-Phott, the last remaining of the medieval commoners' rights. The remains of much larger areas of 'turf' extraction for fuel, such as the Ballaugh/Lezayre curraghs in the north and Greeba curragh in the central valley, are well known.[45] Re-growth of 'turfa' peat, and a subsequent reabsorption into the landscape through lack of a viable modern land use, means that they and much smaller local diggings are not always easily seen as cuttings. The moorland south of Sulby reservoir from Druidale Rheast east towards Beinn-y-Phott preserves extensive evidence for peat cutting and transportation, particularly in the form of trackways and signs of former cuttings, though these are likely to be later manifestations of practices stretching back into the medieval period. The unusual position of the parish boundary between Michael and Braddan, across open ground rather than along watercourses, and indeed the narrow tongue of land belonging to the latter parish extending all the way north to Close Farm, are more probably the result of a deliberate decision to share the peat resources of this area more equitably than would otherwise be the case.

The Isle of Man has been mined for its minerals since prehistoric times and throughout the medieval period. In the modern era, records of mining operations on the Island begin in the mid-seventeenth century. The main concentrations of mine workings were in the south, around Foxdale, Glen Rushen, and Bradda Head, and in the north, in the Laxey valley, and at Maughold and Cornaa. Mining became most successful on the Island during the latter part of the nineteenth century and most of the extant mine workings date to this period.

THE DEVELOPMENT OF TOWNS AND VILLAGES

Towns

The Isle of Man lacks towns in a conventional sense. There are no physical defences, charters, guildhalls, officials, parish churches or resident monastic establishments that would be expected in a functioning medieval or early modern town elsewhere in Europe. The early sixteenth-century rent books suggest that there were only three nucleated settlements of any consequence on the island: Douglas, Castletown, and Peel.[46] By the mid-seventeenth century,

45 P.J. Davey *et al.*, 'The Curragh and other lowland wetlands of the Isle of Man', in M. Atherden (ed), *Wetlands in the landscape: archaeology, conservation, heritage* (York, 2001), 12–40.

46 See J.R. Roscow, 'Appendix 1 – Castletown cottages', in P.J. Davey *et al.*, *Excavations in Castletown, Isle of Man 1989–1992* (Liverpool, 1996), 157, for introduction to and discussion of the *Survey of the Rents in the Isle of Man*, dated 1506, and N.G.

Blundell identified four settlements worthy of being called a town, adding Ramsey to the three previously named.[47]

In general terms, each settlement was characterised by a natural harbour which called for the provision of infrastructure; access routes joining the ports to their hinterland and to the other main centres became essential. Each embryonic town became established between areas of arable field and a zone of unappropriated coastal land (ranking as *manorial waste*) over which development was able to encroach.[48] The early settlements at Ramsey and Douglas were at risk of coastal erosion. Ramsey suffered its most serious damage, including the loss of houses, in the early seventeenth century, and at Douglas some property had disappeared into the harbour at Rings End shortly before 1705.[49] There are various references to the construction of 'fences' protecting the most exposed parts of Ramsey and Douglas. These defences initially comprised little more than mounds of rubble.[50] Eighteenth-century enclosures made at Peel were later damaged by storms and never fully redeveloped.

The early sixteenth-century rentals show that Douglas and Castletown were quite different in character.[51] In 1511 there were probably as few as 13 households resident at Douglas, most of the buildings clustered on the north side of the harbour there being recorded as *camerae* (normally translated as 'chambers'). Of the 64 chambers in Douglas, eleven were held by potential residents, with the remaining 53 held by individuals who were almost certainly residing elsewhere. Where identifiable, these outsiders were men of some substance holding significant property outside Douglas as well as their chamber.[52] It is likely that each chamber was a detached structure, given Roscow's definition of a chamber as

Crowe, 2015, 'The Quinquecentenary of the Manx Doomsday Book', *PIMNHAS (The Antiquarian)* (2011), 4, 6–8 for commentary on the published rentals for 1511 and 1515. Roscow's 1998 paper is extremely useful for the position in Castletown: see J.R. Roscow, 'The Development of Castletown, 1601–1703', *PIMNHAS*, 11:1 (1998), 5–28.

47 Blundell, 'History', vol. 1, 156–57.

48 It became possible to enclose *manorial waste* by virtue of licensees authorized by the governor on behalf of the lord: R. Sherwood, *Manx Law Tenures* (Douglas, 1899), 20.

49 Blundell, 'History', vol. 1, 179; N.G. Crowe, *The Quarterland and Cottage Rents of Douglas c.1705: a Survey* (Douglas, 2001), 13: Block 04.

50 C.K. Radcliffe, *Ramsey 1600–1800* (Douglas, 1986), 26–28 in respect of Ramsey; Crowe, *Quarterland and Cottage Rents*, Introduction: xiii in respect of Douglas.

51 See Roscow, 'Castletown cottages', 157–60, for the Castletown rental; that of Douglas is unpublished. The 1511 rentals appear in Talbot, *Manorial roll*, 13–17 (Castletown) and 32–33 (Douglas).

52 Apparent non-residents holding at least a quarterland (or equivalent) elsewhere included the bishop; Robert Calcote, the lord's receiver in Castletown; Thomas and John Stephenson, probably of Balladoole and Ballakeighen, Arbory; John McPerson of Pulrose, Braddan; Otes McTagart, miller at Mullen Oates (now Union Mills) and other Braddan tenants from Renscault, Castleward and Middle; from Onchan many of the tenants of the largest farms: Ballaquayle, Tromode, Ballakermeen; William More,

'a single room with no internal divisions and an outside door which allowed access without entering another building.'[53] Demand for these chambers was apparently strong, as for some 20 years after 1511, on average another new one was built at Douglas every year.[54] In Castletown, by contrast, there were potentially some 72 households, each occupying either a house, cottage or tenement, many along with a variety of other premises including gardens, chambers and brewhouses. There were some 52 chambers along with 16 cellars.[55] Twenty-four of the holdings included at least one chamber or cellar without any associated house, cottage, or tenement. Interpretation is complicated by the status of garrison employees: soldiers were expected to be single men and were initially forbidden from setting up households in Castletown.[56]

There had been little development at Ramsey by 1511; the rentals speaking of a farmstead, two cottages and at most three chambers.[57] The contemporary position at Peel cannot be reliably established because a large portion of the town fell within the estates of Rushen Abbey, but the later evidence suggests that it probably followed the same lines as Castletown.[58] Records of more chambers at other landing-places in the south (probably where Port Erin and Port St. Mary later grew up) and at Laxey and Cornaa on the east coast suggest that these chambers were likely used to facilitate import and export.[59]

By the mid-seventeenth century, buildings in these urban settlements were still thatched, and constructed 'of small stones and lime'.[60] The townspeople commonly occupied two or even three such buildings, living in one, using another as a shop or workshop and warehouse, and the third as a storehouse with lodging rooms above. While Blundell notes that the houses had '2 stories', the upper storey was clearly under the eaves, poorly lit, yet warm on account of

probably the bishop's tenant, of Ballakilley, Marown and John More, probably from Santon.

53 George Wilye paid 18d. rent for two 'under one roof'; J.R. Roscow, 'The Development of Sixteenth-Century Castletown: Studies from Contemporary Documents', *PIMNHAS*, 10:4 (1996), 306.

54 This rests on the identification, ordering and approximate dating of a number of volumes of Lib. Assed.: MNH MS 10057.

55 Detailed statistics for Castletown compiled in Roscow, 'Sixteenth-Century Castletown', 306–07.

56 The Statute of 1422 states 'no soldier shall hold continually a Leman within a mile' of Castle Rushen or Peel Castle (*Statutes*, vol. 1 (1422), 17 (section 63)), whereas by 1561 the Castle Regulations recognize that soldiers might have 'their own houses' (*Statutes*, vol. 1 (1561), 32–33 (sections 8–10)).

57 Radcliffe, *Ramsey*, 15.

58 For which the earliest rental dates from 1540.

59 Rushen entries: Talbot, *Manorial roll*, 5; for Cornaa; Davey & Roscow, *Rushen Abbey*, 149.

60 Blundell, 'History', vol. 1, 160–61.

the thatch.[61] The contemporary drawings of Daniel King largely confirm this, depicting mainly single-storey buildings with a few dormers, windows in the gables, and clear evidence for roped thatch (see Fig. 1.8 above). His drawings also confirm Blundell's other significant remarks concerning the apparently confused layout of the settlements, 'The houses in all these towns...being not contiguous, much less continuous, in placing of 'em, observing no order either of uniformity or proportion, only Castle Town hath some little formality more than the rest.'[62]

The street frontages were aligned with their ridges parallel to the highway. The influence of this orientation gradually spread backwards as buildings were elaborated and plot boundaries were regularised. In addition to the building types enumerated in Blundell, many townspeople possessed undeveloped parcels of land varying in size. In Douglas, many of them were described as sandy or Sandside gardens.[63] In Castletown, a few, in the region of the Bog Lane, were styled bog gardens.[64]

Each town had a chapel and a market place associated with it. At Peel, there was an ovoid graveyard surrounding the chapel site but this is not attested at Castletown or Douglas where the chapels were sited close to the water's edge.[65] The chapel at Ramsey was well removed from the town's early core.[66] The market place usually occupied a site between the harbour and the arable area and was surrounded by plots. A lane provided access to the rear of these plots and to the arable land. There is evidence of in-filling of the central area by later encroachments, a common feature which suggests failure of the settlement to thrive on the scale originally envisaged. The market place in Castletown doubled as a parade ground for the castle, but the plots flanking this appear to be comparatively late and are more regular than those identified in the other towns. Ramsey's 'Old Cross' was a relatively small space although possibly dignified by the presence of the Sigurd Cross.[67]

61 Blundell, 'History', vol. 1, 161.
62 Blundell, 'History', vol. 1, 160.
63 Crowe, *Quarterland and Cottage Rents (Douglas)*, 21, 27, 29.
64 Roscow, 'Development of Castletown', 15.
65 J. Lewis, *Peel Town: an archaeological and architectural assessment* (Douglas, 1992), 7; A.M. Cubbon, 'The Medieval Chapel of St Mary's, Castletown, later the Castletown Grammar School', *PIMNHAS*, 7:3 (1968–70), 207–42; J.R. Bruce, *The Manx Archaeological Survey, sixth report 1966, keeills and burial grounds in the sheading of Rushen* (Douglas, 1968), 20–21; P.M.C. Kermode (ed), *The Manx Archaeological Survey, fifth report 1918* (Douglas, 1935), 11–12.
66 P.M.C. Kermode, *The Manx Archaeological Survey, fourth report 1915* (Douglas, 1915), 20.
67 Radcliffe, *Maughold*, 333.

Fig. 5.1 *Douglas harbour and south quay, 1789 [part of Fannin map]: MNH P.1304/2 (XX.3.L).*

The development of harbour facilities was slow until 1734, when statutory provision was made for 'the repairing and amending (of) the sea ports and harbours'.[68] In Douglas, the timing and sequence in which the quay walls were constructed is clarified by a licence permitting enclosure of 'a parcel of waste ground near the shore' in 1737.[69] The licensees, Messrs Oates, were permitted only to build on the first four feet of their enclosure, leaving 18 feet for a street and raising stonework between their improvement and the river. By 1750, Douglas had been provided with a length of quay on the rocky south side of the river (Fig. 5.1).

Construction of the North Quay involved the laying down of timber rafts of pitch pine logs upon which the quay wall of Port St Mary limestone rested.[70] Quays were being constructed at Castletown in 1750.[71] In Ramsey, the 'old quay' was constructed in the vicinity of the original market place at the Old Cross, probably in 1744 or 1745.[72] Once quays were constructed, infilling took place further inland to achieve at least the same level. In Douglas, this resulted in the ground floor of older properties disappearing from sight.[73] In Castletown, a similar position occurs where the double pile property, 5 The Parade, has been

68 *Statutes*, vol. 1 (1734), 203–06.

69 MNH MS 10057 (Lib.Assed.), 1725: extracting licence from enquest files.

70 J.P. Shimmin, 'The Development of Manx Habours', *PIMNHAS*, 8:3 (1974), 336-45, 338.

71 MNH MD 15105/MD 10280, Isle of Man Harbours Division List (MS), probably by J.C. Brown c.1955 taken from minutes of Isle of Man Harbour Committee and Commissioners.

72 Radcliffe, *Ramsey*, 23, 65.

73 N.G. Crowe, 'Manx Houses of the Seventeenth Century: A Hidden Heritage?', *PIMNHAS*, 12:1 (2008), 75.

extended forward onto the street and remains of the modest 'original' dwelling may be found at semi-basement level under the rear wing. The basement of 2 Parliament Square in Castletown has a similar origin.

Piers came even later than the quays and are poorly documented. The pier at Douglas, sometimes called 'the Great Mole', was being constructed around 1750 and projected from the Double Corner area for about 250 yards;[74] that at Peel followed in 1765.[75] Ramsey's first pier was a timber jetty constructed approximately in line with the Old Cross. Following storm damage to the original pier at Douglas in 1789, it was later rebuilt with British funds.[76]

The lords of Man had substantial interest in the ports through their entitlement to charge customs payments on imports and exports. Houses were constructed in each of the ports at a distance from Castletown, for the reception of visiting merchants, and adjoining these would usually be a yard, storeroom and other premises. The lord's house at Ramsey can probably be identified with a substantial house remaining on Mona Street; it had a thatched roof and lay alongside the street, on a plot extending out to the rear of the present promenade.[77] Its contents were listed and valued on the death of Governor Chaloner in 1660.[78] In Douglas, the lord's concerns were for a long period located at the Lord's Hill, a harbour front block immediately seaward of the market place.[79] Substantial building operations were carried out to provide new accommodation in the 1660s, with a long range of warehousing being constructed over vaulted store rooms.[80] A further range at right angles to this was added extending towards the harbour. One of these buildings became the Douglas courthouse.

74 MNH M Map (AP), p. 27 and handwritten note on the same by Basil Megaw referred to in W.B. Kinley, 'The Development of Douglas Harbour: A Mariner's view', *PIMNHAS*, 10:2 (1994), 67–68.

75 MNH MD 15105/MD 10280, Harbours List.

76 J. Train, *History of the Isle of Man*, 2 vols (Douglas, 1845), vol. 2, 364: £15,000 was contributed by the Society for promoting and improving the fisheries of Great Britain, and a further £7,000 granted for completing the structure and repairing the rest of the harbour in 1797.

77 Crowe, 'Manx Houses', 86.

78 Radcliffe, *Ramsey*, 20.

79 Crowe, *Quarterland and Cottage Rents (Douglas)*, 17–18, sub block 6.

80 MNH MS 10192 (Disbursements 1660–84), 1669: 'A Book of Sallaries & pettie Disbursements for the year 1669'. The 1660 range was probably represented by the footprint of the low range of buildings running along New Bond Street to the rear of 48 & 49 North Quay (see Fig. 5.2).

Fig. 5.2 *Douglas, New Bond Street. Early 20th century photo by Frowde looking west along New Bond Street. The range of low buildings (left middle distance) represents – and may have incorporated structural elements of – the lord's warehouses of the 1660s.* MNH /PG8224/2/13.

The lord's 'town-house' at Peel, with a frontage to the harbour, was extended and also eventually converted into a courthouse, a function it retained until the present courthouse was constructed in 1893.[81]

The settings of the four towns placed physical restrictions on their growth and development. Until permanent bridges were constructed, Castletown and Ramsey were not free to expand north of their river estuaries. In Douglas, there were few houses south of the river until the old Douglas bridge was replaced by a new one leading from the town centre, around 1758.[82] Castletown was also partly constrained by areas of wetland. In Castletown, Douglas and Peel, the early layout incorporated significant areas of garden land, and for a long period it was possible for growth to be accommodated by more intensive use of the land. By 1750, houses of three storeys or more were being constructed, and new properties were frequently located on areas of garden. In Douglas, the landholders controlling areas of this character first parted with parcels of land for garden purposes and it was often only after a significant time in this use that plots were developed with town houses of varying elaboration.[83]

Castletown

The 1428 Garrison Roll for Castle Rushen notes that by the early fifteenth century, officers associated with the castle lived in the town. The nature of this settlement is unclear. Assuming the northern bailey to the castle was in place from the twelfth century onwards, then early settlement should be around this bailey – but there is no evidence for early property boundaries and almost no archaeological evidence to test.

The relocation of the castle entrance to face the sea in the 1360s to 1380s is the most likely period for the development of settlement on slightly raised land, at the entrance to the river and protected by the castle from inland access. Chapel Lane runs through this area with small and probably medieval plots on either side. The chapel and this area are likely to be of similar date to the new castle entrance and curtain wall.

A zone immediately around the castle was kept clear to provide a field of fire. This allowed the castle to extend its defences to the south and east with an elaborate glacis and rounded turrets in the Tudor period. The town

81 MNH MS 10192, Petty Disbursements, 30 April 1702; G.L. Quilliam, 'Peel on Foot. Tour 1' (Peel, 1986).

82 S. Slack, 'Harbour Bridges at Douglas, 1757–1937', *PIMNHAS*, 9:3 (1984–87), 365–73.

83 First parcel of Parr's rent sold by Deemster John Parr 31 May 1710: MNH MS 09494, Old Deeds and Old Mortgages series: Onchan, bundle 1, 13. First plot of Finch's rent sold by John Vinch 6 August 1717: MNH MS 09494, Onchan, bundle 1, 56. First parcel of Kelly's rent, sold by Thomas Kelly, Jnr, 9 April 1723: MNH MS 09494 (South Side Sales), 1723. First parcel of Nunnery rent sold by Major John Woods and others 21 March 1715: MNH MS 10057 (Lib.Vast.), May 1716.

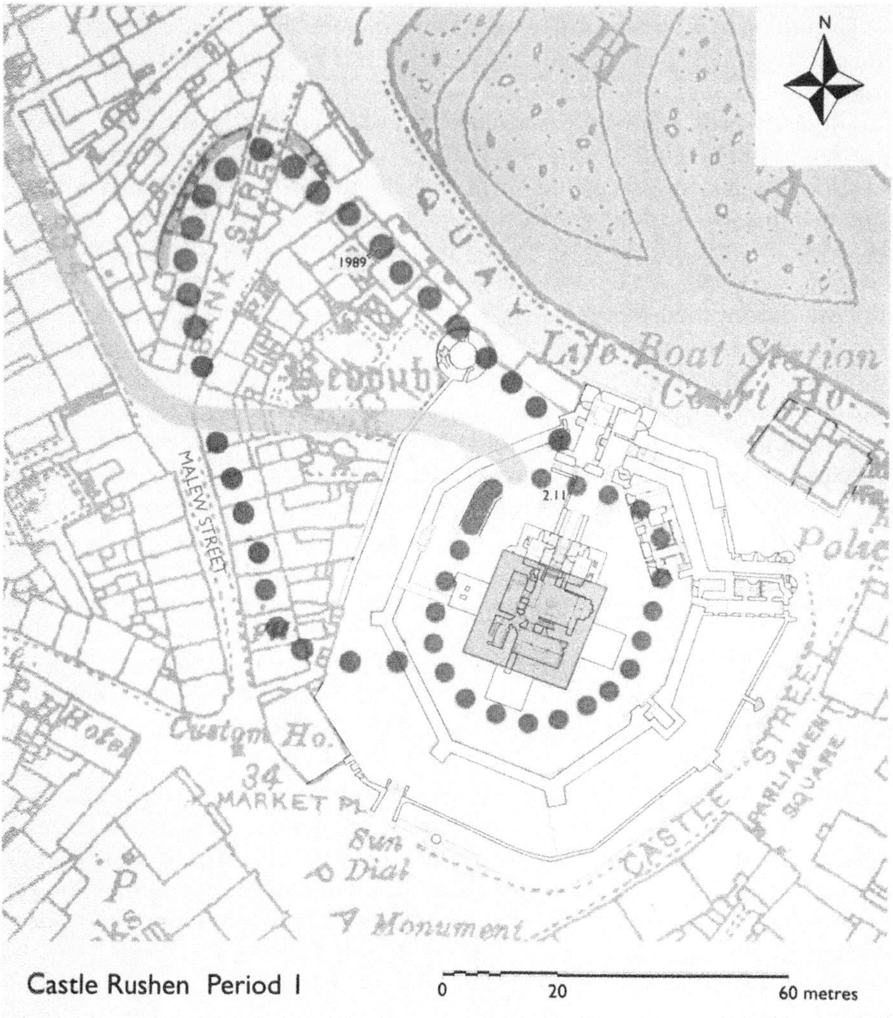

Fig. 5.3 *Plan of Castletown (Paul Drury) – page 34, fig. 17 (MNH: P. Drury and A. McPherson, 'Castle Rushen, Castletown, Isle of Man: conservation plan. Part 1: understanding and significance', (unpubl. report to MNH, June 2012) – MNH.*

subsequently extended along Arbory and Malew Streets, absorbing the former bailey. The Market Square emerges around this time.

The Silverburn meets the sea in a tidal pool and the castle sits with the gatehouse astride the high-water mark. In preparation for the Civil War, the New Worke was constructed in 1645 to protect the castle entrance and subsequently provide footings for a bridge at the narrowest point. In turn this was a catalyst for the development of land across the river in the Georgian period, with Lorne House (built 1827) becoming the Governor's residence, and substantial Victorian housing gradually extending out towards Derbyhaven and King William's College (built 1833) along the coast. The Act of Revestment brought a reduction in the fortification of the castle and the "field of fire" gradually filled in with larger properties such as the Old House of Keys (built 1821).

The late Georgian and Victorian period sees a new mercantile prosperity in the town – still the seat of government. A new quayside against the castle gatehouse dates between 1777 and 1826 when a lifeboat house was built. Warehouses, shipbuilding yards, ropewalks, tanneries, breweries and pubs all followed, mainly around the inner harbour. It was not until 1844 that a new outer harbour and pier to the east were constructed.

Like in many English towns, there was opposition to the railway entering the centre and so the 1874 railway curves elegantly round the town. Its course was largely followed by Alexandra Road, the bypass which turned the town into a cul-de-sac and has arguably preserved the mediaeval road layout of the town centre.

The early approach to the castle was apparently from the north-west and accounts for the otherwise unexplained alignment of Malew Street. There is an area of deflection to the Malew Street plots just beyond the line of Bridge Street which can be interpreted as representing the line of an outer bailey to Castle Rushen (see Fig. 5.3).[84] No further definite sign of this feature can be identified, but its seaward extent must have been a little beyond the plots lining Castle Street which themselves post-date the construction of the glacis (usually held to be early sixteenth century).

The glacis and its associated towers were apparently constructed wholly within the earlier castle complex, although to the north it may have extended further than at present; two corner towers have been removed and its line there may have followed earlier street frontages.[85] To the east of the castle proper, a gun emplacement was constructed facing across the harbour and later fell out of military use. To the south-west, the parade ground and a variety of facilities grew up over a long period, including two houses used for the governor's residence and the lord's stables and outbuildings.

84 P. Drury and A. McPherson, 'Castle Rushen, Castletown, Isle of Man: conservation plan. Part 1: understanding and significance' (unpubl. report to MNH, June 2012), 34: fig. 17.

85 Paul Drury has suggested that the original line of the glacis is marked by Water Street. This is corroborated by the naming of property in the vicinity as Sawny's or Saunder's Bank or Stoney Batter. Broderick, *Place Names*, vol. 6 (2002), 227, 228.

Fig. 5.4 *Castle Rushen as it appears on the south side, c.1656: Daniel King, fol. 10r. © The British Library Board: BL, Add 27362, fol. 10r.*

Documentary research carried out by Jim Roscow established that most of the residential house sites found in the early records were located between the castle and the sea at the point of the promontory.[86] The surroundings of Castle Rushen are generally low-lying and, west of the Silverburn river, the growth of modern Castletown appears to have occurred on medieval arable land. Excavations at Castle Rushen Stores suggested that the plots between Arbory Street and Malew Street had been laid out over agricultural land in the later fifteenth century.[87]

Archaeological evidence establishes the existence of a substantial land division separating a new element of the town plan from land remaining in agricultural use (the later Knock Rushen Flatt).[88] Dating from approximately 1500, this significant feature defined the south-western extent of a further major element in the town plan, the *crofts* of Castletown. This 'overwrote' earlier landscape elements except an 'S' shaped right of way, although it appears to have been closely associated with pre-existing settlement sites now severed from the remainder of the land in large-scale agricultural use. The new element comprised a complex of smallholdings, each consisting of a linear landholding

86 J. Roscow, 'Castletown cottages', 157–60.

87 D.A. Higgins, 'Excavations at Castle Rushen Stores, 1991–1992', in Davey, *Excavations in Castletown*, 58–59, figs 30, 31.

88 Higgins, 'Excavations at Castle Rushen Stores', 58.

aligned obliquely to its frontage on the west side of Malew Street, and perhaps lying opposite an associated house site on the eastern (harbour) side of the street. Groups of buildings on the land between Malew Street and the harbour are depicted in the background of Daniel King's 'Prospective of Castle Rushen as it appears on the South side'.[89]

Douglas

The number of substantial farmers and others from outside the town possessing premises within Douglas had declined substantially by 1705, while the proportion of permanent residents increased.[90] The disproportionate growth of Douglas is noticeable from 1705 onwards. In that year there were some 115 to 120 dwellings at Douglas. In 1730 a listing of occupiers indicated that there were some 210 households.[91] Between 1726 and 1784, Douglas and Castletown together housed almost two thirds of the Island's urban population. However, the population of Douglas increased from 32 per cent of the whole to 45 per cent during this period, with an accompanying decline in the percentage of population residing in Castletown. The population of Peel remained at around one fifth throughout this period, while Ramsey declined in significance from the mid-eighteenth century.

Fig. 5.5 *The population of the four towns as a percentage of the urban population. The percentage of the total urban population for each town is given in brackets.*

Year	Total urban population	Douglas	Castletown	Peel	Ramsey
1726	2530	810 (32)	785 (31)	473 (19)	460 (18)
1757	4416	1814 (41)	915 (21)	805 (18)	882 (20)
1784	6316	2850 (45)	1318 (21)	1254 (20)	894 (14)

Source: Moore, *Isle of Man*, vol. 2, 646–47.

89 J. Roscow, 'Development of Castletown', 11, fig. 4, 12–13; Crowe, 'Manx Houses, 77–78.

90 This rests on the examination and comparison of successive versions of *Liber Assedationis*. Some undated copies have been fitted into the sequence as also done by Roscow in his study of Castletown rentals: Roscow, 'Development of Castletown', 5–28. In 1705, quarterland families with Douglas property included Christian of Milntown (junior branch), Heywood of the Nunnery, Banks of Howstrake, Christian of Bemahague and Oates of Bibaloe (Crowe, *Quarterland and Cottage Rents of Douglas*, *passim*).

91 Probably compiled for an ecclesiastical assessment of the town.

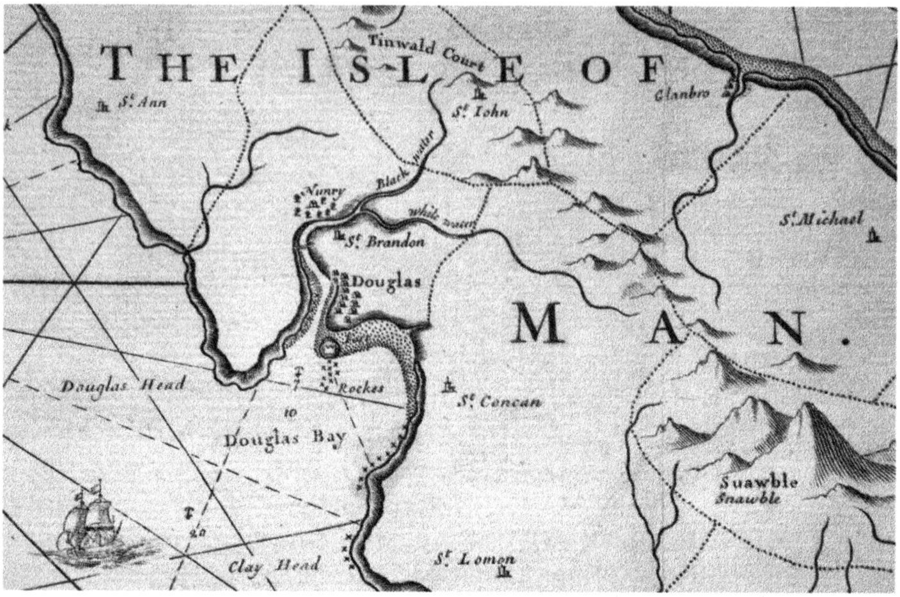

Fig. 5.6 *Douglas: part of Collins' map, 1694 – MNH PXX.41.M (P.2748).*

The development of Douglas has been explored most fully in Crowe's 2001 *Survey of Douglas*.[92] The town grew initially on the raised beach at the foot of the fossil cliff-line. Collins' map of 1694 shows the town situated on the north bank of the river, with houses in two rows, parallel to the harbour.

There are no buildings opposite the town on the south bank. The medieval stone bridge sits to the west of the town, where the river begins to narrow, before reaching the Nunnery.[93] The fort is depicted at the head of the promontory. Daniel King's drawing of Douglas harbour from the mid-seventeenth century shows the houses to the north of the river, and a beacon on the opposite headland (see Fig. 1.8 above). The medieval chapel is also depicted. In 1681, Douglas was described by Thomas Denton as 'a place of ye greatest resort in ye whole Island' due to the wide harbour and safe anchorage.[94]

The agricultural hinterland (much of it open field) was initially farmed by Douglas residents from their steadings within the town itself. Permanent division of this land between the shareholders seems to have occurred in the

92 Crowe, *Quarterland and Cottage Rents of Douglas.*

93 See Slack, 'Harbour bridges', 375; M.J. Hoy, 'Bishop Barrow's Bridge', *PIMNHAS (The Antiquarian)* (2012), 7, 25–31.

94 T. Denton, 'A description of the Isle of Man and its customes, 1681', in G.W. Wood (ed), *Yn Lioar Manninagh*, 3 (1898–99), 441.

Fig. 5.7 *'Douglas from the Nunnery Howe', by James Strutt, c.1830 (with St George's, St Barnabas and harbour with ships): MNH 1960-0013.*

seventeenth century. One by one, those families gradually attaining a status as merchants or gentlemen farmers moved to reside on their own lands. Pressures for growth and development during the eighteenth century were initially absorbed by building on garden land, yards, and replacing low-rise buildings with those of up to five storeys. The town also grew through the addition of ribbons of modest dwellings extending along the road towards Peel, and on the sand-side north along the bay.[95]

Harbour developments throughout the eighteenth century cemented the primacy of Douglas as the Island's trading centre. The first pier was constructed in the 1730s and replaced or extended around 1760. The first lighthouse was built on Douglas Head before 1766 and a light was also provided at the end of the pier. At Revestment, responsibility for the harbours passed to the British authorities, who gave them little priority.

95 Now Duke Street, Strand Street, and Castle Street.

The Stanley and Murray families as manorial lords took no effective interest in the development of Douglas until the arrival of the fourth duke in 1793. He chose to base himself in the hinterland of Douglas and the effect of his interest began to transform some aspects of the town.[96]

Peel

The key topographical features that determined the development of Peel were an off-shore islet at the mouth of the River Neb, providing a sheltered anchorage, the Flandrian cliffs and an emerging land surface formed by both estuarine and wind-blown accretion below them. In human terms, the town has three focal points: the off-shore castle, the waterfront on the east side of the river and the complex on the top of the cliffs formed by St Peter's Church and the Market Place.

Test-pit excavations in 1985 located throughout the town identified domestic horizons dating from the thirteenth century at the north end of Castle Street.[97] These tend to confirm the evidence of the 1428 Garrison Roll that there was a variety of accommodation in the town by that date and suggest that its development was a direct product of the presence of the castle.[98] Elsewhere, including in Market Street and around St Peter's Church, only eighteenth- and nineteenth-century activity was found.

The sixteenth-century rent books give an indication of the size of the settlement then. Part of the town was directly owned by the earl and part by the abbot of Rushen. In 1526 there were 29 'cottage' rent payments to the lord and, in the financial year 1540 to 1541, 21 to the abbey, making 50 in all with a total value of £1 18s. 11d. This contrasts with 86 for Castletown in 1506 and a rent of £9 16s. 9d. The 1985 excavations did not find *in situ* settlement evidence of this period but located sequences of dumping from the sixteenth century to the modern period in a series of test-pits perpendicular to the river, on reclaimed land. Part of a stone harbour revetment dating from around 1500 was identified in the landward-most pit. The undercrofts beneath numbers 27 to 31 Castle Street appear contemporary.[99] Excavations in Shore Road in 2000 on the site of the IRIS pumping station located fragmentary evidence for sixteenth-century buildings, including timber framing and wattle and daub construction, together

96 Architectural development in Douglas is discussed later in this chapter and in J. Belchem (ed), *A New History of the Isle of Man*, vol. 5: *The Modern Period, 1830–1999* (Liverpool, 2000), 364–72.

97 R.A. Philpott & P.J. Davey, 'Peel town sampling project, 1985', and P.J. Davey, 'The topography and chronology of Peel and its economic development', in Lewis, *Peel Town*, 55–62, 66–67.

98 *Crellin* (trans), '1428 Garrison Roll', sec. 5, para 35.

99 Lewis, *Peel Town*, 36–50; Davey, 'Topography and chronology', in Lewis, *Peel Town*, 66.

Fig. 5.8 *Peel castle from the east, c.1656: Daniel King, fol. 28r. © The British Library Board: BL, Add 27362, fol. 28r.*

with a rich domestic assemblage showing that the town had spread eastwards along the shore by that time.

Unlike its Castletown counterpart, the Daniel King view of Peel Castle in 1656 gives no clue as to the nature of the town but does show the islet still separate from the mainland.

The 1784 Corris Map shows the extent of the settlement at that time (see Fig. 5.9). The focus is Castle Street and around St Peter's and ribbon development along Glenfaba Road and Douglas Street with infilling over the eroding cliff edge and new beach deposits below.

Ramsey

Ramsey did not exist as a town in the early sixteenth century. There are records of landholding north and south of the Sulby river, and a significant amount has been written about them, principally by Constance Radcliffe.[100] However, her material does not lend itself to precise reconstruction of the phasing of development. In contrast, the history of the land north of the river as far as St Olave's Church has been studied in considerable depth but remains unpublished.[101]

100 J.W. & C.K. Radcliffe, *Maughold & Ramsey Place-names* (Maughold, 1978); Radcliffe, *Ramsey*.

101 N.G. Crowe & G. Callow, c.2010, ''The Callows and development of North Ramsey including Fayle's Croft or Croit e Squandish and Quayle's Croft or Bridge Croft' (MNH MS 15151).

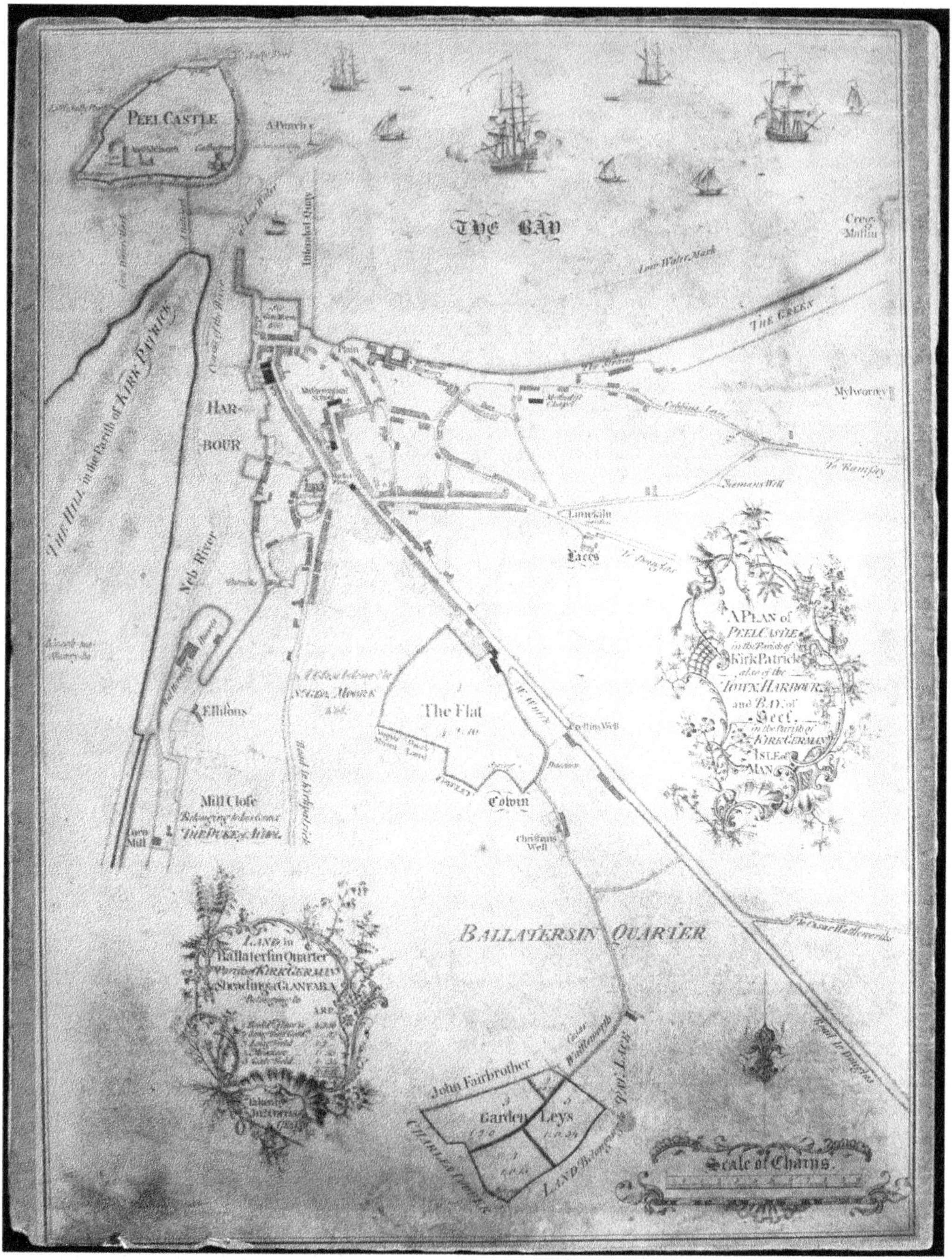

Fig. 5.9 *Peel, 1784: Corris map – MNH P.1526/3 (PE 10/2 S).*

In outline, the site of the earliest growth appears to have centred around the location known as 'Old Cross' from which narrow streets (both since obliterated) ran off to the north-west and south-east.[102] These gave access to enclosures which grew up haphazardly in a linear fashion. This development occurred on the upper part of the shingle beach generally referred to as *The Mooragh* (literally 'land at the seaside'). In tenurial terms, all of this was intack or cottage rent. This portion of the town site was separated by a series of former lagoons which had evolved into loughs or wetland from the agricultural land within the treens of *Ramessay* and *Balywre*, upon which subsequent growth occurred.

Villages

The Island lacks obvious medieval villages, whether deserted or not. Analysis of the distribution of cottages in the early sixteenth-century rent books, show very few outside the towns.[103] Blundell notes in the mid-seventeenth century that rural cottages were spread throughout the landscape 'almost at ye end of every other acre of ground, solely seated and dispersed, yet scarce 2 flightshot distant the one from the other'.[104] He wrote that Manxmen acknowledged only three villages: Ballasalla, Laxey and, probably, Kirk Michael.[105]

In 1755, Bishop Hildesley noted that 'Our villages are made up of scattered parcels of stone-built farmhouses – with certain portions of arable and pasture land about them, occupied chiefly by the owners'.[106] When the clergy were asked in 1774 to comment about settlements within their parishes, Rector Wilks made it clear that there was no village within Ballaugh, 'nor is the term hamlet used among us'.[107] Similar responses were recorded for Andreas and Braddan.[108]

Few Manx villages have yet been provided with a published history. However, dating evidence can sometimes be provided through datestones on bridges, chapels, or other such buildings, or through the presence of milestones of a

102 The Old Cross was located seaward of Lough House, which survives, though in much altered surroundings.

103 Talbot, *Manorial roll*, 84, appendix C.

104 Blundell, 'History', vol. 1, 131.

105 Blundell himself seems to conflate Kirk Michael Village with 'Bala Cury', of which he commented 'though it be the bishop's seat, yet it is no town, but a village': Blundell, 'History', vol. 1, 157.

106 M. Hildesley, letter to a friend, 16 September 1755: transcribed in *The Manx Church Magazine*, 1:9 (September 1891).

107 Warwickshire County Record Office, CR2017/TP17: Pennant Papers CR2017/TP17.

108 Andreas: 2017; Warwick CRO CR2017/TP17.

known date. A careful study of registered deeds can also illuminate the development of the villages.[109]

The sites of the medieval parish churches are not surrounded by cottages but set within the pattern of farm holdings. Ballasalla provides an obvious exception to this. By the time of the Dissolution accounts, it had 25 individuals paying cottage rent. By 1607 this had increased to 34. A sharp rent increase following 1540, which was not repeated in the erstwhile abbey holdings in Peel, suggests that the settlement grew up as partly subsidized accommodation for people who worked the abbey's home farm.[110]

Many of the modern villages were initially focussed on a bridge or crossroads, often near the 'Main Road' or, for example, 'Douglas Street'. Subsequent lateral growth would extend into a 'Glen Road' and a 'Station Road' (for example, Colby, Kirk Michael, and Ballaugh). In some cases, an old settlement was eclipsed. Kirk Michael was unusual in originating as a nucleated settlement close to the parish church. The parochial school was being taught here in 1672.[111] In 1762 the vicar and parishioners acknowledged the bishop's bounty to the parish in 'causing to be erected a handsome and commodious Court-House, in Kirk-Michael village'.

There was no nucleated settlement in Laxey during the sixteenth century. Only one 'small croft' is listed in the 1511 rent book. In contrast, the 1540 monastic rent for Skinscoe lists six cottage rent payers. While the location of these properties is not given, it is likely that they were located on or near the waterfront north of the bridge and east of St Nicholas' chapel. Speed's map of

109 J.H. Caine and William and Constance Radcliffe included church and village within their studies of Bride (see Radcliffe, *Bride: miscellany*). Donald Dugdale's notes on Andreas families (appearing under editorship of S. McCambridge & D.S. Dugdale, *Andreas*, (Douglas, 2005) are arranged geographically, but avoid addressing buildings, landholdings or the layout of the roads. Kermode's *Annals of Kirk Christ, Lezayre* (1954) is not especially focussed on Sulby, and only deals with six family names. Kirk Michael has so far had useful studies made of several topics by R. Kissack, 'The location of a place name: where was Borodaill?', *PIMNHAS*, 10:2 (1991–93), 120; T.L. Cashin, *A Michael Village Trail* (Kirk Michael, 1986); C. Renshaw, 'Words and Deeds in Nineteenth Century Kirk Michael', *PIMNHAS*, 9:4 (1987–89), 543–64; a general survey by J. Grimson, *Kirk Michael, Isle of Man: a guide to village and parish* (Kirk Michael, 1986). Laxey now has the benefit of comprehensive accounts of the mines and railways: A. Scarffe, *The Railways and Tramways of Laxey*, (Douglas, 2014); A. Scarffe, *The Great Laxey Mine* (Douglas, 2004); and F. Cowin *et al.*, *Lady Isabella and the Great Laxey Mine Official Guide* (Douglas, 1989). Onchan has published accounts by N. Mathieson, *Onchan, Isle of Man: the story of a village* (Onchan, 1963), and G.N. Kniveton, *The Onchan Story* (Douglas, 1992).

110 P.J. Davey, 'Towards the 16th-century topography of Ballasalla', *PIMNHAS*, 12:3 (2009–11), 367–86.

111 M.J. Hoy, 'Isaac Barrow: builder of foundations for a modern nation' (PhD thesis, University of Liverpool, 2015), 103.

1605 features 'Laxi Towne' with houses depicted north and south of the bay. The development of Laxey during the seventeenth and eighteenth centuries requires further study.

THE BUILT ENVIRONMENT

Until the Georgian period, the Isle of Man remained, architecturally, something of a cultural backwater with the exception of church and 'state' – the latter represented by the castles and associated administrative infrastructure.

The period covered by this volume was associated with increasing off-shore trade, the importation of construction materials that had previously been in short supply, improved road and bridge construction across the Island, the influx of a cultural mix of people not associated with the insular administration who wished to rent larger houses, and increasing exposure to life beyond Manx waters. These influences led to rising aspirations among the Manx people and brought greater awareness of architectural style, form and quality. This delay in the improvement of construction standards and aspiration for better was also a consequence of the insecure land tenure practices under the Stanley lords, who rarely visited their Manx dominion, preferring to control the Island through an imposed administration, largely staffed by English or Scots personnel based at Peel and Castletown. As a result, the Stanleys did not build fine residences that would provide precedent and example to the Manx people or offer opportunity to the Manx workforce to learn the finer building skills.

The Island's built environment was also determined by the type of building materials available. Historically, the Isle of Man provided an abundance of stone, though most of it was hard to work, and a paucity of timber, thereby limiting the development of any sophistication in insular construction technology. Most structural timber was imported or recycled. Timber, mostly oak, was also salvaged from the peat bogs of the curragh. There have been insufficient known Manx specimens of timber to establish a viable dendrochronological database.

The Island's complex geology provided the Manx 'slate,' a mudstone, limestone (in the south, around Castletown), a small incursion of red Devonian sandstone (Peel), granite (in localized volcanic plugs), and rounded beach and river stones (Kirk Michael and the northern plain).[112] Erratics and fieldstones were also a source of building stone. The predominant mudstone was difficult

112 See www.manxgeology.com (accessed 12 January 2018), also Lamplugh, *Geology*; E. Pickett, *The Isle of Man: foundations of a landscape* (Isle of Man, 2001); V. Robinson & D. McCarroll (eds), *The Isle of Man: celebrating a sense of place* (Liverpool, 1990); and others, culminating in R. Chiverell & G. Thomas (eds), *A New History of the Isle of Man*, vol. 1: *The Evolution of the Natural Landscape* (Liverpool, 2006). Manx

to work and cleave, necessitating the common use of mass rubble walling, often uncoursed and of considerable depth wherever two fair faces were required.

Fortifications

Castle Rushen, probably founded in the late twelfth century as a square tower, is largely a fourteenth-century structure with major and elaborate works carried out during the Montacute lordship following capture and slighting by Robert the Bruce in 1313.[113] The development of Derby House in the inner bailey, the round Tudor gun battery, the glacis, and, lastly, the 'new worke' overlooking the harbour, follow during the sixteenth and seventeenth centuries. The latter structure is prominent in the drawings made by Daniel King in the 1650s.

The additions made to accommodate the English garrison and the prison in the eighteenth and nineteenth centuries were largely removed at the beginning of the twentieth century.

At Peel Castle, most of the curtain wall, linking the already existing interval towers, was built following the Stanley acquisition.[114] The curtain, particularly on the north-west, seaward side, would have been armed with artillery mounted on a rampire, providing a defence against approaching enemy shipping. The need for better protection for Peel Bay was met by the construction of a circular artillery battery on Horse Rock, at the most northerly point of the castle, probably just before the middle of the sixteenth century. Its three guns extended the castle's artillery defences into the bay and as far as the mouth of the harbour. Peel was subsequently significantly modernised during the Civil War with the addition of several loopholed walls for musketeers, and the creation of an irregularly shaped, earthen, artillery sconce which today still fills much of the northern and central part of the walled circuit.

A proportion of the twenty or so promontory forts of Iron Age character around the rockier parts of the coast of the Island have been shown on excavation to have been used in the medieval period.[115] It seems likely that they served several purposes focussed both on the military security of the Island and also policing coastal trade.[116] The concept of a systematic approach

---

'slate' is not a true slate, as it is insufficiently compressed. These stones are generally known as the Manx and Dalby groups of mudstones.

113 B.H.St.J. O'Neil, 'Castle Rushen, Isle of Man', *Archaeologia*, 94 (1951), 22–24.

114 D. Freke, *Excavations on St Patrick's Isle, Peel, Isle of Man 1982–88* (Liverpool, 2002), 166–68.

115 A.C.C. Johnson, 'Watch and ward on the Isle of Man: the medieval re-occupation of Iron Age promontory forts', in P. Davey & D. Finlayson (eds), *Mannin revisited: twelve essays on Manx culture and environment* (Edinburgh, 2002), 63–80.

116 For a recent discussion of their function see P.J. Davey, 'Galley-castles and the Isle of Man?' in P. Martin (ed), *Castles and galleys: a reassessment of the historic galley-castles of the Norse-Gaelic seaways* (Laxey, 2017), 196–207.

Fig. 5.10 *Castle Rushen from the south-east, c.1656: Daniel King, fol. 12r.* © *The British Library Board: BL, Add 27362, fol. 12r.*

to coastal security was clearly already in place by 1417, when the statutes include prominent mention of 'watch and ward'. It is reiterated, with similar prominence in 1422 and 1594. It is last mentioned in official written sources in a document of 1627.[117]

By the mid-seventeenth century, the Island's physical defences are extensive, no longer relying simply on watch and ward and the castles at Peel and Castletown, though these have been transformed over time to meet the changing demands of warfare and the development of gunpowder. The round battery at Peel is reflected in a similar sixteenth-century work on the north side of Castle Rushen, though the latter is intended to protect the castle – and cover the harbour – from landward attack. A similar round fort is constructed at Douglas with four guns to protect the mouth of the harbour on a site approximately beneath the traffic roundabout at the entrance to the modern harbour marshalling yard. Additional guns were mounted in an outerwork during the 1640s and were themselves replaced by an improved gun platform in 1666. A fort was also under construction at Ramsey in 1648, according to Blundell, but its precise location is unknown. The nature of artillery defence at this port is

117 'A pfect Remembrance conteyning all the names of the wardens both of the day and night watches throghout the Isle of Man together with the names of evry pishe and place where the watches are kept': W. Cubbon, 'Watch and Ward in 1627', *PIMNHAS*, 3:4 (1928–30), 258.

confused by later urban development and the shifting nature of the river mouth but was mostly focussed to the south of the modern harbour entrance.[118]

On St Michael's Isle, guarding the entrance to Derbyhaven, lies the largest of these coastal round forts, 24m in diameter and originally mounting eight cannon. Like the other round forts, it appears to have been originally constructed as part of Henry VIII's scheme of coastal defence against his continental enemies, and its size hints at the former importance of Derbyhaven as a port, far safer for sailing vessels than the narrow river mouth of the Silverburn beneath the defences of Castle Rushen. By the seventeenth century the fort was outdated and was rearmed and strengthened by James, seventh earl of Derby's construction of an earthwork battery immediately to the south-west.[119]

Around the time of the Civil War, earthwork defences were the most effective response to the growing power of artillery and, whilst James Stanley's programme of improvements between 1643 and 1651 involved rearming and improving existing fortifications, several other new sites were constructed in the new style.[120] The coastline south of Ramsey was protected by small earthwork batteries at Gob ny Rona and Ballure in 1643, and by another battery of the same date further to the north at Cranstal. Whilst the former two persisted as part of an effective network of coastal defence, the latter was soon found to be ineffective because of its isolation, and by 1656 it was out of use.[121] At the far southern end of the Island, the Calf of Man, the defence of which much preoccupied the earl, was protected by small earthwork batteries at South Harbour and at Fold Point, which may have been completed as early as 1651.[122] In the west, another earthwork battery was constructed at the northern end of Peel Hill, on the advice of the royalist artillery officer Sir Arthur Ashton.[123] A second earthwork nearby suggests that this site may be more complex than hitherto appreciated.

Further inland, a new fort was constructed near Kerroogarrow and Ballachurry, now known by both names.[124] This was of an entirely different scale, and of a similar design to earthwork sconces appearing in England and still seen to good effect, for example, at Newark-on-Trent. The fort is a raised

118 R.A. Curphey, 'The coastal batteries. The Lord's defences: to the revestment', *JMM*, 7:83 (1967), 53–54.
119 Curphey, 'Coastal batteries', 54–56.
120 Curphey, 'Coastal batteries', 50–51: improvements to internal and external splays and arcs of fire.
121 Chaloner, *Treatise*, 44.
122 Curphey, 'Coastal batteries', 56.
123 Ashton (or Aston) was later notoriously murdered in the Parliamentary-led massacre at Drogheda in 1649, and it is tempting to suggest that his advice was given only shortly before.
124 At the time, it was referred to as the 'New Fort', the 'Andrew' or 'Andreas' fort, and possibly also as Fort Loyal.

rectangular earthwork platform protected on all sides by a rampart and at each corner by a projecting, sharply pointed bastion, each of which was designed to serve as a platform for artillery, and giving the fort its characteristic, 'star-shaped' form. The slight remains of a bank are still apparent atop the north rampart, suggestive of a protective raised breastwork for musketeers. Overall, the earthwork measures 110m by 95m, and still stands to a height of 5m. It would originally have appeared more massive, but the surrounding ditch, from which the earthwork was quarried, is now largely filled and the southern rampart distorted by rabbit burrowing and a later entrance. Nevertheless, its well-preserved bastions hint at its original purpose, providing a clear field of fire to the east, north and west, by which route an enemy that landed at Ramsey would have been forced to pass. To the south lies less well-drained land and, beyond, the steep slopes of the hills, neither of them amenable to the easy passing of an invading army. Subtly placed, the fort at Kerroogarrow was designed to command a wide part of the Island's northern plain and frustrate easy cross-country passage from Ramsey to Peel.

Its task was aided by a similar fortification around Bishopscourt. Here, despite later landscaping, the remains of a less regular earthwork are still apparent. The see fell vacant in 1643 following the death of Bishop Parr, and the site was appropriated by Earl James until his own death in 1651. Perhaps the medieval towerhouse at the core of the bishop's residence inspired recollection of the defence of Lathom by Charlotte, countess of Derby in 1644, for the house was surrounded by a raised rectilinear earthwork with corner bastions, perhaps from 1648 onwards. The ramparts survive most clearly on the north-east and north-west sides; the main road lies atop the south-east rampart.

The progressive improvement of castle defences, and the addition of coastal gun batteries and earthen forts transformed the Island into a highly defensible landscape between 1540 and 1651, demonstrating that its lords were well advised in the concepts of peripheral defence and defence in depth. Their successors, once the lordship resumed, were to see that the defence of the Island was maintained in response to subsequent threats until responsibility was passed to the British authorities in 1765.

Religious buildings

At some sites, continuous occupation can be demonstrated from the late Middle Ages even though there is now little architectural detail to show. At Rushen Abbey there is archaeological evidence of new building in the fifteenth century, but only the ravaged core still survives.[125] At Bemaken, the present

125 P.J. Davey, 'Eleven years of archaeological research at Rushen Abbey, 1998 to 2008', *Monastic Research Bulletin* 14, (2008), 11.

farmhouse arguably contains or lies above the domestic accommodation of the Friars. In 1540, no rent was paid as '[n]othing was found there except for the dwelling house duly reserved for the use of the farmer'.[126] Similarly, at the Nunnery, there are no credible medieval buildings, but fragments of the church and nuns' accommodation may still survive in a fragmentary and possibly relocated state.[127] Bishopscourt, with its fourteenth-century tower house at the core, continued to be the residence of the bishop until quite late in the twentieth century.[128]

On Peel Castle, the south aisle of the cathedral was probably reduced, and St Patrick's church extended to the east in this period.[129] The most significant development was the construction of the 'new' hall and vicars choral range to the north of the Cathedral, parts of which still survive.[130] An aisle was added to St Mary's Castletown, probably in the sixteenth century, presumably in response to population growth.[131] The surviving structure at St Peter's in Peel may also belong to this period.[132] New gables were also added to St Trinian's.[133]

Most of the rural parish churches are on, or very close to, the sites of their medieval predecessors, but only a few visibly retain later medieval features such as the second easterly extension of the twelfth-century church at Maughold.[134] These locations instead have high archaeological potential, as shown at Santon when repairs to the foundations of the south wall resulted in the recovery of a repurposed medieval stone cross from the threshold of a redundant doorway.[135]

Bishop Wilson also undertook significant alterations to some churches (including the neo-baroque reworking of the west front at St Mary de Ballaugh with porch and belfry), and had Holy Trinity, Patrick, built between 1708 and 1711 (demolished and rebuilt 1881). Rector James Wilks added galleries to Ballaugh in 1777. These were reached by a double stair, subsequently removed

126 Davey & Roscow, *Rushen Abbey*, 157.

127 C. Corkill *et al.*, 'Archaeological and Documentary Assessment of the Nunnery Estate, Douglas, Isle of Man' (unpubl. report to the Friends of the Chapel of St Bridget at the Nunnery, 2007), 25–26.

128 R.A. Curphey, 'Bishopscourt', *JMM*, 7, No, 88 (1976), 221–4.

129 C.A. Ralegh Radford, 'St Patrick's Isle: the medieval monastic remains', *PIMNHAS*, 11:3 (2004), 379–381; 390.

130 H.G. Slade, 'Architectural interpretation', in Freke, *Excavations on St Patrick's Isle*, 202–20.

131 Davey, *After the Vikings*, 86–89.

132 Davey, *Vikings*, 89–90.

133 P.M.C. Kermode, 'St. Trinian's' (site visit notes), *PIMNHAS*, 1:6 (1911), 328–32; Davey, *Vikings*, 118–120.

134 F. Logan, 2021, 'Maughold Parish Church: an attempt at structural analysis', *Isle of Man Studies*, vol. 17, 33–60.

135 'Avitus' stone cross, Santon: A.M. Cubbon, *The Art of the Manx Crosses* (Douglas, 1971), 5, no. 29.

Fig. 5.11 *Old Kirk Braddan, c.1865: MNH PG 10884.*

in 1849. Wilson's successor Mark Hildesley had major work done at Ballaugh and Andreas, and had galleries added to Bride, Malew and Braddan whilst Onchan was extended.

The limewashed vernacular churches were much admired by John Betjeman for their rustic charm and simplicity.[136] Old Kirk Braddan is a Georgian auditory church with west gallery. It replaced an earlier unsafe and smaller church, and has high box pews, a triple-decker pulpit, clear glass in the windows, pinnacled gables and monuments on the external walls.[137] The earlier church is thought historically to have been demolished and rebuilt from the rubble with quoins of Foxdale granite, but historian Frank Cowin believes that some original twelfth-century walls survive. Unlike many other Island churches, it was probably never whitewashed.[138]

136 J. Betjeman (ed), *Collins Guide to English Parish Churches, including the Isle of Man* (London, 1958), 2 (north), 205–07.

137 It was designed for preaching, with pulpit (in this case, triple-decker) in full view of the congregation. Pre-Reformation, preaching was rare; churches were primarily for the celebration of the Mass, often with the celebrant concealed behind a rood-screen.

138 P. Kelly, *Old Kirk Braddan - short history and tour* (Douglas, 1982).

Fig. 5.12 *St Mary's church in the parade, Castletown, by Thomas Brine, 1823–26. The lantern was removed in 1911. (photo c.1900): MNH PGN 03301.*

St Paul's Church, Ramsey (Thomas Brine, 1822) was initially built in a simple basilican form in rustic Georgian neo-classical style. The West Gallery was added in 1830.[139] The present form includes later additions of the north and south wings, with galleries, the porch and alterations within the sanctuary. St Mary's, Castletown, known as the 'Garrison Church,' was a Pre-Tractarian Georgian church with high pews, galleries, wall tablets and high pulpit (see Fig. 5.12). It accommodated 1,300 people and had special pews for the governor and for the troops.

The early Methodist chapels and schoolrooms were modest in scale, always on roadsides, and often squeezed into a corner of a field, most easily spared by the donor who would be one of the early converts in the area. In 1783 there were 1,758 members in the Manx Methodist connection. The earliest sites betray themselves by their seeming disregard of the main road network, perhaps the oldest being on Glen Road, Ballaugh. The first chapel at Kirk Michael was sited in a seemingly obscure location on a lane accessing the rear of Main Road properties. The acute angle at which this lane meets the Main Road, its modest width, and its trajectory, heading towards the parish church, strongly suggest that it is a fragment of the ancient highway from the south.

139 Floor plan, grant for new church, minutes – Lambeth Palace: ICBS 00076, fols 12ff; rebuilding funded by Church Commissioners: ICBS 00454, fols 23ff.

Vernacular buildings

Relatively few vernacular buildings on the Island can be reliably dated to before the eighteenth century. Early Manx buildings are often difficult to recognize due to substantial alteration, including the construction of additional units to enlarge the house, the heightening of the walls to increase the amount of living space, and the addition of render, thus obscuring the original fabric of the building and any changes to window and door openings.[140] Although no comprehensive survey has yet been undertaken of such on the Isle of Man, recent works by Cannell, Crowe, and Tutt have significantly added to our knowledge of traditional Manx architecture.[141]

The earliest description of Manx vernacular buildings comes from the 1640s. Blundell describes the poorest rural houses of this period as 'mere hovels, compacted of stones and clay for the walls, and thatched with broom, most commonly containing one room only. Very few have 2 rooms, have no upper rooms, - such as in their towns they call lofts, - nor any ceiling but the thatch itself, with the rafters.'[142] Daniel King's drawing of North Quay in Douglas from the same period provides pictorial evidence of such a single-unit house (see Fig. 1.8).[143] The milk cow was originally housed in the single-roomed dwelling, and progressively separated from the family as the house became divided. In the combined dwelling, there was usually a through passage, believed to have been used to obtain a draught for winnowing, as was the practice in England and Wales. As more cattle were acquired, they needed a separate cowhouse, and this was usually attached to the cottage longhouse-style, whilst the small cow space in the dwelling became the bedroom. By 1812, however, most basic houses comprised two rooms, a kitchen (*thie mooar*) and a bedroom (*cuillee*), with a loft above and, according to Thomas Quayle, some houses did have a cowhouse under the same roof.[144] Crowe has identified a possible seventeenth-century longhouse at Glashen farm in Ballasalla.[145] Later farm steadings included a separate cowhouse, as well as a barn and a pigsty and, sometimes, a separate henhouse.

140 Crowe, 'Manx Houses', 65.

141 S. Cannell, *Rural Architecture in the North of the Isle of Man* (Edinburgh: Scottish Vernacular Buildings Working Group, 2001); Crowe, 'Manx Houses of the Seventeenth Century', 65–96; P.A. Tutt, 'An Insular Architecture: The Rural Vernacular Architecture and Landscape of the Isle of Man and the Unique Influencing Factors that have Shaped its Form' (PhD thesis, University of Liverpool, 2012); P.A. Tutt, *An Introduction to the Architecture of the Isle of Man* (Ramsey, 2013).

142 Blundell, 'History', vol. 1, 136.

143 Crowe, 'Manx Houses of the Seventeenth Century', 68. See Fig. 1.8 above.

144 T. Quayle, *Agriculture* (1812).

145 Crowe, 'Manx Houses of the Seventeenth Century', 70.

Fig. 5.13 *James Quayle's (Jemmy Nell's), Jurby: MNH PG/5647/281.*

During this period, the Island's vernacular buildings would have been constructed of whatever suitable material was to hand. In areas where good building stone was predominant, walls were stone-built. Elsewhere, particularly in the north of the Island, walls were often made of turf, clay, or locally produced brick. Shore and river stones were often used and combined with clay or turf to provide extra stability. Walls of earthen dwellings, barns and cowhouses were built from clay or upturned sods and turves. Surfaces were smoothed with a wash of wet clay and dung. Roofs were generally gabled and were thatched with straw or other locally available material at a pitch of 35 degrees. While evidence from the early seventeenth century suggests that pegged thatch 'after the English fashion' was common, by the nineteenth century, roped thatch appears most common with the ropes secured either by 'stones hanging from the end of ropes' or by tying them to pegs, known as *bwid suggane* (usually of stone, but sometimes of timber, brick, or animal bones) projecting from the exterior wall.[146] There was rarely a wall plate. Slate hanging as seen at Bridge House, Castletown, is comparatively rare today, but archive photographs show it was in common use on exposed gables in Castletown and Ramsey and on soft brick gables elsewhere.[147]

146 C. Mackie, 'Observations on the Vernacular House in the Isle of Man', *PIMNHAS*, 12:3 (2009–11), 424.

147 Tutt, *An Insular Architecture*, 151–54.

Fig. 5.14 *Harry Kelly's cottage, Cregneash, interior: MNH PG/0814.*

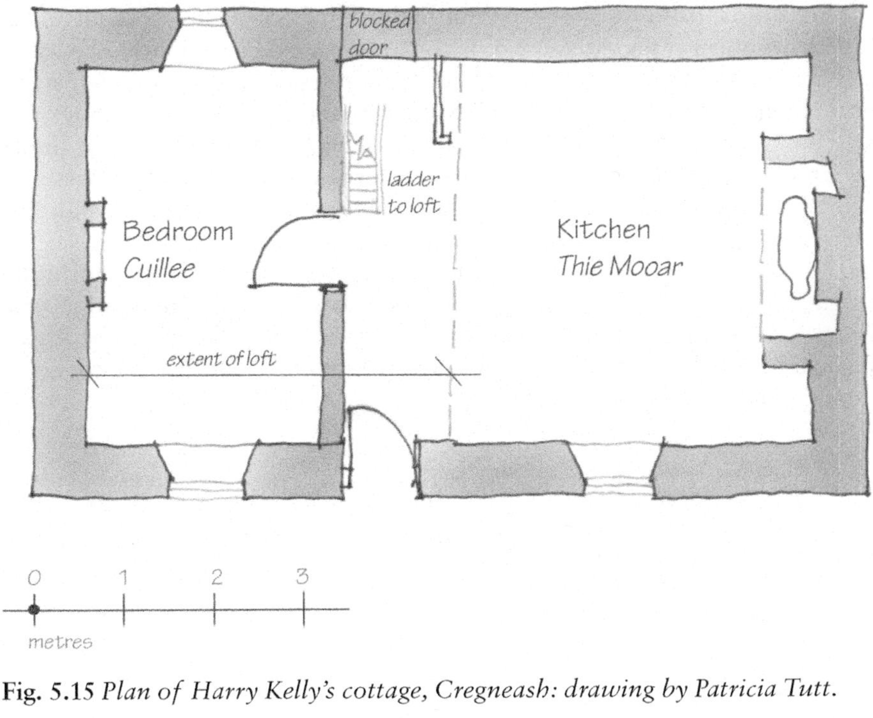

Fig. 5.15 *Plan of Harry Kelly's cottage, Cregneash: drawing by Patricia Tutt.*

While there is no evidence of the prevalence of central hearths in early Manx cottages, the survival, down to the nineteenth century, of what was known as a 'steem', appears to acknowledge this type of house.[148] By the early nineteenth century, the hearth appears to have been placed against a gable wall with the smoke emitting through a small firkin or barrel placed at one end of the roof (see Fig. 5.13).[149] Wattle and daub chimney hoods were common in the north of the Island, while the preponderance of good building stone in the south allowed for the construction of a deep stone fireplace (*chiollagh*), often extending the width of the house, with storage space at either side (see Fig. 5.14). Figure 5.15 shows the layout of Harry Kelly's cottage at Cregneash – a two-unit house with a wide *chiollagh* – now part of an open-air museum managed by Manx National Heritage.[150] The depth of the *chiollagh* results in an asymmetrical façade. The evidence of a cross-passage with opposing doors, as seen here, is commonly considered to be evidence of a former longhouse.

Agricultural buildings

Manx farming remained rudimentary until the late eighteenth century but, by the beginning of the nineteenth century, new landowners had demonstrated how the land could be made profitable by better husbandry and a more structured and scientific approach to farming.

The campaign to 'improve' Manx farms has been well recorded.[151] The initiative in most cases extended only to lands in single ownership. The Manx were remarkably quick in adopting the best of these new practices that suited local conditions, as can be seen in the many 'improved' farm buildings that were built across the island and in the proliferation of lime kilns, for liming the land. Among the most progressive and successful of these improvers were George Moore, at Ballamoore, Patrick (now known as Ballamoar) and Basil Quayle, at The Creggans, Malew.[152]

The enterprising merchant George Moore imported many plants, including hedging shrubs and fruit trees. He appears to have been the key instigator in the use of hawthorn for hedges on Manx lowland farms. It can still be seen in the field boundaries at Ballamoar, where it has mostly grown out into ageing

148 Mackie, 'Vernacular House', 425–29.

149 R. Townley, *A Journal of the Isle of Man*, 2 vols (Whitehaven, 1790), vol. 1, 35; T. Quayle, *Agriculture* (1812).

150 Tutt, *An Insular Architecture*, 185: fig. 6/10.

151 Quayle, *Agriculture* (1794); Quayle, *Agriculture* (1812); F. Radcliffe, *Manx Farming and Country Life 1700–1900: information pack for schools* (Douglas, 1991), 17–28; Curwen, 'The Report for the Isle of Man', in *The Rules & Proceedings of the Workington Agricultural Society* (1810), 105- 68.

152 A.W. Moore, *Manx Worthies* (Douglas, 1901), 193.

hedge trees. Basil Quayle's 1794 description of the typical Manx farm buildings is brief: they were small, poorly constructed and carelessly placed. Recently built farmyards were commodious, better designed, with a good range of offices usually set around a yard where 'young cattle are foddered on the dunghill'.[153] These new buildings were larger and more substantial, stone-built with lime and mortar and mostly under a slate roof. It was the norm to have the barn over the cowhouse, but he noted that the cattle were not kept clean and still tended to be tied to stakes or yoked. Horses, on the other hand, were mostly kept in open stables, and so likely to injure one another. Nearly all the barns standing today are two-storied, with the cowhouse and other offices on the ground floor and grain storage on the upper floor. Although Feltham distinguished between the two, 'barn' has become the generic term for these two combined elements and is used that way in this chapter.[154]

The over-riding impression of the Manx farm is that barns and cowhouses are all attached to the farmhouse (on the smaller farms and smallholdings) or are part of the larger farm yard or street. The cart shed is very much a feature of the improved farm and is generally an element within a bigger linear or yard barn structure. Nearly all Manx cart sheds utilise brickwork to form the arch over the wide opening, as most Manx stone (apart from limestone and sandstone) is too difficult to work into voussoirs.

Milling was carried out for a variety of purposes, using a range of structures, machinery, and tools. Many of the early mills encountered in the manorial records, particularly in the upland valleys, had modest rents and may have been 'little' horizontal mills, operating seasonally or as required. Baldwin Mill is recorded in the 1417 Sheading Roll and by the 1511 and 1515 rent books, there was at least one per parish.[155] By 1540, there were a further ten on monastic land.[156] By 1703 there are 58.[157] In the rent books the mills are often named, and their present location is usually known. Whilst there are no late medieval structures surviving, the sites themselves potentially preserve contemporary evidence. A thirteenth-century corn drying kiln was excavated by Gelling within the shieling complex at Block Eary; it is unclear how far such structures survived in use during the later Middle Ages and early modern periods.[158]

Horse mills (also known as horse-walks, horse engines or horse gins) were particular features of improved farms from the 1790s and were used for

153 Quayle, *Agriculture* (1794), 17.
154 Feltham, *Tour*, 51.
155 Talbot, *Manorial roll*, 82: the table provides a summary of the income from mills by parish.
156 Davey and Roscow, *Rushen Abbey*, 143–52, appendix 1.
157 Talbot, *Manorial roll*, 97–107, appendix K.
158 P.S. Gelling, 'Medieval sheilings in the Isle of Man', *Medieval Archaeology*, 6–7 (1962–63), 164–67.

threshing or grinding grain, or for any purpose requiring power. These were fixed platforms with a central shaft for the horse to circle, pulling a beam to generate power. Some were under cover, usually with circular or multi-sided structures (hexagonal or octagonal) and most of the Manx mills used a single horse. The Balladoole horse-walk, however, which was originally thatched, had four equidistant entrances, and four beams for horses to work the mill. The majority were not covered, however, and most used only a single horse. After threshing or milling, grain was stored in the stone barn alongside. The horse-walk was short-lived, being replaced by mechanical threshing and milling, which came into use in the 1830s.

During the second half of the eighteenth century, newly designed model farms were constructed principally in the lowland plains and the plateau areas.[159] Each typically comprised a significant farmstead together with surrounding enclosures, usually accessed by fenced farm tracks, and clearly forming a single holding. The tracks are straight and generously laid out, and the enclosures are large and surrounded by stone walls or thorn hedgerows. The fields are generally rectilinear as far as compatible with the overall shape of the putative holding to which the steading will often be central.

Polite architecture

By the early seventeenth century, some town houses, quarterland farms and larger gentry houses were venturing beyond the vernacular, but mostly these remained modest and plainly decorated in comparison to equivalent English houses.[160] Blundell notes that, in the mid-seventeenth century, the most affluent inhabitants preferred to live in the country rather than in the towns or villages and, in contrast to the poorer cottages, their dwellings were 'high handsome well-built houses, after the English fashion'.[161] Unfortunately, they are poorly documented: many have been demolished and most that survive have been altered repeatedly, making them difficult to interpret. For example, at Milntown, the house was believed to have its origins in the sixteenth century. However, recently discovered documents date the house to c.1750, with an earlier house located nearby on the estate.[162] Fort Anne (1790s, now lost) is one of the few known to have had a lavish interior, with sophisticated elements and internal

159 Examples (before 1830) include: Middle Farm, Braddan; Leece Lodge, Braddan (both surviving); Howstrake, Onchan; and Ballavoddan, Andreas (both destroyed); Ballacreggan and Ballakilley, Rushen; Loughan y Yeigh, Lezayre (all surviving).

160 Crowe, 'Manx Houses', 65–96.

161 Blundell, 'History', vol. 1, 133.

162 N.G. Crowe, 'Programme for Day 1', in J. Kewley (ed), 'The Isle of Man – Conference Notes' (Society of Architectural Historians of Great Britain, 2014), 55–65 (MNH M 41418).

fittings. The building was castellated, and apparently approached through a conceit resembling a ruined wing.

Small numbers of strangers had been arriving in the Isle of Man since at least the late seventeenth century to take refuge from creditors and taxes and stretch their limited incomes to the maximum. The numbers arriving increased with the outbreak of the French Revolutionary wars. War-time conditions provided impetus for change and by 1810 new residents were bringing 'a very great influx of money' into the Island (reckoned at from £40,000 to £50,000 per annum), the demand for rural property accelerated, and the 'rage for building' prevailed for several years, not only in Douglas but in the surrounding districts.[163] This building boom had a significant visual and economic impact over much of the Island, although the effect outside the towns was largely associated with the recently constructed highway network, particularly where bridges had been constructed. Travelling out of Douglas, before the impact of tree-planting took full effect, visitors to the north saw 'a great many small houses also (all milky white) inhabited by half-pay captains and their families'.[164]

Many of the newly arrived residents sought to occupy a 'cottage', usually possessing paddocks and stabling. Some had sufficient resources to build for themselves, while others were accommodated in housing erected specifically for letting, or which was currently surplus to a family's needs. The obligatory carriage required proximity to the developing highway network. Set back behind walls, drives and lawns, such houses would have had a kitchen garden often accompanied by a miniature range of farm buildings and stabling. However, this building boom was short-lived. The 1814 Act for the More Easy Recovery of Debts, the end of the Napoleonic Wars in 1815, and the temporary repeal of British income tax in 1816 choked off the 'speculations in the building of houses'.[165]

The most notable survivor from this period is the Castle Mona, completed in 1803/4.[166] The estate, which extended to 92 ha, was assembled by John Murray,

163 Curwen, *Isle of Man Report* (1810), 127; MNH X/29 (4th) – 18: 'Minutes of a Meeting of the Legislative Council' held on 11 May 1816, published in A.E. Kelly, 2003: *Documents Relating to Manx Currency* (Douglas, 2003), 57–60; T. Callister, *An accurate, interesting, and peculiarly entertaining description of that lucrative branch of business the Herring fishery of the Isle of Man* (Douglas, 1815), 11.

164 E.C. Wilson (ed), *An Island Bishop: 1762–1838: Memorials of William Ward, D.D. Bishop of Sodor and Mann 1828–1838* (London, 1931), 127: extract dated September 1829 from a holiday journal by M. Barker, house guest of Bishop Ward.

165 *Statutes*, vol. 1, (Douglas, 1897), 371–72 (1814); Kelly, *Manx Currency*, 59, n. 38: Minutes of a Meeting of the Legislative Council, 11 May 1816.

166 M.M. Rix and W.R. Sergeant, 'George Steuart, architect in the Isle of Man', *JMM*, 6:79 (1962), 177–79; S. Goodsir, 'George Steuart in the Isle of Man, and further afield', *PIMNHAS*, 12:4 (2014), 699–720; Tutt, *Architecture of the Isle of Man*, 154–61.

Fig. 5.16 *'Castle Mona', by L. Pollitt: MNH 1954-6963a.*

fourth duke of Athol, from 1793 onwards.[167] His acquisitions wrapped around the north and west sides of the town, where the duke ordered the laying out of 'a great many very fine large fields, with proper drains, hedges, ditches, fences and other improvements'. His initial purchase was Lough House, a seaside property acquired from a family of Douglas merchants.[168] The duke decided to locate his 'marine palace', the Castle Mona, at this level rather than on the cliff tops above and construction took place to the designs of George Steuart between 1801 and 1804 and at a reported cost of up to £36,000 (see Fig. 5.16).[169]

Steuart was a Scottish architect and long-standing acquaintance of the duke, with whom he maintained regular correspondence. He built the Castle Mona using imported materials and labour. Steuart had worked for Robert Adam from whom he drew his style. His work is idiosyncratic, stepping outside the mainstream neo-classical Georgian style with symmetrical planning, volumetric

167 S. Slack, *Streets of Douglas – Old and New* (Douglas, 1996), 33–34.
168 Slack, *Streets of Douglas*, 92.
169 J. Murray (7th duke of Atholl), *Chronicles of the Atholl and Tullibardine Families*, 5 vols (Edinburgh, 1908), 4, 364.

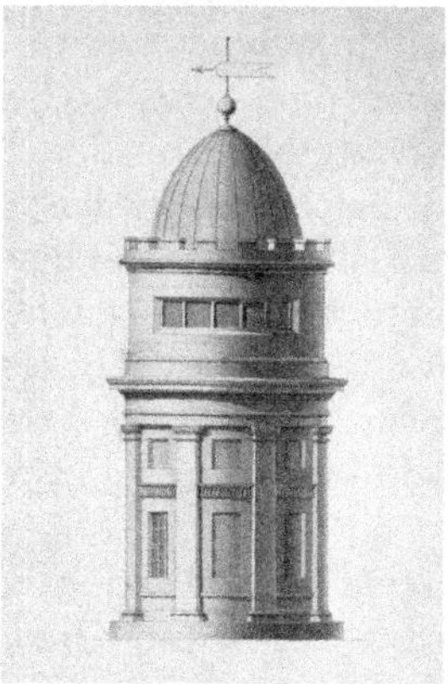

Fig. 5.17 *Steuart's colour-wash drawings of lighthouse and guardhouse on the Red Pier, Douglas: MNH P.6542/5 [lighthouse]; P.6542/6 [guardhouse].*

formalism and perhaps a hint of gendered spaces, such as he used at Attingham Park (1772–1875).[170]

At the Castle Mona the principal room, the saloon, is a double cube with a fine painted ceiling in Adam style. Externally, the parapet is crenelated and there are recessed slender bundled columns and applied decorative swags. Medallions in Coadestone display various iterations of the arms of the duke's Murray family. The bundled columns may have provided precedent for similar columns in works by Thomas Brine at St Mary's RC Church in Bowling Green Road (1823–26), St Mary's Church in the Parade (1826), and Lorne House (1827), all in Castletown.[171]

In addition to the Castle Mona, Steuart also designed the Red Pier in Douglas (1793) (see Fig. 5.17) and the courthouse in Ramsey (1798, with additional work by Thomas Brine in 1822 and 1824).[172] His octagonal guardhouse on the

170 Also used on the Murray Memorial Obelisk, Old Kirk Braddan Graveyard, George Steuart, 1805: Tutt, *Architecture of the Isle of Man*, 161.

171 Lambeth Palace Archives, ICBS, 00454 https://archives.lambethpalacelibrary.org.uk/CalmView/Record.aspx?src=CalmView.Catalog&id=ICBS.

172 C.K. Radcliffe, *Shining by the Sea: A History of Ramsey, 1800–1914* (Douglas, 1989, reprinted 2000), 39.

remains of the Red Pier is now used as an electricity sub-station. His lighthouse and guardhouse on the Red Pier are regrettably long gone, but Steuart's fine colour-washed drawings survive (Fig. 5.17).[173]

Following Steuart's example, the stylistic characteristics of the neo-classical variant of Georgian architecture became dominant in Manx domestic architecture, filtering down to its simplest manifestation in the persistent pattern of the three-bayed, two-storied, chimneyed-gabled vernacular cottage. These features, widely disseminated through pattern books, include symmetry of the principal façade and plan, hipped rooflines with a shallower pitch (enabled by the importation of large, cleanly-riven Welsh slates), more carefully considered fenestration (enabled by the availability of larger panes of better-quality glass) and the use of limewash or stucco. Windows remained small in the cottages due to the scarcity of materials strong enough in compression to act as long lintels. Mimesis in design, whether in farm, large or small rural dwelling, or townhouse, is indicative of an aspiration to conform to the new norm, for the improved farmhouse to match the improved farming methods, and to be occupied by a new type of 'enlightened' family.[174]

The largest manifestations of this neo-classical style are Balladoole, Castletown (1714) (see Fig. 5.18), Kentraugh, Rushen (1815–1820), and Kirby, Braddan (1816).[175]

Bridge House, Castletown, dates from the early eighteenth century. It took on its present form in 1809 when enlarged and raised in height by George Quayle, to block views of the harbour from the earlier Lorne House (the present Lorne House dates from 1827). It is now noteworthy for its slate cladding on the harbour elevation of the main house, the secret bank vault with a complicated locking mechanism designed and made by George Quayle, and the boathouse for the yacht Peggy, which had direct access to the narrow harbour. The latter was housed in what is now the Nautical Museum, and is currently undergoing conservation before being returned to the site.

Stronger stylistic themes emerged in the next decade, such as at the Nunnery (castellated, by John Pinch the Younger, 1823) and Lorne House (Regency, attributed to Thomas Brine, 1827) (see Fig. 5.19).[176] Both these later styles were subsequently copied elsewhere, especially the castellations. Milntown owes its present castellated form, dating from c.1830, to Deemster John Christian.

173 Callister, *Herring fishery*, 14.

174 D. Maudlin, *The Highland House Transformed, architecture and Identity on the Edge of Britain* (Dundee, 2009), 4.

175 Tutt, *Architecture of the Isle of Man*, 275–76, 279–81, 282–83; W. Thwaite, *Directory* (Sheffield, 1863), 425.

176 Tutt, *Architecture of the Isle of Man*, 270–71.

Fig. 5.18 *Balladoole with cast iron portico, subsequently removed: MNH PG/5799.*

Fig. 5.19 *Bridge House, Castletown: Photo Charles Guard.*

Notably, this reworking bears comparison with Ewanrigg Hall in Cumbria.[177] Other significant Georgian houses include 2 Parliament Square, Castletown, 1719, built close to Castle Rushen by James Cornah, steward to the tenth earl of Derby, and the Douglas Hotel in Douglas, c.1759, by Robert Black.[178]

Thomas Brine was prolific in Castletown and Derbyhaven, having impressed John Murray, fourth duke of Atholl some years after the death of George Steuart. He built the new House of Keys in 1821. The design and costs were repeatedly contested and pared down by the Home Office and the resulting modest villa was widely condemned for being inadequate for purpose.[179] This inadequacy, together with the immense difficulty Governor Piggott found in locating a suitable gubernatorial residence in Castletown, contributed to the progressive removal of the whole administrative infrastructure of the Island to Douglas from 1860 onwards. Brine built some, possibly several, of the Georgian houses facing the Parade in Castletown, which date from c.1820, including the George Hotel (now Manannan House), commissioned by the Duke in 1821. He also built the castellated Market House (c.1830), originally as a market and assembly room, which is now Barclays bank. He was also responsible for St Paul's church in Ramsey (1814–1822).[180]

Significant Georgian streets and terraces can be found in most of the Manx coastal towns. While Athol Street, Douglas, began to be laid out by John Taggart from 1810, most other terraces came later. The fourth duke of Atholl built a terrace of four marine cottages *ornées* at Strathallan around 1824 or 1825 for letting as holiday accommodation. Derby Square dates from 1836, and Auckland Terrace, Ramsey, from 1840. Thomas Callister, writing in 1815, describes several streets in Douglas as having 'handsome and genteel' new houses, particularly mentioning Fort Street and Mount Prospect (now Prospect Hill), and Duke Street as being 'the largest and finest old street in the town … being little short of half a mile in length'.[181]

In other, non-domestic secular buildings, some of the largest and most impressive structures are associated with industry and the harbours. The Isle of Man boasts three lighthouses designed by Robert Stevenson: twin lights on

177 See P. de Figuereido, 'Ewanrigg Hall Maryport Cumbria: Heritage Statement' (2015), plates 1, 3 & 4: a 1640 elevation and late nineteenth-century photographs (Cumbria County Council: planning, Allerdale. Carlisle 2015).

178 A. Harrison & N.G. Crowe, 'A Dateable Manx House of the Eighteenth Century', *PIMNHAS*, 11:4 (2007), 553–55. Nigel Crowe notes that internal inspection suggests part of the basement was a pre-existing structure.

179 A.C.C. Johnson, 'The Old House of Keys', *PIMNHAS*, 11:2 (1999–2001), 223.

180 Lambeth Palace Archives, ICBS, 00076 https://archives.lambethpalacelibrary.org.uk/CalmView/Record.aspx?src=CalmView.Catalog&id=ICBS; for Thomas Brine, see H.M. Colvin, *A biographical dictionary of British architects 1600–1840* (New Haven, Conn and London, 1995).

181 Callister, *Herring fishery*, 11.

the Calf of Man and the lighthouse at the Point of Ayre. All were built in 1818, with material imported from Scotland.[182]

CONCLUSION

While this chapter provides an overview of major perspectives, themes, and influences, the need for new focussed research within a multi-disciplinary environment is strongly indicated.

For archaeologists, comprehensive survey of the whole land surface of the island is imperative, in the manner of the British Royal Commissions, so that post-medieval features and landscapes can be identified. Such a survey would transfer into a digital mapping information system, the evidence gleaned from the 1940s RAF air photographs, more recent Isle of Man Government air surveys and LIDAR coverage; and, most importantly, it would identify possible sites on the ground.[183] In a few key cases, excavation would be required to establish chronology and function. Once a comprehensive data set has been established, it can be interrogated from a variety of angles and theoretical positions.

Landscape historians should continue to extend topological and morphological techniques, combined with evidence from rent books, intack records, family names and place names. A full assessment of the extant estate plans, including those subsequently used as tithe maps, would help to illuminate eighteenth-century studies, though with a bias towards the wealthy holdings.[184] The complete archaeological excavation of a farm complex thought to be significant both for its position within the land holding system and for its surviving architecture would be a useful next step.[185]

182 T.A. Bawden, *et al.*, *The Industrial Archaeology of the Isle of Man* (Newton Abbot, 1972), 34–37.

183 MNH PG/14919: 540 & 542 Squadron Aerial Photographs by RAF, 1944–46.

184 As in N.C. Johnson, 'Three quarterland farms in the parish of Santon: change and continuity in field boundaries', in Davey, *Recent archaeological research*, 273–75.

185 A priority too for Viking (D.M. Wilson, *The Vikings in the Isle of Man* (Aarhus, 2008), 100) and medieval studies (Davey, *Vikings*, 178).

Conclusion

CATRIONA MACKIE

This volume sets out the current state of knowledge in a range of areas that were significant to the development of the society and economy of the Isle of Man during the late medieval and early modern periods. The contributions in this volume make a valuable addition to the history of the Isle of Man and its relationship to its closest neighbours. However, our knowledge is limited by both the sources available and the research that has been undertaken to date. Importantly, the chapters in this volume highlight areas where further research would be fruitful.

There are a number of documentary sources that have yet to be fully explored and evaluated. For example, there has been no complete or systematic analysis undertaken of the Island's probate inventories or ecclesiastical court records, both of which would enhance our understanding of daily life and belief, as well as the role of the church in Manx society. Probate inventories from the seventeenth century onwards help to illuminate the material aspects of rural and urban domestic life, although only those with goods to bequeath are represented here. The lives of broader sections of Manx society are represented in the ecclesiastical court records, which are a significant source of information about life on the Isle of Man in the seventeenth, eighteenth, and nineteenth centuries. In addition to providing insight into religious and folk beliefs, they are also a reliable source of evidence of social activities and relationships within communities. In particular, the records elucidate beliefs and practices relating to witchcraft, charming, and cursing. While the Island's rich seam of traditional beliefs, customs, and folklore has long been a source of interest for antiquarians and academics, work still needs to be done to situate the Manx evidence in its wider British and international context.

Our understanding of this period would also be enhanced by a fuller analysis of the corpus of Manx Gaelic sermons dating from the late seventeenth to the mid-nineteenth centuries, and carvals (religious songs written by clergy and laity) from the eighteenth and nineteenth centuries. This would not only contribute to a greater understanding of religious history and daily life on the Island but would aid our understanding of the linguistic development of Manx Gaelic and, perhaps, the relationship between the Isle of Man's intellectual elite and the wider Gaelic world.

There are other areas of the Island's social history that are underexplored for this period, such as crime and its impact on society, experiences of famine and disease, and attitudes towards gender and the role of women in society. This was a period of significant social change in Britain and in Europe, in which social aspiration came to be reflected through food, manners, dress, furnishings, and architecture. Relatively little is known about the way in which this was experienced on the Isle of Man, either by the incoming population or by the new Manx 'middling sort.'

From the seventeenth century onwards, there is a rich tapestry of documentary and pictorial evidence that sheds light on the lives of both rural and urban populations. Sources such as Daniel King's illustrations of the Island, published in 1656, depict scenes, primarily of Castletown and Douglas, featuring buildings, landscapes, and people engaged in daily activities. These can be combined with William Blundell's first hand account of the Island and its people, written in the 1640s, and seventeenth-century maps of the Island, to help elucidate the daily life of the inhabitants. Towards the end of the eighteenth century and into the nineteenth, as the Island began to open up to visitors, an increasing number of first hand observations of the Island appear in print. In addition, John 'Warwick' Smith's watercolour paintings from 1795 provide a snapshot of the Island, both urban and rural, at that time.

Archaeological excavation has shed some light on the daily life of the Island's inhabitants during the late medieval and early modern periods, although the evidence is limited by the number and location of the excavations conducted, and the fragmentary nature of the archaeological record. There is significant scope for archaeology to further contribute to our understanding of this period in Manx history. The Island's medieval ecclesiastical history could be more fully explored through archaeological research at known or suspected medieval sites. More research is also needed on the development of human settlement during this period. Archaeological survey, combined with historical and geographical approaches to settlement morphology would help illuminate the development of field boundaries, routeways, and landholdings. The excavation of at least one significant farm complex would provide insight into daily life over an extended period, particularly when combined with other forms of evidence.

Research into Manx history is constantly evolving, and new publications appear regularly. While the authors of this volume all point to additional sources of information where these are available, it is inevitable that some recent research will have been overlooked. Above all, it is hoped that this volume will provide information and inspiration to future researchers of this period in Manx history.

Appendix I

LORDS OF MAN – 1405–1830

The lords of Man were styled kings in many Island sources and some elsewhere.

Sir John Stanley, lord of Man 1405–14
Sir John Stanley, lord of Man 1414–37
Thomas Stanley, lord of Man and first baron Stanley 1437–59
Thomas Stanley, lord of Man and first earl of Derby 1459–1504
Thomas Stanley, lord of Man and second earl of Derby 1504–21
Edward Stanley, lord of Man and third earl of Derby 1521–72
Henry Stanley, lord of Man and fourth earl of Derby 1572–93
Ferdinando Stanley, lord of Man and fifth earl of Derby 1593–94
Queen Elizabeth I takes back possession of the Isle of Man, 1595–1603
King James I holds possession of the Isle of Man until 1610, when the lordship reverts to the Stanleys
William Stanley, sixth earl of Derby 1610–42 and Elizabeth de Vere, countess of Derby 1610–27 (jointly lords of Man)
James Stanley, lord of Man and seventh earl of Derby 1642–51
Thomas Fairfax, third baron Fairfax of Cameron holds the lordship of Man for the Commonwealth 1651–60
Charles Stanley, lord of Man and eighth earl of Derby 1660–72
William Stanley, lord of Man and ninth earl of Derby 1672–1702
James Stanley, lord of Man and tenth earl of Derby 1702–36 (died without male issue)
James Murray, lord of Man and second duke of Atholl 1736–64 (maternal grandson of James Stanley, seventh earl of Derby)
John Murray, lord of Man and third duke of Atholl 1764–65
By the Revestment Act of 1765 (5 Geo. 3. c. 26) the sovereign rights of the Isle of Man reverted to the British crown

Appendix II

BISHOPS OF SODOR AND MAN – 1405–1830

John Sprotton c.1392–1410
Richard Payl / Pully 1410–33 (Payl and Pully may represent two separate individuals)
John Burwais 1433–c.1455
Thomas Burton 1455–58
Thomas Kirkham 1458–78
Richard Oldham 1483–85
Huan Blackleach 1487–1509
Hugh Hesketh 1513–c.1523
John Howden 1523–c.1540–42
Henry Man 1546–55
Thomas Stanley 1555–69
Vacant 1569–70
John Salesbury 1570–73
Vacant 1573–76
John Meryck 1576–99
George Lloyd 1599–1604
John Phillips 1604–33
William Foster 1633–35
Richard Parre 1635–44
Vacant 1644–61
Samuel Rutter 1661–63
Isaac Barrow 1663–71
Henry Bridgman 1671–82
John Lake 1682–84
Baptista Levinz 1684–93
Vacant 1693–98
Thomas Wilson 1698–1755
Mark Hildesley 1755–72
Richard Richmond 1773–80
George Mason 1780–84
Claudius Crigan 1784–1813
Vacant 1813–14
George Murray 1814–27
William Ward 1827–38

Appendix III

ABBOTS OF RUSHEN – 1408–1540

From the founding of Rushen Abbey in 1187, only fourteen are known by name. Five are recorded in the period 1408 to the dissolution.[1]

Richard 1408–18
Henry Radcliffe 1495–97
John Faragher 1503–07
Thomas Radclyf 1531–32
Henry Jackson 1540

1 Peter Davey, *Rushen Abbey, Isle of Man*, 240–41 (Douglas and Oxford, 2023).

Bibliography: editions of primary sources and earlier printed texts pre-1900

1703 Act of Settlement: Election of Representatives, 25 June 1700 (MNH MS 09782 (CRP)).

A Book containing the Answeare of th'Officers, Deemsters, Viccars Generall and 24 Keyes to certain Articles Objected by John now Bishop of this Isle against John Ireland Esquire Leiutenant and Captaine of the Isle of Man, 1 February 1611 [1610/11]

A Book of Precedents [Quayle's Precedents], by J. Quayle, n.d., c.1725 (Douglas).

A Christian Directory, Richard Baxter, 1673 (London).

A Collection of the Sufferings of the People called Quakers, J. Besse (ed), 1733, reprinted 1753, 2 vols (London), 1.

A Defense of the Charity-Schools, W. Hendley, 1725 (London).

A Description of the Isle of Man and its Customes, Thomas Denton (1681), G.W. Wood (ed), *YLM*, 3 (1898–99).

A Description of the Isle of Man, by George Waldron, W. Harrison (ed), Manx Society, 11, 1865 (Douglas).

A Description of the Isle of Man, by George Waldron, 1731, in T. Waldron (ed), *The Compleat Works, in Verse and Prose, of George Waldron*, 1731, 2nd edn (London).

A Dictionary of the Manx Language, A. Cregeen, 1835 (1984 reprint, Douglas).

A General View of the Agriculture of the Isle of Man, B. Quayle, 1794 (London).

A General View of the Agriculture of the Isle of Man, T. Quayle, 1812 (London).

A Historical Sketch and Descriptive View of the Isle of Man; Designed as A Companion to Those Who Visit and Make The Tour of It, by S. Haining, 1822, 1st edn (Douglas).

A History of St Mark's Chapel, Malew from the Year of Our Lord 1771 to the year 1843, J.T. Clarke, 1861 (Douglas) (MNH MS 00135A).

A History of the Isle of Man, by W. Blundell, 1648–56, 2 vols (unpublished MS: MNH MS 00049 C & MS 00050 C).

A History of the Isle of Man, W. Blundell, 1648–56, 2 vols, Manx Society, 25: vol. 1 and 27: vol. 2, 1876, 1877 (Douglas).

A History of the People called Quakers, J. Gough, 1789, 2 vols (Dublin).

A Journal kept in the Isle of Man, R. Townley, 1791, 2 vols (Whitehaven).

A Maritime Survey of Ireland and the West of Great Britain. M. Mackenzie, vol. 2, 1775 (London).

A Memoir of Mr F.P.D. Geneste, H. Stowell, 1822 (Liverpool).

A New Discovery of the Old Art of Teaching Schoole, C. Hoole, 1600, T. Mark (ed) (Syracuse).

A New Guide, and Visitor's Companion, through the Isle of Man, W. Cannell, 1843 (Douglas).

A Practical Grammar of the Antient Gaelic, or Language of the Isle of Man, usually called Manks, J. Kelly, Manx Society, vol. 2, 1859 (Douglas).

A Short and Plain Instruction for the Better Understanding of The Lord's Supper ... to which is annexed the office of the Holy Communion (*Shibber y Chiarn*), T. Wilson, 1777 (Whitehaven) and 1796 24th edn (London).

A Short Treatise of the Isle of Man, J. Chaloner, J.G. Cumming (ed), Manx Society, vol. 10, 1864 (Douglas).

A Short Treatise of the Isle of Man, digested into six chapters, by James Chaloner, one of the commissioners under Lord Fairfax, for settling the affairs of the Isle of Man in 1652; and afterwards Governor of the island, from 1658 to 1660. Originally published in 1656, as an appendix to 'King's Vale Royal of England; or, the County Palatine of Chester, Illustrated with Severall Prospects of the Island, by Daniel King [written 1653, published 1656] (London) (MNH MS 12587).

A Six Days' Tour through the Isle of Man, J. Welch, 1836 (Douglas).

A spelling book: or, Reading and spelling made easie, the second edition, T. Lye, 1677 (London).

A Summary of the Antient state of the Isle of Man, [1700] (MNH MS 00485C).

A supplement to the method of charity-schools, for Ireland, E. Nicholson, 1714 (Dublin).

A Tour through the Island of Mann, in 1797 and 1798, J. Feltham, 1798 (Bath).

A Tour through the Isle of Man: to which is subjoined A Review of the Manx History, David Robertson, 1st edn (unexpurgated), 1794 (London).

A Tour through the Isle of Man: to which is subjoined A Review of the Manx History, David Robertson (expurgated edn), W. Rollinson (ed), 1970 (Newcastle upon Tyne).

Act of Uniformity 1662 (14 Car 2 c. 4).

An Abridgement or Short Tract of the most usefull Lawes Actes and Ordinances conteyned in the Statute Book of the Isle of Man, J. Parr, 1679 (MNH MD 15040).

An Account of the Diocese of Sodor and Man, W. Harrison, 1879, Manx Society, 29 (Douglas).

An Account of the Isle of Man, (c.1694), William Sacheverell, J.G. Cumming (ed), Manx Society, vol. 1 (1859).

An Account of the Isle of Man, its Inhabitants, Language, Soil, Remarkable Curiosities, the Succession of its Kings and Bishops, down to the Eighteenth Century, (c.1694), William Sacheverell, 1702 (London).

An Account of the Past and Present State of the Isle of Man, G. Woods, 1811 (London & Edinburgh).

An accurate, interesting, & peculiarly entertaining description of that lucrative branch of business the Herring fishery of the Isle of Man, T. Callister, 1815 (Douglas).

An historical and statistical Account of the Isle of Man, from the earliest times to the present date, J. Train, 2 vols, 1845 (Liverpool).

Ardglass, or The Ruined Castles, S. Burdy, 1802 (Dublin).

Athenæ Oxonienses. An Exact History of all the Writers and Bishops Who have had their Education in the University of Oxford [...] to which are added the Fasti or Annals of the said University, by Anthony Wood, 1691–92, 3rd edn, 1813–20, P. Bliss (ed), 4 vols, vol. 2 (London and Oxford).

Bibliotheca Monensis, W. Harrison, 1861, Manx Society, 8. (Douglas).

Britain, or a Chorographicall description of ... England, Scotland and Ireland, by William Camden (1695), E. Gibson (ed), 1st edn (London). [*Britannia sive Florentissimorum regnorum, Angliæ, Scotiæ, Hiberniæ, et insularum adjacentium ex intima antiquitate chorographica descriptio authore Guilielmo Camdeno*, William Camden, 1586 & 1590 (London)].

Britannia Insularum, C. Saxton, 1583 (Birmingham Central Library).

Burke. Selected Works, E.J. Payne (ed), 3 vols, 1874 (Oxford).

Calendar of Entries in the Papal Registers Relating to Great Britain and Ireland: Papal Letters, XI: *1455–1464*, J.A. Twemlow (ed), 1921 (London).

Calendar of State Papers Domestic: Charles II, 1668–9, M.A. Everett Green (ed), 1894 (London).

Carvalyn Gailckagh chyndaait ayns Baarle, marish goan-foshlee giare (*Manx Carols, Translated into English, with a short preface*), A.W. Moore (ed), 1891 (Isle of Man).

Catholic Missions and Registers, 1700–1880, **vol. 5:** *North West England*, M. Gandy (comp), 2nd edn, 1998 (London).

Cavalier. Letters of William Blundell to His Friends, M. Blundell (ed), 1933 (London).

Chronicle of the Kings of Man and the Isles, G. Broderick & B. Stowell (eds), 1973 (Edinburgh).

Chronicles of England, Scotlande, and Irelande, R. Holinshed, 1577, (London), vol. 1.

Chronicles of the Atholl and Tullibardine families, J. Murray (7th duke of Atholl), 1908, 5 vols (Edinburgh).

'Church furniture in Malew church, Isle of Man', *Archaeologia Cambrensis*, 3rd ser., 48, 472–76, E.L. Barnwell, 1866.

Civil and Ecclesiastical Records and Documents of the Isle of Man and Diocese of Sodor and Man, W.P. Ward (ed), 1837 (London).

Commentaries on the Laws of England, W. Blackstone, 4 vols: vol. 1, 442–45, 1765 (Oxford),

De sacra poesi Hebræorum, R. Lowth, 1753 (Oxford).

Description of Ballaugh parish in the year 1774 (MNH MS 00197 C:1–3).

Diocesan Histories: Sodor and Man, A.W. Moore, 1893 (London).
Directory and Topography of the Isle of Man, J. Pigot, 1837 (Douglas).
Ellan Vannin, W.T. Radcliffe, 1895 (London).
Episcopalia, Thomas Wilson, in J. Keble, 1863, *The Life of Thomas Wilson*, 2 vols, 2 (Oxford).
Epitome of some of the chief events and transactions in the Life of Joseph Lancaster, containing an account of the rise and progress of the Lancasterian system of Education ... written by himself, J. Lancaster, 1833 (New Haven).
Fasti ecclesiae anglicanae, or a Calendar of the Principal Ecclesiastical Dignitaries in England and Wales, and of the Chief Officers in the Universities of Oxford and Cambridge, from the Earliest Time to the Year 1715, by J. Le Neve, 1854, T.D. Hardy (ed), 3 vols (Oxford).
Fockleyr Manninagh as Baarlagh, W. Gill (ed), 1866 (Douglas).
Great Britain's Coasting Pilot. The Second Part, G. Collins, 1693 (London).
Hibernia curiosa, J. Bush, 1769 (Dublin).
'History of the Isle of Man', T. Wilson, 1796, in W. Harrison (ed), *The Old Historians of the Isle of Man*, Manx Society, 18, 1871 (Douglas).
History of the Isle of Man, H.A. Bullock, 1816 (London).
History of the Stanleys, J. Seacome, 1741, 1821 edn (Manchester).
'Horn Books', E.B. Savage, *Manx Church Magazine*, March 1895 (Douglas).
Hugh Stowell Brown, A Memorial Volume, W.S. Caine (ed), 1888 (London).
Illiam Dhone and the Manx Rebellion 1651, Records and Proceedings, W. Harrison (ed), Manx Society, vol. 26, 1877 (Douglas).
Isle of Man Directory, W. Thwaite, 1863 (Sheffield).
James Stanley, Earl of Derby, History and Antiquities of the Isle of Man, in F.R. Raines (ed), *The Stanley Papers*, pt 3, vol. 3, Chetham Society, Old Series, vol. lxx (1867).
John Moore's Music Book, J. Moore (comp), 1804 (in private hands).
Journal of the Rev. John Gell, J. Gell, 1789, in *Manx Miscellany*, 2, Manx Society, 30 (1880).
Leabhraiche an t-Seann Tiomnaidh [...] Earrann I 1783 (Dun-Eidin).
Leabhuir na Seintiomna, U. Bedel, 1685 (London).
Legislation by three of the thirteen Stanleys, Kings of Man, W. Mackenzie (ed), Manx Society, 3 (1860).
Letter of the seventh earl of Derby, by J. Stanley, 7th earl of Derby, 1643, in *Desiderata Curiosa: or, a collection of divers scarce and curious pieces, relating chiefly to matters of English History ... A new edition, greatly corrected, with some memoirs of the life and writings of Mr Peck*, G. Peck, 1779 (London).
Letters and Papers Illustrative of the Wars of the English in France during the Reign of Henry the Sixth, King of England, J. Stevenson (ed), 2 vols, 1861–64 (London).

Letters of the Rev. Philip Moore, by P. Moore, c.1763–9, reprinted 1897/8 in *Ramsey Church Magazine*, 1 and 2 (Ramsey) (MNH M 02880).

Lioar dy Hymnyn as Arraneyn Spyrrydoil chyndait gys Gaick veih lioaryn Wesley, Watts as Scriudeyryn Elley, G. Killey (ed), 1799 (Doolish [Douglas]).

'Literacy in England, Scotland and Wales, 1540–1900', W.B. Stephens, *History of Education Quarterly*, 30:4 (1890), 545–71.

Manks and English Carols, 1890, R.E. Christian (ed), 2 vols (Douglas).

Manx Ballads and Music, A.W. Moore (ed), 1896 (Douglas).

Manx Law Tenures, R. Sherwood (ed), 1899 (Douglas).

Memoir of the Rev. Joseph Stowell, H. Stowell, 1821 (Wellington).

Memoirs of Mark Hildesley, DD, Lord Bishop of Sodor and Man and Master of Sherburn Hospital, W. Butler, 1799 (London).

Memoirs: Containing a Genealogical and Historical Account of the Ancient and Honourable House of Stanley: From the Conquest to the Death of James Late Earl of Derby, in the Year 1735; as Also a Full Description of the Isle of Man, &c., J. Seacome, 1741 (Liverpool).

Memorial of the Bishop of Sodor and Man to his Majesty's Commissioners Appointed to Consider the State of the Established Church with Reference to Ecclesiastical Duties and Revenues, Colchester 1837, reprinted in Wilson, E.C., 1931, *An Island Bishop 1762–1838: Memorials of William Ward, DD, Bishop of Sodor and Mann, 1828–1838* (London).

Memorials of 'God's Acre': a tour through the Isle of Man taken in the Summer of 1797 by John Feltham and Edward Wright, J. Feltham & E. Wright, 1797 (Bath), reproduced in W. Harrison (ed), Manx Society, 14, 1868 (Douglas).

Method of Curing Herring in the Isle of Man, in *The Scots Magazine*, 57: 220, 1795.

Mona Melodies, J. Barrow, 1820 (London).

Mona Miscellany a selection of Proverbs, Sayings, Ballads, Customs, Superstitions and Legends peculiar to the Isle of Man, 1st ser., W. Harrison (ed), 1869, Manx Society, 16 (Douglas), and *2nd ser.*, W. Harrison (ed), 1873, Manx Society, 21 (Douglas).

Monumenta de Insula Manniae: Or, A Collection of National Documents Relating to the Isle of Man, 3 vols, J.R. Oliver (ed), 1860–62, Manx Society, vols 4, 7, 9, 1860–62, 1867 (Douglas).

Moses Griffith, 1747–1819, artist and illustrator in the service of Thomas Pennant, 1979, (Exhibition catalogue: Welsh Arts Council).

'Notes of my Life' in *Hugh Stowell Brown His Autobiography His Commonplace Book and Extracts from his Sermons and Addresses*, by H.S. Brown, 1887, W.S. Cain (ed), 2nd edn (Glasgow and New York).

Notes on 'The Supposed True Chronicle of the Isle of Man', in *An Abstract of the Laws, Customs and Ordinances of the Isle of Man, compiled by John Parr, vol. 1*, J. Gell (ed), Manx Society, vol. 12, 1867 (Douglas).

'On the Progress of Elementary Education', W.L. Sargant, *Journal of the Statistical Society of London*, 30:1 (1867), 80–137.

Palatine Anthology: A Collection of Poems and Ancient Ballads Relating to Lancashire and Cheshire, J.O. Halliwell-Phillips (ed), 1850 (London).

Paradise Lost: a Poem by John Milton, Translated into the Manks Language by The Rev. Mr. Thomas Christian [Phargys Callyt], T. Christian (Douglas, 1796).

Pargys Caillt: an abridgement of John Milton's Paradise Lost by Thomas Christian with the anonymous translation of Thomas Parnell's The Hermit, T. Christian, R.L. Thomson (ed), 1995 (Douglas).

Petition to the Commons of Great Britain by the 'Clergy, Landowners and other principal Inhabitants of the Isle of Man', 1780 (MNH MS 15544), transcribed in *JMM*, 3:51 (1937), 195–200 (doc. 181).

Pigot and Co.'s Isle of Man Directory, J. Pigot, 1824 (London & Manchester).

Polychronicon, Ranulph Higden (c.1357), C.J. Babington & J.R. Lumby (eds) (London, 1865–86.

Ramsey Church Magazine, E.C. Paton (ed), 1897, 2 (Ramsey).

Records of the English Province of the Society of Jesus, H. Foley (ed), vols 1–4, 1877–79 (London).

Reliquiæ Baxterianæ: Or, Mr. Richard Baxter's Narrative of the most Memorable Passages of His Life and Times. Faithfully Publish'd from His Own Original Manuscript, by Matthew Sylvester, Richard Baxter, M. Sylvester (ed), 1696 (London).

Report of the Select Committee of the House of Commons on Education of the Poor [Brougham Commission], 1822.

Sacra Privata, T. Wilson, 1792 (Bath).

Society of Bucks: A Candid Enquiry into the Principles and Practices of the most Ancient and Honourable Society of Bucks, P. Dickenson, 1770 (London).

Some Thoughts concerning Education, J. Locke, 1728, 9th edn (Dublin).

The ancient ordinances and statute laws of the Isle of Man, M.A. Mills (ed), 1821 (Douglas).

The Antiquities of England and Wales, F. Grose, 1783, vol. 6 (London).

The Book of Common Prayer [...] translated into Manks, for the Use of the Diocese of Mann, 1765 (London).

The Book of Common Prayer [...] translated into Manks, For the Use of the Diocese of Mann, 1769: the 'Ramsey' Book of Common Prayer (Ramsey, Isle of Man).

The Book of Common Prayer in Manx Gaelic: Being Translations Made by Bishop Phillips in 1610, and by the Manx clergy in 1765, A.W. Moore (ed), assisted by J. Rhŷs, Manx Society, vols 32–33 (1895).

The chronicle of Man and the Sudreys from the manuscript codex in the British Museum, revised, annotated, and furnished with additional documents, and

English translations of the chronica, and of the Latin documents by the right reverend Dr Goss, 2 vols, P.A. Munch (ed), Manx Society, 22 & 23 (Douglas).
The Counties of Britain. A Tudor Atlas by John Speed, Nicholson, N. and A Hawkyard (eds), 1998 (London).
The Crown Garland of Golden Roses, R. Johnson, 1659 (London).
The Description of England, W. Harrison, 1968, reprinted 1994, G. Edelen (ed) (Washington, D.C.).
The Diaries of Thomas Wilson, DD, 1731–7 and 1750, C.L.S. Linnell (ed), 1964 (London).
The Dublin Scuffle, J. Dunton, 1699 (London).
The Folk Lore of the Isle of Man, A.W. Moore, 1891 (Isle of Man and London).
The Geographical and Topographical Guide of the Isle of Man, G. Jefferson, 1824 (Douglas).
The History of Wesleyan Methodism in the Isle of Man: with some account of the Island, and of the life and labours of Bishop Wilson; in a series of letters, J. Rosser, 1849 (Douglas).
The House of Stanley, P. Draper, 1864 (Ormskirk).
'The Isle of Man' in *Ecclesiological Notes on the Isle of Man, Ross, Sutherland and the Orkneys; A Summer Pilgrimage to S. Maughold and S. Magnus*, J.M. Neale, 1848 (London).
The Isle of Man Charities, J. McHutchin & G. Quirk (eds), 1831 (Liverpool).
The Isle of Man, its History, Physical, Ecclesiastical, Civil and Legendary, J.G. Cumming, 1848 (London).
The Lex Scripta of the Isle of Man, G. Jefferson (ed), 1819 (Douglas).
The Life of Adam Martindale, R. Parkinson, 1845 (Manchester).
The Life of the Right Reverend Father in God Thomas Wilson, DD, Bishop of Sodor and Man, J. Keble, 1863, 2 vols (Oxford).
The Life of the Right Reverend Father in God Thomas Wilson, DD, late Lord Bishop of Sodor and Man, H. Stowell, 1819 (London).
The Literary Quixote: or, the beauties of Townley versified, J. Stowell, 1791 (Douglas).
'The Manx Bible' (1771), Philip Moore, in 'Letters of Rev Philip Moore', *Ramsey Church Magazine*, 2.24 (1897).
The Manx Notebook, 3 vols, A.W. Moore (ed), 1886 (Douglas).
The Manx Sketch Book or Beauties of the Isle of Man in a series of Lithographic Engravings, T. Ashe (comp), 1825 (Douglas) http://www.isle-of-man.com/manxnotebook/views/as1825/index.htm.
The Manx Traditionary Ballad, R.L. Thomson (ed), 1962–63 (*Études Celtiques*, 10), 60–87.
The Manxman, H. Caine, 1897 (London).
'The Mylecharaine silver cross', W. Harrison, Manx Society, 21, 1873 (Douglas).
The Principles and Duties of Christianity with Short and Plain Directions and Prayers, Thomas Wilson, 1707 (London).

The Report of the Commissioners of Inquiry for the Isle of Man, 1792, J. Spranger *et al.* (Commissioners of Enquiry into allegations by the John Murray, 4th duke of Atholl), 1805 (London).
The Reverend Richard Baxter's Last Treatise (The Poor Husbandman's Advocate to Rich Racking Landlords), 1691, F.J. Powicke & G. Unwin (eds), 1926 (Manchester).
The Stanley Papers, F.R. Raines (ed), 1853, vol. 2 (Chetham Society, 31) and vol. 3 (Chetham Society, old ser., 70).
The Statutes of the Isle of Man, J.F. Gill (ed), vol. 1 (1417–1824), 1883 (London).
The Theatre of the Empire of Greate Britaine Presenting an Exact Geography of the Kingdomes of England, Scotland, Ireland, and the Iles Adioyning: With the Shires, Hundreds, Cities and Shire-Townes, Within ye Kingdome of England, J. Speed, 1611 (London).
The Universal Dictionary of Trade and Commerce, M. Postlethwayt, 1755 (London): 'Smuggling in relation to the Isle of Man' (MNH, M05329).
The Works of the Right Reverend Thomas Wilson, D.D., Lord Bishop of Sodor and Man, with his Life, 8 vols, C. Cruttwell (ed), edns 1784, 1796 (Bath).
To the Rt. Hon.ble George Canning ... this map of the Isle of Man, J. Drinkwater & B. Smythe, 1826 (Douglas).
Workington Agricultural Society, President's Isle of Man Report, J.C. Curwen, 1808 (Workington).
Workington Agricultural Society's Annual Report for the Isle of Man, 1810, J.C. Curwen, 1810 (Workington).
Yn Vible Casherick (Manx Gaelic Bible), published in three parts, 1771, 1772, 1773; published in one volume, 1775 (Whitehaven).

Newspapers

Caledonian Mercury (Edinburgh).
Chester Chronicle (Chester).
Cumberland Pacquet, and Ware's Whitehaven Advertiser (Whitehaven).
Dublin Intelligence (Dublin).
Gore's Liverpool General Advertiser (Liverpool).
Isle of Man Examiner (Douglas).
Isle of Man Gazette (Douglas).
Lancaster Gazette (Lancaster).
Manchester Mercury (Manchester).
Manks Mercury (Douglas).
Manks/Manx Advertiser (Douglas).
Manx Sun (Douglas).
Rising Sun (Douglas).
Universal Magazine (London).
Whitehaven Weekly Courant (Whitehaven).

Electronic resources

Poly-Olbion, M. Drayton (1622), 2nd edn (London), & University of Exeter for Oxford University Press, electronic resource). http://poly-olbion.exeter.ac.uk/the-text/scholarly-edition/ (accessed 7 October 2017).

Lewin, C, and M.W. Wheeler, *Yn Fer-raauee Creestee çhyndait dys Gaelg liorish Paul Crebbin as prentit 'sy vleïn 1763*, https://www.academia.edu/49260468/ (accessed 2 October 2023).

Lewin, C. and M.W. Wheeler, *Lewis's Catechism in Manx Gaelic, 1769*, https://www.academia.edu/49133139/ (accessed 2 October 2023).

Bibliography: manuscripts

Douglas, Isle of Man Public Record Office

IOMPRO, Braddan tithe map, 58.

Douglas, Manx National Heritage Library and Archive (MNH)

MNH B.162/HIL (3), The Isle of Man District Association of the Royal National Institution for the Preservation of Life from Shipwreck

MNH D126/3, Isle of Man Sisterly Society

MNH D126/3, Ramsey Philanthropic Society

MNH F78/RUL, Laxey Patriotic Society

MNH FLS, Notebook of John Kneen

MNH M 02581, *Yn Vible Casherick*

MNH M 02680, *Manx Gaelic Book of Common Prayer*

MNH M 02880

MNH M 05329

MNH M 07461, E 240f

MNH M 08977, E 205/5(1)

MNH M 11397

MNH M 17096

MNH M 17591, E240

MNH M 17845

MNH M 41418, Conference Notes (Society of Architectural Historians of Great Britain, 2014)

MNH M Map (AP), Douglas harbour

MNH MD 00436

MNH MD 10097

MNH MD 10141/B1

MNH MD 15040, Parr's *Abridgement*

MNH MD 15105, MD 10280, Isle of Man Harbours Division List

MNH MS 00003, Phillips' Manx Gaelic translation of the Bible

MNH MS 00049 C, Blundell, *History*, vol. 1

MNH MS 00050 C, Blundell, *History*, vol. 2

MNH MS 00197 C

MNH MS 00213 A

MNH MS 00268 A, Manx Sermons

MNH MS 00437 A

MNH MS 00482 C (QBHP)

MNH MS 00485 C

MNH MS 00509 (Lib.Canc.)

MNH MS 00510 C (QBHP)

MNH MS 00511 C (QBHP), extracts from 'Liber Cur. Monaster'
MNH MS 00790 C
MNH MS 00791 C
MNH MS 00792 C
MNH MS 00793 C
MNH MS 00794
MNH MS 00794 C
MNH MS 00795 C
MNH MS 00797 C
MNH MS 00798 C
MNH MS 00802 C
MNH MS 00810 C
MNH MS 00876 B, Society of Bucks
MNH MS 00994 C
MNH MS 01147 C
MNH MS 01405 A, Carvals
MNH MS 01507 C
MNH MS 02568 C
MNH MS 02833 C
MNH MS 04283.4c (QBHP)
MNH MS 04284
MNH MS 04600 C
MNH MS 04932 C (QBHP)
MNH MS 04933 C (QBHP)
MNH MS 04952 A, John Quayle's Notebook
MNH MS 05179 C, Onchan Friendly Society
MNH MS 05298/1
MNH MS 05583 A
MNH MS 05668
MNH MS 05690 C
MNH MS 06193
MNH MS 06448
MNH MS 06523 (DP)
MNH MS 06568 MD 436
MNH MS 06575, Stevensons
MNH MS 06679, MD 492
MNH MS 07014, Robert Busk's Journal
MNH MS 09241, '1428 Garrison Roll'
MNH MS 09309, Correspondence
MNH MS 09494, Registered deeds
MNH MS 09562, Curphey
MNH MS 09591
MNH MS 09609, Fitzsimmons, History of the Isle of Man, 1805

MNH MS 09707 (AP)
MNH MS 09709 (AP)
MNH MS 09756
MNH MS 09767, parish registers (Malew)
MNH MS 09782 (CRP)
MNH MS 09820
MNH MS 09862, Rolls Office
MNH MS 09864 (Lib.Irrot.)
MNH MS 09888, parish registers (St Matthew's Douglas)
MNH MS 09946, parish registers (St Paul's Ramsey with Ballure)
MNH MS 09992, parish registers (Andreas)
MNH MS 10052
MNH MS 10057 (Lib.Assed., Lib.Mon., Lib.Vast.)
MNH MS 10058, Ingates and outgates
MNH MS 10071 (Lib.Canc., Lib.Plit., Lib.Scacc.)
MNH MS 10192
MNH MS 10194 (Lib.Caus.)
MNH MS 10216 (EW)
MNH MS 10537, Correspondence
MNH MS 10855
MNH MS 10933, Ann Harrison, 'Associational History of the Isle of Man, 1764–1916'
MNH MS 10974, parish registers (German)
MNH MS 11195
MNH MS 11970
MNH MS 12587, Chaloner, *Treatise*
MNH MS 13144, Carval tradition report
MNH MS 13221
MNH MS 13603
MNH MS 14103, Mona United Service Club
MNH MS 15151
MNH MS 15544
MNH MS 17096
MNH M 12486 (E240/25)

Bodleian Library, Oxford

Bodl Rawl Poet 143.II
Bodl MS Fairfax 33, fols 24r-v.

Borthwick Institute of Historical Research

Borthwick, Bp. C&P XV/7

British Library

BL Sloane 4061, fol. 316.
BL Add MS 11215, Manx Gaelic Songs

BL, Add MS 27362 'A collection of views of the Isle of Man, formerly belonging to Ralph Thoresby, Esq. Leeds, [1650]'
BL Add MS 33589, fol. 238 r
BL Cotton MS Julius F10, fols 125–25
BL Add MS 4149, fol. 331
Cumbria County Archives
Carlisle Archive Centre: CASCAT
Friends House Library, London
Friends House Library, Swarthmore MSS, vol. 1, 128
Hampshire County Record Office
Hampshire Record Office 21M65/B5/1
Knowsley Hall
Knowsley Hall MS H/45 'Leases of the Isle of Man'
Lambeth Palace Archives
ICBS 00454, Church Commissioners' Records
ICBS 00076, Church Commissioners' Records
Lancashire County Record Office
LRO DDKe 84
Liverpool Municipal Archives
Liverpool Municipal Archives ('Town Books'), MS 1 (c.1550–70), fol. 150v.
National Library of Wales
National Library of Wales, B/QA/26
National Library of Wales, B/QA/14
North East Wales Archives – Flintshire, Hawarden
NEWAF D/NA/905 'An account of the Isle of Man [Richard Tyldesley], c.1665'
The National Archives
TNA E190
TNA Wills PROB 11/363/622, fols 413v, 414r.
Vatican Regesta
Vatican Regesta 470: 1459, f 441
Warwickshire County Record Office
Warwick CRO, CR2017/TP17

Bibliography: books and articles

Note: works by A.W. Moore published pre-1900 are listed in Bibliography: primary sources and earlier printed texts.

Acheson, A.R., 1997, *A History of the Church of Ireland 1691–1996* (Dublin).

Akenson, D.H., 1971, *The Church of Ireland: Ecclesiastical Reform and Revolution, 1800–1885* (New Haven and London).

Allwood, D., 2019, 'The Maughold high cross and its symbolism', *Isle of Man Studies*, vol. 16, 39–54.

Archibald, M.M., 1996, 'Coins', in P.J. Davey, D.J. Freke & D.A. Higgins, *Excavations in Castletown, Isle of Man 1989–1992* (Liverpool), 117–18.

Arkell, T., N. Evans, N. & N. Goose (eds), 2000, *When death do us part: understanding and interpreting the probate records of early modern England* (Oxford).

Ashley, A., 1953, 'The claims and needs of children in traditional Manx law and custom', *PIMNHAS*, 5:4, 358–67.

Ashley, A., 1957, 'The spiritual courts of the Isle of Man, especially in the seventeenth and eighteenth centuries', *English Historical Review*, 72:182, 31–59.

Atkinson, A., *et al.*, 2005, 'Woodwork' in 'St Sanctain's Church', and 2017, 'St Cairbre, Belle Abbey Church, Colby, Isle of Man', and 'St Columba, Arbory Parish Church, Ballabeg, Isle of Man', *NADFAS Record of Church Furnishings* (MNH MS 11165).

Aydelotte, F., 1913, *Elizabethan Rogues and Vagabonds* (Oxford).

Baigent, E., 2004, 'Waldron, George (1689/90–1726), antiquary,' *ODNB* (Oxford).

Baldwin, J.R., 2010, 'Harvesting Seabirds and their Eggs on the Irish Sea Islands', pt 2: Mainland of Man, *Folk Life*, 48:2, 144, & 2011, pt 3: The Calf of Man, 49:1, 30.

Barton, R., 1999, 'Manx Granite Tempered Ware', in P.J. Davey (ed), *Recent Archaeological Research on the Isle of Man*, BAR Brit Ser, 278, 221–40 (Oxford).

Bate, J.R., 1924, 'Ormskirk Grammar School: the first Minute Book, 1613–1890', *Historic Society of Lancashire and Cheshire*, 76, 91–114.

Bawden, T.A., *et al.*, 1972, *Industrial Archaeology of the Isle of Man* (Newton Abbott).

Bazin, F.C., 1995, 'Music in the Isle of Man up to 1896' (PhD thesis, University of Liverpool).

Bazin, F.C., 2000, 'Music', in J. Belchem (ed), *A New History of the Isle of Man*, vol. 5: *The Modern Period 1830–1999*, (Liverpool), 383–93.

Bazin, F.C. (ed), 2000, *The Promised Land: thirty-two country anthems from the collection of Edward Quayle* (Douglas).

Bazin, F.C., 2004, '"Mylecharaine": a forgotten call to nationhood', in I. Russell & D. Atkinson (eds), *Folk Song: Tradition, Revival and Re-Creation* (Aberdeen).
Bazin, F.C., 2006, *The Everlasting Hills: Hymns from the Isle of Man* (Isle of Man, 2006).
Bazin, F.C., 2009, *John Moore's Music Book* (Douglas).
Bebbington, D.W., 1989, *Evangelicalism in modern Britain: a History from the 1730s to the 1980s* (London).
Beckerson, J., 2000, 'Statistical Appendix', in J. Belchem (ed), *A New History of the Isle of Man*, vol.5: *The Modern Period, 1830–1999* (Liverpool), 417–36.
Beier, A.L., 1985, *Masterless Men. The vagrancy problem in England, 1560–1640* (London).
Belchem, J. (ed), 2000, *A New History of the Isle of Man*, vol. 5: *The Modern Period, 1830–1999* (Liverpool).
Belchem, J., 2000, 'The Little Manx Nation: Art, Ethnic Identity, and Home Rule Politics in the Isle of Man, 1880–1918', *Journal of British Studies*, 39, 217–40.
Betjeman, J. (ed), 1958, *Collins Guide to English Parish Churches, including the Isle of Man*, 2 vols (London), vol. 2 (north).
Bird, H., 1995, *An Island that Led: the History of Manx Education*, 2 vols (Isle of Man).
Blackwood, B.G., 1965, 'The Lancashire cavaliers and their tenants', *THSLC*, 117 (1965).
Blackwood, B.G., 1976, 'The economic state of the Lancashire gentry on the eve of the civil war', *Northern History*, 12, 53–83.
Blair, C., 1999–2001, 'The Manx Sword of State', *PIMNHAS*, 11:2, 259–74.
Bossy, J., 1975, *The English Catholic Community 1570–1850* (London).
Bowden, P.J., 1990, 'Agricultural prices, farm profits and rents, 1500–1640', in P.J. Bowden (ed), *Economic Change: Wages, Profits and Rents, 1500–1750* (Cambridge).
Braithwaite, W.C., 1923, *The Beginnings of Quakerism* (London).
Bray, G. (ed), 1998, *The Anglican Canons, 1529–1947* (Woodbridge).
Bray, G. (ed), 2005, *Records of Convocation: Sodor and Man 1229–1877*, 2 vols (Woodbridge).
Britnell, R.H., 1993, *The Commercialisation of English Society, 1000–1500* (Cambridge).
Broderick, G., 1981, 'Baase Illiam Dhone', *Celtica*, 14, 105–23.
Broderick, G., 1981, 1982, 'Manx Stories and Reminiscences of Ned Beg Hom Ruy', *Zeitschrift für celtische Philologie*, 38 (1981), 113–78, 39 (1982), 117–94.
Broderick, G., 1984, 'Berrey Dhone: A Manx Caillech Bérri?', *Zeitschrift für celtische Philologie*, 40, 193–210.

Broderick, G., 1984, 'Ec ny Fiddleryn', *Zeitschrift für celtische Philologie*, 40), 211–27.

Broderick, G., 1984, 'Ny Kirree fo Niaghtey', *Celtica* 16, 157–68.

Broderick, G., 1984–86, *Handbook of Late Spoken Manx*, 3 vols (Tübingen), vol. 1, 348–52, 464–65.

Broderick, G., 1990, 'Fin as Oshin', *Celtica*, 21, 51–60.

Broderick, G., 1999, *Language Death in the Isle of Man* (Tübingen).

Broderick, G., 2005, *Place names of the Isle of Man*, 7 vols (Tübingen, 1994–2005), vol. 7.

Broderick, G., 2016, 'Fíanaigecht in Manx tradition', *Scottish Gaelic Studies*, 30, 191–241.

Broderick, G., 2018, 'Fin as Oshin: A reappraisal', *Zeitschrift für celtische Philologie*, 65, 7–25.

Broderick, G., 2022, 'Mylecharaine: A Manx traditional song collected from Manx oral tradition', *Béaloideas*, 90, 26–49.

Broderick, G., 2023, 'The Revival of Traditional Songs and Music in the Isle of Man', *Isle of Man Studies*, 18, 69–84.

Brown, C.G., 1997, *Religion and Society in Scotland since 1707* (Edinburgh).

Brown, S.J., 2001, *The National Churches of England, Ireland and Scotland 1801–1846* (Oxford).

Bruce, J.R., 1957–65, 'John Murrey's Smelt-House, Derbyhaven', *JMM*, 6:78, 152–54.

Bruce, J.R., 1968, *The Manx Archaeological Survey, sixth report 1966, keeills and burial grounds in the sheading of Rushen* (Douglas).

Butler, L.A.S., 1994, 'The Cistercian landscape on the Isle of Man', in L. Pressouyre (ed), *Espace Cistercien* (Paris), 185–89.

Caine, J.B., 1986, 'In the Beginning', in S. Harrison (ed), *100 Years of Heritage: The Work of the Manx Museum and National Trust* (Douglas 1986), 10–16.

Caine, P.W., 1946–50, 'William Blundell and his Manx History', *PIMNHAS*, 5:2, 128–35.

Callow, J., 2014, '"In so shifting a Scene": Thomas Fairfax as Lord of the Isle of Man, 1651–60', in A. Hopper and P. Major (eds), *England's Fortress: New Perspectives on Thomas, 3rd Lord Fairfax* (London).

Callow, J., 2016, '"The Force of Angry Heaven's Flame": Lieutenant John Hathorne and Garrison Government in the Isle of Man, 1651–1660', *Isle of Man Studies*, 14.

Cannell, S., 2001, *Rural Architecture in the North of the Isle of Man* (Edinburgh: Scottish Vernacular Buildings Working Group).

Carswell, C.F., 1997, 'Man & the Quakers: Quakers in the Isle of Man 1655–1735', (undergraduate dissertation, University of East Anglia).

Carswell, C.F., 2019, *Man and the Quakers. A case study of the experiences of early Quakers in the Isle of Man* (Kibworth Beauchamp).

Cashin, T.L., 1986, *A Michael Village Trail* (Kirk Michael).

Chapman, E.V., c.1971, 'The Story of Manx Methodism in the Isle of Man', incomplete interim report for the Manx Methodist Society, revised by F. Coakley (1997), 'Introduction – Early Days', 3.
Chappell, C., 1980, *Island Lifeline. The Isle of Man Steam Packet Co Ltd* (Prescot).
Cheney, C.R., 1984, 'Manx synodal statutes: A.D. 1230(?)–1351 part 1: introduction and Latin texts', *Cambridge Medieval Celtic Studies,* 7 (1984a).
Cheney, C.R., 1984, 'Manx synodal statutes: A.D. 1230(?)–1351 part 2: translation of Latin texts', *Cambridge Medieval Celtic Studies,* 8 (1984b).
Chiverell, R. & Thomas, G. (eds), 2006, *A New History of the Isle of Man*, (5 vols): *The Evolution of the Natural Landscape* (vol. 1) (Liverpool).
Clague, J., 1911, *Cooinaghtyn Manninagh [Manx Reminiscences]* (Castletown).
Clamp, P., 1986, 'Schooling in the Isle of Man, 1650–1950' (PhD thesis, University of Alberta).
Clark, P., 1976, 'The ownership of books in England, 1560–1640', in L. Stone (ed), *Schooling and Society* (Baltimore).
Clarke, W.K.L. & C. Harris (eds), 1932, *Liturgy and Worship: A Companion to the Prayer Books of the Anglican Communion* (London).
Claydon, T. & I. McBride (eds), 1998, *Protestantism and National Identity: Britain and Ireland, c.1650–c.1850* (Cambridge).
Clement, M., 1959, 'Gouge, Thomas', in *The Dictionary of Welsh Biography down to 1940*, J.E. Lloyd, *et al.* (eds) (London).
Cliffe, J.T., 1969, *The Yorkshire Gentry. From the Reformation to the Civil War* (London).
Coakley, F., 1998, 'The 1851 religious and educational censuses', paper given to the Manx Methodist Historical Society, 7 November 1998 (MNH M 17845).
Colman, J.S., and A.B. Bowers, 1968, 'The Marine Biological Station of the University of Liverpool at Port Erin, Isle of Man: A New Wing, and a New Research Vessel', *Journal of the Marine Biological Association of the United Kingdom*, 48, 259–72.
Colvin, H.M., 1978, *A Biographical Dictionary of British Architects 1600–1840* (London).
Corkill, C. *et al.*, 2007, 'Archaeological and Documentary Assessment of the Nunnery Estate, Douglas, Isle of Man' (unpublished report to the Friends of the Chapel of St Bridget at the Nunnery).
Corkill, C., 2005, 'An archaeological survey of Lezayre' (MA thesis, University of Liverpool).
Corkill, U., 2000, 'Nineteenth-century Literature in English Relating to the Isle of Man', in J. Belchem (ed), *A New History of the Isle of Man: The Modern Period 1830–1999* (Liverpool).
Cornwall, J.C.K., 1988, *Wealth and Society in Early Sixteenth Century England* (London).

Coward, B., 1983, *The Stanleys, Lords Stanley and Earls of Derby, 1395–1672: The Origins, Wealth and Power of a Landowning Family* (Chetham Society, 3rd ser., 30).

Cowin, F., 2002, 'Bricks', in D.J. Freke *et al.*, *Excavations on St Patrick's Isle, Peel, Isle of Man 1982–88* (Liverpool), 226–27.

Cowin, F., 2004, *Douglas, Isle of Man, A History and Celebration* (Salisbury).

Cowin, F., *et al.*, 1989, *Lady Isabella and the Great Laxey Mine Official Guide* (Douglas).

Cowin, J., 1902, *Reminiscences of Notable Douglas Citizens and a Review of Manx Men and Manners Fifty Years Ago* (Douglas).

Cragoe, M., 1996, *An Anglican Aristocracy: the Moral Economy of the Landed Estate in Carmarthenshire, 1832–1895* (Oxford).

Craine, D., 1955, *Manannan's Isle* (Douglas).

Craine, D., 1938, 'Mark Anthony Mills: a Tragedy', *JMM*, 4:54, 10.

Craine, D., 1940–42, 'A Manx merchant of the eighteenth century', *PIMNHAS*, 4:4, 640–62.

Craine, D., 1940–42, 'The Potato Riots, 1825', *PIMNHAS*, 4:4, 565–77.

Craine, D., 1942–1946, 'The Dungeon of St. German's. Sidelights on Church Discipline, 1600–1800', *PIMNHAS*, 5:1, 161–88.

Craine, D., 1953, 'Manx Clerical Life, 1600–1800', *PIMNHAS*, 5:4, 368–84.

Craine, L., 1974, *St George's and St Barnabas' Church* (Douglas: pamphlet).

Craine, L., 1976, 'The Castle Mona Estate', *PIMNHAS*, 8:1, 18–26.

Crampton, N.V., 1954–56, 'Schools in Mann', *PIMNHAS*, 5:5, 484–98.

Creer, W., 2017, 'Metalwork' in 'St Columba, Arbory parish church, Ballabeg, Isle of Man' in *NADFAS* Record (MNH MS 11165).

Cressy, D., 1972, 'Education and Literacy in London and East Anglia, 1580–1700' (PhD thesis, University of Cambridge).

Cressy, D., 1976, 'Educational opportunity in Tudor and Stuart England', *History of Education Quarterly*, 16:3, 301–20.

Cressy, D., 1977, 'Levels of illiteracy in England, 1530–1730', *Historical Journal*, 20, 1–23.

Cressy, D., 1980, *Literacy and the social order: reading and writing in Tudor and Stuart England* (Cambridge).

Crosby, A., 2004–05, 'A Chester merchant buys leather from the Isle of Man in 1524', *Cheshire History*, 44, 37–41.

Cross, T.P., 1952, *Motif-Index of Early Irish Literature*, Indiana University Folklore Series, vol. 7 (Bloomington, Indiana).

Crowe, N.G. and G. Callow., c.2010, 'The Callows and Development of North Ramsey including Fayle's Croft or Croit e Squandish and Quayle's Croft or Bridge Croft' (MNH MS 15151).

Crowe, N.G., 1981, 'The Corletts and Ballakoig', *PIMNHAS*, 9:1, 95–124.

Crowe, N.G., 1994, 'The Moores of Ballakilley, Marown', *PIMNHAS*, 10:2, 35.

Crowe, N.G., 2001, *The Survey of Douglas, vol. 1: The Quarterland and Cottage Rents of Douglas, c.1705* (Douglas).
Crowe, N.G., 2008, 'Manx houses of the seventeenth century: a hidden heritage?', *PIMNHAS*, 12:1, 67–70.
Crowe, N.G., 2011, 'The Quinquecentenary of the Manx Doomsday Book', *PIMNHAS (The Antiquarian)*, 4, 6–8.
Crowe, N.G., 2014, 'Programme for Day 1', in J. Kewley (ed), 'The Isle of Man – Conference Notes' (Society of Architectural Historians of Great Britain, 2014), 55–65 (MNH M 41418).
Crowe, N.G., n.d., 'Origins of an Island Port: Douglas before 1705' (MNH: unpublished research papers).
Cubbon, A.M., 1954, *Early Maps of the Isle of Man: a guide to the collection in the Manx Museum* (Douglas).
Cubbon, A.M., 1958, 'Thomas and Ann Durie, An Eighteenth Century Douglas Merchant and His Wife: Two handsome portraits presented by the Friends of the Manx Museum', *JMM*, 6:75 (1958), 41–42.
Cubbon, A.M., 1964, 'The Cap of Illiam Dhone', *JMM*, 6:80, 217–18.
Cubbon, A.M., 1968, 'The Mediaeval Chapel of St Mary's, Castletown, later the Castletown Grammar School', *PIMNHAS*, 7:3, 307–42.
Cubbon, A.M., 1971, *The Art of the Manx Crosses* (Douglas).
Cubbon, A.M., 1982, *Views of the Isle of Man of 1795 by John 'Warwick' Smith* (Reproduction of six watercolours: MNH 1982).
Cubbon, M., 'P.M.C. Kermode: An Appreciation on the Centenary of the Manx Museum', *PIMNHAS*, 9:3, 319–33.
Cubbon, W. (ed), 1933 & 1939, *A Bibliographical Account of Works relating to the Isle of Man*, 2 vols (Douglas).
Cubbon, W., 1925–26, 'Early Schools and Scholarship in Mann', *PIMNHAS*, 3:1, 106–29.
Cubbon, W., 1928–30, 'Watch and Ward in 1627', *PIMNHAS*, 3:4, 258–65.
Cubbon, W., 1935, 'The Baptism of the Castle Mona', *JMM*, 3:45, 75.
Cubbon, W., 1935, 'The Peregrine Falcon in Man', *JMM*, 3:45, 66.
Cubbon, W., 1937, 'Popular Election of the Keys, Demanded in 1780', *JMM*, 3:51, 195–200.
Cubbon, W., 1937, 'The Early Manx Printers', *JMM*, 3:53, 238–40.
Cubbon, W. (ed), 1940, 'The Barony of Saint Trinian in Kirk Marown: A Memorial to Saint Ninian of Galloway', *JMM*, 4:62, 175–77.
Cullen, L.M., 1968, *Anglo-Irish Trade, 1660–1800* (Manchester).
Curnock, N. (ed), 1909–16, *The Journal of the Rev John Wesley*, 8 vols (London).
Curphey, R.A., n.d., 'Bishop Barrow's Trusts' (MNH MS 09562, box 1).
Curphey, R.A., 1976, 'Bishopscourt', *JMM*, 7:88, 221–24.
Curphey, R.A., 1966–68, 'The Castletown Artificers' Friendly Society', *PIMNHAS*, 7:2, 164–80.

Curphey, R.A., 1967, 'The Coastal Batteries. I. The Lord's Defences: To the Revestment', *JMM*, 7:83, 50–57.

Curphey, R.A., 1982, 'Peel Castle', *PIMNHAS*, 9:1, 59–94.

Curry, W., 1906–07, 'A Kingdom Won. The story of Primitive Methodism in the Isle of Man', published in *Primitive Methodist World*.

Danaher, K. & P. Lysaght, 1980/81, 'Supplement to a Bibliography of Irish Ethnology and Folklore', *Béaloideas*, 48/49, 206–27.

Davey, P.J., 1992, 'The topography and chronology of Peel and its economic development', in J. Lewis, *Peel Town: an archaeological and architectural assessment* (Douglas).

Davey, P.J. *et al.*, 1995, *Kerrowdhoo, Bride, Isle of Man: Field Work and Excavations 1992–1994* (Douglas).

Davey, P.J., 1996, 'Molluscs', in P.J. Davey, D.J. Freke and D.A. Higgins, *Excavations in Castletown, Isle of Man 1989–1992*, 151–54 (Liverpool).

Davey, P.J., 1999, 'Medieval and post-medieval continental imports on the Isle of Man', in P.J. Davey (ed), *Recent Archaeological Research on the Isle of Man*, BAR Brit Ser, 278, 241–60 (Oxford).

Davey, P.J., 1999, 'Notes on a collection of post-medieval pottery and glass from 9 Malew Street, Castletown', in P.J. Davey (ed), *Recent Archaeological Research on the Isle of Man*, BAR Brit Ser, 278, 267–72 (Oxford).

Davey, P.J. & D. Allwood, 2017, 'Archaeological Fieldwork and Research Summaries', *Isle of Man Studies*, 15: 176–84.

Davey, P.J. & J.R. Roscow, 2010, *Rushen Abbey and the Dissolution of the Monasteries in the Isle of Man*, IMNHAS Monograph 1 (Douglas), 63–115.

Davey, P.J. *et al.*, 2001, 'The Curragh and other lowland wetlands of the Isle of Man', in M. Atherden (ed), *Wetlands in the landscape: archaeology, conservation, heritage* (York), 12–40.

Davey, P.J., 2002, 'Claypipes', in D.J. Freke, *Excavations on St Patrick's Isle, Peel, Isle of Man 1982–88*, 428–34 (Liverpool).

Davey, P.J., 2002, 'Pottery', in D.J. Freke, *Excavations on St Patrick's Isle, Peel, Isle of Man 1982–88*, 363–427 (Liverpool).

Davey, P.J., 2008, 'Eleven years of archaeological research at Rushen Abbey, 1998 to 2008', *Monastic Research Bulletin 14*.

Davey, P.J., 2009–11, 'Towards the 16th-century topography of Ballasalla', *PIMNHAS*, 12:3, 367–86.

Davey, P.J., 2011, 'Les exportations françaises vers l'Isle de Man du XVème au XVIIème siècles', in A. Bocquet-Lienard and B. Fajal (eds), *A propo(t)s de l'usage, de la production et de la circulation des terres cuites dans l'Europe du nord-ouest (xive-xvie siècle)*, 219–27 (Caen).

Davey, P.J., 2013, *After the Vikings: medieval archaeology of the Isle of Man AD 1100–1550* (Douglas).

Davey, P.J., 2016, 'The ceramic finds from the Peel IRIS excavations', *Isle of Man Studies*, 14: 71–79.

Davey, P.J., 2017, 'Galley-castles and the Isle of Man?' in P. Martin (ed), *Castles and galleys: a reassessment of the historic galley-castles of the Norse-Gaelic seaways (Laxey, Isle of Man)*, 196–207.

Davey, P.J., 2020, 'Monastic landscapes in the Isle of Man: AD 1100 to 1540', in J.C. Sánchez-Pardo, E.H. Marron and M.C. Tiplic, *Ecclesiastical landscapes in Medieval Europe an archaeological perspective*, Oxford: Archaeopress Archaeology, 125.

Davey, P.J., 2023, *Rushen Abbey, Isle of Man* (Douglas and Oxford).

Davidson, J., 1918, 'Presbyterianism in the Isle of Man', *Journal of the Presbyterian Historical Society of England.*

Davies, A., 1968, 'Some aspects of the operation of the old poor law in Cardiganshire, 1750–1834', *Ceredigion*, 6:26, 1–44.

Davies, G., 1990, 'Agriculture, forestry and fishing', in *The Isle of Man Celebrating a Sense of Place*, V. Robinson & D. McCarroll (eds) (Liverpool).

Davies, J., 1992, *The Caroline Captivity of the Church: Charles I and the Remoulding of Anglicanism* (Oxford).

Davies, M.G., 1956, *The Enforcement of English Apprenticeship, 1563–1642* (Cambridge, Mass.).

de Selincourt, E. (ed), 1939, *Journals of Dorothy Wordsworth* (London).

Dempsey, W.S., 1958, *The Story of the Catholic Church in the Isle of Man* (Billinge).

Dickinson, J.R. and J.A. Sharpe, 1999, 'Courts, Crime and Litigation in the Isle of Man, 1580–1700', *Historical Research*, 72, 140–59.

Dickinson, J.R. and J.A. Sharpe, 2004, 'Public Punishment and the Manx Ecclesiastical Courts during the Seventeenth and Eighteenth Centuries', in S. Devereaux and P. Griffiths (eds), *Penal Practice and Culture, 1500–1900: Punishing the English*. (Basingstoke), 138–56.

Dickinson, J.R., 2004, 'Barrow, Isaac (1612/13–1680), bishop of St Asaph', *ODNB* (Oxford).

Dickinson, J.R., 2004, 'Bridgeman, Henry (1615–1682), bishop of Sodor and Man', *ODNB* (Oxford).

Dickinson, J.R., 1991, 'The earl of Derby and the Isle of Man, 1643–1651', *THSLC*, 141, 39–70.

Dickinson, J.R., 1996, *The Lordship of Man under the Stanleys: Government and Economy in the Isle of Man, 1580–1704* (Chetham Society, 3rd ser., 41).

Dickinson, J.R., 2005, 'The overseas trade of the Isle of Man, 1576–1755', *THSLC*, 154, 18–29.

Dodgshon, R.A., 1995, 'Human and historical geography', in F.C. Bazin *et al., Research Review,* Douglas: Centre for Manx Studies, Research Report 1 (Douglas).

Drury, P. & A. McPherson, 2012, 'Castle Rushen, Castletown, Isle of Man: conservation plan. Part 1: understanding and significance', (unpublished report to MNH, Douglas).

Dugdale, D.S., 1998, *Manx Church Origins* (Lampeter).

Dunstan, V.S., 2010, 'Reading habits in Scotland c.1750–1820' (PhD thesis, University of Dundee).

Edie, C.A., 1970, 'The Irish cattle bills: a study in Restoration politics', *Transactions of the American Philosophical Society*, 60, pt 2.

Egan, G., 1996, 'Non-ferrous Metal', in P.J. Davey, D.J. Freke and D.A. Higgins, *Excavations in Castletown, Isle of Man 1989–1992*, 109–17 (Liverpool).

Etchingham, C., J.V. Sigurðsson, M. Ní Mhaonaigh and E.A. Rowe, 2019, *Norse-Gaelic contacts in a Viking world* (Turnhout), 123–96.

Evans, E.J., 1976, *The Contentious Tithe* (London).

Every, G., 1956, *The High Church Party 1688–1718* (London).

Fargher, D., 1979, *Fargher's English–Manx Dictionary* (Onchan).

Farrant, R.D., 1937, *Mann. Its Land Tenure, Lord's Rent and Deemsters* (Oxford).

Farrer, W. & Brownbill, J. (eds), 1907–08, *The Victoria History of the County of Lancaster*, 8 vols, vols 2, 3 & 4 (London: Victoria County Series).

Fel, C., P. Foote, J. Graham-Campbell and R.L. Thomson (eds), *The Viking Age in the Isle of Man* (London, 1983), 169–174.

Fellows-Jensen, G, 2005, 'The Scandinavian Element in the Place-Names of the Isle of Man', in G. Broderick, *Placenames of the Isle of Man*, vol. 7, 357–70 (Tübingen).

Fenton, A., 1978, reprinted 1997, *The Northern Isles: Orkney and Shetland* (Edinburgh & East Linton).

Ferguson, J.P., 1975, *The Parochial Libraries of Bishop Wilson* (Douglas).

Ferris, J.P., 1975, 'A Connoisseur's Shopping-List, 1647', *Journal of the Warburg and Courtauld Institutes*, 38.

Fisher, C.T., 1996, 'Bird Bone', in P.J. Davey, D.J. Freke and D.A. Higgins, *Excavations in Castletown, Isle of Man 1989–1992*, 144–51 (Liverpool).

Fisher, C.T., 2002, 'The Bird Bones', in D.J. Freke, *Excavations on St Patrick's Isle, Peel, Isle of Man 1982–88*, 252–7 (Liverpool).

Flinn, M.W. (ed), 1977, *Scottish Population History from the Seventeenth Century to the 1930s* (Cambridge).

Flynn, J., 2008, 'Thomas Mulliner: an apprentice of John Heywood?', in S. Boynton and E. Rice (eds), *Young choristers, 650–1700, Studies in medieval and renaissance music*, 7 (Woodbridge).

Forster, R.E.C., 1984–87, 'The Pioneering Schools of Peel', *PIMNHAS*, 9:3, 269–91.

Forster, R.E.C., 1989–90, 'Aspects of Manx Emigration: 1750–1850', *PIMNHAS*, 10:1, 26–31.

Freke, D., 2002, *Excavations on St Patrick's Isle, Peel, Isle of Man 1982–88* (Liverpool).

Garrad, L.S., 1967, 'Catherine Halsall's School, Castletown, and the Finigan family', *JMM*, 7:83, 41–43.

Garrad, L.S., 1986, A History of Manx Gardens, 1st edn (Douglas).

Gawne, C.W., 2006, *A History of St George's Church, Douglas, Isle of Man*, church leaflet (Douglas).

Gawne, C.W., 2010, *Isle of Man Hockey* (Douglas).

Gelling, J.D., 1998, *A History of the Manx Church 1698–1911* (Douglas).

Gelling, P.S., 1962–63, 'Medieval sheilings in the Isle of Man', *Medieval Archaeology*, 6–7, 156–72.

Gibson, W., 1994, *Church, State and Society, 1760–1850* (London).

Gibson, W., 1995, *The Achievement of the Anglican Church, 1689–1800: The Confessional State in Eighteenth Century England* (Lampeter).

Gibson, W., 2001, *The Church of England 1688–1832* (London).

Gibson, W., 1998, '"Sully the lawn sleeves": the appointment of Claudius Crigan as Bishop of Sodor and Man, 1784', *Archives: The Journal of the British Records Association*, 23, 41–50.

Gilchrist, J., 1967, *Anglican Church Plate* (London).

Gill, W.W., 1929, *A Manx Scrapbook* (London & Bristol), 121–66.

Gill, W.W., 1943, 'The three relics of Man', *JMM*, 5:69, 125.

Goodsir, S., 2014, 'George Steuart in the Isle of Man, and further afield', *PIMNHAS*, 12:4, 699–720.

Goodwin, G., 1901, 'Manx Annals of Eighty Years Ago: Newspapers', in Peel City Guardian, 28 December.

Grant, I.F., 1930, *The Social and Economic Development of Scotland before 1603* (Edinburgh).

Grass, T.G., 2021, 'The Reformation in the Isle of Man', *Isle of Man Studies*, 17, 89–102.

Gray, C.M., 1963, *Copyhold, Equity and the Common Law* (Cambridge, Mass.).

Gregory, J., 1999, *Restoration, Reformation and Reform, 1660–1828: Archbishops of Canterbury and their Diocese* (Oxford).

Gregory, R.A. *et al.*, 2014, *Archaeology at the Waterfront 1: Investigating Liverpool's Historic Docks* (Lancaster).

Griffin, A.J., 2005, 'The Amateur Competition Movement: Shaping Identity through Participation in the Manx Music Festival 1892–2005' (PhD dissertation, University of Durham).

Griffiths, D.N., 2002, *The Bibliography of the Book of Common Prayer 1549–1999* (London).

Grimson, J., 1986, *Kirk Michael, Isle of Man: a guide to village and parish* (Kirk Michael).

Hams, L.V., 1984–87, 'Tholt-y-Will and the Upland Farms Community', *PIMNHAS*, 9:3, 308–18.

Harris, B. *et al.* (eds), 1979–, *The Victoria History of the County of Cheshire*, 5 vols (London, Oxford and Woodbridge), vol 3.

Harrison, A. & N.G. Crowe, 2007, 'A Dateable Manx House of the Eighteenth Century', *PIMNHAS*, 11:4, 553–55.
Harrison, A., 'Associational Culture, 1830–1914', in *A New History of the Isle of Man* (5 vols), vol. 5, J. Belchem (ed), *The Modern Period 1830–1999* (Liverpool), 393–406.
Harrison, A., 1976, 'The Mathematical School, Peel', *JMM*, 7:88, 212–16.
Harrison, A., 1988, 'Associational History of the Isle of Man, 1764–1916' (MNH MS 10933, thesis prepared in accordance with the regulations of the University of Liverpool for the degree of PhD).
Harrison, A., 2002, 'Sources for the Documentary History of Peel Castle', in D.J. Freke, *Excavations on St Patrick's Isle, Peel, Isle of Man 1982–88*, 15–23 (Liverpool).
Harrison, A.M., 1934, 'New light on Methodism in the Isle of Man', *Proceedings of the Wesley Historical Society*, 19:8, 195–202.
Harrison, A.M., 1982, 'Reform from the North, 1844–47', *PIMNHAS*, 8, 403–12.
Harrison, M.W., 1923, *South Ramsey and its Churches* (Ramsey).
Hasler, P.W. (ed), 1981, *History of Parliament: The House of Commons, 1558–1603*, 2.
Hempton, D, 2005, *Methodism: Empire of the Spirit* (New Haven, Conn. and London).
Henderson, L. & E.J. Cowan, 2001, *Scottish fairy belief: a history* (East Linton).
Higgins, D.A., 1996, 'Excavations at Castle Rushen Stores, 1991–1992: the excavations', in P.J. Davey, D.J. Freke and D.A. Higgins, *Excavations in Castletown, Isle of Man 1989–1992*, 49–64 (Liverpool).
Hindley, R., 1984, 'The decline of the Manx language: a study in linguistic geography', *Bradford Occasional Papers*, 6, 15–39.
Hodgkin, T., 1908, 'Ruillick-ny-Quakeryn: notes of the history of Friends in the Isle of Man', *Friends Quarterly Examiner*, 10, 457–95.
Houlbrooke, R.A., 1996, 'Refoundation and Reformation, 1538–1628', in I. Atherton, *et al.* (eds), *Norwich Cathedral: Church, City and Diocese, 1096–1996* (London), 507–39.
Houston, R.A., 1982, 'The Development of Literacy: Northern England, 1640–1750', *Economic History Review*, 2nd ser., 35:2, 199–216.
Houston, R.A., 1982, 'The Literacy Myth?: Illiteracy in Scotland 1630–1760', *Past and Present*, 96, 81–102.
Houston, R.A., 1983, 'Literacy and Society in the West, 1500–1850', *Social History*, 8:3, 269–93.
Houston, R.A., 1985, *Scottish Literacy and the Scottish Identity: Illiteracy and Society in Scotland and Northern England, 1600–1800* (Cambridge).
Houston, R.A., 1992, *The Population History of Britain and Ireland, 1500–1750* (Cambridge).
Howell, D.W., 2000, *The Rural Poor in Eighteenth-Century Wales* (Cardiff).

Hoy, M.J., 2006, *A Blessing to this Island* (Isle of Man).
Hoy, M.J., 2010, *Isaac Barrow: his Life and Legacy* (Douglas).
Hoy, M.J., 2012, 'Bishop Barrow's Bridge', *PIMNHAS (The Antiquarian)*, 7, 19–32.
Hoy, M.J., 2015, 'Isaac Barrow: Builder of Foundations for a Modern Nation: The Church, Education and Society in the Isle of Man, 1660–1800' (PhD thesis, University of Liverpool).
Hoyle, R., 1987, 'An ancient and laudable custom: the definition and development of tenant right in north-western England in the sixteenth century', *Past and Present*, 116, 24–55.
Hoyle, R., 1990, '"Vain projects": the Crown and its copyholders in the reign of James I', in J.A. Chartres and D. Hey (eds), *English Rural Society, 1500–1800* (Cambridge).
Hoyle, R., 2002, 'The management of the estates of the earls of Derby, 1575–1640: some new sources', *Northern History*, 39, 25–36.
Hunt, M.R., 1996, *The Middling Sort: Commerce, Gender, and the Family in England, 1680–1780* (Berkeley, CA & London).
Hutchinson, A.R. and A.K.G. Jones, 2002, 'The Fish Remains', in D.J. Freke, *Excavations on St Patrick's Isle, Peel, Isle of Man 1982–88*, 258–61 (Liverpool).
Hutchinson, T. & E. de Selincourt (eds), 1936, *The Poetical Works of William Wordsworth* (London & Oxford).
Hutton, R., 1995, 'The English Reformation and the evidence of folklore', *Past and Present*, 148, 89–116.
Hutton, R., 2010, 'The Changing Faces of Manx Witchcraft', *Cultural and Social History*, 7:2, 153–69.
Hutton, R., 2017, *The Witch: A History of Fear, from Ancient Times to the Present* (New Haven and London).
Innes, J., 1998, 'State, Church and Voluntarism in European Welfare, 1690–1850', in H. Cunningham and J. Innes (eds), *Charity, Philanthropy and Reform* (London), 15–65.
Inwood, S., 2004, 'Coffee Shop Society in Seventeenth Century London' (lecture transcript, Gresham College, London).
Jackson, D., 1989, 'Early Manx Methodism and the Eighteenth Century' (BA dissertation, London Bible College).
Jackson, K., 1955, *Contributions to the Study of Manx Phonology* (Edinburgh).
Jacob, W.M., 1996, *Lay People and Religion in the Early Eighteenth Century* (Cambridge).
James, M., 1974, *Family, Lineage and Civil Society* (Oxford).
Jarvis, R.C. (ed), 1954, *Customs Letter-Books of the Port of Liverpool, 1711–1813* (Chetham Society, 3rd ser., 6).
Jessop, A., 1913, *One Generation of a Norfolk House: A Contribution to Elizabethan History*, 3rd edn (London).

Johnson, A.C.C., 1999, 'A preliminary gazetteer of early archaeological remains in the upper Sulby valley', in P.J. Davey (ed), *Recent archaeological research on the Isle of Man* (Oxford), 153–70.

Johnson, A.C.C., 1999–2001, 'The Old House of Keys, Castletown', *PIMNHAS*, 11:2, 223–48.

Johnson, A.C.C., 2002, 'Watch and ward on the Isle of Man: the medieval re-occupation of Iron Age promontory forts', in P. Davey & D. Finlayson (eds), *Mannin revisited: twelve essays on Manx culture and environment* (Edinburgh), 63–80.

Johnson, M., 1996, *An Archaeology of Capitalism* (Oxford).

Johnson, N.C., 1996, 'Coal, Coke, Cinder and Burnt Stone', in P.J. Davey, D.J. Freke and D.A. Higgins, *Excavations in Castletown, Isle of Man 1989–1992*, 120–22 (Liverpool).

Johnson, N.C., 1997, 'Ballamona New Hospital: Recovery of Archaeological Material, Part One: Field Walking' (unpublished report, Douglas).

Johnson, N.C., 1997, 'The built structures in the valley floor', in P.J. Davey, N.C. Johnson & J.J. Woodcock, *Upper Glendhoo, Ballaugh, Isle of Man: field survey, September 1996*, Centre for Manx Studies, Research Report 6 (Douglas), 39–48.

Johnson, N.C., 1999, 'Three quarterland farms in the parish of Santon: change and continuity in field boundaries', in P.J. Davey (ed), *Recent archaeological research on the Isle of Man* (Oxford, 1999): British Archaeological Reports, British Series 278, 273–75.

Johnson, N.C., 1999, 'The pig-sties and thie veg, Church Farm, Cregneash', in P.J. Davey (ed), *Recent Archaeological Research on the Isle of Man*, BAR Brit Ser, 278, 277–80 (Oxford).

Johnson, N.C., 2001, 'IRIS Peel, Pumping Station: Trial Trenching', unpublished report (Douglas).

Jones, E.A., 1907, *The Old Church Plate of the Isle of Man* (London and Derby).

Jones, J.G.R. 1976, 'Multiple estate and early settlement', in P. Sawyer (ed), *Early Medieval Settlement* (London), 15–46.

Jones, M.G., 1938, *The Charity School Movement* (Cambridge).

Jordan, W.K., 1959, *Philanthropy in England, 1480–1660: a study of the changing pattern of English social aspirations* (London).

Joughin, J.J., 1916 & 1917, 'Folk-lore Notes', in S. Morrison (ed), *Mannin: A Journal of Matters Past and Present relating to Mann*, vol. 8 (Douglas 1916), 486–88, & vol. 9 (Douglas 1917), 530–33.

Joughin, J.J., 1924, 'St Peter's Church, Peel', *PIMNHAS*, 2:4, 425–46.

Kelly, A.E., 2003, *Documents Relating to Manx Currency* (Douglas).

Kelly, F., 2000, *Early Irish Farming* (Dublin).

Kelly, I.M., 1987, *'Twas Thus and Thus They Lived'* (Douglas).

Kelly, P., 1982, *Old Kirk Braddan - short history and tour* (Douglas).

Kermode, J., 1996, 'The trade of late medieval Chester, 1500–1550', in R.H. Britnell & J. Hatcher (eds), *Progress and Problems in Medieval England: Essays in honour of Edward Miller*, 286–87 (Cambridge).

Kermode, J. *et al.*, 2006, 'Small Beginnings: Liverpool 1207–1680', in J. Belchem (ed), *Liverpool 800*, 59–112 (Liverpool).

Kermode, P.M.C., (ed), 1915, *The Manx Archaeological Survey, fourth report 1915* (Douglas, 1915) and *fifth report* (Douglas, 1918; reprinted Glasgow, 1968).

Kermode, P.M.C., (ed), 1935, 'The Douglas Chapel', *The Manx Archaeological Survey, fifth report* (Douglas).

Kermode, P.M.C., 1911, 'St. Trinian's' (site visit notes), *PIMNHAS*, 1:6, 328–32.

Kermode, P.M.C., 1918, 'The parish church of Kirk Braddan', in *The Manx Archaeological Survey Fifth Report* (Douglas, 1935; reprinted Glasgow, 1968).

Kermode, R.D., 1937–39, 'Parish of Trinity Ayre now called Kirk Christ Lezayre', *PIMNHAS*, 4:3, 347–59.

Kermode, R.D., 1954, *The Annals of Kirk Christ Lezayre: sometime known as Trinity Ayre* (Douglas).

Kerridge, E., 1953, 'The movement of rent, 1540–1640', *Economic History Review*, 2nd ser., 6:1, 16–34.

Kerridge, E., 1969, *Agrarian Problems in the Sixteenth Century and After* (London).

Kewley Draskau, J., 2000, *Account of the Isle of Man in Song* (Douglas).

Kewley, J., 2014, 'Malew Church', in J. Kewley (ed), *Annual Conference 2014: the Isle of Man Conference Notes,* The Society of Architectural Historians of Great Britain (London).

Kewley, J., 2014, 'The old grammar school', in J. Kewley (ed), *Annual Conference 2014: the Isle of Man Conference Notes,* The Society of Architectural Historians of Great Britain (London).

Killip, I.M., 1971, 'Crofting in the Isle of Man', *Folk Life*, 9:1, 61–78.

Killip, I.M., 1957–65, 'Mrs. Gilrea of the East Nappin', *JMM*, 6:81, plate 277.

Killip, I.M., 1959–60, 'Unwillingly to School', *JMM*, 6:76, 94–96.

Killip, I.M., 1978, 'The development of the Manx nineteenth-century field pattern', in *Man and Environment in the Isle of Man*, P.J. Davey (ed), British Archaeological Reports: British series, 54, 401–02.

Kinley, W.B., 1994, 'The Development of Douglas Harbour: A Mariner's view', *PIMNHAS*, 10:2, 65–85.

Kinvig, R.H., 1975, *The Isle of Man: A Social, Cultural and Political History*, 3rd edn (Liverpool).

Kissack, R., 1993, 'The contribution of Methodism to the culture of the Isle of Man', *Manx Methodist Historical Society Newsletter*, 17 (Port Erin, Isle of Man).

Kissack, R., 1994, 'The location of a place name: where was Borodaill?', *PIMNHAS*, 10:2, 120–22.

Kmec, S., 2010, *Across the Channel: Noblewomen in Seventeenth-Century France and England. A Study of the Lives of Marie de La Tour, Queen of the Huguenots, and Charlotte de La Trémoïlle, Countess of Derby* (Trier).

Kneale, W.T., 1960, 'The Trials of a Manx Radical: The Life and Times of Robert Fargher, 1803–63', *JMM*, 6:76 (Douglas), 89–93.

Kneen, J.J., 1925–26, 'Manx fairs and festivals', *PIMNHAS*, 3:1, 59–80.

Kneen, J.J., 1925–29, *The Place Names of the Isle of Man: with their Origin and History*, Manx Society (Douglas).

Kneen, J.J., 1931, *A Grammar of the Manx Language* (Oxford).

Knight, F., 1995, *The Nineteenth Century Church and English Society* (Cambridge).

Kniveton, G.N., 1992, *The Onchan Story* (Douglas).

Knott, E., 1957, *An Introduction to Irish Syllabic Poetry of the period 1200–1600, with selections, notes and glossary* (Cork).

Lamothe, A.E., 1905, 'Humorous stories of the clergy', in A.E. Lamotte (ed), *Manx Yarns, Witty, Wise and Otherwise* (Douglas).

Lamplugh, G.W., 1903, *Geology of the Isle of Man* (London).

Laqueur, T., 1976, 'The cultural origins of popular literacy in England, 1500–1850', 'History and Education', 1, *Oxford Review of Education*, 2:3, 255–75.

Laslett, P., 1972, 'Introduction: the history of the family', in P. Laslett and R. Wall (eds), *Household and Family in Past Time* (Cambridge).

Latimer, J., *et al.*, 2017, 'Metalwork' in 'St Cairbre, Belle Abbey Church, Colby, Isle of Man' in *NADFAS Record*.

Leece, J.E., 1925–26, 'Philip Christian, Clothworker, of Peel and London', *PIMNHAS*, 3:1, 83–89.

Lewin, C. and P. Ó Muircheartaigh, 2022, 'Manx manuscript sermons, 1696–1863: language and historical context', *Celtica*, 34, 126–78.

Lewin, C., 'Lexical influence of the 1767 Scottish Gaelic New Testament on the Manx Bible translation' (in press).

Lewin, C., 'Manx lexicology and etymology: four case studies', *Éigse* 42 (in press).

Lewin, C., 2011, 'A sermon in Manx translated from the work of Thomas Wilson: Text and Commentary', *Scottish Gaelic Studies*, 28, 175–210.

Lewin, C., 2014, *Lioar-lhaih Ghaelgagh: Original Manx Gaelic Prose 1821–1907* (Douglas).

Lewin, C., 2015, 'A Manx sermon from 1696', *Zeitschrift für celtische Philologie*, 62, 45–96.

Lewin, C., 2016, 'The syntax of the verbal noun in Manx Gaelic', *Journal of Celtic Linguistics*, 17 (2016), 147–239.

Lewin, C., 2017, '"Manx hardly deserved to live": perspectives on language contact and language shift', *Zeitschrift für celtische Philologie* 64, 141–205.

Lewin, C., 2017, 'Scholarship and Language Revival: Language Ideologies in Corpus Development for Revived Manx', *Studia Celtica Posnaniensia*, 2, 97–118.

Lewin, C., 2020, 'Aspects of the historical phonology of Manx' (PhD dissertation, University of Edinburgh).

Lewin, C., 2022, '"An English monstrosity"? Evolution and reception of Manx orthography', *Studia Celtica Posnaniensia*, 5, 35–59.

Lewin, C., 2023, 'Lexical influence of the 1767 Scottish Gaelic New Testament on the Manx Bible translation' (in press).

Lewin, C., T. Grass, and M.W. Wheeler, 'A newly discovered fragment of the Phillips Manx Prayer Book' (in preparation).

Lewis, E.A. (ed), 1927, *The Welsh Port Books, 1550–1603*, Cymmrodorion Record Series, 12 (London).

Lewis, J., 1992, *Peel Town: an archaeological and architectural assessment* (Douglas).

Lewthwaite, P.M., 1986, *Fleece and Flail United: the History of Union Mills Isle of Man* (Braddan, Isle of Man).

Lindert, P.H., 2003–04, 'Unequal Living Standards', in R. Floud & D. McCloskey (eds), *The Cambridge Economic History of Britain since 1700*, 1 (1700–1860) (Cambridge), 357–86.

Ling, J., 2008, *The Ballaugh Elk of 1819* (Isle of Man).

Linnell, C.L.S. (ed), 1964, *The Diaries of Thomas Wilson, DD, 1731–7 and 1750* (London).

Logan, F., 2012, 'Maughold parish church: a structural analysis and subsequent synthesis, periodization and discussion' (BA thesis, University of Chester).

Logan, F., 2021, 'Maughold parish church: an attempt at structural analysis', *Isle of Man Studies*, vol. 17, 33–60.

Lowe, N.G., 1972, *The Lancashire Textile Industry in the Sixteenth Century* (Chetham Society, 3rd ser., 20).

Lythe, S.G.E., 1960, *The Economy of Scotland in its European Setting, 1550–1625* (Edinburgh).

Macauley, J.S., 2004, 'Phillips, John (c.1555–1633), bishop of Sodor and Man', *ODNB* (Oxford).

Mackie, C., 2009–11, 'Observations on the Vernacular House in the Isle of Man', *PIMNHAS*, 12:3, 417–34.

Mandelbrote, S., 2003, 'The English Bible and its Readers in the Eighteenth Century', in Isabel Rivers (ed), *Books and their readers in 18th century England: new essays* (London).

Mann, J.O., 1998, 'Thomas Wilson and Anglicanism: A Study of the Theology, Spirituality and Pastoral Practice of Thomas Wilson, Bishop of Sodor and Man (1698–1755) with reference to his place within the development of

Anglicanism, examined chiefly on the basis of his written works' (MA thesis, Queen's University, Belfast).

Marstrander, C.J.S., 1932, 'Det Norske Landnåm på Man', *Norsk Tidsskrift for Sprogvidenskap*, 6, 40–386.

Mather, F.C., 1992, *High Church Prophet: Bishop Samuel Horsley (1733–1806) and the Caroline Tradition in the Late Georgian Church* (Oxford).

Mathieson, N., 1946–50, 'Sir George Moore and his Sons', *PIMNHAS*, 5:2, 144–68.

Mathieson, N., 1953–54, 'Old Inns and Coffee-Houses of the Isle of Man', *PIMNHAS*, 5:4, 411–33.

Mathieson, N., 1958–60, 'Early Newspapers in the Isle of Man', *PIMNHAS*, 6:2, 208–10.

Mathieson, N., 1963, *Onchan, Isle of Man: the story of a village* (Onchan).

Maudlin, D., 2009, *The Highland House Transformed, architecture and Identity on the Edge of Britain* (Dundee).

McCambridge, S. & D.S. Dugdale, 2005, *Andreas,* (Douglas).

McCarthy, M., 1996, 'Animal Bone', in P.J. Davey, D.J. Freke and D.A. Higgins, *Excavations in Castletown, Isle of Man 1989–1992*, 127–44 (Liverpool).

McClure, P.T., 2013, 'The Archaeology of Manx Church Interiors: Contents and Contexts 1634–1925' (PhD thesis, University of Liverpool).

McFee, C.C., 1972, *Colby Methodism and its Buildings* (Colby, Isle of Man: pamphlet).

McLaughlin, R., 2008, *Early Irish satire* (Dublin), 88.

McLeod, W., 2004, *Divided Gaels: Gaelic Cultural Identities in Scotland and Ireland 1200–1650* (Oxford).

McManners, J., 1998, *Church and Society in Eighteenth Century France,* 2 vols (Oxford), vol. 1.

McMillan, N., 2002, 'The Molluscs', in D.J. Freke *et al.*, *Excavations on St Patrick's Isle, Peel, Isle of Man 1982–88*, 262–63 (Liverpool).

Medhurst, E., 1914, *The Life of Lady Elizabeth Hastings* (Leeds).

Megaw, B.R.S. & E.M. Megaw, 'Early Manx fishing craft', *PIMNHAS*, 5:2, 250–60.

Megaw, B.R.S., 1939, 'The Harvest of the Turbary', *JMM*, 4:58, 95–101.

Megaw, B.R.S., 1943, 'The Manx Pony', *JMM*, 5:68, 100–04.

Miller, S., 2001, 'Norwegian Dead-Child Legends in Mann (ML 4025)', *Béaloideas*, 69, 107–14.

Miller, S., 2007, '"My Misfortunes press so hard upon me": Letters from George and Theodosia Waldron to Sir Hans Sloane', *PIMNHAS*, 11:4, 557–64.

Miller, S., 2007, 'The Mona Melodies are now published and ready for delivery' – a bibliographical note on *The Mona Melodies* (1820), *PIMNHAS*, 11:4, 565–70.

Miller, S., 2015, 'Episcopacy of Bishop Wilson: Presentments for Ballaugh (for Magical Practices)', and '"For giving charm for the ague". Alice Cowley before the Church Courts (1709–13)', *Ballaugh Heritage Trust Newsletter (BHTN)*, 13, 13–17, 18–27.

Miller, S., 2018, 'George Waldron and the Good People', in S. Young and C. Houlbrook (eds), *Magical Folk: British & Irish Fairies 500 AD to the Present*, 165–80 (London).

Moore, A.W., 1900, *A History of the Isle of Man*, 2 vols (London).

Moore, A.W., 1901, 'The early land system of the Isle of Man', *Yn Lioar Manninagh*, 2, 40–44.

Moore, A.W., 1901, *Manx Worthies, or Biographies of notable Manx Men and Women* (Douglas).

Moore, A.W., 1904, *The Isle of Man Steam Packet Company Ltd, 1830–1904* (Manchester).

Moore, R., 1999, 'The origins of the Manx land system debate', in P.J. Davey (ed), *Recent Archaeological Research on the Isle of Man,* Oxford: British Archaeological Reports: British Series 278 (Oxford).

Morrison, S. (ed), 1912, *Wm. Cashen's Manx Folk-lore* (Douglas).

Morrison, S. (ed), 1914, *Mannin: A Journal of Matters Past and Present relating to Mann* (Douglas).

Murray, J. (ed), 1908, *Chronicles of the Atholl and Tullibardine Families,* 4 vols (Edinburgh).

Ó Cuív, B., 1957. 'A poem in praise of Raghnall, king of Man', *Éigse*, 8, 283–301.

Ó hUiginn, R., 2015, 'Éireannaigh, Fir Éireann, Gaeil agus Gaill', in C. Breatnach and M. Ní Úrdail (eds), *Aon don éigse. Essays marking Osborn Bergin's centenary lecture on bardic poetry (1912)* (Dublin), 17–50.

Ó Muircheartaigh, P., 2016, 'Fin as Ossian revisited: A Manx ballad in Belanagare and its significance', *Zeitschrift für celtische Philologie*, 63, 95–128.

Ó Muircheartaigh, P., 2020, 'Pargys Caillit and John Kelly's Manx dictionary', *Celtica*, 32 (2020), 261–63.

O'Day, R., 1982, *Education and Society, 1500–1800. The social foundations of education in early modern Britain* (London).

O'Neil, B.H.StJ., 1951, 'Castle Rushen, Isle of Man', *Archaeologia,* 94, 1–26.

O'Rahilly, T.F., 1932, *Irish Dialects Past and Present with chapters on Scottish and Manx* (Dublin).

Overton, M., 1996, *Agricultural Revolution in England* (Cambridge).

Page, C.J. & D. Viner, 2015, 'Panniers to Stiff Carts: Farm Transport in the Isle of Man', *Folk Life*, 53:2, 126–27.

Page, C.J., 2002, 'Manx Farming Communities and Traditions', *Mannin Revisited* (Edinburgh).

Paton, C. I., 1940, 'Manx Calendar Customs', *Folklore*, 51:1, 43–64.

Payne, E.J. (ed), 2012, *Select Works of Edmund Burke: Thoughts on the present discontents and the two speeches on America* (London).

Peck, L.L., 2005, *Consuming Splendour, Society and Culture in Seventeenth-Century England* (Cambridge).

Perkin, M., 2004, *A Directory of the Parochial Libraries of the Church of England and the Church in Wales* (London).

Philpott, R. (ed), 2015, *The pottery and clay tobacco pipe industries of Rainford, St Helens: new research* (Liverpool: Merseyside Archaeological Society), 67–93.

Philpott, R.A., & P.J. Davey, 1992, 'Peel town sampling project, 1985' in Lewis, J, *Peel Town: an archaeological and architectural assessment* (Douglas).

Pickett, E., 2001, *The Isle of Man: foundations of a landscape* (Isle of Man).

Platten, J.A., 1999, 'Mid-Seventeenth Century Church Court Presentments in the Isle of Man: Social Control or Salvation for Sinners?' (MA thesis, University of Liverpool).

Platten, J.A., 2010, 'The Church Court System: Presentments to the Manx Church Courts 1640–1799' (PhD thesis, University of Liverpool).

Powell, D.M., 2001, '"Considering the extraordinary dearth and scarcity of bread ..." Aspects of life on the Isle of Man in the years, 1647 to 1651' (MA thesis, University of Liverpool Centre for Manx Studies).

Purser, J., 1992, *Scotland's music: a history of the traditional and classical music of Scotland from earliest times to the present day* (Edinburgh).

Quayle, G.E., 1973, *Legends of a Lifetime: Manx Folklore* (Douglas).

Quilliam, G.L., 1986, 'Peel on Foot. Tour 1' (Peel).

Radcliffe, C.K., 1995–97, 'Manx news from Whitehaven 1774–1794 as Read in the *Cumberland Pacquet*', *PIMNHAS*, 10:4, 413–33.

Radcliffe, C.K., 1974–76, 'The Maughold Quakers', *PIMNHAS*, 8:2, 116–29.

Radcliffe, C.K., 1986, *Ramsey, 1600–1800* (Douglas).

Radcliffe, C.K., 1989, 'Mylecharaine: the tune and the treasure', *PIMNHAS*, 10:1, 49–62.

Radcliffe, C.K., 1989, *Shining by the Sea: a History of Ramsey, 1800–1914* (Douglas).

Radcliffe, F., 1991, *Manx Farming and Country Life 1700–1900: information pack for schools* (Douglas), 17–28.

Radcliffe, J.W. & Radcliffe, C.K., 1978, *Maughold & Ramsey Place-names* (Inverness).

Radcliffe, J.W. & C.K. Radcliffe, 1979, *A History of Kirk Maughold* (Douglas).

Radcliffe, J.W. & C.K. Radcliffe, 1982, *Kirk Bride: a miscellany* (Isle of Man).

Ralegh Radford, C.A., 2004, 'St Patrick's Isle: the medieval monastic remains', *PIMNHAS*, 11:3, 379–381.

Ralfe, P.G., 1924, *Parish Church of St Mary, Castletown, pamphlet in bound vol. Castletown* (Castletown).

Renshaw, C., 1987–89, 'Words and Deeds in Nineteenth Century Kirk Michael', *PIMNHAS*, 9:4, 543–64.

Report of the Manx Language Society, *Celtia*, 2, no. 3, March 1902, 44–45.

Rhys, J., 1902, *Celtic Folklore* (Oxford).
Riley, P. (ed), 1995, W. Beamont, *Winwick: its history and antiquities*, by W. Beamont, 2nd edn, 1878 (Warrington) (1995 edn, Runcorn),
Rix, M.M. & W.R. Sergeant, 1962, 'George Steuart, architect in the Isle of Man', *JMM*, 6:79, 177–79.
Roads, F. (ed), 2006, *Ye Boundless Realms of Joy: Forty West Gallery psalms, hymns and anthems from the Colby Manuscripts, collected and used by William Shepherd in the Isle of Man in the early decades of the 19th Century, with 32 added Manx texts* (Isle of Man).
Robinson, V. & D. McCarroll (eds), 1990, *The Isle of Man: celebrating a sense of place* (Liverpool).
Roig-Marín, A., 2021, 'Northern Middle English spelling evidence in the Durham Account Rolls', *Lingua*, 253, 1–19.
Roscoe, T., 1943, 'Dorothy Wordsworth visits the Island, 1828', *JMM*, 5:69, 113–15.
Roscow, J., 1996, 'Castletown Cottages', in P.J. Davey, D.J. Freke & D.A. Higgins, *Excavations in Castletown, Isle of Man 1989–1992*, 157–60 (Liverpool).
Roscow, J.R., 1994, 'The Development of Women's Rights in the Isle of Man up to 1777', PIMNHAS, 10:2, 41–54.
Roscow, J.R., 1998, 'The development of sixteenth-century Castletown: studies from contemporary documents', *PIMNHAS*, 10:4, 301–25.
Roscow, J.R., 2000, 'The development of Castletown, 1601 to 1703', *PIMNHAS*, 11:1, 5–28.
Scarffe, A., 2004, *The Great Laxey Mine* (Douglas).
Scarffe, A., 2014, *The Railways and Tramways of Laxey* (Douglas).
Schofield, R.S., 1968, 'The measurement of literacy in pre-industrial England', in J. Goody (ed), *Literacy in Traditional Societies* (Cambridge).
Schofield, R.S., 1973, 'Dimensions of illiteracy', *Explorations in Economic History*, 10:4, 437–54.
Sharpe, J., 2007, 'Witchcraft in the Early Modern Isle of Man', *Cultural and Social History*, 4:1, 11–28.
Shimmin, J.P, 1974, 'The Development of Manx Harbours', *PIMNHAS*, 8:3, 336–45.
Slack, S., 1984–87, 'Harbour Bridges at Douglas, 1757–1937', *PIMNHAS*, 9:3, 365–73.
Slack, S., 1996, *Streets of Douglas – Old and New* (Douglas).
Slade, H.G., 2002, 'Architectural interpretation', in D.J. Freke, *Excavations on St Patrick's Isle, Peel, Isle of Man 1982–88*, (Liverpool), 202–20.
Smith, P., 1990, 'Rural building in Wales, 1640–1750', in M. Barley (ed), *The Buildings of the Countryside, 1500–1750* (Cambridge).
Spaeth, D., 2016, '"Orderly made": re-appraising household inventories in seventeenth-century England', *Social History*, 41:4, 417–35.

Spufford, M., 1974, *Contrasting communities. English villagers in the sixteenth and seventeenth centuries* (London).
Standring, A., 2012, 'An Introduction to Manx Folk Medicine, the Informal Provision of Community Healthcare in the Isle of Man Before 1899', *PIMNHAS*, 12:3, 435–52.
Stanley, E.G., 'Rhymes in English Medieval Verse: From Old English to Middle English', in E.D. Kennedy, R. Waldron and J.S. Wittig (eds), *Medieval English Studies Presented to George Kane* (Cambridge, 1988), 115–38.
Stenning, E.H., 1978, *Portrait of the Isle of Man*, 4th edn (London).
Stephens, W.B., 1987, *Education. Literacy and Society, 1830–1870* (Manchester).
Stone, L., 1964, 'The Educational Revolution in England, 1560–1640', *Past and Present*, 28, 41–80.
Stone, L., 1969, 'Literacy and Education in England, 1640–1900', *Past and Present*, 42, 69–139.
Stone, L., 1977, *The Family, Sex and Marriage in England 1600–1800* (London).
Stott, R.M., 2000, 'Highways Legislation in the Isle of Man 1736–63: Elements of a New Political Landscape', *PIMNHAS*, 11:1, 79–89.
Stowell, P.L. & B. Osborne (eds and arrs), 1981, *The Leighton Stowell Book of Manx Dances* (Isle of Man).
Stowell, T. n.d. 'The Free Grammar School of Castletown' (MNH MS 06575 (Stevensons of Balladoole), box 3).
Taggart, H.S., c.1923, *The Story of St Matthew's, Douglas, Isle of Man* (Douglas), and 1943, St Matthew's Church, Isle of Man Examiner (MNH MS 09782 (CRP)).
Talbot, T., 1924, *The manorial roll of the Isle of Man 1511–1515* (London).
Tawney, R.H., 1912, *The Agrarian Problem in the Sixteenth Century* (London).
Taylor, A., 2012, *The Songs and Travels of a Tudor Minstrel: Richard Sheale of Tamworth* (York).
Taylor, E.G.R., 1934, reprinted 1968, *Late Tudor and Early Stuart Geography, 1583–1650* (New York).
Taylor, J., 1966, *The 'Universal Chronicle' of Ranulph Higden* (Oxford).
Temperley, N., 1979, *The Music of the English Parish Church*, vol. 1 (Cambridge).
Thirsk, J., 1990, 'Farming techniques, 1500–1640', in J. Thirsk (ed), *Agricultural Change: Policy and Practice, 1500–1750* (Cambridge).
Thompson, D., 1964, *A History of the Parish Church of St Mary's* (Castletown).
Thompson, S., 1955–58, *Motif-Index of Folk-Literature: A Classification of Narrative Elements in Folk-Tales, Ballads, Myths, Fables, Mediæval Romances, Exempla Fabliaux, Jest-Books and Local Legends*, revised & enlarged edn, 6 vols (Copenhagen).
Thomson, R.L. (ed), 1995, *Pargys Caillit, an Arrangement of John Milton's Paradise Lost by Thomas Christian with the Anonymous Translation of Thomas Parnell's The Hermit*, Centre for Manx Studies Research Report 3 (Douglas).

Thomson, R.L. 1953, 'Early Manx. A Contribution to the Historical Study of Manx Gaelic arranged as a supplementary volume to the Moore-Rhys edition of the Phillips Prayer Book' (1610) (BLitt thesis, University of Glasgow).

Thomson, R.L. 1984, 'Manx' in P. Trudgill (ed), *Language in the British Isles* (Cambridge).

Thomson, R.L. and A. Pilgrim, 1988, *An Outline of Manx Language and Literature* (Douglas).

Thomson, R.L., 1954, 1956, 1959, 'A Glossary of Early Manx', *Zeitschrift für celtische Philologie* 24 (1954), 272–307; 25 (1956), 100–40, 264–308; 27 (1959), 79–160.

Thomson, R.L., 1958, 'The date of the Traditionary Ballad', *JMM*, 6:75.

Thomson, R.L., 1960 & 1962, 'The Manx Traditionary Ballad', *Études Celtiques*, 9:1, 521–48 (1960), & 10:1, 60–87 (1962).

Thomson, R.L., 1969, 'The Study of Manx Gaelic: Sir John Rhys Memorial Lecture', *Proceedings of the British Academy*, 55, 177–210.

Thomson, R.L., 1979, 'Introduction' in *Bible Chasherick yn Lught Thie* (Onchan).

Thomson, R.L., 1981, *Lessoonyn Sodjey 'sy Ghailck Vanninagh* (Douglas).

Thomson, R.L., 1990, 'The Revd Dr John Kelly as a Lexicographer', *PIMNHAS*, 9, 443–458.

Thomson, R.L., 1992, 'Manx language and literature', in G. Price (ed) *The Celtic connection* (Gerrards Cross).

Thomson, R.L., 1998, *Yn Fer-raauee Creestee (1763) The Christian Monitor (1686) A Bilingual Edition with Notes and Introduction* (Douglas).

Thornton, T.J., 2021, 'Lordship and sovereignty in the territories of the English crown: Sub-kingship and its implications, 1300–1600', *Journal of British Studies*, 60, 848–66.

Thornton, T.J., 1998, 'Scotland and the Isle of Man, c.1400–c.1625: Noble Power and Royal Presumption in the Northern Irish Sea Province', *Scottish Historical Review*, 77, 1–30.

Tupling, G.H., 1927, *The Economic History of Rossendale* (Chetham Society, new ser., 86).

Tutt, P.A., 2012, 'An Insular Architecture: The Rural Vernacular Architecture and Landscape of the Isle of Man and the Unique Influencing Factors that have Shaped its Form' (PhD thesis, University of Liverpool).

Tutt, P.A., 2013, *An Introduction to the Architecture of the Isle of Man* (Ramsey).

Twemlow, J.A., 1921, *Calendar of Papal Registers Relating to Great Britain and Ireland: volume 11, 1455–1464* (London).

Tyacke, N., 1987, *Anti-Calvinists: the Rise of English Arminianism c.1590–1640* (Oxford).

Venn, J.A. & Venn, J., 1922–54, *Alumni cantabrigienses: a biographical list of all known students, graduates and holders of office at the University of Cambridge, from the earliest times to 1900*, 10 vols (Cambridge).

Vincent, D., 1989, *Literacy and popular culture: England, 1750–1994* (Cambridge).

Virgin, P., 1989, *The Church in an Age of Negligence* (Cambridge).

Vose, R.H., 2002, 'Vessel and Window Glass', in D.J. Freke, *Excavations on St Patrick's Isle, Peel, Isle of Man 1982–88*, 331–38 (Liverpool).

Wallis, P., 2008, 'Apprenticeship and Training in Pre-modern England', *Journal of Economic History*, 68:3, 835–41.

Walpole, S., 1885, 'The Manx Note Book, January 1885', *The Manx Note Book*, 1 (1885), 1–3.

Walsh, D., n.d., *Ireland and the Isle of Man*, Catholic Truth Society of Ireland: rev and enlarged by N. Donnelly (Dublin).

Walsh, J., Haydon, C. and Taylor, S. (eds), 1993, *The Church of England c.1689–c.1833: From Toleration to Tractarianism* (Cambridge).

Ward, W.G., 1972, *Religion and Society in England 1790–1850* (London).

Ward, W.R. (ed), 1995, *Parson and Parish in Eighteenth Century Hampshire: Replies to Bishops; Visitations* (Hampshire Record Series, 13).

Ward, W.R., 1992, *The Protestant Evangelical Awakening* (Cambridge).

Webb, R.K., 1935, *The British Working Class Reader, 1790–1848* (London).

Webber, 'Captain', c.1917, 'An Impartial Enquiry, c.1760', in G.W. Wood, *An Account of Manx Smuggling* (Douglas).

Webster, C. (ed), c.2003, *'Temples … worthy of His presence': the early publications of the Cambridge Camden Society*, Ecclesiological Society (Cambridge).

Welsh Arts Council, 1979, *Moses Griffith, 1747–1819, artist and illustrator in the service of Thomas Pennant*, (Exhibition catalogue).

Wheeler, M.W., *Pargeiys Caillit* (forthcoming).

Whittington, G., 1973, 'Field systems of Scotland', in A.R.H. Baker & R.A. Butlin (eds), *Studies of Field Systems in the British Isles* (Cambridge), 530–49.

Whyte, I.D., 1979, *Agriculture and Society in Seventeenth-Century Scotland* (Edinburgh).

Wilkins, F., 1994, *George Moore and Friends: Letters from a Manx Merchant (1750–1760)* (Kidderminster).

Williamson, K., 1939, 'Paper Making in Man: the Story of a Lost Industry', *JMM*, 4:59, 126.

Williamson, L.E., 1977, *A Short History of Ramsey Grammar School* (Ramsey).

Wilson, D.M., 2004, 'Kermode, Philip Moore Callow (1855–1932), archaeologist', *ODNB* (Oxford).

Wilson, D.M., 1994, 'Philip Kermode and Manx crosses', in P.M.C. Kermode, *Manx Crosses*, 2nd edn (facsimile edn of 1907 edn; Balgavies, Angus 1994), 1–8.

Wilson, D.M., 2008, *The Vikings in the Isle of Man* (Aarhus).

Wilson, E., 2014, *A Book of Prospects: Seventeenth-century prints and drawings of the Isle of Man* (Castletown, Isle of Man).

Wilson, E.C., 1931, *An Island Bishop 1762–1838: Memorials of William Ward, DD, Bishop of Sodor and Mann, 1828–1838* (London).

Woodall, J., 1997, *Portraiture: facing the subject* (Manchester).

Woodcock, J.J., 1997, 'The archaeology of the hills and slopes above Glendhoo', in P.J. Davey *et al., Upper Glendhoo, Ballaugh, Isle of Man: field survey, September 1996* (Douglas), 5–26.

Woodward, D.M., 1967, 'The Chester leather industry', 1558–1625, *THSLC*, 119.

Woodward, D.M., 1970, *The Trade of Elizabethan Chester*, University of Hull Occasional Papers in Economic and Social History, 4 (Hull).

Woolf, A., 2015, 'The Early History of the Diocese of Sodor', in *A New History of the Isle of Man* (5 vols), vol 3, S. Duffy & H. Mytum (eds), *The Medieval Period, 1000–1406* (Liverpool), 328–48.

Wright, S., 2004, 'Meyrick, John (1537/8–1599), bishop of Sodor and Man', *ODNB* (Oxford).

Wrightson, K., 1982, *English Society 1580–1680* (London).

Wrigley, E.A. & R.S. Schofield, 1981, revised edn, 1989, *The Population History of England, 1541–1871* (Cambridge).

Wrigley, E.A., 1985, 'Urban growth and agricultural change: England and the Continent in the early modern period', *Journal of Interdisciplinary History*, 15, 683–728.

Yates, W.N., 2004, 'An Opportunity Missed? The Provision of Education and Training for a Non-Graduate Clergy: Comparative Case Studies of the Dioceses of St David's and Sodor and Man in the Eighteenth and Nineteenth Centuries', *Dutch Review of Church History*, 83, 319–29.

Electronic resources

Brine, T., 'Ramsey, St Paul, Man, Isle of' (Lambeth Palace Church Plans Online, 1818–1826) (accessed 30 May 2012).

Ewanrigg Hall (Maryport, Cumbria) Heritage Statement: Cumbria County Council Planning, Allerdale, Carlisle (2015). http://planning.allerdale.gov.uk/portal/servlets/AttachmentShowServlet?ImageName=327028 (accessed 26 October 2018).

www.manxgeology.com (accessed 12 January 2018).

https://corpus.gaelg.im/ (accessed 27 August 2023).

Wheeler, M.W., 2020, *Psalmyn Ghavid. A critical parallel text edition of the two Manx translations of the Psalms, alongside the English*, https://www.academia.edu/41917797/ (accessed 27 August 2023).

Wheeler, M.W., 2021, *The Book of Common Prayer in Manx Gaelic, 1765/1777* (2021), https://www.academia.edu/49187655/ (accessed 27 August 2023).

https://mannincloud.info/indexes/index_1600-29.pdf (accessed 20 January 2020).

Electronic Dictionary of the Irish Language, s.v. 2 ail https://dil.ie/955 and suthain https://dil.ie/39343 (accessed 28 August 2023).

Lewin, C. and M.W. Wheeler, Lioar dy Hymnyn: A critical edition of the four Manx Gaelic hymn books printed 1795–1846, https://www.academia.edu/38262104/ (accessed 28 August 2023).

Index

Printed and bound by CPI Group (UK) Ltd, Croydon, CR0 4YY
09/11/2026
14999546-0001